Bound 4/1/81

From Freedom to Freedom

From Freedom to Freedom
African Roots in American Soil
SELECTED READINGS

Edited by Mildred Bain and Ervin Lewis
MIAMI-DADE COMMUNITY COLLEGE

Foreword by Alex Haley,
author of **Roots: The Saga of an American Family**

RANDOM HOUSE, NEW YORK

First Edition

98765432

Copyright © 1977 by Random House, Inc.

Library of Congress Cataloging in Publication Data
Main entry under title:

From freedom to freedom.

   1. Slavery in the United States—Addresses, essays,
lectures. 2. Slavery in the United States—Emancipation
—Addresses, essays, lectures. 3. Afro-Americans—
History—Addresses, essays, lectures. 4. Ethnology—
Africa—Addresses, essays, lectures. 5. Africa—History
—Addresses, essays, lectures. I. Bain, Mildred,
1929–   II. Lewis, Ervin.
E441.F8   973'.04'96073   76–54645
ISBN 0-394-32077-8

Designed by J. M. Wall

Manufactured in the United States of America.

SOURCES AND PERMISSIONS ACKNOWLEDGMENTS

CHAPTER ONE

From W. E. B. Du Bois, *The World and Africa.* New York: International Publishers, 1965, pp. 81–92, 94–97. Reprinted by permission.

From Lucile Carlson, "African Landscapes," *Africa's Lands and Nations.* New York: McGraw-Hill, 1967, pp. 3–24. Copyright © 1967 by McGraw-Hill. Reprinted by permission.

From Stanlake Samkange, *African Saga: A Brief Introduction to African History.* Nashville: Abingdon Press, 1971, pp. 47–53. Copyright © 1971 by Stanlake Samkange. Used by permission.

From John I. Clarke, "The Peoples of Africa," in R. J. Harrison Church, John I. Clarke, P. J. H. Clarke, and H. J. R. Henderson, *Africa and the Islands.* New York: Wiley; London: Longmans Green, 1966, pp. 55–61. By permission of the Longmans Group, Ltd.

CHAPTER TWO

From Galbraith Welch, *Africa Before They Came.* New York: William Morrow, 1965, pp. 286–292, 294–301. Copyright © 1965 by Galbreith Welch. Reprinted by permission.

From D. T. Niane, *Sundiata: An Epic of Old Mali.* Atlantic Highlands, N.J.: Humanities Press, 1965, pp. 1–3, 83–86, 95–96. Reprinted by permission.

From Richard E. Leakey, "Hominids in Africa," *American Scientist,* 64, 2 (March–April 1976), pp. 174, 177–178. Reprinted by permission of *American Scientist,* journal of Sigma Xi, The Scientific Research Society of North America.

From Philip D. Curtin, *Precolonial African History.* Washington, D.C.: American Historical Association, 501 AHA Pamphlets, 1974, pp. 3, 5, 9, 14–15, 17, 31.

From J. Spencer Trimingham, *A History of Islam in West Africa.* London: Oxford University Press, 1970, pp. 127–129. Copyright © 1962 by Oxford University Press. Reprinted by permission.

From A. Adu Boahen, "Kingdoms of West Africa (c. A.D. 500–1600)," in Alvin M. Josephy, Jr., ed., *The Horizon History of Africa,* pp. 177, 179–192. Copyright © 1971 American Heritage Publishing Co., Inc. Reprinted by permission.

CHAPTER THREE

Ervin Lewis, "Maturity Rites." Miami-Dade Community College, original material written for this anthology.

From Anna Apoko, "Growing Up in Acholi," in Lorene K. Fox, ed., *East African Childhood: Three Versions.* Nairobi: Oxford University Press, 1967, pp. 45–47, 51–53, 59–75. Reprinted by permission.

From Philip D. Curtin, *Economic Change in Precolonial Africa: Senegambia in the Era of the Slave Trade.* Madison: The University of Wisconsin Press, 1975, pp. 29–37. Reprinted by permission of The Board of Regents of the University of Wisconsin System.

CHAPTER FOUR

From "Language Groups," in Clark D. Moore and Ann Dunbar, eds., *Africa Yesterday and Today.* New York: Bantam Pathfinder Editions, 1968, pp. 26–28. Copyright © 1968 by The George School. Reprinted by permission of Bantam Books, Inc.

From William F. P. Burton, *The Magic Drum.* New York: Criterion Books, 1961, pp. 9–13, 142–144, 146–147. Copyright © 1961 by W. F. P. Burton. Reprinted by permission of Abelard-Schuman, Publisher.

From John S. Mbiti, *The Prayers of African Religion,* pp. 93–97. Copyright © 1975 by John S. Mbiti. U.S. edition, Orbis Books, Maryknoll, New York 10545; by permission of the original publisher, SPCK, London.

From Janet and Alex D'Amato, "Sahara Desert," "Western Grasslands," "Western Forest," *African Animals Through African Eyes.* New York: Julian Messner, 1967, pp. 9–11, 13–16, 18–19, 21–23, 26–27, 29–30, 32–33. Copyright © 1971 by Janet and Alex D'Amato. Reprinted by permission of Simon & Schuster, Inc., Julian Messner Division.

CHAPTER FIVE

From Alexander Von Wuthenau, *Unexpected Faces in Ancient America 1500* B.C.—A.D. *1500: The Historical Testimony of Pre-Columbian Artists.* New York: Crown, 1975, pp. 14–15, 18, 27–29, 58, 78, 82, 135–136, 170, 195. Copyright © 1975 by Alexander Von Wuthenau. Used by permission of Crown Publishers, Inc.

From James Shenton, "Slavery as an Institution," in Inez Smith Reid, ed., *The Black Prism: Perspective on the Black Experience.* Brooklyn, N.Y.: Faculty Press for Summer Institute in Afro-American Studies, Brooklyn College, 1970, pp. 43–49. Reprinted by permission.

CHAPTER SIX

From Eric Williams, *Capitalism and Slavery.* New York: Russell & Russell, 1961, pp. 30–50. Copyright 1944 by the University of North Carolina Press. Reprinted by permission.

From Charles S. Syndor, "The Biography of a Slave," *The South Atlantic Quarterly,* XXXVI, 1 (January 1937), pp. 59–73. Copyright 1937 by Duke University Press. Reprinted by permission.

CHAPTER SEVEN

From Winthrop D. Jordan, *White over Black: American Attitudes Toward the Negro, 1550–1812.* Baltimore: Penguin Books, 1969, pp. 3–11. Copyright © 1968 by the University of North Carolina Press. First published by the University of North Carolina Press for the Institute of Early American History and Culture. Reprinted by permission.

From Eugene Irving McCormac, *White Servitude in Maryland, 1634–1820.* Johns Hopkins University Studies in Historical and Political Science, Series XXII, Nos. 3–4 (March–April 1904), pp. 7–10, 107–111. Reprinted by permission.

From Edgar A. Toppin, *Blacks in America.* New York: David McKay, 1971, pp. 34–47. Copyright © 1969 The Christian Science Publishing Company. Reprinted by permission of the publisher, David McKay Co., Inc.

CHAPTER EIGHT

From Page Smith, *A New Age Now Begins,* Vol. I. New York: McGraw-Hill, 1976, pp. 28–46. Copyright 1976 by Page Smith. Reprinted by permission.

From Harvey Wish, "American Slave Insurrections Before 1861," *Journal of Negro History,* XXII, 3 (July 1937), pp. 299–320. Reprinted by permission of The Association for the Study of Afro-American History Inc.

CHAPTER NINE

From John Woolman, *A Journal of the Life, Gospel Labors, and Christian Experiences of That Faithful Minister of Jesus Christ, John Woolman.*

From Lisa W. Strick, *The Black Presence in the Era of the American Revolution, 1770–1800.* Washington, D.C.: Education Department, National Portrait Gallery, Smithsonian

Institution, 1973, pp. 7–11, 14–19, 21–25, 28, 30–31, 35–37, 39. Derived from *The Black Presence in the Era of the American Revolution, 1770–1800* by Sidney Kaplan. New York: Graphic Society, 1973.

From the *Federalist,* No. 54, 1788.

Peter Williams, "A Discourse Delivered on the Death of Captain Paul Cuffe," 1817.

CHAPTER TEN

From *Slavery in America,* Nos. 1–14, 1836–1837. Westport, Conn.: Negro Universities Press, a division of Greenwood Press, 1970. Reprinted by permission of Greenwood Press, Inc.

From Leslie Howard Owens, *This Species of Property: Slave Life and Culture in the Old South.* New York: Oxford University Press, 1976, pp. 121–129, 136–145. Copyright © 1976 by Oxford University Press. Reprinted by permission.

From *Frederick Douglass' Paper,* 1854; *Southern Episcopalian,* Charleston, S.C., April 1854.

From *Memoirs of a Monticello Slave: As Dictated to Charles Campbell in the 1840's by Isaac, One of Thomas Jefferson's Slaves,* edited by Rayford W. Logan. Charlottesville: The University Press of Virginia, 1951, pp. 3–7, 11–12, 22–23. Reprinted by permission of The University Press of Virginia.

From Gladys-Marie Fry, *Night Riders in Black Folk History.* Knoxville: University of Tennessee Press, 1975, pp. 212–215. Copyright © 1975 by the University of Tennessee Press. Reprinted by permission.

From John H. Lovell, Jr., *Black Song: The Forge and the Flame, The Story of How the Afro-American Spiritual Was Hammered Out.* New York: Macmillan, 1972, pp. 326–335, 340–343, 584–585. Copyright © 1972 by John H. Lovell, Jr. Reprinted with permission of Macmillan Publishing Co., Inc.

CHAPTER ELEVEN

From Carter G. Woodson, ed., *Free Negro Owners of Slaves in the United States in 1830.* New York: Negro Universities Press, a division of Greenwood Press, 1968, pp. v–viii. Reprinted by permission of Greenwood Press, Inc.

From Whittington B. Johnson, "Black Patterns of Employment, 1750–1820." Unpublished manuscript, University of Miami, 1976. Used by permission of the author.

From Charles H. Wesley, "In Freedom's Footsteps: From the African Background to the Civil War," in *International Library of Negro Life and History.* Washington, D.C.: The Association for the Study of Afro-American Life and History, Inc., 1968, pp. 124–125. Copyright © 1968 by Publishers Company, Inc. Reprinted by permission.

From Richard Allen, *The Life, Experience and Gospel Labors of the Rt. Rev. Richard Allen* (Philadelphia: Lee & Yocum, 1888), as reprinted in John H. Bracey, Jr., August Meier, and Elliott Rudwick, eds., *Black Nationalism in America.* New York: Bobbs-Merrill, 1970, pp. 4–10.

CHAPTER TWELVE

From Thomas Wentworth Higginson, "Nat Turner's Insurrection," *Atlantic Monthly,* VIII (August 1861), pp. 173–187 (originally published anonymously).

Frederick Douglass, "Editorial from the *North Star,* Vol. 1, No. 1," as reprinted in Herbert Aptheker, *A Documentary History of the Negro People in the United States.* New York: Citadel Press, 1951, pp. 265–266. Used by permission of Citadel Press (a division of Lyle Stuart, Inc.), 120 Enterprise Avenue, Secaucus, N.J. 07094.

From Kenneth M. Stampp, ed., "William Lloyd Garrison's Prospectus for the *Liberator*, 1831," in Daniel J. Boorstin, ed., *An American Primer*. New York: New American Library, 1968, pp. 276–281. Copyright © 1966 by The University of Chicago. Reprinted by permission of The University of Chicago Press and the author.

From Carter G. Woodson, ed., *The Mind of the Negro as Reflected in Letters Written during the Crisis 1800–1860*. Washington, D.C.: The Association for the Study of Negro Life and History, 1926, pp. 216–219, 508, 509, 607. Reprinted by permission of the Association for the Study of Afro-American Life and History, Inc.

CHAPTER THIRTEEN

From W. E. B. Du Bois, *Black Reconstruction in America, 1860–1880*. Copyright 1935, 1963 by W. E. B. Du Bois; reprinted by Russell & Russell, New York, 1956, pp. 55–83. Used by permission.

From John Hope Franklin, ed., "Abraham Lincoln: The Emancipation Proclamation, 1863," in Daniel J. Boorstin, ed., *An American Primer*. New York: New American Library, 1968, pp. 409–415. Copyright © 1966 by The University of Chicago. Reprinted by permission of The University of Chicago Press and the author.

From Benjamin Quarles, *Lincoln and the Negro*. New York: Oxford University Press, 1962, pp. 239–242. Copyright © 1962 by Oxford University Press, Inc. Reprinted by permission.

CHAPTER FOURTEEN

From La Wanda Cox and John Cox, eds., *Reconstruction, the Negro, and the New South*. New York: Harper & Row, 1973, pp. xiv–xv. Copyright © 1973 by La Wanda Cox and John H. Cox. Reprinted by permission.

From Francis A. Allen, ed., "The Civil War Amendments: XIII–XV," in Daniel J. Boorstin, ed., *An American Primer*. New York: New American Library, 1968, pp. 161–169. Copyright © 1966 by The University of Chicago. Reprinted by permission of The University of Chicago Press and the author.

From Willard E. Rosenfelt, ed., *The Spirit of '76* Minneapolis: T. S. Denison, 1976, p. 87. Reprinted by permission.

From Annjennette Sophie McFarlin, *Black Congressional Reconstruction Orators and Their Orations 1869–1879*. Metuchen, N.J.: The Scarecrow Press, 1976, pp. 27–28. Copyright 1976 by Annjennette Sophie McFarlin. Reprinted by permission.

From Hollis R. Lynch, *The Black Urban Condition: A Documentary History, 1866–1971*. New York: Crowell, 1973, pp. 5–11.

From John H. Lovell, Jr., *Black Song: The Forge and the Flame, The Story of How the Afro-American Spiritual Was Hammered Out*. New York: Macmillan, 1972, pp. 163–167. Copyright © 1972 by John H. Lovell, Jr. Reprinted with permission of Macmillan Publishing Co., Inc.

From Benjamin Quarles, *Lincoln and the Negro*. New York: Oxford University Press, 1962, pp. 3–13. Copyright © 1962 by Oxford University Press, Inc. Reprinted by permission.

CHAPTER FIFTEEN

From Margaret Just Butcher, *The Negro in American Culture*, based on materials left by Alain Locke. New York: Knopf, 1956, pp. 11–37. Copyright © 1956 by Margaret Just Butcher. Reprinted by permission of Alfred A. Knopf, Inc.

From Mabel Morsbach, "Negro Contributions to American Life," *The Negro in American Life*. New York: Harcourt Brace Jovanovich, 1966, pp. 221–226, 228–232, 234–238,

A personal foreword from
Alex Haley
author of *Roots: The Saga of an American Family,*
the book upon which the American
Broadcasting Company's TV
series of the same name
was scheduled for first
showing nationwide
in 1977

FOREWORD

As the author, I have been flattered in the extreme by early reactions from an array of scholars representing institutions across the United States, and even abroad. It appears that *Roots* likely will have an enduring academic role in the teaching of a variety of disciplines: Afro-American history; history of the United States; anthropology; sociology; and some others.

It is a privilege now to offer this foreword to the readers of *From Freedom to Freedom,* who will pursue a structured, academic use of this book. The sections which follow have been organized and developed by a faculty team from Miami-Dade Community College, whose expertise has impressed me as of a high order of capability and objectivity.

Those of you who are studying *From Freedom to Freedom* might have a particular interest in some of the details of how my book *Roots* was produced, because it will serve as collateral reading.

The final chapter of *Roots,* Chapter 118, affords a capsuled account of how I grew up in a small town, Henning, Tennessee, hearing my grandmother's narrative account of our family's history until those stories became indelible in my head, much the same as with the biblical parables I heard in Sunday School. Grandma didn't realize, and most assuredly I didn't, that in fact we were engaged in one of the oldest forms of human communication—the transmission of oral history.

Thirty-odd years later, things my grandmother had told me of events as far back as 200 years before those days would prove to be accurate to an astonishing degree. They were even corroborated by professional oral historians, known as *griots,* and pronounced GREE'os, in West Africa.

Oral history, however, is not peculiarly African, or Afro-American. It is entirely universal. Every living person in this world is descended from ancestors who lived at some time and in some place that had no writing. In that time and in that place, information was transmitted *only* from the memories of elders through their mouths and into the ears of younger persons. Certain elders, such as the *griots,* functioned as professional repositories and transmitters of information. Africa's *griots* had counterparts in every other ethnic culture, the Slavic *guslah* and the English bard being two examples.

But as technology and mobility have performed their work of radically changing cultures, traditions, and customs, the exclusively oral preservation and communication of history have dwindled and atrophied into cultural artifacts, supplemented by the printing press and electronic transmissions, at least for the most part.

It is highly significant that some of the officials whom I met upon my first visit to The Gambia in West Africa smiled when I registered astonishment at their descriptions of the commonplace memory feats of their remaining *griots.* "You are so surprised," they said, "because you come from the Western culture, which has become so conditioned to leaning on the crutch of print that you have forgotten how capable is the memory."

We no longer make anywhere near so much use of human memory as we ought to be doing. Memory still works, however, among people everywhere, in limited ways and settings, as it was working in Henning, Tennessee. Indeed, what made *Roots* possible was the eventual and near-miraculous fusion of a few physically recorded facts in various archives with a few other facts contained only within a narrative which had been passed down by word of mouth across generations of my maternal family.

The student will appreciate that, in the writing of books, a certain architecture of structure must be accomplished before the actual process of writing begins, and that the structuring of *Roots* was particularly complicated.

First, there was about a two-year quest involved in the establishment of the family lineage. This search moved backward in time, from myself of the seventh generation to Kunta Kinte, who was born about 1750 in the village of Juffure in The Gambia, in West Africa. With those ancestral facts in hand, there was some initial temptation simply to produce a long magazine article which would present these facts in a somewhat dramatic manner.

But I was deeply intrigued with what I felt to be an immense need within our culture for some source in the greater depth of a book. Such a book, I hoped, could have a chance to reach and appeal to a wide public, and to illumine, for whomever read it, what had been the *truths* of the long saga of those unique millions of people who are Afro-Americans. This saga has spanned some three centuries, since the time when Africans began being taken on a regular commercial basis for the purposes of their enslavement in the Americas, mainly the United States.

The story of my family would be symbolic of that saga, as would the story, in continuum and detail, of any other black family. No other ethnic grouping on earth has such a common denominator of ancestral pattern: every black American descended from some ancestor who lived in some African village, who got captured in some way, and who crossed the ocean in some slave ship; then to some succession of plantations, up until the Civil War; then the Emancipation; and since then a struggle for *freedom,* in its various facets.

Reflecting further upon this projected book, it seemed to me that a major reason why freedom has to this day remained relatively within quote marks, where Afro-Americans are concerned, in this American nation of immigrant peoples (with the probable exception of the American Indian, all Americans ancestrally came from somewhere on the other side of an ocean, the Afro-American being the only unwilling immigrant) was because Americans, whether black or white or otherwise, really comprehended scarcely anything of the truth about the culture of the African ancestral source of black people, with the result that blacks have tended variously to manifest shame of their heritage and hence of their contemporary selves, while persons of other ethnic groupings have tended to be derisive. Most Americans' images of Africa and Africans had derived from such films as *Tarzan* and *Jungle Jim*—even as Africans whom I have queried told me it was also the cinema which fed their images of black Americans as grinning, shiftless buffoons. These are images which we are struggling yet to disperse.

So what *was* the truth of the African culture, out of which Afro-Americans' ancestors had come? The book *Roots* should portray that culture; the narrative should be woven around the life of the growing Kunta Kinte.

Across the next two years, I researched eighteenth- and nineteenth-century African culture, seeking out the most primary sources available in the middle of this twentieth century. Traveling at irregular intervals to The Gambia, I would make trips into various back country villages, usually with two interpreters. I did not seek out *griots* now, but merely the most senior elders. Through interpreters, I asked these elders a great many questions, always trying to push further back in time; what did they remember *their* fathers' having told them of the time when their fathers had been boys?

How was honey taken from the beehive trees? How were the various crops planted? Harvested? With what ceremony? What were the day-to-day tasks of women? How were girls trained for the roles of wives and mothers? What about the manhood training for boys? How would one best describe the Council of the Elders? And so on, across many hours, in different villages.

Leaving a village, generally I would next fly to London to pore through documents helpful to my search for the threads of African culture, such as *The Travels of Mungo Park* and other adventurers' written accounts, including the extremely detailed personal diaries of Quaker and Wesleyan missionaries—keen observers who wrote candidly of what they saw in The Gambia. Being professionally sympathetic, they tended not to be so supercilious as others. Yet they staunchly cast aspersions upon the Africans' religious practices, especially the Islamic, for they were there to proselytize for their own religion.

Two years of search for this African culture resulted in such a formidable array of material that now the question was how it could be incorporated into a book of popular form. Probably four or five *scholarly* books could have been produced, bearing such titles as "The Cultural History of The Gambia, West Africa, circa 1750–1800." But how on earth to present such a huge pile of static facts without creating essentially a compendium?

An idea was finally arrived at. Kunta Kinte, born in Juffure, remained there, growing up, until he was captured when about sixteen years of age. A purchase was made of sixteen large three-ring binder notebooks, each thickly filled with unlined sheets of paper. I labeled the notebooks "Kunta, Age One," "Kunta, Age Two," and so on, through age sixteen.

The vast array of static, researched, cultural material now was laid out on nearly any flat surface available in my home, on tables and shelves, covering almost every square foot of floor, with only a walkway remaining.

My idea was to siphon into each notebook, representing each successive year, whatever the boy Kunta *plausibly* could have experienced through any one or any combination of the human senses. Starting with notebook "Kunta, Age One," I went through the entire vast array of material distilling for use that which was applicable as the reactions of a baby of that age, as registered through his faculties of sight, sound, smell, feel, and taste.

That notebook filled, I turned to the notebook for age two, and so on. By the time Kunta was four, in my plausible reconstruction, his mental faculties were portrayed as increasing enough that he could comprehend some more involved things.

The sixteen notebooks eventually were thick with materials. The previously intimidating array of static materials had been distributed across the life of a Gambian boy and youth who lived two centuries ago, yet whose life was just as real to him as yours or mine today.

Now my need was for what editors and writers term a "story line"—the skein of successive activities which would move through the succession of years, with cultural material woven in along the way.

Finally, after what had been a lifetime for me since the days at my grandmother's knee, the actual writing began. It would take three years.

The resulting book, *Roots,* has, I hope, achieved the result that a reader will soon become intrigued with a disarming baby—for babies are universal. I hope the reader will continue to be intrigued, as Kunta has successive experiences as a small boy, and then as a youth. I further hope the reader peripherally will be absorbing a huge amount of facts about African culture and become aware of truths which would probably never have become known to him or her except perhaps through the pursuit of more scholarly books.

It is felt that this understanding of the more or less architectural construction and structuring of *Roots* will assist the study of *From Freedom to Freedom* in such a way as to afford better assessment of the cultural and informational contents of *Roots.*

More or less the same procedures were applied to those sections of *Roots* which deal with Kunta's experience on the slave ship. Booking myself as a passenger on a freighter bound from West Africa to the United States, I spent each night of the crossing lying on a plank, stripped to my underwear, down within the dark, cold hold. Even so, my experience was sheerest luxury, by comparison with that of Kunta and 139 others within the slave ship *Lord Ligonier,* but it was the closest I could come in an attempt to sense at least something of their otherwise unimaginable experience.

Still more notebooks of voluminous, categorized materials were drawn upon in order to share with the reader of *Roots* insight and information on the everyday lives of antebellum slaves as exemplified by Kunta, Bell, Fiddler, Kizzy, and others on the John Waller and thence the William Waller plantations, and later the descendant families and their friends on the subsequent Lea and Murray plantations.

Roots takes us through the Civil War, and into the Reconstruction era, when a wagon train took about twenty ex-slave families to establish new and improved free lives for themselves in the small town of Henning, Tennessee. In that wagon train was Cynthia, then aged two, who was to become my grandmother, the one at whose knee I learned true stories that would not leave my consciousness and which I wish to share.

Each character portrayed within *Roots* is felt to symbolize many thousands of persons of similar, general personalities and circumstances . . . who once lived in West Africa . . . who were crew and cargo of slave ships . . . and who lived on plantations within the United States.

ALEX HALEY

PREFACE

This anthology is made up of background readings selected to assist a student to understand the historical background of black Americans. Some readings help the student to become acquainted with Africa; others deal with the ramifications of the institution of slavery in various periods of American colonial and national history. Finally, other selections highlight the presence of black Americans in various periods of history and the contributions of black Americans to many aspects of American life and culture.

A few basic historical documents that are important to various periods and events have been included, as well as selections that acquaint the reader with the feelings of people living in different periods of history. Finally, there is a sampling of writings—some old, some recent—chosen again to reflect the spirit of the times as well as efforts to reinterpret the past.

The compilers believe that these readings will make a significant contribution to understanding the black heritage; likewise, we believe that this material will help readers come to grips with an important part of American history. We hope that these materials, together with Alex Haley's highly acclaimed family chronicle, *Root: The Saga of an American Family,* will broaden the perspectives of all Americans and lead to a more enlightened outlook on race relations in America.

The title of this book, *From Freedom to Freedom,* was suggested by the story line of *Roots.* Kunta Kinte was born free and lived free until he was captured while selecting and cutting wood to make a drum. Outwardly a slave, he retained his pride and dignity and remained free in mind and spirit. He taught his daughter to be proud of her African heritage. Thus was a tradition established that led to Haley's remarkable reconstruction and telling of his family's experiences through two hundred years. With the Emancipation Proclamation and the passage of the 13th Amendment, the members of the fourth and fifth generations of the family were legally free. Although no one would deny that the struggle for full freedom has continued from that time to the present and will continue into the future, freedom remains the goal not only for Kunta's descendents and all blacks, but also for all people. Until all are free, no one is fully free.

ACKNOWLEDGMENTS

The development of a college course, and the subsequent development of instructional materials, was the inspiration of Robert H. McCabe, executive vice-president of Miami-Dade Community College. The course is intended to capture and expand on the wealth of information contained in the best-selling novel *Roots: The Saga of an American Family,* as well as to parallel the Wolper Productions, Inc., television series based on *Roots* to be shown on ABC-TV. The cooperation and contributions of Alex Haley, who wrote *Roots,* were important from the inception of the project to its conclusion. Mr. Haley has kindly written a foreword to this collection of readings. George Sims, the principal researcher for the book *Roots,* was likewise invaluable as the main researcher for the academic materials.

The selected articles were organized by a team of faculty at Miami-Dade Community College under the guidance of the Project Director, Mildred Bain. The faculty were Sharon Thomas, Morris Johnson, and William Primus. Ervin Lewis provided editorial expertise. The clerical support was efficiently handled by Susan Perrotti.

In addition, the help of the Library of Congress and the libraries of Miami-Dade Community College and the University of Miami is acknowledged.

CONTENTS

From Freedom to Freedom

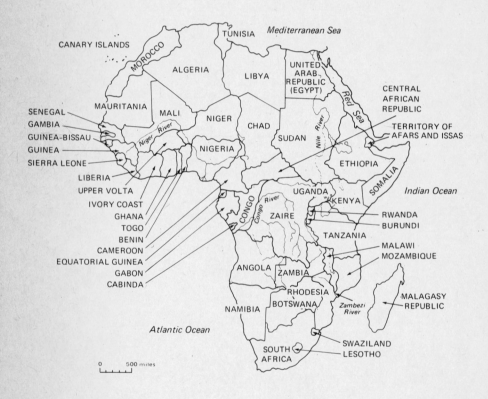

CANARY ISLANDS

TUNISIA

Mediterranean Sea

MOROCCO

ALGERIA

LIBYA

UNITED ARAB REPUBLIC (EGYPT)

CENTRAL AFRICAN REPUBLIC

MAURITANIA

MALI

NIGER

CHAD

SUDAN

Red Sea

TERRITORY OF AFARS AND ISSAS

SENEGAL
GAMBIA
GUINEA-BISSAU
GUINEA
SIERRA LEONE

Niger River

NIGERIA

Nile River

ETHIOPIA

LIBERIA
UPPER VOLTA
IVORY COAST
GHANA
TOGO
BENIN
CAMEROON
EQUATORIAL GUINEA
GABON
CABINDA

CONGO

Congo River

ZAIRE

UGANDA

KENYA

SOMALIA

Indian Ocean

RWANDA
BURUNDI

TANZANIA

MALAWI
MOZAMBIQUE

ANGOLA

ZAMBIA

RHODESIA
BOTSWANA

Zambezi River

MALAGASY REPUBLIC

NAMIBIA

Atlantic Ocean

SOUTH AFRICA

SWAZILAND
LESOTHO

0   500 miles

CHAPTER ONE

AFRICA: Land of Diversity

Africa was probably the first environment to produce the animal we know as man. In fact, archeological findings tend to support the theory that mankind originated in Africa. In addition, civilizations in various areas of the continent attained high levels of artistic, scientific, political, and religious development. As you read this chapter, try to identify the variables (e.g., seasons, animal and mineral resources) that affected the growth of civilizations in Africa and the reasons for their development in different areas of the continent.

The Peopling of Africa

W. E. B. Du Bois

A historian whose writings can escape controversy has yet to be born. History is always subject to interpretation. The historian cannot report all the facts; he selects from among the facts and attempts to interpret them. W. E. B. Du Bois (1868–1963) was a black American scholar and educator whose stature as a historian is internationally acclaimed. The following selection from his book *The World and Africa* on the African environment gives testimony to Du Bois's meticulous research and broad perspectives. The article should serve as a foundation for building an understanding of Africa.

Seers say that for full two thousand million years this world out of fiery mist has whirled about the sun in molten metal and viscous crusted ball. That crust, congealing and separating the solids from the liquids, rose and fell in bulging ridges above the boiling sea. Five times the mass of land called Africa emerged and disappeared beneath the oceans. At last, at least a thousand million years ago, a mass of rigid rock lifted its crystal back above the waters and remained.

Primeval Africa stretched from the ramparts of Ethiopia to where the copper, diamonds, and gold of South Africa eventually were found. More land arose, and perhaps three hundred million years ago Africa was connected with South America, India, and Australia. As the ocean basins dropped, the eastern half of Africa was slowly raised into a broad, flat arch.

The eastern side of this arch gave way, forming the Indian Ocean, and when the roof of the arch fell in there appeared the great Rift valley. This enormous crack, extending six thousand miles from the Zambesi to Ethiopia and Syria, is said to be the only thing that Martians can descry as they look earthward of a starry night. All the great East African lakes lie in the main rift, and doubtless the Red Sea and the Sea of Galilee are also part of this vast phenomenon. Later, about ten million years ago, a second rift occurred, and rifting and tilting kept on until perhaps a hundred thousand years before our era.

Recurrent change came in geography and climate. Europe and Africa were united by land and separated. Lower Egypt was submerged, and the Mediterranean extended to Persia. Finally, what the geologists call the modern world emerged. In Egypt great rivers poured down the hills between the Red Sea, and the Nile found old and new valleys. The Sahara was crossed by a network of rivers, pouring into a vaster Lake Chad and uniting the Niger, the Congo, and the Nile.

Gondwanaland, the ancient united continent of Africa, South America, and Asia, was divided into three parts by the new changes which caused the rift valleys. The radioactivity of the inner earth made the crust break apart. We can see by the map how Africa broke from South America and Europe from North America. Changes in climate were caused by the sun, the earth's inner heat, and by two main glacial periods in Africa. The rainfall varied, bringing periods of flood between the glaciers.

The continent of Africa in its final modern form has been described as a question mark, as an inverted saucer, as the center of the world's continents. Including Madagascar, it is three times the size of Europe, four times the size of the United States; and the whole of Europe, India, China, and the United States could be held within its borders. In actual measurement it is nearly square: five thousand miles long by four thousand six hundred miles wide. But its northern half is by far the larger, with the southern half tapering off. In the middle the equator cuts across Africa, and the whole continent lies mainly within the tropics.

Of the physical aspects of Africa, its relatively unbroken coastline has had the greatest effect upon its history. Although Africa is about three times larger than Europe in area, the coastline of Europe is four thousand miles longer than that of Africa. In other words, Africa has almost no peninsulas, deep bays, or natural harbors. Its low and narrow coast, almost level, rises rapidly to a central plateau with a depression in the center. Thus the great rivers fall suddenly to the ocean, and their navigation is impeded by rapids and falls.

Its five areas include the original Great Plateau with an average elevation of over thirty-five hundred feet, where mountains crowned with snow rise from thirteen to twenty thousand feet. Over these open spaces have always roamed herds of wild animals—elephants, rhinoceroses, and buffaloes.

The second area is the Great Depression, the basin of the Congo River draining nearly a million and a half square miles. Its average altitude is a thousand feet and it is the bed of a former inland sea. As Stanley described it: "Imagine the whole of France and the Iberian peninsula closely packed with trees varying from twenty to a hundred and eighty feet in height, whose crowns of foliage interlace and prevent any view of sky and sun, and each tree from a few inches to four feet in diameter."[1] In this area lies the Belgian Congo and French Equatorial Africa, Liberia and the British West African colonies.

The fourth area is the Sahara, extending from the Atlantic to the Red Sea. It covers three and a half million square miles and is divided into desert and fertile islands. In the past the Sahara was fertile and had a large population. Its surface today is often a hundred feet below sea level. In the east is Egypt and the Egyptian Sudan. North Africa lies on the Mediterranean with Algeria and Tunisia, Libya and Egypt. There are senses in which it is true that "Africa begins at the Pyrenees," and also that "Europe ends at the borders of the Sahara."

We may distinguish in Africa equatorial and tropical climates, and then over smaller areas climates peculiar to specific areas. The equatorial climate is divided into the climate of Central Africa and that of Guinea and East Africa. The first with constant heat, much rainfall, and humidity; the second with constant heat and smaller rainfall. In both these regions there is luxurious growth of plant life and dense forests. The East African climate is hot. There are savannahs and varied vegetation. Of the tropical climate, there is the Sudanese, with heat but less rain, and the desert type, with great heat but wide daily variation and little rain. Besides these, there is the climate peculiar to the Mediterranean, with hot summers and rain in winter; and to the Cape district, with more moderate summers and winters and less rainfall.

This is the climate of Africa today, but it has varied, and probably greatly, in the vast stretches of past time. The changes came with the distribution of land and water, the elevation and subsidence of land, the severance of the continent from Asia and South America, and the rise of the mountains in India and Europe that affect the air and sea currents. The rim of the great inland plateau which forms most of Africa falls to sea level near the coast and falls so steeply that the valleys of the rivers draining it do not spread into broad alluvial plains inviting settled populations. The history of tropical Africa would have been far different if it had possessed a Saint Lawrence, an Amazon, a Euphrates, a Ganges, a Yangtze, or a Nile south of the Sahara. The difference of land level within the continent brings strange contrasts.

Sixty million years ago vast reptiles and dinosaurs wandered over this continent. It became, as the years passed, a zoological garden with wild animals of all sorts. Finally there came domesticated cattle, sheep, and goats and a tremendous development of insects. As Sir Harry Johnston well remarks, "Africa is the chief stronghold of the real Devil—the reactionary forces of Nature hostile to the uprise of Humanity. Here Beelzebub, King of the Flies, marshals his vermiform and arthropod hosts—insects, ticks, and nematode worms—which more than in other continents (excepting Negroid Asia) convey to the skin, veins, intestines, and spinal marrow of men and other vertebrates the microorganisms which cause deadly, disfiguring, or debilitating diseases, or themselves create the morbid condition of the persecuted human being, beasts, bird, reptile, frog, or fish."[2]

Africa is a beautiful land; not merely comely and pleasant, but haunted with swamp and jungle; sternly beautiful in its loveliness of terror, its depth of gloom, and fullness of color; its heaven-tearing peaks, its silver of endless sand, the might, width, and breadth of its rivers, depth of its lakes and height of its hot, blue heaven. There are myriads of living things, the voice of storm, the kiss of pestilence and pain, old and ever new, new and incredibly ancient.

The anthropoid ape with the great brain who walked erect and used his hands as tools developed upon earth not less than half a million years ago. Traces of him have been found in Africa, Asia, and Europe and in the islands of the sea. Many types which developed have doubtless been lost, but one species has survived, driven hither and yon by cold and hunger, segregated from time by earthquake and glacier and united for defense against hunger and wild beasts.

Groups of this species must have inbred and developed subtypes over periods of tens of thousands of years. Of the subspecies thus developed, scientists have usually distinguished at least three, all of which were fertile in their crossbreeding with one another. In course of time they have given rise to many transitional groups and intermediary types, so that less than two-thirds of the living peoples of today can be decisively allotted to one or the other of the definite subspecies. These subspecies include the long-headed dark people with more or less crinkled hair whom we know as Negroids; the broad-headed yellow people with straight and wiry hair whom we call Mongoloids; and a type between these, possibly formed by their union, with bleached skins and intermediate hair, known as the Caucasoids.

No sooner had these variant types appeared in Central Africa, on the steppes of Asia, and in Europe than they merged again. The importance of these types was not so much their physical differences and likenesses as their cultural development. As Frobenius says: "With vast and growing weight there begins to emerge today out of the microscopic spectacles of blind eyes, a new conception among living men of the unity of human culture." Inquiring search has made clear "here Greek, there old Mexican spirituality; here European economic development, there pictures of the glacial age; here Negro sculpture, there shamanism; here philosophy, there machines; here fairy tale, there politics."[3]

Was Africa the cradle of the human race? Did it witness man's first evolution from the anthropoid ape to *Homo sapiens?* We do not know. Charles Darwin thought that "it is somewhat more probable that our early progenitors lived on the African continent than elsewhere." Sir G. E. Smith agrees with this and says that Africa "may have been the area of characterization, or, to use a more homely phrase, the cradle, both of the anthropoid apes and the human family." From Africa, Negroids may have entered Asia and Europe. On the other hand, the human race originating in Asia or even in Europe may have invaded Africa and become Negroid by long segregation in a tropical climate. But all this is conjecture. Of the origin of the Negro race or of other human races, we know nothing. But we do know that human beings inhabited Africa during the Pleistocene period, which may have been half a million years ago.

A memoir presented by a well-known Belgian scientist, Alfred Rutot, just before World War I, to the scientific section of the Académie de Belgique caused some stir. It was accompanied by a series of busts, ten in number, executed under careful supervision, by M. Louis Mascré. The busts were striking. The attempt to reproduce various prehistoric types, beginning with Pithecanthropus erectus, was characterized as "audacious," and, of course, much confirmation is necessary of the facts and theories adduced.

The chief interest of the paper was the reconstruction of the Negroids of Grimaldi, so-called from the finds at Mentone, France, helped out by similar remains found in the Landes and at Wellendorff in Lower Austria. How did specimens of Negroes so intelligent in appearance find themselves in the immediate presence of Caucasians, introducing amongst them the art of sculpture which presupposes an advanced stage of civilization? Science explains this phenomenon by the successive cataclysmic changes on our planet. For the quaternary period, Sicily formed part of the Italian mainland, the Strait of Gibraltar was nonexistent, and one passed from Africa to Europe on dry land. Thus it was that a race of more or less Ethiopic type filtered in amongst the people inhabiting our latitudes, to withdraw later toward their primitive habitat.

From the position of certain Negroid skeletons exhumed in France, some have concluded that this race carried and made use of the bow. This is uncertain; but it is well authenticated that these visitors brought to the white race the secret of sculpture, for their bones are almost invariably found in company with objects sculptured on steatite or stone, in high or low relief. Some of their sculptures are quite finished, like the Wellendorff Venus, cut in a limestone block. Of this Venus, Rutot's Negroid type of man is a replica out of mammoth ivory. The shell net of four rows adorning the head of this artistic ancestor is a faithful reproduction of the ornament encircling the cranium of the skeleton found in the Grotte des Enfants at Mentone. For the ancient Negroid woman, Mascré has gone to a figure in relief found in the excavations at Lausses (Dordogne). The marked horn held in the right hand is that of a bison, the bracelets and armlets are exact copies of the ornaments exhumed at Mentone.

These Negroid busts are most attractive and intelligent looking and have no exaggerated Negro features. The Cro-Magnon man of Dordogne is a Magdalenian, contemporary with the Negroid intrusion. The fine proportions of the skull indicate unmistakable intellectuality. The remains left by this race in the caves of Périgord reveal great skill in the art of sculpting and painting animals, whereas the Negroids of that time specialized in the representation of their own species. The daggers of that epoch, described in *Reliquiae Aquitaniae,* are engraved on reindeer horn, and the weapons underwent perhaps many practical improvements due to the effort, eventually successful, of the Magdalenians to drive out the Negroids, their artistic rivals.[4]

"There was once an 'uninterrupted belt' of Negro culture from Central Europe to South Africa. 'These people,' says Griffith Taylor, 'must have been quite abundant in Europe toward the close of the Paleolithic Age. Boule quotes their skeletons from Brittany, Switzerland, Liguria, Lombardy, Illyria, and Bulgaria. They are universal through Africa and through Melanesia, while the Botocudos and the Làgoa Santa skulls of East Brazil show where similar folk penetrated to the New World.' Massey says: 'The one sole race that can be traced among the aborigines all over the earth or below it is the dark race of a dwarf, Negrito type.' "[5]

It seems reasonable to suppose that Negroids originating in Africa or Asia appeared first as Negrillos. The Sahara at that time was probably covered with rivers and verdure and North Africa was in close touch with Mediterranean Europe. There came upon the Negrillos a wave of Negroids who were hunters and fishermen and used stone implements. The remains of an African stone age are scattered over a wide area with amazing abundance, and there is such a resemblance between implements found in Africa and those in Europe that we can apply, with few differences, the same names. The sequence in culture in Europe resembles the sequence in Africa although they may not have been contemporary.

The most primitive type of stone implement was found in Uganda and is known as the pebble tool. The same pebble industry extended to Tanganyika and the

Transvaal. This gave way to the hand-ax culture, which extended over North Africa, the Sahara, Equatorial Africa, West and South Africa. Superb hand axes and other tools are the evidence. Then the middle Paleolithic flake-tool culture spread over wide areas of Africa and is shown by perfect implements in South Africa and other places. The remains indicate a cave-dwelling people with a great variety of tools as well as beads and pottery.

During the Pleistocene period came a new Stone Age, with agriculture, domestic animals, pottery, and the grinding and polishing of stone tools. Evidence of this culture is found in Egypt and North Africa, the Sahara in West Africa, East and South Africa.

The Neolithic culture is of great significance. In Egypt it is found five thousand years before Christ. A thousand years later it changed from flint to copper. The Predynastic Egyptians who represented this culture were settled folk; they hunted and fished, and cultivated grain; made clothes and baskets, used copper, and were distinctly Negroid in physique. Probably they came from the south, from what is now Nubia. Later there came to Egypt other people of the type corresponding to the modern Beja, who lived in settled communities and used copper and gold. This brown Negroid people, like the modern Beja, Galla, and Somali, mixed increasingly with Asiatic blood, but their culture was African and extended by unbroken thread up the Nile and beyond the Somali peninsula.

The first wave of Negroes were hunters and fishermen and used stone implements. They gradually became sedentary and cultivated the soil and must have developed early artistic aptitudes and strong religious feeling. They built the stone monuments discovered in Negro Africa and the raised stones and carved rocks of Gambia. They did not mix with the Negrillos nor did they dispossess them, but recognized their ancestral land rights and seized unoccupied land. Thousands of years after this first wave of Negro immigrants there came another migration. The newcomers pushed north and west, dispossessed the Negrillos, and drove them toward the central forests and the deserts. They mixed more with the Negrillos, developed agriculture, the use of cattle and domestic fowl. They invented the working of iron and the making of pottery. Also, those who advanced farthest toward the north mixed with the Mediterranean race in varying degrees, so that sometimes the resulting population seemed white mixed with Negro blood and in other cases blacks mixed with white blood. The languages were mixed in various ways. Thus we had the various Libyan and Egyptian populations. All this migration and mixture took place long before the epoch of the first Egyptian dynasty.

There exists today a fairly complete sequence of closely interrelated types of human beings in Africa, leading from Australopithecus to such known primitive African types as Rhodesian Man and Florisbad Man. If these types are affiliated with, if not actually ancestral to, Boskop Man, the common presence of all three in the southern half of Africa is presumptive evidence that they all emerged on this continent from some common ancestral stock.

The name "Negro" originally embraced a clear conception of ethnology—the African with dark skin, so-called "woolly" hair, thick lips and nose; but it is one of the achievements of modern science to confine this type to a small district even in Africa. Gallas, Nubians, Hottentots, the Congo races, and the Bantus are not "genuine" Negroes from this view, and thus we find that the continent of Africa is peopled by races other than the "genuine" Negro.

Nothing then remains for the Negro in the "pure" sense of the word save, as

Waitz says, "a tract of country extending over not more than ten or twelve degrees of latitude, which may be traced from the mouth of the Senegal River to Timbuktu." If we ask what justifies so narrow a limitation, "we find that the hideous Negro-type, which the fancy of observers once saw all over Africa, but which, as Livingstone says, is really to be seen only as a sign in front of tobacco-shops, has on closer inspection evaporated from almost all parts of Africa, to settle no one knows how in just this region. If we understand that an extreme case may have been taken for the genuine and pure form, even so we do not comprehend the ground of its geographical limitation and location. We are here in presence of a refinement of science which to an unprejudiced eye will hardly hold water."[6]

Palgrave says: "As to faces, the peculiarities of the Negro countenance are well known in caricature; but a truer pattern may be seen by those who wish to study it any day among the statues of the Egyptian rooms in the British Museum: the large gentle eye, the full but not overprotruding lips, the rounded contour, and the good-natured, easy, sensuous expression. This is the genuine African model; one not often to be met with in European or American thoroughfares, where the plastic African too readily acquires the careful look and even the irregularity of the features that surrounded him; but which is common enough in the villages and fields where he dwells after his own fashion among his own people; most common of all in the tranquil seclusion and congenial climate of Surinam plantation. There you may find, also, a type neither Asiatic nor European, but distinctly African; with much of independence and vigour in the male physiognomy and something that approaches, if it does not quite reach, beauty in the female. Rameses and his queen were cast in no other mould."[7]

What are the peoples who from vague prehistory emerged as the Africans of today? The answer has been bedeviled by the assumption that there was in Africa a "true" Negro and that this pure aboriginal race was mixed with a mythical "Hamitic race" which came apparently from neither Europe, Asia, nor Africa, but constituted itself as a "white element" in Negro Africa. We may dismiss this "Hamitic" race as a quite unnecessary assumption and describe the present African somewhat as follows:

At a period as early as three thousand years before Christ the people of the North African coastal plains were practically identical with the early Egyptians and present two types: long-headed Negroid people and broad-headed Asiatics. Among the Berber types today are tall and medium long-headed people with broad faces, swarthy skin, and dark eyes. They have many Negroid characteristics, especially toward the south. Beside these there are short, broad-headed people.

These Berbers are the ones who correspond to the ancient Egyptians and who have close relationship to the Neolithic inhabitants of France. Among them today the Negro element is widely represented. It is in every part of Mauritania, where the reigning family itself is clearly of Negro descent. A large strain of Negro blood may also be found in Algeria.

In East Africa we have the Massai, Nandi, Suk, and others, tall, slender, and long-headed. In the case of the Massai the nose is thinner and the color tinged with reddish-brown. The Bari people are tall and the Lutoko very tall. Then there are the Nilotics in the Nile valley, extending south of Khartoum to Lake Kioga. Physically, as in the case of the Shilluk and Dinka, they are tall, very black, long-headed people, often with well-shaped features, thin lips, and high-bridged noses. The Nuba, tall, long-headed men, live in the hills of Kordofan. East of Kordofan are the Fung, with many tribes and with much Asiatic blood; and also broad-headed tribes like the Bongo and the Asande, a mixed people of reddish color with long heads.

On the other side of Africa, the lower and middle portion of the Senegal River forms a dividing line between West African types of Negroes and the Negroes of the Sudan. South of the river are the Jolofs and the Serers. With these are the Senegalese, including the Tukolor and Mandingo tribes. They are dolichocephalic with both broad and narrow noses. They are rather tall, some of them very tall, and their skin is very dark. The Mandingo, or Mandi, are among the most important groups of French Senegal and live between the Atlantic and Upper Niger. They are tall and slender with fine features, beards, and rather lighter skin than that of neighboring Negroes.

Among the most interesting of the West African people south of the Sudan are the Fulani, stretching from the Upper Niger to the Senegal River. They are Negroids, perhaps with Asiatic blood. They are straight-haired, straight-nosed, thin-lipped and long-headed with slender physiques and reddish-brown color. The Songhay are tall and long-headed with well-formed noses and coppery-brown color. The people of Kanem and the Bagirmi cluster around Lake Chad. They are broad-nosed and dolichocephalic and resemble the Negroes on the Nile. In the east and South Africa are the Wachagga and the Fang and especially the Swahili, mixed people whose language dominates East Africa. They have all possible degrees of physical characteristics from Arabic to Negro. In South Africa there are the Bushmen, short, yellow, with closely-curled hair. Beside them live the Hottentots, probably Bushmen with Bantu admixture and later with white Dutch admixture which gave rise to the so-called "coloured" people.

The Negroes in the neighborhood of the Gulf of Guinea can be differentiated at present chiefly by their languages, which have been called Sudanic. Three great stocks prevail: the Twi, Ga, and Ewe. Belonging to these are the Ashanti, moderately tall men, long-headed with some broad heads; the Dahomey, tall, long-headed, and black; the Yoruba, including the peoples of Benin and Ibo, dark brown or black, closely curled hair, moderate dolichocephaly, and broad-nosed. Their lips are thick and sometimes everted, and there is a considerable amount of prognathism. The Kru, hereditary sailors, are typically Negroid with fine physiques. The Haussa of the central Sudan are very black and long-headed but not prognathic and with thin noses.

Finally there are the Bantu, who are a congeries of peoples, belonging predominantly to Central and South Africa and occupying the southern two-thirds of black Africa. The Bantu are defined on purely linguistic criteria. The term "Bantu" primarily implies that the tribes included speak languages characterized by a division of nouns into classes distinguished by their prefixes (usually twelve to fifteen), absence of sex-gender in the grammar, and the existence of alliterative concord, the prefix of each class (noun-class) being repeated in some form or another in all words agreeing with any noun of that class in the sentence. It is the reappearance of the prefix in every word in agreement with the noun that gives the alliterative effect.

The southern Bantu outnumber all other groups of South Africa and are about four times as numerous as the Whites. They are divided into a large number of tribal units, each with its own distinctive name. In social organization and religious system they show broad resemblances to one another, but in details of history there are a number of important differences which permit of their being classified into four groups:

1. The Shona peoples of Southern Rhodesia and of Portuguese East Africa.
2. The Zulu-Xosa, chiefly in the coastal region south and east of the Drakensberg Mountains.
3. The Suto-Chwana occupy the greater portion of the high plateau north of the Orange River.
4. The Herero-Ovambo, in the northern half of Southwest Africa and in southern Angola.

In skin color the range is from the black of the Amaswazi to the yellowish-brown of some of the Bechuana. The prevalent color is a dark chocolate, with a reddish ground tint. The hair is uniformly short and woolly. The head is generally low and broad with a well-formed bridge and narrow nostrils. The face is moderately prognathous, the forehead prominent, cheekbones high, lips fleshy. The Negro facial type predominates in all groups, but side by side with it in the Zulu and the Thonga sections are relatively long, narrow faces, thin lips, and high noses.

The inhabitants of Natal and Zululand, divided originally into more than a hundred small separate tribes, are all now collectively known as "Zulus," a name derived from one of the tribes which, under the domination of Chaka, absorbed and conquered most of the others and so formed the Zulu nation which played so important a part in the political history of South Africa during the nineteenth century.

Tribes vary in size, some having from a few hundred to a couple of thousand members. Others are much larger, for example, the Bakwena, 11,000; the Batawana, 17,500; the Bamagwato, 60,000; the Ovandonga, 65,000; the Ovakwanyama, 55,000; the Amaswazi, again, number 110,000; while the Basuto, by far the largest of all and might be called a nation, number nearly half a million.

The area of the western Bantu includes the Cameroons (French), Rio Muni (Spanish), the Gaboon (French), French Equatoria, the Congo (Belgian), Angola (Portuguese), and Rhodesia, with the fraction of Portuguese East Africa north of Zambesi. This vast area is the true "Heart of Africa," the tropical rain forest of the Congo. Johnston enumerated over one hundred and fifty tribes in this area who speak Bantu or semi-Bantu tongues. The southern limit of the western Bantu is vague; the formation of the Lunda empire, the Yagga raids, and the subsequent encroachments of the Bajokwe (Kioko) have played havoc with tribal organization. The Bateke occupy a vast region on the right bank of the Congo which is now largely peopled by the Fang, who in their various expeditions and conquests have left their mark on most tribes north of the Ogowe River. Finally, in the midst of Africa are the Negrillos or pygmies, small men with reddish-brown or dark skin and brachicepahalic heads.[8]

These are but a few examples of the infinitely varied inhabitants of Africa. There is thus no one African race and no one Negro type. Africa has as great a physical and cultural variety as Europe or Asia.

This is the Africa of which Langston Hughes sings:

I've known rivers:
I've known rivers ancient as the world and older than the flow of
   human blood in human veins.

My soul has grown deep like the rivers.
I bathed in the Euphrates when dawns were young.
I built my hut near the Congo and it lulled me to sleep.
I looked upon the Nile and raised the Pyramids above it.[9]

NOTES

1. Stanley, *op. cit.*, Vol. II, p. 76.
2. Harry H. Johnston, *The Negro in the New World* (London: Methuen & Co., 1910), pp. 14, 15.
3. Frobenius, *op. cit.*
4. Francis Hoggan, "Prehistoric Negroids and Their Contribution to Civilization," *The Crisis*, February 1920, p. 174.
5. J. A. Rogers, *Sex and Race* (New York: published by the author, 1942–44), Vol. I, p. 32.
6. Friedrich Ratzel, *The History of Mankind*, tr. from the German by A. J. Butler (London: Macmillan & Co., 1904), 2nd ed., Vol. II, p. 313.
7. W. G. Palgrave, *Dutch Guiana* (London: Macmillan & Co., 1876), pp. 192–93.
8. In this description of African peoples, I have relied principally on C. G. Seligmann's well-known studies.
9. Langston Hughes, "The Negro Speaks of Rivers," *The Crisis*, June 1921, p. 71.

African Landscapes

Lucile Carlson

The land of every continent determines to a large extent the distribution and livelihood of its human inhabitants. This is especially true in Africa. There we find a vast and continuing dependence on such basics as the variables of the season, with their ensuing crop successes or failures. The extreme ways in which nature blesses and limits mankind in Africa are fully evident in those regions from which most of the slaves for America came. In this selection, Lucile Carlson gives some introduction to the immense diversity of animal, vegetable, and mineral resources that characterize a continent of new nations facing the hazards and the opportunities of technological development.

Africa is the second largest continent in the world, 11,635,000 square miles in area. It straddles four hemispheres, for both the Prime Meridian and the Equator pass over it. In the Gulf of Guinea, below the great African hump, the two lines cross, the Prime Meridian bisecting the bulge, the Equator the continent. Africa extends 37°N and 35°S of the Equator and is the most tropical of the continents.

It is a part of the great "World Island," that vast block of land made up of Eurasia and Africa, and is barely separated from Europe at Gibraltar, and from Asia at Suez. In fact, Africa and Asia were joined by the thread of land across which the Suez Canal now passes until the canal was dug and opened in A.D. 1869. Because of this, Africa is a part of three worlds—Middle Eastern, Mediterranean, and African.

Its interior is difficult of access. Littoral plains abut against plateaus onto which there are no easy routes because the rivers fall to the sea, or the plains merge into the immensity of the Sahara. Once the interior has been attained, it is still a hard land that repulses conquest—hot and humid, or hot and dry, or swinging climatically from extremes of drought to equal extremes of moisture. Huge rifts rend the surface, forming a system of valleys that cuts across well over half of the north-south length of the continent: East Africa was almost split apart from the rest of the continent in the geologic past.

There are mountains in Africa that are capped with eternal snow, one (Mount Kenya) whose flanks touch the Equator. The climates of Africa, therefore, range from some of the hottest on earth to some that, because of altitude, are polar in character. It holds the world's greatest desert, and the most impenetrable swamp. Henry M. Stanley opened up the unknown interior of "Darkest Africa," by tracing the course of the Congo River, less than 4 decades before Robert Falcon Scott was pushing across the snows toward the South Pole in Antarctica.

PATTERNS OF RELIEF AND RIVERS

Africa is a block plateau of notable extent, with edging escarpments whose abrupt fronts, dissected by streams and notched with ravines, resemble angular mountains when viewed from the sea. Once the summits of the escarpments are reached, broad and relatively flat uplands stretch away in many directions. Prominences rise upon the plateau surface, some very high. These are apt to be volcanic in structure or capped by lava. Notable among the interior mountains of nonvolcanic origin, however, is Mount Ruwenzori lying along the rift valley. Some are more like hills, and are likely to be remnants left during periods of intense erosion.

The African plateau has several times been lifted en masse, and as often undergone peneplanation. It is a very rigid piece of the earth's crust on which tectonic forces have had little effect. The relatively flat lying rock strata that form the basement of the continent are, therefore, little crumpled. Only in the extreme northwest in the Atlas Mountains, and in the extreme south in the Cape highlands has extensive folding occurred. In some places warping has left gently undulating surfaces, as in parts of the Sahara; volcanic activity, fairly widespread and yet extremely localized, has constructed mountains whose bold features stand out conspicuously within the landscape. Lava flows were associated with the formation of the central Saharan domes, and the resistant igneous rocks that represent the formerly molten deposits stand up as grotesque and tortured landforms in this arid region. Volcanic activity was associated with the rifting of the East African plateau. The volcanoes thus formed rise as majestic mountains—Kilimanjaro, Kenya, Elgon, the Mufumbiro cluster, and others; a double range of volcanoes forms the linear highlands that run diagonally southwest-northeast through the Cameroons.

The plateau extends without interruption from the bounding escarpments of South Africa northward to the northern Sahara, and from the Guinea coast to Somaliland. The folded regions in the south and northwest lie outside of the plateau.

Since Africa is a plateau, the continent generally stands high with the margins dropping as escarpments to the sea. Some of the most rugged mountains in Africa mark the plateau or rift edges, such as the Drakensberg and Ruwenzori. In general, the plateau rises from the west and north toward the east and south. The eastern and southern portions of the upland stand highest—Abyssinia and north-ward along the Red Sea coast and south, and all of the plateau south of the Congo basin; portions of the ranges of the Guinea lands and the central Saharan massifs also rise high in parts.

Between and among the higher blocks lie wide basins. The central portion of the plateau, cradling the Congo basin, is one such depression. It is separated from the basinlike surface of South Africa by the Benguela swell; in the north, the Congo and Chad basins are separated by the Ubangi-Chari upland, the water divide between Congo and Chad drainage.

THE SAHARA

The Ubangi-Chari swell slopes northward into the Sahara, a vast desert that persists without interruption from one side of the continent to the other through a band of 20° of latitude. It stretches away, a remarkably flat surface averaging from 600 to 2,000 feet in elevation but with mountainlike masses rising above the plateau platform here and there, and basins occurring as shallow, intervening lowlands. Underneath lies the African shield, as rigid and resistant here as elsewhere.

Relief in the Sahara has been controlled both by tectonic and erosion factors, and by the rigidity of the rock base. The mountains—Ahaggar, Tibesti, Ouenat, Aïr, Adrar des Iforas—are structural domes, formed by a combination of warping and symmetrical local uplift due to pressure, and volcanic activity. The latter was particularly important, and the rocks testify that these massifs are essentially eroded lava plateaus; volcanic necks, lava flows, and craters crown the domed surfaces of the ancient structures. Subsequent erosion carved the broad slopes into series of wide encircling lowlands and inward-facing scarps and plateaus rimming the domes, and of barren and forbidding sandstone and rock plateaus that sweep, in places, nearly to the base of the Sahara Atlas. The massifs and their "halos" of erosional forms make up the principal features of the central Sahara. The Tibesti plateau rises the highest; its greatest eminence, Emi Kusi, a still active volcano, mounts to over 11,000 feet elevation.

Surrounding and separating the domes are the *ergs* and *regs,* the sand and gravel surfaces that cover a large part of the central Sahara. The greatest of the sand deserts, the Oriental and Occidental *ergs,* are the immense alluvial fans of rivers; the Grand Erg Oriental of the ancient Irharhar River that flowed north-ward from the Ahaggar to lose itself in the depression of the shotts Melghir and Djerid, the Grand Erg Occidental of the several rivers that flow down the slopes of the Southern Atalas, jointly depositing their alluviums in a series of fans that together form the huge western dune desert of the Erg Occidental, the Erg Iguidi formed by the Daoura River, and the *ergs* Raoui and Chech deposited by the Saoura River.

More forbidding and less known than the central portions, the western Sahara is an immense waste where few transportation lines cross and few oases are found. Structurally it is simple, dominated by the northeast-southwest trending arch of the Yetti–Eglab that is bounded, as in the case of the central Saharan plateaus, by the eroded slopes of the dome. Broad lowlands and rugged escarpments face toward the anticline. At the base of these eroded slopes are two longitudinal synclines, the Tindouf lowland between the Yetti–Eglab arch and the arch of the Anti-Atlas, and the broad depression of the Djouf that blends into the flat and barren Azaouad and Tanezrouft. To the south and east of this syncline lie the Aouker dome and the Adrar des Iforas. The Yetti–Eglab arch stretches westward, as the Mauritanian upland, to the borders of the Atlantic.

Like the western portion of the desert, the eastern Sahara, extending from the Tibesti to the Red Sea ranges, is an immense, little traveled waste except where the Nile River makes possible the long oasis confined within the valley bottom. The strata here are generally flat lying, with slight uplift toward the east in the Arabian–Nubian deserts beyond the Nile; northward, from the Ouenat dome, the Libyan desert slopes gradually down toward the Mediterranean so that eroded scarps face inward and south. In the far north, the scarps of Marmarica mark the edge of the Libyan plateau and, at the foot of the escarpment, lie the Quattara depression and the famed oasis and desert entrepôt of Siwa.

THE GREAT RIFT VALLEY

More spectacular, possibly, than any of the foregoing features are those associated with the eastern plateau, namely, the great rift valleys with their elongate grabens and associated lofty mountains and volcanoes, and the sagging plateau that lies between the western and eastern rifts and within which lies equatorial Lake Victoria.

The upland surface of East Africa is high, edged by escarpments that may present long slopes or resemble bold, serrate mountains. The upland is a broad, level to undulating plateau interrupted here and there by hills and volcanoes, the latter isolated and impressive features. Deep ravines slash through the whole.

Horizontal force of one kind or another caused the formation of the East African rifts, which are a part of a greater rift system with links continuous in a generally north-south direction, across one-sixth of the earth's circumference from the Sea of Galilee–Jordan River–Red Sea depression to and beyond the coastline of Mozambique.

The rift occupied by the Red Sea is intermediary between the Asian and African sectors, and represents a faulted block of the earth's crust. It is bordered by the steep escarpments of the Arabian plateau on the east, and the edges of the Nubian and Abyssinian plateaus on the west. In the north, the Red Sea rift divides to send spurs along the two sides of Sinai Peninsula; in the south, also, it bifurcates, one stem being represented in the southwest-northeast trench of the Gulf of Aden, which is depressed between the precipitous plateau margins of southern Arabia and northern Somalia, the second and more impressive branch striking south and slightly to the west. The latter begins as a wide funnel top between the bisected parts of the Ethiopian massif and narrows to a furrowlike graben about halfway through the massif. The main strike of fracture faulting continues, interruptedly and generally southward, as an eastern branch across the uplands of Kenya and into Tanganyika. In Tanganyika the clear trace of rifting becomes partially lost, but is picked up again somewhat farther south as it recurves to meet the western rift. The latter arcuately outlines the western margin of the Nyanza basin, which therefore occupies a cradled position between the eastern and western rifts. Lake Victoria lies in a gentle dip in the center of this saucer-like upland.

South of the point of juncture the line of faulting passes south to southeast through the cleft of the Lake Nyasa graben, across Malawi and Mozambique to disappear under the ocean waters.

PATTERNING OF CLIMATE, VEGETATION, AND SOILS

Every day of the year, the vertical rays of the sun fall on some part of Africa. There is no landmass on earth that proportionately receives an equivalent amount of sunshine because there is no other continent that is so "symmetrically located"[1] relative to latitude. Most of Africa lies within the tropics; only the extreme northern and southern tips are extratropical. These sectors, subtropical, extend poleward from the Equator far enough to come under the influence of the westerly winds and their accompanying disturbances during the low sun period.

As Africa is a plateau standing moderately above sea level, altitude introduces modifications: the equatorial African lands that lie over and near the Equator, averaging generally between 1,000 and 2,000 feet elevation, are neither so hot nor so humid as are the South American tropics with comparable distances from the Equator. However, where mountains stand athwart winds that are drawn in from the sea onto the continent, as along the Guinea coast, rainfall averages are so high that South America can show no equivalent readings. In South America the equatorial basin lowlands are the wettest lands; in Africa, coasts backed by mountainous highlands received the highest rainfall. Great mountain systems, that act so effectively as climatic divides in North and South America and in Eurasia, are absent in Africa, and transitional zones of climate are characteristic.

PRESSURE, WIND, AND CLIMATE: MECHANICS OF SEASONALITY

Night is the "winter" of tropical Africa. In other words, diurnal ranges of temperature are greater than seasonal ranges. Temperatures are warm the year around, and except as elevations intervene or cold currents send in cooling effects to produce asymmetry, temperatures vary smoothly and transitionally across Africa from the Equator north and south. Belts of climate likewise match outward from the Equator (except in East Africa), the equatorial rainy zone merging into wet and dry tropics which in turn pass into tropical deserts, dry subtropics, and in the southeast, humid subtropics. The basic character of African climate is derived from latitude; varying elevation and trend of the landforms, differentials in continental bulk, proximity to Eurasia, and ocean currents impose the modifications.

The year-round high incidence of sunshine, low pressures, and vigorous convection make the equatorial zone hot and humid. Contrariwise, because the anticyclonic effects of the subtropical high pressure belts north and south of the equatorial areas likewise persist the year around, extensive areas of Africa both north and south of the Equator are desert. Africa is the only continent that feels the effects of the subtropical anticyclonic, high pressure belts in both hemispheres. Transitional between the belts of moisture and drought are the tropical wet and dry lands, or the tropical savannas whose climates derive from the movement inward of the bordering belts at reciprocal seasons: during the high sun period, when the humid equatorial zone with its organized disturbances and high humidity is pulled in, these tropics are wet; they are dry when the sun, shining vertically in the opposite hemisphere, pulls the desert across the land. The alternating seasons are as absolute in character as are the migrating belts that set the climatic frame.

The trade winds, or the tropical easterlies, blow toward the Equator out of the subtropical high pressure belts. Anticyclonic in their source regions, warm, and blowing toward equatorial lands, they are by nature drying winds. Poleward out of the subtropical highs move the westerlies, away from warm tropical regions toward cooler zones, by their very nature moist winds. Dominating a zone 30° or more of latitude in width in each hemisphere, the westerlies alternate their influence seasonally with the arid tropics over intervening areas, producing another wet and dry climate known as the dry subtropical or Mediterranean. In Africa this occurs in the extreme northwest and southwest. The alternating wet and dry periods of these subtropics occur at seasons directly opposite to those of the tropical wet and dry lands, so that the Mediterranean lands have wet winters and dry summers.

GRADATIONS OF TEMPERATURE

Plotting actual seasonal temperatures on maps will bring out several significant factors. It is notable that in the broad belt between 10°S and 23½°N, there are no stations that record average monthly temperatures below 64.4°F except on the East African plateaus. Nairobi, Kenya (altitude 5,450 feet, latitude 1.17°S) may be taken as a typical plateau station. Here, in July and August, the average temperature falls to 62.9 and 63.7°F respectively; on the Abyssinian plateau where elevations reach to above 8,000 feet, the whole temperature curve is thrown several degrees lower than in a lowland area in the same latitude.

North and south of this middle, high temperature zone there are no cold seasons, although both the deserts and uplands have weather during the low sun period that can be called cool. Winters throughout Africa, if the term winter can be applied here as distinct from summers (the high sun period), are to be defined in terms of moisture, not temperature, although with distance from the Equator seasonal temperature differences become greater. Contrasts in temperature between the daylight and nighttime hours may make sensible temperatures seem extreme: in humid lands the diurnal range, although normally low, can be greater than the annual; in dry lands temperatures tend to drop rapidly at night due to radiation cooling, sometimes many degrees within a short time.

These effects of changing humidity conditions, elevation and trend of uplands, situation—marine or inland, windward or leeward—and currents bring an asymmetry into thermal and other elements of climatic distribution in Africa. The contrary effects of cold and warm currents produce a lower thermal curve on west side littorals, where cold currents moving toward the Equator lower temperatures in all months of the year, than on the East coast, where equatorial currents are warming and moistening. The effects of currents upon temperatures are most noticeable right along the coast and in latitudes where cold currents parallel the shore; inland, after a distance of a few miles, the influence of the currents plays out. Warm currents touching warm coasts have only slight temperature effects in tropical lands.

Temperature contrasts between lowlands and uplands in those regions of Africa that have humid climates are sharp and considerable, with consequent greater periodicity of seasons and lower humidity on the plateaus. The Lake Victoria plateau, bisected by the Equator, is equatorial in neither temperature nor moisture; it falls within the wet and dry climate, and the drought-resistant character of the acacia grass and bush savannas reflect the semiaridity and lowered temperatures. This contrasts sharply with conditions throughout most of the Congo basin and the Guinea coast in like latitudes; desert laps along all sides of the green-crested Ethiopian plateau.

Generalized maps bring out only the broad thermal contrasts between the equatorial and tropical lowlands and the uplands of the same latitudes. They do not show the gradations that occur with ascent, as along the slopes of Ruwenzori, Kenya, Kilimanjaro and Elgon where climates pass from equatorial or tropical through a series that terminates in polarlike zones of bare rock and sometimes glaciers. Nor do generalized maps define the pattern of windward, rainy slopes and semiarid to rid lee slopes that occurs in crossing some mountains, as the Atlas from the seaward north to the Saharan south. Such maps do not prepare one for the quick appearance of semiarid vegetation as one departs from the equatorial Congo River basin, as at Yangambi or Kisangani and drives by car, north and east, into the bush savanna of Parc de la Garamba. The savanna seems to appear too soon and too close to the Equator. One is unprepared, after studying a generalized climatic map, for the chill and gusty winds that blow across the plateau veld of South Africa in July and August, at latitudes just beyond the Tropic of Capricorn. One expects the Congo basin to be distressingly hot and humid at all times; but such is not the case because the plateau character of the basin, lifting the basin to a 1,000 to 2,000 foot elevation, ameliorates the equatorial effects. Also not discernible on these maps are the contrasts in daytime temperatures between the equatorial and desert lands: daytime temperatures in the rainy tropics are not so high as are those of the central Sahara, 15 or 20° from the Equator, where, in the afternoon, the mercury can climb to 122°F in the shade, and where average daytime temperatures are not much below this extreme figure. By contrast, people have perished in snowstorms on the Algerian plateaus just north of the Sahara.

PATTERNS OF MOISTURE DISTRIBUTION

Humidity and precipitation follow conditions of temperature, pressure, and winds.

The trade winds are the most persistent winds of Africa. Blowing diagonally from the northeast and southeast out of the cells of subtropical high pressure toward the low pressure belt engirdling the Equator, the trades help to sustain the great tropical deserts that cover a good two-fifths of the continent. Meager rainfall, excessive aridity of the air, and excessive evapotranspiration are characteristic. There is no rainfall in the Sahara except from passing storms, always unpredictable in time, which may drop abundant showers occasionally over limited localities. There is no season of rainfall, no assurance even that rain will fall during the course of a given year except along the fringes where traces of rain may be seasonally predicted at the height of the rainy periods in the adjacent wet and dry lands. There are desert stations that record the passage of several years without rainfall; whatever falls is negligible. It is the heights that draw most of the moisture from the atmosphere in the deserts. But even this usually fails, and desert rivers are ephemeral in the extreme, some merely leaving scars from the past to recall a former more humid era. Such a river is the Irharhar.

Evaporation is high, because in addition to great heat, relative humidity is low. At Tamanrasset in the Ahaggar, relative humidity varies between 4 and 21 percent; while in contrast, relative humidity in New York City varies between 65 and 72 percent.

CLIMATIC PATTERN

The realm of the rainy tropics extends across a belt that is irregular and asymmetric and varies in width from about 4 to 10° of latitude on either side of the Equator; outliers extend along sections of the Guinea coast. Within the basin of the Congo River, the ever-near vertical rays of the sun, heating the earth, creating low pressures, and generating convection provide the requisites for intensified moisture conditions despite the small frontage on the ocean. Heat, high humidity, and year-round rainfall obtain across wide sectors, giving rise to an abundant verdure in most places where conditions of equatoriality occur. These are the equatorial rain forests. The rainy tropics are nature's greenhouse. Although rainfall in central Africa does not compare with the amounts spilled seasonally upon sections of the monsoon lands of Asia, nevertheless the constancy of precipitation and the conditions of high humidity create an environment that is "conservatory" in character. The warm humid air has an earthy scent.

The equatorial climate terminates abruptly in the east along the base of the East African plateau, and is almost absent in East Africa even along the low coast. Only on the lowlands of the eastern Madagascar shore does the wet tropical climate really prevail. West of the East African plateau, the symmetry of the equatorial belt of the interior becomes less marked as the Atlantic shore is approached: the equatorial zone recedes toward the north, especially along the south and markedly along the coast, compressing the span of tropical wet climate to about half the width that it had in the interior basin. The isohyets bend northward so that along the Gulf of Guinea the sectors of heaviest rainfall and the most marked development of equatorial climate occur north of the Equator. This is Africa's rainiest sector.

The rainfall of the tropical wet regions results less from the mechanics of local heating and convection, however, than from winds that originate outside of but penetrate into the equatorial zones. Two circulations of air of contrasting characteristics dominate the Congo basin. One is a southwesterly flow of surface air, present at all seasons, that originates over the South Atlantic Ocean and above the cool Benguela Current off the southwestern coast of Africa. Maritime in its source, it is a humid air current about 3,000 to 4,500 feet in depth that flows into the equatorial zone of low pressure with relative ease. Above these southwesterly maritime air masses blow the tropical easterlies, both from the southeast and the northeast, the latter affecting especially the lands lying in the latitudes north of 5°N. These trades extend down to the surface of the earth, where they flow contrary to the movement of air currents from the southwest along a zone of convergence that fluctuates greatly, changing its position not only with the seasons but "aperiodically as well. Seemingly, the stream of southwesterly maritime air varies considerably in thickness and also in vertical structure, and as a consequence its weather does as well."

There is a wide divergence of opinion as to the functions of the easterly and westerly circulations in Congo weather and also of the relative significance of the Atlantic and Indian Oceans

as moisture sources of this region. . . . Jeandidier and Rainteau . . . look upon the southwesterlies as providing much the greater part of the precipitable moisture, [and state the view that] weather in the Congo Basin depends largely upon the vertical depth and the extent of penetration by the southwest current. Even as far east as Uganda on the East African Plateau the equatorial westerlies appear to play an important role in the precipitation processes. . . . When the westerly flow is weak or absent, rainfall on the western part of the East African Plateau in equatorial latitudes is below normal.

According to Rainteau, the eastern plateau and associated mountains exert a blocking effect upon the southeast trades so that there is no significant contribution of moisture to the Congo basin from the Indian Ocean except "along the corridor" between the Ethiopian and Kenyan highlands, along which small amounts are carried to the interior. Locally the tropical southeasterlies are called monsoons.[2]

Despite the constant high humidity, rainfall in most areas is relatively moderate, although torrential in character. However, where elevations stand in the path of winds drawn in from the sea, as in the Gulf of Guinea, rainfall may exceed 400 inches a year, as in the Cameroon Mountains; Monrovia averages 198.48 inches annually. In these and other instances, topography puts the "orographic squeeze"[3] on the humid monsoonal air masses, causing excessive amounts of moisture to fall.

As distance from the equator increases, marked periodicity of rainfall sets in, and the climate becomes tropical wet and dry. Because these tropics merge on one side with rainy, forested lands and on the other with arid, barren lands, conditions within the realm are transitional. The rainfall pattern ranges from a wet and dry cycle that does not have a really dry season but only one that is less wet and is therefore modified wet tropical as at Lagos, to one where seasons are nearly equal in length as at Kano, to near desert as at Timbuktu, where for 5 months no rain falls and for 4 more months only traces of rain appear. In the southern part of the continent the pattern is much the same, going from a long rainy and short dry season on the equatorial side to a long dry and short rainy season on the desert margin. The belt from Bujumbura to Elizabethville to Bulawayo might be taken as illustrative. The extreme conditions of the two bordering climates typify the seasons in the wet and dry regions: during the months of drought, desert conditions obtain and out of the Sahara the harmattan blows; during the wet period, humid heat and rain are characteristic. Colors change from brown to green, and back to brown with the seasons.

These are the savanna lands. Except along streams, the dry period impairs the growth of tree vegetation other than such drought resistant types as acacias and bush savanna. Tropical grass is characteristic of this zone. It varies from thick elephant grass that grows to heights of 10 and 12 feet on the equatorial edges to low clump steppe along the dry side.

These lands of varying savannas stretch in a horseshoe-shaped belt across what are known as the Sudan, the plateau of East Africa, and southward, the veld, a broad but ill-defined and irregular region extending almost from sea to sea along the southern side of the equatorial rain forests. The zone of savanna is broader in the south than in the north, the more rapid advance toward aridity along the north being due to the greater bulk of the African continent here.

Outward from the deserts and their poleward steppelike fringes are the dry subtropical, or Mediterranean lands, like the wet and dry tropics intermediate between arid and humid belts, the latter in this case being that of the westerlies. Since the Mediterranean lands partake of the characteristics of the bordering zones at alternate seasons, summers are clear, bright, and dry as the desert takes over while winters bring rain as the fringes of the moist westerlies drop across the area.

Only two small sectors of Africa are dry subtropical, the tip of Cape Province in the southwest, and the coastal sectors of the Atlas lands in the northwest. Vegetation is drought resistant because it must endure through a long dry period: the olive tree with its deep taproot, the cork oak with its evaporation resistant bark, and bush (known as maqui and including a large group of sagelike and dwarf plants) live through the dry seasons.

Winters are cool, not cold, and as might be expected, temperature contrasts heighten inland with cooler winter and warmer summer temperatures. Rainfall is moderate, ranging from about 15 to 27 inches. The rainfall pattern is typified in the regimes of Cape Town and Casablanca, at opposite ends of Africa and in different hemispheres and therefore with the wet season in one coming at the time of the dry season in the other.

Most of South Africa, except the southwest corner of Mediterranean climate and the humid Southeast, is steppe or desert. The humid eastern coast of the south (the Natal coast) comprises the African humid subtropics. The warm Mozambique Current washes along this shore, reflecting its influence in both temperature and moisture. Rainfall, while not excessively high, is enough to support a tropical palm and a bush vegetation, and this subtropical Natal coast is sometimes called "the palm belt" in South Africa.

The eastern side of the plateau of the south is more moist than the western two-thirds of the upland in the same latitude, owing to the indrawn humid air from the Indian Ocean. Although the veld lands show the same seasonality in rainfall as do those of the Natal coast, year-round precipitation with a summer maximum, the plateau is semicontinental in climate and vegetation. This means that winters are colder and drier, summers are warm, and temperature ranges are greater than along the coast. This semicontinentality becomes more marked westward as aridity increases.

One other feature of African climate should be mentioned before leaving moisture. This is the effect of the monsoon control upon winds and rainfall in certain parts of Africa. By the monsoon effect is meant that alternation of wind direction controlled by the differential pressures set up seasonally on land and over adjacent seas: during the low sun period north of the Equator, a high pressure center that represents a movement inward of the permanent high pressure belt found in the southern part of the North Atlantic forms over the northern desert and fends off moisture-laden winds from the sea; at the same season, a large center of low pressure forms from approximately the Equator southward. Air moves from the northern high, which is most pronounced in the northwest, mostly south across the Sahara, pulled into the areas of lower pressures off the coast of Guinea and Africa south of the Equator. This southward pull of air across the desert from the dominant high in the north is responsible for the disagreeable harmattans, previously referred to—hot, searing, dusty winds that blow out of the Sahara southward.

During the northern high sun period, opposite conditions of pressure obtain across the northern half of Africa: the dominant Asian low, centered over the Indus valley, extends westward into northern Africa. The effect is to accentuate, along those areas where indrawn winds flow across the coast, the humid conditions brought on by the movement inward of the equatorial belt with its convectional rains. The Guinea coast and the Ethiopian highlands feel strong effects from this summer monsoon.

Preliminary to an analysis of the causes for excessive or meager rainfall we must bear in mind the seasonal patterns of atmospheric circulation over Africa. Except in southern Africa a "marked seasonal reversal of surface winds is conspicuous"—southerly winds when the sun is in the Northern Hemisphere, northerly winds when the sun is south of the Equator. Locally these are called the northeast and the southeast monsoons. "However, the seasonal wind reversal is scarcely the result of differential heating of land and water, but instead represents only a normal migration of pressure and wind systems following the course of the sun. The somewhat elusive and diffuse zone of wind discontinuity and confluence separating the two monsoons is the well-known ITC."[4]

The major controls of climate in West Africa are the seasonal movements of two air masses: tropical continental air that moves down from the Sahara between November and late April, reaching its most southerly extent (5 to 7°N) in January; and tropical maritime air that migrates inland from the west and southwest, beginning in May, to about 17°N along the coast and 21°N inland at the time of its greatest extent (in July or August). Since during the winter months highest pressures lie over the northern Sahara and decrease southward across West Africa, the winds are out of the Sahara, northeasterly or easterly, and are warm and dry. During the summer season the opposite condition obtains: highest pressures are offshore and along the shores, and decrease toward the interior of the desert. Winds drawn in from the sea bring moisture.

The two air masses meet along a front, the maritime air, because of its cooler temperatures and greater density, wedging under the continental air. Rains occur where the wedge of moist maritime air reaches heights of 3,000 feet or more. The front migrates—advances or retreats—with the seasons, and also with daily variations in the depth of the wedge; precipitation seems to be related to these diurnal and seasonal changes. Because dry air overlies the moist, the front itself is not a rain producer; rather, a belt of doldrums develops, the weather is clear with few clouds, and winds are persistently gentle. Thus in West Africa the front acts to screen out rain rather than to generate it. The tropical easterlies, which originate in the Indian Ocean and most of the time overlie the two alternating air masses discussed above, may at times produce line squalls because they are moist.

Orographic precipitation is particularly heavy where uplands run athwart the winds from the sea. This accounts for the excessive rainfall averages in the southwest (Guinea, Sierra Leone, and Liberia especially), and in southeast Nigeria and the highlands of the Cameroons. On the other hand, those lands that lie in the rain shadow of the uplands are drier than would otherwise be the case, as in central Ivory Coast and the coastal sectors of eastern Ghana, Togo, and Dahomey. A further effect of the highlands upon climate is to decrease the overall average temperatures in the upland areas and to increase the daily temperature ranges.

In East Africa "the northerly flow is made up of two unlike air streams, a drier one that has traveled across Egypt and the Sudan, and a more humid one originating in much the same region but which in moving around the eastern side of the Arabian high has had a sea track of modest length. In the equinoctial transition seasons, between the retreat of one monsoon and the advance of the other, winds are fickle and more easterly. Above the surface monsoons the winds of higher altitudes are dominantly from the east.

"In addition to the northerly and southerly surface currents there are also occasional invasions of moist unstable westerlies representing Congo air which probably originated in the South Atlantic" (see beginning of section on Climatic Pattern earlier in this chapter).

Over most of East Africa there is a deficiency of rainfall despite the incidence of the two monsoons. Reasons for this differ among East African meteorologists, but most agree that the origin of the water deficiency is found in not one but several causes. "There is general agreement that both monsoons are divergent and subsident over extensive areas; . . . the surface air flow . . . likewise is not of great depth," in places "too shallow to surmount the escarpment and reach the plateau. . . . In addition, these shallow monsoon currents are capped by another current moving from a somewhat different direction, usually easterly, in which moisture content is low but variable and lapse rates weak and even inverted" in consequence of which, if clouds do form in the lower moisture air strata they are "unable to develop and expand in the dry and stable easterly air aloft."

A further element conducive to moderate rainfall in East Africa, states Trewartha:

is the strongly meridional flow characteristic of both monsoons over the land. The southeasterly current, the moisture of the two, has had a long trajectory across the Indian Ocean before reaching the African coast, but the drier northerly monsoon has a much more meridional than zonal track both over the ocean and the adjoining land. But along the coast and over the land the southerly monsoon likewise becomes strongly meridional, so that at times it is nearly parallel to the coast or even offshore. The result is a much smaller transport of moisture from ocean to land than would be true if the air flow were more nearly normal to the coast while the lifting effect of the eastward-facing plateau escarpment is greatly minimized. It is significant in this respect that it is during the transition seasons between the two monsoons, when the air movement is more zonal and from the east, that rainfall reaches its maximum.[5]

In southern Africa climates and seasons reflect the controls imposed by the great planetary pressure and wind belts except as relief and altitude introduce modifications. Isohyets representing annual rainfall, from the Equator to about 20°S latitude, trend generally east and west; precipitation is greater near the Equator and declines southward, and shows a high maximum during the high sun period. "This expresses the operation of latitudinally migrating zonal controls such as the ITC wind systems, and associated disturbance belts." South of about 20°S the trend of the isohyets is transverse to the east-west direction farther north, running generally north-south and parallel with the coast. Rainfall decreases from east to west, the 16-inch isohyet approximately bisecting the southern sector.

This contrasting meridional alignment of the isohyets south of about 20°S reflects the waning effect on rainfall of zonal tropical controls, and the rapid taking over of subtropical anticyclones and westerly flow, with drought-producing controls in the form of a stable anticyclone and cold waters prevailing on the west side, and weaker subsidence, a warm current and more numerous disturbances, chiefly of westerly origin, on the east.

An exception to the prevailing aridity on the west side is to be found in the extreme southwest, where, in the vicinity of the elevated Cape, cold-season cyclonicorographic rains produce a limited area of Mediterranean climate.[6]

AFRICA'S WATER PROBLEMS

Water problems in Africa swing to extremes, regionally and seasonally, from excess water owing to too persistent rainfall and high humidity, or the flooding of rivers to too little water as a result of low rainfall and high evaporation, to a harsh swinging from one extreme to the other, seasonally, in the wet and dry lands. Only in the humid and dry subtropical parts can the continent be described as not being plagued by a water problem, and even in the Mediterranean lands, irrigation is a necessity for the most part, so the water problem is not absent.

In places where subsurface conditions, aridity, and excessive evaporation have caused salts to accumulate in the upper layers of the soil, a region may have not only the problem of irrigating the land but, because of irrigation, also that of drawing off the salty vadose waters at depths so that they will not accumulate. In parts of North Africa, for example, impervious layers of subsurface clay cause water to be retained at depths varying from 8 to 10 feet. Deep drainage ditches must be dug to draw off these salt-impregnated waters, at the same time that irrigation water is needed to provide moisture at the surface. Nature is lavish—and harsh—in Africa and often both at one and the same time and place. These two features of irrigation and drainage in the African environment accentuate the difficulty of development.

Although swamps undoubtedly cover far wider regions and a greater proportion of the equatorial lands in South America than they do in Africa, along riverine areas of equatorial Africa where lowlands extend away from stream edges, swamps nevertheless stretch outward for miles and miles beneath the tree vegetation. Such inundated lands are a major problem along sections of the Nile River, in the upper Niger delta, and along the Congo River and its tributary streams and lakes. Only fishing peoples occupy these wetlands in the Congo basin: their houses stand precariously along the riverfront, hemmed in on three sides by marshes, on tiny islets of moist land standing but slightly above the water in the midst of these murky swamps. The all-pervading humidity and heat, the ever-present moisture underfoot, and the thick dark drapery of vegetation overhead and all around make these swamp forests extremely dismal and unhealthful. Mangrove swamps make useless large sections of the Guinea coast and the delta lands that build up along the sea, as in the delta area between Port Harcourt and the historic old slaving port of Bonny.

At the opposite extreme are the dry lands. It has already been noted that deserts alone cover two-fifths of Africa, and if the steppelands are included in these water-starved lands, three-fifths of the continent is arid to semiarid. The problem here is to find enough water to irrigate the land, to grow pastures, and to support life. Where rivers like the Nile send their waters from equatorial headstreams across the width of the desert, or, like the Niger, intrude along the arid fringe, or like the Atlas streams rush, short but swiftly, down the Saharan side from moisture heights to water the thirsty land, or where man-made pipes conduct water across miles of arid surface to irrigate such garden spots as Marrakech watered from the distant Atlas, the land is blessed, and with painstaking work flowers and produces.

Where such obvious means are absent, where will the water be obtained to sustain life?

It may be concealed in the porous dunes of sand that billow across the surfaces of the *ergs,* to be tapped by plant roots or by shallow digging, as in the Saharan Suf. Or it may lie deep beneath the surface in the rocks, to be laboriously drawn up from 50 to 100 or more feet by rope and leather bucket, by man or animal or, if modern technology has reached the reservoir, by diesel motor from thousands of feet below the surface. This is occurring in some places in both the Algerian and Libyan deserts in association with oil development. Or water may be trapped between layers of rock—porous rocks that make good reservoirs when resting on impervious layers—and seep out as springs at the base of the reservoir; then oases will be found along the base of the rocks adjacent to the springs, as at Egyptian Siwa situated at the foot of the Marmarica escarpment. Or diligent, perservering men may hollow out cisterns on the surface, the rocks to serve as catchments for the rain that occasionally may fall, or build barrages across wadis to dam the waters of flash floods originating farther upstream. The Algerian Mozabites do this.

Man taxes his ingenuity to meet the challenge of sustaining life in the midst of aridity. A look at the map of the deserts, however, indicates the measure of success that man has had in his efforts to conquer the arid places. The oases are few, far between, and small. Each green spot, set alone and apart, is a haven of security against the cruel lack or insufficiency of water and a harsh, relentless sun. Entire caravans have been known to perish for lack of water.

Modern science and engineering are trying to utilize a small fraction of the desert by impounding water that originates outside of the desert, as in the case of the High and Sennar dams on the Nile, or along the Orange and other rivers. But were the acres reclaimed by such perennial irrigation projects plotted on the breadth of the African arid and semidesert lands, they would look minute in contrast to the area of the water-deficient expanses of the Sahara, the Namib and Kalahari deserts, and the steppes. Their importance, however, can scarcely be calculated.

Water Balance. The amount of rain that falls is not the sole determinant of how well the water needs of any given region are being met. Also involved is the area's potential rate of evapotranspiration: by placing one against the other, a "water balance" is determined from which the water needs can be calculated. This is not a direct or simple process.

Thornthwaite introduced the idea of potential evapotranspiration as a method of climatic classification; from his studies, others have followed. He defined evapotranspiration as "the combined evaporation from the soil surfaces and transpiration from plants," therefore "the reserve of precipitation." The process of evapotranspiration is accomplished by the combination of vaporization by the sun and of the "sink strength (attractive power)" of the atmosphere. The effect of the sun upon vaporization is translated through insolation (sunshine), length of the daylight period, and temperature; that of atmosphere in wind and atmospheric turbulence, and relative humidity. The effectiveness of evapotranspiration depends upon the completeness or incompleteness of the vegetation cover, and upon the moisture that is available.[7]

On the basis of water balance, a possible 36 percent of Africa may be characterized as humid; of the remainder, about 16 percent is true desert, 26 percent arid, and 22 percent semiarid. In other words, nearly two-thirds of Africa is plagued during all or part of the year by a moisture deficiency. Where seasons are based on moisture variation, as throughout most of Africa, the seasonal distribution sets limits on the crops that can be cultivated: those plants that require a growing period that is longer than the season of rains can be cultivated only under irrigation. Where seasonal changes are marked not only by moisture differences but also by temperature change and by a winter maximum of precipitation, as in the northern and southern Mediterranean extremities, evaporation is less critical, and the rainfall, although less than in the tropical lands, will be more effective. In other words, it requires less rain to grow crops in lands of winter rain than in those where rain falls during the warm season and consequently have a higher evaporation rate.

The cultivation mosaic that prevails is greatly influenced by natural conditions of the habitat, reflecting in no small measure the precipitation-evapotranspiration factor. New techniques of cultivation and the stabilization of the water supply through irrigation can, in places and at times, better the water balance even as poor methods may accentuate the rate of moisture loss. How best to procure the maximum good out of this coefficient is a problem for scientific agriculture to solve. In the extensive regions where a deficiency of water exists, there is also greater variability and seasonal fluctuation. Since an accentuation of low moisture conditions in these normally moisture-deficient regions is almost invariably accompanied by high temperatures, thereby raising the rate of evapotranspiration, crop yields show a like fluctuation. Only where irrigation is practiced on a broad scale, as in the Nile valley, can crop yields be held steady in the arid and semiarid lands; only then will yields consistently rise to above continental averages.

SOILS

African soils generally show a remarkably belted distribution closely coincident with climatic and vegetation belts. Since climate, vegetation, and soil impact upon each other, and in the case of soil and vegetation, are basically interdependent, our study of African soils will be largely an interpretation of soils from this viewpoint. This means that we will be speaking largely in generalizations that hold for wide sweeps of territory. As soon as one begins to do detailed soil analyses within small areas, however, this method will break down, because in addition to climate and vegetation, a number of other things such as topography, use and misuse by man, drainage conditions, parent rock material, insects, and animal life have their effects and often create wide soil differences within small areas. Leaching is another basic process, operative especially in humid areas, that affects the soil horizons. In some climates it operates slowly, in others rapidly, but in all places it has a similar effect—soaking out the mineral substances and leaving the soil more or less infertile depending upon the amount, rate, and continuousness of the leaching process. And yet a comparison of the climatic, vegetation, and soil maps of Africa will reveal that vegetation follows climate, and soil follows vegetation (and climate). The process of soil formation is slow. It has operated under all conditions of climate, and throughout all eras of time.

Laterization, which sometimes is applied blanketlike to all humid soils from the equator into the humid subtropics, is by no means so generally prevalent as this. Laterites develop under conditions of tropically hot temperatures and high rainfall, as do also red loams. Both have their red color because of a residual iron constituent. This characteristic of color is so widespread and striking that it has been accepted as "a universal and essential characteristic of laterites. It is always present (also) in red loams."[8] Both soil types occur in Africa. It is perhaps unwise to say, therefore, that the laterites are the soils of the tropical and equatorial zones of Africa. Rather it is better to use terms cautiously, and to speak of characteristics, instead, until further research clarifies the exact types.

Most tropical soils, although deep, wear out rapidly, losing both fertility and structure when continuously cultivated, because cultivation places a greater strain upon soil than does natural growth, luxuriant though the latter may be. Even where tropical lands have a profuse floral complex, and much humus is therefore added to the soil, soils are leached and infertile because the rapidity of decomposition, caused by the persistency of the rains and heat, does not permit the humus to accumulate in the surface horizon. If the organic material could remain for a long time undisturbed, and if the profuse plant association persisted, the soils would be rich because the plants would so continuously feed a supply of organic materials into the soil that they would maintain a supply of the soluble elements, and also support bacteria. However, once the plant cover is removed by burning and clearing for cultivation, the meager residue of organic and inorganic solubles depletes much more rapidly than it does in temperate latitudes. It takes only a few years for a soil that formerly supported a towering three-storied rain forest, whose highest species may have reached 175 to 200 feet, to become exhausted.

Across all the equatorial and wet and dry tropical lands of Africa, the problem of how to preserve soil fertility and structure is insistent. The Africans solved it by engaging in a type of shifting cultivation that is an excellent adaptation to soil conditions as they naturally exist. Two years of cultivation (generally four croppings) will wear out a tropical soil and break down the structure. To counter this, the migratory cultivators practice long periods of fallowing—to restore a vegetation cover that will once more provide humus, and that can be burned to contribute potash, at the beginning at least. The long fallow also allows the roots of trees time to penetrate deeply into the soil and bring up fertilizing chemicals from the zones of alluviation. Shifting cultivation is practiced throughout all of the equatorial and wet and dry tropical lands of Africa. Although a soil preserving technique, it is highly destructive of vegetation.

Overlooking the wasteful aspects of vegetation destruction and/or deterioration, the method of migratory cultivation is suitable where population pressure is not great; but when large populations begin to press on the land, making impossible the long fallow and continuous clearing of new lands, the system becomes impractical and precarious. Cultivation techniques whereby fertility is maintained or restored by shorter periods of fallowing, or fertilization must then be substituted. Fertilization comprises the use of commercial fertilizers, composting, green or animal manuring, cover cropping, crop rotation, or the adoption of integrated farming that involves animal rearing as well as cultivation. Most humid African soils need to be protected and restored.

To prescribe and to practice are, however, two different things, because success depends also upon the solution of many other problems. Plant a leguminous fallow (green manure) and permit animals to graze upon this land? In many parts of the continent animal rearing awaits control of the tsetse fly, a scourge across hundreds of thousands of square miles of African savannas and forests where other environmental conditions would favor animal keeping. Add commercial fertilizer? It is too expensive for most small cultivators.

All African soils are good for short periods of cultivation and long fallow, but as agriculture intensifies, soil analyses and changed techniques are needed. Not only must a right system be used, but also the right soil for the right plant culture. It is a slow process to experiment with soil usage under varying conditions of climate, cropping, and fallowing. In central Africa alone hundreds of tests have been concurrently and constantly carried out under the guidance and financing of Europeans. It is likely that integrated farming, with animals and the restorative manures, in combination with other remedies will be needed to provide the answer to this problem of soil and agriculture in tropical and equatorial Africa.

The problems incident to soils in arid and semiarid lands are completely different from those of the humid hot lands. In deserts, the first need is to obtain water to use the soil at all. Generally, desert soils are relatively rich in inorganic minerals because scant moisture and high evaporation tend to concentrate salts near the surface. An excess of these chemicals may even be harmful. Humus is low, and absent in many parts. Erosion, both by running water and wind, is another problem of immense proportions. When soil and water are properly handled, however, the deserts produce abundantly.

NATURAL FAUNA

Africa has the greatest and most varied reserve of natural fauna on earth, and the combination of African wildlife and the untamed environment that is their habitat leaves an impression of immensity and grandeur. The setting is primeval, and everything is on a grand scale: the animals graze across the vast plains of the savannas, in the valleys of the mighty rifts, up the slopes of mountains and rock faults—profuse in variety and numerous.

A century ago extratropical America was also a vast natural conservatory of wildlife, but with the filling in of the land by humans and with man's encroachment upon the haunts of the wildlife, the picture changed. The herds of bison that had thundered over the plains, supplying meat and furs and horns for the Indians without diminishment, disappeared almost to the point of extinction.

But for the setting aside of reserves for the preservation of the fauna, decades ago Africa would have followed the same way to the near extinction of the faunal species. The wanton killing began later in Africa because the European hunter with his gun did not get into the interior of the continent until the latter years of the nineteenth century, or the destruction of game would have been greater. However, in those parts where he did penetrate Africa at an earlier date, the indigenous animal life was all but exterminated, as in the Maghrib where the Romans wiped out the animals of Mediterranean lands, and when no more were available there, transported wild beasts from below the Sahara for the spectacles in the arenas. The pressure of the native Africans upon faunal life before the advent of the European (as in America) was not so great but that natural replacement was sufficient to replenish the herds; but as "the great hunters" and traders began their trophy killing, hunting by Africans—who wanted to get in on the profits that this rich booty brought—also increased.

Although game reserves and "controlled areas" have been set aside, they have not eliminated illegal hunting and poaching; both are problems. The two most serious forms of poaching are the killing of animals for the traffic in trophies such as ivory, rhino horn, and leopard skins, and commercialized meat hunting. Whereas petty poaching makes only small inroads on the game because the number killed is small, poaching for trophies and commercial meat constitutes a genuine threat to faunal populations. Further, the practice of trophy-hunting takes the "trophy," and leaves the carcass of the animal to rot where it was killed —or, possibly, leaves the animal to die a slow, agonizing death. The circling of vultures indicates the spot of such killings. Clearing of the land for safe occupation, especially in the past, also made great inroads on the reserves of wildlife.

Why is man so destructive of this treasury of wildlife that is so quickly destroyed, so difficult to replenish, and impossible to replace once it is gone? The above is only one side of the wildlife picture; crop damage and conveying contagion are another. Intruding on the farmlands, trampling and tearing up their crops, killing and carrying off their livestock, spreading disease, the natural fauna represent a destructive force that must be held in check. Crop destruction by some marauding mammals, such as elephants and hippos, is considerable; elephants are particularly destructive. Plundering by lions results in considerable loss of livestock; baboons and monkeys are pests.

The wild game are also carriers of disease, the herds constituting "reservoirs of infection"; in the various stages of development of ticks and insects, birds, bats, animals, reptiles, and even amphibians play host to many species of these arachnids and insects that infest extensive areas of Africa and to a greater degree than on any other continent; various sorts of tick fever result from the bite. The fur, feathers, and hides of the wild creatures serve as admirable places for germ carriers to hide and be transported, and the arachnids and insects thus transferred may communicate diseases not only to other animals but also to human beings.

Thus, although the wildlife in their natural habitat may create scenes of haunting beauty, men, cohabiting Africa with the animals, must protect themselves and their property from them.

Nevertheless, this rich faunal heritage should be preserved. Some species are already extinct; some strains have been so decimated that extinction is a possibility; all African wildlife has numerically declined as compared with the prolific populations that existed a century and a half ago, and as the balance that nature created is upset by further changes in the proportions of the faunal population and in the vegetation, the imbalance thus induced may lead naturally to an ungovernable decimation of some species and the ungovernable multiplication of others. Out of this an entirely new faunal complex could emerge. Sanctuaries where the fauna are allowed to live unrestricted and unmolested within an environment natural to their habits are now the only means by which the complex developed by Nature can be maintained; control over population numbers and ratios is also affected by the setting up of reserves.

NOTES

1. Glenn T. Trewartha, *The Earth's Problem Climates,* Madison, Wis.: The University of Wisconsin Press, 1961, p. 91.
2. *Ibid.,* pp. 111–112.
3. Joseph E. Spencer, *Asia, East by South,* New York: John Wiley & Sons, Inc., 1954, p. 49.
4. Trewartha, *op. cit.,* pp. 123–124.
5. *Ibid.,* pp. 124–126.
6. *Ibid.,* p. 138.

7. C. W. Thornthwaite, "An Approach toward a Rational Classification of Climate," *Geographical Review*, vol. XXXVIII, no. 1, p. 55, January, 1948.
8. H. L. Shantz and C. F. Marbut, *The Vegetation and Soils of Africa*, New York: American Geophysical Society, Res. Series 13, 1923, pp. 125–126.

Ancient Egyptians Black

Stanlake Samkange

Prejudices have origins, in many cases, so remote in the past that present research cannot be expected to explain them. Fortunately, there have been discoveries which challenge or flatly discredit one form of bias after another. As Stanlake Samkange points out, recent archeological findings indicate that mankind may have originated in Africa, and that long-lost civilizations in various parts of the continent attained levels of scientific, artistic, and sociological development equal to or exceeding those in other parts of the world during the same eras. There seems no remaining doubt that peoples with a wide spectrum of dark skin were among the governmental and religious leaders of these advanced civilizations.

Before we embark upon an examination of the Neolithic way of life in Egypt, it may be useful to pause briefly and scrutinize the people who inhabited Africa at this time. We have observed three racial types: the Bushmanoids, Negroids, and Pygmanoids as being indigenous to Africa. A fourth type, the Caucasoids, arrived in Africa from Europe and Asia around ten thousand years before the birth of Christ. Thousands of years later, the Mongoloids occupied Malagassy to make Africa a continent inhabited by all races of man.

The migration of Caucasoids from Europe and Asia into Africa in prehistoric times was by no means a one-way traffic, as the remains of Negroids found at Mentone in France, Landes and Wellendorf in Lower Austria, and in other parts of Europe testify. In *The World and Africa*, Du Bois cites several authorities who agree with him that there was once a belt of Negro culture extending from Central Europe to South Africa. These people were probably very numerous in Europe at the close of the Paleolithic Age and their remains have been found in Brittany, Switzerland, Illrya, Bulgaria, as well as other locations. They are, of course, universal throughout Africa and Melanesia, and the Botocudos and the Lagoa Santa skulls of East Brazil show where similar folk penetrated to the New World. This and similar evidence leads to the conclusion that "The one sole race that can be traced among the aborigines all over the earth or below it is the dark race of a dwarf, Negrito type."[1]

In Europe it may well have been Negroid people who introduced the art of sculpture to the Caucasians. Some of their works, such as the Wellendorf Venus cut in a limestone block, have been found intact. The migration of people to and from the African continent occurred at a time when it was still possible to pass from Africa to Europe on dry land because Sicily was then part of the Italian mainland, and the Straits of Gibraltar did not exist.

Although the presence of Negroid remains in Europe has not caused black historians to make extravagant claims on their behalf, white historians have attributed to the people of Caucasoid stock in Africa—whom they now refer to as Erythriotes or Hamites—every worthwhile innovation that has taken place on African soil.[2]

It is interesting to note that before descendants of Caucasoids came to be called Hamites, this name referred to black people. So Hamites are the only people in history who have undergone a metamorphosis, changing their race from Negro to Caucasian, without even trying.

From the sixth century, when a collection of Jewish oral traditions, known as the Babylonian Talmud, appeared stating that the descendants of Ham are cursed, being black because Ham was a sinful man and his progency degenerate, Hamites were identified with Negroes. Throughout the Middle Ages and right up to the end of the eighteenth century, the Negro was seen by Europeans, as a descendant of Ham bearing the stigma of Noah's curse and destined to be, forever, the white man's drawer-of-water and hewer-of-wood. This view suited Europeans very well indeed because it absolved them from any sense of guilt they might nurse concerning the enslavement of fellow human beings and enabled them to exploit and treat Negroes with brutal cruelty without compunction, since it was not for them—good Christians—to interfere with what God had ordained: that Hamites would be servants of servants forever.

As Europeans grew richer and richer from the institution of slavery, they became more and more reluctant to regard the Negro as a human being and yearned for scientific proof to show that the Negro did not share a common ancestry with them. The status of the black man deteriorated in direct proportion to his value as chattel, and the Negro was held to be either depraved and degenerate from his environment or a separate subhuman creation. Du Bois notes that "in the usage of many distinguished writers there really emerged from their thinking two groups of men: Human Beings and Negroes."[3] And his thesis was that this extraordinary result came from the African slave trade to America in the eighteenth century and the capitalistic industry built on it in the nineteenth.

This was Europe's attitude to the Hamites until Napoleon invaded Egypt in 1798, and his archaeologists and scientists found ancient monuments, well-preserved mummies, evidence of the beginnings of science and art. They came to realize that the origins of Western Civilization were much earlier than the Greeks or Romans. Even though the population which Frenchmen found in the country was racially mixed, Napoleon's scientists came to the conclusion that the ancient Egyptians were Negroid. One member of that expedition, Baron Denon, described the people as having "a broad and flat nose, very short, a large flattened mouth . . . thick lips, etc."[4]

Their conclusions coincided with the opinion of a famous French traveler who earlier had spent four years in Egypt and Syria. Constantin Volney wrote, "How are we astonished . . . when we reflect that to the race of negroes, at present our slaves, and objects of our contempt, we owe our arts, sciences, and . . . when we recollect that, in the midst of these nations, who call themselves the friends of liberty and humanity, the most barbarous of slaveries is justified; and that it is even a problem whether the understandings of negroes be of the same species with that of white men."[5] But how could Negroes, the cursed sons of Ham, be originators of a civilization older than that of the West? What justification had Europeans to enslave such people or regard them as a separate race?

It was at this point that white scholars, on both sides of the Atlantic, began their efforts to prove that Egyptians are not Negroes until "it came to pass that Egyptians emerged as Hamites, Caucasoid, uncursed and capable of high civilization. This view became widely accepted and it is reflected in the theological literature of that era."[6] After this Hamites ceased to be black and became Caucasoids—whites, even though some people so designated are as black as six midnights put together. Egypt was completely left out of African history, and to the Hamites was ascribed not only the civilization of Egypt but also anything worthwhile that ever happened in Africa.

Consequently, today "The term 'Hamitic" is highly confusing, and also hedged with racist overtones. It has been used in a variety of ways to denote linguistic, physical and cultural traits, and often more vaguely, reflecting European presumptions that light-skinned peoples are more intelligent than dark-skinned. For the Hamites have commonly been envisaged as the 'more European-like' of Africans—in other words those peoples with lighter skins, thinner lips and straighter noses inhabiting most of northern and north-eastern Africa. To these 'Hamites' have been attributed any remarkable technological feat, any notable political organization, any trace of 'civilization' in black Africa." Old irrigation systems, drystone walling, rock-cut wells, the coming of ironworking, the origins of the interlacustrine kingdoms, have all been ascribed to "Hamitic" invasions or influences. J. H. Speke and C. G. Seligman invented theories of vanished "Hamatic" civilizations, of "conquest of inferior by superior peoples," of Negroes being raised from barbarism by intermarriage and interaction with Hamites, and of Negroes improving themselves by copying the example of Hamites. In fact, Seligman claimed that the civilizations of Africa are the civilizations of the Hamites and the history of Africa could only be written in terms of Hamites and their influences. This, of course, is nonsense.

As Sutton points out, among the so-called Hamites are the least cultured or "civilized" peoples in Africa, pastoralists whose seasonal movement in search of pasture and water does not encourage the development of advanced material cultures of political systems. But the pastoralist, especially if he is light-skinned, has been hailed as innately superior to the Negro.[7]

But what race were Ancient Egyptians? Negro—of course! Even though there were Caucasians in Egypt at this time, there is nothing to suggest they were more numerous than, or drove away, the native black population they found in the country. On the contrary, all the evidence points to the black population's having remained dominant. This was not only the opinion of Napoleon's scientists, it was also the view of contemporaries like Diodorus, Strabo, Pliny, Tacitus, and Herodotus, who visited the country. As Cheik Anta Diop argues, "To show that the inhabitants of Colchida were of Egyptian origin and that they should be considered as a part of the army of Sesostris that settled in this region Herodotus said: The Egyptians think that these people are the descendants of a part of the troops of Sesostris I would suppose the same for two reasons: the first is that they are black and have crinkly hair."[8]

Diop charges that many Negro skeletal remains and mummies were destroyed by white scholars because the facts were too disconcerting, and it was necessary to make them confirm to previously fixed assumptions. Those that have survived, together with paintings and reliefs, confirm the views of ancient writers that the Ancient Egyptians were Negro. Du Bois also concludes "that the Egyptians were Negroids, and not only that, but by tradition they believed themselves descended not from the whites or the yellows, but from the black peoples of the south. Thence they traced their origin, and toward the south in earlier days they turned the faces of their buried corpses."[9] We are, therefore, talking about black people, Negro Africans, when, in the following pages, we discuss the civilization of Ancient Egyptians.

It is because Ancient Egyptians were black that some people believe Moses and Jesus were black. For, "how could the Jewish people be exempt from having Negro blood? During the four hundred years in Egypt they would have increased from seventy individuals to about 600,000 in the midst of a Negro nation which dominated them during that period," argues Diop. "If the Negroid characteristics of the Jews are less apparent today, this is due, it would seem, to their mixing with European elements since their dispersion."[10]

The black man's own experience of slavery in a white-dominated society in America supports Diop's contention. Few black people, if any, in America today can claim to have no Caucasian blood, while their skin color ranges from black to white. This must have been the case with the Jews when they left Egypt and, under such circumstances, it is quite likely Moses and Jesus were black. What we know for certain, however, is that Moses chose a black woman, an Ethiopian, to be his wife (Numbers 12:1). His choice is quite understandable since Moses had been brought up and educated as an Egyptian prince. In a country where the aristocracy was black, it is only natural, in view of his social and cultural background that he should have had more in common with the black aristocratic classes than members of his own enslaved Jewish race. It was presumably because his wife was, by religion, a Gentile and not a Jew that there was opposition to his marriage among some members of his family, opposition which, we are told, did not escape the wrath and punishment of the Lord.

Evidence which points to Jesus' having been black also comes from Europe where black statues of the Virgin Mary are found in several countries, and the author of *Roman Rolland Intermediare des Chercheurs et des Curiex* asks, "Why are the majority of the Virgins that are revered in the celebrated pilgrimages black? At Boulogne-sur-Mer the sailors carry a Black Virgin in the procession. At Clermont, Auvergne, the Black Virgin is revered as also at Einsiendeln, Switzerland, near Zurich, to which thousands of pilgrims—Swiss, Bavarians, Alsatians go to pay her homage. The famous Virgin of Oropa, in the Piedmont, is still a negress, as well as the not less legendary one of Montserrat in Catalonia which receives 60,000 visitors a year. I have been able to trace the history of this one to the year 718 A.D. and it was always black. Tradition says St. Luke, who personally knew the mother of Christ, carved with his own hand the majority of these Black Virgins. It is highly interesting to know, therefore, if the mother of Christ was not a Negro woman; how it happens that she is black in France, Switzerland, Italy and Spain?"[11]

If Mary was black, it stands to reason that Jesus was also black. As a matter of fact, Eisler tells us that according to Josephus, a Jewish historian of the first century, Christ "was a man of simple appearance, mature age, dark skin, short growth, three cubits, hunchbacked, . . . with scanty hair, . . . and with an underdeveloped beard." The prophet Isaiah had said of the Messiah, "He hath no form or comeliness; and when we shall see him, there is no beauty that we should desire him" (53:2), and Eisler maintains that this pen picture of Christ, which appeared in the reconstructed original (Halosis 217: ff.), was accepted by early Christians, including Tertullian and Augustine. But the picture changed when the Halosis underwent the usual corrections at the hands of Christian copyists who embellished it. For when Christians gained power and possessed authority, Christ became King. It was, therefore, no longer fitting to portray him as unimpressive in appearance. Eisler indicates that because it was feared the original text would give offense to believing Christians and their Hellenistic idea of male beauty the pen picture of Christ was changed to make him "ruddy, six feet tall, well-grown, venerable, erect, handsome . . . blue eyes, beautiful mouth, copious beard."[12]

There is thus evidence indicating that both Moses and Jesus were not the blue-eyed blondes white people have pictured and painted them. There is more than humor in the story of a black man who complained to Jesus that white Christians were refusing him admission to a certain church because of his color, and Christ replied, "Don't I know it? I have been trying to enter that church myself all these years. They won't let me in."

NOTES

1. J. A. Rogers as quoted by Du Bois in *World and Africa,* p. 88.
2. I am indebted to Edith R. Sanders for the arguments which underlie the basic thesis of this chapter. Her excellent article, "The Hamitic Hypothesis," in *Journal of African History* 10 (1969), 521–32, traces the developments and transformations in the theory of the Hamites.
3. Du Bois, *World and Africa,* p. 87.
4. Baron V. Denon as cited by Sanders, "Hamitic Hypothesis," p. 525.
5. Count Volney as cited by Sanders, "Hamitic Hypothesis," p. 525.
6. Sanders, "Hamitic Hypothesis," p. 527.
7. Sutton in *Zamani,* pp. 96–97.
8. Cheik Anta Diop, "Negro Nations and Culture," in *Problems in African History,* ed. H. O. Collins (Englewood Cliffs, N.J.: Prentice Hall, 1968), p. 12.
9. Du Bois, *World and Africa,* p. 106.
10. Diop, "Negro Nations," pp. 12–13.
11. G. K. Ogsai, "Fifty Unknown Facts about the African," p. 5.
12. Robert Eisler, *The Messiah Jesus* (London: Methuen & Co., 1931), pp. 411–21, 425–29.

The Peoples of Africa

John I. Clarke

The history of Africa and its people is a fascinating study of individuality and diversity. The origins, language, and cultural characteristics of Africans are highlighted in the following article by John I. Clarke from a book called *Africa and the Islands.* It may be helpful to refer to a map of Africa as the article is read to better identify the regions where the various African tribes live.

There is little doubt that Africa has witnessed the whole evolution of man, and that man existed at a very early period. The growing number of finds in East and South Africa demonstrate a succession from anthropoid apes of the Miocene, through the South African *Australopithecinae (hominidae)* of the Pliocene, to the East African *Zinjanthropus Boisei* and finally *Homo sapiens* of the Pleistocene. Furthermore, differentiation of human ethnic groups occurred before the Upper Pleistocene, a fact which has increased the diversity of Africa's peoples.

THE DIVERSITY OF PEOPLES

Classification of the diverse peoples of Africa is difficult for several reasons: *(a)* insufficient anthropometric, genetic, linguistic and other data; *(b)* the variety of possible criteria; *(c)* confusing racial, linguistic and cultural terminology and nomenclature; *(d)* the shortage of historical records and the 'darkness' of the African past; *(e)* the frequency of intermarriages, migrations and conquests, and consequent mixing of peoples; and *(f)* the influence of Europeans on patterns of peoples, especially the influence of slavery and the growth of towns.

In the past, ethnic classifications of African peoples have rarely been determined by physical characteristics alone; languages have frequently been employed as additional criteria. However, in recent years a mass of data concerning blood groups has been made available which is helping to clarify the ethnic complexity of Africa. In particular, a study of the ABO blood groups has revealed that Negroes have a high O frequency, and that Bushmen and Berbers have a high A frequency. The Pygmies may also offer a clue to the ethnic evolution of Africa, as they possess a chromosome (cDe) of the rhesus (Rh) system which is uniformly distributed in Africa south of the Sahara, but rare or non-existent elsewhere in the world. It has been inferred that Pygmies or a similar stock constitute a basic component of many African tribes. But the next decade is likely to multiply the volume of blood-group data, and possibly transform traditional concepts of racial development.

At present it is appropriate for our purposes to adopt the simple classification used by Seligman, who was influenced by linguistic studies and distinguishes the following main groups: Negrillos, Bushmen-Hottentots, Negroes, Hamites, Hamiticized Negroes (Nilo-Hamites, Nilotes and Bantu), and Semites. To these may be added the Asians and Europeans.

NEGRILLOS

The pygmy Negrillos of the equatorial rain forests are certainly among the oldest of African peoples, and their distinctive physical traits justify their consideration as a race separate from the Negroes. The skin colour of Pygmies may be reddish, yellowish-brown or very dark, but their most characteristic feature is diminutive stature. Adult males average 4 feet 9 inches in height, weigh only 88 pounds, and have brown body hair and protruding abdomens. The Pygmies, who live as nomadic hunters and collectors, number 150,000 in all, but estimates are bedevilled by racial mixing with the surrounding peoples, who exercise some control over the Pygmies. The material culture of the Pygmies is small, their condition primitive, and they live in scattered and isolated communities.

BUSHMEN AND HOTTENTOTS

The Bushmen are also an old African people, found in the remote parts of South West Africa, Angola and the adjacent countries. Like the Pygmies, they were formerly more widely distributed, and their ancestors may have occupied a large part of northern and eastern Africa as well as the whole of southern Africa. They are a race of nomadic hunters and collectors, driven south by the Bantu and confined to the Kalahari by the northward-moving Europeans. The Bushmen nearly suffered extinction at the hands of the Bantu, Hottentots and Europeans, and they now number no more than about 55,000. Bushmen are only a few inches taller than Pygmies, but differ from them by their yellowish wrinkled skin and narrow eye slits. An unusual physical characteristic of the women is their prominent buttocks, or steatopygia. Bushmen practice neither cultivation nor animal husbandry, and have a very low level of culture. Brushwood shelters are their only dwellings, and possessions are few. Yet the ancestors of the Bushmen are famous for their rock-paintings and drawings, which help in the determination of their distribution.

The Hottentots are almost certainly a race derived from the mixing of Bushmen with early Hamitic invaders, perhaps in the Great Lakes area. After moving south they occupied a large area of the western part of South Africa south of the Kunene River. Today, only about 35,000 nomadic pastoralists in South West Africa maintain the old tribal traditions; the remainder have lost their former customs, and many have mixed with Europeans and Asians to form the half-caste peoples known as 'Cape Coloured', 'Griqua' and 'Rehoboth'. The more secure existence of the pastoral Hottentots has probably been the cause of their physical superiority over the Bushmen; they are 4 or 5 inches taller.

NEGROES

Black Africa begins south of the Sahara and Ethiopia, and includes almost three-fifths of the total population of the continent and nearly three-quarters of the Negroes in the world. But the term Negro covers a wide variety of peoples, many of whom have been affected by an admixture of Hamitic blood and an absorption of Hamitic culture.

True Negroes are found in West Africa between the Senegal River and Cameroon. Possibly the purest types of Negroes are found along the Guinea Coast, and are noted for their black skins, moderately tall structure, spiral hair, flat noses, thick lips and lack of prognathism (protrusion of the jaws). They are grouped in a vast and varied array of tribes, which have some common cultural features, notably their gable-roofed huts, types of weapons, secret societies, artistic ability, and former propensity for human sacrifice. These were the peoples who established powerful and extensive kingdoms such as those of the Ashanti, Yoruba and Wolof.

In the savanna zone, which stretches from Senegal in the west to Kordofan in the east, the Sudanese Negroes are much taller, darker and more prognathous. Hamitic influence is still prominent despite continuous negritization. Here, tribal units are almost innumerable, but at the same time the powerful Fulani emirates and Hausa kingdoms once dominated much of the zone. From this zone came many of the Negroes who live in the Saharan oases.

In the Ubangi-Welle Basin, between the Nile and Congo, are found another group of Negroes, distinct from the Nilotic peoples and from the Bantu to the south. They are smaller than the true Negroes, mesocephalic, and usually have a dark reddish-brown skin. Among them are the Azande of the southern Sudan and northern Congo.

Other Negro peoples exist, including the tall Nuba of southern Kordofan and the short Bergdama of South West Africa, who have long been under the sway of the Hottentots.

HAMITES

The Hamites are white peoples who are thought to have penetrated into northern Africa from a source area around the Red Sea. They are proud and warlike nomads who have played a very important role in the history of Africa. Their thrusts southward brought them into contact with the other two basic African peoples, the Negroes and the Bushmen, with whom they have greatly mixed. Establishing their superiority, of which they are very conscious, the Hamites founded many of the large African states. The Hamites are properly a linguistic group; but, in general, they are quite tall and light-skinned, and have narrow faces, straight noses and dark wavy hair. They are frequently divided into two branches:

 (i) the Northern Hamites, including the Berbers of Libya, the Maghreb and the Sahara and the Fulani of the Sudan;
(ii) the Eastern Hamites, including the Egyptians, the Beja, the Berberines, the Somali and many Ethiopians.

Not surprisingly, these branches embrace a wide range of physical characteristics, despite the common anthropological base.

HAMITICIZED NEGROES

The mixing of Negro and Hamitic blood has varied greatly regionally, and there has arisen an immense variety of peoples who owe their origin to this process. They have been broadly classified, again on the basis of language, into three groups; Nilotes, Nilo-Hamites and Bantu.

The Nilotes live in the basin of the Upper Nile, in the Sudan. They are very tall, slender and dark, but their facial features are more Hamitic than Negro. The pastoral Dinka of the Sudd are an example, although Hamitic features are probably stronger among the Shilluk.

The Nilo-Hamites occur in East and East-Central Africa in Kenya, eastern Uganda and northern Tanzania. More Hamitic than either the Nilotes or the Bantu, the Nilo-Hamites also speak Nilotic languages with Hamitic elements. Again, tall slender and dark, they have few Negro features. The predominantly pastoral tribes include the cattle-herding Masai.

The Bantu are a broad linguistic group of central and southern Africa, among whom the root -ntu means man. Bantu means 'the men (of the tribe)'. Found south of the so-called 'Bantu line', which runs roughly from the Nigeria–Cameroon border east-south-eastwards to the environs of Mombasa, the Bantu have experienced different degrees of infusion of Hamitic blood, producing considerable physical variety. Hamitic features are most obvious among the tribes of East and South Africa. In fact, different linguistic groups of the Bantu tend to have different physical features.

Like the West African Negroes, the Bantu number about 60 million. Despite fairly advanced political and military organization, as seen for example in the Bantu Kingdom of the Baganda, they were, on the arrival of the Europeans in Africa, much less advanced economically than the West African Negroes, as well as in trade, weaving, pottery and metal-work. Most Bantu tribes are pastoral, and place great value on cattle, but many have suffered some disintegration with the movement of people to the towns.

SEMITES

The Semites are the Arabs, who first entered North Africa from the east as conquerors in the seventh century, but whose main invasions were between the eleventh and fourteenth centuries. They brought Arabic and Islam, and in places mixed so much with the Berbers that tribal origins are confused. Today it is practically impossible to tell Arabs and Berbers apart by physical characteristics alone. Unfortunately, the term 'Arab' is often loosely used to denote a Moslem, a native of North Africa, or merely someone who speaks Arabic. The term now has more of a cultural than a racial connotation, but it would be wrong to assume that Arabs are attached to one mode of life. Although the original conquerors of North Africa were predominantly nomads, their successors also comprise semi-nomads, cultivators and town-dwellers. The purest Arabs tend to be nomads, but they are not exclusively so. They have been active traders along the East African coast, and played a great part in the struggles for its control in the sixteenth, seventeenth and eighteenth centuries. Naturally, they have left their mark in the racial composition.

ASIANS

Apart from the Arabs, other peoples from Asia have penetrated into Africa, especially into Madagascar and South and East Africa. Madagascar poses a problem of racial origins, for archaeological evidence is lacking to help in deciphering the evolution of the complex mixture of Negro, Caucasian and Malayan peoples. Negroes prevail in the coastal zone and Malayan in the interior, while the smaller Caucasian groups are located wherever there is evidence of European or Arab settlement. The culture and language of Madagascar are principally Malayan, although the culture and language of the Arabs are also strongly represented, far more than those of the Bantu. Theories are numerous about the origins of the Malagasy peoples, but it is likely that the early inhabitants until about A.D. 1000 were almost entirely from Indonesia.

Asia is represented in South Africa by the Indian community, numbering nearly 477,000 in 1961. Unlike the Arabs, the Indians seldom mix with the native peoples. Asians from India and the Levant are found throughout East Africa where they form important urban minorities active in trade and crafts; in 1961, Kenya, Uganda and Tanganyika contained 350,000 Indians, Pakistanis and Goanese as well as 76,000 Arabs. Kenya has over 217,000 Asians, whose numbers have multiplied many times in this century. In West Africa, on the other hand, Asians are mainly restricted to several thousand traders, generally known as Syrians but coming from Lebanon.

EUROPEANS

There are over 4½ million people of European descent living in Africa. The two largest concentrations occur in the northern and southern extremities where temperate and subtropical conditions prevail: over 3 million in the Republic of South Africa, and about 1 million in North Africa. In the latter the Europeans are mostly from southern Europe, especially Frenchmen (particularly from southern France and Corsica), Italians and Spaniards; in South Africa, the white settlers have been principally Dutch and British. The differences in the origins of the European settlers, and in the period of occupation, have produced contrasts in political evolution, modes of life and cultural values. In both of these regions Europeans are deeply implanted and constitute important minorities with considerable economic power, as they did formerly in the Rhodesias and Kenya, despite their smaller numbers (300,000 and 68,000 respectively in 1960).

North Africa has received European immigrants at least since the second century B.C., although the main waves came in the nineteenth and early twentieth centuries. An important feature of the modern immigrants is that they have mixed very little racially with the native white peoples, despite the lack of ethnic contrasts. On the other hand, in South Africa the mixing of coloured and white peoples has produced a half-caste people generally known as the Cape Coloured, who numbered nearly 1½ million in 1961. Mixing has also occurred in Angola and Mozambique, but has been of little importance in the former Belgian Congo or in the Rhodesias and Malawi, where there were 304,000 Europeans in 1961.

The only other area of European colonization is in East Africa, but the 100,000 Europeans in Kenya, Uganda and Tanganyika are greatly outnumbered by Asians, as well as by the indigenous population. Elsewhere in tropical Africa Europeans were repelled at first, not merely by the climate but also by the difficulties of penetration from the coast into the interior, and by the uncertainty of rich material rewards to be found there. The vast majority of Europeans are town-dwellers; their activities have been largely in administration, commerce and industry, and their numbers in some countries have diminished rapidly after political independence.

CHAPTER TWO

AFRICA: Land of a Glorious Past

The real story of African beginnings is only now emerging. A quick glance at a political map of Africa drawn as recently as 1950 would reveal a crazy-quilt pattern of boundaries established by European nations during 500 years of colonial expansion. The boundaries and the names bear only incidental relation to the rich and varied cultural heritage they overlie.

Three disciplines have contributed greatly to the new history of Africa that has emerged.

Archeologists shifted their search for the beginnings of man to sub-Saharan Africa. In 1924 anatomist Raymond Dart had discovered the skull of a five- or six-year-old child in a place called Taung in southern Africa. Dart's contention was that the physical structure of the skull suggested an upright posture, a distinct departure from other primates. The teeth were small and square, not the large tearing teeth of the ape. These, he concluded, were the teeth of a creature who must forage with his hands and perhaps make primitive stone tools. It was man.

Dart's evidence was not widely accepted until much later, when additional and independent discoveries corroborated his early findings. North, in the Olduvai Gorge of Tanzania, Louis S. B. Leakey and his wife, Mary, made complementary discoveries in the 1950s. Recent discoveries in Ethiopia have further established the fact that men, virtually indistinguishable from modern man, walked the earth in Africa more than two million years ago.

Anthropologists sought to understand the cultural wholeness of African tribal units. This understanding was largely buried in the songs, ritual, and oral histories of the people. Linguists provided the key to this understanding by opening up a wide range of language-based material for careful examination and inclusion. The rediscovery of indigenous histories, particularly those written in Arabic, added more information. These describe a series of feudal states each having a form and substance rivaling their European equivalents.

In this chapter you will be introduced to this emergent history and to a few of the sources of the discovery.

The Authors Who Talked

Galbraith Welch

It is doubtful that any region on earth has been richer in literature than Africa. This may be surprising since the written history of this immense continent is relatively new. The explanation lies in oral literature, which was originated and perpetuated by men long before the first printed word or perhaps even before the earliest engravings on stone. These preservers of historic heritage were not mere chroniclers. They went behind the facade of facts to discern, recall, and interpret the reasons why, as well as the what and the when of events.

To the dimension of human happenings they added a rich tapestry of imagination, praise, criticism, and even mythology, insofar as myths portrayed the gamut of emotions, fears, and traditions as far back as the story of the Garden of Eden.

Reciting chapters of oral literature could take days, not just hours, and while varying with the community and the occasion, became so familiar to audiences (including crowds ever renewed with the addition of young children), listeners insisted on inclusion of any significant episode or favorite phrase which the *griot* (pronounced GREE-o), or local historian, might have overlooked. There was also much joining in for song or poetry, so that literature as spoken belonged to all.

The following article by Galbraith Welch may make the reader wonder if something has not been lost wherever oral literature has been drowned in the soundless, impersonal flood of words from the mechanical *griot* we call the printing press.

Where some wrote so brilliantly but most could not write at all literature had two manifestations. In contrast with the authors who could and did write there were the non-writers who were the designers—the wise observers, the imaginers, the dispensers of praise and criticism—the revisers and editors, and the transmitters and repeaters through the centuries of traditions and history, legends and marvels —in short, the "writers who talked."

The oral literature which these nameless, non-writing and bookless authors have given us is both a record of the past and a picture of Africa's thought and fancy and desires and fears, and it has in both phases great value to us today. It was the essence of Africa's mind.

In the bookless regions and in the old pre-colonial days the recital by a specialist was a big element in popular life. These official talkers astonished early European travelers, who reported how the speaker or bard would deliver an historical discourse for days on end, his narrative interspersed with apropos songs and pantomimes.

Such performers had power. They were the press and the drama, the literature, the history, the libraries of the people, their inspiration and sometimes their criticism. Ibn Battuta tells how at the court of Mali he observed an old custom dating from the country's days before Islam displaced bookless paganism which permitted on certain feast days a bard in disguise—he wore a feathered dress and a mask like a bird's head—to deliver a hortatory address, almost a rebuke, direct to the king. The king was reminded of the fine actions of his predecessors, admonished and urged to live up to their high example.

Experts among the bards were said to carry along traditions of their tribe and its rulers for hundreds of years, trained by retired practitioners in the art and inheriting and embellishing their memories. They operated across sub-Saharan Africa, their caste variously named in regional languages. Laing in Sierra Leone heard the bard called a *jelle;* Major Gray, his near contemporary in Senegal, speaks of him as *jallikea,* or *joulah.* Elsewhere he was sometimes *dyeli.* The term *griot* was very common and covered the history teller, the entertainer and a lot of activities, including sometimes that of a blackmailer who threatened unless he received a bribe to recite details damaging to an individual or a family. The official talker was a big man in the community in the days when the glamour of tribal institutions was untarnished by foreign influence.

Now the authority and prestige of the recited has diminished, but what survives of the narratives of these picturesque historians has been the source indirectly for almost all of our history of pagan sub-Sahara. People who cannot write provide no documents or inscriptions. The detailed past of the wide sweep of bookless Negroland must be based on verbal information.

It is regrettable that modern historians and anthropologists could not hear the tribal reciters in their pre-colonial swagger and almost sacred power and conviction. It is an art and a tribal property which has dwindled and lost authority. Students who seek to draw memories from aged folk who remember the tales they used to hear or who listen to the younger folk who attempt to imitate the old professionals meet snags and disappointments. They meet the talker who consciously or unconsciously tries to tell a fine tale, the talker who artlessly introduces some item from general history that he has picked up under colonialism's teachings—a dashing deed or phrase pillaged from far parts which he hitches to a former local hero or regional drama.

Jan Vansina, expert in the method of sifting and evaluating oral history—especially in the Congo region—warns that "there is the possibility of conscious falsification [by the reciters] out of fear, prestige and other reasons." Meyer Fortes complains that in some cases "myths and legends counterfeit history; they do not document it." Captain Urvoy, who worked over the past of the central Sudan, which includes the Republic of Niger and Bornu—now in Nigeria—noted in the old recitals which are handed down orally that the career of a popular king would be garnished with all the fine deeds of his predecessors. I quote these remarks from some of Africa's thoughtful historians and anthropologists as revealing that the study of oral history under today's conditions is a hard one, and as J. D. Fage says, "There are limits to the value of oral traditions."

But, for all that, Dr. Vansina repudiates with a snort the suggestion that "written sources are better than oral ones." He says, "This is the maxim of the non-historian." And despite the disappointments and snags oral history in bookless Africa is sometimes the only kind there is.

We can view with more ease that sort of Africa's oral literature which does not claim to recount the actual annals of kings and tribes but offers a revealing picture of Africa's thoughts and fancies and desires and deeper emotions through the ages. These help us far more than scraps of local history to an understanding of that puzzling continent now in the throes of rebirth. I wish to speak about a few of the mass of creations and revisings of Africa's talking authors—some items which seem especially characteristic of Africa's mentality—such as their imaginative handling of tribal origins, often associated with wicked reptiles and giant heroes, their revamping of the adventures of some personages made familiar by the Old Testament and the Koran.

These tales are not factually true, but they are truer than history in another sense. They show the sentiment of the people. Oral history has been a photograph considerably touched up. Tales and legends are a psychological portrait. Authors they surely had, some individual who invented or who gave circumstance to some instinctive longing or fear or vanity, or imported into the local setting some renowned name or personage.

Sprinkled across the continent one may find legends of Old Testament and Koran heroes who came in person to Africa. One was allegedly born there— Noah, in Nigeria—to say nothing of Moses, who was of course, by birth an African.

Noah, who according to the myth cited by Ibn Khaldun first taught carpentry to the world, had presumably a post-Deluge residence in the western Sudan, while another legend lands him in Morocco, where he settled down and founded a town at Salé. Salé still stands. It is across the river from the capital city of Rabat. Two of Noah's children were buried in Morocco. His son Shem, who founded Ceuta at the Strait of Gibraltar, was buried in Cairo. One of the anchors of the Ark is a treasure, still displayed at Kairwan in Tunisia.

Thus Africa's imaginative storytellers scattered and conserved Noah's memory. These were not Deluge stories about the adventures and escapes of native heroes such as are distributed across the world. They were specific references to the African performances of the individual Noah and his family. And they are not post-colonial tales. They do not come from the Christian colonial influence.

Jonah also came to Africa, though not by intent. His first glimpse of Africa was the Atlantic coast of Morocco. It was on the beach where was located the ancient city of Massa that the whale spewed Jonah up and the people of Massa revered Jonah's memory. Upon that beach, says Leo, who was there (Massa is now extinct), was a particularly sacred mosque partially built of whales' ribs, such building material being abundant because great numbers of dead whales were washed ashore. Any whale which attempted to swim in the Atlantic along this special coastline was instantly and miraculously deprived of life. This was in punishment, we infer, because one of their ancestors had swallowed Jonah, an event which evidently affected local people profoundly and inspired very imaginative local authorship.

We are told that there is symbolism in the Jonah story which interests psychologists. The folk of Massa were probably moved simply by retroactive indignation against an animal which had misused a man. A contrasting and very domesticated monster figures in a Christian legend of Ethiopia. A saintly monk and some companions traveling on a pious mission mistook one night the open mouth of a gigantic boa serpent for a cave and went inside to sleep. The boa had a drink and swallowed them. Instinctively understanding the sacred mission of his passengers, the boa took them to their destination, spewed them up, waited and carried them home again and re-spewed them. This happened, according to a legend told by Doresse, to St. Abiya-Egzi.

King Solomon was the traditional grandfather of Ethiopian royalty, the supposed founder of a Moroccan Jewish colony and the creator of a hell on earth for disobedient jinn in Algeria. It was in this last locality that Ibn Khaldun shut himself away from distractions for four years and conceived the scheme for his great history. This coincidence must have delighted thoughtful Africans of his times. There was an Arabic literary tradition that great authors had been inspired by the jinn. Sir Hamilton Gibb in his *Arabic Literature* frequently speaks of this and cites by his name and its title a Spanish Arabic writer's work consisting of "a series of imaginary interviews with jinn who inspired [according to the ancient Arab conception] the great poets of the past." There at Kalaa, the jinn place of imprisonment, possibly impregnated by their influence, Ibn Khaldun, the greatest of Africa's authors in Moslem times, was inspired.

Moses was naturally a pet of Africa's storytellers. He was African-born, traveled far in Africa—way up the Nile into Nubia and even, some said, across to Gibraltar. He was by marriage to an Ethiopian woman the legendary ancestor of Lalibela, the great Ethiopian church builder. And some even believed the tradition that he was himself a black man. It was from Gao on the Niger that the Pharaoh imported a group of magicians he met competitively.

Africa's imaginative storytellers would so interpret the Koran as to have it that Moses traveled to the western extremity of Morocco. His companion was a mysterious unknown and immortal personage, Ahmed El-Khadir, who had taken of the Fountain of Life and who enters into history as aid and counselor through the ages—he was the reputed vizier of Doul Karnein (the mythical Alexander the Great). His earliest appearance seems to be as traveling mate and adviser of Moses. They went to "the confluence of the two seas," which some in Africa have called the meeting of the Mediterranean and Atlantic, and they visited a city which was, so says an African legend, Tlemcen near the Algerian-Moroccan frontier.

We ask ourselves on what and how did the storytellers base these and many other tales about Old Testament and Koran heroes.

Was there even before the Arabs came the nucleus of parallel stories in Africa's mind which, under the influence, direct or indirect, of the Old Testament or the Koran, was amalgamated with some heroic name or circumstance in the books?

A very simple instance of how myths can shift their African dress is the story of the helpful ants, which was so old that Apuleius hitched it to Psyche and which reappeared later attached to the Virgin Mary. (The ants helped Psyche, the victim of Venus, to sort seeds of grain; ants helped the Virgin to find the needle with which she had been mending the clothes of the Baby Jesus and which she had lost in the sand.)

Did central Africans have a far older flood tradition which was subsequently mingled with the fame of Noah when they heard of his adventures and then combined with a giant of their own invention—Oudj, mentioned earlier in this book—who in his turn was combined with Moses and the Exodus from Egypt, which Oudj sought to impede and whom Moses killed?

Or did word of the adventures and heroes of Israel, of which yet more ancient counterparts have in some cases been discovered in the East and Near East, come into Africa originally from some yet earlier communications than the Jewish and Arabic book-based teachings?

There has been endless speculation, in which anthropologists, missionaries and Islamists have joined, about Africa's adoption of what we class as Old Testament or Koran heroes and Africa's rearrangement of their adventures.

If Africa's main source was the Koran some maintain that the Koran had merely copied passages inaccurately from the Old Testament.

Islam responded that it was the Koran which first told the traditions correctly and that the Jewish book had previously botched them. Islam claims to be a restatement of the true religion revealed by God to Abraham "before Israel ever was." Moslem scholars using the term "Israelite stories" to indicate Old Testament narratives, looked upon them, as a rule, as "mere fiction presented as history." I quote from a note by Rosenthal on a passage in *Muqaddimah* where Ibn Khaldun cites an "Israelite story" as correct.

Bearing out Islam's confidence in the unique authenticity of the Koran is the tradition that Mohammed said, "If Moses were alive he would have no choice but to follow me."

That the Koran actually copied the Old Testament, albeit inaccurately, is impossible, for the compiler of the Koran, according to orthodox Moslem belief, could not read (some non-Moslems differ), and furthermore the Old Testament was not put into Arabic until some centuries after Mohammed's death. But Mohammed might have heard from Jews in Arabia stories about the careers of Jewish heroes, possibly garbled.

Goldziher tells that the Jewish Bible was a mysterious thing to earlier Arabs and offers a quaint item. According to a Moslem tradition the Jewish sacred books were made up of a thousand chapters of a thousand verses each, that was to say seventy camel loads of books. It took a year to read through one part, and only Moses, Joshua, Ezra and Jesus had studied them in totality.

Africa's storytellers absorbed in various ways about which we cannot tell, and accepted uncritically, altered and to their notions improved these tales from the East. All over Africa—Moslem northern Africa, Christian Ethiopia, sub-Saharan Moslem and semi-pagan localities—legends have been invented and retold about those familiar heroes.

The authors who adopted these heroes and combined them with romances of their own designing and imported these heroes in person into an African setting performed an interesting bit of unwritten authorship.

*   *   *

To Africa in general a giant ancestor or local hero was an almost essential tribal heritage, for Africa held to a high degree the universal reverence for the gigantic. A giant represented strength. He was the early symbol of greatness and success in the days when the world seemed spacious. A ninety-two-foot statue of Ramses II overlooked Egypt. Even New York has its Statue of Liberty! This delight in the images of enormous males and females seems inherent in mankind. Jewish writings tell of an Adam of vast size. A Moslem tradition even caused his forehead to brush the skies. There seems to have been a belief even to relatively recent times that early humans were huge. The eighteenth-century Puritan divine, Cotton Mather, sent to the Royal Society, so Tylor tells us, an account of the discovery in New England of some bones which, he argued, were remains of antediluvian giants.

Africa expressed this fascinated preoccupation with giants in her oral literature, and the giants her storytellers invented made Goliath (six ancient cubits and a span tall—nearly twelve feet) seem like a pygmy. They use the familiar imagery of their homeland—giant heroes or villains who carried elephants with ease or who ate five hippos at a meal. There was one who carried four elephants suspended to a tree trunk and as he walked along ate another, which he held in his hand. There was one who bore several elephants on each shoulder, and when he sneezed uprooted the strongest tree.

These details delighted the listeners and caught attention. But beneath the grandeur of the giants was by implication the history of a people. As an example, giant episodes dealing with the Niger region are recorded by an interesting person —an ex-Catholic missionary father, part anthropologist and linguist, part lusty liver and part French colonial official—who spent almost all his life at Timbuctoo, by name Dupuis-Yakouba. (William Seabrook wrote a book about him, *The White Monk of Timbuctoo,* 1934; and I myself saw him when I was there.) Yakouba's legends take up almost seventy pages as appendix to Lieutenant Desplanges book about the same region.

A huge female called Fatimata Belle—no one had ever seen a woman so big, for her a year's sleep meant a night's rest—typified the Bellah, Tuareg vassals, who invaded the country of the Sorko, a part of what was to become the great Songhai Empire. The sandal of one of Fatimata Belle's giant sons was so heavy that a strong man could not lift it off the ground. The Sorko were dominated by Fatimata Belle until they, too, bred a giant, Farang, who slew her and her giant offspring. Farang was an immortal hero; the stories of his adventures and victories continue into the days when firearms came to the region—bullets had no effect on him. His name even became a synonym of power to such degree that in one of the Senegalese legends I find "Farang" given as the name of a Pharaoh who by insistent *corvées* drove to flight out of Egypt a group who became the original inhabitants of Senegal.

These pieces of oral literature, still unforgotten, are the overall, revised and improved repetition of history told by symbolism. Such is a legend included in the *Tarikh es-Soudan* about the beginning of the Songhai power. There came from a far place a savior who conquered the demon fish with a ring in his nose which tyrannized over them, the savior becoming the first king of an empire which endured for eight hundred years. The interpretation, albeit the pious author of the *Tarikh* gives it a religious twist, would seem to be that a vigorous newcomer vanquished the pillaging river folk—the fish with a ring in his nose— who had been the torment and ruin of the farmers and village dwellers.

Farang the giant personalized history. His adventures were the dangers through which they had passed; he himself was the surge of force with which over and over they had resisted. Deathless Farang fought giants and men and beasts and magic, each of these opponents a symbol of an enemy across the years.

It is a fine way to tell history, though it lacks the literal value of chronicles— no specified times or dates, no individual names, no definite localities. It thrilled the young and bred courage and roused patriotism.

The lively parts entertained the ribald element, such as the girl wife's lament at the physical discomfort she suffered from a giant husband who was extra-uxorious: "Do you think that a woman on whom rests a leg like his [and there the narrator attributed to her other plaints which are not printed] is not ready to die?" Or on account of Farang's attack on Fatimata Belle. He and his followers in a big pirogue traveled rapidly along the Niger and came so suddenly upon the huge woman straddling the river, one foot on each bank and bending forward to fill her water bucket, that they drove straight into "the noble parts of Fatimata." They entered into her belly without knowing it and reached the barrier of her heart. "We can go no farther!" they cried in amazement. "We have reached the end of the river!"

Eventually by nature's process the pirogue and its paddlers and the giant Farang emerged, Fatimata untroubled by the intrusion. Later Farang and the giantess battled and Farang won. Her surprising posture is supposed to signify that the Bellah invaders, whom she typified, held both banks of the Niger.

There was humor too: the giant suitor Farang stood back politely in the village street as an act of respect to the father of the girl and knocked down a house. And Farang as a decorous person was disturbed because his drawers, to the making of which had gone 333 measures of cloth (the measures equal to a man's forearm, say a generous half yard), would cover only one of his legs.

But to the sober, wise and proud old folks every detail had serious significance. They listened to the repetition of the Farang legends, which they had heard so often dramatically told and enacted by the professional storyteller, with head noddings and exchange of glances of comprehension. A color, a locality, Farang's precious guitar, which a hyena stole and died for his pains—cut into pieces with Farang's little fingernail—all this and the rest had important concealed meaning in their history. The giant was themselves. The animals which the giant fought were the tribal emblems of their enemies. The eel and hippo, the hyena, serpents, birds and the crocodile—all were associated with tribal groups and clans. It was jumbled, non-factual, non-chronological history, but very much their own.

It was a vision of history untrammeled by cold actuality, inaccurate but never sodden, quite non-photographic, but with a wider suggestion than the flat truth of the photograph and leading the listener into the past by a pathless route, the route of the emotions. Sometimes the art of pagan Africa has seemed to us similarly to possess power through its very disregard of the exact. And so perhaps the recital of these sweeping memories of a past that was nebulous but marked with their own character, vague in the habits of history—dates and names—and often supernatural, but true in its spirit, spoke to them directly and unhampered, and they understood as a person is carried along by his own identity, not the consciousness of his experiences, but the feel of himself, the "I am I."

I should imagine that one of those who listened to the legends of Farang or to many of such others in bookless Africa felt closer to the past of his people, though certainly without the slightest factual knowledge, than does any reader of history as it is written, closer than those who listened to the court recitals of dynastic chronicles. It was useless stuff as history, but rather fine art. It was history as bookless Africa sometimes knew it in pre-colonial days—not "a land without a history," as some have said, but a land where history could leapfrog facts yet mirror the truth.

Other stories were told besides those of the past. All over Africa there was a profusion of folklore and fables. Europeans listened, and many regional collections of such tales have been made and published in an assortment of European languages, also an anthology of the folklore of all Africa by René Basset, which has been called the only outstanding complete collection. (Delafosse says so in *L'Ame Nègre*.) Basset gives stories translated from ninety-eight different African languages plus a few African folk tales as imported by Negroes into the United States and West Indies, including the familiar Anansie spider stories. His anthology gives tales from all over the continent, from the Berbers and Arabs of the north to the Bantu, Hottentots and Bushmen.

Folk tales, though imaginative and sometimes containing wisdom and warning, were of limited scope and did not show the mind of Africa in its spaciousness, as did tribal oral literature. Folklore dealt with individual humans and animals, often with the interrelationship of the two. Perhaps in this regard it was the most revealing. As Rodney Needham has said, the social anthropologist when studying primitive peoples must, among other things, "accept a common nature of mankind and animals." Basset includes quaint tales about this animal-human relationship—such as the story of a Moroccan girl who lived with gazelles, a Tuareg boy who became the pet of the ostriches, an instance of a lion-human friendship in East Africa, the experiences of a woman in the upper Nile region who indirectly learned manners from a hyena, and many tales of animal-human marriages.

In the historic tribal stories animals appear not as mere individual beasts but as symbolic of important actions or emblematic of big human groups.

Animals in exalted or powerfully villainous situations, the newcomer from some far place who becomes the leader or savior, or else the coming of the whole tribe from some remote place—these elements seem to be the outstanding features in the legends of tribal origins. Often the three elements mingle in the same legend.

The conviction that they come from some far land is deeply planted in the African mind. It is said that few think their present location is their original home. Their migratory past was a proud heritage and they liked to say, "Once we came from afar off!" Alternately they celebrated the powerful personage who came from afar and organized the local people, often marrying a local female. This was probably an idealized memory of an invasion. Perhaps he was a giant. Often there is mention of some animal either as hero or villain of the episode, or as a mystic influence.

Although groups took animal emblems indiscriminately it seems as if the animals upon which the imagination of Africa's legend builders fixed as heroes, villains or expressions of mystic force were often chosen from two extreme opposites in the social order of the animal world, either reptiles or that most respectable of beasts, the domestic cow.

Here are two tales about the legendary renown of individual cows. The sacred white cow came out of the Nile and gave birth to a male child. Such to the Shilluk on the upper Nile was the creation of the human race. The first conversion to Islam was brought to Sudan by the Niger by a mysterious couple, a cow behind which walked a man.

Cattle in some tribes had a mystic value. The so-called "Cattle Fulani," to distinguish them from those Fulani who were not pastoralists but preachers and conquerors, had a conviction almost of kinship with their herds. Neighboring Negro tribes would say, "When his father dies he does not cry, but on what sorrow when he loses a cow!" and it was believed that the Fulani pastoralist could converse with his cow, could speak her language. There is a fable that a Fulani long ago rubbed his body against a newborn calf, was adopted and suckled by the calf's mother, since when the "Cow Fulani" and cattle are brothers.

In the upper Nile region there existed what Seligman called "almost religious esteem" for cattle, and between man and beast an attachment to which he gave the psychological term "identification." More recently Evans-Pritchard has carefully and sensitively described the same sentiment in his *Nuer Religion.* I like his phrase, "an enduring relationship between a social group and its ancestral herd."

The animal-human closeness in Africa may seem to us to show deplorable savage simplicity, a manifestation of that inability to distinguish between man and beast which is a characteristic of what older anthropologists like Tylor called "the lower races." It is contrary to the ideas of all three of the "book religions." To some of us it may seem to suggest, although crudely expressed, a great wisdom that we have lost.

Ancient Egyptians, who were no simple savages, attached religious significance to animals. An explanation of this which might be stretched to cover other Africans through the ages is in Henri Frankfort's *Ancient Egyptian Religion.* He wrote, "We assume that the Egyptian interpreted the nonhuman as superhuman, in particular when he saw it in animals—in their inarticulate wisdom, their certainty, their unhesitating achievement, and above all their static reality. With animals the continual succession of generations brought no change . . . the animals never change, and in this respect they appear to share—in a degree unknown to man—the fundamental nature of creation."

Africa's interest in animals centered particularly upon snakes, a preoccupation which goes against our taste but which we must view tolerantly, given our recognition of serpents in religious literature, in mythology and as an emblem of medicine.

Africa was snake land. Snakes appeared in her rock art. Her storytellers repeated tales with reptilian heroes and villains. To the snake was attributed in some parts of the continent a value akin to deification. And from antiquity her snakes were celebrated in classical literature.

Strabo told about snakes in what is now Morocco so huge that they grew plots of grass on their backs—possibly an honest report from an observer who saw the grass moving as a giant serpent slithered through.

A Latin poet who lived in the time of Nero and whose name was Lucan wrote a long account of what was to him recent history—the exploits of Caesar, Pompey and Cato—and offered a list of Africa's snakes which is said to have been "a celebrated passage," much studied by medieval readers. He lists by name and with frightening details nearly twenty varieties of serpents encountered by Cato in his march across what is now the Kingdom of Libya. Cato, seeking to protect his men, engaged members of the local tribe of Psylli, who were themselves immune to harm from snake bites and were able to cure others who had been bitten. The Psylli had in their bodies "by nature a certain kind of poison which was fatal to serpents and the odor of which overpowered them with torpor," says Pliny.

It is striking and rather puzzling that Pliny, writing about a day when Negro Africa was unknown, tells about a peculiar immunity claimed into modern days by certain sub-Saharans. Wilfred Hambly, who conducted a study of African snake beliefs on the spot in 1929–30, reports claims to such immunity as attributable to family heritage, or to membership in a secret society, or to self-immunization with an anti-venom, and lists localities where such claims are made in West Africa, northern Nigeria, among the Hottentots and Bushmen, in Rhodesia, Ethiopia and many other regions.

An African snake was the father of Alexander the Great, according to his mother's alleged confession to her husband, the snake being the physical guise worn by the god Ammon for the seduction. Alexander when he visited the Oasis of Siwa to check his supposed Ammon-via-snake parentage was led into the desert by two serpents "hissing as they went." This Arrian attributes to Ptolemy, later to be Egypt's king.

This story of the snake in the royal bedchamber is a recurrence of a very old myth about the snake's association with conception and the snake as a tempter of women. The snake which while a woman slept and was unaware had intercourse with her has been the innocent girl's fear and the guilty woman's excuse —the obvious reason, a phallic resemblance, to which add the instinctive morbid fascination snakes have had for women ever since the birth of mythmaking.

Hambly notes that there have been snake fecundity beliefs across the sub-Sahara: Mandingo, Ashanti, Yoruba, Swahili. Hottentot girls sometimes went to bed with a weapon at hand in snake fear, sexual fear.

An interest which Africans and others took in snakes and in which the serpent occupied a dignified intellectual position rather than one of lascivious suggestiveness was that of the Ophite sect, a Gnostic group already mentioned, which revered the memory of the snake in the Garden of Eden because it tried to introduce Adam and Eve to knowledge—the thwarted serpent-teacher.

The Words of the Griot Mamadou Kouyaté

D. T. Niane

The fact that *griots* have been Africa's oral historians since eras far predating the printed word might give the impression that they disappeared with the coming of books. Their numbers are indeed declining, but those who remain are as proud of their role in life as ever. They continue to guard zealously the knowledge passed on to them by their *griot* forefathers, only part of which they convey to their enthralled audiences. The *griot's* memory is so remarkable that it baffles experts on human information storage and retrieval. *Griots* were the human taperecorders of their time, and it's a good thing they were. Without them, much or even most of the world's knowledge of one of the oldest civilizations on earth would have been lost. In the following selection from *Sundiata: An Epic of Old Mali,* we can at least read, even if unfortunately we cannot hear, the words of someone who was a living history book, entertainer, poet, and musician.

I am a griot. It is I, Djeli Mamoudou Kouyaté, son of Bintou Kouyaté and Djeli Kedian Kouyaté, master in the art of eloquence. Since time immemorial the Kouyatés have been in the service of the Keita princes of Mali; we are vessels of speech, we are the repositories which harbour secrets many centuries old. The art of eloquence has no secrets for us; without us the names of kings would vanish into oblivion, we are the memory of mankind; by the spoken word we bring to life the deeds and exploits of kings for younger generations.

I derive my knowledge from my father Djeli Kedian, who also got it from his father; history holds no mystery for us; we teach to the vulgar just as much as we want to teach them, for it is we who keep the keys to the twelve doors of Mali.[1]

I know the list of all the sovereigns who succeeded to the throne of Mali. I know how the black people divided into tribes, for my father bequeathed to me all his learning; I know why such and such is called Kamara, another Keita, and yet another Sibibé or Traoré; every name has a meaning, a secret import.

I teach kings the history of their ancestors so that the lives of the ancients might serve them as an example, for the world is old, but the future springs from the past.

My word is pure and free of all untruth; it is the word of my father; it is the word of my father's father. I will give you my father's words just as I received them; royal griots do not know what lying is. When a quarrel breaks out between tribes it is we who settle the difference, for we are the depositaries of oaths which the ancestors swore.

Listen to my word, you who want to know; by my mouth you will learn the history of Mali.

By my mouth you will get to know the story of the ancestor of great Mali, the story of him who, by his exploits, surpassed even Alexander the Great; he who, from the East, shed his rays upon all the countries of the West.

Listen to the story of the son of the Buffalo, the son of the Lion.[2] I am going to tell you of Maghan Sundiata, of Mari-Djata, of Sogolon Djata, of Naré Maghan Djata; the man of many names against whom sorcery could avail nothing.

THE FIRST KINGS OF MALI

Listen then, sons of Mali, children of the black people, listen to my word, for I am going to tell you of Sundiata, the father of the Bright Country, of the savanna land, the ancestor of those who draw the bow, the master of a hundred vanquished kings.

I am going to talk of Sundiata, Manding Diara, Lion of Mali, Sogolon Djata, son of Sogolon, Naré Maghan Djata, son of Naré Maghan, Sogo Sogo Simbon Salaba, hero of many names.

I am going to tell you of Sundiata, he whose exploits will astonish men for a long time yet. He was great among kings, he was peerless among men; he was beloved of God because he was the last of the great conquerors.

Right at the beginning then, Mali was a province of the Bambara kings; those who are today called Mandingo,[3] inhabitants of Mali, are not indigenous; they come from the East. Bilali Bounama, ancestor of the Keitas, was the faithful servant of the Prophet Muhammad[4] (may the peace of God be upon him). Bilali Bounama had seven sons of whom the eldest, Lawalo, left the Holy City and came to settle in Mali; Lawalo had Latal Kalabi for a son, Latal Kalabi had Damul Kalabi who then had Lahilatoul Kalabi.

Lahilatoul Kalabi was the first black prince to make the Pilgrimage to Mecca. On his return he was robbed by brigands in the desert; his men were scattered and some died of thirst, but God saved Lahilatoul Kalabi, for he was a righteous man. He called upon the Almighty and jinn appeared and recognized him as king. After seven years' absence Lahilatoul was able to return, by the grace of Allah the Almighty, to Mali where none expected to see him any more.

Lahilatoul Kalabi had two sons, the elder being called Kalabi Bomba and the younger Kalabi Dauman; the elder chose royal power and reigned, while the younger preferred fortune and wealth and became the ancestor of those who go from country to country seeking their fortune.

Kalabi Bomba had Mamadi Kani for a son. Mamadi Kani was a hunter king like the first kings of Mali. It was he who invented the hunter's whistle;[5] he communicated with the jinn of the forest and bush. These spirits had no secrets from him and he was loved by Kondolon Ni Sané.[6] His followers were so numerous that he formed them into an army which became formidable; he often gathered them together in the bush and taught them the art of hunting. It was he who revealed to hunters the medicinal leaves which heal wounds and cure diseases. Thanks to the strength of his followers, he became king of a vast country; with them Mamadi Kani conquered all the lands which stretch from the Sankarani to the Bouré. Mamadi Kani had four sons—Kani Simbon, Kamignogo Simbon, Kabala Simbon and Simbon Tagnogokelin. They were all initiated into the art of hunting and deserved the title of Simbon. It was the lineage of Bamari Tagnogokelin which held on to the power; his son was M'Bali Nènè whose son was Bello. Bello's son was called Bello Bakon and he had a son called Maghan Kon Fatta, also called Frako Maghan Keigu, Maghan the handsome.

Maghan Kon Fatta was the father of the great Sundiata and had three wives and six children—three boys and three girls. His first wife was called Sassouma Bérété, daughter of a great divine; she was the mother of King Dankaran Touman and Princess Nana Triban. The second wife, Sogolon Kedjou, was the mother of Sundiata and the two princesses Sogolon Kolonkan and Sogolon Djamarou. The third wife was one of the Kamaras and was called Namandjé; she was the mother of Manding Bory (or Manding Bakary), who was the best friend of his half-brother Sundiata.

*   *   *

ETERNAL MALI

How many piled-up ruins, how much buried splendour! But all the deeds I have spoken of took place long ago and they all had Mali as their background. Kings have succeeded kings, but Mali has always remained the same.

Mali keeps its secrets jealously. There are things which the uninitiated will never know, for the griots, their depositaries, will never betray them. Maghan Sundiata, the last conqueror on earth, lies not far from Niani-Niani at Baland-ougou, the weir town.[7]

After him many kings and many Mansas reigned over Mali and other towns sprang up and disappeared. Hajji Mansa Moussa, of illustrious memory, beloved of God, built houses at Mecca for pilgrims coming from Mali, but the towns which he founded have all disappeared, Karanina, Bouroun-Kouna—nothing more remains of these towns. Other kings carried Mali far beyond Djata's frontiers, for example Mansa Samanka and Fadima Moussa, but none of them came near Djata.[8]

Maghan Sundiata was unique. In his own time no one equalled him and after him no one had the ambition to surpass him. He left his mark on Mali for all time and his taboos still guide men in their conduct.

Mali is eternal. To convince yourself of what I have said go to Mali. At Tigan you will find the forest dear to Sundiata. There you will see Fakoli Koroma's plastron. Go to Kirikoroni near Niassola and you will see a tree which commemorates Sundiata's passing through these parts. Go to Bankoumana on the Niger and you will see Soumaoro's balafon, the balafon which is called Balguintiri. Go to Ka-ba and you will see the clearing of Kouroukan Fougan, where the great assembly took place which gave Sundiata's empire its constitution. Go to Krina near Ka-ba and you will see the bird that foretold the end to Soumaoro. At Keyla, near Ka-ba, you will find the royal drums belonging to Djolofin Mansa, king of Senegal, whom Djata defeated. But never try, wretch, to pierce the mystery which Mali hides from you. Do not go and disturb the spirits in their eternal rest. Do not ever go into the dead cities to question the past, for the spirits never forgive. Do not seek to know what is not to be known.

*   *   *

Men of today, how small you are beside your ancestors, and small in mind too, for you have trouble in grasping the meaning of my words. Sundiata rests near Niani-Niani, but his spirit lives on and today the Keitas still come and bow before the stone under which lies the father of Mali.

To acquire my knowledge I have journeyed all round Mali. At Kita I saw the mountain where the lake of holy water sleeps; at Segou, I learnt the history of the kings of Do and Kri; at Fadama, in Hamana, I heard the Kondé griots relate how the Keitas, Kondés and Kamaras conquered Wouroula.[9] At Keyla, the village of the great masters, I learnt the origins of Mali and the art of speaking. Everywhere I was able to see and understand what my masters were teaching me, but between their hands I took an oath to teach only what is to be taught and to conceal what is to be kept concealed.

NOTES

1. The twelve doors of Mali refer to the twelve provinces of which Mali was originally composed. After Sundiata's conquests the number of conquests increased considerably. Early Mali seems to have been a confederation of the chief Mandingo tribes: Keita, Kondé, Traoré, Kamara and Koroma. D.T.N.
2. According to tradition Sundiata's mother had a buffalo for a totem, namely the fabulous buffalo which, it is said, ravaged the land of Do. The lion is the totem and ancestor of the Keitas. Thus, through his father Sundiata is the son of the lion, and through his mother, the son of the buffalo. D.T.N.
3. I have used this word 'Mandingo' to mean the people who inhabited Mali and their language, and as an adjective to mean anything pertaining to these people, though the adjective 'Mandingan' exists too. Old Mali, where much of the action of this story takes place, is a vaguely defined area between the Niger and Sankarani rivers and should not be confused with the modern Republic of Mali of which it is only a fraction. G.D.P.

The inhabitants of Mali call themselves Maninka or Mandinka. Malli and Malinke are the Fulani deformations of the words Manding and Mandinka respectively. 'Mali' in the Mandingo language means 'a hippopotamus' and it is not impossible that Mali was the name given to one of the capitals of the emperors. One tradition tells us that Sundiata changed himself into a hippopotamus in the Sankarani river. So it is not astonishing to find villages in old Mali which have 'Mali' for a name. This name could have formerly been that of a city. In old Mali there is one village called Malikoma, i.e. New Mali. D.T.N.
4. Bilali Bounama was the first muezzin and the Companion of the Prophet Muhammad. Like most medieval Muslim dynasties, the Mali emperors were careful to link themselves with the Prophet's family, or at least with someone near to him. In the fourteenth century we will see Mansa Moussa return to Mali after his pilgrimage with some representatives of the Arab tribe of Qureish (Muhammad's tribe) in order to bring down the Prophet of God's blessing on his empire. After Kankan Moussa, several princes of Mali were to imitate him, notably Askia Muhammad in the sixteenth century. D.T.N.

This Askia Muhammad (1493–1528) ruled the Songhay Empire which overran that of Mali, but Muhammad's surname—Touré—indicates his Mandingo origin and in this sense he can be styled a 'prince of Mali'. G.D.P.
5. The Mandingo word is 'Simbon' and it literally means 'a hunter's whistle', but it is also used as an honorific title to denote a great hunter, a title which Sundiata later bore. The funeral wake which the hunters of a district organize in honour of a dead colleague is called 'Simbon-si'. D.T.N.
6. Kondolon Ni Sané is a dual hunting deity. Kondolon is a god of the chase and has Sané as an inseparable companion. These two deities are always linked and they are invoked as a pair. This dual deity has the property of being everywhere at once and when it reveals itself to the hunter the latter frequently comes across game. The guardianship of the bush and forest devolves on this deity and it is also the symbol of union and friendship. One must never invoke them separately at the risk of

incurring very severe punishments. The two deities sometimes rival each other in skill but never fall out. In Hamana (Kouroussa) Mamadi Kani is accredited with the oath which the hunter takes before being received as a Simbon. Here is the oath: (a) Will you resolve to satisfy Kondolon Ni Sané before your own father? (i.e. one should opt for the Master Hunter when confronted with an order from him and a conflicting order from one's own father.) (b) Will you learn that respect does not mean slavery and give respect and submission at all times to your Master Hunter? (c) Will you learn that cola is good, tobacco is good, honey is sweet, etc.—and give them over to your Master? If the answer is 'yes' the apprentice hunter is accepted. In certain provinces of Siguiri, this oath is attributed to a certain Allah Mamadi who was not a king. D.T.N.

7. Here Djeli Mamadou Kouyaté declined to go any further. However, there are many accounts of Sundiata's end. The first says that Sundiata was killed by an arrow in the course of public demonstration in Niani. The second, very popular in Mali, is rendered feasible by the presence of Sundiata's tomb near the Sankarani. According to the second account Sundiata was drowned in the Sankarani and was buried near the very place where he was drowned. I have heard this version from the mouths of several traditionists, but following what events did Sundiata meet his death in the waters? That is the question to which a reply must be found. D.T.N.

8. Here Djeli Mamadou Kouyaté mentions several kings of Mali. Hajji Mansa Moussa is no other than the famous Kankan Moussa (1307–1332) made for ever illustrious by his celebrated pilgrimage in 1325. The Dioma tradition attributes to Kankan Moussa the foundation of many towns which have now disappeared. D.T.N.

9. Griot traditionists travel a great deal before being 'Belen-Tigui'—Master of Speech in Mandingo. This expression is formed from 'belen', which is the name for the tree-trunk planted in the middle of the public square and on which the orator rests when he is addressing the crowd. 'Tigui' means 'master of'. There are several famous centres for the study of history, e.g. Fadama in Hamana (Kouroussa), situated on the right bank of the Niandan opposite Baro; but more especially Keyla, the town of traditionists; and Diabaté near Kangaba (Ka-ba), Republic of Mali. Mamadou Kouyaté is from the village of Djeliba Koro in Dioma (south of Siguiri), a province inhabited by the Keitas who came from Kita at the end of the fourteenth century and the beginning of the fifteenth century (see my *Diplôme d'Etudes Superieures*). D.T.N.

Hominids in Africa

Richard E. Leakey

Few mysteries intrigue man more than the source and scene of his origin. Viewpoints ranging from those of religious fundamentalists to strictly objective scientists may differ indefinitely as to the creation. But the *area* of man's origin seems increasingly to be above disagreement. It was Africa, in the opinions of many archeologists and anthropologists. One of these is Richard E. Leakey, son of Louis and Mary Leakey, director of the National Museums of Kenya and a paleoanthropologist well known for his fossil discoveries in eastern Africa. The following is from an address given by Leakey in November 1975.

The existing fossil evidence supports the contention that Africa was the crucible of human origins and development. African sites yield evidence illustrating many phases of the human story from the earliest stages. . . .

TOOLS AND HABITATIONS

The most impressive record of tools and habitation sites is from Olduvai Gorge, where numerous localities have been excavated over the past 30 years. The progression from simple "pebble tools" to intricate and perfect bifacial implements is well documented in this one area. There are also inferences to be drawn on the probable social organization, in the sense of community size and hunting preferences. At one locality, remains of a stone structure—perhaps the base of a circular hut—were uncovered; there is an excellent date of 1.8 million years for this. The threshold of technological ability is difficult to pinpoint exactly, and at best one could only suggest that it occurred during the Pliocene, perhaps in relation to the adaptive response embodied by the differentiation of *Homo*.

During the early Pleistocene, circa 1.6 million years ago, bifacial tools such as crude handaxes make their appearance. This development can be traced in situ at Olduvai and is supported by findings from other East African sites. The first record of stone implements in Asia and Europe is of handaxes, but, unfortunately, no absolute dates are known for them at the present time. In my opinion, the evidence available could suggest a migration of the "handaxe" people—perhaps *Homo erectus*—from Africa into Europe, Asia, and the Far East during the early Pleistocene, or a little earlier. The subsequent development of stone implements is complex, with impressive late Pleistocene and Holocene records from most of the world. It is not proven but can be postulated that the post-Acheulean, or handaxe, technologies can be related to the emergence of *Homo sapiens* and the subsequent success of this species. The association of stone implements with early hominid remains is rare, and many mid-Pleistocene and subsequent sites contain only one or two specimens, with certain impressive exceptions. The earliest record of *Homo sapiens* remains a problem because of the limitations imposed both by the small samples and by the dating techniques that can be employed.

It is clear that extraordinary advances have been made in recent years in our data records, and continuing investigations will presumably provide further evidence. There is now obvious evidence for considerable morphological diversity in the Plio/Pleistocene hominids of Africa, which has been interpreted as a consequence of a Pliocene radiation with different evolutionary experiments persisting into the early Pleistocene. The presence of at least three contemporary species in East Africa may be established on both cranial and postcranial material, and any review must incorporate the analysis of the entire fossil collection. The problem of whether two closely related and competing species could live side by side will be better understood when further studies are completed on paleoecological evidence, including palynology and micropaleontology under closely documented stratigraphy. It is known that several closely allied and morphologically similar ceropithecoid monkeys live alongside one another in African forests today, with no suggestion of mutual exclusion.

Darwin seems to be vindicated for his prophesy on the African origin for man. Many great scientists—Robert Broom, Raymond Dart, and Louis Leakey among them—were pioneers in the field which today has so captured the popular imagination. As the ancient record builds up with each new fossil find, we are reminded that extinction is a common phenomenon in vertebrate evolution—and modern man may be no exception.

Precolonial African History

Philip D. Curtin

Western involvement in World War II provided the beginnings of a global view of history by a largely isolationist United States and a perpetually interventionist Europe. That catastrophic conflict, with its inter-hemispheric air attacks, forced a realization that other continents were vital not merely for exploitation but as sources of manpower, materials, and morale. The historic shift in attitude is reported in this article by Philip D. Curtin, from a pamphlet of the American Historical Association entitled "Precolonial African History."

THE EMERGENCE OF AFRICAN HISTORY

America's new position in the world after 1945 called for a new perspective. Before the Second World War we could take a sea-based view of the world. Maps showed a Western Hemisphere, conveniently isolated behind a moat of oceans. But in terms of the air age these maps were seriously distorted. They were not even centered on the United States but on a point in the Pacific Ocean near the Galapagos Islands. After the war a new look at the globe showed that the bulge of Africa and the bulge of Brazil were about equally far away. Viewed from New York, Timbuktu, that ancient symbol of inaccessibility, was shown to be closer than Buenos Aires.

Our earlier view of world history was equally distorted. It, too, needed a change of perspective that would show more accurately how the modern world came to be as it is. Like the hemispheric map of an isolated America, the older history showed only part of the truth. Many human societies remained beyond the horizon. Instead of trying to explain the modern world in terms of its past or even tracing the rise of human civilizations, the older "world history" began with the United States and then searched for the roots of American civilization. It was, in effect, "history taught backward"—back to the colonial period on this continent, then back to Europe, and still further back to the Western Middle Ages, Rome, Greece, and the ancient civilizations of the Near East. . . .

The change that took place between about 1750 and 1900 was, of course, the Industrial Revolution. Before the marvels of steam and steel Europeans and Americans were likely to think of their own civilization as one among many. They thought, perhaps naturally, that it was the best civilization in the world, but they could not ignore the others altogether. European overseas expansion before 1750 was largely commercial, and the time when Europe would conquer the world was still to come. With industrial technology, however, and economic growth at unprecedented rates, the Western self-image began to change. Europeans and Americans began to place a much higher value on their accomplishments. When they thought of progress they thought of their own rapid progress over recent decades. By contrast the pace of historical change in other societies seemed slow, and Europeans began to talk about the "changeless East." In fact the East was far from changeless; only the very rapid European changes of the nineteenth century made it appear to be so. But the new rate of European change altered the Western concept of history: if history is the study of change, then societies thought to be static had no history worth speaking of. The new pattern of historical thought began with Europe and concentrated on European achievements. Americans easily took it over and extended it to their own country.

The rise of this attitude, which can be labeled "cultural chauvinism," had other side effects that helped bring about the neglect of African history. . . .

The prevalence of racial interpretations in otherwise-respectable books of the recent past poses a special problem in understanding early works on African history. It is not easy for the specialist, conscious of the probable racial bias of these works, to make adjustments accordingly, and a strong presumption exists that any work of African history published before 1935 will be racist to some degree, if only in ways of which the author was unconscious. . . .

THE DISCOVERY OF HISTORICAL AFRICA

The turning point for African history came with the Second World War. Some of the generation that fought in the war returned to the universities, where they combined an interest in the discipline of history with an active experience in places many older historians had barely heard of. Other men, too young for active duty, also had a feeling in the postwar years that traditional "world history" failed to explain the modern world. The first historians to turn their attention to Africa were mainly either African themselves or Europeans from one of the colonial powers. By the 1950s Britain was recruiting scholars to staff the new African universities. The French and Belgians began to support more active social-science research institutes that included research in history. Both universities and research institutes were part of a broader change in policy that looked forward to African independence. In this context the emergence of African history was a minor theme in the decolonization of the continent. . . .

NEW TECHNIQUES AND NEW SOURCES

The most spectacular features of the new postwar boom in African history have been the development of new techniques for investigation and the application of older techniques to the African past. The result has been to stretch our knowledge much further back through time.

Before 1945 archeology on the African continent was virtually unknown outside of North Africa, southern Africa (as far north as Rhodesia), and the Nilotic Sudan. After the war the spread of universities in tropical Africa brought a new impetus. So, too, did the movement of African states toward independence. Many set up antiquities services and began government sponsorship of archeological research. During the 1960s, as the waters began to rise behind the Aswan Dam, an international effort was made by archeologists to recover as much as possible from the Nile Valley on either side of the frontier between Egypt and the Sudan. Other important excavations at Igbo Ukwu in eastern Nigeria and at Ife and Benin in the west have added greatly to knowledge about early African art in bronze, terracotta, and stone. These discoveries are pushing back the time horizons for tropical West Africa, where some of the finest bronze may date from the ninth century A.D. Radiocarbon dating has been the most important new archeological technique in the decades after the Second World War, but it is far from foolproof, and the best recent archeology has used a combination of techniques for dating the distant past. This allows a cross check against possible errors in any one kind of evidence.

The common pattern in European, Middle Eastern, and North African history is a long, early period where archeological evidence is virtually alone, followed by relatively short periods where archeological and written evidence exist side by side, and then another long period where written evidence stands alone. The evidence for sub-Saharan history is not in this pattern, mainly because sub-Saharan societies were often nonliterate. Even where they were literate the natural destruction of paper in a wet tropical climate has annihilated much of the evidence. This produces special problems for historical research in precolonial history, problems peculiar to an "oral" society. It is possible to know some things about its past; but the things that are knowable are often different from what is knowable about Western history, and the techniques for discovering them are different. Archeological investigation is needed alongside written evidence and oral traditions for all periods, even though written evidence goes back more than a thousand years for many parts of sub-Saharan Africa and much longer for North Africa. Both archeology and writing can be supplemented by other kinds of evidence, so that the well-trained historian of Africa finds that he needs to know something about a variety of other disciplines.

Linguistics is one of the most important. Language is especially useful as a clue to the migrations of peoples within the African continent. If two groups of people speak related languages, we can assume that sometime in the past their ancestors spoke the same language and lived in the same part of the world. The degree of linguistic separation will also indicate the lapse of time since the original group divided. To measure the extent of linguistic change and translate it into a measure of time, linguists have developed a method known as "glotto-chronology," a technique still at an experimental stage. All we know at present is that the degree of linguistic separation will have some relationship to the duration of physical separation. Nor is linguistic evidence always foolproof. People can, for example, change their language, just as many immigrants to America dropped their original language after a generation and turned to English. Linguistic evidence nevertheless provides many valuable clues that can then be checked against other kinds of evidence, such as physical measurements or blood types that are known to be inherited. . . .

For recent periods the most valuable new technique for discovering African history is the critical use of oral tradition. Oral evidence in the form of myths, legends, and sagas has long been used in the investigation of early European history. We know that Homer's epic poetry cannot be accepted as the literal truth. Still it tells a great deal about the way people lived before the age of written documents. Through Homer archeologists were led to the site of Troy, and other valuable information came to light.

Traditional histories in Africa, however, are different from those of Homeric Greece in one very important respect: African traditional histories are still remembered and repeated by living people. Often a professional class of minstrels, drummers, or praise singers still has its old function of remembering and repeating dynastic or epic poetry, long stories about the deeds of past rulers, or long recitations of the traditional history of the nation. The quantity of such material is very large. In some of the more complex African states one form of tradition is preserved by the royal court, another in the major provincial centers, and still another in each village. These may be checked against one another and against the traditions of neighboring peoples. At times they can be checked against written versions taken down by early explorers, administrative officers, or anthropologists. Present-day historians work with tape recorders, which make it possible to record and then to transcribe in the original language with far greater care than amateur historians could use in the past, but many of the formal traditions that were still known a half century ago are now lost, and others are disappearing rapidly.

However the traditions are collected, the most important step is critical evaluation. This is not so much a question of finding the best version of a particular tradition but of finding what truth it may contain. Most formal traditions, repeated from memory, were preserved because they served political ends. They are "official history," no more worthy of complete credence than a Pentagon press release. . . .

Europe was free of barbarian invasions after the tenth century. It was also able to rebuild its civilization through the mediation of Byzantium and Islam. By the time of the Crusades northwest Europe was fully within the zone of intercommunication between world civilizations. Overland trade linked the Baltic and North seas with the Mediterranean. Seaborne trade soon ventured regularly into the Atlantic. The Sudan, on the other hand, remained cut off behind the barrier of the Sahara.

There is no need here to trace the rising technical prowess of the Europeans or the way they borrowed and assimilated techniques of other civilizations, added their own discoveries, and finally produced modern science and the Industrial Revolution. The point, for present purposes, is simply this: the lag in African development, as seen in the nineteenth-century confrontation with Europe, had two components. One was the ancient lag behind the Near Eastern civilization, which was shared for a time by northwest Europe. The second was the European advance, which carried the West further ahead technologically than either the Sudan or the Near East. This second component has no direct relation to African history. It was produced by unusual achievements in Europe, not by unusual failures outside Europe. The Sudan has progressed steadily during the past millennium. There is no cause to ask why it did not progress as fast as Europe: it moved ahead at about the same rate as most other human societies in the period between the first civilizations and the Industrial Revolution. Only Europe's unusual dynamic in its own breakthrough into industrialism made Africa and other civilizations of the world appear static.

The Phases of Islamic Expansion and Islamic Culture Zones in Africa

J. S. Trimingham

Islam, also called Mohammedanism, Moslemism, and Muslimism, is one of the world's major religions. It maintains that there is but one God, Allah, and that Mohammed, whose revelations are collected in the Koran, was his prophet. Islam has experienced varied degrees of acceptance throughout Africa, as described in the following selection by J. S. Trimingham, from *A History of Islam in West Africa.*

THE SPREAD OF ISLAM

The spread of Islam in Africa is marked by four phases, which also represent methods and depths and correspond to types of contemporary Islam.

1. THE WINNING OF NORTH AFRICA (A.D. 638–1050)

The first stage is the conquest by the early Muslim Arabs of all the Mediterranean littoral from Egypt to Morocco; then there followed a period of pacification, quickly succeeded by a break-up of the short-lived political unity into many Muslim states. Islam slowly won over the Berbers, but their Arabization took place during the next stage, following a new break-in of Arab nomads.

2. THE SPREAD OF ISLAM INTO THE SUDAN BELT (1050–1750)

This period witnessed the slow and largely peaceful spread of Islam southwards across the Sahara and up the valley of the Nile into the Hamitic and Black Africa of the Sudan belt. Across the Red Sea and by way of East Africa sea-routes it spread into the plains of the Eastern Horn, where it gained the 'Afar and Somali. Settlements were formed along the East African coast, where a new cultural group—the Swahili—was formed, but Islam had no effect upon the Bantu and other peoples of the region.

This phase began with the upsurge of the Berber Murabitun (from 1056) and the dispersion throughout North Africa of Arab nomads of the Bani Hilal (from 1045). These events principally affected the desert and North Africa, for though the Murabits conquered the Negro state of Gana on the edge of the southern desert, they were soon expelled. The Arab tribes did not spread Islam, but their conquest of the Berbers of Mauritania, south of Morocco, led to their Arabization. The Berbers of central Sahara, the Tuareg, were neither conquered nor Arabized.

The spread of Islam across the Sahara into the northern Sudan came through the work of Berber traders and clerics in the west and an influx of Arab tribes (A.D. 1300–1500) in the east, where the Christianity of the Nilotic Sudan disappeared.

The feature of this period is the adoption of Islam as a class religion—the imperial cult in the Sudan states like Mali and Kanem and as the cult of the trading and clerical classes. Just as various religious strata existed side by side in the mosaic of Sudanese religion, so when Islam came on the scene there was no feeling that it was incompatible with an African religious outlook, and, strange though it may seem, Islam was incorporated into the Sudanese religious scheme. Religious life was characterized by accommodation or, more correctly, by a dualism or a parallelism of the old and the new—the African idea of the harmony of society maintained itself over against any idea of Islamic exclusiveness. Consequently, Islam's elements of challenge to traditional life were largely neutralized.

The next period witnessed the triumph of Islam throughout the Sudan belt in a form which claimed its exclusiveness, while the modern period has seen the emergence among new converts of a secular Islam different from traditional African Islam.

3. THE ERA OF THEOCRACIES AND OF STATES WHERE ISLAM IS THE STATE RELIGION (1750–1901)

The nineteenth century was characterized by the appearance of a new, intolerant and militant Islam. Clerics made their appearance (the first in Futa Jalon in 1725) who waged the *jihad* or holy war and formed a number of theocratic states as they are usually called though they should really be called divine nomocracies, since they all claimed to be ruled by divine law. These states appeared throughout the Sudan belt from Guinea (Futa Jalon, 1776) and Senegal (Futa Toro, 1776), through Masina (1818) and Sokoto (1802) to the Mahdia of the Nilotic Sudan (1881). These states degenerated, and most of them were conquered or came under the rule of a new type of despot, for example, alhajj 'Umar (1854–64) in western Sudan and 'Abdallah al-Ta'aishi in Nilotic Sudan (1885–98).

The great change introduced by the nineteenth-century reformers lay in the stress placed on the uniqueness and exclusiveness of Islam and its incompatibility with worship within the old cults. These reformers brought an intensity into the former unchallenging Islam, so Africanized as to be at the point of losing its identity, which drove Islam into the centre of life as a transforming factor, whereby the very equilibrium of society was changed. Although under their successors this exclusive reference waned, yet sufficient had been done to bring Islam forward as the supreme arbiter of life and dominant in spite of all the accommodation with pagan practices which was in fact allowed in life.

The conquests of the reformers resulted in a great expansion of nominal allegiance to Islam, but their greatest contribution to the implanting of Islam came from the way they broke up social and tribal groups (prisoners, slave-villages, forcible removals) and destroyed organized cults, leaving Islam as the sole cement for new or reconstituted organizations. This process was accelerated during the next phase, when all these territories came under European occupation.

Kingdoms of West Africa

A. Adu Boahen

West Africa is neither a precisely bounded nor a politically defined area, so perhaps the terms "west Africa" or "western Africa" would be more apt and less misleading. Similarly, the kingdoms of this vast region of the African continent have been imprecise, changing, and contested. But where and while they lasted, they embraced some of the most picturesque, powerful, rich, just and unjust administrations of all time. Incidentally, it is worth noting that slaves in Africa were generally treated as human beings and not as the chattels they were considered to be in colonial and postcolonial America. The following excerpt from A. Adu Boahen's book *Kingdoms of West Africa* can touch on only a few of the realities of the period from A.D. 500 to 1600, but these are enough to make a Westerner marvel at the stages of development reached in this region of Africa long before the voyages of Christopher Columbus.

In West Africa, the area bounded to the north by the Sahara desert, to the south by the Atlantic Ocean, and to the east by Lake Chad and modern Cameroon, a number of independent states and empires evolved in the period between A.D. 500 and 1470. Among them were Ghana, Mali, Songhai, Kanein-Bornu, and the Hausa states, which were clustered along the southern frontier of the Sahara. Still farther south, between these states and the forest region, arose the Mole-Dagbane states and the Mossi states. Finally, in the forest and coastal zones of Guinea emerged the states of Takrur and Wolof in the region of the Senegal and Gambia rivers, or Senegambia; the Akan, Fante, and Ga states in the area of modern Ghana; and the states of Ife, Oyo, and Benin in Nigeria.

The questions that we shall attempt to answer here are: When did these states and empires crystallize and when did each attain its peak of greatness? How and why were they formed, and how were they governed? And what cultures and civilizations did they develop before the arrival of the Portuguese?

It is significant that the earliest of these states to grow into large kingdoms and empires were those in the savanna immediately to the south of the Sahara. Of these three, namely Ghana, Mali, and Songhai, the first to reach maturity was Ghana, peopled by the Soninke. It is not known for certain when it took form as a state. However, if there were as many as twenty-two kings before the rise of Islam in A.D. 622, as the oral traditions of Ghana tells, and if by the time the Persian geographer Al-Fazari was writing in A.D. 773–774 Ghana was already well known to North African and Middle Eastern traders as the Land of Gold, it is not unreasonable to suppose that it emerged as a full-fledged state in the fifth or sixth century A.D.

There is no doubt that by A.D. 1000 Ghana had attained the peak of its power, an empire ruling over a number of smaller tribute-paying states and monopolizing West Africa's enormous and valuable gold trade to North Africa and Europe. This meant that Ghana and its formidable armies also dominated the roads of the Sahara and the savanna. Ibo Hawqal, the first known Arab explorer of the western Sudan, offers in his tenth-century *Book of Ways and Provinces* his impression of the Ghanaian sovereign: "the wealthiest of all kings on the face of the earth on account of the riches he owns and the hoards of gold acquired by him and inherited from his predecessors since ancient times." He based his estimate on the quantity of goods he saw being shipped through the Moroccan entrepôt of Sijilmasa.

Ghana's capital city was then Kumbi Saleh, which the Arab writer Al-Bakri described in 1067 as consisting of "two towns situated on a plain, one principally inhabited by Muslim traders, the other settled by the emperor and the local populace." The Muslim town was "large and possessed twelve mosques; in one of these mosques they assembled for the prayers on Fridays. There were imams and muezzins as well as jurists and scholars."

Ghana, however, began to decline during the second half of the eleventh century. Saharan Berbers, driven by territorial ambitions and inspired by Almoravid zeal, succeeded in disorganizing trade and stirring up rebellion among Ghana's tributaries. The empire was overthrown in 1235 by one of its former vassal states, the Susu kingdom, under its ruler Sumanguru Kante.

Mali, which succeeded Ghana, had emerged as a rather small principality by the end of the ninth century A.D. Between the eleventh and the thirteenth centuries it was dominated first by Ghana and then by the Susu kingdom, and it was not until the reign of Sundiata (1230–1255) that Mali embarked on its career of conquest. Building upon the administrative model of Ghana, it extended its trading empire over large parts of the western Sudan, and through the leadership of Mansa Kankan Musa, who reigned from 1312 to 1337, it absorbed such centers as Timbuktu, Gao, and Walata. Ibn Battuta, visiting Mali two decades after Mansa Musa's death, was astounded by the peace, order, and racial tolerance that prevailed in the empire:

> The Negroes possess some admirable qualities. They are seldom unjust and have a greater abhorrence of injustice than any other people. Their Sultan shows no mercy to any one guilty of the least act of it. There is complete security in their country. Neither traveler nor inhabitant in it has anything to fear from robbers or men of violence. They do not confiscate the property of any white man who dies in their country, even if it be uncounted wealth. On the contrary, they give it into the charge of some trust-worthy person among the whites, until the rightful heir takes possession of it.

Although the Portuguese, when they first came ashore in 1441, found that most of the states on the coast as well as in the immediate hinterland were still under the control of Mali, the state was already in a period of decline and Songhai was on the rise.

The Songhai people, with the city-state of Gao, or Al-Kawkaw, as their political center, had become active in the trans-Saharan trade by the end of the ninth century. Al-Yaqubi described Gao in 871 as "the greatest of the realms of the as-Sudan, the most important and most powerful, and all the other kingdoms obey its rulers." However, until the last quarter of the fourteenth century, it was controlled first by Ghana and then by Mali. Ibn Battuta, visiting Gao during the era of its vassalage to Mali, described it as "one of the finest towns in the Negroland. It is also one of their biggest and best provisioned towns with rice in plenty, milk and fish. . . ."

In 1375, however, Gao broke away from Mali, though it did not grow into an empire until the reign of Sunni Ali, the celebrated politician, soldier, and administrator who reigned from 1464 until 1492. The empire was consolidated and its frontiers further extended by the second of its most famous rulers, Askia Muhammad the Great. It was during his reign, which lasted from 1493 to 1528, that Songhai attained its peak, controlling the entire central region of the western Sudan.

Leo Africanus, a Christianized Arab geographer who visited Songhai in about 1510, has left us some vivid accounts of its intellectual and commercial life. For example, Gao was a town full of "exceeding rich merchants: and hither continually resort great store of Negroes which buy cloth here brought out of Barbarie and Europe. . . . It is a woonder to see what plentie of Merchandize is dayly brought hither, and how costly and sumptuous all things be."

However, during the last decade of that very century, for reasons to be discussed later, this sprawling and famous empire completely disintegrated. Its rulers were forced to retreat south along the Niger into their ancestral home in the region of Dendi.

In conformity with the Hamitic hypothesis, scholars of the 1930's and 1940's attributed the foundation of these three states, as well as that of Kanem-Bornu and the Hausa states (which will be discussed in greater detail in Chapter Six), simply to some white-skinned invaders from the north. More recently, the introduction of the use of iron has been emphasized as the determining factor. To the present writer, their ascendance was the result of several major developments. The first was the rapid growth of population in the area immediately to the south of the Sahara and especially in the regions of the Niger Bend and the Senegambia. The second was the development of the caravan trade and the subsequent activities of wealthy and therefore powerful and ambitious families. The third was the spread of Islam.

The steady increase of the savanna's population between 1000 B.C. and A.D. 300 or 400 was caused in part by the Neolithic revolution (that is, the change from the hunting of wild animals and the collection of wild fruits to the cultivation of food crops and domestication of animals). Historians and ethnobotanists are still hotly debating whether or not there was an independent Neolithic revolution among the Mande peoples in the region of the Niger Bend in about 5000 B.C. But even if this revolution was introduced into Africa from Asia via Egypt, there is no doubt that the area between the Niger Bend and the middle Senegal River as well as the areas around Lake Chad proved a superior environment for the cereal crops, especially sorghum and millet, which were among the first crops to be cultivated. The Mande and the Kanuri peoples of those areas must, therefore, have obtained an early lead over all the others. Since they could also supplement their diet through fishing, these peoples must have been able to produce food in such quantities that their numbers multiplied. As the contemporary British Africanist J. D. Fage has pointed out, this Neolithic revolution must have also led to "the beginnings of urbanization and of organized government and administration, and, even, perhaps, the flourishing of the idea of a king as a god-like being supreme over all his subjects."

This increase in population must have been further accelerated by the steady desiccation of the Sahara from about 3000 B.C. onward. As the Sahara slowly assumed its barren look, a process that was complete by 1500 B.C., some of its inhabitants began to drift into the savanna belt.

The use of iron tools must also have had its effect on population growth in that it facilitated agriculture, but surely it was not, as some scholars have argued, the principal factor in the rise of the western Sudanese states. If this were so, it would follow that the states would have emerged much earlier—nearer 300 B.C., when iron technology is thought to have reached the Nok culture on the lower Niger —and first in the east rather than in the west as, in fact, happened.

It would seem then to this writer that by about the last century B.C. or the first century A.D. the whole of the savanna in general, and the regions of Lake Chad, the Niger Bend, and Nok in particular, must have been occupied by large populations living in family, lineage, or clan groups, in villages bound together by kinship ties or even in city-states and small kingdoms ruled possibly by "divine" kings. Something else must have been needed to stimulate one or more of these nuclei to develop into larger kingdoms and, eventually, empires, and this stimulus must have been provided by the caravan trade. From rock paintings of two-wheeled horse-drawn war chariots and from other archeological data, it is clear that by 1000 B.C. the caravan trade was well established along two main routes. These were a western route through Morocco to the Niger Bend and a central route through the Fezzan, Ghat, and Adrar des Iforas, possibly to the region of Gao on the Niger. The main beasts of burden were bullocks and, after 1200 B.C., horses. It is equally clear from the fifth-century B.C. accounts of Herodotus and from other ancient Greek and Roman sources that both the Carthaginians and the Romans were trading with the people of the savanna belt through Berber intermediaries settled in the Fezzan and the western Sahara.

However, this trade could not have been very extensive until the introduction of the camel. The use of this singularly endowed beast of burden spread westward and then southward into the Sahara, and as a result, a complicated network of caravan routes across the Sahara was developed between about A.D. 200 and 500. To the Morocco-Niger route and the old Garamantes' route from Tripoli to Chad and to Gao was added a caravan route from Egypt to Gao by way of the Saharan oases, including Ghat and the future site of Agadès.

As trade expanded with the use of the camel, not only did more and more people grow wealthy but handicrafts, mining, and agriculture were stimulated. So, too, urban centers grew in size and influence. Wealth, of course, generates among individuals and families still greater ambition and the desire to control more and more trading activities and trade routes. It is the activities of the talented members of these families (especially of such men as Sundiata and Mansa Musa of Mali and Sunni Ali and Askia Muhammad of Songhai) and not the mere use of iron that bring about the creation of large states and empires.

The people who would be the first beneficiaries of this increasing trade would naturally be those living in the border zone between the Sahara and the savanna, an ideal position from which to play the lucrative role of the middleman. The Soninke of Ghana and the Kanuri of the old state of Kanem were the peoples at the crossroads of the Sahara and the savanna, and they were among the first to develop kingdoms and then empires. The fact that no large kingdoms emerged in Hausaland until the fourteenth century, when the north-south trade began there, provides a further indication of the importance of caravan trade in state-building.

The final factor, which did not cause, but rather accelerated or facilitated to some extent the growth of the empires of Mali and Songhai, as well as Kanem-Bornu and the Hausa-states, must have been the introduction of Islam. This religion penetrated the Sahara via the caravan routes and reached the savanna in the ninth and tenth centuries.

Islam is not just a body of doctrines, but a complete way of life, having its own laws, its own system of taxation and administration of justice, its own statecraft, and its own language and traditions of scholarship. Islam's adoption by the rulers of Gao in the tenth century and of Mali and Kanem in the eleventh century must have given them access to all these sciences as well as the means by which to create an educated bureaucracy. A more intense exposure to Islam was gained by those who took the hadj, or pilgrimage, to the Islamic civilization of the Middle East.

It is known, for instance, that on Mansa Musa's celebrated pilgrimage to Mecca in 1324–1325, he met the Spanish scholar, poet, and architect As-Sahili, whom he successfully persuaded to go with him to Mali. It is also known that not only did As-Sahili insist on a strict observance of Islam, but he revolutionized architecture of Mali and of the western Sudan in general by introducing brick as the building material for mosques and palaces. Similarly, during his equally famous hadj to Mecca in 1497 Askia Muhammad the Great also met and befriended great scholars such as Abd ar-Rahman as-Suyuti and Muhammad al-Majhili, with whom he began a lifelong correspondence. The latter actually visited him in Songhai and gave him as well as the king of Kano a great deal of advice on religion and politics.

Nevertheless, the governments of all these early Sudanese empires were of the divine-kingship type, a typically African conception, indicating that these states did not derive their political institutions from Islam, but possibly from ancient Ghana or, in any case, from indigenous Mande institutions. At the head of each was a hereditary monarch. He was assisted by a council of ministers, whose members, following the introduction of Islam, were mostly literate Muslims. Al-Bakri, writing in 1067, tells us that even though the king of Ghana held animistic beliefs, the official in charge of his treasury and the majority of his ministers were Muslims. Unfortunately, we do not have the titles of the ministers of Ghana, but they were probably similar to those of Songhai, whose cabinet included the *hi-koy* (the commander of the navy), *dyina-koy* (commander in chief of the army), *hari-farma* (minister in charge of navigation and fishing), *fari-mundyo* (minister of taxation), *waney-farma* (minister in charge of property), *korey-farma* (minister in charge of foreigners), and *sao-koy* (minister in charge of forests).

The divine-kingship nature of the government is further borne out by descriptions that we have of their court protocol and ceremonial. According to Al-Bakri:

> The king [of Ghana] adorns himself like a woman wearing necklaces round his neck and bracelets on his forearms, and when he sits before the people he puts on a high cap decorated with gold and wrapped in a turban of fine cloth. The court of Appeal is held in a domed pavilion around which stand ten horses covered with gold-embroidered materials. Behind the king stand ten pages holding shields and swords decorated with gold and on his right are the sons of the vassal kings of his country wearing splendid garments and their hair plaited with gold. The governor of the city sits on the ground before the king and around are ministers seated likewise. At the door of the pavilion are dogs of excellent pedigree who hardly ever leave the place where the king is, guarding him. Round their necks, they wear collars of gold and silver studded with a number of balls of the same metal. The audience is announced by the beating of a drum which they call daba, made from a long hollow log. When the people who profess the same religion as the king approach him, they fall on their knees and sprinkle dust on their heads for this is their way of showing respect for him. As for the Muslims, they greet him only by clapping their hands.

Ibn Battuta, who visited and had an audience with Mansa Sulaiman, the brother and successor of Mansa Musa, describes another court ritual:

> On certain days the Sultan holds audience in the palace yard. . . . The Sultan comes out of a door in a corner of the palace, carrying a bow in his hand and a quiver on his back. On his head he has a golden skull cap . . . [he] is preceded by his musicians. . . . As he takes his seat the drums, trumpets and bugles are sounded. . . . Two saddled and bridled horses are brought, along with two goats which they hold to serve as a protection against the evil eye. . . . The Negroes are of all people the most submissive to their king and the most abject in their behavior before him. They swear by his name.

... If he summons any of them while he is holding an audience in his pavilion, the person summoned takes off his clothes and puts on worn garments, removes his turban and dons a dirty skull-cap, and enters with his garments and trousers raised knee-high. He goes forward in an attitude of humility and dejection, and knocks the ground hard with his elbows, then stands with bowed head and bent back listening to what he says. If any one addresses the king and receives a reply from him, he uncovers his back and throws dust over his head and back for all the world like a bather splashing himself with water. I used to wonder how it was they did not blind themselves.

And finally, from Leo Africanus' eyewitness account of the court of Songhai at Timbuktu:

The rich king of Tombuto hath many plates and scepters of gold, some whereof weigh 1300 poundes . . . and he keepes a magnificent and well furnished court. When he travelleth any whither he rideth upon a camell, which is led by some of his noblemen; and so he doth likewise when hee goeth to warfar, and all his souldiers ride upon horses. Whosoever will speake unto this king must first fall downe before his feete, & then taking up earth must sprinkle it upon his owne head & shoulders: which custom is ordinarily observed by them that never saluted the king before, or comes as ambassadors from other princes.

The drums, the linguists, the praise singers, the gold swords and caps, the prostrations and the removal of sandals in the presence of the king are closely observed to this very day in some courts of African kings (for example, among the Akan of modern Ghana). It is true that both Mali and Songhai added such Muslim trappings as banquets and Turkish and Egyptian bodyguards to their courts, while some of their symbols of investiture—the tunic, turban, and sword —were certainly Islamic. But the basic court ceremonial and protocol, and the position of the king in both Mali and Songhai, were definitely pre-Islamic and African in origin, most probably deriving from those of ancient Ghana.

However, some differences appear in the system of royal succession. It is clear from Al-Bakri's account that like the present practice among the Akan people, royal succession in Ghana was matrilineal, whereas in the later Mali and Songhai empires it was patrilineal. Al-Bakri was informed that Tunka Manin succeeded not his father but his maternal uncle. And as if to dispel any doubts, he added: "This is their custom and their habit, that the kingdom is inherited only by the son of the king's sister." He goes on to give an explanation of what appeared to him to be a most odd and non-Muslim practice: "He the king has no doubt that his successor is a son of his sister, while he is not certain that his son is in fact his own, and he does not rely on the genuineness of this relationship."

Although the fourteenth-century Tunisian historian Ibn Khaldun did report that one of the kings of Mali, Abu Bakr, was the son of a daughter of Sundiata, and although it has been inferred from this that royal succession in Mali at times went through the female line, a recent authority has shown that this was an exception to the rule. It would appear then that royal succession in both Mali and Songhai generally followed the patrilineal rather than the matrilineal rule. This difference might well be due to the impact of Islam.

The systems of provincial government in these Sudanese empires show some differences, but in degree rather than in kind. In all three cases the kings were directly responsible for the administration of the core, or metropolitan part, of the empire, which they divided into provinces ruled by governors. In the case of both Mali and Songhai, these governors either were members of the royal family or former generals. The governors in turn appointed district chiefs to administer a number of villages, each of which was ruled by a village chief.

The other parts of the empire, consisting of states conquered and reduced to vassal or tributary status, were governed in a variety of ways. In Ghana it would appear that the states remained under their own rulers and that their main obligations were to pay annual tribute and to supply contingents to the king's army when called upon to do so. Sons of vassal rulers were occasionally kept at the king's court to ensure their fathers' continued allegiance. In Mali the same system prevailed, with some minor improvements: the sovereigns of the conquered states retained their right to rule, but only after being invested by the Mansa and given a Mande title; the swearing of allegiance and the payment of tribute were seen as proofs of loyalty.

The kings of Songhai, especially Askia Muhammad, made still greater improvements toward centralizing the administration of government. Askia Muhammad ruled metropolitan Gao directly, but he reduced the status of the conquered rulers further by placing governors and minor governors over them. As was the case in Mali, these were court favorites or members of the royal family. Above this structure he created four viceroyalties, or regions, each under a viceroy, or commissioner, who was in charge of a cluster of provinces. These viceroyalties were Dendi, Bal, Benga, and Kurmina. Since most of these administrative posts were appointive rather than hereditary, Songhai must have had a much more tightly controlled and more effective system of provincial administration than the other two.

Arabic sources do not throw much light on the system of justice in these states. For the most part, the kings were directly responsible for its administration. We are told by Al-Bakri that the kings of Ghana went out on horses everyday to summon those people who had been wronged or had suffered any injustice to come and lodge a complaint. Trial by wood was also practiced in ancient Ghana. According to Al-Bakri, "When a man is accused of denying a debt or having shed blood or some other crime, a headman takes a thin piece of wood, which is sour and bitter to taste, and pours upon it some water which he then gives to the defendant to drink. If the man vomits, his innocence is recognized and he is congratulated. If he does not vomit and the drink remains in his stomach, the accusation is accepted as justified." The kings held what seem to have been courts of appeal in their palaces. Cases were initially heard, especially in the towns, by *qadis,* who obviously administered justice in accordance with the Koran and the Sharia (Muslim law). These judges also wielded great influence at the court of the kings. Ibn Battuta's main contact with the king of Mali was a *qadi,* whom he described as "a negro, a pilgrim, and a man of fine character." The chroniclers of the Timbuktu *Tarikh* indicate that the *qadis* of that town were all from the Aqit family and wielded considerable influence over the Askias. One of them, Al-Aqib, who died in 1583, was noted for his frankness. "He was of stout heart," wrote one of the chroniclers, "bold in the mighty affairs that others hesitate before, courageous in dealing with the ruler and those beneath him. He had many conflicts with them and they used to be submissive and obedient to him in every matter. If he saw something he thought reprehensible, he would suspend his activities as *qadi* and keep himself aloof. Then they would conciliate him until he returned."

These high-ranking officials appear to have been rewarded for their services. Most of them, certainly those of Mali and Songhai, were given fiefs, or serf domains, as well as valuable goods. According to Al-Umari, some of the provincial governors of Mali received as much as "1500 mithqals [a unitary measure equal to one eighth of an ounce] of gold every year besides which he the king keeps them in horses and clothes." To encourage civil servants and military men, the kings of Mali instituted various decorations, such as the award of golden bracelets, collars, and anklets. The highest of all the awards, presumably given to soldiers, was the Honor of the Trousers. An eyewitness told the fourteenth-century writer Al-Umari: "Whenever a hero adds to the list of his exploits, the King gives him a pair of wide trousers, and the greater the number of a knight's exploits the bigger the size of his trousers. These trousers are characterised by narrowness in the leg and ampleness in the seat."

It is interesting to note that the Scottish explorer Alexander Gordon Laing, who visited among the Mandingos of Solimana in 1822, observed: "The width of the trousers is a great mark of distinction." This is true of the Dagomba and Mamprusi of northern Ghana to this day.

For the maintenance of law and order, and for defensive as well as offensive purposes, each of these west Sudanese empires had an army. Mali and Ghana had no standing armies; they, like many African kingdoms, depended on contingents contributed upon demand by vassal states. According to Al-Bakri, the kings of Ghana could raise an army of 200,000, of whom 40,000 were archers; and Mansa Musa of Mali could call up 100,000, a tenth of whom were cavalrymen. Songhai also relied on levies until the reign of Askia Muhammad, who instituted a professional army. It was this new army that enabled him not only to ensure stability and order, but to extend the boundaries of the empire that he had inherited from Sunni Ali. The armies of all these empires used the same weapons and were organized in the same way. They were divided into cavalry and infantry, their main weapons being spears, swords, javelins, and bows and arrows. Firearms were completely unknown until the Moroccan invasion late in the sixteenth century.

It would appear that both Mali and Songhai established diplomatic relations with the Maghreb and Egypt and kept up regular contacts with the sultan of Morocco. Mansa Sulaiman, Mansa Musa's brother and successor as king of the Mali, exchanged deputations with Morocco's Marinid sultans, and on the occasion of a new sultan's enthronement, sent an embassy to do him honor. Sulaiman's successor is also known to have sent gifts to the new sultan of Morocco. Among them was a giraffe, which the Moroccans talked about for a long time "because of the various adornments and markings which it combined in its body and attributes."

The complex administrative machineries of these states must have been expensive to run. Three main sources filled the royal treasury: tribute from vassal states, import and export duties, and imperial domains. Details of the annual levies have not been preserved, but of the duties collected in Ghana, Al-Bakri writes, "for every donkey loaded with salt that enters the country, the king takes a duty of one gold dinar, and two dinars from every one that leaves. From a load of copper the king's due is five mithqals and from a load of other goods ten mithqals." We are also told that in Ghana any gold nugget found by anybody had to be surrendered to the king. Both Mali and Songhai imposed similar duties on goods coming to and fro. In fact, Songhai had a minister solely concerned with taxation.

The third, and probably the greatest, source of revenue was from the royal estates. Ghana's records are quite silent on this; but it is clear from the accounts of Mali and Songhai that the kings had royal domains—some hereditary and some acquired by war—in different parts of the empire. After his victory over Mali, Askia Muhammad is said to have added twenty-four fiefs to his holdings. These were occupied and worked by slaves whose overseers, or *fanfa,* were charged with raising a fixed quantity of produce every year for the kings.

"Some of these *fanfa,*" says the chronicler of the Askia dynasty, "had under them 100 slaves employed in cultivation, whilst others had 60, 50, 40, or 20." Each estate had a special function: some had to provide such commodities as yams, grain, or fish; others had to manufacture such goods as bows and arrows. Before the reign of Askia Muhammad the Great, the quantity of articles or provisions to be produced by each fief was not fixed, but Askia the Great set rigid quotas. Thus the Abda estate in the province of Dendi had to produce 1,000 sunhas (6,500 bushels) of rice annually. A chronicler reported: "This was fixed, which could neither be increased nor reduced." The Dyam Tene and Dya Wali estates had to supply 100 iron spears and 100 arrows per family per year. As the personal property of the kings, the estates were often given away as presents to trusted courtiers and friends.

The principal exports of Ghana, Mali, and Songhai were gold, ivory, slaves, and later, from the thirteenth century onward, kola nuts, a stimulant highly prized among Muslims. Most of these commodities, especially gold and kola nuts, came from the forest regions along trade routes controlled mainly by the Diula, a Mande people. The chief imports from the north were salt, horses, textiles, linen, books, writing paper, swords, and knives.

Ghana, situated as it was in the borderlands between the Sahara and the savanna, was most dependent upon the caravan trade; its people played the leading role as middlemen between producers and merchants. Al-Yaqut says of thirteenth-century Ghana: "From here, one enters the arid waste when going to the land of gold, and without the town of Ghana, this journey would be impossible."

Elsewhere Al-Yaqut adds that merchants from the north took with them Ghanaians as interpreters and go-betweens in negotiating with gold miners to the south. (It would appear that only small amounts of gold were mined in Ghana itself.) Ghana was also able to control the crucial and very lucrative trade in salt imported from the Taghaza mines of the western Sahara, "the source of an enormous income," according to Al-Bakri.

Since both Mali and Songhai successively gained direct control over some of the southern gold-producing regions, Wangara in particular, and since they were able to establish peace and order along the caravan routes, they must have derived even more income from trade than had Ghana. It is quite clear from Maghrebin, Egyptian, and Sudanese sources that from the thirteenth to the fifteenth centuries, when Europe and the Muslim world were facing an acute shortage of precious metals, the western Sudan was their chief source of gold. The enormous quantities of gold that both Mansa Musa and Askia Muhammad took with them on their pilgrimages to Mecca, in 1324 and 1497 respectively, leaves no doubt about the wealth their states possessed in gold.

However, other commodities also contributed to the income of Mali and Songhai. Both were favorably situated to practice agriculture, cattle breeding, and fishing. Ibn Battuta and Leo Africanus indicate that a certain amount of rice and millet was exported great distances. Fishing was quite important among the Sorko clans of Songhai, and some of the royal estates had their quota of fish to catch. Numerous craftsmen, tailors, blacksmiths, and cloth weavers attracted traders, too. Leo Africanus reports that Timbuktu had "many shops of artificers and merchants and especially such as weave linen and cotton cloth." Another chronicler wrote that there were as many as twenty-six tailors' workshops in the crossroads city, each with between fifty and one hundred apprentices.

Society in the Sudanese states was highly stratified. At the top was the ruling aristocracy, consisting of the royal families, officials, and Muslim scholars. The second and major part of the population consisted of merchants, farmers, fishermen, and cattle breeders. At the bottom were the slaves, who constituted only a small percentage of the population. It should be emphasized that the status of a slave in these early states, as indeed in almost all African societies, was fundamentally different from that which would prevail in the Americas. Not only was the number relatively small but slaves were treated as human beings rather than as chattel.

Although Islam had remained essentially the religion of foreigners in ancient Ghana, superficial changes reflecting the influence of the new faith began to appear in Mali and Songhai. The administration of justice and the system of taxation in those states were based on the Koran. The architecture of the principal buildings, the mosques, and the palaces was Islamic, as was the attire of the town dwellers. Al-Umari wrote that "they wear turbans with ends tied under their chin like the Arabs, their cloth is white and made of cotton which they cultivate and weave in a most excellent fashion." Ibn Battuta was also impressed by the attention paid to religious worship. "They are careful to observe the hours of prayer," he noted, "and assiduous in attending them in congregations, and in bringing up their children to them."

By the late fifteenth century Timbuktu had developed into the educational and commercial metropolis of the western Sudan, or rather, as one writer called it, the Queen of the Sudan. Its university, in the Sankore district of the city, produced such scholars and historians as Mahmud al-Kati, author of the *Kitab al-Fattash,* a chronicle of Songhai's Askia dynasty, and Abd al-Rahman as-Sadi, author of the *Tarikh as-Sudan,* a chronicle of the Sudan. Even the West African historian J. Spencer Trimingham, who is rather skeptical about Sankore as a university, admits that there were as many as one hundred fifty Koranic schools in Timbuktu alone. Leo Africanus also talks of "the great store of doctors, judges, priests, and other learned men that are bountifully maintained at the King's cost and charges. And hither are brought diverse manuscripts or written books out of Barbarie which are sold for more money than any other merchandise."

Mahmud al-Kati pays tribute in the *Kitab al-Fattash* to his colleagues: "The scholars of this period were the most respected among the believers for their generosity, their force of character, and their discretion." We also have the names of scholars who went on lecture tours and set up schools in different parts of the western Sudan, and especially in Hausaland. Mahmud Ibn Umar, for instance, lectured in Kano in 1485 to large and reverent crowds of people. Indeed, the Timbuktu tradition of learning dominated the cities of the western and central Sudan until the beginning of the nineteenth century.

But if the towns in Mali and Songhai assumed an Islamic hue, it would appear that the rural areas of both empires stuck to their traditional ways. They maintained their animistic beliefs, their traditional cults and indigenous African way of life, their initiation rites, their sorcerers, and their family and clan heads and chiefs, who administered justice in accordance with customary law.

It should be obvious from the above that, in spite of the skepticisms of certain European writers, the early empires of the western Sudan were true states, with all the fundamental attributes of government that statehood implies. They had paid bureaucracies, strong economies based on trade, mining, agriculture, and political machinery capable of ensuring law, order, security, and diplomatic exchange.

The fall of all these states was due to both internal and external factors. The internal factors were usually the rivalries among members of the royal family. The external factors were for the most part foreign attacks. With the possible exception of Songhai, none of these empires had a really durable provincial administrative structure. As pointed out earlier, the conquered states and kingdoms within each empire were governed by their own rulers and were held to the central authority mainly by military might. Moreover, each empire was composed of different ethnic and linguistic groups, hence it lacked cultural and ethnic homogeneity. Some of the rulers of both Mali and Songhai did attempt to use Islam to provide cohesion, but only with very limited success. Both Ghana's central authority and its army were weakened as a result of the defeats they suffered between 1054 and 1076 by the adherents of the Almoravid movement. As described more fully in Chapter Four, this was an Islamic movement that arose in the eleventh century among the Sanhaja Berbers who occupied the western Sahara. Although Ghana did reconquer its capital from the Almoravids after 1087, it never really recovered from those earlier blows, and its vassal states broke away. The coup de grâce, however, was delivered in 1203 by an external force, the rulers of the Susu kingdom to the south.

Mali fell victim principally to the internal breakdown of the central government, as a result of the inordinate ambition and frivolity of its royal family. The trouble began at the end of the reign of Mansa Sulaiman in 1359–1360. The history of the kings of Mali for the next several decades was a sordid record of regicides, civil wars, contested successions, and coups d'état. Indeed, within the brief period from 1360 to 1390 as many as seven people were enthroned, four of them between 1387 and 1390. Central authority collapsed, anarchy and instability came in its wake, and as in Ghana, the vassal states began to break away. The demise of the empire came after Mali had been attacked from three sides: the Tuareg attacked from the north, the Mossi from the south, and the Songhai from the east. By 1433 the Tuareg had captured Arawan, Walata, and Timbuktu, and in the 1460's and the 1470's the Mossi took arms against the southern and even the central regions of Mali. The rulers of Mali appealed to Portugal for assistance in the 1490's and again in the 1530's. The Portuguese could do nothing but send words of encouragement. The Songhai attacks delivered the final blow, and by the fourth decade of the sixteenth century Mali had shrunk again into the tiny Mande principality of Kangaba.

Songhai's glory lasted little more than a century after its victories over Mali. The establishment of the Askia dynasty in Songhai in 1493, a result of the military coup organized and led by Askia Muhammad, was the beginning of the internal division of the country. Being of the Soninke rather than the Songhai people, he tried to replace the animistic beliefs of the Songhai with Islam, as indeed Sunni Ali, his predecessor, had done in an effort to unify the empire. Though Askia Muhammad's attempts only alienated the Songhai people, he was shrewd and strong enough to contain these internal differences. His successors could not. As had been the case in Mali, a series of disputed successions, revolts, and usurpations broke out among members of his family. In the sixty years after his deposition as many as eight people mounted the throne. However, it would appear that at least one of the rulers, Askia Daud, was quite competent, and during his long reign from 1549 to 1582 the fortunes of Songhai improved. Although disputed successions broke out again after Daud, and as many as three rulers came to the throne between 1582 and 1591, the central authority would appear to have remained intact.

It was the decisive defeat inflicted by the forces of Sultan Al-Mansur of Morocco that precipitated the disintegration of the empire. Led by Judar Pasha, a young Spanish eunuch, the sultan's army crushed the Songhai army at the battle of Tondibi in 1591 and marched south in search of Songhai's fabled riches. The Songhai army was estimated by Al-Kati to have been a huge one consisting of 18,000 cavalry and 9,700 infantry, while the Moroccans are said to have numbered only 4,000. The Moroccan victory was in some measure due to the fact that the Songhai fought with spears, swords, and bows and arrows, whereas the Moroccan army was equipped with harquebuses and cannon. When the advisers of Al-Mansur tried to dissuade him from undertaking what they considered to be a crazy enterprise, the sultan is said to have replied:

> You talk of the dangerous desert we have to cross, of the fatal solitudes, barren of water and pasture, but you forget the defenseless and ill-equipped merchants who, mounted or on foot, regularly cross these wastes which caravans have never ceased to traverse. I, who am so much better equipped than they, can surely do the same with an army which inspires terror wherever it goes. . . . Moreover, our predecessors would have found great difficulty if they had tried to do what I now propose, for their armies were composed only of horsemen armed with spears and of bowmen; gunpowder was unknown to them, and so were firearms and their terrifying effect. Today the Sudanese have only spears and swords, weapons which will be useless against modern arms. It will therefore be easy for us to wage a successful war against these people and prevail over them.

Following Al-Mansur's military success, however, anarchy broke out in the area of the Niger Bend, and it would continue intermittently until the late nineteenth century.

And what was happening in the regions to the south of the empires of Ghana, Mali, and Songhai? As has been already pointed out, a simultaneous process of state formation was at work. Arising just to the west in the regions of the Senegambia was the kingdom of Wolof; to the south emerged the Mole-Dagbane states and the Mossi kingdoms. Still farther south arose a number of forest and coastal states: Ife, Oyo, and Benin in Nigeria; the Ga kingdom and Akan states in modern Ghana. Their emergence was due to factors similar to those that gave birth to Ghana, Mali, and Songhai. Of first importance was the extension of the caravan trade routes southward into the savanna, the forest, and the coastal regions; of second was the development within the region of trade among the coastal peoples; and of third were the activities of the wealthy and ambitious families or clan groups who were stimulated by those commercial activities.

As has already been pointed out, the mainstays of the caravan trade—gold, kola nuts, ivory, and slaves—could all be obtained in the regions of the southern savanna and forest. From evidence rapidly accumulating today, it is certain that by the end of the fourteenth century, at the height of Mali's power, the trade routes from the Sahara, which had earlier stopped at the savanna cities of Walata, Timbuktu, Jenne, and Gao, had now been extended westward and southward.

The people who were responsible for the development of this trade between the forest regions and the states of Mali and Songhai were certainly the Diula group of the Mande people. They founded a number of caravan posts, including Bobo-Dioulasso (in modern Upper Volta), Kong and Bouna (in modern Ivory Coast), and Wa and Begho (in modern Ghana). Begho, the last of them, was established just north of the forest zone in about 1400. From Begho, routes radiated directly south to the coastal regions of Axim (in southwest Ghana) and southeastward through Asante to the coastal region of modern Cape Coast and Elmina.

Proof of the extension of northern trade routes to the coast can be taken from the fact that two items of clothing, *lanbens* (shawls) and *aljaravais* (dressing gowns) that were manufactured in Morocco and Tunis were in great demand on the coast of modern Ghana before the arrival of the Portuguese. Describing that trade in 1500, the Portuguese agent Pacheco Pereira also mentions peoples from the interior: "Boroes, Mandingoes, Cacres, Andeses, or Souzos." Here again, the "Boroes" are obviously the Bono of northern Asante, the "Cacres" are possibly the Kasena-Grusi of northern Ghana, and the "Mandingoes" and "Souzos" are readily identifiable as the Mandingos and the Susu of the larger family of Mande peoples.

The Portuguese and later the Dutch traders found the coastal peoples enjoying very lucrative salt and fish trade with the inland peoples. The Dutchman Pieter de Marees, writing in 1601 about one of the Akan settlements, states that "the inhabitants of the sea-side, come also to the markets with their . . . fish, which their husbands have gotten in the sea, whereof the women buy much and carrie them to other townes within the land, to get some profit by them, so that the fish which is taken in the sea, is carried at least one hundred or two hundred miles up into the land, for a great present." William Bosman, an official of the Dutch West India Company who came to the coast during the second half of the seventeenth century, made a similar observation. There is no reason to think that trade in salt and fish was not going on prior to the arrival of the Portuguese. Salt has always been an indispensable commodity and has generated contact between people who produce it and those who do not, and we know that salt is not found in the forest region and can be produced only in very small quantities in the savanna regions to the north.

It also seems clear that the Mande were responsible for the extension of the routes eastward from Timbuktu and Gao into the Hausa states, probably in the fourteenth century. From these Hausa states, trade routes radiated southwestward across the Niger and through the Mole-Dagbane areas into the gold- and kola-producing areas of Asante in modern Ghana. The Kano Chronicle states that kola nuts reached Hausaland from northern Ghana during the first half of the fifteenth century. Other routes also led southward through the regions surrounding the confluence of the Benue and Niger rivers and into the Yoruba and Benin areas to the southwest. Ibn Battuta talks of copper from the Takedda mines being exported southward into Nigeria, and judging from the bronze works of Ife and Benin (to be discussed later), it is not unlikely, as the British ethnographer Frank Willett has suggested that "some of this Takedda ore eventually found its way even farther south."

Pre-European trade also existed between east and west via the sea, especially between the coasts of modern Ghana and Nigeria. Evidence for this conclusion is found in the oral tradition, very widely held among the Ga and the people of Asebu (one of the Akan states), that they migrated from Benin by sea into the coastal regions of modern Ghana and that the Ga kingdom was in fact a part of the empire of Benin. However, on the basis of linguistic and other ethnological data, it is exceedingly unlikely that the Ga and the Asebu did in fact originate from Benin. Rather, the oral tradition seems to be an echo of the old trading contacts between the people of Benin and those of the coast of modern Ghana. The fifteenth- and early sixteenth-century accounts of the Portuguese traders suggest that they merely exploited a pre-existing pattern of trade to their own advantage. Pacheco Pereira, who was there in the 1500's, says that they bought slaves at the port of Benin for "twelve or fifteen brass bracelets each, or for copper bracelets which they prize more; from there the slaves are brought to the castle of S. Jorze da Mina [the extant fortress of São Jorge at Elmina on the Ghana coast] where they are sold for gold." He also says that they traded on the Niger near the coast of the Bight of Benin, "principally in slaves, in cotton stuff, some leopard skins, palm oil, and blue beads with red stripes which they call 'coris'— and other things which we are accustomed to buy here for brass and copper bracelets. All these commodities have value at the castle of S. Jorze da Mina. The Factor of our prince sells them to Negro traders in exchange for gold."

Pereira goes on to describe the local people's manner of travel: "At the mouth of the River Real [the Bonny River] . . . there is a very large village, consisting of about 2,000 souls. Much salt is made here, and in this country are to be found the largest canoes, made of a single trunk, that are known in the whole of Ethiopia of Guinea; some are so large that they hold 80 men. They travel distances of a hundred leagues and more down the river, and bring many yams, which are very good here and make a tolerable diet, many slaves, cows, goats and sheep."

Writing early in the next century, Pieter de Marees also describes the canoes in use on the coast of Ghana. He notes that the people of Accra had large canoes "to fish or go to sea withall," and that he saw one "cut out of a tree which was five and thirty foot long and five foot broad and three foot high, which was as big as a shallop, so that it would have held thirty men." In the same century Jean Barbot, agent general of the French Royal Africa Company, also saw canoes on the coast of Ghana of sizes ranging from fourteen to forty feet long, and he added that the largest of them could "carry above ten tons of goods with eighteen or twenty blacks to paddle them." He stated further that the best canoe men were the Elmina blacks, who "drive a great trade along the Gold Coast, and at Wida by Sea [Ovidah, a seaport in the area of modern Dahomey], and are the fittest and the most experienc'd men to manage and paddle the canoes over the bars and breakings, which render this coast, and that of Wida so perilous and toilsome to land either men, goods or provisions." One may conclude from these descriptions that going to sea in large canoes was already well established on the eve of the Portuguese arrival. Indeed, it probably dated as far back as the first millennium A.D., when the coastal areas began to be occupied by peoples from the interior, and commercial and cultural contacts were initiated.

As was the case farther north, the West African peoples who were geographically situated to play the role of middlemen would be those who could develop large states and kingdoms. To the south of Ghana and Mali, the first states to become sizable kingdoms were the Wolof kingdom to the west, the Mole-Dagbane and Mossi states to the south in the Volta River Basin, and the Ife, Oyo, and Benin kingdoms to the southeast. All except Benin were situated in the southern savanna belt. The Wolof people could control not only the lucrative salt trade from the sea, but could share in the gold trade with Morocco. The Mole-Dagbane states and the closely related Mossi states—all of which were founded during the first half of the fifteenth century—expanded mainly to establish a firm control over the trade routes linking the Niger Bend and Hausaland with the Akan's gold fields and kola-tree groves.

The oral traditions of the Akan peoples indicate that the first Akan states to emerge early in the fifteenth century were Bono-Manso in the region between the savanna and the forest and Adansi and Assin in the region where gold was obtained. Later on, different groups migrated northward to establish city-states, which were all within a few miles of where the routes that led from the Niger Bend terminated. It was these states that would later form the nucleus of the famous Asante empire.

The other Akan states of Aguafo, Fetu, Asebu, Fante, Agona, and the Ga kingdom—the so-called Gold Coast states—were created mainly in response to the demands of the transoceanic as well as the overland north-south trade. Their failure to develop into powerful kingdoms prior to the arrival of the Portuguese can be explained by the fact that they were one step further removed from the source of gold, trading through the intermediary of their sister Akan states in the interior. The Gold Coast states were also hampered by being crowded into a relatively short stretch of coast—the five Akan states occupied no more than one hundred miles.

Primarily by virtue of its geographical position, Benin became a center of both overland and sea trade, the latter by way of Ghana. Of the Yoruba states that later developed to the northwest of Benin, between 1380 and 1420, the first to develop into a sizable kingdom was Oyo. This northernmost Yoruba state was situated in the savanna region just below the Niger and, by the end of the fifteenth century, was able to claim the dominant share of trade between Hausaland and the Niger Bend and the other Yoruba states to the south. However, since Oyo had as rivals other centralized states to the south and west, its expansion could not be as rapid as that of Benin. Indeed, it was not until the seventeenth and eighteenth centuries that, using guns, Oyo's army extended its frontiers to the Guinea coast.

What then were these kingdoms like when the Portuguese first established contact with them? Pacheco Pereira reported in 1505: "Here at the Senegal you find the first black people. This is the kingdom of Wolof, a hundred leagues long and eight broad. The kingdom of Wolof can put into the field an army of about 10,000 cavalry and 100,000 infantry." It would appear from the early sixteenth-century accounts of Alvise da Cadamosto, a Venetian explorer in the service of Prince Henry of Portugal, that the kingdom consisted of five polities, all under a single ruler. Valentine Fernandes, a Lisbon printer of Moravian origin, writing in the same period, furnishes us with further details. He says the king had many subjects under him and administered his state with the aid of Muslim "dignitaries after the fashion of dukes and counts" and "white bischerigs who are priests and preachers of Mahomet, and can read and write." He adds that some of the ordinary people had embraced Islam, though the majority of them were sticking to their animistic beliefs. It is not surprising that some of the people should be

Muslims, since the kingdom was situated to the south of Takrur, into which Islam had penetrated as early as A.D. 1000.

The Portuguese found the fifteen-hundred-mile-long stretch from Gambia to the borders of modern Ghana only sparsely settled; it appears that no state of any size emerged along that coast before the end of the fifteenth century. But in the area of modern Ghana, between the Pra and Volta rivers, the explorers-traders came upon the cluster of Akan states described earlier.

The three contiguous Akan states of Aguafo, Fetu, and Asebu were similar in organization: at the head of each state was a king (he lived in a capital a few miles from the coast), who was assisted by a council of elders. Eustace de la Fosse, writing in 1479, reports taking security from the "Mansa and Caramansa," who, he adds, "are the king and viceroy of Aguafo," and it was with the viceroy that Don Diego de Azambuja negotiated for the plot at Elmina, on which the castle São Jorge was built in 1482. Each of these states had trading villages or outlets, some of which became European settlements.

In contrast, the Fante state seems to have been composed of a series of inland townships, or quarters, within about three to five miles of one another. Collectively, they made up the capital district of Mankessim (alternatively Fantyn), and each quarter was under a chief, or *braffo,* who was advised by the family or clan heads. One *braffo* was recognized as overall leader, though his authority was limited, and he had to consult the others before he could declare war or make peace. It is also evident from the oral traditions and from a shrine that has survived near Mankessim that all the Fante recognized one national god, whom they called Nanaam. Orders emanating from the chief priest of Nanaam were binding on all the Fante. Thus, the government of the Fante was a sort of theocracy with political power being controlled by the chief ruler and the chief priests. Like the other states, the Fante also had some coastal outposts; these were Anomabu, Little Fantyn, and Kormantin. The Fante remained in Mankessim until the last three decades of the seventeenth century when, probably as a result of population pressure, they began to move out of the townships to establish kingdoms within a twenty- or thirty-mile radius of the capital.

No sizable states had emerged in the area between the mouth of the Volta River and Yorubaland by the middle of the fifteenth century, but in the western and midwestern regions of Nigeria, the Portuguese found the Yoruba and Edo peoples living in what were probably the most advanced and certainly the most interesting states of the Guinea coast: Ife, Benin, and Oyo. The oldest of these was Ife. Indeed, the Yoruba-speaking peoples regard Ife as the center of the world and the cradle of their civilization. According to one of their traditional accounts, it was there that God's children landed and set about to create the world. The most senior of these children was Oduduwa, whom they regarded as the first ruler, or *oni,* of Ife. He is said to have had sixteen children, whom he sent out to found the Yoruba states.

From a careful analysis of these oral traditions and the terra-cotta art of Ife, Willett has concluded that these oral traditions represent the arrival of "a small, but influential group of people," probably from the east or northeast. He postulates further that these people found the indigenous Yoruba and Igbo peoples already working in terra cotta, and that they introduced the art of bronze casting and the ideas of divine kingship, and that these new arrivals founded Ife, from which place the other Yoruba kingdoms would be created. Whether founded by the Yoruba or by invaders from the east, Ife never developed into a kingdom, for reasons that are still not apparent. It remained throughout essentially a city-state ruled by a "divine" king, who, as a Portuguese observer put it, was held "in great reveration as is the Supreme Pontiff with us." Nevertheless, Ife is of vital interest because it has remained from its foundation the religious center of all the Yoruba peoples and because it was there that the Yoruba's world-acclaimed sculpture in bronze, wood, and terra cotta was first developed.

From there this unique art spread to the whole of West Africa. The bronze sculptures, their supreme achievement, were made by the lost-wax process. The best of these were created in the classical period of Ife art, which conventionally has been said to have lasted from the beginning of the thirteenth to the middle of the fourteenth century. However, in view of the bronze sculptures recently discovered at Igbo-Ukwu, which have been dated by the radiocarbon process to the ninth century A.D., many scholars are beginning to accept an earlier date for Ife's classical period, probably before our millennium, bringing it closer to the Nok culture.

To the southeast of Ife, in the forest area, Benin emerged. Whereas Ife remained a city-state, Benin had developed into a sizable kingdom by the middle of the fifteenth century. Pereira, who visited Benin four times, wrote in 1505:

> A league up this river on the left two tributaries enter the main stream: if you ascend the second of these for twelve leagues you find a town called Huguatoo [Gwato], of some 2,000 souls: this is the harbor of a great city of Beny [Benin], which lies nine leagues in the interior with a good road between them. Small ships of fifty tons can go as far as Huguatoo. This city is about a league long from gate to gate; it has no wall but is surrounded by a large moat, very wide and deep, which suffices for its defense. . . . Its houses are made of mud walls covered with palm leaves. The Kingdom of Beny is about eighty leagues long and forty wide; it is usually at war with its neighbors. . . .

It seems clear from the traditional accounts of Benin that there are at least two periods of Benin history. All that can be pieced together is that during the first period Benin was a city-state under the rule of the Ogiso dynasty and that this family was replaced by the Oba dynasty sometime before 1300. Establishing themselves among the Edo-speaking peoples, who were organized only into clans, lineages, and village groups, the new Oba kings claimed supernatural powers. They soon succeeded in converting the city-state into the sizable and thriving kingdom that the Portuguese found on their arrival in the 1470's.

The oral traditions of Benin, Ife, and Oyo shed some light on how the Oba dynasty came to power. The histories of all three kingdoms agree that after a period of anarchy, the people of Benin beseeched the *oni* of Ife, Oduduwa himself, for a ruler, and he sent his son Oranmiyan. But believing that it would be better for a native of Benin to rule there, Oranmiyan married a daughter of one of the local chiefs and shortly thereafter had a son, Eweka, to whom he gave the throne. Oranmiyan then returned to Ife and from there went on to establish the kingdom of Oyo. Eweka thus became the first *oba* of Benin, but he had to obtain his insignia of office from the *oni* of Ife. It seems obvious from this account that the founders of the Oba dynasty of Benin, like the founders of Oyo, came from Ife.

To govern this kingdom, it would appear that the Oba kings developed certain political institutions that were an amalgam of Ife traditions and local political and social ideas. At the head of the kingdom was the *oba,* who, like the rulers of the early Sudanese states and those of Ife, was a "divine" king. As the English explorer Thomas Wyndham observed in 1553: "And here to speak of the great reverence they give to their king, it is such, that if we would give as much to our Saviour Christ, we should remove from our heads many plagues which we daily deserve. . . ."

The king was assisted by three ranking classes. The first class was the *uzama,* or king makers, whose position dates from Benin's early dynastic era. They had to perform certain important state rituals, including the installation of the *oba.* The second group was the *eghaevbo n'ogbe,* or palace chiefs, who were responsible not only for the *oba's* regalia, his wives and children, his personal relations, and his doctors and divine men but also for the administration of the provinces, or fiefs. The third estate was the *eghaevbo n'ore,* or town chiefs, whose leader was the *iyase,* the prime minister and commander in chief of the army, and from whom other war leaders as well as other governors of provinces were chosen. Since most of these officials were appointed by the *oba* himself, he enjoyed considerable powers, though he still had to ensure his position by playing one group against another.

Provincial Benin, that is the conquered territories, was divided into three administrative units. At the base was the village under a village head; at the intermediate level was the chiefdom made up of a number of villages, each administered by a chief appointed by the king; at a higher level were the fiefs, or provinces, each consisting of a number of chiefdoms and directed by either a town or palace chief. This system of administration remained without any fundamental changes until the late nineteenth century.

Regarding Benin's achievements in art, the local oral tradition admits to learning the art of bronze casting from Ife. It is related that Oguola, the fifth *oba* of the second dynasty, who reigned during the end of the fourteenth century, sent to the *oni* of Ife for a bronzesmith to teach his people. The *oni* is said to have agreed and sent Iguegha, who is worshiped to this day in Benin as the patron of bronzesmiths. In fact, the style of the early Benin bronzes is quite similar to that of Ife, but by the sixteenth century, using the same lost-wax process known in Ife, Benin artists had evolved a distinctive style of their own, which was less naturalistic and more formal. As in Ife, the people of Benin also worked in wood, ivory, and raffia.

Despite the widespread tradition that attributes the founding of both Benin and Oyo to Oranmiyan, it is now generally agreed that Oyo's founding occurred nearly a century later, between the last two decades of the fourteenth and the first three decades of the fifteenth centuries. That it had grown into a fairly large kingdom by the end of the fifteenth century through expansion northward must have been due partly to the ability of Oyo's founding kings and partly, as we have seen, to its position in an area best suited for the domination of the trade routes from the north. Their art was derived from Ife, but as Frank Willett has pointed out, it shows "gradually declining naturalism, as if the social pressures which produced the naturalism of Classical Ife have gradually weakened."

Oyo's political institutions were based, as in the other kingdoms of West Africa, upon a "divine" king. The *alafin* ruled the kingdom with the advice of a council composed of seven notables known as the *oyo mesi* under the leadership of the *bashorun,* or prime minister. The *oyo mesi* was not only responsible for the election of the *alafin,* but according to a historian of Yoruba tradition, Samuel Johnson, its members "represent the voice of the nation, on them developed the chief duty of protecting the interests of the kingdom." The *alafin* could not declare war or peace without their consent. Moreover, should the *bashorun* ever declare three times, "the gods reject you, the people reject you, the earth rejects you," the *alafin* was obliged to commit suicide. However, some safeguards were instituted against the abuse of this power. Firstly, one of the members of the *oyo mesi,* known as "the *alafin's* friend," had to die with the *alafin.* Secondly, both the *alafin* and the council were controlled by the *ogboni,* a secret earth cult consisting of all members of the *oyo mesi,* heads of the other cults, rich traders, and prominent diviners. This society had to ratify certain decisions of the *oyo mesi,* among them the rejection of the *alafin* by the *bashorun.* It seems clear that the people of Oyo devised a system that had checks and balances built into it to eliminate arbitrary or dictatorial exercise of power.

In summation, the people of West Africa, stimulated by trade and ruled and inspired by talented leaders, did form states and develop political institutions that were truly unique and truly African between 500 and 1450. Some of them also developed artistic skills, which in their aesthetic sensitivities were comparable, if not superior, to those of contemporary Europe.

AFRICA: A Rich Cultural Heritage I

"Growing up" has been a subject for research and theorization in disciplines such as psychology, sociology, and cultural anthropology. The concept of growing up marks the transition from childhood to adulthood. The selections included in this chapter focus on growing up in African societies. Africa's rich cultural heritage derives from a number of factors related to survival, to existence. The high disease and death rate, the complicated system of social rank, the erosion of African culture by the introduction of Western technology—all contributed to both the content and the media for the communication of cultural values and heritages. The extended family, the close-knit neighborhood, and the role of rituals in growing up are some of the features in African society that will be of interest to readers because of novelty, or comparison, or both.

Maturity Rites

Ervin Lewis

There is in Africa frequently a high incidence of disease and death among children, and simple development of the young assumes an uncommon importance, not only for the children's sake but for the perpetuation of the group and support of the family in its older years. These harsh facts may help to explain the trials and the rituals associated with mere survival to puberty. The following article by Ervin Lewis deals briefly with the significance of attaining child-bearing age in various African communities.

Tribal or other community life in much of Africa is often sufficiently isolated and concentrated as to call for modes of conduct that might seem strange to many populations on other continents. Puberty, for example, is regarded as so important as to merit detailed instructions by adults for boys and girls, ranging in subject matter from everyday and casual deportment to premarriage or postmarriage sex. Circumcision is a memorable event, among major and minor groups, even as it is with some religious faiths in and beyond Africa. Songs have been composed and sung for the particular benefit of boys facing circumcision, not only to support courage in the physical ordeal but to offer promise of the pleasures of sex to come and to warn of the dangers of excesses and promiscuity. It is felt that singing, by the boys themselves or the attendant adults, has psychological and social values at this stage of life for pubescent males. With the Mandinkas, an entire repertoire of songs is available, as the occasion justifies. The following is one example, and it should be borne in mind that the song might be repeated time and again, as a kind of mesmeric chant:

Kunu fing, kunu koi o!
Kunolu benta fara baa le.
Fara dibongo le teeta banko la tai,
Kunu foro lonta jee le.[1]

Black bird, white bird o!
The birds gathered in the big rice swamp.
The dibong bird of the swamp crashed on the ground;
The true bird is known there.[2]

Explanation: When boys are circumcised, the first one to heal up is called "the true bird." In the context of the shed where circumcision takes place, the song would mean that the first boy to heal up is thereby distinguished as of a superior nature to the others. The song would be used to encourage the boys to do their best in ensuring proper attention to their surgical wound in order that they recover quickly. The boy who does so achieves considerable prestige, and all are anxious to avoid the stigma of being last. Later in life, the same song would be used in different context. It might be sung where some person has been distinguished by passing an examination or being chosen for a job. Thus it can be sung either to praise the successful or to rub salt in the wounds of the unsuccessful. As with many African songs, the meaning is deliberately disguised in the words chosen, not only for subtlety and symbolism but for adaptability to more than one occasion.

Alex Haley's *Roots* provides a dramatic example of the psychological approach to the maturing of young males in The Gambian precolonial village of Juffure. Kunta was one of the group of adolescents confused and resentful at the severity of the elderly Kintango, who supervised this process during four months of intensive disciplining. Yet, when the ordeal ended, including circumcision as one of its many trials, there was unanimous and unabashed gratitude, even affection, for Kintango. He and his assistants has skillfully guided Kunta and the others into early manhood. And they had done so with speed and sophistication, long before the recognition of psychology as a science of mental processes and behavior. Obviously, a primitive setting did not mean a community of savages, except perhaps in Western eyes.

NOTES

1. Gordon Innes, "Mandinka Circumcision Songs," *African Language Studies,* XIII (1972), p.106.
2. *Ibid.,* p. 107.

Growing Up in Acholi

Anna Apoko

The following article is entitled "Growing Up in Acholi," but it might well be subtitled "Acholi Grows Up." This large tribe in eastern Africa has been entering the age of what is casually labeled "progress" for more than a decade, and obviously not all the changes are for the better. The dilemma for the Acholis is much the same as for many other communities in Africa and elsewhere, with technology eroding culture as it eases physical labor. The flavor of tribal life is being diluted by an appetite for modernity that is whetted by outside contacts and the mass-communications media. Ironically, much of the fascination comes from the same New World that drew from Africa the slave labor that helped to create the technology. Could this be a new and subtle form of enslavement by similarly selfish masters?

VILLAGE BIRTHPLACE

The Acholi people live in the north of Uganda. To the west of the District, the River Nile marks their boundary with the West Nile District. To the east there lies Karamoja, to the south Lango District; to the north, the boundary of the Sudan cuts across, leaving some of the Acholi in Sudan.

The Acholi people were originally divided into several chiefdoms. The most important of these were Payira, Patiko, Puranga, and Koich, my own chiefdom with which I am mainly concerned. Each chiefdom has many clans and each clan has many families. Groups of families, who are very often related to one another, live together in a village. The population of a village often drinks from the same well, and groups all the crops in the same place every year. A village with many people can also have a dancing field, with a high pole in the centre for the drum. (Acholi dancers have been famous throughout Uganda for many years.) People living in the same village have a lot in common. When the rainy season approaches, the men often gather together and go to open one another's new cotton, simsim, groundnut or millet fields in turn. This makes digging easier and more enjoyable than if one man tries to work alone on his field. The man whose new cotton field is to be opened always arranges a big beer party for the workers. The women also work in groups, helping one another weed in their gardens.

Within each village family in Acholi, there is a strict division of labour between the father and the mother, or husband and wife. The father or husband is the head of the family. He has the decisive voice on all matters concerning the family. Acholi people follow the patrilineal system of inheritance. Every father makes it a point to train his son to become a strong-willed man, who cannot be dominated by a woman. The husband's work is the cutting of wood for building a house and the actual building of the house. The wife's work is to cut grass for thatching the roof. The man also digs the field and sows the seed, but it is the work of the woman to keep the garden clear of weeds and to harvest the crops like millet, simsim, peas and beans. All domestic work concerned with cooking is the work of the woman. It is a disgrace for a grown up man or even a boy to go to the well and carry water. That is the work of a woman. Grinding is also the work of a woman; no man in Acholi must grind. Anything concerned with babies and young children is a woman's work.

A man who has so many acres of cotton, millet, and simsim, so many grain stores full of millet, simsim, and peas, who has so many cows or goats; a man whose houses are big and strong; a man who is brave in hunting and fighting—is considered a good and successful man in rural Acholi and is respected by society. A lot of songs are often composed, especially by women, for such men. For example, this one:

Odai we ye,
Odai latin acel pire tek,
Obutu kicel long gang oling tik.

Our Odai,
The only great one.
He was absent for a day
   and the house went to pieces.

Likewise, a woman whose house is well smeared with black soil and kept clean; who has a lot of food in her home; who cooks and gives generously to visitors (according to the Acholi custom requiring the wife to cook or at least give food to any visitor who comes at any time); a woman whose gardens are well kept; who mixes freely and happily with other women in the village; and who has children—is considered a good woman. Such a woman can be called to join a meeting of village elders to give some talks and advice. Very often such things as this are said about her: *Dako pa Okot dako ki cumun. Dako man minne opwongo ada.* 'Mrs. Okot is a woman and a half. She must have had really good training from her mother.'

Such are the Acholi's ideal people, those who are liked and valued by the whole community. The aim of traditional education or of bringing up children in Acholi is to produce such citizens. People take great care to see that children are given all the necessary training in order that they will be hard-working and useful men and women in the society; men and women who will not have to starve because they cannot cultivate for themselves. Great attention is paid to all aspects of children's 'moral' development. They must learn to obey those who are older than they are. A boy, particularly, has to grow up obeying his father's brothers, who are just as important and influential to him as is his own father. He must respect his mother's brothers, who may curse him and cause ill luck for him if he disrespects them. He must also grow up in close contact with the gods of his grandfathers and must know how to keep *abila,* the shrine.

Everybody who is closely related to the child takes part in, and contributes, towards the child's education. Uncles, aunts stepmothers, elder brothers and sisters, all are members of staff. Teaching takes place through teasing *(ngala),* songs, educative stories *(ododo)* and practical work. . . .

THE FEEDING AND CARE OF CHILDREN

Feeding a child at the breast is the common practice in Acholi. All village mothers breast-feed their babies. There is no regular time for feeding babies. Whenever a baby cries, it is given the breast. If a mother is unable to breast-feed her baby, or if she dies, usually some suckling mother takes over and feeds the two babies together as if they were twins. Otherwise the baby may be fed on cow's milk.

As soon as a mother has given birth to her baby, if she does not have older children of her own, she looks around among her relatives for *lapidi,* a selected young child, preferably a girl from six to ten years old, to act as the baby's 'nurse.' During a recent vacation I met a woman who was once my classmate; she had come sixty-five miles from where she was living with her husband, back to her father's home, looking for *lapidi.* She found a little girl, five years old, who went back with her.

The very young baby, from one to three months old, is tied on *lapidi's* back. *Lapidi,* carrying the baby in this way, goes with the mother to the field where she may be working for most of the day. If the baby wakes up from its sleep and begins to cry, the mother unties it from the child's back and breast-feeds it. By the time the baby is four months old, it may be left at home with *lapidi,* who again follows after the mother as soon as the baby is hungry and begins to cry. Nurses have many lullaby songs which they sing when the babies cry. For example,

Latin kok ngo?
Meni otedo aluri ki kwon.

Baby, why do you cry?
Your mother has cooked a fowl and some millet.

Sometimes the nurse becomes so tired, poor child, that she may begin wearily singing a song about the mother of the child, such as: *Min latin do tedo dyerwor.* . . . 'The child's mother cooks so late in the night.' If the mother has the food nearly ready she calls, 'Bring me my baby! Do not break its back!' But when she realizes that she has not yet cooked the millet, she will say to *lapidi,* 'Take the baby and play with it, out of my sight!' If the baby goes on crying, the nurse will again tie it on her back and follow the mother about the house.

I was *lapidi* for my little cousin for about a year. How I loved that baby! I wanted to be with him all the time. Perhaps this was because I had requested to be *lapidi.* The duty had not been forced on me. By the time the baby was able to walk well and firmly, and another little girl cousin was old enough to be his nurse, I had to give him up so that I could go to school.

A mother who does not have *lapidi* is bound to carry her baby about wherever she goes and whatever she does. Such mothers often sing this lullaby to their babies:

Nynyu ka ikok ngo?
Lapidi meri peke.
Onyu ling.
Lapidi meri obeno.

Why do you cry, my baby?
You have no *lapidi?*
Obeno is your nurse.
Keep quiet, baby, you have no nurse.

Thus *lapidi* is the second mother to the baby; and there are some babies who are fonder of their *lapidi* than of their own mothers.

Only in the homes of rich educated parents are babies fed on cow's milk, in addition to breast milk. The Acholi are not pastoral people; and milk is scarce and expensive. An ordinary family in the village, unless they have cows of their own, cannot afford to use milk. So from birth to seven months the baby is fed on breast milk alone. After that the child begins to take solid food, usually millet porridge, which the mother instructs the nurse to make for the child in her absence. The baby is also fed on roasted ground simsim or groundnuts, of which, incidentally, children are very fond. By the time the baby is one year old, he can eat in small quantities whatever adults eat.

Weaning takes place as soon as the mother discovers a new pregnancy. At this time the milk is said to be bad for the child. Before this, most women see no reason for weaning. Unless they are pregnant, they usually go on breast-feeding their babies until long after the babies can walk or run. Some lastborn children are known to suck for four or five years, until they leave off voluntarily as a result of other people's scornful words. *Irii icak toki golle.* 'If you suck for a long time you develop a hole at the back of your head.' This hole is supposed to be caused by constant bending of the head in order to reach the breast.

Because they lose their favourite food and their mother's close attention and love in the same abrupt process, weaning can be the most painful experience of childhood for many children. Often Acholi mothers will wean their babies by putting bitter herbs or hot pepper on to the nipples. This discourages the child from sucking. Some mothers wean the children by going away on a visit, staying for two or three days so that the baby will become accustomed to doing without breast milk. Weaned children are fed on whatever adults eat, with peas, beans, meat, groundnuts and simsim as their favourite foods. If a mother roasts groundnuts or simsim and begins grinding it, she always gives some of it to the young children to eat. This is one of the reasons, perhaps, why Acholi children do not seem to suffer from malnutrition, as much as do children in Buganda, for instance.

At meal time all the children eat with the mother, sitting on the kitchen floor, while the father eats alone. It is common in the villages to find a group of two or three families eating together, each woman having cooked two separate dishes, one for the men and one for the women and children. If there are a large number of children, one separate dish can be served to the children only. The two or three men, heads of the different families, will sit together near a fire outside or inside a house. They put each woman's dish in their midst and eat them in turn.

It is considered very important that when children are eating, they sit up straight, without supporting themselves on the arm. This leaning on the arm is considered a sign of laziness in the child, and mothers cannot tolerate it. Most mothers want their children to eat quickly, taking big mouthfuls of food. They do not want them to take a long time, eating so slowly that the food is finished by other people before they, the children, are satisfied. This, most women think, tempts children to go back to the cooking pot to steal more food. Again, children are made to keep quiet when they are eating. 'You haven't got two mouths,' they are often told, 'that you can eat with one and talk with the other.'. . .

GROWING FROM PLAY INTO WORK ACTIVITIES

After weaning, the child sees less of his mother and more of his nurse, whose job is now to keep him company and to play with him. Very often, the nurse, with the child on her hip or back, will join the company of other nurses and children. Together they form a play group. A large part of the day may be spent by the nurse in this group play while the mother and father of the baby are at work in the home or the field. As said before, when the mother has to be away from the house, she will leave cooked food for the children and tell the nurse where to find it.

Toys are few among Acholi village children. Commercial toys, like dolls, ducks, building bricks, little motor cars, are not given to Acholi children, except in the relatively few homes in which the parents have had a school education and can afford to buy them. Most children are responsible for finding their own play materials. Almost anything can be made into a useful toy by children. Leaves, old tins, maize-cobs, broken pieces of pottery, fruits, seeds, anything they can pick up, will be used by the children as toys. This constant eagerness for toys, on the part of younger children in particular, often leads to the destruction of valuable possessions of the family. Finding at home such fascinating objects as ball-point pens, for example, or even the grown-ups' shoes, young children, having little else to play with and not being allowed to wander about very far, will often put such objects to use in their play. They may afterwards leave them thrown round the courtyard where parents, upon finding them perhaps in bad condition, may punish the children severely.

Acholi children spend much of their time playing out to their own satisfaction the roles of adults. Little girls can be often observed playing the part of their mothers. They pick up maize-cobs, sticks or bottles, pretending that these are their babies. Sometimes they will sit on the ground, stretching their legs out straight and holding the little 'babies' on their laps. They will take pieces of cloth and tie these make-believe babies on their backs as they see their mothers do. Not long ago I observed one of my sister's children, two and a half years old, carrying her baby. She picked up a tea spoon, and pretended to give some quinine to the doll, 'because the baby is ill', she said. Children of this age, too, particularly the girls, like playing the game of cooking. They will pick up little stones, in place of millet, and start grinding them on the sand. Then, putting together three little stones, they will pretend to make the fire. Old tins and broken pieces of pots are their cooking utensils.

Young boys, already aware of the work of their sex, often like to pull grasses and build little huts. They model motor cars and lorries out of clay. Sometimes they will break off a branch full of leaves, perhaps a big branch, which they use for a motor car. With two or three children astride, they 'drive' rapidly along the ground. Young children want to be active. They like running informal races on their own, climbing trees, singing and dancing. There is no strict grouping of girls and boys in these earlier years. Much of the time they will be seen, and heard, playing together.

A growing number of village children of six to ten now go to primary school. There are still some, however, who do not go, either because their parents cannot afford or do not want to send them to school, or because the nearest school may be four or five miles away, too far for the young child to walk every day. In the latter case, the children may start school when they are older. By this time boys and girls usually stay strictly in their own groups. The separation is encouraged by parents, especially mothers, who feel that it is not proper for their daughters to play among boys. The children themselves have abusive songs which they sing to a child of the opposite sex who may try to join their group. *'Labed, kin litino co!'* 'The girl who stays among boys', they will sing, or vice versa. Such songs will usually force the child to leave that company and join the proper one.

For the girls of primary school age their time of playing is nearly over. Home training and stricter discipline begin. At this age the girls must stop eating chicken or any kind of fowl. (An Acholi village woman does not eat any part of a fowl.) The child now has real duties to perform. If she has younger sisters or brothers, she will be a nurse. If she does not have a younger child to look after, and in some cases even if she does, the little girl is expected to make two or three journeys to the well, carrying a small container on her head in which to fetch water. She may be told by her mother who is cooking beans or meat to keep the fire burning. It may be her job also to look after the millet or peas spread out in the sun to dry, keeping the chickens away, collecting and putting the food in the house if it rains. A girl of eight or nine may be expected to grind millet or simsim with her mother, or to accompany her mother into the field to help dig. If her father is away at meal time, the little girl may be asked to take the responsibility of cooking for him, having the food ready by the time he comes back. There is a dual purpose for this thorough training of the girl. It is partly to prepare her for her future duties as a housewife and a mother, and partly to help the mother who, in the Acholi village, has many pressing jobs to do.

The girls who go to school, of course, have much less time for doing any household chores. Many girls have to leave their homes at seven in the morning, returning as late as half-past seven in the evening. From Primary Three, if the school is several miles distant, they cannot come home for lunch. Thus they have little time to practise cooking and other household duties. But some Acholi parents still reserve certain tasks which their primary school girls must perform anyway.

Since most of the secondary schools are boarding schools, the older girls who attend them are away from their homes for the full nine months of the year, and so are out of reach of further traditional training by their mothers. For this reason schools are often considered by Acholi parents to be making their daughters lazy. There is conflict between the school girls and their mothers when they do return home. At school, the girls are taught to be clean and smart, with heavy school assignments but little if any manual work to be done. When they come home they resent having to spend the whole day in the hot sun, weeding in fields with their hands. They dislike having to grind large amounts of millet on the grinding stone. How can they keep clean and smart, they ask, with all these dirty jobs to do? Further, the fact that most of their schools are mixed schools makes many Acholi mothers reluctant to send their daughters to school. They fear that by mixing so much with boys, by learning and speaking English all the time, and by having no practice in traditional manners and housekeeping, the girls are likely to become *malaya* (prostitutes) in the towns. This is one of the reasons why the education of women in Acholi has tended to lag behind.

The boys, on the other hand, are freer from adult attention until a much later age. From the age of five years, after the separation from the girls, the boys usually play in a gang. They play much wilder games now, too. Shooting or trapping birds is one of their favourite pastimes. They make for themselves *abutidda* or catapults, small Y-shaped twigs of a tree, with rubber strings attached. With these they shoot stones at birds, often going as far as a mile or so from the home to hunt. This takes much of their time. Almost every day, too, they will go in a group to the river to wash their bodies and take a swim.

Another favourite game for Acholi boys at this age is *cobo lawala*. A *lawala* is a willow, bent and tied like a ring about one foot in diameter. Each boy cuts himself a beautiful thin stick about six feet long to use as a spear. The gang divides into two teams. A boy from one team will throw the *lawala* spinning through the air to the other team with all his might, when all of the boys in that team, standing in line, will try to thrust their spears into the centre of the ring. So long as one boy in the team succeeds in spearing and bringing down the *lawala,* the other team will keep throwing it for them to spear. A boy who is an expert at *lawala* is always very good at hunting, too. He will seldom miss the running animal when he goes hunting. Because boys who go to school do not have the time required for practising *lawala,* they can never hope to be really good hunters with spears. As more and more Acholi boys now go to school, the game of *lawala* is gradually dying out.

THE ACHOLI PARENTS AS TEACHERS

Children's relationships with their parents depend, first of all, on the age of the children. Young babies are very close to their mothers or nurses. Most fathers in Acholi do not have a close relationship with babies. It is a woman's job to look after them, as said earlier. Moreover, Acholi men spend most of the day away from their homes. After digging in the morning, they eat their meal, then go off to visit their friends or attend beer parties.

After weaning, even the mother-child relationship breaks considerably. The child now spends most of his time with the nurse. If the mother has no nurse, she may take her child to join some other group of children, where she will leave him to play until she returns. This happens when the child has become too heavy to be carried about, or the mother has another baby to take his place. Sometimes such children are taken to their grandmothers' to be looked after. There is a tendency, however, for grandparents to 'spoil' children by over-feeding and perhaps carrying them on their backs even if they are too heavy. For this reason, mothers hesitate to send their children to stay for long periods with their grandparents.

Child-parent relationships also depend on the sex of the child. After weaning, boys do not have a close relationship with their mothers any more. From two to six years old, a boy spends most of his time with a nurse, and then with a gang of other boys. When a boy is about eight years old, he can accompany his father to the garden to dig, although very often he is excused to come home earlier than his father. His mother will give him food and, after eating, off he goes to play. In the early evenings he may go with his father for a walk round the fields or into the jungle to collect some logs. These logs are burned in the courtyard fire which the family gathers to sit around in the evening. The boy is usually told to sweep the compound before he lights the evening fire.

When he grows a little older, the father will show him the total area of his field, where it starts and where it ends, so that in future nobody can take it from him. During their walks in the evening, father and son carry spears. A father will tell his son to carry a spear or two whenever he goes to the jungle, in case an animal or an enemy appears. He tells the young boy all he knows about the behaviour of certain dangerous animals, and what to do when they appear. He shows him which trees are good, or bad, for building houses or grain stores, for making a hoe, and so on. Gradually, as the boy grows older, he is able to fetch the logs and make the fire without being told or helped.

The expansion of school education, and especially of boarding schools, has seriously weakened this father-son relationship. Day school boys do come home in the evening, when they are expected to sweep the compound and light the evening fire. In the evening the boy sits outside by the fire with his father while the mother is still preparing supper.

The girls, on the other hand, spend more time with their mothers from the beginning. Almost as soon as the girl passes the breast-feeding stage, she is given little jobs to do. She goes to the garden with her mother, perhaps helping or pretending to help with a very small hoe. She also goes with her mother to fetch firewood. Acholi mothers pay great attention to the development of their little daughters. If even the young child shows a tendency towards being lazy in doing these small home duties, the mother may become very worried about her. She may even beat the girl for it. (I remember my own mother slapping me on the face because at ten years of age I had not learned to grind millet well.) In the late evening, when father and brother are sitting out by the fire, the little girl stays inside, helping her mother get the food ready. Again, girls who go to school have less time with their mothers. They are therefore considered lazy and inefficient house-workers by traditional Acholi standards.

Child-parent relationships depend, thirdly, on whether or not the father has other wives. A man with many wives may decide to build all the wives' houses together around one compound or, to avoid too much quarrelling between the co-wives, he can scatter their homes over fairly great distances. In the latter case all of the children tend to have too little attention from their fathers. The young boy has to go and dig with his mother in her small garden instead of accompanying his father. Boys in such homes, because they hardly know their father except when he punishes them, often dislike their father, and tend to build up fear and ill feeling towards him. When quarrels or fights occur between the parents, the children will usually side with the mother against the father.

Children whose mothers are dead or divorced and some children of *luk* or unmarried women, are usually taken, sometimes unwillingly, into the houses of stepmothers. If the stepmother dislikes them, the children may have very harsh treatment, and perhaps be underfed. Surprisingly enough, some girls brought up in this way become very efficient housewives by Acholi standards. By making them work too hard, the stepmothers often train them to be very tough and strong.

As I have said before, it is the concern of all the relatives, not only the parents, to bring up the child properly and make him fit into and be useful in the village community. It is, therefore, a duty of the growing child to obey all his relatives. He is strictly taught by his parents to say nothing rude to anybody, including relatives. A little girl can be asked by any woman in the village to grind some millet, fetch some water, or cook something for her. Any male relative can request a little boy to run an errand, or help him in some other way. Children are expected to do all of these things without complaining. Those who do not obey will always have a bad reputation in the village. They are often told the proverb, *Lalek camo wi ogwang mutwo*. 'The child who cannot do any favour for people, eats the bony skull of a wild cat.' Or the other proverb, *Okwero pwony cito ki cet pa maro*. 'If you do not listen to people's advice, you will go mannerless to your mother-in-law's home.' This would be a disgrace, of course. The place where every man or every woman should show the best behaviour is in a mother-in-law's house.

DISCIPLINE IN TRIBAL EDUCATION

There is a constant attempt on the part of the adults, then, to mould the character and behaviour of children. A child who talks too much or asks too many questions is discouraged by the adults from so doing. A child who cries often without a real cause is whipped by the father, mother, or a relative until he keeps quiet.

The girls from the earliest years tend to be more disciplined and restricted than the boys. In the ordinary village home in Acholi, children often go about naked. For this reason mothers are very particular about the way in which little girls sit. From one and a half years onwards, the girl is repeatedly told and warned to sit down smartly with her knees together. If even a small girl sits carelessly, she may be whipped by the mother. I have twin nieces, aged two and a half, who already are so particular about their sitting habits that they keep reminding each other to sit properly. They often tell the adults to see how well they sit.

Another strict rule for the girls is that they should keep close to the homestead. No mother wants her four to six-year-old daughter wandering from home to home. This is considered a very bad and dangerous practice, which may lead to poisoning, as already said, or to future prostitution of the girl. Nevertheless a group of girls are permitted to go together to the well or out to fetch firewood.

Girls also have to obey their big brothers, who have authority over their younger siblings. A fifteen-year-old boy may order his sister to cook quickly for him because he is in a hurry to go to a dance. He may order her to clean his house or to fetch him some water for washing his clothes. The girl must respond to these orders in perfect obedience. Failure to do so often leads to a fight between the two children, almost always to the disadvantage of the girl, who may be the smaller or physically weaker of the two. Parents tend to ignore or even encourage these incidents, since the role of the Acholi female is to be obedient. 'You will suffer great blows from somebody's son if you do not practise obedience now,' the girls are often told.

Older brothers are also very particular about the way their grown up sisters behave in the presence of their boy friends. If a boy sees his sister misbehaving in any way, he is authorized by his parents to give her a good beating. The sisters are very important to the brothers, whose future can largely depend on them. A brother whose sister has good manners and is married is sure to have a wife himself. The money paid to his father as his sister's bride price is the money he will use for his own marriage. Since he cannot marry until his sister is married, it is his real concern to see that she is well behaved enough to be married early.

Acholi parents do not like their children to steal things. If even a young child shows a tendency towards stealing, he is severely punished by beating; he may be denied his meals for a whole day, or until he confesses and promises to steal no more.

THE ADOLESCENT YEARS

From the age of fifteen years onwards, children are treated in a much more respectful manner. Everybody in the village accepts the fact that the child *odoko dano,* has become a person. No mother wants to beat her daughter at this age. It would be considered a shameful disgrace. If the girl does anything wrong the mother corrects her in words only. Or, she may refer her to an aunt or some older relative who will give her advice.

By this time an Acholi village girl is highly accomplished by traditional standards. She does most of the cooking in the home now, doing everything without being told. She knows, or ought to know, exactly what her duties are. A mother with a grown up girl is very lucky. For almost the first time, in many cases, the Acholi mother can go and relax with her friends, knowing that the daughter is performing the household duties well in her absence. When the mother is at home, she can sit and instruct the girl as she works. No good girl can sit and do nothing while the mother is working. This would give her a bad reputation, which could make her marriage difficult. There are many songs composed to warn such girls.

Min anyaka too ka rego
Colo nyaka pe
Nyako obedo kilao
Min anyaka too yo kulu
Calo nyaka pet
Nyako obedo kilao.

The mother of the girl
Suffers all the way
Going to the well
Grinding and so on
As if she has no daughter to help her.
This girl is hopeless.

The Acholi girls at this stage, educated or not, are usually very particular about cleanliness, of their bodies and of the house. On entering any home in the village one can tell, from the appearance of the house, whether there is an adolescent girl in the family. A house where there is such a girl is usually kept constantly and smartly smeared with black soil. Along the wall, the girl will hang rows of clean white calabashes, very cleverly decorated. Some have *adungu,* a musical instrument played by girls, hanging up there, too. Outside, somewhere behind the house, one sees a heap of firewood neatly tied up into bundles. These are the signs of the presence of a wonderful girl in the home. Such a girl is likely to have a lot of suitors coming and going.

The adolescent boy is treated respectfully, too. The presence of an adolescent boy, or boys, in the home is indicated by an extra house or houses, in the compound, the bachelor huts. Each grown up boy is entitled to a hut of his own. He is highly respected by his mother, who keeps a separate dish for him whenever she cooks. Each year, the boy must, by himself or with the help of his father, open an acre of cotton for his own use. My brother, who is sixteen, has got the first acre of cotton to which he is entitled.

Boys of this age spend a lot of their time away from the home. Nobody minds where they go nor at what time of night they come back to their huts. At this age it is considered normal and proper for a boy to go out looking for a wife. Any father would be worried, and suspect that something was wrong with his son, if he did not show these signs. In case of any misconduct by the boy—for example, if he gets a girl into trouble—the father always pays the necessary fine for it, and does so without much complaint. The mother, contrary to what one would suppose, tends to be happy when her son does this. She expects, and it does happen, that the girl who is in trouble will soon come and spend a few months with her until the illegal baby is delivered. During her stay with the boy's family, she will relieve his mother of her household duties. This is a time of trial for the girl, however. Just like a student teacher on teaching practice, she must show her talents if she hopes to get married into the family, and the whole society approves of this. The result is that such girls tend to be over-worked in the boy's, or what turns out to be the mother-in-law's, home.

POSTSCRIPT

In Acholi today there are hundreds of families who live exactly as I have explained above. This includes most of the people in my own clan, although changes are beginning to affect them also. Our old clan forest, beginning several miles outside of Gulu, extends for some twenty-eight miles. Many family farms are included in this stretch, a few of them very progressive. My father's farm is one of these. We raise cotton, millet, maize, simsim, cassava, groundnuts and all our own fruits and garden vegetables. My four sisters and I, my brother, my late mother, my present stepmother, my father and some of his brothers, all worked in the fields when I was growing up. We still love farm life. My sister, who has just returned from almost two years of Infant Teacher Training in England, tells us how she used to miss the work in the fields, especially during the long vacations. Her British friends could hardly believe that this was true. I myself, when I was home for the recent Easter break from Makerere College, sowed our entire groundnut crop, and was proud to do it. Now several months later, the groundnuts have matured and are ready to be harvested. My sister, my cousins, or my father perhaps, will pull the groundnut plants in my absence, leaving them in the field to dry in the sun. We can do this because, as my sister remarked, the population of our area are still good people. There is no stealing yet. It is sad to think that only as civilization comes to Acholi communities are the people beginning to steal, so that farmers soon will not be able to leave their groundnuts or maize or other crops safely in the fields to dry.

For this is a period of rapid development in East Africa. The old economic and social structure is disintegrating in many ways. Gradually it is being replaced by a money economy. There are Acholi fathers who go from the village now to earn money in the towns. Some of these men leave their wives in the village, there to produce the food for their families, while the men work for money in the towns. When they have earned what they feel is enough, these fathers come back to the village. Some of the younger men who, having received some Primary or Junior

Secondary education, find work in the towns, may take their wives and young children with them. They are able to buy more or less permanent homes on the outskirts, or rent houses provided in quarters or housing estates inside the towns. This class of men is increasing rapidly in Acholi. Most of them work as clerks, office messengers, and such. They are joined by the growing number of teachers, better educated, who also leave their homes or villages to teach in whatever schools they are assigned to. In this class of people, the men or women will earn money and that is all. Their farming or food production is limited to small vegetable gardens. Most of the family food is bought at the market.

Other changes in the practices I have described are gradually, sometimes rapidly, taking place in Acholi villages. These days, for example, more and more children are born in maternity centres or hospitals where none of the old tribal traditions are kept. The placenta and the umbilical cords of babies born in hospitals, instead of being buried in certain places to insure their good health in the future, are destroyed at once. It is nurses now, instead of mothers or mothers-in-law, who look after the women in labour. This is a choice that a gradually growing number of Acholi village women are making, realizing that maternity centres and hospitals offer more security against the many dangers traditionally involved in childbirth. In the centres too, the mothers are given instructions on better ways to look after their babies.

This means also that the special ceremonies for pregnant women are slowly dying out. But one thing still exists, strongly. A young married woman is expected to become pregnant within the first few months of her marriage. If she does not, she will begin to get scornful words or ill treatment from the relatives of her husband.

A few other changes affecting the care of Acholi children should be mentioned. Take eating practices. The custom by which several families have their meals together is restricted to villages now where it is still quite common, especially among the uneducated or less-educated families. Village families which go to the towns will usually eat their own food. It is still common practice, however, even in the towns, for the children to be given their meals separately. Many town wives eat separately too, their working men unable to come home for food in the middle of the day. The men are often too late in returning home in the evenings also for their wives and the children to wait. There are some Acholi families, especially the families of teachers, where husband and wife eat together at a table.

Sleeping facilities for children are improving. In most educated Acholi homes now, babies and other children have beds of their own. Most working men living in towns have proper beds for their children as well as for themselves. In a few very advanced homes, the mothers have prams in which their babies can be pushed and can sleep. It is usually only when these families come back to visit their village relatives that the mats are again spread out on the floor for their sleeping.

Many of these improvements are coming about because of the changing attitudes of Acholi villagers towards school education. The Uganda Ministry of Education figures for June 1965 indicate that eighty per cent of the school-age children in Acholi attend Government schools. Even in the villages, the number is growing rapidly. This has been a tremendous development, bringing improvements in many aspects of living. In the primary school, for example, all children are given health training. They are taught to wash their bodies every day, to keep their nails and hair short, to brush their teeth. And to make sure that they do all of this, some teachers require the children to do it in school every day. This is bound to have a good effect on the school-age children. Already there is a striking difference in the young village child who goes to school and the one who does not. Recently my young cousin, a first-born about to start primary school, said to his mother, 'From next month onwards, you are going to have trouble. Who do you think then will have the awful job of caring for your crying baby?'

The changing attitudes of Acholi villagers towards the school education of girls is especially important. So often I think how well my elder sisters would have done in life if they had been given opportunities for education similar to mine. In their childhood, though, as I have said earlier, it was almost unthinkable for girls to be sent to school. I remember that even in my junior secondary school days, a group of us were taken with a travelling show into villages for fifty miles round, to try to teach the villagers the value of sending their daughters to school. By now many Acholi parents have seen that educated girls can become nurses, teachers or secretaries, and can earn a good livelihood. An increasing number then are sending both sons and daughters to school, with the hard-working mothers especially making sacrifices to pay the school fees. It is most likely that in a few years the Acholi will have many women going on to the University Colleges. I have the honour of being the first. Two others will be joining me at Makerere in the near future.

So it is that with the growing cash economy, the trend towards the towns, and the spread of school education for both men and women, the horizons of Acholi children and young people, even in the villages, are gradually growing wider. Improved transportation facilities are used by more and more people. Better roads are being built all over Uganda, some of them in Acholi going from village to village. Many families in once remote village homes have their night's sleep interrupted, until they become accustomed to the sound, by the constant line of huge lorries that go grinding up and down the slopes at night taking produce to market. The whistle and rumble of trains breaks the silence in many places, since two years ago the railway line was extended across Acholi. From time to time an aeroplane will fly high over Acholi towns and villages. Then even the very young children may look up and, pointing to the moving object, merely remark, 'Aeroplane, Mummy!' Swift and comfortable buses cover the distance between Acholi towns and Kampala in a matter of hours, a journey which in my own childhood took days.

The first time I travelled by bus, I remember, was in 1948, when I was seven years old. I cannot forget that first ride. I was travelling with my mother to my grandmother's house, about thirty-five miles away. I can still hear the noise of the engine and feel the bumping of the bus. It all seemed strange and frightening to me then, especially when I made a remarkable discovery. Wondering if we would ever get to Grandmother's house, I turned round to look at the passengers behind me. They were not moving at all. Everyone in the bus was sitting still, remaining in exactly the same position. When I looked out of the window I saw that it was the trees and the grass and the houses along the road that were moving, not the people on the bus! To me this was an amazing sight. I was still wondering and trying to figure it all out, when the bus stopped. 'Come out, Apoko, come out!' my mother was saying. For we had reached my grandmother's home.

Again, some Acholi children come from rich families who, instead of using bicycles, can own their own cars, thus making it possible for the families to do much more travelling. Motor cars from the towns and cities go whizzing by on the main roads, past the schools and homes and market places where children can always be found. Along these same roads, still, there will always be a constant stream of people walking, especially on market days. Men and boys can be seen with their bicycles, frequently carrying a friend or a wife or child, and sometimes both, or a heavy load of produce up hill and down. The women will be carrying headloads of firewood, perhaps, containers of water, or large loads of market produce. Often they will have babies tied on their backs, with sometimes another child or two clinging to their skirts as the cars flash by. For the Acholi village men, except for the few like my father who truly like to do farm work, are still prone to follow more leisurely pastimes—hunting, chatting in the market, attending funerals, drinking beer—leaving their women to carry the brunt of the heavy work. My Acholi classmate, a man, always argues with me about this. But I have observed much too much of the respective responsibilities carried by the men and boys and the women and girls in my tribe, even nowadays, to feel that I can agree with him. Many times on market days, one will see adolescent girls carrying their headloads along the road, quite obviously annoyed by boys of about their own age who may follow or taunt them. The market place is still a popular place for Acholi adolescents to make friends of the opposite sex.

Children and young people, at school and sometimes at home, are having more access to radio. The primary child who can still tell an old Acholi folk tale in dramatic detail, singing the songs in the story with gusto, also knows how to sing and twist to some of the current 'pop songs'. Dr. Obote is the President of Uganda, of course. And even the youngest child, where there is a radio in the home, will want to twist to this song, *Ye yekka Obote waffe,* or 'He alone, our Obote.' Children also pick up stories from the radio, for Radio Uganda broadcasts children's programmes in most Uganda languages now. The older children, along with their parents, often listen to the news. Thus with the increasing number of radio and even, as time goes on, television sets accessible to Acholi families and schools, it is likely that our children in the future will have better facilities for learning. Already they are becoming increasingly accustomed to modern changes and improvements. More and more of them are learning many of the old tribal customs by word of mouth from their elders, not through experience as we did. Often it seems to be only the oldest villagers who ponder and treasure the past. The children and youth are more apt to enjoy the modern and look to the future.

Senegambia in the Era of the Slave Trade

Philip D. Curtin

It is hard for Westerners, especially Americans, to understand the complexity of social rank that prevailed in the region of the Senegal and Gambia rivers of western Africa before white men turned that hapless area into one of their richest sources of slave labor for the Americas. When compared to today's relatively classless society in the United States, the people of Senegambia either enjoyed, or endured, a system of ranks that was certainly complex. In the following article, Philip D. Curtin shows how birth, kinship, sex, religion, caste, occupation, superstition, and bondage, among other factors, determined an individual's place in the community and whatever chance there was for improving it. An African's life status meant nothing, of course, to European slave traders, who reaped a harvest of human misery from among the high and the low of Senegambia and other countries of mainly western Africa.

SENEGAMBIAN SOCIETY

Just as the new state structure of the late sixteenth century was comparatively stable, the social patterns were also comparatively stable. As a result, recent field studies are in broad agreement with historical records, and this congruence makes it possible to use both sources in reconstructing the patterns of past society. Some of the detail is inevitably lost in this process, and much of the change through time that might be apparent from better historical evidence is simply not visible, but the main outlines are clear enough.

Almost everywhere, the fundamental social division was tripartite. First, the free men, *jambuur* in Wolof, *riimbe* (sing. *diimo*) in Pulaar, *horo* in Malinke. Then came the so-called caste people belonging to endogamous occupational groups such as blacksmiths, leather workers, or minstrels, called collectively *ñe-ño* in Wolof, *ñeeñbe* in Pulaar, or *ñamahala* in Malinke. Finally came the class of servile bondsmen, sometimes called slaves (*jam* in Wolof, *maacube* in Pulaar, *joo* in Malinke). In a broad sense, the three major divisions were a hierarchy of rank, but wealth, status, and power did not line up neatly in the ranked order. Many finer lines and divisions could exist within any of the three divisions, so that in fact they overlapped. Those who were best off in either of the lower groups, in terms of wealth, status, and power, were better off than the lowest ranks of free men.

Several distinctions were drawn among the free men. The mere fact of being free might mean no more than belonging to the mass of the Wolof peasantry, the *baadolo*. It was thus a neutral status, a zero point, to be added to or subtracted from. Some men had less, by virtue of membership in the occupational "castes" or being bondsmen. Others had more, by virtue of office or personal reputation, and above all by membership in a privileged lineage. The root of the free man's self-identity and the framework for his day-to-day relations with others was kinship. In pre-Islamic times this meant a matrilineage for the Wolof, Sereer, and Fuulbe—inheritance passed from male to male, but following the female line. For the Malinke, the normal form of reckoning descent was in the male line, though either system could change to the other. The Fuuibe who converted to Islam changed to the Muslim patrilineage, though traces of matrilineage remain in Fuuta and among the pastoral Fuulbe down to the present. Patrilineal descent also gained a great deal of ground in Wolof territory, though it never replaced the important matrilineages. At the same time, the patrilineal Malinke who became the rulers of the Sereer states and of Kaabu changed over to a system that emphasized matrilineage, though keeping some patrilineal elements.[1]

Whether patrilineal or matrilineal, the largest kind of lineage group in Senegambia, sometimes called a clan, was one made up of all people who traced their descent back to a common ancestor (usually a male ancestor, even when traced through the female line). The members of this clan had (and still have) a common surname called *jaamu* in Malinke, *yetoode* in Pulaar, *sant* in Wolof, but there are more lineages than surnames, so that quite separate lineages may have the same surname. In any event, the whole clan was not an effective social unit. It was usually scattered in villages hundreds of miles apart, and its distribution cut across linguistic, ethnic, and state boundaries, though most prominent surnames have a known original ethnic identity. All the people of a clan were linked by the belief that they were kin and by common totemic animals. One, called *tana* in Malinke, was the totemic animal proper, associated with the ancestors and never to be harmed in any way. The other animal symbol was called *bemba* in Malinke, *ele* in Pulaar, and it was repugnant rather than attractive or protective. This system of dual animal symbols extended far beyond the Senegambia. In spite of the coming of Islam, it was found in recent years from Wolof country on the Atlantic coast, through Fuuta, and on east into the whole of the greater Manding region.

But the clan was too broad to be an effective political or social unit. The effective lineage was the segment living together in a single town or village, often having contiguous compounds of a ward belonging to that clan alone. This local unit (*lu* or *kabilo* in Malinke, *gale* in Pulaar) had an active head, normally the oldest member, who represented its interests to higher officials, settled internal quarrels, and sometimes acted as a central agent for receiving and redistributing income from the group's economic efforts. This local unit usually included the bondsmen subordinate to members of the lineage of free men, and might include some clients and especially some of the associated "caste" people. In this way, the position of the free lineage often determined the status of subordinate ranks as well.

But the "caste" people were not set in a social hierarchy so much as set aside from the rest of society. This is one reason why the Portuguese-Indian term *caste* tends to be confusing in the West African setting. Like Indian castes, the West African ñeeñbe were endogamous and they were associated with particular occupations, but there the similarity ends. The West African caste groups were not separated by religious prohibitions, either Muslim or pre-Muslim. They were defiling to others through sexual contact but not necessarily through social contact, such as common dining. Caste rules in this respect differed from place to place. While the free people everywhere thought of them as separate, they were not necessarily inferior. Whether they were or not depended on the particular caste. Blacksmiths, for example, were feared, but also respected for their technical expertise—not for skill or virtuosity alone, but because they had to deal with the tree spirits to make charcoal and with the earth itself to extract ore for making iron. These dealings required special ritual and spiritual contacts that ordinary people were well advised to stay clear of.

Minstrels were a group with variable status. People looked down on some of them as mere entertainers, just as Europeans of the seventeenth and eighteenth centuries placed "players" at the bottom of the social hierarchy along with domestic servants. But the Senegambian minstrels were not merely at the bottom of a social hierarchy; they were outside it, and their potential for defilement was so strong that they were formerly buried in trees to avoid polluting the soil. At the same time, many were close to the nobility and the centers of power. Not only could they have informal influence through their advice, they often had a formal political role as well, especially in diplomacy and above all in diplomacy between factions within the same lineage. Leatherworkers and woodworkers, on the other hand, were craftsmen whose work itself was defiling. Woodworkers dealt with trees, which were the home of the spirits in the pre-Islamic religion. It was therefore necessary for them to deal with the supernatural in ways that could be dangerous in the same way that it was for blacksmiths, while leatherworkers were defiled by the necessity of breaking certain blood taboos.[2]

The institution of the ñeño or ñamahala is at its most complex, strongest, and probably oldest along the Senegal valley, especially with the Wolof and the Fuulbe. The Wolof in the seventeenth century distinguished five separate occupations as the basis for endogamous social groups—fishermen *(cubaalo)*, weavers *(rabb-ser)*, woodworkers *(lawbe)*, smiths *(tegg)*, and minstrels *(gewel)*. This would be a maximal list of occupations, even though some societies counted two or even three different kinds of minstrels. Approximately the same complexity of caste division still survives in the middle and lower Senegal valley.[3]

The number of divisions and the strength of the institution then tends to diminish with distance from the mouth of the Senegal, but the diminution is not directly proportional to distance. It weakens rapidly to the north and the south, for example, but it stretches far to the east. In Fuuta, the fishermen shift into the group of free men, but a small group of potters is added to the Wolof list. In Bundu and in some parts of Fuuta the weavers tended to be grouped with minstrels, and weavers drop from the list altogether among the Malinke both in the Gambia valley and the Manding heartland. Otherwise, the core of the institution, distinguishing smiths, leatherworkers, woodworkers, and minstrels of two kinds, persists into the whole of the Manding culture area.[4] It begins to weaken sharply only with movement still further east—for example in Mossi country of the present-day Upper Volta, where only blacksmiths persist as a separate "caste."

With movement north or south of the Senegal, on the other hand, the number and importance of the ñeeñbe also decreases sharply. To the north, the Moors of the Mauritania distinguish only two endogamous groups, minstrels and praisers on one hand *('iggawan*, sing. *'iggiw)*, and a group of all the craftsmen on the other, including smiths, soapmakers, leatherworkers, and so on (called *m'allmin*, sing. *m'allam)*.[5] To the south, even the Sereer borrowed the institution from their Wolof and Fuulbe neighbors within recent centuries, and in many instances the "casted" people themselves were immigrants from the north. The institution is strong with the Gambia Malinke, but here it is intrusive and reflects its strength in the Manding region to the east. South of the Gambia, caste distinctions drop off altogether. The Bajaraanke, Koñagi, and Basari of southeast Senegal, who once lived much further north, believe that blacksmiths have a special relationship with the supernatural, but the smiths are not endogamous.[6]

Whatever its origin and cause of diffusion, the institution of "casted" occupations is not coterminous with other aspects of culture. It exists among sedentary people speaking West Atlantic languages, as it does among nomads speaking Afro-Asiatic languages like Arabic and Berber. It appears strongest among West Atlantic speakers like the Wolof and Halpulaar, but it stops short of other West Atlantic speakers like the Bajaraanke, and it has only recently reached the Sereer, who are close linguistic relatives of the Fuulbe. It corresponds somewhat better to the region that has a long historical experience of elaborate political institutions of the state type, but even there the correspondence is far from perfect.

The presence of the ñeeñbe as an institution affected society at large. Where ñeeñbe were important, a strong sense of occupational solidarity was often found among free men, and members of particular lineages tended to follow the same occupation generation after generation. Interest groups or professional groups that came into existence in particular historical circumstances could be frozen by inheritance and then separated somewhat from the rest of society by the tendency toward endogamy. A recent example is the Toorodbe of Fuuta, who began as a religious party which strongly supported Islamic purity in the eighteenth century; many were Muslim clerics by profession. They then won power in the religious revolution during the last quarter of that century, tended to become a hereditary aristocracy, not truly endogamous, but enough so to make some authorities identify them as a "caste." In a somewhat different way, some Moorish tribes tended to be identified as clerical or *zwāya,* while others were military. In fact, both kinds had some Muslim clerics, both had to fight, and both contained "casted" occupational groups of minstrels and smiths.[7]

The boundaries between ñeeñbe and riimbe were not always absolute. Smiths and minstrels were clearly and permanently ñeeñbe, but others have changed status within historical memory. The *jawaanbe* (sing. *jawaando*), for example, were something like minstrels in Fuuta; they too were courtiers and advisors to the rulers, though they were sometimes merchants. In Bundu and Fuuta alike, they were usually considered to be ñeeñbe in the nineteenth century, but in recent decades they have begun to take wives from the class of free men. In much the same way, the *subaalbe* (pl. of *cubaalo*) were fishermen in Fuuta and among the Wolof, but in Fuuta they were considered riimbe, though the seventeenth century Wolof called them ñeeñbe.[8] Subtle shifts with time and place make the historical role of Senegambian castes especially liable to misunderstanding.

The third major group, slaves or *captifs,* is also liable to misunderstanding for other reasons, especially so because the West itself recently had a social category called slave, marked by the legal right of one person to sell another person at will, like any other chattel. The key was the property right, the salability that distinguished the owned from the owner. Purchase was the mechanism for transferring African slaves to the Americas, but it was really a shift of institutions more than a simple change of geography. Senegambian slaves were not property in the Western sense, and most of them could not be sold at all without judicial condemnation. The distinguishing mark of slaves as a social group was the fact that they were foreigners or descendents of foreigners who had entered the society in which they found themselves by capture in war or by purchase.

But these African "slaves" fell into three quite distinct categories. First, there were trade slaves who had themselves been captured or purchased. They were called *jam sayor* in Wolof, *pad okob* in Sereer, *jiaado* in Pulaar, and a variety of different names in different regional dialects of Malinke. Trade slaves had no legal rights at all. Second came the category of slaves born in captivity or accepted as members of the household of the master, called *jam juundu* in Wolof, *pad bin* in Sereer, *maccuudo* (sing. of *maacube*) in Pulaar. From the moment of purchase, a trade slave began gradually to change status as he was assimilated to the new society. For those born in the new society, the status was that of a subordinate membership, including a fictitious quasi-kinship relationship to the master's lineage which carried with it a complex web of rights and obligations. The slave's general well-being depended a great deal on the kind of work he did. Some were settled in slave villages, where they did the work of ordinary peasants and had much the same kind of life, except that they owed a portion of the harvest to the owner. Others served the master more directly in his own fields. Still others were allowed to follow crafts like weaving. Some females were taken as concubines by their masters, or even as wives, since the slaves were not set apart from the rest of society by sexual prohibitions like those against the ñeeñbe. In several Senegambian societies, marriage to a free man that ended after a child was born automatically shifted the mother into the ranks of the free, since it would not be proper for the mother of a free child to marry a slave.

In a separate category came royal slaves used for military or administrative purposes. These were called *ceâdo* in Wolof, Sereer, and the Pulaar singular (*sebe* in the plural and often spelled *thiedo* in French).[9] The potential power and wealth of a royal slave was enormous, and the chief among them sometimes were second only to the king himself. In most Senegambian kingdoms they were the only people available to serve as bureaucrats, because all others had obligations to their own lineages standing in the way of efficiency and loyalty to the king. In the same way, the royal slaves were usually the only standing army, in much the same tradition as the Janissary corps in Turkey, the Mamluks in Egypt, or the corps of black slave-soldiers in eighteenth-century Morocco. This position gave them access to power that could be used to influence the choice of the ruler, or to lord it over the peasantry or even over civilian officials. By the early nineteenth century, the slave-soldiers in the Wolof states and some Malinke Gambian kingdoms had become a branch of the ruling class who happened to be military specialists, and they fell more and more outside of royal control. Their habit of pillaging the countryside, with or without the king's agreement, made them increasingly unpopular with the peasantry. In the second half of the nineteenth century, this unpopularity combined with reformist Islam in a series of insurrections that overturned the political order from the lower Gambia northward to Kajor and Jolof.[10]

The numerical balance of class and caste differed greatly from one place to another, and from one time to another, influenced by the rise and fall of states, the incidence of warfare, or the political success of particular lineages. In recent Fuuta Tooro, a sample of sedentary Fuulbe showed 20 per cent descended from "slaves" (maccube), 6 per cent in the occupational "castes" (ñeeñbe), and 74 per cent riimbe.[11] This may be close to the general pattern in the Wolof and Sereer states as well, but the upper Senegal had a different pattern. Administrative estimates in 1904 put two-thirds of the population of Bundu and lower Gajaaga in slave status at that time. Travelers on the Gambia toward the end of the eighteenth century also guessed that three-quarters of the population of the Malinke states were slaves. Other Malinke in Bambuhu, on the other hand, kept no slaves at all in some regions, and very few in others. On balance, the administrative estimate for all of French West Africa in 1906 was about 25 per cent slave.[12]

One final institution cut across the lines of status, descent, and kinship. This was an age-grade organization, grouping all men or women who were initiated to adulthood at about the same time. In many African societies, the age grades were a crucial cement joining those who were otherwise split into jealous and competing kinship groups. In Senegambia, their importance was uneven. It was greatest in the Manding culture area to the east of Senegambia proper. There, the age grades helped to work across the grain of separate lineages that competed within the framework of the small Malinke state, or *kafu*. A new age grade was created each seven years, and the previous grade promoted for a total of six promotions, yielding a cycle of forty-nine years in all. The Gambia Malinke, however, did not preserve the full force of this system; rather than having a cycle of seven named grades repeated over and over they kept only four. Even so, this was a more important age-grade system than was found in most of Senegambia. Age grades had some importance among the Sereer, but they dropped to insignificance with the Wolof. The Wolof, however, had a related institution, the *mbar* or circumcision group; and it could have importance later in life, as it did when those men who had passed through circumcision with a potential Damel would later become the core of his military support. The sedentary Fuulbe kept only an unimportant age association, while the Soninke of Gajaaga had age associations for adolescents but not for adults.

GOVERNMENT

As elsewhere in West Africa, the essential element of political life in Senegambia was kinship; lineages were the building blocks out of which a constitutional order had to be made. Lineage determined eligibility for office, and some states had a single royal lineage from which the ruler was chosen—the Denankoobe in Fuuta, the Baacili (Bathily) in Gajaaga, the Sisibe (Sy) in Bundu, the Geiwar in the Sereer states, and the Naanco (Nantio or Nyancho) in Kaabu. Others had a number of different lineages that were eligible for office in a multidynastic system of rotation as in Kajor, Waalo, and most of the Gambia Malinke states. Whether one dynasty or several, all Senegambian political constitutions were in the nature of a compromise between the most powerful lineages. The terms of the compromise were privileges or favors promised to other powerful lineages in return for their acquiescence in a one-lineage monopoly of the monarchy.

NOTES

1. For the upper class or free people generally see C. A. Quinn, "Traditionalism, Islam, and European Expansion: The Gambia 1850–90" (Ph.D. diss., University of California, Los Angeles, 1967), pp. 71–73, recently published as *Mandingo Kingdoms of the Senegambia: Traditionalism, Islam, and European Expansion* (London, 1972); Wane, *Les toucouleur,* pp. 29–34; Diagne, *Pouvoir politique,* pp. 56 ff.; Barry, "Royaume du Walo," pp. 45 ff.; Cissoko, "Kabou," pp. 12–13; Y. Person, *Samori: Une révolution Dyoula,* 3 vols. (Dakar, 1968–).
2. For the origins of the ñeeñbe generally see H. Zemp, "La légende des griots malinké," CEA, 6:611–42 (1966); L. Makarius, "Observations sur la légende des griots malinké, CEA, 9:622–640 (1969); P. Smith, "Notes sur l'organization sociale des Diakhanké: Aspects particuliers à la région de Kédougou," *Bulletin et mémoires de la Société d'anthropologie de Paris,* 8 (11th ser.): 263–302 (1965), pp. 290 ff.
3. Barry, "Royaume du Walo," pp. 34–42; Wane, *Les Toucouleur,* passim.
4. Person, *Samori,* 1:54–58.
5. Miské, Ahmed Baba, "Al-Wasît: Tableau de la Mauritanie à la fin du xixe siècle," *BIFAN,* 30:117–64 (1968).
6. D. P. Gamble, *The Wolof of Senegambia* (London, 1957), p. 101; Diagne, *Pouvoir politique,* pp. 71 ff.; W. S. Simmons, *Eyes of the Night: Witchcraft among a Senegalese People* (Boston, 1971); M. de Lestrange, *Les Coniagui et les Bassari* (Paris, 1955); M. Gessain-de Lestrange, *Les migrations des Coniagui et Bassari* (Paris, 1967).
7. H. T. Norris, "Znāga Islam during the Seventeenth and Eighteenth Centuries," *Bulletin of the School of Oriental and African Studies,* 32:496–526 (1969); Wane, *Les Toucouleur,* pp. 34–38; Robinson, "Abdul Bokar Kan."
8. A. Raffenel, *Voyage dans l'Afrique occidentale exécuté en 1843 et 1844* (Paris, 1846), p. 204; F. Brigaud, *Histoire traditionelle du Sénégal* (Saint Louis, 1962); P. Cantarelle, "L'endogamie des populations du Fouta sénégalais," *Population,* 4:665–76 (1960), p. 671; Wane, *Les Toucouleur,* pp. 42–50.

9. The importance of this group differed greatly from place to place in Senegambia, and the terminology also differed. In the Malinke kingdoms, a term cognate with *ceddo* included slave administrators as well as slave soldiers. (Quinn, "The Gambia," p. 88.) The Pulaar *ced̂d̂o* had a variety of different meanings. In Fuuta, even today, it refers to free men descended from the Deñanke dynasty and its followers. In Bundu, however, the original meaning slipped still further, and the word became the generic term for foreigners, especially for Wolof or the Soninke of Gajaaga. (Wane, *Les Toucouleur,* pp. 29–34.) In much the same way, the current meaning in Wolof and Sereer is also extensible in certain usages to mean non-Muslims generally, or simply a member of the precolonial ruling class. (Klein, *Islam and Imperialism,* p. 9.)

10. Colvin, "Kajor," pp. 41–45; Klein, *Islam and Imperialism,* and Quinn, "The Gambia," passim.

11. In this case the jawaanbe, often counted as riimbe, were counted as ñeeñbe, but they were only 1.8 per cent of the total, so that the change is not significant. (Cantarelle, "Endogamie," p. 671.)

12. "Questionnaire sur le sujet de la captivité," 1904, ANS, K 18; J. B. L. Durand, *Voyage au Sénégal,* 2nd ed. in 2 vols. (Paris, 1807), 1:129 (first published An X [Sept. 1802–Sept. 1803]); M. Park, *Travels in the Interior Districts of Africa,* 2 vols. (London, 1816–17), 1:32–33; Boucard, "Relation de Bambouc," June 1729, AM, mss. 50/2, f. 61; Deherme, "L'esclage en AOF," ANS, K 25, p. 218.

CHAPTER FOUR

AFRICA: A Rich Cultural Heritage II

Africa's cultural heritage has utilized a variety of media, some of which are more familiar to us than others. In most cases, the selected medium of expression related closely to the values and needs of the particular African group. For example, African art tended to focus on the beasts of land, water, and air for areas of content and veneration. Religious activity, and in particular prayer, was occasioned by any circumstance of life. One of the most interesting areas of activity, the oral perpetuation of African heritage, is probably the least understood medium of expression. Africa may be viewed as lacking in literary heritage because writing was not emphasized in many African cultures. How many languages were spoken in Africa? How did this diversity affect communication and commerce within the continent? What current educational practices have been suggested by the activities of African civilizations?

African Language Groups

One of the reasons why much of the world has wrongly viewed Africa as lacking in literary heritage is becoming rather well known: that oral literature was preserved by *griots,* or native historians, for possibly thousands of years before Africa's history began to be printed. Less known, perhaps, is the fact that Africa is a continent with an astounding number of languages. By comparison, each of the fifty states of the United States would have an average of sixteen languages apiece, if it were to balance with the more than eight hundred languages indigenous to Africa. And this does not include the half a dozen or more languages that Africa imported from Europe! As will be deduced from the following selection from *Africa Yesterday and Today,* the wonder is that a continent could produce linguists sufficiently versatile to assure communications and commerce among the African nations. It certainly explains why no single African language could have a numerical following equal to any of the relatively few languages of Europe or the Americas.

One of the first and most basic cultural characteristics any individual acquires is his language. For our purpose, it is practical to look briefly at the language classifications of Africa to determine how complex can be the problem of inter-group communication and hence how extensive the political organization.

A language family is a group of languages stemming originally from a single source. English is a member of the Indo-European family of languages. Among the other members of that family are German and the other Teutonic languages, French and the other Romance languages, Russian and other Slavic languages, Latin, Greek, and Sanskrit. Scholars estimate that it has taken about 6000 years for the Indo-European family to reach its present stage of differentiation.

There are over 800 indigenous languages spoken on the African continent, in addition to English, French, Spanish, Portuguese, and Italian. The African languages can be grouped into four major language families: Congo-Kordofanian, Nilo-Saharan, Afro-Asiatic, and Khoisan. "Bantu," a term frequently associated with African languages, can legitimately be applied only to a subdivision of one of the branches of the Congo-Kordofanian family. This and other linguistic designations are often misused, however, to refer to racial rather than language groups. The Bantu languages are widely dispersed, extending from parts of north-western Cameroon to east, central, and southern Africa. Swahili, spoken as both a first and second language by people in East Africa and parts of the Congo, is a Bantu language.

Another interesting type of language to be found in Africa is Pidgin, which is spoken only as a second language. In West African coastal areas Pidgin developed as the result of trading between Europeans and Africans. It appears to be a blend of a simplified form of the grammar of some African languages and English vocabulary. Currently in some areas it is the common language between neighboring villages which speak different languages, and in cities between speakers of different languages who do not have English in common.

There are frequently many different languages within the boundaries of a modern African state. Nigeria in West Africa contains over 200 languages representing three of the major African language families. Hausa, an Afro-Asiatic language, is spoken in the northern region. Because many Hausa have been traders for hundreds of years, that language can be heard in many other parts of West Africa as well. The other two major languages of Nigeria—Yoruba and Ibo —are both Congo-Kordofanian languages. Each of these three languages is used in major newspapers, on the radio, and in novels, plays, and poems in its respective region.

Since language is a vehicle for the transmission of culture, the choice of a national language has crucial implications for the development of education and the mass media. This decision is often one of the most important political acts of a newly independent nation. Language diversity is one of the most interesting and challenging features in the development of modern African countries.

The Magic Drum

William F. P. Burton

Surrounded by night sounds, Luban villagers in the Congo sit around campfires and listen to the myths and stories told by the *bamfumu.* Buried in his chants and couplets is the essence of environmental understanding and the survival of the culture. Through repetition, Luban children acquire specific knowledge of plants, seasons, animals, illness and cures, as well as social guidance. Burton's preface compares the Luban teaching system with Western fables and sets the stage for "The Magic Drum," one example of the wisdom and knowledge imparted by the Luban *bamfumu.*

PREFACE

The following fables will doubtless come as a surprise to some who think that everyone who has not been educated by European standards is an "uncivilized" barbarian. For our standard of education is supposed to indicate the degree of a nation's civilization.

For centuries the Congo native has had a most accurate and efficient teaching system. It fits a native for adult life and is the product of the needs of the Central African environment and the demands of Central African youth. It shows him the part he should play in his relations with other people and his responsibility to the community. It gives him an accurate knowledge of the trees, animals and insects of the forests in which he lives. He receives the rudiments of geography, tribal history, medicine and many other branches of knowledge and handicrafts.

Of course much of the work of the blacksmith, gardener, builder, fisherman, hunter and canoe carver is learned by imitation. The son makes his tiny bow and arrows and follows his father to the forest or to the lakeside. The little girl takes her hoe and accompanies her mother to the plantations, or, during the heat of the day, lends a hand in rendering palm oil, weaving baskets and preparing food.

But quite apart from "education by imitation" there is a beautiful system of instruction which is applied in the quiet of the evening about the fireside.

Luban village life is most efficiently organized. Each chief has his counsellors or *bamfumu,* often up to twenty-five in number, and each counsellor has his title and duties. Order of precedence and respect for superiors are most punctiliously observed, and the whole of court etiquette has evolved from age-long custom.

The *bamfumu* once held the power of death, and even today they are regarded as far above the ordinary villagers. They are to a large extent entrusted with advising the chief, regulating village life, and instructing the young.

Before they will display their stores of lore and learning, the dignity and reserve of some of these old aristocrats must be melted by gifts from the younger generation. Others, however, delight in interesting the children, and talk round the fireside is as much a source of satisfaction to them as to their listeners. They deliberately select the most attractive forms of teaching, wrapping up an otherwise objectionable pill in so much sugar-coating that their hearers are unaware of how much sound teaching they are assimilating.

The *bamfumu* often specialize in one particular branch of learning. Thus the *balute,* or "men of memory" as the village historians love to be called, can go back over two or three centuries of Luban history and tell of successions and wars, early customs and tribal boundaries, migrations and changes.

Careful enquiry from native historians in villages as much as a month's journey apart shows how remarkably the historics agree, and how accurate are the memories of these old men, although, as their records are entirely oral, it is only to be expected that they should differ on minor details.

Others pride themselves on their proverbs and sayings, and are so apt with them that they are the staple of almost all their conversation. To the uninitiated, it sounds like a strange and unintelligible form of "stump oratory." There are thousands of proverbs, each consisting of two parts. In law cases and similar proceedings the orator throws out the first part of his proverb as a sort of challenge, and his listeners shout back the second in reply.

Much geography and natural history is learned by memorizing short couplets. Every tree and animal, every hill and stream, has an appropriate couplet describing its main features.

Thus, just as an English child naturally thinks of a sheep, cat or frog in connection with the nursery rhymes "Ba ba black sheep," "Pussy-cat, pussy-cat, where have you been?" and "A frog he would a-wooing go," so a Luban child can unhesitatingly repeat hundreds of couplets describing, for instance, the villages beyond the Luvidyo River, the uses of the mulolo tree, the weather to be expected in February, the dangers of the kongolo snake, or the best bait for catching sendji rats.

These couplets have been heard over and over again until they have become part of the child's nature. A Luban boy of twelve can readily distinguish between two hundred different trees and describe the various uses of their leaves, bark, fruit, wood or roots, just as he can name as many different birds at sight or from their notes. He can also describe many of the habits of the more common animals, and the kind of trap with which they may be caught. He can give native remedies for a dozen different maladies, and knows the right month for sowing and harvesting the various crops. In fact these fireside chats give him a thorough and efficient start in his forest life.

In addition to the kind of teaching I have just described, there are various modes of social intercourse which most white people learn either from religious precept or from the hard knocks of life. The old *bamfumu* know that to teach such things in dry, formal platitudes, would be neither agreeable nor effective, so they give them the more palatable form of the fable.

Even in England, to make a point we do not need to recite the whole fable. When we call someone a "dog in the manger," or declare that a financier has "killed the goose that laid the golden eggs," the fables are so well known that the titles alone are enough to indicate the meaning. Similarly, in Lubaland the bare mention of "the dove's eggs in the gale," or of "the nightjar's big mouth," will often carry a point home far more forcibly than an hour's reasoning.

The African is the prince of fabulists, and students of native language and lore have done excellent service in collecting his tales. But in reading some of these collections one gets the impression that they are like a bouquet of beautiful flowers without the foliage, or a handful of loose gems without a setting. The real purpose of instruction, which originally called forth the fables, has been neglected. In retelling some of them in colloquial English I have therefore tried as far as possible to preserve the object their narrators had in mind when they originally told them across the logs of the open fire.

I have been tempted to delete much of the repetition with which the stories abound, but to do so entirely would be to rob them of one of their strongest attractions, at least in native minds. The little, wide-eyed, shivering youngsters round the village fires wait as eagerly for the inevitably repeated call of the lion to dinner, or the lame excuse of the tortoise, as we ourselves did for the "Fee fi fo fum, I smell the blood of an Englishman," which made so deep an impression in the giant stories of our own childhood.

These fables are not the isolated product of a few local celebrities. They are as well known in Lubaland as "The Three Bears" or "Cinderella" in the nurseries of England, and may be heard any evening round the fires of any Luban village.

My only regret is that in our stereotyped, cut-and-dried English I cannot express all the beauties that are brought out by a native story-teller. To be heard at their best, the fables must be told by the old, half-naked, Luban *bamfumu* through the smoke of a village fire, with the dark forest trees as a background, and to the accompaniment of chirping crickets, the croaking of frogs in the stream, and the distant call of the jackal and hyena.

THE MAGIC DRUM

The three younger boys prided themselves on their quick wits and were always taking a mean advantage of the oldest, who was slow, good-natured, and immensely strong. They would say, "Umpume, whatever would you do without us?" To which he would reply with a smile, "Perhaps some day you may even be glad of my help. At least you're glad to dance to my drumming." For he was a marvellous drummer.

They all went into the forest to hunt, putting up a temporary lodge of poles and grass in which to sleep and store the meat as they dried it on racks over slow fires.

They would select the lightest loads, such as the legs of the animals killed, and would leave him to bring in the rest of the carcass. Then they would cut the daintiest portions to cook for themselves, leaving him to gnaw the scraps off the bones. He only smiled.

One night as they slept there was a commotion outside the hunting lodge, and they looked out to find the paramount chief with his warriors.

"Who is there?" he called.

"We are huntsmen," replied the younger men, leaving Umpume apparently asleep.

"Whose is all this meat?"

"It belongs to our children."

"Give it all to me."

"We cannot give away what is not ours."

"Then I will eat all your children," threatened the chief.

"Rather take the meat," they said, and the chief's warriors carried away every scrap.

In the morning they accused Umpume and thrashed him, but he said, "If I read the tracks in the dust aright, the chief was here in the night, and he nearly ate you." He had silently listened to all that had taken place.

After next day's hunting they decided to mount guard at night over the meat that was drying on the racks. Once more the chief came, and finding the three younger men sitting round the fire he went to see who was in the hut, whereupon Umpume, reaching out from the darkness, seized a glowing brand and pushed it into the chief's face. The chief fled, declaring furiously, "I'll fetch my warriors, cut you all up and dry your meat over those racks. You've burned the whiskers off my face."

"Umpume, what shall we do?" they asked in terror. "You have insulted his majesty with your fire-brand and we are all doomed to die."

"Don't worry," said Umpume, smiling, "I will save you." And while they hid the dried meat in a hollow tree, he carved a great drum. Then he put them into it, stretched a skin over the top, and taking a pointed digging stick and gourd in one hand and the drum under the other arm, as soon as light dawned he set out for home.

After a time he came face to face with a lion. "Where are you going?" said the lion.

"I come from home and I'm going home."

"Why do you carry these things?"

"The digging stick is for rooting out wild sweet potatoes and the gourd is for drinking-water."

"And why carry a drum?"

"So that if anyone is sad-hearted I can drum for his dancing and send him away happy." With this Umpume sat down and rapped the drum so skilfully that the lion danced all round him in a circle and went away saying, "That is a nice fellow. He has put me in a good temper."

Then Umpume met a leopard. "Where are you going?" asked the leopard.

"I come from home and I'm going home."

"Why carry the digging stick and gourd?"

"The stick is for rooting out sweet potatoes and the gourd for drinking-water."

"And why carry the drum?"

"So that if anyone is agile he can dance to my drum." And Umpume sat down and rapped the drum so skilfully that the leopard danced all around him in a circle, and then went away saying, "That is a charming fellow. He has recognised my agility."

Soon Umpume came face to face with an elephant, who demanded, "Where are you going?"

"I come from home and I'm going home."

"Why carry the digging stick and gourd?"

"The stick is for unearthing wild sweet potatoes and the gourd for drinking-water."

"What purpose does the drum serve?"

"So that if anyone is stiff in the knees he may dance to my drumming and loose his joints."

With this he put down his drum and played it so well that the elephant danced all round him in a circle and went away saying, "That is a splendid fellow. He has cured my stiff knees."

The same thing occurred with the buffalo, the wart-hog and the crocodile.

Finally Umpume came face to face with the paramount chief and his warriors, all in a terrible rage. The chief did not recognise him as the man who had poked the glowing fire-brand in his face, for that had occurred at night and in the darkness of the hunting lodge.

"Where are you going?" asked the chief.

"I come from home and I'm going home."

"Then why carry the digging stick and the gourd?"

"To provide myself with sweet potatoes for dinner and water to drink."

"What purpose does the drum serve?"

Umpume did not say that he had three trembling brothers inside the drum, but setting it down he said, "I drum for those who are in a rage, that they may give vent to their feelings and go home in peace."

With this he started to beat out a war dance, while the chief and his warriors leapt all round him in a frenzied circle of revenge, declaring that they would gnaw the very bones of those who had singed the chief's beard.

Gradually Umpume changed his measure until they danced around him in an ecstasy of rhythm, and finally his drum took on a tone of peace and satisfaction so that when he ceased to drum, the warriors ceased to dance, and the chief was so charmed that he quite forgot that he was on an expedition of revenge. He rewarded Umpume with a gun and sent him on his way remarking, "That is a delightful fellow. He has soothed my feelings."

When he arrived home, Umpume undid the drum-skin and let his brothers out. They saluted him by rubbing earth on their chests in abject respect and said, "Umpume, you have saved us from the lion, the leopard, the elephant and all the other animals, and finally from the wrath of the king and his warriors. We are ashamed for having treated you so meanly, and henceforth we will give you your rightful place as head of the family."

Umpume did not say, "I told you so!" for that would not have been polite. He just kept on smiling.

The Prayers of African Religion

John S. Mbiti

Belief in the effectiveness of prayer is a prominent characteristic of Africans of various faiths. Almost any stage or circumstance of life can be the occasion for praying, as evidenced by the following set of examples, taken from *The Prayers of African Religion*.

FERTILITY AND CHILDBIRTH

124 'GRANT CHILDREN TO HER' [LITANY FOR FERTILITY]

LEADER: Thou, Jouk [God], who art our Father and hast created all of us,

Thou knowest this woman is ours, and we wish her to bear children—

Life's journey

ALTOGETHER: Grant children to her!
LEADER: Should we die tomorrow, no children of ours will remain—
ALTOGETHER: Grant children to her!
LEADER: If she bears a son, his name will be the name of his grandfather.
 If she bears a daughter, her name will be the name of her grandmother.
ALTOGETHER: Grant children to her!
LEADER: Would it be displeasing to thee if many children surrounded us?
 Spirit of the father, spirit of the grandfather, you who dwell now in the skies,
 Are you displeased that we ask for children?
ALTOGETHER: Grant children to her!
LEADER: Should we die without them, who will guard the family?
 Your name and ours shall be forgotten upon the earth.
ALTOGETHER: Grant us this night good dreams,
 That we will die leaving many children behind us.

125 'GRANT ME A SON'

I pray to you, grant me a son.
If you grant my prayer, I will show you my gratitude and offer a
   goat up to you.

126 FOR A SAFE DELIVERY

ALL ASSEMBLED: O fathers and ancestors, and all who are of the near and far
 past, bear witness: we cry to thee [God] to let this child be safely born.
HUSBAND: If I have sinned, be merciful, and if thou canst not be merciful then
 punish me, slay me: but heal this woman and let this child live.
FATHER *of the woman:*   This is my daughter: she is in your hands: spare her life,
 and give her a living child.

127 A MIDWIFE'S PRAYER

I take you out of the world of the spirits. Do not be sick, settle down, and may
you have work. Here is this cloth for you, and now a pillow and now a bed: receive
these to take you out of the world of the spirits. Settle down, and may you have
work.

128 PRAYER FOR TWINS

Thou, Nhialic [God], it is thou alone who created them,
Thou alone didst bring them: no man hates them.

Thou, Nhialic, look on life mercifully;
No man is mighty, thou art mighty.
Accept the bull, I have paid you the wage,
Let them live!

129 'GOD, STAY WITH US FAVOURABLY'

Pu! Thou, God, hast come upon us. We accept thee. Stay, stay thou with us favourably. May the children be well; may their mother be well. Any animal that comes before us, let our spears fall on its body. Any man who seeks us, let us kill him and rejoice.

130 AT THE CEREMONY OF WASHING AN INFANT

God! give us health.
God! protect us.
And you our spirits, protect for us this child.

To the child:

Become a man! throw away the cough.

NAMING AND INITIATION

131 AT THE NAMING CEREMONY

Father and divinity Bosomtwe (or whichever), my child so-and-so has begotten a child and he has brought him to me, and I now call him after myself naming him so-and-so; grant that he grow up and continue to meet me here, and let him give me food.

132 LITANY FOR THE INITIATION CEREMONY

(*The Gazelles* is the name of the newly initiated group: *The Mountains* is the name of the inducting group. Ngipian is the territorial section.)

LEADER:	GROUP RESPONSE:
The Gazelles. I say the Gazelles.	
There are Gazelles.	There are!
These people, the Gazelles which are here, they have become big (i.e. grown up).	They have become big!
The Mountains also. There are Mountains.	There are!
There are!	There are!
The Karimojong also, they are.	They are!
There are Karimojong.	There are!
Cattle as well. The cattle of the Mountains. They are.	They are!
The cattle, the cattle of the Mountains, they become fat.	They are fat!
They become fat. Do they not become fat?	They are fat!
The land. This land here. Does it not become good?	It is good!
In this country there are Gazelles.	There are!
The Mountains also, they are.	They are!
Ngipian also. They are here, are they not?	They are!
In this land here, they are.	They are!
There is well-being in our country, is there not?	There is!

It is here.

Yes. Evil is going away.

It is leaving.

Well-being is with us.

It will always be with us, will it not?

It will.

Will it not?

God has heard.

He has heard.

The sky, the cloud-spotted sky here, it has heard!

It is!

It has gone!

It has gone!

It is!

It will!

It will!

It will!

He has heard!

He has heard!

It has heard!

133 TO HIM WHO IS DEATHLESS

Thou who art deathless,
Who knowest not death,
Who livest always,
Never feeling the cold sleep,
Thy children have come
To gather around thee.

O Father, gird up thy strength,
Penetrate them (the young initiates) with thy shadow,
O Father of our race,
O Father who never dies.

134 INVOCATION AT CIRCUMCISION OFFERING

Wele [God], you bless this cock which I am holding. I'm giving it to all those who have passed on for their use. Come, this is your [plural] white cock. You may use it. I'm placing it here in the basket.

135 AT THE FIRST MENSTRUATION CEREMONY

Nyankonpon Tweaduapon Nyame [Supreme Sky God, who alone
 is great], upon whom men lean and do not fall, receive this wine
 and drink.
Earth Goddess, whose day of worship is a Thursday, receive this
 wine and drink.
Spirit of our ancestors, receive this wine and drink.
This girl child whom God has given to me, today the Bara state has
 come upon her.
O mother who dwells in the land of ghosts, do not come and take
 her away, and do not have permitted her to menstruate only to die.

136 FOR FERTILE PUBERTY

Receive this loin cloth, and sponge, and eggs, and do not let this infant have come to puberty [only] to die.

137 AT THE ENGAGEMENT OF A CHIEF'S DAUGHTER

O father, forebear of my daughter, this is the ox that we are sacrificing for you. Go up to the mountains, call your servants, assemble all your people for this banquet, all your warriors. This is your ox, chosen for you by your people. Sit and eat it, you and your people.

DEATH

138 AT THE DEATH OF AN INFANT

O Mother who dwells in the land of spirits, receive this *eto* and eggs and eat. We thank you very much that you permitted this one to come, but we beg you for a new one. And you infant who are gone, receive your eggs and give to your old mother saying: 'Let one come again but permit it to remain.'

The MOTHER *of the dead child says:*
Spirit, eat on the path, do not eat in my belly.

139 COMMENDING A DYING PERSON

Our God, who has brought us [to this world],
May she take you.

140 PRAYER OF A DYING MAN

And though I behold a man hate me,
I will love him.
O God, Father, help me, Father!
O God, Creator, help me, Father!
And even though I behold a man hate me,
I will love him.

141 FUNERAL RECITATION

LEADER: GROUP RESPONSE:

The creature is born, it fades away, it dies,
And comes then the great cold.

> It is the great cold of the night, it is the dark.

The bird comes, it flies, it dies,
And comes then the great cold.

> It is the great cold of the night, it is the dark.

The fish swims away, it goes, it dies,
And comes then the great cold.

> It is the great cold of the night, it is the dark.

Man is born, he eats and sleeps. He fades away,
And comes then the great cold.

And the sky lights up, the eyes are closed,
The star shines.

Man is gone, the prisoner is freed,
The shadow has disappeared.

Khmvoum [God], Khmvoum, hear our call.

It is the great cold
of the night, it is
the dark.

The cold down
here, the light
up there.

The shadow has
disappeared.
Khmvoum,
Khmvoum,
hear our call.

African Animals Through African Eyes

Janet and Alex D'Amato

Animals hold a special and complex place in African life. They are viewed as not only sources of food, drink, clothing, medicine, and weapons but even, in some communities, as reincarnations of human souls. Artists, both primitive and sophisticated, have made the beasts of land, water, and air the subjects of their religious veneration. In so doing, they have told us much about the people of Africa, as illustrated in the following selection from *African Animals Through African Eyes* by Janet and Alex D'Amato.

FOREWORD

Since the earliest times, people and animals have shared the continent of Africa. Much of the history of Africa before the arrival of the first Europeans is now lost to us. Little is known because nothing was *written* that described those times or the life of the people who lived there.

But there are clues to tell us how men lived long ago and how they felt about the animals around them. Some of these clues can be found in bones of animals and pieces of ancient carvings that archeologists have dug up from sand and soil. Other clues are in cave paintings done long ago which show scenes of farming, cattle-raising, fishing, and hunting.

Still another way we learn of African beliefs is through myths, legends, and folktales. We are very fortunate that some stories from the past have survived to tell us about African customs, culture, and religion.

The animals of Africa play a big part in tribal religious beliefs. Most tribal religions agree that there is a supreme god, who made the world and everything in it. But they also believe the affairs of the world were left to lesser gods, or were taken over by evil spirits. The weather, the seasons, the crops, and the lives of the people were all controlled by these lesser gods. The name and character of each god varied greatly from tribe to tribe. Some tribes believed these gods appeared on earth in animal form.

There was also the belief that when someone died, his spirit took another form. Often, a dead ancestor was believed to dwell in an animal or in a carved figure. But no matter what form they appeared in, the people believed that the gods and spirits lived very close to them and took a large part in their affairs. Rituals, ceremonies, and magic were used by the people to please or influence these spirits and were part of almost every act in their daily life.

Like stories and religious beliefs, carvings give some clues to the past. The methods and styles used in making a carved figure were handed down from father to son. Thus, for many generations, animal carvings were done much the same way, not to make a work of art but usually for a religious purpose. Sometimes carvings were made for adornment of a king's court. Wood carvings, as well as sculptures in metal, clay, and stone were not meant to be exact copies of the animals they represented. Instead, they often represented a god or spirit who was believed to have taken the form of an animal. Their art was a link from the people to their gods or ancestors.

Of course, Africans also used animals in many practical ways. Animals provided a major source of food, and hides and furs were made into clothing and household items. Horn and bone were sometimes used in musical instruments or carved tools and ornaments. Even the teeth and claws of animals were put to use, for the people made decorations and jewelry from them.

The various tribes thought of the same animal in different ways. To one tribe, a particular animal was merely a source of food. But another tribe might believe this same animal represented a god or ancestor, and so members of that tribe were not allowed to harm it.

From their myths and fables, carvings and paintings of animals, we have some idea of what the plentiful animals and other creatures meant to these African peoples of the past.

THE SAHARA DESERT: AN ANCIENT WELL-POPULATED GRASSLAND

Very long ago, when men were just beginning to live together in groups, the large parts of North Africa that are now desert were covered by grassy plains. Vast herds of wild animals lived in the Sahara, the area west of the Nile River. The people farmed, raised cattle, and fished in the rivers. We know this because archeologists have found the bones of these people and animals in the sands of the desert.

Clues to what life was like in the ancient Sahara have been found in the form of paintings made by men on the rock walls of caves. These paintings portray lively scenes of hunting, cattle-herding, and family life. In these scenes are many pictures of animals. Giraffes, rhinoceros, fish, and many kinds of gazelles appear in life-like detail. Scientists believe the paintings were done as long ago as 5000 B.C.

However, the people who made the Sahara cave paintings were not able to continue living on the land. By 2000 B.C., their crops had become poor, and the rivers had begun to dry up. No one knows why. Perhaps, worldwide changes in climate had cut down the rainfall in the area. Perhaps, the cattle had grazed the grass too short and left the ground bare. In any case, by 1500 B.C., the Sahara was already becoming the desert it is today. The people and animals moved south to land that was less dry. But they left behind the cave paintings that tell us how important animals were in the Africa of this ancient period. For centuries, the hot, dry Sahara made travel between East and West Africa difficult. Then, about 600 B.C., the camel was brought to Africa by traders from the Middle East, the lands at the eastern end of the Mediterranean Sea. This beast, the one-humped dromedary or camel, was able to live in the desert whereas horses or cattle could not. These camels were very tough, and they could travel tirelessly with little food or water for many days. They could also carry heavy loads.

The arrival of the camels made it possible to cross the Sahara once again. Soon, caravan routes opened up communication between West Africa and the lands to the east. West African gold and ivory were traded for salt and other products from Egypt and other areas.

Centuries later, the great empire of Mali occupied a large part of the western grassland. Like the previous local kingdoms, Mali depended largely on the camel for trade and for transportation. In 1352 A.D., Mali's most famous king, Mansa Musa, made a religious pilgrimage across the Sahara to the holy city of Mecca in Arabia. He rode at the head of a camel caravan, which carried sixty thousand people and one hundred camel-loads of pure gold!

THE WESTERN GRASSLANDS: OF KINGDOMS, CATTLE, AND AN ANIMAL TRICKSTER

Between the western Sahara and the forests along the coast of the Gulf of Guinea lies a wide area of grassland. Most of these areas are now parts of the nations of Mali and Niger, but the grasslands were once much larger.

In ancient times, the plentiful animals of the grasslands were hunted by men who used weapons of wood or stone. When the people of this area learned to make iron (no one knows exactly when or how), their lives changed considerably. Sharper weapons and stronger tools made it easier both to hunt animals and to farm. The people had more time to develop skills and to trade, and they began to live together in towns. By 300 A.D., some of the towns had grown into powerful kingdoms. The people of these kingdoms used iron weapons to conquer other peoples.

The rulers of these kingdoms had courts of great splendor. Iron had not only brought increased trade and conquest, but also better ways of carving. The royal courts were often decorated with statues of men and animals that had been carved with iron tools. Sometimes, the statues themselves were made of iron.

The common people of the time lived in grass-roofed houses in villages. They were mainly farmers, fishermen, and skilled tradesmen. The iron-workers, wood-carvers, and other craftsmen of these villages made statues and masks which were often shaped like animals. Usually, these objects were used for religious purposes. They are the only things which have survived to tell us about the life of the kingdoms of the grasslands.

Statues and masks were made according to traditions which were handed down from parent to child for many generations. The people believed that the tree whose wood was going to be carved was a living thing, like an animal or a human being. Therefore, they felt that the tree had to give them permission to cut it down and carve it. To these Africans, animals, plants, and men were joined together in a world of regularly changing times and seasons. Throughout the year, they celebrated natural events such as springtime, harvest, and birth in special ceremonies.

A myth of the Bambara tribe of Mali tells of Chi Wara, the god of growth. One day, Chi Wara came to earth in the form of an antelope, a very common animal in the grasslands. As an antelope, this god showed men how to grow their food, rather than having to hunt for it. Thereafter, a dance was held each spring in honor of Chi Wara, in the hope that he would grant his people a good growing season. The leader of the dance wore on his head a carved figure of the god in antelope form. Chi Wara was also honored by a dance during the fall harvest season. During both these ceremonies, the dancers leaped high in the air, imitating the graceful bounds of the antelope. Another hoofed animal which lived in the grasslands was the evil-tempered African buffalo. This beast was both feared and respected by the people. In Buganda, when a man killed a buffalo, he built a small hut and put the head of the dead animal inside. In that way, he hoped to satisfy the angry spirit of the buffalo so it would not follow him back to his village.

CATTLE

The herding of cattle is a very old occupation in western Africa. Even today, some tribes, such as the Fulani, count a man's wealth by the number of cattle he owns. The Fulani have no permanent homes, and they constantly follow their cattle to new grazing lands. The Fulani raise cattle for milk rather than meat, and their entire way of life is centered around their herds. One of their legends tells about the first herdsmen.

Way back at the beginning of time, a young boy was walking by a river when he heard the water god call out to him: "Do you want to help your people?" The boy nodded.

"Then you must walk away from the river and never look back," said the water god.

So the boy began walking in the direction he had been told. He heard strange noises behind him, but he knew he must not look back. He walked on and on. The sounds grew even louder and the earth began to shake. Finally, the boy could not resist looking back. He saw a herd of strange beasts coming out of the river and following him. As soon as he turned to look at them, the cattle stopped coming out of the river. But a vast herd had already gathered, so the boy took them home to his people. Ever since, the men of that tribe have been cattle herders.

The Fulani have a proverb: He who harms cattle harms the Fulani.

THE HORSE

Cave pictures indicate that the horse has been in Africa since at least 1200 B.C. The early kingdoms of the grasslands depended on horses to carry their warriors into battle. In 1067 A.D., one of these armies had two hundred thousand mounted warriors!

The ancient West African kingdoms were well known for their mounted troops, whose horse-trappings were often covered with gold. One clan did nothing but care for the horses and their luxurious stables.

Since it was horses which carried the warriors to victory, it is easy to see why horses were valued so highly in these lands. Statues of men on horseback were usually the figures of kings or important leaders. Sometimes the mounted figure was that of a spirit, sometimes even a god.

THE HARE

Smaller animals also appear in the tales and carvings of the grasslands. A favorite type of African fable is one in which a weak creature, such as the hare, overcomes a larger and stronger one by cunning. These stories express the feelings of every human being who has ever felt himself helpless when faced with problems he cannot solve.

There are countless tales about a hare's pranks and the mischief he gets himself into. A lazy beast, the hare often talks other animals into doing his work for him. Sometimes, he steals things and then easily convinces the owners that someone else is guilty. The hare is a practical joker too. He may muddy up a water hole (a serious thing in a dry country) and then see that another animal, such as a lizard or a baboon, is punished for it.

The hare's role is not always the same in these tales. Sometimes, he is the only animal that is able to overcome a beast as fearsome as the lion—always by using sly tricks. At other times, his tricks are cruel, and he may be punished in the end. Yet he is always a weakling who uses his wits instead of his strength.

THE WESTERN FORESTS: ROYAL LEOPARDS, BRONZE SCULPTURES, AND SACRIFICES

In the bulge of western Africa are forests, which vary in kind from dense woodland to steamy rain forest. The people of these western forests produced some of the finest animal sculpture of Africa. Their skill in working with wood, metal, and clay has given us unforgettable pictures of the life and customs of times past.

The earliest animal figures that have come down to us from the western forest were made as long ago as 1000 B.C. by the people who lived along the Niger River. Later, in the same area, the kingdom of Ife arose, which brought the art of bronze sculpture to new heights. It is known that in about 1300 A.D., a messenger came to Ife from the kingdom of Benin (further south), asking for a craftsman to teach the workers of Benin how to cast bronze.

This casting was a complicated process. First, the figure had to be shaped in wax. Then it was covered with clay. When the clay hardened, the wax was melted out, leaving a mold. Next, molten bronze was poured into the mold. When the metal had cooled, the clay was broken away. The final step was to file and finish the bronze. This method is known as the lost wax process, and it is used today by sculptors throughout the world.

The craftsman from Ife who taught the lost wax process to the people of Benin was named Igueghae. In gratitude, Benin's guild of bronze-makers made him a national hero. They later produced beautiful bronzes which were alive with birds, animals, and fish, as well as kings and warriors.

Along the Volta River were gold mines so rich that the region became known as the Gold Coast. Among the people called the Ashanti, the form of money used was gold dust. This fact led to the development of an interesting art form. The custom was to weigh out quantities of gold dust using bronze weights. The earliest weights were merely lumps of bronze of the right size. Later, however, the weights were made so as to be decorative. They were cast into all sorts of fanciful shapes by the use of the lost wax method. Many were no more than two inches high, but they had the form of animals, plants, or people. Some of the weights illustrated scenes from fables.

THE LEOPARD

A very fierce and beautiful animal once common in the forests of western Africa was the leopard. In Benin, he was a symbol of royalty. Throughout the king's residence, there were statues of leopards in ivory, bronze, and wood. The ceremonial jars used for pouring water for the king were also in the shape of leopards, as were the gold or ivory ornaments and the jewelry worn by the members of the court.

In other parts of Africa, such as Gaboon, and among the Fon tribes of Dahomey, the leopard was a sign of terror rather than of power. Secret groups called Leopard Societies committed acts of murder and cannibalism. A man was required to kill a member of his own family in order to join one of these societies. The members dressed in leopard skins and carried claw-shaped knives.

THE FIRE-SPITTER

The Senufo tribe of the Ivory Coast created a ceremonial mask which combined the features of several animals in order to be as terrifying as possible. This mask was called the fire-spitter. It had the powerful jaws of the crocodile, the tusks of the warthog, and the horns of the antelope. Often, other creatures such as birds, chameleons, and snakes were shown crawling on the mask. Some of the masks were two-sided, with jaws both front and back.

The fire-spitter was so fearful-looking that it was thought to be dangerous just to touch the costume worn with it. The mask was supposed to frighten away evil spirits or witches that were threatening the people. The men of the tribe kept the mask in a secret grove except when it was in use. Then, on a dark night, drums would beat and a horrifying figure would appear. Running and stomping, the fire-spitter would chase away evil spirits.

The most impressive part of the ceremony was that the figure really appeared to spit fire. Inside the mask's huge jaws was a clever arrangement of glowing coals and bits of grass coated with resin. When the person inside the mask blew on the coals, a stream of orange sparks shot out into the night. The people believed that this sight was sure to frighten away the demons, so no harm would come to the village.

THE GOAT AND THE CHICKEN

Another way these people kept themselves safe from evil spirits was by making a sacrifice. For that purpose, the animals most often used were the goat and the chicken. Both have been domesticated in Africa since ancient times. Therefore, they were available when needed. The purpose of the sacrifice was to win the favor of the gods by giving them something of value. If the gods were pleased, they would not send such disasters as floods, famines, and disease. A goat was the usual sacrifice, but a chicken might be used for less important problems.

In addition to being used for sacrifices, chickens sometimes served to tell whether a man was guilty or innocent of a crime. The medicine man, who acted as judge, first questioned the suspect. Then he gave a dose of poison to a chicken. If the chicken died, it was considered a sign from the gods that the man was guilty. This method was thought to be more fair than if the people had just asked the opinion of the medicine man, who might have personal reasons for his answer. However, the medicine man could have varied the dosage of the poison in such a way that the chicken would die only if he believed that the suspect was guilty.

In one story from Nigeria, the chicken plays a role in the creation of the world. The creator god, Olorun, had made the world and the many lesser gods who lived in heaven. But down below, there was nothing but watery marshes. Olorun sent a god named Obatala down to make some dry land. Obatala dumped a huge snailshell full of dirt into the water, and on the mound of dirt he set sixteen sacred chickens. For four days, the chickens scratched about, and they made the dry land on which was located the center of the world, the city of Ife. The fifth day was set aside for praising the creator, Olorun. Then, in the next four days, Olorun created the other birds, trees, people, and animals. And that is how the world was made.

The importance of the chicken in African life is shown by the fact that it was the subject of so many proverbs. For example: "A blind chicken scratches what others will eat." Also: "Rooster, don't make so much noise; your mother was only an egg."

Many West African fables are about the spider. His web is said to stretch from earth to heaven, so he carries messages from gods to men.

In the stories of the Ashanti people, the spider hero, Anansi, is very clever. He is the one who brought the art of story-telling to the people from the gods. Like the hare in the stories from the grasslands, Anansi is a trickster. In spite of his small size, he often outwits men and other larger creatures.

THE RAM

Another animal of western Africa that was known for its power was the ram. The ram was most often associated with Shango, the thunder god. The sound of thunder was believed to be either the voice of the ram or the stamping of his feet. Shango was feared because he was a god of storms. But he was also considered helpful in that he brought rain.

Worshippers of Shango were sometimes portrayed with a double-headed axe. The axe represented lightning, which also splits trees. Among the Yoruba people of West Africa, there was a ceremony in which Shango was worshipped by pouring ram's blood over a carved figure with a double-headed axe.

AFRICA to AMERICA: The Beginnings of Slavery

A great variety of people visited and settled in America before Columbus's historic voyage. However, if you were to query average citizens on the first appearance of black persons in America, they would most likely reply that they appeared as a direct consequence of slavery. Nothing could be further from the truth. There is very strong archeological and anthropological evidence to support the fact that black people were present in ancient America. Nevertheless, there is no doubt that most present-day black Americans are, in fact, descendants of Africans who were involuntarily relocated as a consequence of the slave trade. In addition, some contemporary black Americans are related to Africans who came to America with European explorers. Whatever the reasons for the black migration, the fact remains that many blacks call America their home because greedy and callous people found "black gold" and engaged in the inhumane but profitable international enterprise of slavery.

Unexpected Faces in Ancient America

Alexander von Wuthenau

There are many who claim that the New World was visited by those of the Old World prior to the arrival of Columbus. It is conceivable that humans migrated to the New World not only via land or ice bridges, but also by traversing the Pacific and Atlantic Oceans. There is evidence of very early contacts between Africa and America and that black persons inhabited America long before Columbus. This article, from *Unexpected Faces in Ancient America,* explores pre-Columbian art among other supportive evidence existing today which strongly suggests the presence of black people in ancient America.

ETHNIC DIFFUSION AND CULTURAL DIFFUSION

I was reluctantly drawn into new investigations centered on the theories of the so-called diffusionists who claim that long before Columbus voyaged to the New World contacts took place between the Old and New World. These scholars argue that many ethnic and cultural developments in the New World could not be explained otherwise. Teaching at the same college as Don Pablo Martinez del Rio, I almost had to keep these heretical theories of mine a secret. The charming old gentleman became very violent if anybody had ideas like that. Furthermore I ran right into the antagonistic views of practically every archaeologist and anthropologist of Mexico, who all followed the undisputed leadership of Alfonso Caso. Every schoolchild and every student was told to be proud of the extraordinary cultural achievements arrived at by the sole efforts of the Indian race without any contacts whatsoever from the outside world before Columbus.

The first question that arises is: What was the so-called Indian race, now named Amerindians, composed of to begin with? What elements were necessary to form the vast American population during the millennia preceding the arrival of the European conquerors? Two distinct problems, which always seem to be mixed up indiscriminately, have to be kept separate. One is ethnic diffusion and the other is cultural diffusion. Since my investigations are primarily based on the physical appearance of American man as portrayed by his contemporaries, my chief concern is ethnic diffusion. The question of cultural and technical diffusion is less relevant for this specific study. Of course both types of diffusion may be interconnected, but that is not absolutely necessary.

When I implied in my pre-Columbian terracotta book *The Art of Terracotta Pottery*[1] that white and even Negro people existed in America long before Columbus, I immediately was challenged with the argument "But what about the wheel, the absence of the wheel?" At this point I am inclined to ask: "What on earth has the wheel to do with the adventure of a white man or a Negro having intercourse with an aborigine girl on this continent?" The man might have been killed before he had time to tell his amorous partner all about the wheel, or perhaps he just never got around to describing this marvelous invention to her before he became sick and died. One also might presume that he was not quite sure himself how to make a wheel or how to use it in the proper way. Nevertheless, one fact is relatively certain. After nine months, another American arrived on the continent who looked different from his brothers and sisters and who did not know anything at all about the wheel.[2]

At the time my above-mentioned terracotta book was reviewed by Mr. Karl E. Meyer in *Life* magazine, sure enough, the argument of the wheel was brought up and I received several letters relating to it. It is strange how many people seemed to be concerned about the absence of the wheel in America. There was an almost fanatic urge to have this phenomenon explained. According to one source, the native population considered it improper to use the wheel in an ordinary way because it was a holy symbol. According to another source this attitude was given a slightly dramatic explanation. In a Catholic country like Spain or Italy, an iron crucifix, though handy, could never be used to drive a nail into a wall.

How far the antidiffusionists go in their arguments is sometimes quaint. I was told that it was quite impossible for Phoenicians to have arrived in America because no glass was made here. We know what beautiful little bottles and glass beads were used in profusion in Carthage. They were never made in America. The attitude of a Phoenician sailor with respect to a wheel is understandable. Aside from his primary concern with ships, oars, sails, ropes, anchors, and the like, he might not have had a special interest in wheels. But to expect a concise knowledge of glassmaking from him is going too far. . . .

TRANSPACIFIC, TRANSANTARCTIC, AND TRANSATLANTIC CONTACTS

The above-mentioned earliest contacts are not essentially important for our fundamental concept of ethnic diffusion. Much more interesting is the question: How did the different ingredients of the pre-Columbian melting pot arrive on the shores of this continent? Apart from the land or ice bridge of the Bering Strait, which presumably served as the primordial route of human migration to the New World, there remain the possibilities of *transpacific* and *transatlantic* contacts. To suggest transantarctic contact is not quite as eccentric as one might think. Anyone will understand what I am saying who knows Charles H. Hapgood's study of the old Turkish Piri Reis map (1513), which shows not only the accurate rendering of the east coast of South America but also the shoreline of the Antarctic, a polar region that has been covered with ice for millennia. This demonstrates a surprisingly advanced geographical knowledge. Hapgood's study, now being republished in London, is well described in Charles Berlitz's *Mysteries from Forgotten Worlds*. For our investigation, however, these exceedingly remote events of over 6,000 years ago are not of immediate interest.

Truly important, however, is the question of *transpacific* contacts. Thirty-five years ago one could not even hint at such a possibility in Mexico. But now officially accepted books dealing with the origin of man in America appear with illustrations of little ships and rafts traversing the Pacific Ocean from west to east and from east to west, as well as of miniature figures tramping over the Bering Strait. . . .

SOME PERIPHERAL INDICATIONS SUPPORT THE PROBABILITY OF TRANSATLANTIC CONTACTS AND CONFIRM ETHNIC DIFFUSIONS AS REPRESENTED PICTORIALLY IN PRE-COLUMBIAN ART

Another reason to examine the probability of early transatlantic contacts is afforded by the work of the famous African explorer Leo Frobenius (1873–1938). His opinions were revealed to me in 1966 when I was invited by the government of Senegal to take part in the first International Festival of Negro Art in Dakar. At the festival the Leo Frobenius Institute of Frankfurt, Germany, presented a splendid exhibition of all the works of the eminent explorer, and I was able to examine his writing closely.

Frobenius was deeply interested in Phoenician contacts with Nigeria, but he also stated clearly that there must have been very early contacts between Africa and America.[3]

During the German anthropological expedition in Nigeria (1910–1913) Frobenius excavated a substantial number of terracotta heads, partly from Ebolokun and partly from Ilife. The British archaeologist Flinders Petrie assigned these Nigerian heads to the fifth century B.C. because of their "extremely close affinity" with the pottery heads from the foreign quarters of Memphis in Egypt, which

Petrie himself had excavated in the 1880s.[4] In 1966, I photographed many Memphis heads in the Petrie Collection in London. These heads have a remarkable variety of racial types and show a great diversity in craftsmanship. This diversity leads me to believe that they were not manufactured at the same time but that some of them were made long before the Persian invasion of Egypt (525 B.C.) and some probably later. The Memphis collector, whoever he was, obviously had the same kind of interest in finding "unexpected faces" in ancient Egypt, as I have in finding "unexpected faces in ancient America." In this context we might recall an aphorism of the so-called weeping Greek philosopher Heraclitus (fifth century B.C.). "If you do not expect it, you will not find the unexpected, for it is hard to find and difficult."[5]

Among the heads excavated by Frobenius in Nigeria was a representation that was practically identical with a Phoenician clay mask (Humbaba) from Sardinia. . . .

In connection with the question of Negroes in America, I should mention also the investigations conducted by the Mexican scientist Dr. A. de Garay on the presence of Negro blood in one of the oldest and most secluded tribes in Mexico, the Lacandones. Dr. de Garay is the director of the Genetic Program of the National Commission of Nuclear Energy in Mexico. His report includes a reference to the sickle cell, a malaria resistant mutant gene usually found only in the blood of black people.

During the first International Festival of Negro Art in Dakar, I was invited to exhibit my material of early representations of Negroes in pre-Columbian America. I displayed 64 photographs and 25 artifacts, which I had brought with me from America, in the library of the Assemblée Nationale. I had investigated this unexpected phenomenon for many years, but in Dakar I was able for the first time to present my findings to Africans, who obviously know what a Negro is and what he looks like. My point of view that these ancient American sculptures could be considered truthful representations of Negroes was amply confirmed by everyone, including the President of Senegal, Leopold Sedar Senghor.

Clearly Negroid representations in America can be identified as early as 1200 to 650 B.C., at least in terracotta and other materials known at present. This time would extend in the Old World from the reign of Ramses III and the later Libyan rulers in Tanis (Lower Egypt) to the epoch of the Ethiopian or Nubian domination of Egypt including the Twenty-fifth Dynasty and the Negro king Taharka.[6] It would of course also include the period of Assyrian thrusts against the Phoenician city-states in Asia Minor. Since nobody can believe that Negroes ever tramped all the way through Siberia and crossed the Bering Strait and Alaska to arrive very much later in the warmer parts of the American continent, the only acceptable interpretation for their presence here at the above-mentioned time would be transatlantic voyages, a phenomenon that sooner or later will have to be explained. At this point, it might be appropriate to recall the navigation skill of the Phoenicians and the excellent quality and magnificent organization of their ships given us by contemporary eyewitnesses. The prophet Ezekiel, around 590 B.C., describes the marvel of the Phoenician ships as follows:

They made all thy ship boards of fir trees from Senir; They have taken cedars from Lebanon to make masts for thee . . . of the oaks from Bashan have they made thine oars; they made thy benches of ivory . . . [Ezekiel 27:5]

The Greek writer Xenophon, born in 430 B.C., tells the following story in his book *Ischomacus:*

The best and most accurate arrangement of things I ever saw was when I went to look at the great Phoenician ship. For I saw the greatest quantity of tackling separately disposed in the smallest stowage. You know that a ship comes to anchor or gets under way by means of wooden instruments and many ropes, and sails by means of many sails and is armed with many machines against hostile vessels and carries with it many arms for the crew, and all the apparatus which men use in dwelling houses, for each mess. Besides all this, the vessel is apart filled with cargo which the owner carries for his profit. And all that I have mentioned lay in no much greater space than would be found in a chamber large enough to hold conveniently ten beds. All the things too lay in such a way that they did not obstruct one another, so they needed no one to seek them, and should easily be got together, and there were no knots to be untied, and cause delay if they were suddenly wanted for use. I found the mate of the steersman who is called the prow's man, so well acquainted with the place of each article that even when absent he could tell where everything lay, and what their number was, as one who has learned to read could tell the number and order of letters in the name of Socrates. I saw this man examining, at an unoccupied time, everything that is of use on board of a ship; and on my asking him the reason, he replied: Stranger, I am examining whether anything is difficult or out of order; for it will be no time to look for what is wanting, or put to rights what is awkwardly placed, when a storm arises at sea.[7]

Descriptions like these make us wonder about the wide discrepancy between actual ancient seagoing ships and the historically interesting but strange contraption of papyrus that Thor Heyerdahl was not afraid to use on his heroic trips across the Atlantic Ocean. Yet the historically well founded choice made by Heyerdahl has been vindicated by his success.[8] His choice was especially rewarding. It led to the correct interpretation of a Maya Campeche stela in the National Museum in Mexico City and one of the rock drawings in the Jewish necropolis of Beit She'arim, both mentioned in the following chapter.

The type of vessel used to reach America for the first time is not important; what really counted concerning the Heyerdahl enterprise is the unique spirit behind it. The same can be said of the Phoenicians and their adventures of thousands of years ago. Their well-attested nautical skill and craftsmanship in shipbuilding was not enough. What really counted is the vigorous spirit of a remarkable race. . . .

By far the most important one is the intrinsic art value of the sculptural objects presented here for the first time to a public that is becoming more and more aware of the artistic aspects of all cultures. The second reason is the generally growing interest in the ancient history of the whole American continent in its global setting. The third reason, we might say, is the great concern shown by so many people about all questions relating to the racial and ethnological background of America from every conceivable human and historical angle.

With reference to the last reason, the startling fact is that in all parts of Mexico, from Campeche in the east to the south coast of Cuerrero, and from Chiapas, next to the Guatemalan border, to the Panuco River in the Huasteca region (north of Veracruz), archaeological pieces representing Negro or Negroid people have been found, especially in Archaic or pre-Classic sites. This also holds true for large sections of Mesoamerica and far into South America—Panama, Colombia, Ecuador, and Peru.

In view of the fact that so many present-day inhabitants of Meso and South America have Asiatic-looking features, the presence of their Asiatic ancestors on American soil in antiquity has to be considered a historical fact. That will surprise nobody. Surprising, however, is the competence of pre-Columbian artists to render these features in realistic detail, whether re-creating the purest Mongoloid characteristics or a complex racial mixture. These artistic testimonies, executed with incredibly skillful craftsmanship, are first present in pre-Classic Olmec times and appear in all periods of ancient American history.

The white types, chiefly with Semitic characteristics, were probably numerous within the pre-Columbian population. I have already stressed this point of view in my terracotta book, with many illustrations, including those of figures resembling Etruscans, Greeks, Caucasians, Ainus, and Vikings.

Whereas the classification of white men in ancient America is relatively easy, the selection of the items that demonstrate definitely Semitic features is more difficult. The tentative argument I am making in this book is by no means meant to be conclusive, but at least it should serve the purpose of elucidating a real ethnic question. The same holds true for the selections in the Negroid part of this book.

For a real understanding of the historical message of pre-Columbian artists, the enumeration of dry facts is not enough. An intimate involvement of modern man, and emotional if not passionate personal effort, is necessary to open the door to the world of ancient American art. I would like to close this chapter with a quotation from a speech given by André Malraux at the Congress of Writers in Paris in 1935.[9] "Every work of art is created to satisfy a need, a need so passionate as to give it birth. When the need expires or is withdrawn as the blood from the body, then its mysterious transfiguration begins; it enters the sphere of shadows. Then, only our own needs, our own passions, can revive it again.

"Every work of art dies when love is withdrawn. A heritage does not transmit itself. It has to renew itself."

. . . The all-important ethnic variations and crossbreedings in the pre-Classic period of Mesoamerica . . . show an assembly of a preponderantly pre-Classic "Humanitas Americana." . . . The true ethnic situation in those ancient times is well described by one of the great scientific philosophers of our day, Buckminster Fuller. He believes that over a thousand years ago "a widely crossbreeding Mongolian-Polynesian-African-South American people already existed" in the New World. In *Utopia or Oblivion* (1966) Fuller makes the following observation:

Just to the south of us, in Mexico, we have the earlier world encirclement of highly crossbred people. These people probably came millenniums ago into the Central America area of Mexico, from all around the world, by drifting, paddling, and sailing across both the Atlantic and the Pacific on rafts, and climbing mountains and crossing the Bering Strait. You will find in Mexico every shape of face, eye, and lip, every shape of head, and you will find any and every one of these shapes and faces in every grade of color, from very dark to very light. The people of Mexico constitute a highly crossbred man of yesterday. He has no unique color identity. The new and second-degree stage of world-encircling crossbreeding is now taking place a little bit further to the north.

With Buckminster Fuller one does not know what to admire most, the master-mind of modern technology or the unflinching spirit of a man of extremely lucid common sense.

THE ABSORPTION OF THE NEGROES: THEIR SPORADIC REPRESENTATION DURING THE ENTIRE PRE-COLUMBIAN EPOCH IN ALL REGIONS FROM MESOAMERICA TO PERU

An attentive study of Negroid portrayals in pre-Columbian art leaves us little doubt about the presence of black people in ancient America. This paramount reality is even more surprising as soon as we examine the chronological and geographical extent of a racial phenomenon that was practically ignored in the past by professional investigators and the general public alike.[10] In former chapters we have seen that this remarkable racial incident can be traced back to the remotest history of America. Michael Coe's last carbon dating (1966) of San Lorenzo, going back to almost 1200 B.C., gives us an unmistakable clue to the great antiquity of the colossal "Olmec" heads. George Kuebler describes these monumental witnesses as manifesting, on the part of their creators, "a Pharaonic desire for eternity, for physical survival beyond all the accidents of time." I believe Kuebler is right, and I am beginning to believe that he is also right in introducing the word Pharaonic even if it means the vindication of the often-laughed-at explorer Count Waldeck. Waldeck (1766–1875) was a close friend of Lord Kingsborough. Kingsborough believed in the early Semitic background of America's population, but Waldeck stuck to his ideas of ancient Egyptian contacts. They never quarreled. Now we may assume that both of them did not go so far astray in their respective stubborn convictions!

One piece of new archaeological evidence that has made a most lasting impression on me is the terracotta figurine excavated by MacNeish in Techuacan. . . . There is no escape. It is one of the oldest specimens of its kind and it is definitely Egypto-Nubian in looks. Other early dated Negroid or semi-Negroid pieces come from Guerrero (Xochipala and Pacific coast), La Venta, Tlatilco, Tlapacoya, Guatemala, El Salvador, and so on. Among them is a great favorite of mine, an exquisite "Nilotic" girl, who in her well-bred distinction and negritude can rival the Egyptian boy-king Tutankhamen. Incidentally, the most accurate and convincingly lifelike portrayals of racial distinctions in antiquity can be found among the archaeological objects from the tomb of Tutankhamen. The features of this Egyptian king, whose mother was of pure black stock, are almost as Negroid looking as the ones of his captured Nubian "enemies," so admirably portrayed by the royal artists, commemorating the death of their sovereign.

It is strange that some people still believe that all the Negroid images in this book were "accidental" creations of the American "Indians." A severe blow to this erroneous belief was given during the XLI International Congress of Americanists in Mexico (September 1974) by Andrzej Wiercinski, the well-known craniologist from the University of Warsaw. Dr. Wiercinski was kind enough to lend me the manuscript of his contribution to the Congress, which I included in my paper also read at the Congress. Wiercinski says:

It appeared that some of the skulls from Tlatilco, Cerro de las Mesas and Monte Albán (all pre-Classic sites in Mexico) show, to a different degree, a clear prevalence of the total Negroid pattern that has been evidenced by the use of two methods: a) multivariate distance analysis of average characteristics of individual fractions distinguished cranio-scopically; b) analysis of frequency distributions of Mean Index of the position between combinations of racial varieties.

To this long list of implausible "accidental creations" another very dramatic one can be added. Recently an incredible rock carving was discovered on a mountaintop in the state of Morclos, Mexico, near the small village of Chalcat-zingo. The Olmec stone reliefs of Chalcatzingo were already mentioned in Chapter Eleven. They are mentioned also in the new book by Carlo Gay illustrated by Francis Pratt (*Chalcatzingo,* Graz, Austria, 1972). For us the most unexpected surprise was a big stone face carved out of the living rock, situated above all the other reliefs in the same place. For almost 3,000 years this face has been gazing over the vast valleys of Morelos in the direction of the snow-covered peak of Popocatepetl, Mexico's famous volcano. The features of this face are indisputably Negroid. . . .

Pedro Martir was the trusted friend of Isabela la Católica and Fernando, the man whom they put in charge of the education of their children; he had firsthand contacts with all explorers during the age of the discovery of America, and he reported conscientiously all the facts that came to his knowledge to the Pope and his friends among the Cardinals in Rome. In his third Decade, Chapter II, dealing with the exploration of Vasco Nuñez de Balboa of the Isthmus of Panama and under the heading "Ethiopian tribes," he writes:

There they met Negro slaves from a region only two days in distance from Caruaca, where nothing else but Negroes are bred, who are ferocious and extraordinary cruel. They (the explorers) believe that in former times Negroes, who were out for robbery navigated from Ethiopia and, being shipwrecked, established themselves in those mountains. The inhabitants of Caruaca have internal fights full of hatred with these Negroes. They enslave each other mutually or just kill each other.

Similar testimony is given by the Dominican Fray Gregorio Garcia (1554–1637), who in the latter part of the sixteenth century spent nine years in Peru and three in Mexico. In his book *Origen de los Indios en el Nuevo Mundo* (Madrid, 1607 and 1729), which is practically unknown and hardly ever cited by historians, he mentions that the Spaniards saw Negroes for the first time on an island off the shore of Cartagena, Colombia. "Here were slaves of the chief, Negroes, which were the first ones our people saw in the Indies."

In addition to these two virtually irrefutable sources concerning the presence of black people in America prior to the arrival of the Spaniards, we now have the work of Professor M. D. W. Jeffreys of Johannesburg University, mentioned in Chapter Ten. Jeffrey's theories on Arabian voyages to America and the introduction of American corn into West Africa by Arabian merchants prior to the arrival of the Portuguese dovetail with the preceding historical documents. They help explain the presence of the fine terracotta heads of late post-Classic times, which show North African features. The voyages by the Arabians might also account for the presence of African "guanin" metal in the West Indies before 1492. Frederick J. Pohl, author of *Amerigo Vespucci, Pilot Major* (New York: Columbia University Press, 1944), is convinced that there were direct overseas contacts made by black people. He writes thus:

Columbus was probably preceded in reaching the shore of South America by Phoenicians (ca. 1000 B.C.) and certainly by natives of Guinea, who crossed from Africa in canoes from time to time. After his first voyage Columbus said that "Guanines," or "Goanines," had been handed to him by the natives of Española who told him "that there had come to this island, from the direction of the south and the southeast, black people, and that they had the point of their spears made of metal which they call "guanin." "Guanines" was a native African name. African guanines were alloys of gold containing copper for the sake of its odor, for it seems that the Negroes liked to smell their wealth. The guanines brought home by Columbus were assayed in Spain and were found to contain the same ratio of alloy as those in African Guinea, for "of the 32 parts, 18 were gold and 6 silver and 8 copper." On his third voyage Columbus learned that in the Cape Verde islands there "had been found canoes which set out from the coast of Guinea and steered to the west with merchandise," and on his return he reported the presence of Negroes in lands he had visited. In the proper season it is quite feasible to cross the Atlantic near the Equator from Africa to South America in small, open boats.

This statement by a scholar and investigator refers principally to the latest pre-Columbian contacts of black people with America. The earliest contacts with blacks, on the other hand, are described by Alfonso Medellin Zanil, director of the Archaeological Museum of the State of Veracruz in Jalapa and one of the few Mexican archaeologists who had an unbiased approach to this subject, as follows:

Kinky hair, broad chubby noses, thick lips and other less definable corporal features, belong to the ethnic group of Negroes, alien to Amerindian man. It is possible that at the end of the pre-Classic period a small group of Negroes arrived on the Atlantic shores of America, though they could not perpetuate their biological inheritance, on account of their small numbers. Memory, legend and myth would surely deify them or endow them with the character of cultural heroes depicted in terracotta figurines and who were immortalized in monumental stone sculptures.

NOTES

1. *Altamerikanische Tonplastic, Das Menschenbild der Neuen Welt* (Baden Baden: Holle Verlag, 1965); *Terres Cuites Precolombiennes, L'Image Humaine du Nouveau Monde* (Paris: Albin Michel, 1970); *Pre-Columbian Terracottas* (London: Methuen, 1970); *The Art of Terracotta Pottery in Pre-Columbian Central and South America* (New York: Crown Publishers, 1970).
2. The eagerness of Mesoamerican women to have sexual intercourse with foreign men is well documented, at least for the fifteenth century, in Amerigo Vespucci's letters and the writings of Pedro Martir d'Angliera. See Germán Arciniegas's *Amerigo and the New World,* and Frederick J. Pohl's *Amerigo Vespucci, Pilot Major.*
3. Leo Frobenius, *The Voice of Africa* (London, 1913).
4. W. M. Flinders Petrie, *Ancient Egypt* (London, 1914).
5. Loren Eiseley, *The Unexpected Universe* (New York, 1969).
6. The beautiful black stone head of the Egyptian king Taharka (680 B.C.) who joined the fight with the Israelites against the Assyrians is still one of the showpieces in the Cairo Museum.
7. *Concise Encyclopedia of Explorations* by Jean Riverain (English edition, Collins, Glasgow; Follett, Chicago, 1969), page 211.
8. It is interesting to note that the ancient migration myths of the Hopi Indians in North America contain a detailed description of the hollow stems of papyrus for the manufacture of seagoing rafts (*Book of the Hopi* by Frank Waters. New York: Viking Press, 1972).

9. From Gustave Regler's autobiography, *Le Glaive et le Fourreau* (Paris: Plon, 1960), page 262. Regler was one of Malraux's friends and comrades in arms in the Spanish Civil War.
10. In the scholarly book *Blacks in Antiquity* by Frank M. Snowden, Jr. (Harvard University Press, 1970), there is no mention of the presence of blacks in American antiquity. This unfortunately reflects the attitude of many North American writers as well as the posture of the general public, namely, to ignore the history of an ancient America south of the border of the United States. The minute study of Mr. Snowden is, however, very interesting for us since it shows many parallels in his research work on "Greco-Roman" material; similar investigation procedures are used in my book.

Slavery as an Institution

James Shenton

According to author James Shenton, slavery was a well-developed institution in antiquity and cannot be excluded from a comprehensive treatment of history. He contends that slavery worked, as a system of labor, and thus he presents information supportive of his position. Analyze the article carefully and determine for yourself whether or not the author adequately defends his contention that slavery was a successful institution. Whether one concludes in the affirmative or the negative, the article is intended to help the reader assess the impact of the institution of slavery on blacks as well as whites.

In my 19th-Century course at Columbia, when I assert that slavery worked, the students look at me rather strangely as if somehow I've made a slight betrayal of the faith. But my assumption is that the purpose of a lecture on slavery is to try to provide a general framework in which to place the institution of slavery, and I have come to believe that the best and easiest way to begin is to emphasize that slavery as a system of labor has existed for time immemorial, and that, if one were to look just simply at its role in a historical context, one would have to begin by knowing that slavery was a well-developed institution in antiquity, and that it would be almost impossible to deal with any portion of ancient history without coming at some point to grips with the institution.

I think the critical difference, of course, is that the nature of slavery in antiquity was never racially defined; that is, the concept of slavery was something which usually involved the definition of the "other" as a non-person who belonged to another society typically defined as barbarian. In effect, they were the strangers and were, therefore, to be enslaved if that suited your purpose.

Nonetheless, the institution of slavery in antiquity had distinct characteristics which set it off from modern slavery. Nowhere was this more apparent than in the view that slavery was not to be treated as a condition of life which precluded access of the slave to the normal institutions of the society. Thus, for example, not infrequently slaves were among the most learned men of a given society; not infrequently, Greeks who found themselves enslaved served as tutors to young Romans.

The critical shift of emphasis, however, within the nature of the institution of slavery came, of course, with the discovery of the New World and for reasons which are fairly specific. If one were to take a map of the New World and look at what is best described as the Afro-American world, one discovers a world which extends from the northern areas of South America beginning with northeastern Brazil, stretching up into and around the Caribbean and finally including the southern part of the United States. Within this particular region, when the Europeans launched their explorations, there emerged almost immediately a fundamental problem: if you were to exploit the resources of the region, you had to have a labor supply. In other areas where there was a large indigenous Indian population which had developed within itself a structured society accustomed to disciplined labor procedures, slavery as a rule did not emerge; rather, a form of compulsory labor such as peonage, which is a variation of serfdom, developed. In many areas of the New World the indigenous Indian population were unable to adjust to a systematic utilization of the labor force: perhaps the most graphic example of this is in the West Indies where the Carib Indians were widely established. However, the Spaniards' effort to impose upon them labor discipline culminated in what is best defined as the original example, at least in the New World, of genocide. The Carib Indian was exterminated by the process. His cultural conditioning makes it almost impossible for him to adjust to demands for organized labor. Thus what you find is that insofar as there is an indigenous population in the region which are the areas of Afro-American dominance, one of two things happens: either it is destroyed, or it retreats, as in the case of the northeastern Brazil, into the interior. Thus, anyone who wants to develop the region's resources must bring their labor supply from outside.

Specifically the development of slavery in the New World arose out of the slave institutions that had already developed in western Europe, particularly in the areas of Europe which were directly influenced by Portugal's importation of Blacks. I might add there's a rather curious aspect of this which is spelled out, I think, most distinctly in Gilberto Freyre's study of *Masters and Slaves,* which is a study of the emergence of a distinctive Brazilian life and Brazilian society. The original enslavement of Blacks by the Portuguese occured, in part, as a result of the Portuguese male viewing of the dark-skinned woman as a more attractive sexual object than fair skinned women. Now the explanation for this is quite simply that traditionally, during much of Portuguese history, the dominant population of Portugal were the Moorish conquerors. The dark-skinned woman was the woman, the wife, of the ruler. She was the inaccessible one. Subsequently, Portuguese, travelling along the coast of Africa, come upon what was a characteristic of some African social systems; that is, some African societies took much the same attitude that antiquity had taken towards neighbors, and treated the "others" as susceptible to enslavement. It was not a system which had developed to the extent of becoming in any way a major aspect of the economy of Africa, but enslavement amongst Africans existed. The Portuguese suddenly had an opportunity to obtain a form of gratification which had been previously viewed as beyond his grasp. The existence of this source of slaves was to suggest to the European colonizers almost automatically that slavery could provide needed labor as the settlement of the New World began.

In northeastern Brazil, where the Portuguese established themselves shortly after the first voyages of Columbus, there developed the first major staple crop agriculture in New World history, specifically, sugar. If one were to exploit this crop, a labor source had to be found. Portugal itself was a country whose population was simply inadequate to supply the necessary labor even if such had been desired. The nearest and most available source of labor, with which the Portuguese were thoroughly familiar, was the market immediately across the Atlantic from the Brazilian bulge along the Calabar-Guinea coast. And the availability of this labor force was to prove one of the most critical aspects of European history for the next three centuries—specifically, the question of the control of the *asiento*. I might suggest, at this point, for any of you who are interested in pursuing the subject of the significance of the slave trade to the West in detail, that the book to read is Eric Williams' *Slavery and Capitalism,* which contends, and I think rather powerfully, that in many respects the original capitalization which was subsequently utilized for the development of western capitalism was derived from the profits obtained from this particular trade. The right of *asiento* was essentially the right to supply slave labor to the Spanish New World empire.

The introduction of slavery into the western hemisphere led to organizing the slave trade. It began as a reciprocal accommodation between certain African elements, particularly settlements along the Calabar coast and White slave traders, but, generally speaking, it was increasingly dominated by whites who, along the entire coast, began to develop what were known as "factories." The function of these factories was to provide points of concentration for the large numbers of captives brought in from the interior of Africa. One of the intentions of these factories was to begin a process which has in some way been most effectively defined by Stanley Elkins as a process of total disorientation and disintegration of the normal social patterns that existed among the Black captives. What frequently happened in the factories was a systematic effort to create a compliance or passivity among the captives by intermixing them in such a way as to preclude any maintenance of previous cultural or social patterns within a group being processed at a factory. Thus, for example, one of the things exploited in the factory was the ethnicity of the African, specifically as a means of precluding organized opposition. As increasingly, the slaves were thrown together without reference to their pasts, slavery as an institution began to negate the ethnic and cultural differences amongst Africans. Within the factory system itself, the aspect that made it so effective at the outset was the possibility of exploiting, and at that rather effectively, historical antipathies and long-sustained hostilities, among the various African peoples. In a very basic way, therefore, Africans were victimized, as they were prepared for a slavery, by the variety of their social attitudes, the variety of their cultural commitments, the variety of their identifications, in a way by the very nature of their previous historical experience.

In the process of preparing individuals for their subsequent transportation across the Atlantic, there developed what is known as the "middle-passage," the journey from the factory system to the point in the New World where they slaves were to be put to work on what was generally defined as a plantation. The journey across the Atlantic Ocean represents by any measurement one of the most horrendous episodes in human history. To look at the middle passage and to understand it is in some way to understand something of the very horror of the whole experience. The way in which a slave ship was usually identified at sea into the nineteenth century was very simple. If one were downwind fifteen or twenty miles away, one could smell the ship even before it was sighted. The usual conditions on a slave ship were such that it was taken as a given that if one could successfully transport one third of his cargo across the ocean, one would have covered the total cost of the entire expedition with somewhere between a 200 or 300 percent profit.

The ships themselves were specifically structured or organized so as to minimize the possibility of any slave uprising on the ship itself. Thus, for example, the usual deck was divided into three layers. Assuming, for example, that a deck was approximately nine feet high, there would be compartments three feet high into which a slave was placed, with both arms and legs shackled. Once or twice a day, depending upon the conditions of the trip, groups of slaves would be taken out to walk the deck, this to prevent complete paralysis because of sustained confinement in a small place. Not infrequently the ships were swept by epidemics. To understand the full implications of the journey, it should be remembered that in the middle passage, during the period between 1500 and 1850, perhaps 11 to 13 million people were transported; some one third to two thirds of whom may have perished in the journey.

Thus the impact of the journey itself was devastating. The original "seasoning", the term used for the process of preparing the captives in the "factory" for the journey, was usually completed by the time they had journeyed across the ocean. Not infrequently, by the time they reached dry land again, the survivors were so thoroughly disoriented that there was a kind of almost built-in responsiveness— by that I mean an unquestioning willingness to accept direction from their masters in the utterly unfamiliar environment, with a sense, at least temporarily induced, of utter powerlessness in many areas.

The diversity of the slave institution is best understood in terms of how, over time, the slavers themselves learned to accentuate differences among slaves. For example, whereas originally many of the earlier cargoes actually had been drawn substantially from a single area of Africa, the emphasis as time proceeded, upon diversifying the source of supply to accentuate differences and therefore to induce even more effective controls became a powerful method of retaining dominance over the slave once on the other side of the ocean.

There are a number of other points that ought to be noted. The comparative evaluation of slavery systems, is generally speaking, one of the areas where one runs into a curious argument, such as the contention that Latin American slavery was less brutalizing than Anglo-Saxon. There is no question that, in a sense, there were aspects of Latin American enslavement which were less destructive. But I think it would be a catastrophic error to assume from this that, because it was less destructive, it becomes in some way more defensible. The trouble with the comparative approach is the need to recognize that in a sense the differences are differences of degree, and most certainly before anyone goes off cavalierly to support the argument that Portuguese enslavement was somehow more preferable to say Anglo-Saxon enslavement, bear in mind that the Portuguese developed the seven-year system. Perhaps the best way to illustrate the seven-year system is to deal with that aspect of it which was most certainly as brutal as any which ever emerged under any other system of slavery. Sugar, as you may know, dictates certain labor conditions. It is a crop which normally has an eight-month growing period in which the labor force is essentially non-utilizable. Thus, for example, in any discussion of a predominantly sugar economy, something to keep in mind is that, since the actual sowing of the sugar is followed by a growing season which requires little labor, there is an uneconomic use of the labor force. The labor process however becomes one which increases in intensity during the harvest season. Normally, where sugar is grown, the harvest season has a twenty-hour work day; thus, there are four months of intensive labor, seven days a week which averages from eighteen to twenty hours a day. To resolve this problem the Portuguese developed a system of multiple fields. They would first clear one and prepare it, and the crop would begin to grow. While this crop was growing, the slaves would be put to work preparing a second field, so that at the end of the eight-month growing period, a second crop would be maturing. Next a third field would be set up, the result of all this being a twelve-month cycle of intensive labor seven days a week, twelve months of the year, averaging eighteen to twenty hours a day. The seven-year system was based upon the principle that in seven years you would work your slave population to death. However, in the first two harvests, the entire capital investment would be recouped. The Portuguese system worked, and particularly as it developed on northeastern Brazil, precisely because of the nearness of that region to Africa. What the Portuguese assumed was that you could go across the ocean whenever you needed slave replenishments, and bring them across. One of the consequences of the acceleration of demand for slave labor forces was the introduction into Africa of a disruptive force which was to have catastrophic consequences on the whole social fabric of those areas of Africa directly exposed to the depredations of the seekers after slave labor.

Now beyond the Portuguese system there are other emphases that ought to be made. For instance, the question as to whether Spanish enslavement was preferable to Anglo-Saxon enslavement is one which has to take into consideration the Spaniards' deep involvement in *asiento*. This came about because much of their original labor force, the Carib Indians, has been decimated by its incapacity to adjust to enslavement. Anyone who wants to understand the implications of the tragic plight of the Carib Indians ought to read the class confrontation of Las Casas and Sepulvada, two churchmen who appeared before the Spanish King: Las Casas arguing the humanity of the Indian, Sepulvada arguing the reverse. Interestingly enough, Las Casas blundered into what he subsequently himself regretted. In his effort to save the Indian population from total destruction, he called for the utilization of Black labor.

But the essential point is that the question of what precisely was the nature of the individual who was being enslaved was one of the large overriding questions that permeated the institution of slavery. It would seem that in focusing then upon the Anglo-Saxon variety of slavery, we ought to emphasize that in any discussion of slavery as it existed elsewhere in the new world, the mitigating circumstances were not sufficiently strong to prevent what was in Brazil a constant, endless series of massive slave uprisings. Brazil was not alone, the Caribbean islands also witnessed massive uprisings. The problem of dealing with the question of the seeming paucity of uprisings in the southern part of the United States or in the colonies before the establishment of the American Republic should be understood in the following context: slave uprisings were possible in proportion to the existence of bases of operation which would provide fugitive slaves with a sanctuary. One of the basic explanations of the history of the southeastern part of the United States in the early nineteenth century—and the classic example of this is Andrew Jackson's use of the war of 1812 to undermine the Creek federation—was the elimination of an area where the Blacks could successfully sustain their flight to freedom. Specifically, one of the major targets of Jackson's campaign was the destruction of lower Alabama, lower Mississippi, northern Florida, of enclaves of fugitive slaves who had managed to develop an autonomous independent existence. They were in effect what will be known in the Caribbean islands as a "maroon" population, dissidents who have broken out of the framework of the slave institution. One of the constants in southern history, through to the Civil War, is the imperative of pushing back, as much as one can, any area where there was a possibility of a slave establishing an independent existence or a sanctuary.

But this in itself, however, isn't sufficient to explain what made the American variety of slavery peculiar and distinct. First and foremost, in Latin America, the definition of race was in the context of one's proportion of White ancestry. Thus in Brazil if you're Black, you're at the bottom, as a rule, of the social heap: there are differentiations based upon the intermixing of races. In Anglo-Saxon slavery, a difficulty arises in defining a Negro or a Black because assignment to the racial category of Negro is without concern for the proportion of Black ancestry to White. To illustrate the point: every state in the United States until this day defines a Black as being either one sixteenth or one thirty-second Black. There are also rather interesting kinds of differentiation which involve the coloration of the skin. But differentiation brings no advantage, if you look as if you are a Negro, you are so defined, and if it can be established that you have Negro ancestry, you are also so defined. But when you look at this practically its absurdity becomes obvious. Let's begin by noting that an individual with two parents, one of whom was Black, is defined as a mulatto. An individual one of whose grandparents was Black is defined as a quadroon. An individual one of whose great-grandparents was a Black is defined as an octoroon. A person who had one great-great-grandparent who was Black is a sextaroon. The ultimate lunacy, of course, is when one gets to one thirty-second. If one thinks in terms of only generations of thirty years, in theory at least, an American can be defined as a Negro if he or she had a great-great-great-grandparent who was Black, some one hundred fifty years ago.

Now the problem of defining what constitutes a Negro in the United States is complicated further by the emergence of the definition of the legal context which emphasized the condition of motherhood, the assumption being one which is, if you contemplate its implications for a traditional family structure, most devastating. The assumption is that the Black slave woman is more likely than not unable to defend herself against the demands of a White master. Enslavement, therefore, involves sexual accessibility for the White male of the Black female slave, but the ultimate twist in the law is that issue born of that relationship is born, therefore, into the condition not of the father, but into the condition of the mother. Needless to say there was no effort made, for example, to provide under law separate conditions of treatment for children in order to mitigate the resulting enslavement. The consequences of this situation were perhaps best summarized by that extraordinary entry in Mary Chesnut's Diary from Dixie. Mary Chesnut, wife of a South Carolina senator on the eve of the Civil War, maintained a diary which remains unquestionably one of the most extraordinary source materials for understanding the nature of the impact of the Civil War upon the ruling class of the South. In one entry she notes her response to a woman who expressed envy at her condition as a mistress of a plantation, in it she says approximately the following: any person who envies a mistress of a plantation is really envying the mistress of a harem. And then in one of those explosive entries which crops up in her diary, she adds, "Our men live like patriarchs of old, surrounded by their wife, family, and concubines." And then she says, "the young woman who waits on me at morning is my niece. The young man who drives my coach is my children's half brother." And then she adds, "You can go to any plantation and the mistress of that plantation can name the father of every child on every plantation but her own." She ended with a comment, "Ours is a monstrous system."

Let me add that the definitive statement on the subject is that of Winthrop Jordan in *White Over Black,* a book with which one should become thoroughly familiar because it describes how the Americans defined the superiority of White over the Black. But even more significantly, it deals with the whole incongruity within the American system, a system which was built upon assumed natural rights while it concurrently maintained its absolute contradiction in slavery. And what greater contradiction than that of Thomas Jefferson, who fathered five quadroon children.

Now in a very basic sense, the essential problem of how to come to grips with American history is complicated by the unwillingness of people to begin looking at men like Jefferson as men who were born into a system which took slavery as a norm, which nurtured him to put forth very succinctly in his "Notes on Virginia" as a central proposition that which asserted there was an innate inferiority of the Black to the White. I might add for the purpose of making this view even sharper that anyone who has been traditionally accustomed to teaching a course in American history will come out with a disastrously different interpretation of the confrontation between Jefferson and Hamilton if we just consider the fact that Hamilton was one of the founders of the emancipation society in New York, and that the vehicle for emancipation and the end of slavery in the North was the Federalist Party. It is going to be very hard to sustain that marvelously neat little dichotomy between the villain Hamilton and the hero Jefferson. The fact is that if one just looks at the practical position of the Federalists versus Republicans, the critical point is that the Federalists led the fight against slavery in the North: they mobilized northern sentiment to bring about what was the culminating acts of emancipation in the North by 1804. But in all of this, the system itself becomes one in which not only Blacks were being enslaved, but also Whites, because by any logical measurement, when one gets to one eighth, one sixteenth, one thirty-second, it would be very difficult to say that you're dealing with the enslavement of Blacks alone. You're dealing with an enslavement of people who are *believed* to be Negro; and I suppose that nothing better illustrates the depth and intensity of the Anglo-Saxon conviction of the innate inferiority of the Black than the assumption that Black ancestry, no matter how small the measurable proportion, has a corroding effect.

Now within the development of slavery in the colonial United States, there is a point that has to be borne in mind always: slavery was not exclusively a Southern institution, at least not until the post-Revolutionary period. If there was one significant social consequence of the American Revolution which might well be singled out, it was that the American Revolution served to begin and focus a campaign against slavery in the North. Now I don't mean at this point to suggest in the slightest that this campaign meant the elimination of the racial attitudes which were so characteristic of antebellum Americans—and by the way, postbellum Americans also. The critical point is, however, that slavery as it existed became increasingly a colonial institution which flourished most effectively in areas where there were grown staple crops, and that generally speaking there existed a rule of thumb which ran as follows: where rice was grown, slavery was a characteristic of the labor force; where sugar was grown, slavery was a characteristic of the labor force; where indigo was grown, the same held true. So also was the case with tobacco. Now again, in those areas of the colonial South where those staple crops, that is, rice and tobacco, were most widely grown, there developed a divergent attitude toward slavery. In Virginia and the Chesapeake region generally, tobacco demanded two things: constant unremitting labor, with a considerable amount of sophistication and skill because of the problems of processing the crop. Secondly, tobacco was characteristically destructive of the soil; this means that in a country where land seemed to be inexhaustible, efforts to preserve it from this destructive impact were the exception rather than the rule. Thus it was normal to find in the Chespeake region a rather striking attribute of slavery: it was nomadic. The assumption was that the slave population would be uprooted at fairly regular four to five year intervals and moved to new land as the old land was exhausted. The second point is that the tobacco crop tended to be particularly subject to erratic price fluctuations, and that, generally speaking, by the eve of Revolution, one of the characteristics of the Virginia planters was that they were a group of people involved in an economic endeavor which was becoming less and less economically feasible. Consequently, one of the antipathies expressed in Virginia against the existence of slavery was based upon the inability to make immediate use of the labor supply. For example, Jefferson's legendary antipathy to slavery was also complemented by a corollary, and that corollary was that slavery could end in Virginia only if the Black population were expatriated. And it's within the framework of this emphasis upon expatriation that one finds the first developing agitation for the end of slavery in Virginia which called for colonization, or a return of the slave to Africa. But still one of the terms of the proposition was that if one could not eliminate Blacks one must maintain them in slavery. Thus, for example, in Virginia where an examination of slavery from the perspective of tobacco profits showed it economically unfeasible in many areas, the new legitimation of slavery was as a social necessity, and Jefferson again on this is extraordinarily effective. In his "Notes on Virginia," written in 1780, and in his famous letter to Holmes on the Missouri Compromise of 1820, there was a constant theme: slavery must be maintained, as he put it, "in one scale is justice, in the other as self-preservation", and the latter consideration was preeminent; he said also that the natural reaction of the Black, if granted freedom, would be automatically to seek retribution for the slights, the humiliation, the abuse, they had suffered in slavery. Now in terms, therefore, of looking at Virginia as a slave society, I think the critical thing to keep in mind is that slavery became in Virginia, by the eve of Revolution, an institution in which economically at least there was a large question as to its justification. There was no question about its serving an essential social necessity. Slavery became in Virginia a medium of police control.

Within the framework of the rice economy of South Carolina, (where the demand for South Carolina rice in the West Indies and in the Mediterranean regions was so large that supply never seemed to equal demand), what one finds was the existence of slavery consistently justified as an economically sound system. No one, for example, should forget that when the Declaration of Independence contained within itself the original indictment against slavery, it was deleted at the demand of South Carolina and Georgia, neither of whom were prepared to acknowledge that slavery as an institution must go. What one found the South Carolinian arguing was an economic legitimation accentuated by a fear characteristic of South Carolina. The proportion of Black to White was, even on the eve of Civil War, 60 percent to 40 percent. The proportion is even more accentuated when one examines the tidewater region, where rice was the predominant crop; there the proportion was about 80 to 20, the bulk of the twenty being located in the city of Charleston.

To accept emanicipation would have meant for the White who accepted the principles of natural rights, the possibility that South Carolina would pass under Black domination. The South Carolinians were in a position where the emergence in the formulations by John C. Calhoun of a logical rejection of the natural rights theory was an effort to make theory and practice concur. Eventually they contended that not only economically and socially, but politically, enslavement was essential. Thus, in the South, there began to develop a systematic definition of the Blacks' status under law as one of a submerged inferior race which used all kinds of complex rationalizations to justify it.

The tendencies inherent in the South before the revolution took final form once the final crop was introduced, cotton. The largest problem of interpretation that emerged was essentially that of U. B. Phillips, an argument which has been reformulated by Eugene Genovese, who is essentially a neo-Phillipsian, that slavery in the South was a way of life, as opposed to that of Lewis B. Grey, the author of a classic study of Southern agriculture before 1860, which in a certain sense has been restructured and restated by Kenneth Stampp, which contends that slavery was essentially a form of capitalistic exploitation. Once cotton was introduced as the chief southern staple, one enters into a realm best summarized by using the year 1859 as a base. By 1859, the South was producing five and a half million bales of cotton. A bale of cotton averages in weight about 500 pounds. The average price in the period from about 1830 through to 1860 was twelve cents a pound. The average return on a bale of cotton was about sixty dollars. The maintenance cost of a slave, a fully adult slave, was eleven dollars in cash for a year, plus $25 in terms of kind, that is, the food consumed which might in many instances have been actually produced by the slave on the plantation after his normal work day. The total annual maintenance cost of the slave would be $36; this for a fully adult field hand. In terms of the distribution of the profitability of the cotton crop, let me make a number of very general statements. First and foremost, by 1860 the largest single capital investment in the United States was found in the institution of slavery. Its total evaluation on the eve of the Civil War was more than two billion dollars, which was twice the amount of the total investment in railroads. Secondly, the largest single component in international trade of the United States was cotton, averaging between 60 and 70 percent of total foreign earnings. Looking at this in the context of southern presumptions about the role of King Cotton, the southern argument essentially asserted that the whole structure of industrialization in Western Europe and the northern part of the United States, particularly within the textile industry, was rooted in the exploitation of the cotton crop being produced by an enslaved population.

Two characteristics of slavery were striking—and can be seen in books, like Sellers study of slavery in Alabama—where cotton was grown; there was a steadily increasing concentration of holdings of slaves and land in fewer and fewer hands. Thus, on the eve of the Civil War, one tenth of one percent of the White population of the state of Alabama owned one third of all the slaves or about 130,000. They owned 30 percent of all the assessed valuation of the property of the state of Alabama. In fact they owned some $250 million worth of property. Their per capita income totalled somewhere in the general area of $25,000 per year. One of the problems of dealing with this development is to recognize that one of the striking characteristics of slavery was that in the process of expanding cotton culture, there developed a system of rational distribution of the labor supply designed to perform a repeated pattern of tasks. The slave was assigned a role in which he became part of an assembly line kind of agricultural production; certain jobs had to be performed every day in a certain way. In this process, there was a significant secondary development; that each of the individuals enslaved became progressively, as the cotton crop expanded, an article of commerce of growing value. When I use the term "article of value" bear in mind that the critical shift of emphasis within slavery by the last three decades of the pre-Civil War period was the ultimate dehumanization of the individual slave by asserting that a slave was preeminently property. By utilizing the logic of the Bill of Rights, which provides that no man can be deprived of his property without due process of the law, an assertion that the individual slave was a form of property, in effect, eliminated the slave from the governance of any of the assumptions of the natural rights doctrine. The Dred Scott decision's fundamental impact was to complete this effort by making the categorical assertion that nothing in the Constitution or any of the other documents of the Founding Fathers was to be interpreted as applying to the slaves. The conversion of humanity to property was consumated in 1857.

Now in looking at what this meant to the South generally, the thing which ought to be emphasized most strongly is: as the system of slavery expanded in the South, and as the demand for slave labor began to grow in the South, a crisis began to develop after 1808 when the external slave supply, at least in theory, was closed; I say "in theory" because although the Constitution enjoins against further importations of slaves, illegal importations continued. It is extremely important for any individual interested in this aspect of slavery to look at the old but still in many ways the best single description of the struggle to suppress the slave trade, that of W. E. B. Du Bois. The book makes it perfectly clear that the importation of slaves was a continuing phenomenon through to the eve of Civil War, that the numbers may well have run into the tens of thousands. But simultaneously, what one also finds, probably best suggested in a remarkable interchange in the debate in the state of Virginia over the ratification of the Constitution, was the emergence of a domestic effort to meet the demand for slaves. George Mason was a man who opposed ratification because it allowed continuation of the slave trade, and at first reading, one might almost say, "How impressive!", except for a slight twist. As John Marshall, a Federalist, pointed out, the question was, did George Mason in fact oppose the closing of the slave trade because of the horrendous nature of the trade, or because as one of the largest slaveholders in Virginia he was interested in creating in that state a closed market for his commodity. In fact, what happened with the development of the cotton economy was the emergence of a growing demand for slaves which created a reciprocity between the upper and the lower South in which states like Virginia, Maryland, Kentucky, Tennessee became breeding houses designed to supply a continuing inflow of slave labor to meet the seemingly endless demands of the deep South. What occurred therefore was a solidification of Southern sentiment around the emergence of a marketable product or of what was at least, supposedly in the 1780's and '90's, a property that could not be disposed of. One of the major aspects of 19th century slavery was the emergence within the South itself of a system of marketing slaves, who, increasingly the evidence indicates, were being bred specifically for the purpose of their sale into the lower South.

The implications of this are perhaps best suggested by the following: one third of the income of Virginia in 1850 has been estimated as derived from the sale of slaves into the lower South. Slavery had become, therefore, by the eve of the Civil War, an institution which had reached a climactic development in the United States. It was the ultimate application of "the iron law of wages"—David Ricardo's proposition that the individual laborer could never hope to receive more than what was essential to his survival. Slavery on the eve of Civil War had reduced the Black labor force, the slave labor force, to a system of total exploitation. Whatever mitigating conditions existed were the capricious decisions of individual owners. Within the framework of law, there was nothing that obliged them to maintain those conditions. The slave stood helpless before a system which had usurped his humanity and stole his property. It was as Mary Chesnut had noted, "a monstrous system."

I presume that this afternoon, when you move on into the subject of slave resistance, there will be, I would presume, a further development of certain points which I have raised.

CHAPTER SIX

SLAVERY: The Birth of the Industrial Revolution

One of the ironies of the slave trade was that its principal advocates represented the best of European society. Even outspoken defenders of the rights of the poor were apparently oblivious to the inconsistency of their perspectives. Slavery was, however, a large and profitable international business, and this fact alone transcended all other considerations.

Great Britain recognized the revenue-generating potential of the slave trade and tried through its foreign policy to dominate the world market. Initially, the British followed a monopolistic policy. Later, with colonies established around the world, they became the recognized leader in the slave trade by endorsing free trade. The development of a triangular trade route—by which England, France, and the American colonies supplied exports and ships; Africa contributed its human cargo, and the colonies fed raw material to the growing industrial plants in Europe—contributed to rapid commercial expansion and the accumulation of wealth.

There were many who condoned the practice of slave trading and profited handsomely. More important, however, were the many lives shattered by the process. Nevertheless, the prosperity that came contributed greatly to the rise and expansion of industrializing Europe.

In the following readings you will have the opportunity to examine the events that shaped the time and evaluate their impact on innocent individuals.

The Development of the Negro Slave Trade

Eric Williams

Until 1783 a primary objective of Britain's foreign policy was to preserve and improve upon the slave trade. At the beginning, Britain's slave-trading efforts were nothing more than buccaneering expeditions, but that nation soon gained international dominance because of the emergent demands of the sugar and tobacco industries in the colonies of the New World. Also contributing to its dominance was the end of the monopoly in the slave trade by a single company in Britain. The policy of monopoly fell during the last decade of the seventeenth century, thereby ushering in the principle of free trade and bolstering Britain's slave trade enormously. Unchallenged by the English people, slave trading became an important part of the triangular trade arrangements principally among England, Africa, and the mainland colonies. Wealth accrued by England from triangular trade helped to finance the Industrial Revolution. All the details associated with these historical events are explained in an interesting and appealing manner in the following article, by Eric Williams, excerpted from his book, *Capitalism and Slavery*.

The Negro slaves were "the strength and sinews of this western world." Negro slavery demanded the Negro slave trade. Therefore the preservation and improvement of the trade to Africa was "a matter of very high importance to this kingdom and the plantations thereunto belonging." And thus it remained, up to 1783, a cardinal object of British foreign policy.

The first English slave-trading expedition was that of Sir John Hawkins in 1562. Like so many Elizabethan ventures, it was a buccaneering expedition, encroaching on the papal arbitration of 1493 which made Africa a Portuguese monopoly. The slaves obtained were sold to the Spaniards in the West Indies. The English slave trade remained desultory and perfunctory in character until the establishment of British colonies in the Caribbean and the introduction of the sugar industry. When by 1660 the political and social upheavals of the Civil War period came to an end, England was ready to embark wholeheartedly on a branch of commerce whose importance to her sugar and her tobacco colonies in the New World was beginning to be fully appreciated.

In accordance with the economic policies of the Stuart monarchy, the slave trade was entrusted to a monopolistic company, the Company of Royal Adventurers trading to Africa, incorporated in 1663 for a period of one thousand years. The Earl of Clarendon voiced the enthusiasm current at the time, that the company would "be found a model equally to advance the trade of England with that of any other company, even that of the East Indies." The optimistic prediction was not realized, largely as a result of losses and dislocations caused by war with the Dutch, and in 1672 a new company, the Royal African Company, was created.

The policy of monopoly however remained unchanged and provoked determined resistance in two quarters—the merchants in the outports, struggling to break down the monopoly of the capital; and the planters in the colonies, demanding free trade in blacks as vociferously and with as much gusto as one hundred and fifty years later they opposed free trade in sugar. The mercantilist intelligentsia were divided on the question. Postlethwayt, most prolific of the mercantilist writers, wanted the company, the whole company and nothing but the company. Joshua Gee emphasized the frugality and good management of the private trader. Davenant, one of the ablest economists and financial experts of his day, at first opposed the monopoly, and then later changed his mind, arguing that other nations found organized companies necessary, and that the company would "stand in place of an academy, for training an indefinite number of people in the regular knowledge of all matters relating to the several branches of the African trade."

The case against monopoly was succinctly stated by the free traders—or inter-lopers as they were then called—to the Board of Trade in 1711. The monopoly meant that the purchase of British manufactures for sale on the coast of Africa, control of ships employed in the slave trade, sale of Negroes to the plantations, importation of plantation produce—"this great circle of trade and navigation," on which the livelihood, direct and indirect, of many thousands depended, would be under the control of a single company. The planters in their turn complained of the quality, prices, and irregular deliveries, and refused to pay their debts to the company.

There was nothing unique in this opposition to the monopoly of the slave trade. Monopoly was an ugly word, which conjured up memories of the political tyr-anny of Charles I, though no "free trader" of the time could have had the slightest idea of the still uglier visions the word would conjure up one hundred and fifty years later when it was associated with the economic tyranny of the West Indian sugar planter. But in the last decade of the seventeenth century the economic current was flowing definitely against monopoly. In 1672 the Baltic trade was thrown open and the monopoly of the Eastland Company overthrown. One of the most important consequences of the Glorious Revolution of 1688 and the expul-sion of the Stuarts was the impetus it gave to the principle of free trade. In 1698 the Royal African Company lost its monopoly and the right of a free trade in slaves was recognized as a fundamental and natural right of Englishmen. In the same year the Merchant Adventurers of London were deprived of their monopoly of the export trade in cloth, and a year later the monopoly of the Muscovy Company was abrogated and trade to Russia made free. Only in one particular did the freedom accorded in the slave trade differ from the freedom accorded in other trades—the commodity involved was man.

The Royal African Company was powerless against the competition of the free traders. It soon went bankrupt and had to depend on parliamentary subsidy. In 1731 it abandoned the slave trade and confined itself to the trade in ivory and gold dust. In 1750 a new organization was established, called the Company of Merchants trading to Africa, with a board of nine directors, three each from London, Bristol and Liverpool. Of the slave traders listed in 1755, 237 belonged to Bristol, 147 to London, and 89 to Liverpool.

With free trade and the increasing demands of the sugar plantations, the volume of the British slave trade rose enormously. The Royal African Company, between 1680 and 1686, transported an annual average of 5,000 slaves. In the first nine years of free trade Bristol alone shipped 160,950 Negroes to the sugar plantations. In 1760, 146 ships sailed from British ports for Africa, with a capac-ity for 36,000 slaves; in 1771, the number of ships had increased to 190 and the number of slaves to 47,000. The importation into Jamaica from 1700 to 1786 was 610,000, and it has been estimated that the total import of slaves into all the British colonies between 1680 and 1786 was over two million.

But the slave trade was more than a means to an end, it was also an end in itself. The British slave traders provided the necessary laborers not only for their own plantations but for those of their rivals. The encouragement thereby given to foreigners was contrary not only to common sense but to strict mercantilism, but, in so far as this foreign slave trade meant the Spanish colonies, there was some defence for it. Spain was always, up to the nineteenth century, dependent on foreigners for her slaves, either because she adhered to the papal arbitration which excluded her from Africa, or because of a lack of capital and the necessary goods for the slave trade. The privilege of supplying these slaves to the Spanish colonies, called the Asiento, became one of the most highly coveted and bitterly contested plums of international diplomacy. British mercantilists defended the trade, legal or illegal, with the Spanish colonies, in Negroes and manufactured goods, as of distinct value in that the Spaniards paid in coin, and thus the supply of bullion in England was increased. The supply of slaves to the French colonies could plead no such justification. Here it was clearly a clash of interest between the British slave trader and the British sugar planter, as the trade in the export of British machinery after 1825 led to a clash of interests between British shippers and British producers.

The sugar planter was right and the slave trader wrong. But in the first half of the eighteenth century this was noticed only by the very discerning. Postlethwayt condemned the Asiento of 1713 as scandalous and ruinous, an exchange of the substance for the shadow: "a treaty could scarce have been contrived of so little benefit to the nation." During the nine months of British occupation of Cuba in the Seven Years' War, 10,700 slaves were introduced, over one-sixth of the importations from 1512 to 1763, over one-third of the importations from 1763 to 1789. Forty thousand Negroes were introduced into Guadeloupe by the British in three years during the same war. The Privy Council Committee of 1788 paid special attention to the fact that of the annual British export of slaves from Africa two-thirds were disposed of to foreigners. During the whole of the eighteenth century, according to Bryan Edwards, British slave traders furnished the sugar planters of France and Spain with half a million Negroes, justifying his doubts of "the wisdom and policy of this branch of the African commerce." Britain was not only the foremost slave trading country in the world; she had become, in Ramsay's phrase, the "honourable slave carriers" of her rivals.

The story of this increase in the slave trade is mainly the story of the rise of Liverpool. Liverpool's first slave trader, a modest vessel of thirty tons, sailed for Africa in 1709. This was the first step on a road which, by the end of the century, gained Liverpool the distinction of being the greatest slave trading port in the Old World. Progress at first was slow. The town was more interested in the smuggling trade to the Spanish colonies and the tobacco trade. But, according to a historian of the town, it soon forged ahead by its policy of cutting down expenses to a minimum, which enabled it to undersell its English and continental rivals. In 1730 it had fifteen ships in the slave trade; in 1771 seven times as many. The proportion of slave ships to the total shipping owned by the port was slightly over one in a hundred in 1709; in 1730 it was one-eleventh; in 1763, one-fourth; in 1771, one-third. In 1795 Liverpool had five-eighths of the British slave trade and three-sevenths of the whole European slave trade.

The "horrors" of the Middle Passage have been exaggerated. For this the British abolitionists are in large part responsible. There is something that smacks of ignorance or hypocrisy or both in the invectives heaped by these men upon a traffic which had in their day become less profitable and less vital to England. A West Indian planter once reminded Parliament that it ill became the elected representative of a country which had pocketed the gains from the slave trade to stigmatize it as a crime. The age which had seen the mortality among indentured servants saw no reason for squeamishness about the mortality among slaves, nor did the exploitation of the slaves on the plantations differ fundamentally from the exploitation of the feudal peasant or the treatment of the poor in European cities.

Mutinies and suicides were obviously far more common on slave ships than on other vessels, and the brutal treatment and greater restrictions on the movements of the slaves would doubtless have tended to increase their mortality. But the fundamental causes of this high mortality on the slave ships, as on ships carrying indentured servants and even free passengers, must be found firstly in epidemics, the inevitable result of the long voyages and the difficulty of preserving food and water, and secondly in the practice of overcrowding the vessels. The sole aim of the slave merchants was to have their decks "well coverd with black ones." It is not uncommon to read of a vessel of 90 tons carrying 390 slaves or one of 100 tons carrying 414. Clarkson's investigations in Bristol revealed a sloop of twenty-five tons destined for seventy human beings, and another of a mere eleven tons for thirty slaves. The space allotted to each slave on the Atlantic crossing measured five and a half feet in length by sixteen inches in breadth. Packed like "rows of books on shelves," as Clarkson said, chained two by two, right leg and left leg, right hand and left hand, each slave had less room than a man in a coffin. It was like the transportation of black cattle, and where sufficient Negroes were not available cattle were taken on. The slave trader's aim was profit and not the comfort of his victims, and a modest measure in 1788 to regulate the transportation of the slaves in accordance with the capacity of the vessel evoked a loud howl from the slave traders. "If the alteration takes place," wrote one to his agent, "it will hurt the trade, so hope you will make hay while the sun shines."

The journal of one slave dealer during his residence in Africa admits that he had "found no place in all these several countrys of England, Ireland, America, Portugall, the Caribes, the Cape de Verd, the Azores or all the places I have been in . . . where I can inlarge my fortune so soon as where I now live." Money made the man. The prodigal who returned home empty-handed would have to be content with the common name of "the Mallato just come from Guinea." If, however, he returned with his pockets well stuffed with gold, "that very perticular hides all other infirmities, then you have hapes of frinds of all kinds thronging and wateing for your commands. Then your known by the name of 'the African gentleman' at every great man's house, and your discource is set down as perticular as Cristopher Culumbus's expedition in America."

About 1730 in Bristol it was estimated that on a fortunate voyage the profit on a cargo of about 270 slaves reached £7,000 or £8,000, exclusive of the returns from ivory. In the same year the net return from an "indifferent" cargo which arrived in poor condition was over £5,700. Profits of 100 per cent were not uncommon in Liverpool, and one voyage netted a clear profit of at least 300 per cent. The Lively, fitted out in 1737 with a cargo worth £1,307, returned to Liverpool with colonial produce and bills of exchange totalling £3,080, in addition to cotton and sugar remitted later. The Ann, another Liverpool ship, sailed in 1751 with an outfit and a cargo costing £1,604; altogether the voyage produced £3,287 net. A second voyage in 1753 produced £8,000 on a cargo and outfit amounting to £3,153.

An eighteenth century writer has estimated the sterling value of the 303,737 slaves carried in 878 Liverpool ships between 1783 and 1793 at over fifteen million pounds. Deducting commissions and other charges and the cost of the outfit of the ships and maintenance of the slaves, he concluded that the average annual profit was over thirty per cent. Modern scholarship has tended to reproach contemporary observers with undue exaggeration. But even taking the reduced estimates of Professor Dumbell, the net profit of the *Enterprise* in 1803, estimated on cost of outfit and cost of cargo, was 38 per cent, while that of the *Fortune* in 1803, for a cargo of poor slaves, was over 16 per cent. Again with these reduced estimates the profit of the *Lottery* in 1802 was thirty-six pounds per slave, the *Enterprise* sixteen pounds, and the *Fortune* five. The slave trade on the whole was estimated to bring Liverpool alone in the eighties a clear profit of £300,000 a year; and it was a common saying in the town of the far less profitable West Indian trade that if one ship in three came in a man was no loser, while if two came in he was a good gainer. On an average only one ship in five miscarried.

Such profits seem small and insignificant compared with the fabulous five thousand per cent the Dutch East India Company cleared at times in its history. It is even probable that the profits from the slave trade were smaller than those made by the British East India Company. Yet these trades were far less important than the slave trade. The explanation lies in the fact that from the mercantilist standpoint the India trade was a bad trade. It drained Britain of bullion to buy unnecessary wares, which led many at the time to think that "it were a happie thing for Christendome that the navigation to the East Indies, by way of the Cape of Good Hope, had never bene found out." The slave trade, on the contrary, was ideal in that it was carried on by means of British manufactured goods and was, as far as the British colonies were concerned, inseparably connected with the plantation trade which rendered Britain independent of foreigners for her supply of tropical products. The enormous profits of the Dutch spice trade, moreover, were based on a severe restriction of production to ensure high prices, whereas the slave trade created British industry at home and tropical agriculture in the colonies.

The "attractive African meteor," as a contemporary Liverpool historian called it, therefore became immensely popular. Though a large part of the Liverpool slave traffic was monopolized by about ten large firms, many of the small vessels in the trade were fitted out by attorneys, drapers, grocers, barbers and tailors. The shares in the ventures were subdivided, one having one-eighth, another one-fifteenth, a third one-thirty-second part of a share and so on. "Almost every man in Liverpool is a merchant, and he who cannot send a bale will send a band-box . . . almost every order of people is interested in a Guinea cargo, it is to this influenze that (there are) so many small ships."

The purchase of slaves called for a business sense and shrewd discrimination. An Angolan Negro was a proverb for worthlessness; Coromantines (Ashantis), from the Gold Coast, were good workers but too rebellious; Mandingoes (Senegal) were too prone to theft; the Eboes (Nigeria) were timid and despondent; the Pawpaws or Whydahs (Dahomey) were the most docile and best-disposed. The slaves were required for arduous field work, hence women and children were less valuable than robust males, the former because they were liable to interruptions from work through pregnancies, the latter because they required some attention until able to care for themselves. One Liverpool merchant cautioned his agents against buying ruptured slaves, idiots or any "old spider leged quality." A West Indian poet advised the slave trader to see that the slave's tongue was red, his chest broad and his belly not prominent. Buy them young, counselled one overseer from Nevis; "them full grown fellers think it hard to work never being brought up to it they take it to heart and dye or is never good for any thing. . . ."

But the slave trade was always a risky business. "The African Commerce," it was written in 1795, "holds forward one constant train of uncertainty, the time of slaving is precarious, the length of the middle passage uncertain, a vessel may be in part, or wholly cut off, mortalities may be great, and various other incidents may arise impossible to be foreseen." Sugar cultivation, moreover, was a lottery. The debts of the planters, their bankruptcies and demand for long credits gave the merchants many worries. "As you know," wrote one of them, "quick dispatch is the life of trade, I have had many anxious hours this year, I wou'd not wish the same again for double the profits I may get if any." From 1763 to 1778 the London merchants avoided all connection with the Liverpool slave traders, on the conviction that the slave trade was being conducted at a loss; between 1772 and 1778 the Liverpool merchants were alleged to have lost £700,000. Of thirty leading houses which dominated the slave trade from 1773, twelve had by 1788 gone bankrupt, while many others had sustained considerable losses. The American Revolution seriously interrupted the trade. "Our once extensive trade to Africa is at a stand," lamented a Liverpool paper in 1775. Her "gallant ships laid up and useless," Liverpool's slave traders turned to privateering, anxiously awaiting the return of peace, with never a thought that they were witnessing the death rattles of an old epoch and the birth pangs of a new.

Prior to 1783, however, all classes in English society presented a united front with regard to the slave trade. The monarchy, the government, the church, public opinion in general, supported the slave trade. There were few protests, and those were ineffective.

The Spanish monarchy set the fashion which European royalty followed to the very last. The palace-fortresses of Madrid and Toledo were built out of the payment to the Spanish Crown for licences to transport Negroes. One meeting of the two sovereigns of Spain and Portugal was held in 1701 to discuss the arithmetical problem posed by a contract for ten thousand "tons" of Negroes granted the Portuguese. The Spanish queen, Christina, in the middle of the nineteenth century, openly participated in the slave trade to Cuba. The royal court of Portugal, when it moved to Brazil to avoid capture by Napoleon, did not find the slave atmosphere of its colonial territory uncongenial. Louis XIV fully appreciated the importance of the slave trade to metropolitan France and France overseas. The plans of the Great Elector for Prussian aggrandizement included the African slave trade.

Hawkins' slave trading expedition was launched under the patronage of Queen Elizabeth. She expressed the hope that the Negroes would not be carried off without their free consent, which "would be detestable and call down the vengeance of Heaven upon the undertakers." But there was as much possibility that the transportation of the Negroes would be effected in democratic fashion as there was of collective bargaining. The Company of Royal Adventurers and the Royal African Company had, as their names imply, royal patronage and, not infrequently, investments by members of the royal family. According to Wilberforce, George III later opposed abolition, and great was the joy of the Liverpool slave traders and Jamaican sugar planters when the royal Duke of Clarence, the future William IV, "took up the cudgills" against abolition and attacked Wilberforce as either a fanatic or a hyprocrite.

The British government, prior to 1783, was uniformly consistent in its encouragement of the slave trade. The first great rivals were the Dutch, who monopolized the carrying trade of the British colonies. The bitter commercial warfare of the second half of the seventeenth century between England and Holland represented an effort on the part of England to break the commercial net the Dutch had woven about England and her colonies. "What we want," said Monk with military bluntness, "is more of the trade the Dutch now have." Whether it was nominal peace or actual war, a sort of private war was maintained, for thirty years, between the Dutch West India Company and the Royal African Company.

England's victory over Holland left her face to face with France. Anglo-French warfare, colonial and commercial, is the dominant theme in the history of the eighteenth century. It was a conflict of rival mercantilisms. The struggle was fought out in the Caribbean, Africa, India, Canada and on the banks of the Mississippi, for the privilege of looting India and for the control of certain vital and strategic commodities—Negroes; sugar and tobacco; fish; furs and naval stores. Of these areas the most important were the Caribbean and Africa; of these commodities the most important were Negroes and sugar. The outstanding single issue was the control of the Asiento. This privilege was conceded to England by the Treaty of Utrecht in 1713 as one result of her victory in the War of the Spanish Succession, and produced popular rejoicings in the country. It was the proud boast of Chatham that his war with France had given England almost the entire control of the African coast and of the slave trade.

Colonial assemblies frequently impeded the slave traders by imposing high duties on imported slaves, partly to raise revenue, partly out of their fear of the growing slave population. All such laws were frustrated by the home government, on the insistence of British merchants, who opposed taxes on British trade. The Board of Trade ruled in 1708 that it was "absolutely necessary that a trade so beneficial to the kingdom should be carried on to the greatest advantage. The well supplying of the plantations and colonies with a sufficient number of negroes at reasonable prices is in our opinion the chief point to be considered." In 1773 the Jamaica Assembly, for the purpose of raising revenue and to reduce the fear of slave rebellions, imposed a duty on every Negro imported. The merchants of London, Liverpool and Bristol protested, and the Board of Trade condemned the law as unjustifiable, improper and prejudicial to British commerce. The governor was sharply reprimanded for his failure to stop efforts made to "check and discourage a traffic so beneficial to the nation." As counsel for the sugar planters later argued: "in every variation of our administration of public affairs, in every variation of parties, the policy, in respect to that trade, has been the same. . . . In every period of our history, in almost every variation of our politics, each side and description of party men have, in terms, approved this very trade, voted its encouragement, and considered it as beneficial to the nation."

Parliament appreciated the importance of slavery and the slave trade to Britain and her plantations. In 1750 Horace Walpole wrote scornfully of "the British Senate, that temple of liberty, and bulwark of Protestant Christianity, . . . pondering methods to make more effectual that horrid traffic of selling negroes." Parliament heard many debates in its stately halls over abolition and emancipation, and its records show the doughty defenders the slave traders and slave owners possessed. Among them was Edmund Burke. The champion of conciliation of America was an accessory to the crucifixion of Africa. In 1772 a bill came before the House of Commons to prohibit the control of the African Committee by outsiders who were not engaged in the slave trade. Burke protested, not against the slave trade, however, but against depriving of the right to vote those who had legally purchased that right. Only a few, he argued, were so accused. "Ought we not rather to imitate the pattern set us in sacred writ, and if we find ten just persons among them, to spare the whole? . . . Let us not then counteract the wisdom of our ancestors, who considered and reconsidered this subject, nor place upon the footing of a monopoly what was intended for a free trade." Bristol could well afford to share in the general admiration of the great Liberal.

The Church also supported the slave trade. The Spaniards saw in it an opportunity of converting the heathen, and the Jesuits, Dominicans and Franciscans were heavily involved in sugar cultivation which meant slave-holding. The story is told of an old elder of the Church in Newport who would invariably, the Sunday following .the arrival of a slaver from the coast, thank God that "another cargo of benighted beings had been brought to a land where they could have the benefit of a gospel dispensation." But in general the British planters opposed Christianity for their slaves. It made them more perverse and intractable and therefore less valuable. It meant also instruction in the English language, which allowed diverse tribes to get together and plot sedition. There were more material reasons for this opposition. The governor of Barbados in 1695 attributed it to the planters' refusal to give the slaves Sundays and feast days off, and as late as 1823 British public opinion was shocked by the planters' rejection of a proposal to give the Negroes one day in the week in order to permit the abolition of the Negro Sunday market. The Church obediently toed the line. The Society for the Propagation of the Gospel prohibited Christian instruction to its slaves in Barbados, and branded "Society" on its new slaves to distinguish them from those of the laity; the original slaves were the legacy of Christopher Codrington. Sherlock, later Bishop of London, assured the planters that "Christianity and the embracing of the Gospel does not make the least difference in civil property." Neither did it impose any barriers to clerical activity; for his labors with regard to the Asiento, which he helped to draw up as a British plenipotentiary at Utrecht, Bishop Robinson of Bristol was promoted to the see of London. The bells of the Bristol churches pealed merrily on the news of the rejection by Parliament of Wilberforce's bill for the abolition of the slave trade. The slave trader, John Newton, gave thanks in the Liverpool churches for the success of his last venture before his conversion and implored God's blessing on his next. He established public worship twice every day on his slaver, officiating himself, and kept a day of fasting and prayer, not for the slaves but for the crew. "I never knew," he confessed, "sweeter or more frequent hours of divine communion than in the last two voyages to Guinea." The famous Cardinal Manning of the nineteenth century was the son of a rich West Indian merchant dealing in slave-grown produce. Many missionaries found it profitable to drive out Beelzebub by Beelzebub. According to the most recent English writer on the slave trade, they "considered that the best way in which to remedy abuse of negro slaves was to set the plantation owners a good example by keeping slaves and estates themselves, accomplishing in this practical manner the salvation of the planters and the advancement of their foundations." The Moravian missionaries in the islands held slaves without hesitation; the Baptists, one historian writes with charming delicacy, would not allow their earlier missionaries to deprecate ownership of slaves. To the very end the Bishop of Exeter retained his 655 slaves, for whom he received over £12,700 compensation in 1833.

Church historians make awkward apologies, that conscience awoke very slowly to the appreciation of the wrongs inflicted by slavery and that the defense of slavery by churchmen "simply arose from want of delicacy of moral perception." There is no need to make such apologies. The attitude of the churchman was the attitude of the layman. The eighteenth century, like any other century, could not rise above its economic limitations. As Whitefield argued in advocating the repeal of that article of the Georgia charter which forbade slavery, "it is plain to demonstration that hot countries cannot be cultivated without negroes."

Quaker nonconformity did not extend to the slave trade. In 1756 there were eighty-four Quakers listed as members of the Company trading to Africa, among them the Barclay and Baring families. Slave dealing was one of the most lucrative investments of English as of American Quakers, and the name of a slaver, *The Willing Quaker,* reported from Boston at Sierra Leone in 1793, symbolizes the approval with which the slave trade was regarded in Quaker circles. The Quaker opposition to the slave trade came first and largely not from England but from America, and there from the small rural communities of the North, independent of slave labor. "It is difficult," writes Dr. Gary, "to avoid the assumption that opposition to the slave system was at first confined to a group who gained no direct advantage from it and consequently possessed an objective attitude."

The Navy was impressed with the value of the West Indian colonies and refused to hazard or jeopardize their security. The West Indian station was the "station for honour," and many an admiral had been feted by the slave owners. Rodney opposed abolition. Earl St. Vincent pleaded that life on the plantations was for the Negro a veritable paradise as compared with his existence in Africa. Abolition was a "damned and cursed doctrine, held only by hypocrites." The gallant admiral's sentiments were not entirely divorced from more material considerations. He received over £6,000 compensation in 1837 for the ownership of 418 slaves in Jamaica. Nelson's wife was a West Indian, and his views on the slave trade were unequivocal. "I was bred in the good old school, and taught to appreciate the value of our West Indian possessions, and neither in the field nor the Senate shall their just rights be infringed, while I have an arm to fight in their defence, or a tongue to launch my voice against the damnable doctrine of Wilberforce and his hypocritical allies."

Slavery existed under the very eyes of eighteenth century Englishmen. An English coin, the guinea, rare though it was and is, had its origin in the trade to Africa. A Westminster goldsmith made silver padlocks for blacks and dogs. Busts of blackamoors and elephants, emblematical of the slave trade, adorned the Liverpool Town Hall. The insignia and equipment of the slave traders were boldly exhibited for sale in the shops and advertised in the press. Slaves were sold openly at auction. Slaves being valuable property, with title recognized by law, the postmaster was the agent employed on occasions to recapture runaway slaves and advertisements were published in the official organ of the government. Negro servants were common. Little black boys were the appendages of slave captains, fashionable ladies or women of easy virtue. Hogarth's heroine, in *The Harlot's Progress,* is attended by a Negro boy, and Marguerite Steen's Orabella Burmester typifies eighteenth century English opinion in her desire for a little black boy whom she could love as her long-haired kitten. Freed Negroes were conspicuous among London beggars and were known as St. Giles blackbirds. So numerous were they that a parliamentary committee was set up in 1786 for relieving the black poor.

"Slaves cannot breathe in England," wrote the poet Cowper. This was licence of the poet. It was held in 1677 that "Negroes being usually bought and sold among merchants, so merchandise, and also being infidels, there might be a property in them." In 1729 the Attorney General ruled that baptism did not bestow freedom or make any alteration in the temporal condition of the slave; in addition the slave did not become free by being brought to England, and once in England the owner could legally compel his return to the plantations. So eminent an authority as Sir William Blackstone held that "with respect to any right the master may have lawfully acquired to the perpetual service of John or Thomas, this will remain exactly in the same state of subjection for life," in England or elsewhere.

When, therefore, the assiduous zeal of Granville Sharp brought before Chief Justice Mansfield in 1772 the case of the Negro James Somersett who was about to be returned by his owner to Jamaica, there were abundant precedents to prove the impurity of the English air. Mansfield tried hard to evade the issue by suggesting manumission of the slave, and contented himself with the modest statement that the case was not "allowed or approved by the law of England" and the Negro must be discharged. Much has been made of this case, by people constantly seeking for triumphs of humanitarianism. Professor Coupland contends that behind the legal judgment lay the moral judgment and that the Somersett case marked the beginning of the end of slavery throughout the British Empire. This is merely poetic sentimentality translated into modern history. Benjamin Franklin pointed scornfully to "the hypocrisy of this country, which encourages such a detestable commerce, while it piqued itself on its virtue, love of liberty, and the equity of its courts in setting free a single negro." Two years after the Somersett case the British government disallowed the Jamaican Acts restricting the slave trade. In 1783 a Quaker petition for abolition was solemnly rejected by Parliament.

In 1783, moreover, the same Mansfield handed down a decision in the case of the ship *Zong*. Short of water, the captain had thrown 132 slaves overboard, and now the owners brought an action for insurance alleging that the loss of the slaves fell within the clause of the policy which insured against "perils of the sea." In Mansfield's view "the case of slaves was the same as if horses had been thrown overboard." Damages of thirty pounds were awarded for each slave, and the idea that the captain and crew should be prosecuted for mass homicide never entered into the head of any humanitarian. In 1785 another insurance case, involving a British ship and mutiny among the slaves, came before Mansfield. His Daniel judgment was that all the slaves who were killed in the mutiny or had died of their wounds and bruises were to be paid for by the underwriters; those who had died from jumping overboard or from swallowing water or from "chagrin" were not to be paid for on the ground that they had not died from injuries received in the mutiny; and the underwriters were not responsible for any depreciation in price which resulted to the survivors from the mutiny.

The prosecution of the slave trade was not the work of the dregs of English society. The daughter of a slave trader has assured us that her father, though a slave captain and privateer, was a kind and just man, a good father, husband, and friend. This was probably true. The men most active in this traffic were worthy men, fathers of families and excellent citizens. The abolitionist Ramsay acknowledged this with real sorrow, but pleaded that "they had never examined the nature of this commerce and went into it, and acted as others had done before them in it, as a thing of course, for which no account was to be given in this world or the next." The apology is unnecessary. The slave trade was a branch of trade and a very important branch. An officer in the trade once said that "one real view, one minute absolutely spent in the slave rooms on the middle passage would do more for the cause of humanity than the pen of a Robertson, or the whole collective eloquence of the British senate." This is dubious. As it was argued later about the Cuban and Brazilian slave trade, it was no use saying it was an unholy or unchristian occupation. It was a lucrative trade, and that was enough. The slave trade has even been justified as a great education. "Think of the effect, the result of a slave voyage on a youngster starting in his teens. . . . What an education was such a voyage for the farmer lad. What an enlargement of experience for a country boy. If he returned to the farm his whole outlook on life would be changed. He went out a boy; he returned a man."

The slave traders were among the leading humanitarians of their age. John Cary, advocate of the slave trade, was conspicuous for his integrity and humanity and was the founder of a society known as the "Incorporation of the Poor." The Bristol slaver "Southwell" was named after a Bristol parliamentarian, whose monument depicts him as true to king and country and steady to what he thought right. Bryan Blundell of Liverpool, one of Liverpool's most prosperous merchants, engaged in both the slave and West Indian trades, was for many years trustee, treasurer, chief patron and most active supporter of a charity school, the Blue Coat Hospital, founded in 1709. To this charity another Liverpool slave trader, Foster Cunliffe, contributed largely. He was a pioneer in the slave trade. He and his two sons are listed as members of the Liverpool Committee of Merchants trading to Africa in 1752. Together they had four ships capable of holding 1,120 slaves, the profits from which were sufficient to stock twelve vessels on the homeward journey with sugar and rum. An inscription to Foster Cunliffe in St. Peter's Church describes him thus: "a Christian devout and exemplary in the exercise of every private and publick duty, friend to mercy, patron to distress, an enemy only to vice and sloth, he lived esteemed by all who knew him . . . and died lamented by the wise and good. . . ." Thomas Leyland, one of the largest slave traders of the same port, had, as mayor, no mercy for the engrosser, the forestaller, the regrater, and was a terror to evil doers. The Heywoods were slave traders and the first to import the slave-grown cotton of the United States. Arthur Heywood was treasurer of the Manchester Academy where his sons were educated. One son, Benjamin, was elected member of the Literary and Philosophical Society of Manchester, and was admitted to the Billiard Club, the most recherché club Manchester has ever possessed, which admitted only the very best men as regards manners, position and attainments. To be admitted to the charmed circle of the Forty meant unimpeachable recognition as a gentleman. Later Benjamin Heywood organized the first of the Manchester exhibitions of works of art and industry.

These slave traders held high office in England. The Royal Adventurers trading to Africa in 1667, a list headed by royalty, included two aldermen, three dukes, eight earls, seven lords, one countess, and twenty-seven knights. The signatures of the mayors of Liverpool and Bristol appear on a petition of the slave traders in 1739. The Bristol Committee set up in 1789 to oppose abolition of the slave trade included five aldermen, one an ex-captain of a slaver. Many a slave trader held Liverpool's highest municipal dignity. The slave traders were firmly established in both houses of Parliament. Ellis Cunliffe represented Liverpool in Parliament from 1755 to 1767. The Tarleton family, prominent in the slave trade, voiced Liverpool's opposition to abolition in Parliament. The House of Lords, traditionally conservative, was confirmed in its instinctive opposition to abolition by the presence of many ennobled slave traders. It gave sympathetic hearing to the Earl of Westmorland's statement that many of them owed their seats in the Upper House to the slave trade, and that abolition was Jacobinism. No wonder Wilberforce feared the Upper Chamber. Not without confidence did the Assembly of Jamaica state categorically in 1792 that "the safety of the West Indies not only depends on the slave trade not being abolished, but on a speedy declaration of the House of Lords that they will not suffer the trade to be abolished."

Some protests were voiced by a few eighteenth century intellectuals and prelates. Defoe in his "Reformation of Manners," condemned the slave trade. The poet Thomson, in his "Summer," drew a lurid picture of the shark following in the wake of the slave ship. Cowper, after some hesitation, wrote his memorable lines in "The Task." Blake wrote his beautiful poem on the "Little Black Boy." Southey composed some poignant verses on the "Sailor who had served in the Slave Trade." But much of this eighteenth century literature, as Professor Sypher has shown in an exhaustive analysis, concentrated on the "noble Negro," the prince unjustly made captive, superior even in bondage to his captors. This sentimentality, typical of the eighteenth century in general, more often than not carried the vicious implication that the slavery of the ignoble Negro was justified. Boswell on the other hand stated emphatically that to abolish the slave trade was to shut the gates of mercy on mankind, and dubbed Wilberforce a "dwarf with big resounding name."

Two eighteenth century merchants, Bentley and Roscoe, opposed the slave trade before 1783; they were more than merchants, they were Liverpool merchants. Two eighteenth century economists condemned the expensiveness and inefficiency of slave labor—Dean Tucker and Adam Smith, the warning tocsin, the trumpeter of the new age. The discordant notes went unheeded. The eighteenth century endorsed the plea of Temple Luttrell: "Some gentlemen may, indeed, object to the slave trade as inhuman and impious; let us consider that if our colonies are to be maintained and cultivated, which can only be done by African negroes, it is surely better to supply ourselves with those labourers in British bottoms, than purchase them through the medium of French, Dutch, or Danish factors."

On one occasion a Mauritius gentleman, eager to convince the abolitionist Buxton that "the blacks were the happiest people in the world," appealed to his wife to confirm his statement from her own impressions of the slaves she had seen. "Well, yes," replied the good spouse, "they were very happy, I'm sure, only I used to think it so odd to see the black cooks chained to the fireplace." Only a few Englishmen before 1783, like the good spouse, had any doubts about the morality of the slave trade. Those who had realized that objections, as Postlethwayt put it, would be of little weight with statesmen who saw the great national emoluments which accrued from the slave trade. "We shall take things as they are, and reason from them in their present state, and not from that wherein we could hope them to be. . . . We cannot think of giving up the slave-trade, notwithstanding my good wishes that it could be done." Later, perhaps, some noble and benevolent Christian spirit might think of changing the system, "which, as things are now circumstanced, may not be so easily brought about." Before the American Revolution English public opinion in general accepted the view of the slave trader: "Tho' to traffic in human creatures, may at first sight appear barbarous, inhuman, and unnatural; yet the traders herein have as much to plead in their own excuse, as can be said for some other branches of trade, namely, the *advantage* of it.

. . . In a word, from this trade proceed benefits, far outweighing all, either real or pretended mischiefs and inconveniences."

The Biography of a Slave

Charles S. Sydnor

Abduhl Rahahman, son of Alman Ibrahim, King of Futa Jallon, West Africa, was educated in a manner befitting a young prince. At an early age, he was placed in the cavalry by his father and sent out to protect the kingdom and wage war. It was during one of his encounters with an encroaching tribe that he was captured, traded to the captain of an English slave ship, and eventually sold to a Mississippi plantation owner. Toward the end of his life, and following prolonged negotiations, he and his wife were allowed to return to his African birthplace, where he hoped to be reunited with his family. Abduhl's life was filled with fascinating twists and turns of fate that generally were more tragic than fortunate. Charles S. Syndor re-creates the life of this African slave in the following selection, reprinted from *The South Atlantic Quarterly.*

In the year 1788 there poured down from the rugged and beautiful mountains of Futa Jallon, West Africa, an army of seventeen hundred Fulbes, mostly horsemen. These were a proud people, a mixture probably of Negro and Berber stock, who dominated the darker Negroes among whom they lived. This army was being launched against the Hebohs, a coast tribe of Negroes, who had been disturbing the trade of the Fulbe by destroying vessels that came to the coast.

At their head rode Abduhl Rahahman, a tall young man of twenty-six years. After seven years of service among the horsemen he had now advanced to the command of this important expedition. The responsibility was great, but his courage was sustained by pride of rank and of race and by the thought that he was following a course which had brought much success and power to his father.

His father was Alman Ibrahim, King of Futa Jallon, and his grandfather had been King of Timbuktu. Thus he was descended from the Moorish invaders who had conquered Timbuktu back in 1591. Because of this, Abduhl considered himself even better than the proud Fulbe, for he claimed to be of pure Moorish blood. Had not his father passed over his first-born son, begotten at Futa Jallon by a Soosoo Negress, and chosen Abduhl as his heir because Abduhl's mother was one of his Moorish wives at Timbuktu?

This remarkable city, the birthplace of Abduhl, was far in the interior of Africa on the northern edge of the great bend of the Niger River, where the jungle of central Africa jutted out into the desert of northern Africa. It was the meeting place of the canoe and the camel, of gold, wax, and ivory from the Niger country and of salt from the Sahara. By an act of nature it was the "port of the Sudan in the Sahara"; it was the great interior market-town of western Africa. Although the inhabitants did some weaving of cotton, working of leather, and making of earthenware, most of them were traders, serving as middlemen between the pagan woolly-haired Negroes from the south and the Mohammedan Arabs, Berbers, and fierce Tuaregs who came with their caravans out of the desert. Most of the inhabitants were Mohammedans; none were Christians with the exception of an occasional slave. The first European traveler to reach Timbuktu came in 1824, and he was promptly murdered.

Five years after Abduhl's birth Alman Ibrahim moved his family from Timbuktu to Timbo, the capital of Futa Jallon. When Abduhl was twelve years old his father sent him back to Timbuktu to be educated in a manner befitting the heir to a throne. In later years Abduhl described the school he attended as containing "upwards of two hundred pupils under four masters. They read the Alcoran, wrote on boards, attended to what they called Geography, to Astronomy, to calculation, to the Mohammedan Religion, and to the laws of the country." At the age of seventeen he once more made the long journey to his father's kingdom, and two years later was placed with the cavalry and sent out to war.

It was within that year that Abduhl first saw a white man. This stranger was John C. Cox, the English surgeon of a ship that dropped anchor off the coast of Sierra Leone, West Africa, in 1781. While waiting for the time of sailing Cox went on a hunting expedition and became lost; when he at last found his way back to the coast, he discovered that his ship had sailed. Seeking to escape, he began traveling northward toward the Gambia River where English ships frequently came to buy slaves. By the time he reached Futa Jallon his plight had become desperate, for an injured leg had made him so lame and sick that he could scarcely travel. In this condition he was found and brought before Alman Ibrahim. Cox had no reason to hope for hospitable treatment. In fact, cannibalism was practiced by various tribes of that part of Africa. But Alman Ibrahim invited him to remain until he should be able to travel again, and he placed him under the care of a woman who nursed him back to health. While Cox was recovering he had an opportunity to become well acquainted with the king and the son who was expected to succeed to the kingship.

The curiosity which first drew the young Moor to the Englishman soon changed to friendship. While Cox's wounded leg was healing he lived in Abduhl's house, which adjoined that of the king. To be taken into the royal family of one of the tribes in the interior of Africa was an interesting experience for an adventurous young Englishman; but as health returned, Cox began to long for his family and friends back in England, and he wanted to go home. However, Timbo was almost one hundred and fifty miles from the coast; Cox knew little or nothing of the country through which he would have to pass; the tribes along the coast were less civilized and would doubtless be less benevolent than the people of Futa Jallon; nor was it certain where and when he could find a ship.

At the end of about six months Alman Ibrahim asked Cox whether he wanted to return to his own country. When the latter said, "Yes," Ibrahim asked the reason, reminding him that he was being well treated. Cox replied that that was so, but he explained that his mother and father had doubtless thought him dead when his ship returned without him, and that he would like to return to them. Such a plea could be understood among almost any people, and preparations began to be made for his departure. Ibrahim detailed a guard of fifteen armed men to escort Cox to the coast, provided gold and ivory to pay for his passage, and bade him farewell. The guard was instructed to bring Cox back if no ship could be found; but should one be found, the warriors were warned not to go on board. Evidently Ibrahim had heard of English slave-ships and the methods of their masters.

Cox and his guard reached the coast in safety. After some delay they found the same vessel on which Cox had come to Africa, and on it he returned to England.

As Abduhl led his army westward down into the coast country he may have remembered his white friend who had sailed off seven years before over the same great sea he was approaching. And he may have remembered how his father had in his youth led an army westward from Timbuktu to win the kingdom of Futa Jallon. Now he in his turn was leading an army to conquest.

After putting the Hebohs to flight and ravaging their country, Abduhl began his triumphal march back to his mountainous country. When the dismounted warriors, leading their horses, were half way to the top of a steep mountain the Hebohs began firing down upon them. They had quickly rallied and by forced marches gone in advance of the Fulbe army. Abduhl at once ordered his confused men to charge up the mountain as best they could and there to assemble and fight. He led the way; but on reaching the top he found that only his guard had followed. Since they were too few to make a stand, they gave ground, fighting as they went. Retreat soon changed to flight, but Abduhl, refusing to humble himself by running from a Negro, dismounted and sat down. One of the Hebohs approaching him from behind shot him in the shoulder. Another came in front and raised his gun to kill him; but seeing his clothes, ornamented with gold, he cried out that this was the king. They therefore lowered their guns and rushed in to bind him. The first Abduhl killed with the sword on which he had been sitting. At almost the same moment another Heboh, standing behind, knocked him unconscious with a gun.

His captors revived him by dipping him into a nearby pond. Then he was bound, his shoes were pulled off, and he was made to walk barefooted over the hundred miles back to the country of the Hebohs. While his feet were being bruised, his eyes watched his own horse being led before him—the horse on which he had just ridden at the head of his conquering army.

When the remnant of Abduhl's force straggled home, his father at once collected an army and set out to rescue him. But the Hebohs hid their captive in the jungle until Ibrahim gave up the search, burned their villages, and returned home. Abduhl was then taken into the Mandingo country. He offered his captors a large amount of gold and many sheep and cattle if they would release him. Instead, they sold him with about fifty other slaves to an English ship on the Gambia River.

At this time the English bought scarcely a thousand slaves a year on the Gambia; fifteen or twenty years earlier they had purchased nearly three times as many. In the course of this trade Abduhl was purchased for two powder horns, two muskets, two bottles of whiskey, a handful of tobacco, and a few other articles of trade. He was placed in irons and taken on board; for the drag-net of this great trade was no respecter of race, religion, or rank.

What were the thoughts and emotions of the young prince can only be imagined, nor indeed can his physical surroundings be described with exactness; but the current practices of English slave vessels bound for America are well known. About ten shillings' worth of plantains, bananas, yams, potatoes, rice, bread, and wheat was considered ample for each slave on the voyage to American ports, which was seldom made in less than two months. During that time the slaves were crowded in the space between the first and second decks. Except during storms, light and air filtered in through portholes and grated hatchways. On one well-known slaver, the height between decks was five feet and eight inches, and around the sides a platform was built cutting this space in half. Slaves were packed on this platform, on the floor under it, and on the floor of the unplatformed center as closely as they could lie.

So many slaves died on the passage that the British Parliament, by an act passed in the same year that Abduhl was captured, provided a bonus for the captain and surgeon of each ship that reached the West Indies without losing on the passage over 3 per cent of the human cargo. And insuring against losses by death while at sea was prohibited because this had led some captains to dump overboard and collect insurance on slaves who seemed likely to die or remain hopelessly diseased after the vessel docked. Also, in spite of the protests of the merchants of Liverpool, Parliament ordered that floor space six feet long and one foot and four inches wide should be allowed for each grown man. The surface of the platform was counted as part of the floor. Women and children were allowed less than the men.

Abduhl survived the crossing and with his fellow-slaves was unloaded into the sunshine and fresh air of the English island of Dominica, one of the Leeward group. He was then reshipped to New Orleans, and from there he was taken up the Mississippi River and sold to Thomas Foster, a planter who lived near Natchez.

Possibly his most humiliating experience was having his head shaved, for he was a Mohammedan. He was put to work in the cotton fields by the side of other Africans, most of whom he considered his inferiors, but in time he took a Negro slave woman for his wife. Gradually he learned to speak the language of the new country but not to write it, and he must have claimed that he was the son of a king in his own country because he came to be called by the name Prince. He made the best of life as a slave in Mississippi; in time he became highly valued by his master; but he never forgot the life he had lived in Futa Jallon, nor Allusine, the two-year old son he had left in Africa.

One day, about seventeen years after he was made a slave, Prince's master sent him to the village of Washington, six miles east of Natchez, to sell sweet potatoes. There he met a fellow-slave, Sambo. While they were talking by the roadside, one of the most respected physicians in the Natchez region came on horseback in their direction. After watching him a moment Prince said to the other slave:

"Sambo, that man rides like a white man I saw in my country. See when he comes by; if he opens but one eye, that is the same man."

Suddenly realizing that the basket of sweet potatoes on his head could be made an excuse for a closer examination of the rider, he walked out to him and asked: "Master, you want to buy some potatoes?"

The rider stopped, asked what kind of potatoes he had, and began to look them over. Meanwhile Prince looked closely at his eyes and was sure that this was Cox. "Where did you come from?"

Naming his master, Prince replied: "From Colonel Foster's." But this was not the information Cox was seeking; he also was struggling to bring into clear focus memories that had blurred in the passing of almost twenty-five years. Suddenly he exclaimed: "He did not raise you: you came from Timbo! Your name is Abduhl Rahahman!"

Springing from his horse, he embraced the slave, told him to put down his load and to come to his house. But Prince was a well-trained slave and would not desert his master's property until a Negro woman had been summoned to take charge of the potatoes.

Cox at once sent for Nathaniel Ware, Acting Governor of the Mississippi Territory, to come to his house. When he came, Cox told him that he wanted to aid his enslaved friend to return to his own country. However, an arrangement satisfactory to his owner would have to be made, for neither the governor nor anyone else could take a slave from his master.

The next morning, accordingly, Cox went to Foster's plantation and told him of his desire to send Prince back to Africa. But Foster was not given to sentimentality. Prince, he pointed out, was an industrious and faithful servant who was still in the prime of life. He had never known him to be intoxicated, he was honest, and his influence over his fellow-slaves gave him a value far beyond that of an ordinary laborer. Cox replied that he was willing to pay whatever Prince was worth and offered a thousand dollars, which was a handsome price at that time. But Foster absolutely refused, adding that he doubted whether the man would be any happier if his freedom were given to him.

For the remaining ten years of Cox's life no change occurred. After his death on December 15, 1816, his son William Rousseau Cox, likewise a physician, took up the task of trying to free Prince. But Foster continued adamant, and in time William Cox also died leaving master and slave bound to each other as though that relationship was the one changeless element in the drama.

Another decade passed, and another attempt was made toward freedom. For some years Prince had known Andrew Marschalk, who many years before had brought the first printing press to the old Natchez region. As a newspaper editor and as a politician Marschalk had learned something of how to get things done. Accordingly, he had the old slave write a letter pleading for his freedom. This, written in Arabic characters, he sent on October 3, 1826, to Thomas Buck Reed, United States Senator from Mississippi. Marschalk added a brief note stating that Prince "claims to belong to the royal family of Morocco" and hoped to return home. He asked Reed to do what he could toward satisfying "the old man's wishes." The first statement, fortunately for Prince, was a mistake. Although he claimed to be a Moor and to belong to a royal family, he did not claim to be close kin to the ruling family of Morocco.

Senator Reed read Marschalk's letter, looked at Prince's Arabic letter, and then turned them both over to the Department of State. The latter, being misled by Marschalk's error, sent them to the American consul at Tangier. After conferring with the Bashaw, the consul urgently advised the government of the United States to send Prince to him, adding that this would make it easier to secure the release of American sailors who were occasionally wrecked on the Moroccan coast. Neither the consul nor the Bashaw detected the error which had caused the case to be brought to them, nor were they enlightened when Prince's letter was read, for instead of being autobiographical it was made up of quotations from the Koran so pieced together as to constitute a plea for help. Only the signature was personal, and if the Bashaw had never heard of any member of the royal family having such a name, he kept his suspicions to himself.

When the consul's dispatch reached the Department of State it was placed before Secretary Henry Clay, who was so impressed that he submitted the matter to President John Quincy Adams with the recommendation that Prince be purchased and sent home. Adams concurred, and on July 12, 1827, a letter was sent to Marschalk requesting him to act as the government's agent in this case.

Accordingly, he visited old Colonel Foster and asked whether he would sell Prince. As the slave was now too old to have much if any value, Foster was fortunate to receive an offer; and by failing to make the best of it he proved that his interest in Prince was not entirely mercenary. He told Marschalk that four years before he had informed the slave that he would release him if he could arrange to return to his native land but that he would make no contribution toward defraying the costs of the journey; he declared that he was still willing to carry out this promise. However, he added that he would do this only on the condition that Prince would not be set free until he reached Africa, fearing that his children and other fellowslaves might be restive if they saw him a free man.

Marschalk also talked with Prince before writing to the Department of State. Prince told him that if he could return, he would take with him "feelings of the most profound friendship and respect to all the white men of America: but most particularly those of the State of Mississippi—and of Natchez." Although Prince was by birth and education a strict Mohammedan, he seemed well informed about the moral precepts of Christianity and was very anxious to secure a New Testament in Arabic. When Marschalk expressed the wish that he would become a Christian, Prince promptly replied that he thought he would. In fact, his chief objection was that Christians did not follow the excellent precepts of their religion.

A report of his conversations with Foster and Prince was sent by Marschalk to Secretary Clay on August 20, 1827, and for a time that seemed to end the matter. Weeks and then months passed and no answer came, but nearly every day Prince came to ask Marschalk whether the letter had come that would take him home. He was impatient, but not to escape from hard labor; for after thirty years Foster had lightened his duties and treated him indulgently. But Prince wanted to revisit the places he had known in his youth, to see once more his friends and relatives in Futa Jallon, and to be a free man. There was not much time to waste if he was to die in his own country, for he was now sixty-five years old. Even Marschalk began to grow impatient, and on December 18 he sent Clay a duplicate of his earlier letter. While Marschalk was writing this, Prince came to ask whether there was any news. When he was told what Marschalk was doing, he borrowed the pen and at the end of the letter he wrote in Arabic who he was.

Whether Prince's note turned the scale or not, Marschalk's letter was answered almost at once. On January 12, 1828, Clay instructed him to take charge of Prince, under the conditions imposed by Foster, and to send him to Washington either up the Mississippi River and thence overland, or down the river to New Orleans and then by sea. Marschalk was further authorized to draw at sight on Clay for a sum not exceeding $200 "to defray the expense of decently, but plainly clothing him, if it should be necessary" and to pay his expenses on the journey to Washington. Clay explained that the object of the government in restoring Prince to his family and country was "for the purpose of making a favorable impression in behalf of the United States."

As the time drew near for Prince to set out for Washington, he began to realize that to break away from his life as a slave in Mississippi would not be entirely pleasant. Though he boasted that there was no Negro blood in his veins and though he considered his own race infinitely superior to that to which his slave-wife belonged, the thought of leaving her and their five children and eight grandchildren began to overshadow the pleasure he felt at the prospect of returning to Africa.

Foster stated that although he valued the woman at three hundred dollars, he would release her for two hundred dollars. This was written out at the top of a subscription paper which was circulated in Natchez. In less than twenty-four hours 140 subscribers contributed enough to purchase her. In fact, there was a surplus which was invested in supposedly Moorish robes, and when Prince departed with his wife he was costumed to fit the part of a returning prince. He took with him the manumission papers of his wife, a letter to the American Colonization Society from Cyrus Griffin, who had written once before in his behalf, and a number of testimonials as to his character and conduct from persons in and about Natchez who had known him many years. Among the signers of such documents were Andrew Marschalk, Woodson Wren, who was Clerk of the Adams County Court, Henry Tooley, John Henderson, and former Governor Nathaniel Ware.

The old couple reached the capital of the United States in the spring of 1828. But when Prince was interrogated about his life in Africa and when the lengthy letters of Cyrus Griffin were read, it was evident to the Department of State that Morocco was not his native land; and though he knew much about the geography, government, and customs of the regions south of the Great Desert, he had never traveled north of it.

The Department was thus in a quandary. With the facts now before it and the error in Marschalk's letter made evident, there was no reason why it should be officially interested in this old African. The government of the United States had no diplomatic relationship with or interest in the mountainous and nearly unknown country of Futa Jallon from which he had come. But here was the old man with his wife, his Moorish costume, his testimonials, and his high hopes of going home.

As it happened, the Secretary of State was well acquainted with the work of the American Colonization Society. He was one of its vice-presidents, and his interest in the organization was so well known that it was sometimes whispered that the society was a part of the Clay political machine. The purpose of the colonization society was to return Negroes from the United States to Africa, and, as quixotic as it may appear, some of its adherents had hopes of doing a thorough job. Before the Civil War over eleven thousand Negroes were colonized on the west coast of Africa a little below Sierra Leone where they eventually created the independent state of Liberia.

The society was in its infancy when Prince reached Washington, and it was sometimes accused of being an anti-slavery organization. But no objection could be raised against transporting Prince to Africa. Though a slave, his master had consented to his return to Africa, and the current argument that the Negro race was unfit for freedom could not be used against Prince who claimed that he was not a Negro. It must be said, however, that those who were befriending him had to make much of the effect of hard labor and Mississippi sunshine on the complexion and the texture of hair to explain why he looked so much like a Negro.

Not only was Prince an unobjectionable case for the colonization society to take under its wing; he was, indeed, something of a windfall. Real princes did not often come to hand, and this one fitted the part. His appearance was good, he was "intelligent, modest, and obliging," and "his manners are not merely prepossessing, but dignified." Nor could his behavior while a slave be criticized, for it was said on good authority that "though born and raised in affluence, he has submitted to his fate without a murmur, and has been an industrious and faithful servant." In short, the society quickly saw the advantages to be gained by pushing him into public view and making of him something of a test case of its work.

Accordingly, Prince was transferred from the Department of State to the American Colonization Society. He, of course, was well pleased at the change. The little colony of Liberia was only ten or fifteen days journey from Timbo. He stated, possibly after some persuasion by the officers of the Society, that he would remain in Liberia and not attempt to take up his old life in his native land. Of what had happened there during his forty years of exile he was ignorant. His father was said to have died long before, which was reasonable to suppose. There were several reports as to whom the present ruler was; some said his older brother, some said another kinsman. Nor was it certain what had become of the infant son Prince had left in Africa. At any rate, he had lost during his long term of slavery the thirst for power, and he declared that instead of seeking to gain the throne of his land he preferred to spend his remaining days as a private citizen in the colony of Liberia.

This profession removed the last argument that might be used against him. Only an excuse for putting him in the limelight was needed, and this was easily supplied. He wished to take his children and grandchildren with him, and funds were needed to purchase them from slavery and transport them to Africa. Accordingly, he was sent through the North on a money-raising tour, which was doubtless an infraction of the agreement made with Foster but was excellent publicity for the colonization movement. Whether he wore his Moorish costume is unknown.

Prince's impresario on most of his tour was the Reverend Thomas H. Gallaudet, a warm-hearted and public-spirited man who had founded at Hartford, Connecticut, the first free school in America for the deaf. Gallaudet devoted several weeks to speaking in Prince's behalf in the New England states, for after leaving Washington Prince visited Baltimore, Philadelphia, Providence, New Bedford, Springfield, Suffield, Windsor, Hartford, and New Haven. Finally they reached New York, where Gallaudet "appealed powerfully in his behalf to the generous and the wealthy of that city—at a large and most respectable meeting in the Masonic Hall." By this meeting the fund for the purchase of Prince's family was swelled to two thousand five hundred dollars. A committee of five was appointed at its conclusion to continue the canvass. Gallaudet, to aid this committee, wrote a brief history of Prince's life, which was published as an eight-page pamphlet in October, 1828.

In the meantime, the American Colonization Society was giving publicity to the case by printing the letters of Cyrus Griffin and several other articles in its monthly journal known as the *African Repository*. Some of these were copied or summarized in newspapers and thus reached a wider audience.

In these writings "the case of this venerable old man and his affectionate wife" was placed before the public with a plea for their help, which was supported by appeals to logic and to sentiment. The kindness of Prince and his family to Dr. Cox, "a sick, wandering, friendless stranger in Africa," was described. It was argued that Prince's return would help to spread Christianity in Africa. Luckily for this argument Prince, his wife, and their oldest son had joined the Baptist Church shortly before he departed from Natchez. And supposing Prince did not prove to be an active missionary himself, the mere fact of his return would prove, so it was claimed, the evidence of a Christian spirit in the United States. The deed itself would be a sermon preached to Africa.

The claim was also made that Prince's return would help destroy the slave trade in Futa Jallon and increase the prosperity of Liberia: Futa Jallon would cease exporting men when it was learned that other products could be sold to great profit through Liberia. Prince's connection with the royal family of his country would help to create this economic union. Indeed, some of the more optimistic dared to hope that trade might be developed between Liberia and the great interior market-town of Timbuktu.

The editor of the *Journal of Commerce* declared: "We are soberly convinced, that if Great Britain had possession of Abduhl Rahahman, and he stood in the same relation to her that he does to us, she would prize her good fortune beyond almost any sum. . . . It is more than probable, that within two years, we should hear of a thriving commerce with the whole of that vast interior; we should have an accurate description of the habits, origin, and resources of the people; an accurate geography of the country, containing the whole unexplored course of the Niger; and what is more weight still with the Christian and philanthropist, a way would be opened for the entrance of Charity and the Christian Religion. We really hope that an expedition will be fitted out, if not by government, at least by the enterprise of individuals to accompany the Prince to his native country."

By the end of 1828 the total contributions had been increased to approximately four thousand dollars. This was not enough to purchase his five children and eight grandchildren whose cost, so the American Colonization Society estimated, would amount to about ten thousand dollars. Therefore, the decision was made to send Prince and his wife on instead of delaying their passage until their children could go with them.

Early in 1829 the aged couple sailed out of Hampton Roads on the ship *Harriet*, Captain Johnson commanding. The *African Repository* celebrated the event by printing a three-stanza poem inspired by the occasion. In all, there were one hundred and sixty emigrants aboard bound for the small colony at Liberia, where a new state was being created on the African coast. Two of the lot were ministers, and most of those on board were from Virginia. Prince doubtless found his companions more agreeable and his lot infinitely better than it had been on the slave ship forty years earlier.

After the sailing of Prince and his wife, efforts were continued in behalf of their children and grandchildren, and eight of them were purchased for $3,100. The others presumably remained in slavery. These eight were sent by boat from New Orleans to New York, where they were placed in the home of a colored family in Brooklyn. Later, they were taken to Norfolk, Virginia, whence they sailed, October 26, 1830, on the *Carolinian* with ninety-nine other emigrants bound for Liberia.

Meanwhile, Prince had reached Liberia. He had been sent to fill many and great purposes. He was expected to have a large share in the development of trade with the interior parts of Africa, in the Christianizing of the inhabitants of these regions, and in securing for the struggling settlement at Liberia the friendship of Futa Jallon. While he doubtless felt these responsibilities to some extent, his own thoughts were of his family: those he had left in Mississippi, and those whom he had hoped to see in Africa after the lapse of forty years.

A glimpse into his heart is gained through the following letter, which he wrote soon after landing, to one of the officers of the American Colonization Society.

MONROVIA, May 5, 1829

REVEREND SIR:

I am happy to inform you that I arrived safely in Africa, with my wife, and found the people generally in good health. You will please inform all my friends that I am in the land of my forefathers; and that I shall expect my friends in America to use their influence to get my children for me, and I shall be happy if they succeed. You will please inform my children, by letter, of my arrival in the Colony.

As soon as the rains are over, if God be with me, I shall try to bring my countrymen to the Colony, and to open the trade. I have found one of my friends in the Colony. He tells me we can reach home in fifteen days, and promises to go with me. I am unwell, but much better.

I am, with much respect, your humble servant.

ABDUHL RAHAHMAN.

About two months after this letter was written a small band of Fulbe set out from Timbo. They had received a letter from Abduhl Rahahman whom the old men remembered as the prince whom the Hebohs had captured in battle many years ago. He was writing to tell them that he was now free but that his children and grandchildren were slaves in a distant country, and he asked for money to ransom them. In response to this plea the band of Fulbe were bringing seven thousand dollar's worth of gold dust through the wilderness to Liberia.

On their journey they met a trader who had recently been in Liberia. While telling them the news he mentioned the fact that among the recent immigrants there was an old man named Abduhl Rahahman who claimed to be a Fulbe. Since his hearers seemed especially interested in this person he went on to tell them that Abduhl, like most newcomers, had been attacked by the coast fever. He had recovered, so the trader said, but soon afterward he had suffered another attack and had died on July 6. When they heard this news the Fulbe at once returned with their gold to Timbo.

CHAPTER SEVEN

SLAVERY: Its Development in Colonial America

The initial reaction of white colonists to the skin color of those who were brought into the colony of Virginia after 1619 was one of surprise. The blacks' color greatly influenced the racial attitudes that whites developed. Baptized blacks were at first assigned the same status as white indentured servants. However, as the labor needs of the colonists grew, skin color alone soon served as the basis for permanent enslavement in Virginia and Maryland.

First Impressions: The English Confrontation with Africans

Winthrop D. Jordan

The most impressive characteristic of Africans to the English was their blackness. In England the concept of blackness was loaded with emotional, negative meanings. Africans were perceived to be different in their manner of living, un-Christian in their religious practices, and libidinous. Even centuries before any physical contact with Africans, English writers expressed some of their more ingrained emotional values on the concepts of blackness and whiteness. Winthrop D. Jordan catalogues some of these statements in the following excerpt from his book, *White over Black*.

When the Atlantic nations of Europe began expanding overseas in the sixteenth century, Portugal led the way in Africa and to the east while Spain founded a great empire in America. It was not until the reign of Elizabeth that Englishmen came to realize that overseas exploration and plantations could bring home wealth, power, glory, and fascinating information. By the early years of the seventeenth century Englishmen had developed a taste for empire and for tales of adventure and discovery. More than is usual in human affairs, one man, the great chronicler Richard Hakluyt, had roused enthusiasm for western planting and had stirred the nation with his monumental compilation, *The Principal Navigations, Voyages, Traffiques and Discoveries of the English Nation.* Here was a work to widen a people's horizons. Its exhilarating accounts of voyages to all quarters of the globe (some by foreigners, in translation) constituted a national hymn, a sermon, an adventure story, and a scientific treatise. It was these accounts, together with ones added during the first quarter of the seventeenth century by Hakluyt's successor Samuel Purchas, which first acquainted Englishmen at home with the newly discovered lands of Africa.

English voyagers did not touch upon the shores of West Africa until after 1550, nearly a century after Prince Henry the Navigator had mounted the sustained Portuguese thrust southward for a water passage to the Orient. Usually Englishmen came to Africa to trade goods *with* the natives; the principal hazards of these ventures proved to be climate, disease, and the jealous opposition of the "Portingals" who had long since entrenched themselves in forts along the coast. The earliest English descriptions of West Africa were written by adventurous traders, men who had no special interest in converting the natives or, except for the famous Hawkins voyages, in otherwise laying hands on them. Extensive English participation in the slave trade did not develop until well into the seventeenth century. The first permanent English settlement on the African coast was at Kormantin in 1631, and the Royal African Company was not chartered for another forty years.[1] Initially, therefore, English contact with Africans did not take place primarily in a context which prejudged the Negro as a slave, at least not as a slave of Englishmen. Rather, Englishmen met Negroes merely as another sort of men.

Englishmen found the natives of Africa very different from themselves. Negroes looked different; their religion was un-Christian; their manner of living was anything but English; they seemed to be a particularly libidinous sort of people. All these clusters of perceptions were related to each other, though they may be spread apart for inspection, and they were related also to circumstances of contact in Africa, to previously accumulated traditions concerning that strange and distant continent, and to certain special qualities of English society on the eve of its expansion into the New World.

1. THE BLACKNESS WITHOUT

The most arresting characteristic of the newly discovered African was his color. Travelers rarely failed to comment upon it; indeed when describing Negroes they frequently began with complexion and then moved on to dress (or rather lack of it) and manners. At Cape Verde, "These people are all blacke, and are called Negros, without any apparell, saving before their privities."[2] Robert Baker's narrative poem recounting his two voyages to the West African coast in 1562 and 1563 first introduced the natives with these engaging lines:

And entering in [a river], we see
  a number of blacke soules,
Whose likelinesse seem'd men to be,
  but all as blacke as coles.

Their Captaine comes to me
    as naked as my naile,
Not having witte or honestie
    to cover once his taile.[3]

Even more sympathetic observers seemed to find blackness a most salient quality in Negroes: "although the people were blacke and naked, yet they were civill."[4]

Englishmen actually described Negroes as *black*—an exaggerated term which in itself suggests that the Negro's complexion had powerful impact upon their perceptions. Even the peoples of northern Africa seemed so dark that Englishmen tended to call them "black" and let further refinements go by the board. Blackness became so generally associated with Africa that every African seemed a black man. In Shakespeare's day, the Moors, including Othello, were commonly portrayed as pitchy black and the terms *Moor* and *Negro* used almost interchangeably.[5] With curious inconsistency, however, Englishmen recognized that Africans south of the Sahara were not at all the same people as the much more familiar Moors.[6] Sometimes they referred to Negroes as "black Moors" to distinguish them from the peoples of North Africa. During the seventeenth century the distinction became more firmly established and indeed writers came to stress the difference in color, partly because they delighted in correcting their predecessors and partly because Negroes were being taken up as slaves and Moors, increasingly, were not. In the more detailed and accurate reports about West Africa of the seventeenth century, moreover, Negroes in different regions were described as varying considerably in complexion. In England, however, the initial impression of Negroes was not appreciably modified: the firmest fact about the Negro was that he was "black."

The powerful impact which the Negro's color made upon Englishmen must have been partly owing to suddenness of contact. Though the Bible as well as the arts and literature of antiquity and the Middle Ages offered some slight introduction to the "Ethiope," England's immediate acquaintance with black-skinned peoples came with relative rapidity. While the virtual monopoly held by Venetian ships in England's foreign trade prior to the sixteenth century meant that people much darker than Englishmen were not entirely unfamiliar, really black men were virtually unknown except as vaguely referred to in the hazy literature about the sub-Sahara which had filtered down from antiquity. Native West Africans probably first appeared in London in 1554; in that year five "Negroes," as the legitimate trader William Towrson reported, were taken to England, "kept till they could speake the language," and then brought back again "to be a helpe to Englishmen" who were engaged in trade with Negroes on the coast. Hakluyt's later discussion of these Negroes, who he said "could wel agree with our meates and drinkes" though "the colde and moyst aire doth somewhat offend them," suggests that these "blacke Moores" were a novelty to Englishmen.[7] In this respect the English experience was markedly different from that of the Spanish and Portuguese who for centuries had been in close contact with North Africa and had actually been invaded and subjected by people both darker and more highly civilized than themselves. The impact of the Negro's color was the more powerful upon Englishmen, moreover, because England's principal contact with Africans came in West Africa and the Congo where men were not merely dark but almost literally black: one of the fairest-skinned nations suddenly came face to face with one of the darkest peoples on earth.

Viewed from one standpoint, Englishmen were merely participating in Europe's discovery that the strange men who stood revealed by European expansion overseas came in an astounding variety of colors. A Spanish chronicle translated into English in 1555 was filled with wonder at this diversity: "One of the marveylous thynges that god useth in the composition of man, is colour: whiche doubtlesse can not bee consydered withowte great admiration in beholding one to be white and an other blacke, beinge coloures utterlye contrary. Sum lykewyse to be yelowe whiche is betwene blacke and white: and other of other colours as it were of dyvers liveres."[8] As this passage suggests, the juxtaposition of black and white was the most striking marvel of all. And for Englishmen this juxtaposition was more than a curiosity.

In England perhaps more than in southern Europe, the concept of blackness was loaded with intense meaning. Long before they found that some men were black, Englishmen found in the idea of blackness a way of expressing some of their most ingrained values. No other color except white conveyed so much emotional impact. As described by the *Oxford English Dictionary,* the meaning of *black* before the sixteenth century included, "Deeply stained with dirt; soiled, dirty, foul. . . . Having dark or deadly purposes, malignant; pertaining to or involving death, deadly; baneful, disastrous, sinister. . . . Foul, iniquitous, atrocious, horrible, wicked. . . . Indicating disgrace, censure, liability to punishment, etc." Black was an emotionally partisan color, the handmaid and symbol of baseness and evil, a sign of danger and repulsion.

Embedded in the concept of blackness was its direct opposite—whiteness. No other colors so clearly implied opposition, "beinge coloures utterlye contrary"; no others were so frequently used to denote polarization:

Everye white will have its blacke,
And everye sweete its sowre.[9]

White and black connoted purity and filthiness, virginity and sin, virtue and baseness, beauty and ugliness, beneficence and evil, God and the devil.[10]

Whiteness, moreover, carried a special significance for Elizabethan Englishmen: it was, particularly when complemented by red, the color of perfect human beauty, especially *female* beauty. This ideal was already centuries old in Elizabeth's time,[11] and their fair Queen was its very embodiment: her cheeks were "roses in a bed of lillies." (Elizabeth was naturally pale but like many ladies then and since she freshened her "lillies" at the cosmetic table.)[12] An adoring nation knew precisely what a beautiful Queen looked like.

Her cheeke, her chinne, her neck, her nose,
This was a lillye, that was a rose;
Her hande so white as whales bone,
Her finger tipt with Cassidone;
Her bosome, sleeke as Paris plaster,
Held upp twoo bowles of Alabaster.[13]

Shakespeare himself found the lily and the rose a compelling natural coalition.

'Tis beauty truly blent, whose red and white
Nature's own sweet and cunning hand laid on.[14]

By contrast, the Negro was ugly, by reason of his color and also his "horrid Curles" and "disfigured" lips and nose.[15] As Shakespeare wrote apologetically of his black mistress,

My mistress' eyes are nothing like the sun;
Coral is far more red than her lips' red:
If snow be white, why then her breasts are dun;
If hairs be wires, black wires grow on her head.
I have seen roses damask'd, red and white,
But no such roses see I in her cheeks.[16]

Some Elizabethans found blackness an ugly mask, superficial but always demanding attention.

Is *Byrrha* browne? Who doth the question aske?
Her face is pure as Ebonie jeat blacke,
It's hard to know her face from her faire maske,
Beautie in her seems beautie still to lacke.
Nay, she's snow-white, but for that russet skin,
Which like a vaile doth keep her whitenes in.[17]

A century later blackness still required apology and mitigation: one of the earliest attempts to delineate the West African Negro as a heroic character, Aphra Behn's popular story *Oroonoko* (1688), presented Negroes as capable of blushing and turning pale.[18] It was important, if incalculably so, that English discovery of black Africans came at a time when the accepted standard of ideal beauty was a fair complexion of rose and white. Negroes not only failed to fit this ideal but seemed the very picture of perverse negation.[19]

From the first, however, many English observers displayed a certain sophistication about the Negro's color. Despite an ethnocentric tendency to find blackness repulsive, many writers were fully aware that Negroes themselves might have different tastes. As early as 1621 one writer told of the "Jetty coloured" Negroes, "Who in their native beauty most delight,/And in contempt doe paint the Divell white"; this assertion became almost a commonplace and even turned up a hundred and fifty years later in Newport, Rhode Island.[20] Many accounts of Africa reported explicitly that the Negro's preference in colors was inverse to the European's.[21] Even the Negro's features were conceded to be appealing to Negroes. By the late seventeenth century, in a changing social atmosphere, some observers decided that the Negro's jet blackness was more handsome than the lighter tawny hues; this budding appreciativeness was usually coupled, though, with expressions of distaste for "Large Breasts, thick Lips, and broad Nostrils" which many Negroes "reckon'd the Beauties of the Country."[22] As one traveler admiringly described an African queen, "She was indifferently tall and well shap'd, of a perfect black' had not big Lips nor was she flat Nos'd as most of the Natives are, but well featur'd and very comely."[23] By this time, the development of the slave trade to America was beginning to transform the Negro's color from a marvel into an issue. In what was surely a remarkable complaint for the master of a slaving vessel, Captain Thomas Phillips wrote in 1694 that he could not "imagine why they should be despis'd for their colour, being what they cannot help, and the effect of the climate it has pleas'd God to appoint them. I can't think there is any intrinsick value in one colour more than another, nor that white is better than black, only we think it so because we are so, and are prone to judge favourably in our own case, as well as the blacks, who in odium of the colour, say, the devil is white, and so paint him."[24] During the eighteenth century the Negro's color was to come into service as an argument for "diversitarian" theories of beauty;[25] Europe's discovery of "blacks" and "tawnies" overseas helped nurture a novel relativism. More important so far as the Negro was concerned, his color was to remain for centuries what it had been from the first, a standing problem for natural philosophers.

NOTES

1. Kenneth G. Davies, *The Royal African Company* (London, 1957), 38–46; John W. Blake, trans. and ed., *Europeans in West Africa, 1450–1560; Documents to Illustrate the Nature and Scope of Portuguese Enterprise in West Africa, the Abortive Attempt of Castilians to Create an Empire There, and the Early English Voyages to Barbary and Guinea (Works Issued by the Hakluyt Society,* 2d Ser., 87 [1942]), II, 254–60.

2. "The voyage made by M. John Hawkins . . . to the coast of Guinea and the Indies of Nova Hispania . . . 1564," in Richard Hakluyt, *The Principal Navigations, Voyages, Traffiques and Discoveries of the English Nation . . . ,* 12 vols., 1598 ed. (Glasgow, 1903–05), X, 15. See Katherine Beverly Oakes, Social Theory in the Early Literature of Voyage and Exploration in Africa (unpubl. Ph.D. diss., University of California, Berkeley, 1944), 120–23.

3. "The First Voyage of Robert Baker to Guinie . . . 1562," in Richard Hakluyt, *The Principall Navigations, Voiages and Discoveries of the English Nation . . .* (London, 1589), 132. The entire poem was omitted in the 1598 edition.

4. "The Voyage of M. George Fenner . . . Written by Walter Wren" (1566), Hakluyt, *Principal Navigations,* VI, 270. All ensuing references are to this reprinted 1598 edition unless otherwise indicated.

5. Warner Grenelle Rice, Turk, Moor and Persian in English Literature from 1550–1660, with Particular Reference to the Drama (unpubl. Ph.D. diss., Harvard University, 1926), 401–2n; Robert R. Cawley, *The Voyagers and Elizabethan Drama* (Boston, 1938), 31; Samuel C. Chew, *The Crescent and the Rose: Islam and England during the Renaissance* (N.Y., 1937), 521–24; Wylie Sypher, *Guinea's Captive Kings: British Anti-Slavery Literature of the XVIIIth Century* (Chapel Hill, 1942), 26.

6. An early instance is in "The Second Voyage to Guinea . . ." (1554), in Hakluyt, *Principal Navigations,* VI, 167–68. See the associations made by Leo Africanus, *The History and Description of Africa and of the Notable Things Therein Contained . . . ,* trans. John Pory [ca. 1600], ed. Robert Brown, 3 vols. (London, 1896), I, 230.

7. Hakluyt, *Principal Navigations,* VI, 176, 200, 217–18. Just how little Europeans knew about Africa prior to the Portuguese explorations is evident in T. Simar, "La géographie de l'Afrique central dans l'antiquité et au moven âge," *La Revue Congolaise,* 3 (1912), 1–23, 81–102, 145–69, 225–52, 288–310, 440–41.

8. Francisco López de Gómara, in Peter Martyr (D'Anghera), *The Decades of the Newe Worlde . . . ,* trans. Richard Eden (London, 1555), in Edward Arber, ed., *The First Three English Books on America . . .* (Birmingham, Eng., 1885), 338.

9. Thomas Percy, *Reliques of Ancient English Poetry . . . ,* ed. Robert A. Willmott (London, 1857), 27 (Sir Cauline, pt. 2, stanza 1).

10. Numerous examples in Middle English, Shakespeare, the Bible, and Milton are given by P. J. Heather, "Colour Symbolism," *Folk Lore,* 59 (1948), 169–70, 175–78, 182–83; 60 (1949), 208–16, 266–76. See also Harold R. Isaacs, "Blackness and Whiteness," *Encounter, 21* (1963), 8–21; Caroline

F. E. Spurgeon, *Shakespeare's Imagery and What It Tells Us* (Boston, 1958), 64, 66–69, 158; Arrah B. Evarts, "Color Symbolism," *Psychoanalytic Review,* 6 (1919), 129–34; Don Cameron Allen, "Symbolic Color in the Literature of the English Renaissance," *Philological Quarterly,* 15 (1936), 81–92; and for a different perspective, Francis B. Gummere, "On the Symbolic Use of the Colors Black and White in Germanic Tradition," *Haverford College Studies,* 1 (1889), 112–62.

11. Walter Clyde Curry, *The Middle English Ideal of Personal Beauty: As Found in the Metrical Romances, Chronicles, and Legends of the XIII, XIV, and XV Centuries* (Baltimore, 1916), 3, 80–98.

12. Elkin Calhoun Wilson, *England's Eliza* (Cambridge, Mass., 1939), 337; Charles Carroll Camden, *The Elizabethan Woman* (Houston, N.Y., and London, 1952), chap. 7; Cawley, *Voyagers and Elizabethan Drama,* 85; Elizabeth Jenkins, *Elizabeth the Great* (London, 1958), 62, 100, 159, 296; Gamaliel Bradford, *Elizabethan Women,* ed. Harold O. White (Boston, 1936), 82, 212; Violet A. Wilson, *Queen Elizabeth's Maids of Honour and Ladies of the Privy Chamber* (N. Y., n.d.), 4–5. Hugh Plat, *Delightes for Ladies, Written Originally by Sir Hugh Plat, First Printed in 1602, London, England,* ed. Violet and Hal W. Trovillion (Herrin, Ill., 1939), 87–94, 99, 102–3, contains advice on cosmetics.

13. [George Puttenham?], *Parthenaides* (1579), quoted in Wilson, *England's Eliza,* 242.

14. *Twelfth Night,* I, v, 259–60. W. J. Craig, ed., *The Complete Works of Shakespeare* [London, N.Y., Toronto, 1943]. For other expressions of this ideal, *A Midsummer-Night's Dream,* I, i, 128–29; III, i, 98–99; III, ii, 137–44.

15. *Love in Its Ecstacy,* quoted in Cawley, *Voyagers and Elizabethan Drama,* 86*n;* "A Letter written from Goa . . . by one Thomas Stevens . . . 1579." Hakluyt, *Principal Navigations,* VI, 384. Curry, *Middle English Ideal of Personal Beauty,* 64–66, 113–14, indirectly makes abundantly clear how very far Negro women were from matching prevalent English ideals for beautiful noses, lips, and breasts.

16. Sonnet CXXX; see also nos. CXXVII, CXXXI, CXXXII. Shakespeare's "Dark Lady" is discussed by George B. Harrison, *Shakespeare under Elizabeth* (N. Y., 1933), 64–67, 310.

17. Harrison, *Shakespeare,* 310–11, quoting Weever, *Epigrams* (1599), Third Week, Epig. 12, *In Byrrham.*

18. Aphra Behn, *Oroónoko; Or, the Royal Slave,* Montague Summers, ed., *The Works of Aphra Behn,* V (London, 1915), 145.

19. In the Middle Ages a man's "complexion" was conceived as revealing his temperament because it showed his particular blend of humors, each of which was associated with certain colors: Lynn Thorndike, "De Complexionibus," *Isis,* 49 (1958), 398–408. Yet Englishmen seem not to have made efforts to link the Negro's skin color specifically to his bile or dominant humor and hence to his temperament.

20. P[eter] H[eylyn], *Microcosmus, or a Little Description of the Great World. A Treatise Historicall, Geographicall, Politicall, Theologicall* (Oxford, 1621), 379; Peter Heylyn, ΜΙΚΡΌΚΟΣΜΟΣ. *A Little Description of the Great World,* 3d ed. (Oxford, 1627), 735; *The Golden Coast, or a Description of Guinney . . . Together with a Relation of Such Persons, As Got Wonderful Estates by Their Trade Thither* (London, 1665), 3; Thomas Phillips, *A Journal of a Voyage Made in the Hannibal of London, Ann. 1693, 1694, from England to Cape Monseradoe, in Africa; and Thence Along the Coast of Guiney to Whidaw, the Island of St. Thomas, and So Forward to Barbadoes. With a Cursory Account of the Country, the People, Their Manners, Forts, Trade, etc.,* in John and Awsham Churchill, comps., *A Collection of Voyages and Travels, Some Now First Printed from Original Manuscripts, Others Translated Out of Foreign Languages, and Now First Published in English . . . ,* 6 vols. (London, 1704–32), VI, 219; Thomas Browne, "Of the Blackness of Negroes," Charles Sayle, ed., *The Works of Sir Thomas Browne,* 3 vols. (London, 1904–07), II, 383–84; *Newport* [R.I.] *Mercury,* Jan. 11, 1768. See Karl Pearson, E. Nettleship, and C. H. Usher, *A Monograph on Albinism in Man* (Department of Applied Mathematics [or Statistics], University College, University of London, *Drapers' Company Research Memoirs,* Biometric Ser., 6, 8, 9 [6 vols.] [London, 1911–13]), I, 48.

21. Peter Martyr (D'Anghera), *De Orbe Novo: The Eight Decades of Peter Martyr D'Anghera,* trans. Francis A. MacNutt, 2 vols. (N.Y. and London, 1912), II, 39; Morgan Godwyn, *The Negro's and Indians Advocate . . .* (London, 1680), 21; *The Works of Michael Drayton, Esq.,* 4 vols. (London, 1753), III, 1177; W. Gifford, ed., *The Works of Ben Jonson,* 9 vols. (London, 1816), VII, 11; Cawley, *Voyagers and Elizabethan Drama, 32n.* Cf. Katherine George, "The Civilized West Looks at Primitive Africa; 1400–1800. A Study in Ethnocentrism," *Isis,* 49 (1958), 62–72.

22. Francis Moore, *Travels into the Inland Parts of Africa: Containing a Description of the Several*

Nations for the Space of Six Hundred Miles up the River Gambia . . . (London, 1738), 131.
23. Nathaniel Uring, *A History of the Voyages and Travels of Capt. Nathaniel Uring* . . . (London, 1726), 40–41. Also Behn, *Oroonoko,* 136; John Barbot, *A Description of the Coasts of North and South-Guinea; and of Ethiopia Inferior, Vulgarly Angola* . . . in Churchill, comps., *Voyages,* V., 100; William Snelgrave, *A New Account of Some Parts of Guinea, and the Slave-Trade* . . . (London, 1734), 40–41; Moore, *Travels into the Inland Parts,* 29–30, 214.
24. Phillips, *Journal,* in Churchill, comps., *Voyages,* VI, 219.
25. Sypher, *Guinea's Captive Kings,* 51.

White Servitude in Maryland

Eugene Irving McCormac

White indentured servitude in the colonies was a modified form of the system of apprenticeship used in England for centuries. The white indentured servants in the colonies came from the prisons and the lowest socioeconomic levels of society. Sometimes they came willingly, but at other times they were forced to serve. For many years these involuntary servants outnumbered those who came to the colonies of their own free will. When slavery became firmly established in the colonies, the demand for indentured servants declined. After the Revolutionary War, the number of voluntary servants brought into the colonies gradually diminished.

In the following selection from Eugene Irving McCormac's book, *White Servitude in Maryland,* the origins and development of the system of indenturing are explored.

INTRODUCTION

White servitude as it existed in Maryland and the other colonies was only a modified form of the system of apprenticeship which had been in vogue in England for several centuries preceding. The wide use of this system of labor during the fifteenth and sixteenth centuries accounts in a great measure for the readiness with which persons in later years entered into a contract of servitude in order to reach the New World. Not only were persons regularly bound out to masters for the purpose of learning various trades, but it was customary in the early part of the sixteenth century for parents of all classes to apprentice their children to strangers at an early age.[1] Used at first for training tradesmen and domestics, the system was extended to agricultural laborers during the reign of Elizabeth. The condition of the laborer had become so reduced by the debasement of the currency, the change from tillage to sheepfarming and the numerous enclosures of land during the preceding reigns[2] that vagrancy and crime were met with on every hand. Attempts were made to better the conditions by compulsory apprentice laws[3] and by forced contributions for the poor.[4] Work was to be provided for those who were able to do it, and relief for those who were not. Poor children were to be trained for some trade and the idle were to be punished. In the reign of James I, the statutes of Elizabeth for binding children were made use of for sending them to the plantations.[5] But statutory remedies failed to afford adequate relief, and, in spite of the general prosperity during Elizabeth's reign, the condition of the poorer classes was deplorable.[6] In the latter part of the reign and during that of James, attempts were made to relieve England of her surplus population by founding colonies in America. The early expeditions were ill-planned and ill-managed. No systematic methods were adopted for supplying the plantations with laborers and failure was inevitable. In order to maintain a permanent and profitable settlement, a constant supply of laborers from the mother country was indispensable, but without pecuniary assistance the poor of Europe were unable to emigrate.

Various schemes were proposed for promoting emigration, the most successful of which was the system of apprenticeship. It was successful not only in furnishing emigrants with free transportation to America, but in profitably employing them when they reached there.

Sir George Peckham, partner in the colonization schemes of Sir Humphrey Gilbert, seems to have been the first who conceived the idea of sending out apprentices to the plantations. In a treatise on the benefits to be derived from colonization written in 1582, he says: "There are at this day great numbers . . . which live in such penurie & want, as could be contented to hazard their liues, and to serue one yeere for meat, drinke and apparell only, without wages, in hope thereby to amend their estates." He urges that in this way the kingdom will be greatly enlarged and strengthened, the poor relieved, and "all odious idleness from this our Realme vtterly banished."[7]

During the reign of James I, the apprenticeship system was adopted by the Virginia and London Companies as well as private adventurers. Servitude as established by these Companies differed in many respects from the indentured servitude of later years. The servant was in theory a member of the Company and served for a term of years to repay the Company for his transportation and maintenance.[8]

In order to carry out the scheme of colonization, money was raised by subscription to assist those who were willing to embark, and many who were unwilling to go were impressed as servants for the plantations. The practice of apprenticing poor children to the Virginia Company began as early as 1620. In that year, Sir Edwin Sandys petitioned Secretary Naunton for authority to send out one hundred children who had been "appointed for transportation" by the city of London, but who were unwilling to go.[9] By making use of the apprenticeship statute of Elizabeth this difficulty was removed, and both children and vagrants were regularly gathered up in London and elsewhere, and contracts made with merchants for carrying them to America. To this number were added persons who were convicted of capital offences, but pardoned and transported by the order of the king.

For a number of years the involuntary emigrants probably outnumbered those who went of their own free wills;[10] but when the colony became firmly established, men and women willingly bound themselves to serve for a term of years in order to obtain free transportation to America.

The system of servitude thus early established in Virginia was adopted by Lord Baltimore as a means of settling and developing the colony of Maryland. Too poor to send out settlers himself, he induced others to transport servants in return for grants of land in the new colony. Many who did not wish to go in person furnished Baltimore money for transporting servants and received their pay in lands.

The servants usually signed a written contract called an indenture, which bound them to serve a master for a specified number of years in return for free transportation, food, clothing and fifty acres of land. From this contract, whether they signed it or not, all servants came to be called "indented servants."

* * *

THE EARLY LAND SYSTEM IN MARYLAND

The land system in Maryland during the life of the second Lord Baltimore was very closely connected with the enterprise of importing white servants into that colony. Land was parcelled out to the adventures directly in proportion to the number of servants brought with them from England.

Concerning the motives which led Lord Baltimore to found the colony of Maryland there has been much dispute among writers on toleration. By confining their attention to this religious controversy, they have apparently lost sight of the underlying principle in Baltimore's plans which overshadowed all others, viz., that of revenue. There is very little evidence to support the theory that Maryland was founded as a home for persecuted Catholics. A majority of the first settlers sent out were Protestants;[1] the privileges of the Catholics were limited at a very early date and their religion was not publicly allowed.[2] On the other hand, the financial difficulties of the proprietor, his instructions to his deputies, his various proclamations, and his whole scheme of colonization seem to indicate that the planting of the colony was largely a business enterprise by which Baltimore hoped to recoup his fortunes and erect for himself and his posterity a monument in the New World. When through his brother he offered land and privileges to the people of Masachusetts, he was very careful to have it understood that the new comers were to pay "such annual rent as should be agreed upon."[13]

* * *

CONCLUSION

Importation of servants into Maryland from Great Britain and Ireland seems to have reached its height about the middle of the eighteenth century. From that time down to the Revolution the number of voluntary servants brought into the colony gradually diminished. Convicts, on the other hand, came in ever-increasing numbers, and during the twenty years which preceded the Revolution, Maryland received nearly all that were transported. As slavery was firmly rooted in Virginia, there was little demand for convict labor, and laws were enacted to exclude them.[14] In Pennsylvania, the German immigrants more than supplied the demand for servants, and the convict element there was insignificant. But in Maryland the contractors always found a ready market for his Majesty's passengers, in spite of the sentiment against them.

After the convict trade was terminated by the Revolution, very few English-speaking servants came to the new state. Various travelers speak of the difficulty of obtaining white servants. Cooper,[15] who traveled in Maryland in 1793, says that it is impossible to procure any servants "but Negro-slaves." Two years later, Weld[16] writes that "it is a matter of the utmost difficulty to procure domestic servants of any description." These remarks apply only to English and Irish servants, as the Germans and Swiss at that time were seldom purchased for domestics.

The falling off in the number of servants from Great Britain and Ireland was due to several causes. None now found it necessary to emigrate on account of religious persecution. The social and economic conditions at home were much better than in the preceding centuries, and a greater proportion of the immigrants were able to pay for their transportation. Modern improvements had shortened the voyage and greatly reduced its cost.

Another thing which tended to reduce the number imported was the stigma which attached to the institution. So many convicts were annually sent to expiate their crimes by servitude in the plantations that America came to be looked upon as a sort of penal colony, and those who were unable to pay their way preferred to remain at home rather than to cast their lot with the seven-year passengers from Old Bailey and Newgate. This impression was encouraged by the British officials and writers whose desire it was to discourage emigration.

The servant trade was entirely stopped by the war, and was never revived with any great vigor.[17] Now that America had become a separate state, still greater efforts were made to restrain British subjects from going there. Writers never tired of depicting the new republic as a land of barbarism and wretchedness. Lord Sheffield, writing in 1784, represents emigration as the resource only for the culprit and of those who have made themselves the objects of contempt. "It is generally calculated that not above one emigrant in five succeeds so as to settle a family. . . . Irishmen just emancipated in Europe, go to America, to become slaves to a negro. . . . The better sort of emigrants are begging about the streets." [18] The British reviews were equally zealous in their denunciations of America and their warnings to emigrants.[19]

But what was more effectual still in reducing the number of servant immigrants was the restriction put upon emigration to America by the British government. In 1794, the emigration of all skilled laborers was prohibited. By the navigation law of 1817, vessels bound for the United States were permitted to carry but one passenger for every five tons of the vessel, while those going to other countries were allowed to carry twice that number.[20] With these regulations in force, no contractor could profitably transport servants to America.

The German and Swiss redemptioners continued to come in large numbers long after the Revolution. There was no appreciable falling off in the number till after the year 1817. The records for that year, given in Niles' Register, show that the emigration from both Germany and Switzerland was very large. May 24, fourteen vessels are reported as preparing at Amsterdam to bring 5000 emigrants to the United States. From the first to the sixteenth of May, 5817 emigrants passed Mayence on the way to America.[21] It was estimated that the number of Germans who left Baden for America during the summer of 1817 was 18,000.[22] The proportion of servants cannot be safely affirmed.

But in the years 1817 and 1819, measures were adopted on both sides of the Atlantic which dealt a death blow to the institution of servitude by rendering it unprofitable for contractors to longer engage in the traffic. In 1817, steps were taken in both Holland and Switzerland to investigate the condition of emigration and to prevent the passengers from being crowded in ships by contractors and carried to America. Switzerland refused to grant passports to the United States to any emigrant who was unable to present a bill of exchange of at least 200 florins payable at Amsterdam.[23] This practically prohibited the emigration of all who were unable to pay for their transportation. Holland also sent out an ambassador to study the emigration problem and to devise remedies for protecting the emigrants. These regulations did much to reduce the number of emigrants who found it necessary to bind themselves into servitude when they reached America.

While these restrictions were being put upon emigration by the European governments, laws were enacted in the United States which were still more effectual in bringing the institution to an end. The German Society of Maryland, which was incorporated in 1817, set vigorously to work to purge the system of the abuses which had long been practiced upon the poor and ignorant redemptioners. They secured the passage of a law which compelled ship-masters to provide wholesome food for the immigrants and to care for the sick at their own expense. No person could be held to pay for the passage of a deceased relative or friend no matter what contract had been previously made. The term of servitude was reduced to four years. Armed with this law the society at once set to work to strictly enforce its provisions and to bring offenders to justice. It was soon found, however, that state laws did not have adequate jurisdiction in dealing with foreign ships and the matter was laid before Congress. In March, 1819, Congress passed a law which limited the number of passengers to two for every five tons of the vessel. A penalty of $150 was imposed for every passenger that was carried in excess of that number, and if the excess amounted to twenty passengers the vessel was forfeited to the United States.

Official reports show a remarkable falling off in the number of German immigrants after the passage of these laws. From October 1, 1819, to September 30, 1820, the whole number of German and Swiss immigrants landing at Baltimore was only 299, while only 20 came to Philadelphia during the same period.[24]

Indenture of white servants in Maryland practically ceased at this time. There is no entry relating to redemptioners in the books of the German Society after September, 1819.[25] Private individuals continued to import persons under such a contract for a few years longer and isolated cases are mentioned as late as 1835, but the number is insignificant.

For nearly two centuries white servitude played a very important part in the industrial history of Maryland. Employed at first as a means of building up a landed aristocracy, it developed later into an institution approaching in some respects chattel slavery. Its efficiency as a system of labor in colonial days was far superior to either free labor or negro slavery. No other system could have supplied a sufficient number of laborers at so little cost to the planters. The long and certain term of service made it possible for planters to profitably cultivate extensive plantations and build up a lucrative foreign trade. It supplied the colony not only with agricultural laborers, but with tradesmen and professional men. Its superiority over Negro slavery retarded the growth of that institution.

In general, the effect of this system of labor on the servant himself was beneficial. Five years' experience under the rule of an exacting master converted many an indolent immigrant into an industrious and prosperous citizen.

As a means of promoting emigration, this system was equally successful. It afforded relief to thousands of the oppressed and starving peasants of Europe by providing a way of reaching America without paying for their passage in advance. By drawing off the superfluous population of Europe it did more to lessen pauperism and crime than all the laws on the statute books.

But the time came when this stimulus to emigration was no longer necessary. The social and economic conditions which had called the system into existence had passed away, and its continuance was of interest only to those who were engaged in the transportation. The abuses practiced by these dealers in men at last became so flagrant that public opinion was aroused against the institution and measures were adopted which brought it to an end.

NOTES

1. The following contemporary account illustrates how common this custom was in the first part of the sixteenth century. "The want of affection in the English is strongly manifest toward their children; for after having kept them at home till they arrive at the age of 7 or 9 years at the utmost, they put them out, both males and females, to hard service in the houses of other people, binding them generally for another 7 or 9 years. And these are called apprentices, and during that time they perform all the most menial offices; and few are born who are exempted from this fate, for every one, however rich he may be, sends away his children into the houses of others, whilst he, in return, receives those of strangers into his own."—Italian Relation of England, Camden Society, 1847.
2. Gibbins, Industry in England, p. 256.
3. 5 Eliz. cap. 4.
4. 43 Eliz. cap. 2.
5. Cal. St. Pap. Col. Feb. 18, 1623.
6. Gibbins, p. 260.
7. Hart's Contemporaries, I, p. 157.
8. Ballagh, White Servitude in Virginia, p. 13.
9. Cal. St. Pap. Col. Jan. 28, 1620.
10. Hammond, Leah and Rachell, p. 7.
11. Johnson, Foundation of Maryland, pp. 31, 32, 73, 74; Records Eng. Prov. of Soc. of Jesus, p. 362.
12. Rec. of Soc. of Jesus, pp. 362, 365.
13. Winthrop's History of New England, II, 149.
14. Eddis Letters, p. 66.
15. Some Information respecting America, p. 20.
16. Travels in the United States, p. 29.
17. Hildreth, IV, p. 93.
18. Observations on the Commerce of the American States, pp. 195, 196.
19. See Walsh's Appeal, Secs. VII and VIII.
20. See Walsh's Appeal, Secs. VII and VIII.
21. Niles' Register, July 19, 1817, p. 333.
22. Niles' Register, Aug. 16, 1817, p. 397.
23. Ibid. Aug. 2, 1817, XII, p. 365.
24. Report of the Secretary of State, Washington, Feb. 1821.
25. Hennighausen, Redemptioners, p. 21.

Slavery in the British Colonies 1619–1763

Edgar A. Toppin

An historic civil court decision was handed down in Northampton County Court in 1655. A runaway black indentured servant was sentenced to slavery for life. Ironically, Anthony Johnson, the master, was himself a black man. The baptized blacks who were brought to the colonies before 1682 could claim indentured servant status. However, beginning in the 1630s the status of blacks gradually changed from indentured status to slavery for life. Edgar A. Toppin describes the gradual change in the status of colonial blacks in the following selection from his book, *A Biographical History of Blacks in America Since 1528.*

Anthony Johnson was furious because Samuel Goldsmith and Robert and George Parker had deprived him of the services of John Casor. Johnson filed suit in Northampton County Court in 1654.

Casor, a black, resident in Virginia since 1640, told the court that "he came unto Virginia for seven or eight years of Indenture, yet . . . Anthony Johnson his Master . . . had kept him his servant seven years longer than he should or ought." Johnson claimed that he had never seen Casor's indenture papers, insisting that "he had the Negro for his life."

The litigation originated in November, 1653, when Goldsmith visited Johnson and Casor sought Goldsmith's help. Goldsmith brought in the Parkers, who backed Casor's story saying that "they knew that the said Negro had an Indenture." Johnson still refused to release Casor. Goldsmith and the Parkers warned that Casor could be awarded Johnson's cows for damages. Thereupon, yielding to the pleas of his fearful wife, sons, and son-in-law, Johnson released Casor.

What made him angry was that Casor then indentured himself to Robert Parker. Johnson brought suit against Parker claiming that "he detains one John Casor a Negro the plaintiff's servant under pretense the said John Casor is a free man."

In March, 1655, came the judgment: "The court . . . do find that . . . Robert Parker most unrightly keeps the said Negro John Casor from his right Master Anthony Johnson. . . . Be it . . . ordered that . . . Casor . . . shall forthwith return into the service of his said Master Anthony Johnson. . . ." The court made Parker pay all expenses of the suit.

This historic decision was the first civil case in which a Virginia court made a black indentured servant a slave. Casor was returned on the terms on which Johnson brought suit, that Casor was his servant for life.

The strangest thing of all about this case was that Anthony Johnson, the master, was himself a black man. Goldsmith and the Parkers were white, but Robert Parker lost the case.

Although he is properly obscure, Johnson symbolizes a neglected aspect of life among Negroes in colonial Virginia: some were free citizens. Johnson came to Jamestown, Virginia, in 1621 as an indentured servant but became a free man and a land owner upon completing his term. He married another black, Mary, who had entered on the ship *Margarett and John* in 1622. In 1651, Johnson imported five indentured servants and was granted 250 acres of land along the Pungoteague River in Northampton County as head-rights (50 acres per person) on them. Other free Negroes settled nearby, forming the first black community in America.

Early the next year a disastrous fire impoverished the Johnsons, and they petitioned the county court for tax relief. Accordingly, on February 28, 1652, the court issued an order that in "consideration . . . of their hard labor & honored service" as county residents for thirty years, the Johnsons "be disengaged and freed from payment of Taxes and levies in Northampton County for public use." Grateful for this but embittered by his financial reverses, Johnson was in a mood to defend his ownership of Casor, thus winning the suit that made Casor his slave.

When Johnson sued Parker in 1654, blacks had been living in Virginia for thirty-five years. Writing in January, 1620, to Sir Edwin Sandys, Treasurer of the London Company that established Jamestown, John Rolfe (husband of Pocahontas) reported that

About the latter end of August, a Dutch man of War with the burden of 160 tons arrived at Point Comfort, the commander's name, Captain Jope, his pilot to the West Indies, one Mr. Marmaduke, an Englishman. They met with the *Treasurer* in the West Indies and determined to hold consort ship hitherward, but in their passage lost one the other. He brought not anything but twenty and odd negroes, which the Governor in Cape Marchant bought for Victuals, (whereof he was in great need, as he pretended) at the best and easiest rates they could. He had a large commission from his Excellency, to arrange and take purchase in the West Indies.

There are some misconceptions about these Africans who entered in August, 1619, twelve years after the founding of Jamestown. First, many people assume that these were the earliest blacks in the New World, but as has been shown earlier, the history of blacks in North and South America began more than a hundred years before.

Second, some people assume that the Africans who came to Virginia in 1619 were slaves. Although John Rolfe's letter stated that the colonists brought some twenty Africans, this is no certain indication that they were made slaves. Such words as "sold," "bought," and "servant" were utilized in the Jamestown colony to apply to almost all individuals who were not in the status of officers of the company. Most of the colonists were servants of the company, and these twenty-odd Africans imported in 1619 might have been in the same status. Some writers argue that these blacks were indentured servants, because Virginia lacked laws on slavery before 1660. Others have argued that they were slaves almost from the outset, that the attitudes and outlook of the colonists reduced blacks to a distinctly inferior status, below that of all other inhabitants.

The ship *Treasurer,* mentioned in the letter of Rolfe to Sandys, dropped off some Africans in Bermuda before coming to Jamestown later in the year 1619 to drop off still one more African. In the next few years, other ships brought in several more Africans. In the temporary census of 1624–1625 taken in the Colony of Virginia, the twenty-three Negroes then residing there were listed as servants, not as slaves. Evidently some, if not all of them, were treated as indentured servants, who served a limited term and then became free, as in the case of Anthony Johnson.

Although the first statutory recognition of slavery in Virginia did not take place until 1660, there were many indications that slavery was developing prior to that time. From 1619 to 1640, there were some black indentured servants, but, apparently, also some being held as slaves. In the period from 1640 to 1660, slavery was becoming increasingly the status of black Virginians. From 1660 to 1682, laws gradually evolved that gave legal sanction to slavery, making all blacks who entered after 1682 slaves. Nonetheless, there was always a class of free Negroes in Virginia. Those blacks who were free before the basic slave codes were enacted between 1660 and 1682 generally remained free. Others were set free by their masters after slavery became the law of the land in Virginia. Consequently, from the 1620s to the end of slavery in 1865, there were always some blacks in Virginia who were free men.

The first recorded case of enslavement in Virginia came in a criminal case in 1640. Three indentured servants, two white and one black, had run away. The three runaways were captured and put on trial for the crime of deserting their lawful masters who had bought their contracts and were entitled to the full period of service that the indentures had contracted for. As punishment, the General

Court, in which the cases were tried, added four years to the terms of each of the two white runaways. But the court then ruled that "the third, being a negro named John Punch shall serve his said master or his assigns for the time of his natural life. . . ." Thus, the black man, John Punch, became a slave unlike the two white indentured servants who merely had to serve a longer term. This was the first known case in Virginia involving slavery. The 1654–1655 case involving John Casor and Anthony Johnson was the first known civil case enslaving a man in Virginia. The fact that such casual mention was made of the General Court's making John Punch a slave in the 1640 criminal case would seem to indicate that enslavement of blacks was not a startling new departure from the existent practices in Virginia. It is this criminal case of 1640 that causes some scholars to assume that slavery existed in practice in Virginia long before the passage of slave laws.

There were other indications of slavery in Virginia before 1660. County records of the 1640s indicate that some Negroes were being sold for life indentures. Thus, slavery began to develop covertly as black indentured servants had their terms lengthened to life. Also, records of estates probated in the 1640s and 1650s indicate frequently that black indentured servants were listed as being of much greater value than white indentured servants. For example, a young male white indentured servant with six years' service remaining was sold in one probated estate at half the value of an old Negro woman indenture who could not possibly have been as productive as the young white man. She must have been listed at twice his value only because she was a servant for life, in effect a slave, while he had a limited term to serve. Thus, as early as the 1640s, there were blacks in Virginia living in virtual slavery, even in the absence of slave legislation. Yet it is also important to note that there were blacks in Virginia as late as the 1670s and 1680s who were bringing suits that limited their indentures or won their freedom.

Slavery in Virginia evidently antedated slave laws. In 1660, law caught up with custom. Virginia passed a law then stating "That in case any English servant shall run away in company with any negroes who are incapable of making satisfaction by addition of time . . . the English so running away . . . shall serve for the time of the said negroes absence as they are to do for their own. . . ." This law recognized that there were Negroes who could not be punished for running away by being forced to serve more time because they were already serving lifetime indentures, or in other words were slaves. Another step toward legalizing slavery came in 1662 when the General Assembly of Virginia passed a law stating that "all children born in this country shall be held bond or free only according to the condition of the mother. . . ." In England under the common law, by contrast, the child took the status of the father. But in Virginia a child born of a slave woman by her master or any other white man remained a slave.

In 1667 the colonial legislature passed a law that would encourage slave-owners to convert their slaves to Christianity without fear that the newly baptized Christian brother would therefore cease to be a slave. This statute enacted by the General Assembly stated that "the conferring of baptism does not alter the condition of the person as to his bondage or freedom; that divers masters, freed from this doubt, may more carefully endeavor the propagation of christianity. . . ." In contrast to Christianity, the practice among Moslems was to emancipate any slave who converted to the Islamic faith. Moslems would not hold their coreligionists as slaves, as Christians did.

These laws of the 1660s paved the way for the statutes passed by the Virginia legislature in 1670 and 1682 that enslaved all blacks coming to the colony. The law of 1670 provided that "all servants not being christians imported into this colony by shipping" were to be slaves for life. The phrase "all servants not being christians" referred to blacks imported from Africa, almost all of whom were pagans or Moslems. This law had a loophole, however, in that such persons who entered Virginia by land from neighboring colonies were to "serve, if boys and girls until thirty years of age, if men or women, twelve years and no longer." Another loophole arose because some Africans were converted to Christianity before reaching Virginia and thus, under the terms of the law of 1670, had to be limited to a service of thirty years if children or twelve years if adults. As a result, the General Assembly, in 1682, repealed the law of 1670 and passed a new law closing both loopholes. The act of 1682 made slaves of all persons of non-Christian nationalities (which meant persons from Africa) coming into Virginia, whether they came by land or by sea, and whether or not they had been converted to the Christian faith after being captured in their homeland.

A final step in this process of degrading the black man was taken in 1705. In that year, the General Assembly of Virginia passed a law that stated: "all negro, mulatto, and Indian slaves, in all courts of judicature, and other places, within this dominion, shall be held, taken, and adjudged to be real estate. . . ." Thus, a slave became chattel, a piece of property, losing his inherent dignity and value as a human being.

Which came first, prejudice or slavery? Were whites initially prejudiced against blacks, therefore enslaving them? Or did prejudice develop gradually after whites observed blacks living in slavery? Historians disagree. Carl Degler and Wesley Frank Craven adopt the view that whites were prejudiced against blacks from the outset because of their color, therefore regarding them as different and inferior, hastening the process by which blacks were pushed into slavery. Oscar and Mary Handlin and Kenneth Stampp have argued that the English colonists were not prejudiced initially, but that prejudices developed as they observed blacks serving as slaves.

In his recent Pulitzer Prize-winning book, *White Over Black,* historian Winthrop Jordan takes a middle ground between the Degler-Craven and the Handlin-Stampp points of view. Jordan cites many evidences that whites in the English colonies had prejudices even before slavery was fully developed and legally sanctioned. He points to the fact that restrictions were placed on the right of blacks to bear arms, that black female indentured servants customarily worked in the fields while white female indentured servants generally were not required to do so, that strenuous efforts were made by laws and criminal court cases to prevent cohabitation of blacks and whites, and that more severe penalties were meted out to blacks than to whites for committing identical offenses. Therefore, Jordan concluded that:

Rather than slavery causing "prejudice" or vice versa, they seem rather to have generated each other. Both were, after all, twin aspects of a general debasement of the Negro. Slavery and "prejudice" may have been equally cause and effect, continuously reacting upon each other, dynamically joining hands to hustle the Negro down the road to complete degradation.

Slavery developed only gradually in Virginia, evolving almost absentmindedly, Professor Jordan observed. In Virginia, as in Latin America, efforts were first made to use Indian slaves to solve the New World's problem of a shortage of labor. But the Indians proved unsatisfactory because they were not skilled farmers as were the Africans; the Indian braves had concentrated on hunting and fighting, leaving farming to the squaws. Unaccustomed to the hard, laborious drudgery involved in mining and farming and used to a more carefree existence, many Indians succumbed in slavery.

White indentured servants could have solved the New World's labor problem in the English colonies as they did in Australia, if there had been enough of them. But although Europe scraped the bottom of the jails and brothels, and although kidnappers worked feverishly to seize children and adults, there were never enough to fill the needs of employers. Moreover, as capitalists in England and other European countries realized the need for surplus labor there in order to hold down wages in the rising domestic industries of nascent capitalism and the forthcoming factories of full-fledged capitalism, they saw to it that brakes were applied to retard the draining off of white labor. Laws passed in England late in the seventeenth century, for example, made kidnapping of persons for indentured servitude much more difficult. As the supply of white indentured servants dwindled accordingly, the competition for their labor increased. This resulted in their contracts being sold for shorter terms and for higher "freedom dues" at the end of their service. Freedom dues were the grants in land, goods, and money provided an indentured servant at the end of his term, under the specifications of his contract. The rising expenses, therefore, made white indentures more costly and thus less desirable.

Africa, with a vast supply of slaves to offer, became vital to development of the New World. Since a slave served for life, with his children also being slaves, African slavery proved far more profitable than European indentures. Also, black slaves could be more easily detected and apprehended on running away than white indentures who could melt into the general population. Being black and pagans, Africans could be disciplined (whipped) with fewer pangs of conscience than white Christian servants.

In 1649, Virginia's population was estimated to be 15,000 whites and only 349 blacks. By 1671, despite the slave laws of the 1660s and 1670, white indentures outnumbered black slaves three to one, or 6,000 to 2,000. As late as 1683, there were about 12,000 indentured servants to 2,700 slaves. Thereafter, slavery increased rapidly. One reason slavery now outstripped indentured servitude was the passage of the laws in England hampering kidnapping of persons for indentures noted above. Another was the formation of the Royal African Company in England in 1672. Granted a monopoly by King Charles II, this company vigorously pushed the slave trade. When Virginia colonists became alarmed at the great increase in the slave population, by 1772 this company had used its influence to get the king to veto some twenty-three laws that the Virginia assembly passed from time to time to discourage the slave trade. So, with the aid of the Royal African Company, slavery grew in Virginia. In 1708, there were 12,000 slaves to 18,000 whites. In 1756, the 120,000 blacks (less than 3,000 of whom were free) constituted 41 percent of the total population in Virginia of 293,000.

African slaves were a vital labor force on the tobacco farms and plantations of Virginia and of the neighboring colony of Maryland. Maryland was unlike Virginia in that the blacks who entered soon after the colony's founding in 1634 were apparently regarded as slaves from the outset. Yet, as in Virginia, the first law in Maryland recognizing slavery did not come until later in 1664. This law of 1664 in Maryland stated that

All negroes or other slaves already within the province and all negroes and other slaves to be hereafter imported into the province shall serve during their lives and all children born of any negro or other slave shall be slaves as their fathers were for the term of their lives, and forasmuch as several freeborn English women forgetful of their free condition and to the disgrace of our nation do intermarry with negro slaves . . . be it further enacted . . . that all the issue of such free-born women so married shall be slaves as their fathers were.

By 1750, the colony of Maryland had 40,000 black residents, or 29 percent of the total population of 140,000.

Settled about 1654 by poorer migrants coming out of Virginia, the colony of North Carolina had the smallest percentage of blacks among Southern colonies. More of North Carolina's people tended to be small, independent farmers than in the neighboring colonies of Virginia and South Carolina. Thus, there were fewer large plantations and fewer slaves. In 1760, the 16,000 blacks in North Carolina constituted only 17 percent of that colony's total population of 93,000.

Throughout the colonial period and on until the end of the Civil War, Virginia had a larger number of Negroes in its population, in absolute figures, than any other colony or state. South Carolina, however, was the only colony with a black majority. In 1763, a century after it was chartered, South Carolina had a population of 70,000 blacks and 30,000 whites, making Afro-Americans 70 percent of the total population.

Slavery was sanctioned in South Carolina from the start. The eight proprietors who received a charter from King Charles II in 1663 selected John Locke to draft a constitution for their colony. The man who was to become the famed political theorist of the doctrine of human liberty provided in Article 110 of The Fundamental Constitutions of Carolina that "Every freeman of Carolina, shall have absolute power and authority over his negro slaves. . . ." However, this constitution of 1669 was too elaborate and feudalistic in nature, and was not put into effect.

The first settlement in the colony was established at Charleston in 1670. The cultivation of rice was introduced in 1694. The colony had a great need for slave labor on its extensive rice plantations. Since four of the eight proprietors were also directors of the Royal African Company formed in 1672 to monopolize the slave trade, they had a vested interest in pushing the institution of slavery in their colony.

Fears developed, however, because of the large number of blacks in the population. Laws were passed to keep the slaves under control. These laws, similar to slave codes in other English colonies and in Latin America, placed restrictions on the movements of slaves, sought to prevent them from assembling and plotting, denied them the right to possess weapons, and provided severe penalties for any insubordination. For example, the South Carolina Slave Code of 1712 provided that "every master . . . shall cause all his negro houses to be searched diligently and effectually once every fourteen days for fugitive and runaway slaves, guns, swords, clubs, and any other mischievous weapons." This code also provided:

That if any negroes or other slaves shall make mutiny or insurrection, or rise in rebellion against the authority and government of this Province, or shall make preparation of arms powder, bullets or offensive weapons, in order to carry on such mutiny or insurrection, or shall hold any counsel or conspiracy for raising such mutiny, insurrection or rebellion, the offenders shall be tried by two justices of the peace and three freeholders . . . who are hereby empowered and required to try the said slaves so offending, and inflict death, or any other punishment, upon the offenders. . . .

The passage of such a severe slave code, however, did not stop the Negroes from rebelling. One such insurrection was the Cato Conspiracy that took place in 1739 at a plantation called Stono some twenty miles from Charleston. According to one account: "A number of negroes having assembled together at Stono first surprised and killed two young men in a warehouse, and then plundered it of guns and ammunition. Being thus provided with arms, they elected one of their number captain . . . marching towards the south-west with colours flying and drums beating. . . . In their way they plundered and burnt every house." These blacks were marching toward freedom in Florida where the Spaniards provided liberty for slaves fleeing from the English colonists. Militia forces caught up with them, however, stopping them before they could make good their escape. They had marched some twelve miles before being halted. Some thirty whites were killed by the black rebels, and some forty-four blacks perished in the fighting or were executed after trials.

James E. Oglethorpe (1696–1785) founded Georgia in 1733 to give worthwhile imprisoned debtors a new start in life. He planned to have his colonists concentrate on products that England had to import from tropical countries, including silk, oranges, grapes, and olives. He and his fellow proprietors forbade slavery and black residents; prohibited rum, brandy, and other strong drinks; and restricted landholding.

Oglethorpe was not opposed to slavery; he was a director of the Royal African Company formed in 1672 to monopolize English slave-trading. But blacks and slavery had no place in his utopia. Slavery would lead to dissension and inequality among white settlers. Slaves would have to be guarded, diminishing Georgia's role as a military buffer for Carolina against attacks from Spanish Florida. Without a staple crop like tobacco or rice or sugar, slave labor was not needed; even women and children could tend the silkworms and mulberry trees. And if Georgia had no Negro residents, runaway slaves from South Carolina could be more easily detected.

From the outset, the colonists complained about these restrictions and petitioned for their removal. They evaded them by smuggling in strong "spirits" and by hiring blacks from South Carolina for 100-year terms. Oglethorpe relented, ending his experiment: alcohol was permitted in 1742, slave-holding in 1749, and unrestricted land ownership in 1750. By 1760, one-third of Georgia's 9,000 residents were black.

Southerners felt that they needed slaves; some New Englanders also yearned for them. In 1645, Emanuel Downing of the Massachusetts Bay Colony wrote to his brother-in-law, John Winthrop, who was the Governor of Massachusetts:

I do not see how we can thrive until we get in a stock of slaves sufficient to do all our business, for our children's children will hardly see this great Continent filled with people, so that our [white indentured] servants will still desire freedom to plant for themselves, and not stay but for very great wages. And I suppose you will very well see how we shall maintain 20 moors [Negro slaves] cheaper than one English servant.

All of the New England colonies had slaves, Massachusetts as early as 1638. The Puritans rationalized that heathen blacks would learn from Christian masters. Most of the slaves in New England were household servants, dockworkers, or urban laborers. Rhode Island had the most Negroes among the four New England colonies: by 1760, blacks were 12 percent of the population of Rhode Island (4,700 blacks to 36,000 whites), 3 percent in Connecticut (3,600 blacks to 128,000 whites), 2 percent in Massachusetts (4,500 blacks to 195,000 whites), and only 1 percent in New Hampshire (633 blacks to 52,000 whites).

The New England colonies, especially Rhode Island, were involved in the slave trade. Vessels returning with unsold Africans added to Rhode Island's black population. The Brown brothers of Providence, Rhode Island, Nicholas and Moses, were merchants and manufacturers who at one time engaged in the slave trade. Moses Brown (1738–1836) was a partner in America's first factory, set up in Pawtucket, Rhode Island, in 1790. By then, he had become a Quaker, had stopped participating in the slave trade, and had helped establish an abolition society. As a result of the generosity of Nicholas Brown and other members of his family, Rhode Island College was moved from Warren to Providence and was later renamed Brown University.

Slavery was much milder in New England than in the other colonies. Nonetheless, slave plots and insurrections took place there also at such places as Hartford, Connecticut, in 1658, and Charlestown, Massachusetts, in 1741.

New York had the largest black population among Middle Atlantic colonies. In 1756, its 13,500 blacks constituted 14 percent of the 96,500 residents. New Jersey, with 4,700 Negroes and 57,000 whites, was 8 percent black in 1745. Afro-Americans were only 2 percent of Pennsylvania's population: 10,300 blacks to 424,000 whites in 1790.

Delaware may be classified with either the Middle Atlantic or the Southern colonies. Geographically and politically, it belonged with the Middle Atlantic colonies. Founded by the Swedes in 1638, seized by the Dutch in 1655, and taken over by the English in 1664, Delaware was granted to William Penn in 1682, making it part of the colony of Pennsylvania. In 1701, Delaware was granted a separate legislature, but it continued to have the same governor as Pennsylvania until 1776, when it became completely separated. But its climate and its tobacco economy made Delaware a Southern colony. Hence, it is no surprise that Delaware developed a large slave population. By 1790, Delaware was 22 percent black, with 12,800 Negroes to 46,000 Caucasians.

When New York was the Dutch colony of New Netherland, from 1624 to 1664, "half-freedom" grants elevated some slaves to a contractual status. This is described in *A History of Negro Slavery in New York*, by Dr. Edgar McManus, Professor of History at Queens College of the City University of New York. Professor McManus pointed out that

the system of half-freedom under which slaves were conditionally released from bondage . . . was introduced into New Netherland by the [Dutch] West India Company as a means of rewarding slaves for long meritorious service. Slaves who enjoyed half-freedom enjoyed full personal liberty in return for an annual tribute to the Company and a promise to perform labor at certain times. . . . the half-freedmen were given passes which certified them to be free and at liberty on the same footing as other free people.

The system, he continued, "enabled slave owners to be free of the cost and petty nuisances of slave holding while reserving the right to specific labor from their former bondsman." The system worked because it was provided in the half-freedom passes "that freedmen who defaulted" by failing to live up to the terms of the agreement "lost their freedom and returned back into the said Company's slavery." The system was convenient for the masters and was popular among the slaves because "Half-freedom was better than no freedom, and there were few slaves indeed who did not prefer it to absolute servitude." This pragmatic and flexible form of slavery showed that there were alternatives to slavery as it developed among the thirteen English mainland colonies and the United States. The English, when they gained control of the Dutch colony in 1664, dropped this interesting experiment that blurred the line between freedom and slavery and that converted slavery into a contractual obligation.

New Yorkers feared slave plots. In 1712, rebellious slaves set a fire on the outskirts of New York City and then ambushed whites racing to the scene. Although the revolt was crushed and twenty-one slaves executed, panic prevailed. In 1741, a robbery investigation led to a white tavern owner, John Hughson, who included blacks among his patrons and who evidently helped black burglars dispose of their stolen goods. Hughson's Irish indentured servant, Mary Burton, told investigators of plots being hatched in the tavern to overthrow the government of New York, with Hughson to become king and a black named Caesar to become governor.

The authorities believed her incredible tale, especially because of mysterious fires that broke out in various parts of the city at this time. They arrested persons she named. These cooperated, accusing others to save themselves. After trials in an atmosphere of hysteria, without any defense lawyers to assist the defendants overcome the unfair and prejudicial prosecution tactics, thirty-five persons were executed, including Hughson and his wife. Of those given the extreme penalty, eighteen blacks and four whites were hanged and thirteen blacks were burned alive. Another seventy blacks were deported from the colony. Far fewer persons were executed in the well-known Salem witch trials of 1692 than in this New York panic of 1741. At Salem, only twenty were executed, nineteen by hanging and one by being pressed to death. Officials finally realized that Mary Burton was lying when she began to accuse prominent persons who could not possibly have been involved. To save face, however, the city council passes a resolution thanking her for saving the city from this slave plot. Moreover, when she stepped forward to claim the reward that had been offered, they had to give it to her to prevent their gullibility from being revealed.

But, although English colonists became fearful of the mass of blacks in the thirteen colonies after adopting African slavery as the most profitable solution to their labor problem, in the revolutionary atmosphere of the last third of the eighteenth century, whites would develop a new appreciation for individual blacks.

CHAPTER EIGHT

SLAVERY: As Practiced in the Thirteen Colonies

Slavery as an institution had a de facto or de jure status in all of the thirteen colonies. In the southern colonies blacks were permanently enslaved very early because a labor force for the tobacco and rice fields was needed. In the middle colonies blacks were not legally enslaved but worked in the mines and fields and in the lumber industry under slavelike conditions. The blacks of New England also were assigned a de facto slave status as workers in the construction and maritime industries. The treatment of blacks varied in each colony. The presence of Quakers and educated whites had a moderating impact on slavery in most of the original colonies.

Who Came?

Page Smith

The inhabitants of the thirteen colonies came from a variety of places and backgrounds in western Europe. These people represented every class and condition of humanity. The Europeans came to America for a variety of reasons. Some came voluntarily for adventure, wealth, or freedom from religious persecution, and some came involuntarily. The early settlements of these colonists could be found from the rocky, frigid shores of Massachusetts to the sunny beaches of South Carolina and Georgia.

The indentured servants, many of whom were from prisons, crossed the Atlantic from Europe under the most severe conditions. Former convicts were chained below deck and lived under crowded conditions that were described as being "just a little better" than living conditions on slave ships. Many who had already settled here believed that the prosperity and safety of the colonies were endangered by the continuous stream of transported felons.

Page Smith's lively account of the diverse classes of people who came to the New World, excerpted from his book, *A New Age Now Begins*, follows.

The American colonists came from a variety of backgrounds, as we have seen. What united them was the wilderness to which they came, a vast land inhabited by two hundred thousand or so aborigines—native tribes of different languages and social customs to whom the settlers from the Old World gave the general and misleading name of "Indians." The land to which they came was, literally, incomprehensible; it reached beyond the mind's imagining, threatening and promising, larger than all of Europe: coastal shelf and then mountains and endless plains and more mountains and, finally, the Pacific. No one could measure its extent. The English settlers for their part clung to its eastern margins, to the seacoast strip that faced the ocean highway to the Old World. Even here there were terrains, climates, and topographies as dramatically different as one could imagine—from the rocky, frigid shores of New Hampshire to the sunny beaches of South Carolina.

There was a kind of mad presumption about the whole venture: a few thousand, and then a few hundred thousand, and finally a few million souls scattered along almost two thousand miles of coastline. And in truth it could be said that those who made this strange odyssey to the New World were as diverse as the land they inhabited. Those from England itself represented every class and condition of men. And then there were the Swedes, who settled on the Delaware long before William Penn and his followers arrived, and the stolid and intractable Dutch, reputed to have bought Manhattan from the aborigines for a few strings of beads —the most famous real estate deal in history. And the French Huguenots, Protestants fleeing from persecution in a Catholic country; the Catholics of Maryland, fleeing persecution in a Protestant country; the Quakers, fleeing the harassments of the Anglican establishment, the Church of England; and Germans from innumerable principalities, fleeing military draft and the various exactions of petty princes.

Within the British Isles themselves—Ireland, Scotland, England, and Wales— there was striking diversity among the New World emigrants. The Separatists— the Pilgrims under William Bradford—wanted, in essence, to be separate; the Puritans wanted to found a Bible Commonwealth and redeem a fallen world. When Cromwell and the Puritans dominated England and beheaded Charles I, certain Royalists found refuge in Virginia and New York. When the restoration of the monarchy brought Charles II to the English throne and re-established the Stuart line, the regicides—those involved in the execution of Charles I—found refuge in Puritan New England. When the Scottish Covenanters, or Presbyterians, so akin in spirit to the Puritans of New England, rose against the highhanded and tyrannical actions of the re-established monarchy, they were crushingly defeated by the Duke of Monmouth at Bothwell Bridge in 1679 and cruelly repressed. Many, in consequence, came to America. And they continued to come for a hundred years.

When the Stuart dynasty was succeeded by the Hanoverian line, beginning with the reign of George I in 1714, the Scottish Highlanders, a very different breed from the Lowland Covenanters, took up the cause of the Stuart claimants to the throne of England. Finally, in 1745, the supporters of the so-called Young Pretender, Charles Edward, rallied to his cause; but after three initial victories they were destroyed at Culloden in April of 1746. In the aftermath of this disaster, many of the Scottish Highlanders found refuge in America on the Carolina frontier.

And then there were the Irish. They were a special case. They fled famine and rent-wracking landlords. They fled Cromwell and his Roundheads; then they fled Charles II as they had earlier fled Cromwell. A Catholic people, they fled their Protestant masters. But above all they fled poverty, the poverty of a ruthlessly exploited peasantry. Generation after generation, the Irish came to the American colonies, primarily to Maryland and Pennsylvania, where they gravitated to the frontier areas. In addition to the Catholic Irish, Scotch-Irish Presbyterians came in substantial numbers to the colonies throughout the eighteenth century. The Scotch-Irish were those Covenanters, or militant Presbyterians, who had been forced by the bitter divisions in Scotland itself to seek the protection of the English armies in Northern Ireland (hence Scotch-Irish). For many of them, Ireland was little more than a way station to the colonies, where they showed a marked preference for Pennsylvania and settled, typically, on the frontier.

Like the Scotch-Irish, the Welsh, many of them Quakers, made Penn's colony their common destination. There they founded prosperous communities and took a leading role in the affairs of the colony.

So the immigrants came in an ever-growing tide—the hungry, the oppressed, the contentious, the ambitious, those out of power and out of favor, the losers, whether in the realm of politics or of economics. And America could accommodate them all: Irish peasant and his land-poor master, Scottish Highlander and Lowlander, persecuted Protestant and persecuted Catholic, fortune-seeker and God-seeker, they found their places, their kinfolk, the familiar accents of their home shires or counties or countries.

But the essence of them all, of all that human congress, the bone and marrow, the unifying principle, the prevailing and pervasive spirit was English. Like the others who came, the English came, as we have already noted, for a number of reasons. Most of them shared some particular expectation, whether for spiritual or material betterment or, happily, both. Many of those who came later shared, of course, the hopes of the original settlers. Many more came because conditions were desperately hard in England and Ireland for poor people, even for those who had not yet sunk into the pit of abandoned hopelessness that was the lot of the most wretched.

It has been estimated that London in the eighteenth century had 6,000 adult and 9,300 child beggars. In the entire country of some 10,000,000 persons, there were estimated to be 50,000 beggars, 20,000 vagrants, 10,000 idlers, 100,000 prostitutes, 10,000 rogues and vagabonds, 80,000 criminals, 1,041,000 persons on parish relief. Indeed, over half the population was below what we would call today "the poverty line," and many, of course, were profoundly below it—below it to the point of starvation. An estimate of the different classes—and class lines were almost impassable—in 1688 suggests that nobility, gentry, merchants, professionals, freeholders (those who held land on their own), craftsmen, and public officials constituted 47 per cent of the population; while common sailors and soldiers (recruited, for the most part, from the lowest levels of British society and enduring desperately hard conditions of service), laborers, servants, paupers, and all those other remarkable subdivisions that we have listed above such as rogues and vagrants made up 53 per cent of the population. The colonies, for their part, had a virtually inexhaustible demand for labor. Anyone willing to work could be put to worthwhile labor, and might (and often did) in a few years establish himself as an independent farmer or artisan.

Yet it was one thing to be an undernourished London apprentice who hated his master and another to find a way to get to America. Some indication of the situation of the working class in the larger cities may be discerned from the condition of pauper children in London in the early eighteenth century. Orphaned, or more frequently illegitimate and abandoned at birth, they were sent to workhouses and to parish nurses. A Parliamentary study found that of all such infants born or received in London's workhouses in a three-year period, only seven in every hundred were alive at the end of that time. As part of the "surcharge of necessitous people," orphaned and impoverished children who were public charges were sporadically dispatched to the colonies as indentured servants. People worked, typically, from six in the morning until eight at night for a pittance that barely supported life. They had no holidays except at Christmas, Easter, and on hanging days, when everyone might be entertained and edified by watching wretches hanged for crimes that, in many instances, would be classed as misdemeanors today.

Despite the cruelty of punishments, London had a large criminal class and was infested with prostitutes. The working class drowned its miseries in bad gin and beer. There were some 7,000 ginshops in the suburbs of London and, by 1750, 16,000 in the city itself (only 1,050 of which were licensed); most of them were in the poorest sections of the city, whose horrors are vividly recorded in Hogarth's etchings of Gin Lane. The hard liquor consumed in one year (1733) in London alone amounted to 11,200,000 gallons, or some 56 gallons per adult male.

Next to public hangings, the principal entertainments available to the poor—and enjoyed by the rich as well—were cockfighting, bullbaiting, and badger baiting. In such circumstances there was ample incentive to emigrate almost anywhere. In the words of a seventeenth-century historian of Virginia: "Now let me turn back and look upon my poore spirited countrymen in England and examine first the meanest, that is the poore ploughman, day labourer and poore Artificer [it is doubtful, indeed, if they were "the meanest"] and I shall find them labouring and sweating all dayes of their lives; some for fourteen pence, others for sixteen, eighteen, twenty pence or two shillings a day; which is the highest of wages to such kind of people, and the most of them to end their dayes in sorrow, not having purchased so much by their lives labour as will scarce preserve them in their old days from beggery." But to the penniless, the question was: How? The growing need for labor in the colonies supplied the answer, and a system of indenture, based on the long-established apprenticeship, was devised. Agents paid for the ship's passage of improvident men and women who were willing to contract themselves in America to work off the cost of their transportation. By this means, tens of thousands of English and Irish workers of both sexes found their way across the ocean.

The system was easily and often abused. A class of men "of the lowest order," called spirits and crimps, arose, who spirited away unwilling lads and sold them into bondage. A contemporary wrote: ". . . there are always plenty of agents hovering like birds of prey on the banks of the Thames, eager in their search for such artisans, mechanics, husbandmen and labourers, as are inclinable to direct their course for America," Another man wrote, "Well may he be called a spirit, since his nature is like the devil's, to seduce any he meets withal, whom he can persuade with allurements and deluding falsities to his purpose." One spirit boasted that he had been spiriting persons for twelve years at a rate of five hundred persons a year. He would give twenty-five shillings to anyone who would bring him a likely prospect, and he could sell such a one to a merchant at once for forty shillings. Often spiriting was a profitable sideline for a brewer, hostler, carpenter, or tavern keeper. The tavern keeper was in an especially advantageous position, since a drunken patron was an easy victim. So dreaded were these dismal agents that mothers frightened their children into obedience by warning them that a spirit would carry them off if they were bad. It was no idle threat. In 1653 Robert Broome secured a warrant for the arrest of a ship's captain charged with carrying off his son, aged eleven, who had been spirited aboard. A few years later, a commission going aboard the *Conquer* found that eleven out of nineteen servants had been "taken by the spirits." Their average age was nineteen. Not all spirits were depraved men, however, and even the worst of them often performed a useful service in arranging transportation for a servant who wished to emigrate to the colonies against the wishes of parents or a master. In the words of the historian Abbott Smith: "A much larger proportion of our colonial population than is generally supposed found itself on American soil because of the wheedlings, deceptions, misrepresentations and other devices of the 'spirits'; a very small proportion indeed were carried away forcibly and entirely against their wills."

Hugh Jones, in *The Present State of Virginia,* published in 1724, put the matter succinctly: "What shoals of beggars are allowed in Great Britain to suffer their bodies to rust and consume with laziness and want?" England was "over-stocked . . . with vast numbers of people of all trades and professions." But few of them were ready to try their fortunes in America. These people were ideal material for the colonies, but they had a "home fondness" and a suspicion of foreign lands that made them reluctant to leave the mother country. This sentiment had "retarded the plantations from being stocked with such inhabitants as are skillful, industrious, and laborious. . . ." Instead, America had received, for the most part, "the servants and inferior sort of people, who have either been sent over to Virginia, or have transported themselves thither, have been, and are, the poorest, idlest, and worst of mankind, the refuse of Great Britain and Ireland, and the outcast of the people." It seemed ironic to Jones that "the vilest of mankind" must be utilized for the "noblest and most useful undertakings."

For a time it proved easier to get women servants than men servants (or as they were called earlier, before the word began to be associated with blacks in permanent servitude, "slaves"). Mathew Cradock, captain of the *Abraham,* sailing for Virginia, made elaborate preparations for carrying a shipload of servants, men and women alike, to Virginia on a four-year indenture. On his ship's arrival in various English ports, he "caused the drume to be Betten, and gave warning to all those that disposed to goe servants for Virginea. . . ." By such means, he rounded up forty-one men and twenty women, the latter "from 17 to 35 yeares and very lustye and strong Boddied which I will hopp," the captain wrote, "be meyns to sett them of to the best Advantiag . . . and for women they are now Reddear to goe then men, whereof we ar furnished with as many as we have rome."

Clothing, "peppar and Gingar," and three-and-a-half pounds of tobacco for the men were all purchased before the ship set sail, and a midwife was hired to make sure none of the women were pregnant. Soon after the ship sailed it was driven into the harbor of Cowes, and it was a month before it got favorable winds. By that time, three of the women were pregnant and were sent home; some who were put ashore to do the washing ran away and had to be tracked down at a cost of ten shillings; and another was found "not fette to be entertained havinge the frentche dizeas," and was sent packing.

If a female indentured servant became pregnant during her service, her misdeed represented a loss to her master, so that an indentured servant guilty of bastardy was required to pay the usual charges levied against unwed mothers as well as to indemnify her master for the loss of her services during the later stages of her pregnancy and her lying-in. Not infrequently, the master was the culprit. In Maryland, Jacob Lumbrozo, a Portuguese Jew, alias Dr. John, was charged with having made persistent overtures to his maid, Elisabeth Weales, and when rebuffed, "hee tooke her in his armes and threw her upon the bed she went to Cry out hee plucked out his handerchif of his pocket and stope her mouth and force her whether shee will or noe when hee know that she was with Child hee gave her fickes to distroy it and for anything shee know hee would distroy her too. . . ." By the time the case came to court, Lumbrozo had married Elisabeth Weales, who became a prominent if contentious figure in the affairs of the county. In Virginia, a statute was passed to prevent a master who had impregnated his servant girl from claiming extra service from her beyond her indenture: "Late experiments shew that some dissolute masters have gotten their maides with child, and yet claime the benefitt of their service." However, the maid got off no better. After the end of her indenture she was to be sold by the church wardens for the use of the parish for two years.

One depot for the collection of servants to be sold in the colonies was at St. Katherine's, near the Tower of London. Here a kidnaper would bring his victim, who might be forcibly detained for a month before the master of a ship would carry him off. We have a contemporary account of such a dive. After the kidnaper asked his intended victim "many impertinent questions, he invited me to drink with him. . . . He brought into a Room where half a score were all taking Tobacco: the place was so narrow wherein they were, that they had no more space left, than what was for the standing of a small table. Methought their mouths together resembled a stack of chimneys, being in a manner totally obscured by the smoak that came from them: for there was little discernable but smoak, and the flowing coals of their pipes. . . . After I had been there awhile, the Cloud of their smoak was somewhat dissipated, so that I could discern two more in my own condemnation: but alas poor Sheep, they ne'er considered where they were going, it was enough for them to be freed from a seven years Apprenticeship, under the Tyranny of a rigid master . . . and not weighing . . . the slavery they must undergo for five years amongst Brutes in foreign parts, little inferior to that which they suffer who are *Gally-slaves.* There was little discourse amongst them, but of the pleasantness of the soyl of that Continent we were designed for, (out of design to make us swallow their gilded Pills of Ruine), & the temperature of the Air, the plentry of Fowl and Fish of all sorts; the little labour that is performed or expected having so little trouble in it, that it may be accounted a pastime than anything of punishment; and then to sweeten us the farther, they insisted on the pliant loving natures of the women there; all which they used to bait us silly Gudgeons. . . ."

In the words of the mayor of Bristol, "Among those who repair to Bristol from all parts to be transported to his majesty's Plantations beyond seas, some are husbands that have forsaken their wives, others wives who have abandoned their husbands, some are children and apprentices run away from their parents and masters, often times unwary and credulous persons have been tempted on board by men-stealers, and many that have been pursued by the hue-and-cry for robberies, burglaries or breaking prison, do thereby escape the prosecution of law and justice."

The terms of indenture required the master to provide food and clothing for his servants and, often in the case of German or Swiss servants, to take the responsibility for seeing that they learned English during the term of their indenture. At the end of their terms they were to be provided with a stated sum of money and a suit of presentable clothes so that they could make a proper start in life. South Carolina required that a female servant at the expiration of her service be given a waistcoast and petticoat, a new shift of white linen, shoes and stockings, a blue apron and two white linen caps. In some colonies, indentured servants received land at the end of their term of indenture. Thus in North Carolina during the proprietary period a servant's "freedom dues" were fifty acres of land and afterward three barrels of Indian corn and two new suits of a value of at least five pounds. Maryland made generous provision for "one good Cloth suite of Keirsy or broad cloth a Shift of white linen one new pair of stockings and Shoes two hoes one axe 3 barrels of Corne and fifty acres of land . . . women Servants a Years Provision of Corne and a like proportion of Cloth & Land."

It was also true, according to one John Hammond, writing in 1656, that some servants received these benefits before the end of their indenture. "Those servants that will be industrious," Hammond wrote, "may in their time of service gain a competent estate before their freedoms, which is usually done by many, and they gain esteem and assistance that appear so industrious. . . . He may have cattle, hogs, and tobacco of his own, and come to live gallantly; but this must be gained . . . by industry and affability, not by sloth nor churlish behavior."

That there was another side of the coin is indicated by a letter from an indentured servant to her father in 1756: "What we unfortunat English People suffer here is beyond the probability of you in England to Conceive, let it suffice that I am one of the unhappy Number, am toiling almost Day and Night, and very often in the Horses druggery, with only this comfort that you Bitch you do not halfe enough, and then tied up and whipp'd to that Degree that you'd not serve an Animal, scarce anything but Indian Corn and Salt to eat and that even begrudged nay many Negroes are better used, almost naked no shoes nor stockings to wear . . . what rest we can get is to rap ourselves up in a Blanket an ly upon the Ground."

Whether wickedly abused or treasured and rewarded—and certainly they experienced both cruelty and kindness—indentured servants made up more than half the immigrants to the middle and southern colonies. During the twenty-five-year period between 1750 and 1775, some 25,000 servants and convicts entered Maryland, and a comparable number arrived in Virginia. Abbott Smith estimates that during the same period at least twice as many servants and redemptioners entered Pennsylvania, of whom perhaps a third were German and the rest, in large part, Irish. The Irish, in addition to being contentious, dirty, and strongly inclined to drink, were Catholics. To Protestants, this fact made the Irish the least desirable of all immigrant groups. The more substantial class of immigrants, especially the Germans and the Swiss, came as redemptioners. Redemptioners were carried to America by a ship captain with the understanding that after they reached the colonies, they would undertake to sell themselves to the highest bidder and then pay the captain the cost of their passage. Most of the redemptioners were craftsmen whose skills were much in demand in the colonies and who could thus sell themselves on favorable terms to a master. If they could not sell themselves, it was the shipmaster's right to undertake to sell them, often at highly disadvantageous terms. Since a master could buy much cheaper from a ship captain, collusion between prospective buyers and the captain was not uncommon.

The story of indentured servants is one of the most dramatic in colonial America. While many of those who came under indenture were the "scum and offscourings of the earth"—convicts, paupers, runaway apprentices, prostitutes, and the like—many, particularly among the non-English, were respectable and decent people who had fallen on hard times or simply wished to improve their fortunes. We also know that in the rude conditions of colonial life, many of the dissolute were redeemed.

In seventeenth- and eighteenth-century England, crime was endemic. The alarm of the more prosperous classes was expressed in cries for law and order. The penalty of death was prescribed for all felonies. In seventeenth-century England, almost three hundred crimes were classed as felonies; a conviction for anything, indeed, from house-breaking and the theft of goods worth more than a shilling must result in the sentence of death by hanging, since the judge had no discretionary power in felony cases. The benefit of clergy and royal pardon were the only mitigations. A convicted felon could "call for the book," usually a Bible, and if he could read it, he was freed of the penalty of death, branded on the thumb, and released. The practice stemmed from medieval times, when generally speaking only those in holy orders were able to read, and they were subject to their own ecclesiastical courts. The benefit of clergy was undoubtedly a great incentive to the development of a literate criminal class, but in a time when the vast majority of the poor were illiterate, it had little else to recommend it. The simple fact was that if you were poor and illiterate you might be hanged for stealing a few shillings' worth of cloth, while a villainous cutpurse who could decipher a simple text would be branded and then would go free.

In 1705, Parliament, conscious of the absurdity as well as the injustice of the practice, came up with a typically English solution that permitted a felon to plead benefit of clergy even though he could not read, but at the same time set forth a list of some twenty-five felonies that were "nonclergyable," among them petty treason, arson, murder, burglary, stealing more than the value of a shilling, and highway robbery. Other offenses were added periodically until by 1769 there were 169 crimes classified as felonies for which there was no relief in pleading benefit of clergy.

The royal pardon was the only amelioration of a murderous system. Again in a typically English accommodation, judges who thought sentences too severe could send up a list of those convicted felons they considered worthy of mercy, and these would be pardoned by the king. For many years more than half of those sentenced to hang were pardoned, and increasingly it came to be the practice to issue such pardons on the condition that the culprit agreed to leave the country. From the middle of the seventeenth century until early in the eighteenth, thousands of convicts left England under this arrangement. Of these, a substantial majority found their way to the English colonies in the West Indies and in North America. In 1717, Parliament passed a law permitting the "transportation" out of the realm of certain classes of offenders "in clergy." From 1619 to 1640 all felons reprieved by royal pardon were transported to Virginia to help make up the toll of those settlers lost by disease, and between 1661 and 1700 more than 4,500 convicts were dispatched to the colonies. In the years from 1745 to 1775, 8,846 convicts, 9,035 servants, and 3,324 slaves landed at Annapolis, Maryland.

Convicts were certainly not ideal settlers. In one contingent, twenty-six had been convicted for stealing, one for violent robbery, and five for murder. Stephen Bumpstead stole a grey gelding worth forty-six shillings and was sentenced to death, Richard Enos stole a silver cup, Jacob Watkins removed a necktie from a victim in Thames Street at ten o'clock at night, and Charles Atley, a young child, stole twenty-eight shillings and eleven pence. The character of such settlers is indicated by the career of Jenny Voss, who was eventually hanged at Tyburn after having been transported to the colonies, where "she could not forget her old Pranks, but used not only to steal herself, but incited all others that were her fellow Servants to Pilffer and Cheat," so that her master was glad to be rid of her, the more so since "she had wheadled in a Son of the Planters, who used to Lye with her and supply her with Moneys. . . ."

Virginia and Maryland, which had been the principal outlets for transported felons, had passed laws forbidding their importation by the end of the seventeenth century. The Virginia House of Burgesses reported "the complaints of several of the council and others, gent. inhabitants . . . representing their apprehensions and fears lest the honor of his majesty and the peace of this colony be too much hazarded and endangered by the great numbers of felons and other desperate villains sent hither from the several prisons in England. . . ." But despite such protests, Parliament in 1717 passed a statute that overrode colonial efforts to stem the tide of undesirables. A total of thirty thousand convicted felons were shipped from England in the fifty-year period prior to the Revolution, of whom the greater number apparently went to Maryland and Virginia. Since convicts were bound into servitude for seven or fourteen years, which often proved to be a lifetime, the colonists usually bid actively for the most likely ones. The men sold for from eight to twenty pounds or, roughly, twenty-five to fifty dollars. Women brought slightly less, while the old and infirm were given away or, if no taker could be found, a subsidy was paid to anyone who would take them in.

It was not a humane or enlightened system, and the most that can be said for it is that the majority of the transported felons who were sold into white semislavery were slightly better off alive than dead. For those who escaped their masters, fled to other colonies, and established themselves as respectable citizens, it was a handsome bargain. Those willing to work, and fortunate enough to have a kind master, had a far better life than the one they had left behind in England. It is safe to surmise that a substantially higher proportion of women than men were redeemed to a decent life—from which it would presumably follow that a substantial number of Americans who trace their line of descent back to colonial times have an ancestress or two who arrived here as a convicted felon, a sneak thief, or a prostitute.

Three or four times a year, the convicts to be transported were marched in irons through the streets of London from Newgate Prison to Blackfriars. This procession provided, like hangings, a popular form of entertainment for mobs who would hoot at the convicts and, when the convicts replied with obscene epithets, sometimes pelt them with mud and stones. The more prosperous convicts could buy special privileges. Thus in 1736, four felons rode to the point of embarkation in two hackney coaches, and another, "a Gentleman of Fortune, and a Barrister at Law," convicted of stealing books from the Trinity College library, had a private coach to carry him in style. These men paid their own passage and shared a private cabin.

Besides the large number of convicted felons, there were many other Englishmen who fell in the rather commodious category of "rogues and vagabonds." Although they came from a very different economic stratum, these were the hippies and dropouts of seventeenth- and eighteenth-century English society, the men and women so alienated from the dominant culture that they had devised their own. They lived on the margins of the law, devoted to preying in a thousand ingenious ways on the public. A statute of Parliament defined them as "all persons calling themselves Schollers going about begging, all Seafaring men pretending losses of their Shippes or goods on the sea going about the Country begging, all idle persons going about in any Country eyther begging or using any subtile Crafts or unlawfull Games and Playes, or fayning themselves to have knowledge in Phislognomya Palmestry or other like crafty Scyence, or pretending that they can tell Destenyes Fortunes or such other like fantasticall imagynacons; all persons that be or utter themselves to be Proctors Procurers Patent Gatherers or Collectors for Gaoles Prisons or Hospitalls; all Fencers Bearewards comon Players of Enterludes and Minstrells wandring abroade . . . all Juglers Tynkers Pedlers and Petty Chapmen wandring abroade; all wandring persons and comon Labourers . . . loytering and refusing to worcke for such reasonable wages as . . . comonly given in such Parts where such persons do . . . dwell or abide . . . all such persons as shall wander abroade begging pretending losses by Fyre or otherwise; and all such persons not being Fellons wandering and pretending themselves to be Egipcyans, or wandering in the Habite Forme or Attyre of counterfayte Egipcians." What services "counterfayte Egipcians" might have offered that should have made them such a menace, the statute does not reveal, but it does summon up an extraordinary picture of life in the latter part of the sixteenth century, when England was beginning to feel most acutely the results of the rural enclosures. Punishments were meant to be exemplary and painful. All beggars were to be stripped to the waist and whipped until they were bloody, then sent home or to the grim confines of a house of correction. Moreover, any rogue who appeared to be a hardened and dangerous character would be sent to such places beyond the seas as the Privy Council might designate.

By these provisions, incorrigible lawbreakers could be shipped out of the mother country even more readily than convicts throughout the colonial period. How "manie Drunkards, Tossepottes, whoremoisters, Dauncers, Fidlers and Minstrels, Diceplaiers, & Maskers" were dispatched to the colonies is not revealed by British court records. On the other hand, we know of enough charlatans, fortunetellers, minstrels, jugglers, tinkers, and actors in the colonies to assume that a good many of these roguish varieties made their way to America and provided lively if not always discreet entertainment for the less sophisticated colonists. What seems remarkable is that the colonies (like Virginia and Maryland) receiving the largest numbers of indentured servants and convicted felons were not utterly submerged and demoralized by these successive waves of human flotsam. Vicious and depraved as many of them must have been, the great majority made the adjustment to colonial life with reasonable success. Otherwise it is hard to see how these colonies could have survived, let alone prospered in their material and spiritual endeavors.

The transatlantic voyage from England to America was a terrible ordeal for most of those who made the crossing. Indentured servants signed up by crimps and spirits embarked on small, poorly equipped, and often dirty sailing vessels that took from one to as much as five months, depending on prevailing winds, to make the crossing. The *Sea-Flower,* with 106 passengers aboard, took sixteen weeks; forty-six of her passengers died of starvation, and of these, six were eaten by the desperate survivors. The long crossing meant bad food; the water stank and grew slimy, meat spoiled, and butter turned rancid. If the captain or owner was a profiteer, the food was often rotten to begin with. In small boats tossed by heavy seas, seasickness was commonplace. One passenger on such a crossing wrote a crude verse describing the effects of a storm on his fellow voyagers: Soon after the storm began, "there was the odest scene betwixt decks that I ever heard or seed. There was some sleeping, some spewing . . . some damning, some Blasting their legs and thighs, some their liver, lungs, lights and eyes. And for to make the scene the odder, some curs'd Father, Mother, Sister, and Brother."

A French Protestant named Durand sailed for Virginia after the revocation of the Edict of Nantes and the resumption of active persecution of the Huguenots. There were fifteen prostitutes on board ship, headed, hopefully, for a new life in the New World. During the passage, they spent their time singing and dancing and making love with the sailors and the indentured servants aboard. Durand, kept awake by their revels, wrote: "Certainly their insolence wrought a change in my nature, for my acquaintances would no doubt impute to me, as my greatest failing, an exaggerated love of the fair sex, & to tell the truth I must admit that in my youth there was no injustice in this accusation. Not that I was ever low enough or coarse enough to feel an affection for prostitutes, but I am obliged to confess I did not abhor their debauchery as I should have. . . . But when I saw those wenches behave so shockingly with the sailors and and others, in addition to the distress caused by their songs and dances, it awakened within me so intense a hatred of such persons that I shall never overcome it." Durand's wife died at sea, the food ran out, and the captain proved to be a knave and a bully. Their voyage took nineteen miserable weeks, long enough for weakness and hunger to quiet the gaiety of the prostitutes.

In the German principalities, the counterparts of the English "spirits" were the Newlanders, agents who tried to persuade guileless countryfolk to set sail for America. Gottlieb Mittelberger, a German immigrant from Enzweiningen who arrived in Philadelphia in 1750, gave a vivid account of his crossing of the Atlantic. He was bitter about the "sad and miserable condition of those traveling from Germany to the New World, and the irresponsible and merciless proceedings of the Dutch traders in human beings and their man-stealing emissaries— I mean the so-called Newlanders. For these at one and the same time steal German people under all sorts of fine pretexts, and deliver them into the hands of the great Dutch traffickers in human souls." The trip meant "for most who undertake it the loss of all they possess, of freedom and peace, and for some the loss of their very lives and, I can even go so far as to say, of the salvation of their souls." Mittelberger's journey took six months, the people "packed into the big boats as closely as herring. . . ." The water distributed to thirsty passengers was often "very black, thick with dirt and full of worms." Mittelberger's description of conditions on the ship refers to "smells, fumes, horrors, vomiting . . . boils, scurvy, cancer, mouthrot . . . caused by the age and the highly-salted state of the food, especially of the meat. . . . Add to all that shortage of food, hunger, thirst, frost, heat, dampness, fear, misery, vexation, and lamentation . . . so many lice

. . . that they have to be scraped off the bodies. All this misery reaches its climax when in addition to everything else one must suffer through two to three days and nights of storm . . . all the people on board pray and cry pitifully together." Under such circumstances, what little civility there might have been collapsed completely. People grew so bitter "that one person begins to curse the other, or himself and the day of his birth, and people sometimes come close to murdering one another. Misery and malice are readily associated, so that people begin to cheat and steal from one another." It is hardly surprising that America, when the immigrants reached it, seemed a land of deliverance: "When at last after the long and difficult voyage the ships finally approach land," Mittelberger wrote, "for the sight of which the people on board had longed so passionately, then everyone crawls from below to the deck, in order to look at the land. . . . And the people cry for joy, pray, and sing praises and thanks to God. The glimpse of land revives the passengers, especially those who are half-dead of illness. Their spirits, however weak they had become, leap up, triumph, and rejoice. . . ."

As difficult as were the conditions under which indentured servants and re-demptioners crossed the Atlantic, the circumstances of the prisoners were, as might be imagined, substantially worse. They were chained below decks in crowded, noisome ranks. One observer who went on board a convict ship to visit a prisoner wrote: "All the states of horror I ever had an idea of are much short of what I saw this poor man in; chained to a board in a hole not above sixteen feet long, more than fifty with him; a collar and padlock about his neck, and chained to five of the most dreadful creatures I ever looked on." Living conditions were little better than those obtaining on slave ships, and before the voyage was over it was not uncommon to lose a quarter of the human cargo, most frequently to the ravages of smallpox. (Only half as many women as men died on these hell ships, a fact attributed by merchants in the convict trade to their stronger consti-tutions.) Convicts so often arrived in the colonies more dead than alive that Parliamentary statutes finally set minimum allowances of bread, cheese, meat, oatmeal, and molasses per passenger—with two gills of gin issued on Saturdays.

The feelings of the colonists concerning the apparently endless stream of tran-sported feions and vagabonds are indicated by a passage in the *Virginia Gazette* of May 24, 1751: "When we see our Papers fill'd continually with Accounts of the most audacious Robberies, the most cruel Murders, and infinite other Vil-lanies perpetrated by Convicts transported from Europe," the correspondent wrote, "what melancholy, what terrible Reflections must it occasion! What will become of our Posterity? These are some of thy Favours, Britain! Thou are called our Mother Country; but what good Mother ever sent Thieves and Villains to accompany her children; to corrupt some with their infectious Vices and murder the rest? . . . In what can Britain show a more Sovereign contempt for us than by emptying their Jails into our Settlements. . . ." Whatever the colonists' feelings, the English were delighted with the practice of transporting their convicts to America. By such a procedure, the criminal was separated from evil companions and from the usually deplorable conditions that had induced him to take up a life of crime.

Not all convicts appreciated, by any means, the opportunity afforded them to start life over in the colonies. Not a few found their way back home (risking certain death, if caught) and declared that they would rather be hanged than return to America.

Servants and convicts who had served out their indentures often drifted to the frontier areas of the colonies, particularly to the southern frontier. Some took up cattle ranching in western Carolina, where the cattle were turned loose to graze, rounded up yearly into pens (hence Cowpens, South Carolina), and driven to the seacoast markets for meat and hides. Some, like the Hatfields and the McCoys, would in time feud with each other for decades; others lived lives of lawlessness and banditry, preying on staid planters in more settled areas and becoming, in some instances, the ancestors of the Southern mountain folk, who for successive generations resisted the incursions of tax collectors.

A number, of course, gathered in the seaport towns of Baltimore, Philadelphia, New York, Charles Town, and Boston, where they drank excessively, did occasional labor, committed petty crimes, rioted, and formed the nucleus of revolutionary mobs. The truth was that with few exceptions, they belonged to that class of people whose feelings lie very close to the surface. Violent and passionate by nature, they were peculiarly susceptible to both religious conversion and revolutionary ardor. Restless and rootless, they were readily swept up by any emotional storm. Many of them were converted at the time of the Great Awakening into pious Presbyterians, Methodists, and, somewhat later, Baptists. These denominations, with their emphasis on personal experience, were perfectly suited to the psychological needs of such individuals. Thus a substantial number of servants and ex-convicts accommodated themselves to the Protestant Ethic and became in time indistinguishable from their orthodox neighbors.

Less colorful, but equally important, were those settlers who came on their own initiative and at their own expense. By a process of natural selection, such individuals were usually aggressive, ambitious, and, as we would say today, highly motivated. Prominent among them were the Scotch-Irish, typically those Covenanters who had fled Scotland to escape the devastating and constant warfare with the Highland lairds supporting the cause of the Stuart Pretenders, and who had found Northern Ireland inhospitable. They sprang from the Lowland Scots —independent yeoman farmers who were stout Presbyterians, often shared a common Scottish aversion to the British, and were now removed in turn to the congenial atmosphere of the colonies, particularly Pennsylvania. Hardy, enterprising Calvinists, they made their way in large numbers westward, where land was plentiful and cheap. There, serving as "the guardians of the frontier," they were constantly embroiled with eastern land speculators or various Indian tribes over ownership of land.

There was a special affinity between native Lowland Scots and the inhabitants of the middle and eastern colonies. This led to a substantial immigration of Scotch-Irish in the middle years of the eighteenth century preceding the Revolutionary crisis. Never large in numbers, the Scots nonetheless, like the Jews and Huguenots, played a disproportionately important role in colonial affairs and were prominent in the patriot cause.

The Rhineland country in present-day Germany was in the eighteenth century divided into a number of principalities, including the Rheinpfalz or Rhenish Palatinate, Württemberg, Baden, and Brunswick. These petty states were constantly embroiled in European conflicts, and many German peasants, most of them pious Lutherans, fled from the exactions of their princes: from conscription, heavy taxes, and a condition of chronic insecurity. The majority came to Pennsylvania, with some in New York, Virginia, and the Carolinas. In Penn's colony, they established tight-knit, self-contained farming communities, where they clung to their language and their folk traditions. Travelers noted that they were stolid, hard-working, and usually more tidy than their English or Scotch-Irish neighbors. From *Deutsch,* they became Pennsylvania Dutch, developing their own patois and, by clinging stubbornly to their folk traditions, making their villages into small fortresses of cultural separatism. The most conspicuous and long-lived of the German immigrant groups that came to America were the Moravians, a pietist sect that traced its spiritual descent from John Huss. This group settled primarily in Salem, North Carolina, and Bethlehem, Pennsylvania, and to this day they preserve a rich tradition of church music, especially that of Johann Sebastian Bach. The Dunkers, who excelled in choral singing and bookmaking, and their close cousins the Mennonites also came largely to Pennsylvania. Today, forbidden by their religion to wear clothes with buttons, to drive cars, to use electricity, radios, or television, the Mennonite men with their chin hair, plain black clothes, and broad-brimmed black hats, and the women with their long skirts and bonnets, still farm the rich and carefully tended soil of central Pennsylvania and are frequently embroiled with the state over their determination not to send their children to public schools.

The Welsh, most of them Quakers, also came in substantial numbers to Pennsylvania, where they prospered strikingly. In France, under Henry V, Protestantism put down substantial roots in the mercantile middle class, but the French people remained overwhelmingly Catholic. As Protestant England had persecuted its Catholics, so Catholic France persecuted its Protestants (known as Huguenots). In consequence many Huguenots looked to the New World. Since they were denied entry into New France, a number were strung out from Boston to Charles Town, favoring the toleration and commercial opportunities offered by these port towns. Peter Faneuil, the rich merchant who built Faneuil Hall, Boston's "Cradle of Liberty," and who was both a good patriot and a public benefactor, was of Huguenot ancestry, as were Paul Revere and—in South Carolina—the Rhetts, the Gadsdens, the Ravenels, the Laurenses, the Deveaux and the L'Enfants.

A handful of Jews came to the American colonies in the seventeenth and eighteenth centuries, with Pennsylvania and Rhode Island as the preferred locations. The first American synagogue was built in Providence, Rhode Island. Aaronsburg, Pennsylvania, was founded by Jewish settlers, and in Philadelphia the wealthy Gratz family contributed generously to the patriot cause. A Jewish scholar taught Hebrew at Harvard in the middle of the eighteenth century.

American Slave Insurrections Before 1861

Harvey Wish

Black slave plots and revolts took place in all of the New England, middle, and southern colonies. Sometimes white indentured servants joined with blacks against their masters. The inhumane treatment of slaves and the large slave population caused more slave plots and uprisings in South Carolina than in any other slave colony. Significant uprisings in New York—which involved free whites, Catholic priests, and black slaves—caused a retaliation by whites that was unusually barbaric. The struggle of blacks for their liberty was not sporadic in nature but an ever-recurrent battle, waged with desperate courage against the bonds of slavery. The following article by Harvey Wish, reprinted from *The Journal of Negro History,* details some of the slave revolts prior to the Civil War.

The romantic portrayal of *ante-bellum* society on the southern plantation, which depicts the rollicking black against a kindly patriarchal background, has tended to obscure the large element of slave unrest which occasionally shook the whole fabric of the planter's kingdom. Even the abolitionist, eager to capitalize upon such material, could make only vague inferences as to the extent of Negro insurrections in the South. The danger of inducing general panic by spreading news of an insurrection was a particularly potent factor in the maintenance of silence on the topic. Besides, sectional pride, in the face of anti-slavery taunts, prevented the loyal white Southerner from airing the subject of domestic revolt in the press. "Last evening," wrote a lady of Charleston during the Denmark Vesey scare of 1822, "twenty-five hundred of our citizens were under arms to guard our property and lives. But it is a subject not to be mentioned; and unless you hear of it elsewhere, say nothing about it."[1] Consequently, against such a conspiracy of silence the historian encounters unusual difficulties in reconstructing the true picture of slave revolts in the United States.

* * *

Slave outbreaks and plots appeared both North and South during the Colonial period. Sometimes the white indentured servants made common cause with the Negroes against their masters. This was the case in 1663 when a plot of white servants and Negroes was betrayed in Gloucester County, Virginia.[2] The eastern counties of Virginia, where the Negroes were rapidly outnumbering the whites, suffered from repeated scares in 1687, 1709, 1710, 1722, 1723, and 1730.[3] A patrol system was set up in 1726 in parts of the state and later extended. Attempts were made here as elsewhere to check the importation of slaves by high duties.

Two important slave plots, one a serious insurrection, disturbed the peace of New York City in 1712 and 1741. In revenge for ill-treatment by their masters, twenty-three Negroes rose on April 6, 1712, to slaughter the whites and killed nine before they were overwhelmed by a superior force. The retaliation showed an unusual barbarous strain on the part of the whites. Twenty-one Negroes were executed, some were burnt, others hanged, and one broken on the wheel.[4] In 1741 another plot was reported in New York involving both whites and blacks. A white, Hewson (or Hughson), was accused of providing the Negroes with weapons. He and his family were executed; likewise, a Catholic priest was hanged as an accomplice. Thirteen Negro leaders were burnt alive, eighteen hanged, and eighty transported.[5] Popular fears of further insurrections led the New York Assembly to impose a prohibitive tax on the importation of Negroes. This tax, however, was later rescinded by order of the British Commissioner for Trade and Plantations.[6]

The situation in colonial South Carolina was worse than in her sister states. Long before rice and indigo had given way to King Cotton, the early development of the plantation system had yielded bumper crops of slave uprisings and plots. An insurrection, resulting in the deaths of three whites, is reported for May 6, 1720.[7] Ten years later an elaborate plot was discovered in St. John's Parish by a Negro servant of Major Cordes'. This plan was aimed at Charleston, an attack that was to inaugurate a widespread war upon the planters. Under the pretense of conducting a "dancing bout" in the city and in St. Paul's Parish the Negroes gathered together ready to seize the available arms for the attack. At this point the militia descended upon the blacks and killed the greater number, leaving few to escape.[8]

Owing partly to Spanish intrigues the same decade in South Carolina witnessed many more uprisings. An outbreak is reported for November, 1738.[9] The following year, on September 9, the Stono uprising created panic throughout the southeast. About twenty Angola Negroes assembled at Stono under their captain, Tommy, and marched toward Spanish territory, beating drums and endeavoring to attract other slaves. Several whites were killed and a number of houses burnt or plundered. As the "army" paused in a field to dance and sing they were overtaken by the militia and cut down in a pitched battle.[10] The following year an insurrection broke out in Berkeley County.[11] Charleston was threatened repeatedly by slave plots.[12] These reports are confirmed officially in the petition of the South Carolina Assembly to the King on July 26, 1740. Among the grievances of 1739 the Assembly complained of:

> . . . an insurrection of our slaves in which many of the Inhabitants were murdered in a barbarous and cruel manner; and that no sooner quelled than another projected in Charles Town, and a third lately in the very heart of the Settlements, but happily discovered in time enough to be prevented.[13]

Repercussions of slave uprisings in South Carolina sometimes affected Georgia as well. This was particularly true in 1738.[14] In 1739 a plot was discovered in Prince George County.[15] To many slaves St. Augustine on Spanish soil seemed a welcome refuge from their masters.

Indications of many other insurrections in the American Colonies may be inferred from the nature of early patrol laws: The South Carolina law of 1704 for example contains a reference in its preamble to recent uprisings in that Colony.[16] In the British and French possessions to the south, particularly in the West Indies, affairs were much worse and put the planter of the North in constant fear of importing rebellious slaves and the contagion of revolt.

In considering the insurrections of the national period, it is at once evident that abolitionist propaganda played a relatively minor role despite the charges of southern politicians after 1831. The genealogy of revolt extends much further back than the organized efforts of anti-slavery advocates. It is true, however, that white men played an important role in many Negro uprisings, frequently furnishing arms, and even leadership, as well as inspiration.[17] The motives for such assistance varied from philanthropy to unadulterated self-interest. As might be expected, insurrections tended to occur where King Cotton and his allies were most firmly entrenched and the great plantation system established.

Slave unrest seems to have been far greater in Virginia rather than in the states of the Lower South. Conspiracies like those of Gabriel in 1800 and Nat Turner in 1831 attained national notoriety. The Gabriel plot was developed in the greatest secrecy upon the plantation of a harsh slavemaster, Thomas Prosser, several miles from Richmond. Under the leadership of a young slave, Gabriel, and inspired by the examples of San Domingo and the emancipation of the ancient Israelites from Egypt, some eleven hundred slaves had taken an oath to fight for their liberty. Plans were drawn for the seizure of an arsenal and several other strategic buildings of Richmond which would precede a general slaughter of all hostile whites. After the initial successes, it was expected that fifty thousand

Negroes would join the standard of revolt. Beyond this point, the arrangements were hazy.[18] A faithful slave however exposed the plot and Governor James Monroe took rapid measures to secure the cooperation of the local authorities and the federal cavalry. Bloodshed was averted by an unprecedented cloudburst on the day set for the conspiracy and the utter demoralization of the undisciplined "army." Writing to his friend, President Jefferson, the Governor declared:

> It (the Gabriel plot) is unquestionably the most serious and formidable conspiracy we have ever known of the kind. While it was possible to keep it secret, which it was till we saw the extent of it, we did so. . . .[19]

With the opening of the slave trials, hysteria swept the South and many innocent blacks were compelled to pay for this with their lives. Rumors of new plots sprang up everywhere much to the distraction of Monroe. The results of the Gabriel incident were significant. An impetus was given to the organization of the American Colonization Society which took definite form in 1816. The slave patrol laws became very stringent, and the example was copied elsewhere in the South. The incipient feeling of sectional diversity received a new impetus.

Between Gabriel's abortive plot and the Nat Turner uprising, several more incidents occurred which disturbed the sleep of Virginians. In January, 1802, Governor Monroe received word of a plot in Nottaway County. Several Negroes suspected of participation were executed.[20] That same year came disclosures of a projected slave uprising in Goochland County aided by eight or ten white men.[21] Several plots were reported in 1808 and 1809 necessitating almost continuous patrol service.[22] The War of 1812 intensified the apprehensions of servile revolt. Petitions for troops and arms came during the summer of 1814 from Caroline County and Lynchburg.[23] Regiments were called out during the war in anticipation of insurrections along the tidewater area. During the spring of 1816 confessions were wrung from slaves concerning an attack upon Fredericksburg and Richmond. The inspiration for this enterprise was attributed to a white military officer, George Boxley. The latter claimed to be the recipient of divine revelations and the instrument of "omnipotence" although he denied any intention of leading an insurrection. His relatives declared that he was insane, but his neighbors in a complaint to the governor showed serious misgivings on this point:

> On many occasions he has declared that the distinction between the rich and the poor was too great; that offices were given to wealth than to merit; and seemed to be an advocate for a more leveling system of Government. For many years he has avowed his disapprobation of the slavery of the Negroes and wished they were free.[24]

Boxley was arrested but escaped. About thirty Negroes were sentenced to death or deportation in consequence.

The years preceding the Nat Turner insurrection brought further news of plots discovered. During the middle of July, 1829, the governor received requests for aid from the counties of Mathews, Gloucester, the Isle of Wight and adjacent counties.[25] The ease with which "confessions" were obtained under duress casts doubt upon the reality of such outbreaks, but the reports are indicative of the ever-present fear of attack.

Nat Turner's insurrection of August 21, 1831, at Southhampton, seventy miles from Richmond, raised fears of a general servile war to their highest point. The contemporary accounts of the young slave, Nat, tend to overemphasize his leanings towards mysticism and under-state the background of unrest.[26] As a "leader" or lay preacher, Nat Turner exercised a strong influence over his race. On the fatal August night, he led his followers to the plantations of the whites killing fifty-five before the community could act. The influence of the Southhampton insurrection upon the South was profound. Gradually the statesmen of that section began to reexamine their "peculiar" institution in the rival aspects of humanitarianism, the race problem, and the economic requirements for a cheap labor supply. How the friends of emancipation failed is familiar history. The immediate results were also far-reaching. Laws against the free Negro were made more restrictive, the police codes of the slave states were strengthened, and Negro education became more than ever an object of suspicion.[27] Virginia's lucrative business of supplying slaves to the lower South was gradually undermined by the recurrent insurrections. Frederic Bancroft, the historian of the domestic slave trade, has written:

> Believing that as a result of actual or feared insurrections Virginia and other States were taking pains to sell to the traders the most dangerous slaves and criminal free Negroes, Alabama, Mississippi, Louisiana, and other States passed laws forbidding all importations for sale.[28]

Rumors of slave plots continued to disturb Virginia up to the era of emancipation. During 1856, the state, in common with other slaveholding states, shared in the general feeling that a widespread conspiracy, set for December 25, was maturing. Requests for aid came to the Governor from the counties of Fauquier, King and Queen, Culpeper, and Rappahannock; and particularly from the towns of Lynchburg, Petersburg, and Gordonsville.[29] As for John Brown's visionary deed at Harper's Ferry in the autumn of 1859, the aftermath can be easily imagined. The spectre of a general insurrection again haunted the minds of the white citizenry and large patrols were kept in constant service to prevent Negro meetings of all types.[30]

Maryland and North Carolina, although more fortunate than their slave-ridden neighbor, did not escape unscathed. The news of Nat Turner and John Brown brought panic to the other states. In Maryland, baseless rumors of conspiracies, rather than actual outbreaks, seemed to be the rule. In 1845 a plot was "disclosed" in Charles County, Maryland, and a number of Negroes were subsequently sold out of the state.[31] Ten years later there was general excitement over alleged uprisings in Dorchester, Talbot and Prince George's Counties. Resolutions were adopted at the time by various citizens asking that slaveholders keep their servants at home.[32] The reaction to John Brown's raid of 1859 was more intense than had ever before been experienced over insurrections in Maryland. The newspapers for days were full of nothing else but the Harper's Ferry incident. Large patrols were called out everywhere and talk was general of a concerted uprising of all the slaves in Maryland and Virginia. A martial atmosphere prevailed.[33]

In 1802 an insurrection was reported in Bertie County, North Carolina, necessitating an elaborate patrol system.[34] A decade later, another outbreak in Rockingham County was narrowly averted;[35] and in 1816 further plots were discovered at Tarboro, New Bern, Camden and Hillsboro.[36] Several minor disturbances occurred in 1821 among the slaves of Bladen, Carteret, Jones, and Onslow Counties.[37] On October 6, 1831, a Georgia newspaper reported an extensive slave conspiracy in North Carolina with ramifications in the eastern counties of Duplin, Sampson, Wayne, New Hanover, Lenoir, Cumberland, and Bladen.[38]

Slave plots in South Carolina during the national period seem to have been abortive for the most part, but several of the projects could easily have been uprisings of the first magnitude. During November, 1797, slave trials in Charleston disclosed a plot to burn the city. Two Negroes were hanged and three deported.[39] The Camden plot of June, 1816, was a very serious affair and envisaged a concerted attempt to burn the town and massacre its inhabitants. A favorite slave reported the plot to his master, Colonel Chesnut, who thereupon informed Governor Williams. Six of the slave leaders were executed and patrol measures were strengthened.[40]

The outstanding threat of insurrection in the State was the Denmark Vesey plot of 1822. The leader, Denmark, was a free Negro of Charleston, a native of St. Thomas in the West Indies, who had purchased his freedom in 1800 from the proceeds of a lottery prize and had since worked in the city as a carpenter. He desired to emulate the Negro leaders of St. Domingo and win the freedom of his people. Preaching that conditions had become intolerable for the slave, he urged a war against the slave-holder. A white man was to purchase guns and powder for his proposed army; Charleston was to be captured and burnt, the shipping of the town seized, and all would sail away for the West Indies to freedom. Again a "faithful slave"—or spy—exposed the plot and severe reprisals were instituted. Thirty-five Negroes were executed and thirty-seven sold out of the state.[41]

Because of the number of free Negroes involved, the Legislature passed an act preventing such persons from entering the state. To avoid, as far as possible, the contagion of abolitionist and kindred ideas, the purchase of slaves was forbidden from the West Indies, Mexico, South America, Europe, and the states north of Maryland. Slaves, who had resided in these forbidden areas, were likewise denied entrance into South Carolina.[42] A Charleston editor, Benjamin Elliott, penned a sharp reply to the Northern accusations of cruelty, by pointing out that New York in the insurrection of 1741 had executed thirty-five and deported eighty-five. He demanded that the Federal Government act under its power to suppress insurrection.[43] In July, 1829, another plot was reported in Georgetown County[44] and in 1831, the year of Nat Turner's attack, one in Laurens County.[45]

Georgia, like South Carolina, was able to avert the worst consequences of repeated slave plots. One was reported in Greene County in 1810;[46] a plan to destroy Atlanta came to light in May, 1819;[47] during 1831, disquieting rumors came from Milledgeville and Laurens County;[48] four years later, a plot for a general uprising on the Coast was disclosed;[49] in 1851 another plot in Atlanta was reported;[50] and in 1860, similar reports came from Crawford and Brooks Counties.[51]

Florida experienced an uprising in March, 1820, along Talbot Island which was put down by a detachment of federal troops.[52] Another was reported in December, 1856, in Jacksonville.[53] Alabama discovered a plot in January, 1837, believed to have been instigated by a free Negro, M'Donald.[54] Mississippi seems to have been the central area of a widespread slave plot in July, 1835, threatening the entire Cotton Kingdom. Far-reaching plans of revolt had been drawn up by a white, John A. Murrell, who enjoyed a reputation as a Negro kidnapper and land pirate. Ten or fifteen Negroes and a number of whites were hanged for participation in the plot.[55]

Next to Virginia, Louisiana had the greatest difficulty among the southern states in coping with repeated attempts at insurrection. Governor Claiborne of the Mississippi Territory received frequent letters concerning plots in various parts of Louisiana. In 1804, New Orleans seems to have been threatened.[56] Several months later another alarm came from the plantations at Pointe Coupee.[57] In 1805, the attempt of a Frenchman to teach the doctrine of equality to slaves, led to general fears of an uprising.[58]

An actual outbreak occurred in January, 1811. Beginning from a plantation in the parish of St. John the Baptist, about thirty-six miles above New Orleans, a concerted slave uprising spread along the Mississippi. The Negroes formed disciplined companies to march upon New Orleans to the beating of drums. Their force, estimated to include from 180 to 500 persons, was defeated in a pitched battle with the troops.[59] According to one historian many of those executed were decapitated and their heads placed on poles along the river as an example to others.[60]

Another uprising took place in the same area in March, 1829, causing great alarm before it was suppressed. Two leaders were hanged.[61] Other plots were reported in 1835, 1837, 1840, 1841 and 1842.[62] An uprising occurred in August, 1856, at New Iberia.[63]

The situation in Tennessee, Kentucky, and Texas may be briefly summarized. In Tennessee, plots were disclosed during 1831, 1856, and 1857.[64] Kentucky, in December, 1856, hanged several ringleaders of an attempted insurrection at Hopkinsville, in which a white man was involved.[65] That same year, two Negroes were punished by being whipped to death in Texas for an alleged conspiracy at Columbus, Colorado County.[66]

Owing to the nature of such a study any claim to an exhaustive treatment would be mere pretense. An analysis of slave patrol history alone would suggest the existence of far more conspiracies and outbreaks than those already mentioned. It is clear however that *ante-bellum* society of the South suffered from a larger degree of domestic insecurity than the conventional view would indicate. No doubt many Negroes made the required adjustments to slavery, but the romantic picture of careless abandon and contentment fails to be convincing. The struggle of the Negro for his liberty, beginning with those dark days on the slave-ship, was far from sporadic in nature, but an ever-recurrent battle waged everywhere with desperate courage against the bonds of his master.

NOTES

1. T. W. Higginson, "Gabriel's Defeat," *The Atlantic Monthly,* X (1862), 337–345.

2. Ulrich B. Phillips, *American Negro Slavery* (New York, 1918), 472.

3. William P. Palmer (ed.), *Calendar of Virginia State Papers* (Richmond, 1875), I (1652–1781), 129–130; also James Curtis Ballagh, *A History of Slavery in Virginia* (Baltimore, 1902), 79–80; also Coffin, *Principal Slave Insurrections,* 11.

4. Letter of Governor Robert Hunter to the Lords of Trade, in E. B. O'Callaghan (ed.), *Documents Relative to the Colonial History of the State of New York* (Albany, 1855), V (1707–1733), 341–2.

5. *Gentleman's Magazine,* XI (1741), 441.

6. *D.S.T.,* III, 409. Joshua Coffin also reports plots and actual outbreaks in other slaveholding areas in the Northern Colonies. East Boston is said to have experienced a minor uprising in 1638. In 1723, a series of incendiary fires in Boston led the selectmen to suspect a slave plot and the militia was ordered to police the slaves. Another plot was reported in Burlington, Pennsylvania during 1734. Coffin, *Principal Slave Insurrections,* 10, 11, 12.

7. Coffin, *Principal Slave Insurrections,* 11.

8. Edward Clifford Holland, *A Refutation of the Calumnies Circulated Against the Southern and Western States Respecting the Institution and Existence of Slavery* (Charleston, 1822), 68–9, 81.

9. Ralph Betts Flander, *Plantation Slavery in Georgia* (Chapel Hill, 1933), 24.

10. *Gentleman's Magazine,* X (1740), 127–8.

11. See the Constable's bill in the *Magazine of American History,* XXV (1891), 85–6.

12. Edward McGrady, *The History of South Carolina Under the Royal Government* (1719–1776) (New York, 1899), 5.

13. Appendix to Holland, *A Refutation of the Calumnies,* —, 71. Another plot of December 17, 1765, is mentioned in *D.S.T.,* IV, 415.

14. Flanders, *Plantation Slavery in Georgia,* 24; similarly, South Carolina's slave plots sometimes required the assistance of North Carolina as in the scare of 1766. William L. Saunders (ed.), *Colonial Records of North Carolina* (Raleigh, 1890), VIII (1769–1771), 559.

15. Jeffrey R. Brackett, *The Negro in Maryland* (Baltimore, 1889), 93.

16. H. M. Henry, *The Police Control of the Slave in South Carolina* (Vanderbilt University, 1914), 30.

17. One aspect of this subject is discussed in James Hugo Johnston's article, "The Participation of White Men in Virginia Negro Insurrections," *Journal of Negro History,* XVI (1931), 158–167.

18. Details of the Gabriel Plot are in the *Calendar of Virginia State Papers,* X (1808–1835), 140–173, *et passim;* T. W. Higginson, "Gabriel's Defeat," *The Atlantic Monthy,* X (1862), 337–345; Robert R. Howison, *A History of Virginia* (Richmond, 1848), II, 390–3.

19. Monroe to Jefferson, September 15, 1800; S. M. Hamilton (ed.), *Writings of James Monroe* (New York, 1893–1903), III, 201. Much of the Gabriel affair can be followed from the letters of Monroe.

20. Hamilton (ed.), *Writings of James Monroe,* III, 328–9.

21. James H. Johnston, "The Participation of White Men in Virginia Negro Insurrections," 161.

22. *Calendar of Virginia State Papers,* X (1808–1835), 31, 62.

23. *Ibid.,* 367, 388.

24. *Calendar of Virginia State Papers,* X, 433–6.

25. *Ibid.,* 567–9.

26. Thomas Gray (ed.), *Nat Turner's Confession* (Richmond, 1832); Samuel Warner (ed.), *The Authentic and Impartial Narrative of The Tragical Scene of the Twenty Second of August, 1831,* New York, 1831 (A Collection of accounts by eye witnesses); and William Sidney Drewry, *Slave Insurrections in Virginia, 1830–1865* (Washington, 1900), *passim.*

27. The immediate results of the Nat Turner affair are summarized in John W. Cromwell's "The Aftermath of Nat Turner's Insurrection," *The Journal of Negro History,* V (1920), 208–234.

28. Frederick Bancroft, *Slave-Trading in the Old South* (Baltimore, 1931), 18.

29. *Calendar of Virginia State Papers,* XI (1836–1869), 50. Other rumors of unrest during 1856 came from the towns of Williamsburgh and Alexandria, and from Montgomery County. See Laura A. White, "The South in the 1850's as seen by British Consuls," *The Journal of Southern History,* I (1935), 44.

30. Brackett, *The Negro in Maryland,* 97–99.

31. Brackett, *The Negro in Maryland,* 96.

32. *Ibid.,* 97.

33. *Ibid.,* 97–99.

34. John Spencer Bassett, *Slavery in the State of North Carolina,* Johns Hopkins University Studies in Historical and Political Science, XVII (Baltimore, 1899), 332. The nature of North Carolina laws during 1777–1788 regarding insurrections indicates the keen fears entertained of slave uprisings. One preamble of 1777 begins "—Whereas the evil and pernicious practice of freeing slaves in this State, ought at this alarming and critical time to be guarded against by every friend and well-wisher to his country——." This idea is repeated in the insurrection laws of 1778 and 1788. Walter Clark (ed.), *The State Records of North Carolina* (Goldsboro, N. C., 1905), XXIV (1777–1788), 14, 221, 964. The laws regulating manumission were made increasingly stringent for fear of creating a dangerous class of free Negroes.

35. *Calendar of Virginia State Papers,* X (1808–1835), 120–2.

36. A. H. Gordon, "The Struggle of the Negro Slaves for Physical Freedom," *Journal of Negro History,* XIII (1928), 22–35.

37. Hugh T. Lefler (ed.), *North Carolina History told by Contemporaries* (Chapel Hill, 1934), 265.

38. Milledgeville (Georgia) *Federal Union,* October 6, 1831, quoted in *ibid.;* The repercussion of the Nat Turner insurrection at Murfreesboro, Hertford County, has been graphically described by an eye witness, "It was court week and most of our men were twelve miles away at Winton. Fear was seen in every face, women pale and terror stricken, children crying for protection, men fearful and full of foreboding, but determined to be ready for the worst." Quoted from the Baltimore *Gazette,* November 16, 1831, by Stephen B. Weeks, "The Slave Insurrection in Virginia," *American Magazine of History,* XXV (1891), 456.

39. H. M. Henry, *The Police Patrol of the Slave in South Carolina,* 150.

40. Holland, *A Refutation of the Calumnies,* — , 75.

41. J. Hamilton (ed.), *An Account of the Late Intended Insurrection* (Boston, 1822) also Holland, *A Refutation of the Calumnies,* — , 77–82; *Niles Register,* XXIII (1822–3), 9–12.

42. *An Act of the Legislature of South Carolina Passed at the Session in December to Prevent Free Negroes and Persons of Color from Entering This State* (Charleston, 1824).

43. Appendix to Holland, *A Refutation of the Calumnies,* 81.

44. *J.C.N.,* 340.

45. Henry, *The Police Control of the Slave in South Carolina,* 153

46. Flanders, *Plantation Slavery in Georgia,* 274.

47. *Niles Register,* XVI (1819), 213.

48. Flanders, *Plantation Slavery in Georgia,* 274.

49. *Niles Register,* XLIX (1935–6), 172.

50. Flanders, *Plantation Slavery in Georgia,* 275. Georgia suffered in common with the other southern states during the scare of 1856; White, "The South in the 1850's as Seen by British Consuls," 43.

51. Flanders, *Plantation Slavery in Georgia,* 275–6, 186. The abolitionists were accused of organizing the slave plots of the thirties and thereafter. One New England abolitionist, Kitchel, who opened a school for Negroes in Tarversville, Twigg County, Georgia, in 1835, was driven out of the community because he was said to have incited the slaves to revolt. *Ibid.,* 275.

52. *J.C.N.,* III, 327.

53. James Stirling, *Letters from the Slave States* (London, 1857), 299.

54. *J.C.N.,* III, 141. Alabama had two rumors of slave plots reported in 1860, White, "The South in the 1850's as Seen by British Consuls," 47.

55. *Niles Register,* XLIX (1835–6), 119; also Elizur Wright (ed.), *Quarterly Anti-Slavery Magazine* (New York, 1837), II, 104–11.

56. Dunbar, Rowland (ed.), *Official Letter Book of W.C.C. Claiborne* (Jackson, 1917), II (1801–1816), 337–8.

57. *Ibid.,* III (1804–1806), 6.

58. *Ibid.,* 187.

59. *Ibid.,* V (1809–1811), 93–142.

60. Francois Xavier Martin, *The History of Louisiana* (New Orleans, 1829), II, 300–301. During the fall of the following year another plot was reported. *J.C.N.,* III, 449.

61. *Niles Register,* XXVI (1829), 53.

62. *Ibid.,* LIII (1837–8), 129; LX (1841), 368; LXIII (1842–3), 212.

63. V. Alton Moody, *Slavery on the Louisiana Sugar Plantations* (Univ. of Michigan Press, 1924), 41; also Phillips, *American Negro Slavery,* 486. *J.C.N.,* III, 648.

64. Caleb P. Patterson, *The Negro in Tennessee,* Univ. of Texas Bulletin No. 225 (Austin, February 1, 1922), 49; *J.C.N.,* II, 565–6; Stirling, *Letters from the Slave States,* 294.

65. *J.C.N.,* 299.

66. Frederick Law Olmsted, *A Journey Through Texas* (New York, 1857), 513–4; Stirling, *Letters From the Slave States,* 300.

Revolutionary Philosophy: Its Impact on Slavery

Few of us realize that at the time of the War of Independence at least one-fifth of the American population was black. Despite their numbers, and despite the fact that the Declaration of Independence stipulates life, liberty, and the pursuit of happiness for all Americans, black and white, few blacks enjoyed full participation in American life. In fact, the American colonists were criticized by other countries for maintaining a system of slavery while requesting freedom from Great Britain. Yet many blacks volunteered their services in the war hoping to achieve both freedom for the thirteen colonies and freedom for the American Negro. Some were rewarded for their efforts, but most remained in slavery, an institution legitimized by the Constitution, which, paradoxically, referred to the American blacks as both "people" and "property."

The many dichotomies that existed in our society during the period of the American Revolution are the subject of this chapter. One of the most interesting aspects of the readings that follow is the description provided of some American blacks whose efforts in the Revolution were recorded and valued at that time. Also described are the activities of some white Americans with a strong commitment to the abolition of slavery.

The Quakers and Slavery

John Woolman

The Colonies justified the War of Independence by an appeal to the natural rights of man—a position that was based upon both their religious beliefs and a spirit of humanitarianism. But it was clear, particularly to nations abroad such as Great Britain, that the liberties the colonists sought would not necessarily be extended to blacks, even if achieved for whites.

Early in the struggle to free slaves, Quakers firmly established their position for total abolition. The following selection by a New Jersey Quaker, John Woolman (1720–1772), presents the argument that a person's color must not be a factor in the determination of his or her rights. While the language may be somewhat difficult for today's readers, it should be read carefully. The social problem as it existed while the colonies argued and fought for freedom is clearly related to social problems yet to be solved.

It is our Happiness faithfully to serve the Divine Being, who made us. His Perfection makes our Service reasonable; but so long as Men are biassed by narrow Self-love, so long an absolute Power over other Men is unfit for them.
. . .

Placing on Men the ignominious Title, SLAVE, dressing them in uncomely Garments, keeping them to servile Labour, in which they are often dirty, tends gradually to fix a Notion in the Mind, that they are a Sort of People below us in Nature, and leads us to consider them as such in all our Conclusions about them. And, moreover, a Person which in our Esteem is mean and contemptible, if their Language or Behaviour toward us is unseemly or disrespectful, it excites Wrath more powerfully than the like Conduct in one we accounted our Equal or Superior: and where this happens to be the Case, it disqualifies for candid Judgment; for it is unfit for a Person to sit as Judge in a Case where his own personal Resentments are stirred up; and, as Members of Society in a well framed Government, we are mutually dependent. Present Interest incites to Duty, and makes each Man attentive to the Convenience of others: but he whose Will is a Law to others, and can enforce Obedience by Punishment; he whose Wants are supplied without feeling any Obligation to make equal Returns to his Benefactor, his irregular Appetites find an open Field for Motion, and he is in Danger of growing hard, and inattentive to their Convenience who labour for his Support; and so loses that Disposition in which alone Men are fit to govern.

       * * *

He who reverently observes that Goodness manifested by our Gracious Creator toward the various Species of Beings in this World, will see, that in our Frame and Constitution is clearly shown, that innocent Men, capable of managing for themselves, were not intended to be Slaves.

       * * *

Through the Force of long Custom, it appears needful to speak in Relation to Colour. Suppose a white Child, born of Parents of the meanest Sort, who died and left him an Infant, falls into the Hands of a Person who endeavours to keep him a Slave, some Men would account him an unjust Man in doing so, who yet appear easy while many Black People, of honest Lives and good Abilities, are enslaved in a Manner more shocking than the Case here supposed. This is owing chiefly to the Idea of Slavery being connected with the Black Colour, and Liberty with the White: and where false Ideas are twisted into our Minds, it is with difficulty we get fairly disentangled. . . .

Selfishness being indulged, clouds the Understanding; and where selfish Men, for a long Time, proceed on their Way without Opposition, the Deceivableness of Unrighteousness gets so rooted in their Intellects, that a candid Examination of Things relating to Self-interest is prevented; and in this Circumstance, some who would not agree to make a Slave of a Person whose Colour is like their own, appear easy in making Slaves of others of a different Colour, though their Understandings and Morals are equal to the Generality of Men of their own Colour.

The Colour of a Man avails nothing in the Matters of Right and Equity. Consider Colour in Relation to Treaties; by such, Disputes betwixt Nations are sometimes settled. And should the Father of us all so dispose Things, that Treaties with black Men should sometimes be necessary, how then would it appear amongst the Princes and Ambassadors, to insist on the Prerogative of the white Colour?

Whence is it that Men, who believe in a righteous Omnipotent Being, to whom all Nations stand equally related, and are equally accountable, remain so easy in it; but for that the Ideas of *Negroes* and Slaves are so interwoven in the Mind, that they do not discuss this Matter with that Candour and Freedom of Thought, which the Case justly calls for?

To come at a right Feeling of their Condition, requires humble, serious Thinking; for, in their present Situation, they have but little to engage our natural Affection in their Favour.

Had we a Son or Daughter involved in the same Case in which many of them are, it would alarm us, and make us feel their Condition without seeking for it. The Adversity of an intimate Friend will incite our Compassion, while others, equally good, in the like Trouble, will but little affect us. . . .

The Blacks seem far from being our Kinsfolks; and did we find an agreeable Disposition and sound Understanding in some of them, which appeared as a good Foundation for a true Friendship between us, the Disgrace arising from an open Friendship with a Person of so vile a Stock, in the common Esteem, would naturally tend to hinder it. They have neither Honours, Riches, outward Magnificence nor Power; their Dress coarse, and often ragged; their Employ Drudgery, and much in the Dirt: they have little or nothing at Command; but must wait upon and work for others to obtain the Necessities of Life: so that, in their present Situation, there is not much to engage the Friendship, or move the Affection of selfish Men. But such who live in the Spirit of true Charity, to sympathize with the Afflicted in the lowest Stations of Life, is a Thing familiar to them.

The Black Presence in the Revolution, 1770–1800

Lisa W. Strick

The Declaration of Independence, in which the thirteen American colonies declared themselves to be free of Great Britain, stipulates "life, liberty and the pursuit of happiness" for all Americans. In fact, of the 2½ million people in the American colonies at the time of the Revolution, at least one-fifth were black. In addition, American blacks, both free and slave, served in the War for Independence.

The following article, reprinted from a booklet written by Lisa Strick, describes the distribution of the black population in the thirteen colonies. The article emphasizes that only a small percentage of blacks lived in the northern colonies primarily as free Americans and that a far greater number lived as slaves on plantations in the southern colonies. It also describes the great embarrassment over the existence of slavery felt by Americans such as Thomas Jefferson and the resistance to attempts at abolition by the very persons who were soliciting freedom from Great Britain.

Although it is known that many blacks fought for American independence, not much is known about them as individuals. This article describes the involvement in the American Revolution of several blacks. Although they exemplified all the fine qualities of patriots, they encountered a variety of rewards at the end of the war. Many, in fact, were forced to return to slavery.

PRELUDES TO THE DECLARATION: BEING BLACK IN THE COLONIES

We hold these truths to be self-evident, that all men are created equal, that they are endowed by their Creator with certain unalienable Rights, that among these are Life, Liberty and the pursuit of Happiness.—That to secure these rights Governments are instituted among Men, deriving their just powers from the consent of the governed.—That whenever any Form of Government becomes destructive of these ends, it is the Right of the People to alter or to abolish it.

With these bold words the thirteen American colonies declared themselves independent from England. Not everyone in the colonies was in favor of breaking off America's ties with England at this time, but few were left unaffected by the patriots' decision to do so. Seven years of fighting followed the Declaration of Independence, and as those years wore on it became harder and harder to avoid getting involved in the conflict in some way.

There were two and a half million people in the American colonies at the time of the Declaration. At least half a million of them were black. The fact that most of these black Americans were slaves did not prevent them from becoming involved in the War of Independence—far from it. It was a war that was being fought in the name of liberty, and black men and women were no strangers to *that* cause—many had been engaged in a determined struggle for their own liberty for years. Where there was hope for freedom, Blacks were ready to volunteer, and the Revolution offered this hope to many. Thousands of American Blacks, both slave and free, entered the conflict. Some fought for their country's freedom and some for their own. Many fought for both.

Few of the names and faces of the Blacks who served during the Revolution find their way into conventional histories of the era. But there are records indicating that the role Blacks played in the Revolution was often an important one. . . .

But first, let us take a look at what it was like to live in the American colonies as the War for Independence drew near. By 1776 the colonies were no longer the wilderness they had been when English settlers first set foot on the continent. Americans had built whole cities, especially in the North where bustling trade centers had grown up around the harbors of Newport, Boston, New York, and Philadelphia. The busiest places in these cities were the docks, where sailors and sea captains, merchants and traders, laborers and craftsmen, buyers and sellers of all kinds crowded the wharves to meet the ships that were constantly coming and going. Away from the coast, northern America was a land of farms and small towns. But the cities were the centers of commercial activity and also the centers of opinion, fashion, and "society."

Moving farther south, both the look of the land and the way of life were different. The rich soil and warm sun of the southern colonies were perfect for growing things, so southern colonists did not crowd together in cities, but spread themselves out on farms and plantations. Many kinds of crops were grown in the southern colonies, but tobacco, rice, and indigo were the important "cash crops." In some parts of the South, fields of tobacco or indigo stretched as far as the eye could see, and as fast as southern settlers could clear the forests away they planted more. Most of these crops were exported to England, and in good years profits from their sale were high. Even farmers who owned very small plots of land tried to get some of these crops in the ground. A few planters made enough from tobacco or indigo to build themselves great houses, which they filled with the best furniture and luxury articles from America and Europe.

Building cities and plantations in the American wilderness had taken a century and a half of backbreaking labor. Much of it had been forced labor performed by Blacks. As early as the 1620s white colonists had started importing Africans to clear their land, plant their crops, build their houses, and wait on their families. As the colonies expanded, so did the need for laborers. Trading in slaves became a profitable business. Between 1750 and 1770 the black population of the American colonies more than tripled.

Because there was no great demand for slave labor in the northern colonies the number of Blacks there never became large. Blacks made up only three percent of the population in New England at the time of the Revolution, for example, and in New Jersey, New York, and Pennsylvania Blacks were fewer than one in ten. Not all of them were slaves. In places like Boston, New York, and Philadelphia there were quite a lot of free Blacks who had either been emancipated by their owners, purchased their own liberty, or run away and managed to escape capture long enough for their masters to give up looking for them. These black freemen competed with white laborers for available jobs and made their livings as farm hands, house servants, dockworkers, sailors, ropemakers, carpenters, bakers, barbers, and blacksmiths, among other things. Northern slaves often worked at the same occupations.

The destination of the great majority of Africans who were brought to American shores during the colonial period, however, was the sprawling plantations of the South, where thousands of hands were needed to plant, harvest, and process the tobacco, rice, and indigo crops. By 1750 one out of every three people in Maryland and Virginia was black. In South Carolina, Blacks rapidly outnumbered Whites.

Southern plantation slaves had little hope of gaining their freedom. Strong measures were taken to keep slaves from running away, and dreadful punishments often awaited those who tried and got caught. The planters were not just worried about losing their labor force. Fear of slave rebellion was widespread throughout the southern colonies, and in addition to making every effort to keep the Blacks captive, the planters actively prevented slaves from getting any kind of education that would put dangerous ideas of liberty into their heads. Even religious teaching was often discouraged because it was thought that the knowledge that their souls were equal with whites' before God would make the slaves rebellious.

There were few free Blacks in the southern colonies. Free Blacks were considered a dangerous example to slaves, and in many parts of the South a slave could legally be freed only if he promised to leave the area. Also, there were few ways in which a free Black could make a living in the South—not many southerners were willing to *pay* for black labor. The southern slaves who did manage to win their freedom, therefore, often moved north and started new lives.

Slavery did not take root in the American colonies without opposition. From the start there were colonists in both the North and the South who thought it a hateful practice. As the numbers of Blacks in America grew, so did guilt about slavery and concern that something be done to end it.

The group that pursued this goal most consistently over the years was the Quakers. Located mostly in Pennsylvania, they opposed slavery on both humanitarian and religious grounds. First, the Quakers banned slavery among themselves, and then some of them went to work trying to convince other colonists to do the same, arguing the sinfulness of human bondage. Some Quakers were also ready to take on those who seemed to feel that slavery was excusable because the Blacks were an inferior race, unfit for anything *but* labor. Quaker John Woolman argued that if you took a white man and gave him no education, made him work all his life under the hardest conditions, deprived him of the comforts of family, and in general gave him no reason or opportunity to advance himself, you would see no difference between that white man and a black slave. Give Blacks the opportunity to acquire property and allow them the advantages of education, Woolman insisted, and they would prove to be the equals of Whites in every way.

Such views were very unpopular among colonial slaveholders, especially in the South. Not all white southerners believed that Blacks were naturally inferior. But by the mid-18th century the planters, at least, needed slavery too much not to *act* as if they believed it. Without slaves there was no way they could grow crops on a large scale and turn the kind of profits they were becoming used to. Simply put, many slaveowners *wanted* to believe that Blacks were inferior, and turned a deaf ear to all arguments to the contrary. The protests of the early antislavery crusaders were loud, but they had little effect because few slaveowners were willing to listen to them.

During the 150 years that slavery had existed in America the Blacks had not been idle in seeking their own freedom. As soon as the colonial settlers started printing newspapers, those papers carried advertisements for runaway slaves. There were also several slave rebellions reported in the colonies before 1776. While some of these were probably no more than desperate mass runaway attempts, others showed signs of planning and organization, suggesting that the colonists' fear of slave conspiracy had foundation. As the Revolution drew near, however, slaves found themselves presented with new opportunities for pursuing their liberty. The trouble that the colonies were having with England gave many Americans—black and white—a new perspective on their slavery problem.

*   *   *

At this early stage, the patriots were not seeking independence. They were looking for compromise—a promise that they would be permitted to run at least some of their own affairs in return for their continued loyalty and support. Elaborate and high-sounding arguments were advanced to explain *why* the King should let the colonists rule themselves. Some patriots asserted that the British Constitution itself guaranteed their rights to liberty and self-government. Others, however, declared that these rights derived from an even higher source. *"The sacred rights of mankind are not to be rummaged for among old parchments and musty records,"* wrote Alexander Hamilton in 1775. *"They are written, as with a sunbeam . . . by the hand of divinity itself, and can never be erased or obscured by any mortal power. "* The colonies would come to rely on this point of view more and more in their protests against the British. If God gave men a natural right to liberty, the patriots were beginning to ask, what could be wrong in refusing to obey a King who tried to take that right away?

It was hard for the colonists to ignore the fact that all this talk about God-given rights to liberty did not square too well with the fact that there were Americans in all the colonies who owned black slaves. Antislavery spokesmen were quick to turn the patriot rhetoric against slaveholders: *"The Colonists are by law of nature free born,"* said James Otis of Massachusetts, *"as indeed all men are, white or black. . . . Does it follow that 'tis right to enslave a man because he is black?"* Another antislavery writer of this time stated flatly: *"That all black persons should be slaves . . . is as ridiculous as . . . that all red-haired persons should be hanged. "*

American Blacks quickly recognized that they could use this argument themselves. In 1773—the same year in which a group of Bostonians, in indignation over a tax on tea, dressed themselves as Indians and dumped all the tea waiting to be unloaded from a British ship into Boston Harbor—Caesar Hendrick, a Massachusetts slave, took his master to court and sued for his freedom. As he was held in slavery against his will, Hendrick claimed, he was being deprived of his natural right to liberty. An all-white jury not only freed Hendrick but also demanded that his former master pay him court costs and damages. Between 1773 and 1779 there were several such "freedom suits" in New England, and in each case the Negro bringing suit won. Massachusetts courts seemed willing to admit that slaves, like other men, were born with a right to freedom.

Yet few Blacks actually sought their liberty from the courts. There were too many problems with the process. Going to court was very expensive, and how were most slaves to get the money? The courts also persisted in treating each suit as an individual case. This meant that freedom suits could not liberate large numbers of slaves, but only one at a time. Blacks were anxious to find other methods that would strike a blow for *all* slaves in America.

Encouraged by what appeared to be increased willingness to deal with Blacks fairly, groups of slaves in New England began to petition the colonial governments to set them free. A not insignificant fact on their side was that a fugitive slave, Crispus Attucks, had already become a hero among American patriots as one of the first Americans to "die for freedom" during the "Boston Massacre" —a mass demonstration in which five Americans had been killed by British soldiers.

In these petitions, the Blacks used much the same kind of language that white colonists were using to protest the way they were being treated by the King. In 1773 a petition arrived at the Massachusetts legislature that began: *"The humble Petition of many slaves; living in the Town of Boston and other Towns in the Province . . . who have had every day of their lives imbittered with this most intollerable Reflection, That, let their behaviour be what it will, nor their Children to all Generations, shall ever be able to do, or to possess and enjoy any Thing, no not even Life Itself. . . . "* A 1774 freedom petition stated *". . . your petitioners apprehend that we have in common with all other men a natural right to our freedoms without being depriv'd of them by our fellow men as we are a feeborn Pepel and have never forfeited this Blessing by aney compact or agreement whatever. "* It is as if these Blacks were taunting the patriots, saying "You who make great talk of liberty, look in your own backyards! Can what the King is doing to you compare with what you are doing to us?"

No one knows very much about the Blacks who wrote these petitions, but they were certainly men of courage. Many colonists realized they had a good point. Some also feared that if petitions failed, the slaves would resort to more radical methods. *"There has been in Town a conspiracy of the negroes,"* Abigail Adams wrote to her husband John in 1774. *"At present it is kept pretty private. . . . They conducted it in this way . . . to draw up a petition to the [royal] Governor, telling them that they would fight for him provided he would arm them, and . . . liberate them if he conquered. . . . I wish most sincerely there were not a slave in the Province,"* Mrs. Adams concluded, adding *"it always appeared a most iniquitous scheme to me to fight ourselves for what we are daily robbing and plundering from those who have as great a right to freedom as we have."*

But the colonial assemblies did not act on the slaves' petitions. By this time, the troubles between England and the colonies were serious enough for some colonists to be talking about independence. They knew that a declaration of independence would mean war, and that if they were to hope to defy England all of them—northerners and southerners, New Yorkers and Carolinians, Philadelphians and Bostonians, rich men and poor men, merchants and planters— would have to stand by each other. In fact, the patriots were not worried only about England. They knew that there were large numbers of *Americans* who wanted nothing to do with them and their plans for independence, Americans who would help the British if it came to fighting. Still, the rebellious colonists were having a hard time sticking together, and arguments over slavery did not help them get along. Protests against the slave system were becoming a threat to colonial union. And when the patriots started talking about risking all and taking radical action, union meant everything.

Thomas Jefferson, a patriot leader and a southerner who was deeply troubled over slavery, made a famous eleventh-hour attempt to settle the issue when he wrote the Declaration of Independence. The original version of the Declaration contained a passage condemning the slave trade. It was included in the section in which Jefferson itemized the colonists' grievances against the King. In it Jefferson appears to be suggesting that England actually *forced* the slave system on the unwilling Americans. *"He [the King] has waged cruel war against human nature itself, violating its most sacred rights of life and liberty in the persons of a distant people who never offended him, captivating and carrying them into slavery in another hemisphere, or to incur miserable death in their transportation thither,"* Jefferson wrote; *". . . determined to keep open a market where MEN should be bought & sold he has prostituted his negative for suppressing every legislative attempt to . . . restrain this execrable commerce. . . ."*

Jefferson surely knew that the blame for slavery was not deserved only by the King; that *Americans* had blocked many attempts to end the slave trade. But he was also aware that the presence of black slaves in a country where white people were complaining that their liberty was being denied was a weakness in the colonial argument—not to mention a huge embarrassment. By shifting the blame for slavery to the King, Jefferson hoped to make it appear that the patriots were in favor of liberty for *everyone* in America. But southern colonists argued so fiercely against Jefferson's statement on the slave trade that it was stricken out of the Declaration.

The final version of the Declaration of Independence did include one reference to Blacks, however. Toward the bottom of the list of grievances that the patriots had against the King, George III is accused of encouraging "domestic insurrection" in the colonies. What this statement referred to was the fact that the British had begun to expand their army in the South by inviting slaves to desert their masters and join the royal fighting forces.

REVOLUTION

Historian Benjamin Quarles explains the position of the black Revolutionary soldier this way: ". . . *his major loyalty was not to a place nor a people, but to a principle. Insofar as he had freedom of choice, he was likely to join the side that made him the quickest and best offer in terms of those 'inalienable rights' of which Mr. Jefferson had spoken. Whoever invoked the image of liberty, be he American or British, could count on a ready response from the blacks.*"

In other words, of the thousands of Blacks who became involved in the Revolution many fought a "war within a war" for their *own* independence. About 5,000 Blacks rallied when the patriots called for men to fight for the freedom of their country. But when the British—in a shrewdly calculated move that they hoped would cripple the revolutionary effort in the South—offered liberty and protection to slaves who would fight with them, many thousands more offered their services to the King. In some Revolutionary battles, American Blacks could be found fighting on both sides.

Both the Americans and the British started with doubts about using Blacks during the Revolutionary War. Neither side really wanted to use them as fighting men. Despite plain evidence of the black man's bravery and skill in battle, English and American armies usually assigned black volunteers to work as orderlies, carpenters, cooks, wagoners, blacksmiths, messengers, and laborers. A commander would only give his black soldiers guns if he were desperate—and some commanders would not do it then.

But as the war dragged on, both British and American commanders *became* desperate. The British were at first caught short of men, and couldn't wait for new troops to be shipped across the Atlantic to start fighting. The Americans, on the other hand, were faced with the need to raise an entire army almost from scratch, and they were having a difficult time finding men. In both cases, the Blacks were there—a huge, strong, and available force of men who had very little to lose and possibly something to gain from the war. It was inevitable that they would end up in the action.

FIGHTING WITH THE PATRIOTS

Who were the Blacks who fought on the patriot side of the Revolutionary War? Why did they fight? These are difficult questions to answer. There is no question that many Blacks were true patriots. To them, the feelings expressed in the Declaration of Independence meant a great deal. "All men are created equal," the Declaration said, with rights to "Life, Liberty and the pursuit of Happiness." These were words worth fighting for. Some Blacks embraced the revolutionary cause as their own, and volunteered purely out of a commitment to the principles of freedom and democracy.

But there were many other ways for a black man to become involved in the war. For example, throughout the colonies (or "states" as they were soon called) there existed a "substitution system" in which a man called up for the army could avoid service if he could find a *substitute* to take his place. In the northern and middle states Blacks—both slave and free—were often used as substitutes. Northern slaveowners sometimes sent their own slaves to war instead of going themselves. Only in some states was it necessary for a master to free his slave before doing this. In others, it could be agreed that the master would get the slave soldier's pay, or be reimbursed by the state if his "property" were killed. Northern Whites who did not own slaves often found it easier to hire a black substitute than a white one.

Some slaves entered the war simply because their masters had enlisted and they were taken along. Others used the war as a means of running away—they would represent themselves as freemen to recruiting officers and march as far away from their masters as the army would take them. At times when men were hard to find, recruiting officers did not always check a black volunteer's background too carefully.

Most of the Blacks who served with the patriots came from the North. Virginians armed some slaves who volunteered to fight in exchange for promises of freedom, but throughout most of the South, Blacks were not wanted in the Continental Army. Southerners had gone on record about the use of Blacks for military service as early as 1715, when a group of Carolinians declared that "there must be great caution used . . . our slaves when armed might become our masters."

While many black men fought for American Independence, too little is known about who these people really were. Often, the only record we have of a black soldier's existence is a name on a muster roll, or an entry in a ship's log. Now and then we find an account of a battle in which a Black has been singled out for special service or daring. One report praises a Negro named Jupiter who "saved four guns during the time the enemy were in Richmond. . . ." in 1781. Another says that Saul Matthews, a slave, ". . . *during the campaign of the British in the vicinity of Portsmouth [Rhode Island] . . . at the risk of his life, was sent into the British garrison. . . . He brought back military secrets of such value to Colonel Parker that on the same night, serving as a guide, he led a party of Americans to the British garrison. . . .*" Jupiter and Saul are but two of the many Blacks who fought bravely for the patriot cause. What follows are the stories in words and pictures of a few more who helped America win independence.

FIGHTING THE FIRST BATTLES

The earliest battles of the war were fought at Concord, Lexington, and Bunker Hill a year before the Declaration of Independence was signed. America had not yet raised a national army. Responsible for the defense of these places were local Massachusetts "minutemen," who had been secretly getting ready to fight the British for months.

These minutemen were among the few experienced troops George Washington could count on when he took command of the Continental Army in 1775. A number of them were black. On the list of those wounded at Concord we find the name of "Prince Easterbrooks, A Negro Man"—he was a member of the first military company to get into the fight. At least nine other Blacks were among the Americans who fired "the shot heard round the world" in 1775.

Two months after the battles at Concord and Lexington, black soldiers were at Bunker Hill, waiting to see the whites of the enemy's eyes before they fired their flintlocks. (The Americans on Bunker Hill had to wait—they were very low on ammunition and couldn't afford to waste any.) Among them was Peter Salem who, in a critical moment, reportedly killed an important British officer and became a hero of the day. (Peter Salem had been at Lexington, too, and he continued to serve with the patriots throughout the war.) Also present was 28-year-old Salem Poor, a free Negro who showed such extraordinary courage at Bunker Hill that fourteen officers sent a special report of his actions to the Continental Congress in Philadelphia. They wrote *". . . under Our Own observations, Wee declare that a Negro Man Called Salem Poor . . . in the late Battle at Charleston [Bunker Hill], behaved like an Experienced Officer as well as an Excellent Soldier . . ."* and asked that the Congress give Poor *"The Reward due to so great and Distinguisht a Character."*

A TRIO WITH THE GENERALS

Three of the most important generals the Americans had during the Revolution —George Washington, the Marquis de Lafayette, and Tadeusz Kosciuszko—had black orderlies to whom they entrusted the most important and confidential military information.

The face of William Lee, a slave of George Washington's who served at his master's side throughout the war, can be seen in several Revolutionary portraits of the general. It was a fashion of the time to paint black "servants" with their masters, and they are often shown wearing turbans and exotic costumes. Lee served as Washington's orderly throughout the entire seven years of the war, and saw America become free. He did not receive his own freedom, however, until sixteen years later. When Washington died in 1799, Lee was emancipated in his will. *". . . this I give him as a testimony of my sense of his attachment to me, and for his faithful services during the Revolutionary War,"* Washington wrote.

In James Armistead, General Lafayette found not only a faithful servant and companion, but also an excellent spy. After the war Lafayette wrote that James —a Virginia slave who had enlisted with the permission of his master—had become an important member of his forces. *"His intelligence from the enemy's camp were industriously collected and more faithfully delivered,"* Lafayette testified. *"He perfectly acquitted himself with some important commissions I gave him and appears to me entitled to every reward his situation can admit of."* On this evidence, the Virginia assembly bought James from his master and set him free. The black veteran from that point on called himself James Armistead Lafayette.

General Lafayette, a Frenchman, had always had great faith in American black soldiers. In 1781 he tried to raise 400 Blacks for the patriots, writing to George Washington that *"nothing but a Treaty of Alliance with the Negroes can find us dragoon horses . . . it is by this means the enemy have so formidable a Cavalry."*

*   *   *

Agrippa Hull, a free-born black man from Massachusetts, enlisted with the patriots in 1777 at the age of 18. He served four of the six years of his enlistment with General Tadeusz Kosciuszko, a Polish patriot who believed in the American cause and fought for it. During part of his service, Hull was assigned to a unit of military surgeons, and he remembered for the rest of his long life the bloody operations in which wounded soldiers' arms and legs were removed.

*   *   *

Rhode Island, the smallest state, had trouble raising the number of men it was expected to send to the Continental Army. So in 1778 the state passed a law declaring that any slave who volunteered for the army would become free. The result was the nearly all-black regiment that . . . two French observers admired.

The Rhode Island black regiment saw its first action at the Battle of Rhode Island, which General Lafayette later said was the "best fought action of the war." In this battle, Greene and his black volunteers held off an army of professional German soldiers (Hessians) who had been hired by the British. The resistance they put up was so fierce that the Hessian commander refused to make his men face the Blacks again the next day—he instead asked for a transfer to another field of battle.

Boston also raised a black regiment, the members of which called themselves "The Bucks of America." Their commander, Colonel Middleton, was himself a Negro. Still a third black regiment came to fight for America from the far-off Caribbean. In 1778 the Americans made an alliance with the French, and French soldiers were sent to America to help the patriots. Some of these soldiers were raised in Haiti, a predominantly black country that was then French territory. Five hundred forty-five black Haitian volunteers arrived in time to participate in the bloody battle of Savannah, Georgia. Among them was 12-year-old Henri Christophe who would grow up to help Haiti unite and wage a war for her own independence from France. Christophe then became Haiti's king.

Some of the Blacks who helped America win independence fought out of choice, some out of necessity, and some because the war offered a chance of personal freedom. Black soldiers in the Rhode Island regiment, for example, were clearly prepared to risk death in battle in order to escape a life of slavery. There were also Blacks who fought because they believed that an independent United States of America offered the greatest hope of freedom for themselves and their people. In the North, where most of the black patriots came from, liberty for America and liberty for Blacks were seen as compatible goals. But in the South this was not necessarily so. There, a situation developed that convinced many slaves that fighting for the British was the surest road to freedom.

IN THE SERVICE OF THE KING

In November 1775, Lord Dunmore, British Governor of the colony of Virginia, issued a proclamation in which he said that he would guarantee freedom to any slave belonging to an American "rebel" if that slave would volunteer to fight with the British. Inside of a week, 500 slaves presented themselves to Dunmore offering their services. He gave them guns as fast as they came in, and outfitted them in uniforms that had the words "Liberty to Slaves" inscribed across their breasts. This army of Blacks became known as "Lord Dunmore's Ethiopian Regiment," and it was the first black regiment to be raised on either side during the Revolution.

Dunmore went after Blacks because he badly needed men. King George— alarmed by such events as the Boston Tea Party—had been building up his forces in America, but most of the King's soldiers had been sent to the North; there were less than 300 British troops in Virginia when the fighting started. Dunmore saw calling up local Blacks as a quick way of building up his army. The Governor also knew that many southern patriots could not successfully run their plantations without slaves, and so his proclamation struck a blow at his enemies' economic system as well.

To southern Whites who had lived with the vision of armed slave rebellion for years, Dunmore's "Ethiopian Regiment" was like a nightmare come to life: their own slaves were going to be given guns and turned against them. Virginia, where the famous proclamation was issued, was the area most urgently threatened, and white patriots in that colony reacted immediately. *The Virginia Gazette* published frantic appeals that the slaves remain loyal to their masters and ignore Dunmore's offers: "be not then, ye negroes, tempted by this proclamation to ruin your selves" ran one article, implying that awful punishments awaited any slave who was caught trying to join the British. Virginian Patrick Henry—already famous for his "Give me liberty or give me death!"—showed a different stripe when he wrote that Dunmore's action was "fatal to the publick safety" and called for "early and unremitting Attention to the Government of the Slaves."

*   *   *

There were other Blacks who were highly regarded by the British. One report of a 1776 naval battle notes that *"as soon as the action began, the Commodore [of a British ship] ordered to be put into a place of safety, negro Sampson, a black pilot."* Apparently Sampson, with his knowledge of the Carolina shoreline, was too valuable a man to risk his getting hurt in the fight.

No one knows exactly how many slaves found their way to the British lines —only that the figure was in the thousands. They fought bravely from the first battles to the last. Many died. But when the peace between England and America was finally signed in 1783—a peace that declared America the winner—there were still thousands of American Negroes under British protection.

What should be done with these Blacks almost immediately became an issue between the English and the Americans. The English, who were beginning to remove their troops from American soil, felt an obligation to fulfill the promises of freedom they had made to their Negro soldiers, and wanted to take those who were willing away with them to British territory, including Canada and the West Indies. But one of the rules of the peace agreement was that the defeated British could not take any American property with them when they left. George Washington, prodded by Americans with slave interests, insisted that the Blacks who had fought for the British were still the property of American citizens—as were the wives and children the black veterans wanted to take away with them. As such, Washington said, they could not be evacuated, but would have to be turned over to the Americans and returned to their former owners.

Nevertheless, 4,000 Blacks left with the British from Savannah before the Americans could stop them. Six thousand sailed away from New York on British vessels and 4,000 were carried off from Charleston, South Carolina. These Blacks were taken to many places—to Halifax (Canada), Jamaica, Nassau, and Europe —where they started new lives as free men and women. Hundreds of other Blacks who had served with the British fled America on their own—they headed for Canada or for East Florida, which was still British territory at the time. At least one group of 300 black veterans decided to stay. Calling themselves "The King of England's soldiers," they banded together in an armed village in the Georgia backwoods and declared themselves ready to fight anyone who came to re-enslave them.

Not all of the Blacks who served with the British got safely away. Some—most often the old and sick—were deliberately abandoned. Others were captured before they could be evacuated and returned to their former masters or sold. Perhaps the bitterest fate of all was that suffered by some Blacks who escaped with the British to the West Indies—only to be illegally seized and sold as slaves there. There is evidence that some of the veterans returned to slavery in this manner were sold with the help of their British "protectors."

The Blacks who served with the patriots also met with varied rewards at the war's end. Those who had been promised freedom in exchange for wartime service usually got it. There were a few cases—notably in Virginia—in which masters who had freed their slaves to fight tried to re-claim them after the war, but these actions caused such a public uproar that few were able to get away with this sort of thing. Even in the South, state assemblies defended the rights of black veterans who had been promised liberty.

* * *

But many slaves who fought for the Americans had been given no promises of freedom. Often the war's end brought them no choice but to return to their owners and to a life of slavery. For them, the Revolution had been little more than a period in which the kind of service expected of them had been different.

But American Blacks would not forget the Revolutionary experience. The defeat of the British had settled the question of the colonists' right to self-government, but there was another important question that had to be faced: when would the United States of America extend to Blacks the rights and freedoms that black and white patriots had fought so hard to win?

The Slave Compromise

The Federalist, No. 54

One of the issues facing the Constitutional Convention of 1787 was whether to count the slaves in the apportionment for taxes and for members in the House of Representatives. Southern delegates favored counting the slaves for the purpose of apportioning members of the House, thereby increasing the number of representatives from their states; however, these delegates did not favor counting the slaves for the purpose of direct taxation. Northern delegates took the opposite position. Some delegates noted the inconsistency of considering slaves as persons for one purpose while considering them as chattels, or property, for another.

Alexander Hamilton, John Jay, and James Madison wrote *The Federalist,* a collection of essays, in an effort to enlist support for the adoption of the Constitution. The essay excerpted briefly below deals with the compromise that later became part of the Constitution. Strangely, in that compromise slaves were described as being both persons and property.

Following the quotation from *The Federalist* is a sentence from Article I, Section 2 of the Constitution of the United States. This sentence was nullified by section 2 of the Fourteenth Amendment.

THE FEDERALIST, NO. 54

We subscribe to the doctrine, might one of our southern brethren observe, that representation relates more immediately to persons, and taxation more immediately to property, and we join in the application of this distinction to the case of our slaves. But we must deny the fact that slaves are considered merely as property, and in no respect whatever as persons. The true state of the case is, that they partake of both these qualities; being considered by our laws, in some respects, as persons, and in other respects, as property. In being compelled to labor not for himself, but for a master; in being vendible by one master to another master; and in being subject at all times to be restrained in his liberty, and chastised in his body, by the capricious wil of another, the slave may appear to be degraded from the human rank, and classed with those irrational animals, which fall under the legal denomination of property. In being protected on the other hand in his life & in his limbs, against the violence of all others, even the master of his labor and his liberty; and in being punishable himself for all violence committed against others; the slave is no less evidently regarded by the law as a member of the society; not as a part of the irrational creation; as a moral person, not as a mere article of property. The Fœderal Constitution therefore, decides with great propriety on the case of our slaves, when it views them in the mixt character of persons and of property. This is in fact their true character. It is the character bestowed on them by the laws under which they live; and it will not be denied that these are the proper criterion; because it is only under the pretext that the laws have transformed the negroes into subjects of property, that a place is disputed them in the computation of numbers; and it is admitted that if the laws were to restore the rights which have been taken away, the negroes could no longer be refused an equal share of representation with the other inhabitants.

THE CONSTITUTION, ARTICLE I, SECTION 2

Representatives and direct Taxes shall be apportioned among the several States which may be included within this Union, according to their respective Numbers, which shall be determined by adding to the whole Number of free Persons, including those bound to Service for a Term of Years, and excluding Indians not taxed, three fifths of all other Persons.

In Praise of Paul Cuffe

Peter Williams

The following article is an address delivered in 1817 by Peter Williams, a New York Negro studying for the priesthood. In it Williams praises Paul Cuffe, an American shipbuilder, merchant, and sea captain, for his efforts to obtain voting privileges for Massachusetts blacks. Paul Cuffe was an American deeply committed to fighting for the equality of his black brothers. He acted upon this commitment in both the use of his own resources (ships, money, etc.) and his efforts to convince public officials that the status of blacks needed improvement.

In his person, Capt. Cuffe was large and well proportioned. His countenance was serious but mild. His speech and habit, plain and unostentatious. His deportment, dignified and prepossessing; blending gravity with modesty and sweetness, and firmness with gentleness and humility. His whole exterior indicated a man of respectability and piety. Such would a stranger have supposed him to be at the first glance.

To convey a further idea of him, it is necessary to recur to his history. He was born in the year 1759, on one of the Elizabeth Islands, near New Bedford. His parents had ten children—four sons and six daughters. He was the youngest of the sons. His father died when he was about 14 years of age, at which time he had learnt but little more than his alphabet; and having from thence, with his brothers, the care of his mother and sisters devolving upon him, he had but little opportunity for the acquisitions of literature. Indeed, he never had any schooling, but obtained what learning he had by his own indefatigable exertions, and the scanty aids which he occasionally received from persons who were friendly towards him. By these means, however, he advanced to a considerable proficiency in arithmetic and skill in navigation. Of his talent for receiving learning, we may form an estimate from the fact, that he acquired such a knowledge of navigation in two weeks as enabled him to command his vessel in the voyages which he made to Russia, to England, to Africa, to the West India Islands, as well as to a number of different ports in the southern section of the United States. His mind, it appears, was early inclined to the pursuits of commerce. Before he was grown to manhood, he made several voyages to the West Indies, and along the American coast. At the age of 20, he commenced business for himself, in a small open boat. With this, he set out trading to the neighboring towns and settlements; and, though Providence seemed rather unpropitious to him at first, by perseverance, prudence and industry, his resources were so blessed with an increase, that, after a while, he was enabled to obtain a good sized schooner. In this vessel he enlarged the sphere of his action; trading to more distant places, and in articles requiring a larger capital; and thus, in the process of time, he became owner of one brig, afterwards of 2, then he added a ship, and so on until 1806, at which time he was possessed of one ship, two brigs, and several smaller vessels, besides considerable property in houses and lands.

*   *   *

In the year 1780, Capt. C. being just then of age, was with his brother John, called on by the collector to pay his personal tax. At that time the coloured people of Massachusetts were not considered as entitled to the right of suffrage, or to any of the privileges peculiar to citizens. A question immediately arose with them, whether it was constitutional for them to pay taxes, while they were deprived of the rights enjoyed by others who paid them? They concluded, it was not; and, though the sum was small, yet considering it as an imposition affecting the interests of the people of colour throughout the state, they refused to pay it. The consequence was, a law-suit, attended with so much trouble and vexatious delay, that they finally gave it up, by complying with the requisitions of the collector. They did not, however, abandon the pursuit of their rights; but at the next session of the Legislature, presented a petition, praying that they might have the rights, since they had to bear the burden of citizenship; and though there was much reason to doubt of its success, yet it was granted, and all the free coloured people of the state, on paying their taxes, were considered, from thenceforth, as entitled to all the privileges of citizens. For this triumph of justice and humanity over prejudice and oppression, not only the coloured people of Massachusetts, but every advocate of correct principle, owes a tribute of respect and gratitude to John and Paul Cuffe.

In 1797, Capt. Cuffe, lamenting that the place in which he lived was destitute of a school for the instruction of youth; and anxious that his children should have a more favorable opportunity of obtaining education than he had had, proposed to his neighbors to unite with him in erecting a school-house. This, though the utility of the object was undeniable, was made the cause of so much contention, (probably on account of his colour) that he resolved at length to build a school-house on his own land, and at his own expense. He did so, and when finished, gave them the use of it gratis, satisfying himself with seeing it occupied for the purposes contemplated.

*   *   *

But it was in his active commiseration in behalf of his African brethren, that he shone forth most conspicuously as a man of worth. Long had his bowels yearned over their degraded, destitute, miserable condition. He saw, it is true, many benevolent men engaging in releasing them from bondage, and pouring into their minds the light of literature and religion, but he saw also the force of prejudice operating so powerfully against them, as to give but little encouragement to hope that they could ever rise to respectability and usefulness, unless it were in a state of society where they would have greater incentives to improvement, and more favorable opportunities than would probably be ever afforded them where the bulk of the population are whites.

Under this impression, he turned his thoughts to the British settlement at Sierra Leona; and in 1811, finding his property sufficient to warrant the undertaking, and believing it to be his duty to appropriate part of what God had given him to the benefit of his and our unhappy race, he embarked on board of his own brig, manned entirely by persons of colour, and sailed to the land of his forefathers, in the hope of benefitting its natives and descendants.

Arrived at the colony, he made himself acquainted with its condition, and held a number of conversations with the governor and principal inhabitants; in which he suggested a number of important improvements. Among other things, he recommended the formation of a society for the purposes of promoting the interests of its members and of the colonists in general; which measure was immediately adopted, and the society named "The Friendly Society of Sierra Leona." From thence he sailed to England, where, meeting with every mark of attention and respect, he was favored with an opportunity of opening his views to the board of managers of the African Institution, who cordially acquiescing in all his plans, gave him authority to carry over from the U. States a few coloured persons of good character, to instruct the colonists in agriculture and the mechanical arts. After this he returned to Sierra Leona, carrying with him some goods as a consignment to the Friendly Society, to encourage them in the way of trade; which having safely delivered, and given them some salutary instructions, he set sail and returned again to his native land.

*   *   *

Scarcely had the first transports of rejoicing, at his return, time to subside, before he commenced his preparations for a second voyage; not discouraged by the labours and dangers he had past, and unmindful of the ease which the decline of life requires, and to which his long continued and earnest exertions gave him a peculiar claim. In the hope of finding persons of the description given by the African Institution, he visited most of the large cities in the union, held frequent conferences with the most reputable men of colour, and also with those among the whites who had distinguished themselves as the friends of the Africans; and recommended to the coloured people to form associations for the furtherance of the benevolent work in which he was engaged. The results were, the formation of two societies, one in Philadelphia, and the other in New York, and the discovery of a number of proper persons, who were willing to go with him and settle in Africa. But unfortunately, before he found himself in readiness for the voyage, the war commenced between this country and Great Britain. This put a bar in the way of his operations, which he was so anxious to remove, that he travelled from his home at Westport, to the city of Washington, to solicit the government to favor his views, and to let him depart and carry with him those persons and their effects whom he had engaged to go and settle in Sierra Leona. He was, however, unsuccessful in the attempt. His general plan was highly and universally approbated, but the policy of the government would not admit of such an intercourse with an enemy's colony.

He had now no alternative but to stay at home and wait the event of the war. But the delay, thus occasioned, instead of being suffered to damp his ardor, was improved by him to the maturing of his plans, and extending his correspondence, which already embraced some of the first characters in Great Britain and America. After the termination of the war, he with all convenient speed prepared for his departure, and in Dec. 1815, he took on board his brig 38 persons of the dispersed race of Africa; and after a voyage of 55 days, landed them safely on the soil of their progenitors.

It is proper here to remark that Capt. C. in his zeal for the welfare of his brethren, had exceeded the instructions of the institution at London. They had advised him not to carry over, in the first instance, more than 6 or 8 persons; consequently, he had no claim on them for the passage and other expenses attending the removal of any over that number. But this he had previously considered, and generously resolved to bear the burden of the expense himself, rather than any of those whom he had engaged should be deprived of an opportunity of going where they might be so usefully employed. He moreover foresaw, that when these persons were landed at Sierra Leona, it would be necessary to make such provision for the destitute as would support them until they were enabled to provide for themselves.

For this also he had to apply to his own resources, so that in this voyage he expended out of his own private funds, between three and four thousand dollars, for the benefit of the colony.

CHAPTER TEN

Plantation Life: Emergence of a Culture

The selections in this chapter direct the reader's attention to a vivid description of slavery as it existed in the period between the Revolution and the Civil War. They are presented with the hope that the act of reading these descriptions can provide a vicarious experience for the reader of the black experience of a past era. Is it important for people of the present day to sense the feelings of blacks in slavery? For those who seek an understanding of the human experience, as it has emerged at different times and as it continues to evolve, encompassing a multiplicity of people, the answer is likely to be yes.

Slavery in America, 1836–1837

In the following selection the description of the black experience is made poignant with direct quotations from an American lawyer, a clergyman, and George Washington's will. Together, these quotations bring to the surface the American people's divided feelings about slavery when it existed. The feelings they evoke at the present time are predictable in terms of the divergent opinions expressed.

CHARACTER OF AMERICAN SLAVERY

Of all the anomalies existing on the face of the earth, that of American slavery is the most perplexing and criminal. Whether viewed in relation to the civil institutions of the country, or to the professedly Christian character of the population, it awakens emotions of astonishment and disgust. It is a satire on the constitution which proclaims that men are born free and equal, and gives the lie to the religious profession of the community. The contact of slavery with republicanism and Christianity in America, instead of ameliorating its character, has added to its horrors, and rendered it more loathsome and abominable than it is elsewhere found. Its extenuators may plead the moral worth and sacred calling of its patrons, but we point in mournful triumph to the atrocious code, in which its character is depicted, and pronounce it to be the masterpiece of Satanic barbarity and fraud. The following description was given by Mr. Loring, in a learned speech lately delivered in one of the civil courts of America, on behalf of a slave child, whom it was sought to return to bondage. Reader, look upon the picture, and then say what should be thought of clergymen and theological professors who dare to defend it, or to observe an avowed neutrality. "Before looking for the lights of our own jurisprudence on the subject," says the American barrister, "I ask leave to define, in a more special manner, what is slavery, as it exists among us?

For this purpose I shall read from 'Stroud's Sketch of the Laws relating to Slavery' (an accurate and valuable compendium), the following propositions, describing the incidents of American slavery. For the most ample proof of each, I refer to the work itself, where the codes, statutes, judicial decisions, &c. of the several states, on slavery, are digested.

Prop. 1. The master may determine the kind, and degree, and time of labour, to which the slave shall be subjected.

Prop. 2. The master may supply the slave with such food and clothing only, both as to quantity and quality, as he may think proper or find convenient.

Prop. 3. The master may, at his discretion, inflict any punishment upon the person of his slave.

Prop. 4. All the power of the master over his slave may be exercised not by himself only in person, but by any one whom he may depute as his agent.

Prop. 5. Slaves have no legal rights of property in things, real or personal; but whatever they may acquire belongs, in point of law, to their masters.

Prop. 6. The slave, being a personal chattel, is at all times liable to be sold absolutely, or mortgaged or leased at the will of his master.

Prop. 7. He may also be sold by process of law for the satisfaction of the debts of a living, or the debts and bequests of a deceased master, at the suit of creditors or legatees.

Prop. 8. A slave cannot be a party before a judicial tribunal, in any species of action, against his master, no matter how atrocious may have been the injury received from him.

Prop. 9. Slaves cannot redeem themselves, nor obtain a change of masters, though cruel treatment may have rendered such change necessary for their personal safety.

Prop. 10. Slaves being objects of *property*, if injured by third persons, their owners may bring suit, and recover damages for the injury.

Prop. 11. Slaves can make no contract.

Prop. 12. Slavery is hereditary and perpetual.

I hold in my hand another brief delineation of American slavery. It is accurate and most expressive, but its plainness of speech is so remarkable, that I hesitate to read it, before I shall have premised that its author is the Rev. Robert J. Breckinridge, a southern clergyman of great eminence, at this moment a representative from the Presbyterian churches of the United States to those of England and Scotland, but perhaps principally distinguished as an uncompromising opponent of the immediate abolitionists. In a speech delivered by Mr. B., he asks:—

What, then, is slavery? for the question relates to the action of certain principles on it, and to its probable and proper results; what is slavery as it exists among us? We reply, it is that condition enforced by the laws of one-half the states of this confederacy, in which one portion of the community, called masters, is allowed such power over another portion called slaves; as

1. To deprive them of the entire earnings of their labour, except only so much as is necessary to continue labour itself, by continuing healthful existence; thus committing clear robbery.

2. To reduce them to the necessity of universal concubinage, by denying to them the civil rights of marriage; thus breaking up the dearest relations of life, and encouraging universal prostitution.

3. To deprive them of the means and opportunities of moral and intellectual culture—in many states making it a high penal offence to teach them to read; thus perpetuating whatever of evil there is that proceeds from ignorance.

4. To set up between parents and their children an authority higher than the impulse of nature and the laws of God; which breaks up the authority of the father over his own offspring, and, at pleasure, separates the mother at a returnless distance from her child; thus abrogating the clearest laws of nature; thus outraging all decency and justice, and degrading and oppressing thousands upon thousands of beings created like themselves in the image of the most high God!

This is slavery as it is daily exhibited in every slave state."

WASHINGTON'S WILL

Upon the decease of my wife it is my will and desire that all my slaves, which I hold in my own right, shall receive their freedom. To emancipate them during her life, would, though earnestly wished, be attended with such insuperable difficulties, on account of their intermixture by marriages with the dower negroes, as to create the most fearful sensation, if not disagreeable consequences from the latter, while both descriptions are in the occupancy of the same proprietor; it not being in my power under the tenure by which the dower negroes are held to manumit them. And, whereas, among those who will receive their freedom according to this clause, there may be some who, from old age, or bodily infirmities, and others who, on account of their infancy, will be unable to support themselves; it is my will and desire that all who come under the first and second descriptions shall be comfortably clothed and fed by my heirs while they live; and that such of the latter description as have no parents living, or, if having, are unable or unwilling to provide for them, shall be bound by the court until they shall arrive at the age of twenty-five years; and, in cases where no record can be produced whereby their ages can be ascertained, the judgment of the court, upon its own view of the subject, shall be adequate and final. The negroes, thus bound, are by their masters and mistresses to be taught to read and write, and to be brought up to some useful occupation, agreeable to the laws of the commonwealth of Virginia, providing for the support of orphans and other poor children.

And I do hereby expressly forbid the sale or transportation out of the said commonwealth, of any slave I may die possessed of under any pretence whatever. And I do, moreover, pointedly, and most solemnly enjoin it upon my executors hereafter named, or the survivor of them, to see that this clause respecting slaves, and every part thereof, be religiously fulfilled at the epoch at which it is directed to take place, without evasion, neglect, or delay, after the crops which are then on the ground are harvested. Particularly as it respects the aged and infirm, seeing that a regular and permanent fund be established for their support, as long as there are subjects requiring it, not trusting to the uncertain provisions to be made by individuals. And to my mulatto man William (calling himself William Lee), I give immediate freedom, or, if he should prefer it on account of the accidents which have befallen him, and which have rendered him incapable of walking, or of active employment, to remain in the situation he now is, it shall be optional for him to do so; in either case, however, I allow him an annuity of thirty dollars during his natural life, which shall be independent of the victuals and clothes he has been accustomed to receive, if he chooses the last alternative, but in full with his freedom if he prefers the first. And this I give him as a testimony of my sense of his attachment to me, and for his faithful service during the revolutionary war.

The Black Slave Driver

Leslie Howard Owens

How does one feel if one is a slave and a boss at the same time? If the slave has to please both his master and his wards? If one is driven to prove his excellence as a boss but also drawn with compassion to his wards, without whose help he cannot prove his excellence? These are some of the paradoxes that are described in "The Black Slave Driver," a chapter from Leslie Howard Owens' book, *This Species of Property.* The article points to the irony of the black experience, which arose from the paradoxical position that many blacks occupied.

Among those slaves most important to the functioning and harmony of plantation life, the slave driver (foreman) held a slight edge. His hut, perhaps a little larger and better furnished than those of his neighbors, sometimes stood in the center of the slave community. On farms with only a few bondsmen, although there might be no slave known officially as a slave driver, there was usually one who served from time to time as a field leader. His duties in the fields could have considerable impact on the behavior of fellow bondsmen and were crucial to the economic well-being of the slaveholder. One master wrote: "A man would do better to have a good Negro driver, than to have an overseer. . . ." Another noted: "The head driver is the most important negro on the plantation."

What manner of men were these foremen? One ex-driver said simply: "I allers use my sense for help me 'long; jes' like Brer Rabbit. 'Fo' de wah ol Marse Heywood mek me he driber on he place. . . ." Slaveholders' comments provide some other insights. "Nearly every large plantation further South," wrote J. D. B. De Bow, "has a driver, who is a negro advanced to the post from his good character and intelligence." Good character meant any variety of things depending on the situation; most important, however, the driver maintained his position only if he also had the ability to extract work from fellow slaves. James Henry Hammond of South Carolina noted in his plantation book that the driver "is to be treated with more respect than any negro by both master and overseer."

Carefully conceived, the rule recognized the need to attach prestige to the driver's position. Hammond further commented on the unique relationship he thought a driver ought to have with master and overseer. "He is a confidential servant and may be a guard against any excesses or omissions of the overseer."[The driver was thus part of the checks and balances by which careful slaveholders looked out for all their interests.]

Was the driver really so important to the slave scene? The death of Ismael, the slave foreman of Thomas Butler of Louisiana, elicited Butler's recognition that while Ismael was alive there was little fear that the plantation could have "suffered from the mismanagement of an injudicious overseer . . . for he was the best driver I ever knew." The loss of a slave foreman prompted another master to fear that "his services . . . cannot be replaced."

To be sure, slaves' responses to black drivers ran the full spectrum of contacts between men. The position was an important but ambiguous one,[for the effective slave driver had to tread a path between master and slave, serving both whenever he could.]Often this was not possible, leading frequently to driver versus slave or driver versus master-overseer confrontations. The driver might be the plantation "tough," but it was best if he stood up to bullies while forsaking that role himself. Besides, if he bullied the wrong slave there was no telling how the ensuing conflict might end. In one encounter recorded by the driver, a bondsman being disciplined "flong down his cradle and made a oath and said that he had as live die as to live and . . . he then tried to take the whip out of my hand. . . ." In a more serious case, in October 1838 a planter wrote hastily—so his penmanship reflects—to a friend from his West Baton Rouge, Louisiana, plantation that "a few days ago a favorite Negro [a neighbor's driver], . . . was murdered by one of the other negroes he is said to have been horribly cut to pieces, the one that killed him has run away."

Such incidents occurred now and then because in order to save his own back, remarked Francis Fedric, "the slave overseer very often behaves in the most brutal manner to the niggers under him." The experience of another slave confirms this observation. He decried his treatment during one year when, as he emphasized, "he [the master] had a *colored slave foreman,* who had to do as he was commanded, and I hardly had so much consideration as from a white overseer."

There were, quite naturally, many rules to regulate the driver's behavior. But often these rules were only as good as the man. His responsibilities were sometimes nerve-racking, and his temper flared, not unnaturally, when slaves failed to accomplish their tasks. He could be blamed for their shortcomings, and since all the hands knew this any one of them might deliberately antagonize him, compromising his position just as bondsmen regularly compromised the position of overseers.

The Reverend Peter Randolph, an ex-slave writing in the 1890's, set forth an interpretation of drivers which, with minor variations, has passed from the pens and, it seems, through the minds of various scholars unchanged almost to the present. He observed that by placing blacks in the position of foreman, planters were able to point to them as co-initiators of cruelty on plantations. Yet for Randolph the driver was more like a soldier carrying out his orders. The actions of James Williams, himself at one time a slave foreman, are partially illustrative of Randolph's position. Placed in charge of 160 slaves, Williams had "orders to supply the whip unsparingly to every one, whether man or woman." Failure to comply, he explained, left "myself subject at any moment to feel the accursed lash upon my own back. . . ." He admitted whipping a pregnant slave brutally: "I . . . gave her fifty lashes." Although at one point in his narrative he informs his readers, perhaps to ease a troubled conscience, that he "used to tell the poor creatures [females], when compelled by the overseer to urge them forward with the whip, that I would much rather take their places and endure the stripes than inflict them," he seldom seemed to hesitate in carrying out his instructions to the letter. In Frederick County, Virginia, still another driver confided, "I was harder on the servants than he [his master] wanted I should be." His owner punished him for his cruelty, but his self-initiated disciplining of other bondsmen indicates how seriously he took his job.

These statements support the charges of those who describe the driver's relationship with other slaves as despotic. Clearly, this side of the relationship did exist. It is worth mentioning, however, that it does not seem to have been the most prevalent side. The driver also served in another and far more important capacity —as confidant and mediator.

It is true that while some drivers nagged other slaves into making careless mistakes which they might then agree to cover up in exchange for small favors and even a portion of the slave's already meager weekly rations or hunting fortunes, others attempted to be helpful. The southern novelist William Gilmore Simms advanced an interesting, though limited, portrayal of the slave foreman in his 1845 story "The Loves of the Driver." The slave in question is Mingo, a many-sided figure. Simms describes him as of "not uncomely countenance" and as "brave as Julius Caesar in his angry mood." Throughout the story Simms' characterization of Mingo is generally complimentary. He shows Mingo's ability to maintain tranquility in the quarters and to sustain the respect of bondsmen by his conduct before the master. Though Simms' characterization of Mingo is often historically flawed, it stands as an honest portrayal of the driver's functions as Simms saw them.

Mingo's multi-faceted personality angered many literary critics in both the Old South and the North who thought that Simms had overstepped the boundaries of artistic license by making a slave the hero of his tale. Simms apparently was bothered by the criticisms, for in none of his later works do slaves play other than token, undeveloped roles. Nevertheless, his brief descriptions of plantation life and of black bondsmen demonstrate that at least for him slaves were more complex than the stereotypic bondsmen readers often encounter.

A driver's job was difficult, for despite the power granted him, the wise driver understood that he gained the trust or enmity of his companions from his associations with them in private just as much as in the fields. It was probably in these private moments that slaves made those agreements that help to explain bondsman Solomon Northup's and others' observations that the lashes of some drivers came close to but never touched the backs of certain slaves, even when the drivers had been ordered to work them vigorously and lay on the whip.

The driver did, according to the testimony of one planter, have his "perquisites of office—and the privilege of bestowing small benefits . . ." upon his fellows. The ex-slave Baskin, a slave driver, perhaps made other uses of the office. He bragged that when he went courting among the slave women, despite his small stature, "I alers carry off de purties gal, 'cause you see, Missus, [along with being the driver] I know how to play de fiddle [for some drivers this was an important management asset] an allers had to go to obery dance to play de fiddle for dem."

Though this admission is innocent enough, a few drivers sexually assaulted slave women, though we can only speculate about how frequently this occurred. Drivers also worked out arrangements by which certain females were not required to work too hard at times and were given a few minutes' extra rest. Within the shadow of the plantation a variety of agreements were grabbed at to help ease the conditions of bondage.

How was it possible for many of these agreements to come about?[For one thing, many masters gave slave drivers great responsibilities and left important matters to their discretion.]Walter S. Harris, who was born a slave in Virginia in 1847, reflected back in 1910 on the old days in a letter to his former master's son. He remembered that his "father (until we left in May 1864) was your Fathers head man on the home place." But most revealing are his remarks about his father's duties: "he sowed all the wheat, had charge of the hogs, in fact Master never at anytime know how many sheep or hogs he had." Here is part of the answer. A driver might neglect to mention the precise number of livestock, allowing himself one or more head to trade on or off the plantation in exchange for favors or items of use for himself.

It is difficult, in fact, to explain extensive slave plantation maneuverings not in the interest of masters without positing driver complicity with bondsmen in a wide range of activities. For example, in the Parrysburgh district of South Carolina in 1787, according to planter John L. Bourquin, runaways were at his "Swamp plantation, & . . . they left us with the loss of our Driver fellow [who ran off with them], ten Barrels of clean Rice & myself slightly wounded in the hip. . . ." Slave foreman George Skipwith recognized leaders in "resistance" among the field hands under his care in Alabama. He also knew that just because he was the leader chosen by his master he was not necessarily the one chosen by his fellows.

The possibilities for personal development within slavery stretched before slave foremen as for few other bondsmen. For purposes of slave community harmony he was usually a married man, and his household shared in the "perquisities" granted him as well as in the scorn he might receive from companions. Many drivers were married to domestic slaves—cooks or maids—thus setting up additional and important links between the field and the Big House. With each added privilege some drivers grew less amenable to assault, less receptive to direct challenges "for daring to think." When a slaveholder's support was withdrawn drivers often reacted in extreme ways—they ran off, sabotaged the estate, or turned on their masters physically. The ex-slave Walter S. Harris recalled that his driver "father disobeyed your father [a master] in a matter while he was in Charles City in May 1864, which caused an unpleasantness and one dark night, father taken us [his family] an' slipped away." This conversion to rebel was not a simple reflex. The driver's perception of himself had much time to develop as he carried out his duties. He could easily see that although society discriminated against him he was certainly as qualified as many whites to direct the course of his destiny. It is interesting too that often he did not see himself as unique in this regard among "field" slaves.

James Henry Hammond of South Carolina wrote a revealing sentence about drivers in the plantation book he kept. The driver, he stressed, "is on no occasions to be treated with any indignity, calculated to lose the respect of other negroes, without breaking [being especially cruel to] him. . . ." Hammond conceived of the black foreman as a liaison between master and slave, plantation house and slave quarters. The driver could convey the complaints of bondsmen to the master; but he could do this accurately only if he had a sound understanding of specific individuals. He was not usually a spy, a dupe of the slaveholder, although he could become that. But if he breached too many confidences he found his management of slaves increasingly difficult and his private life somewhat censored. It was best to stay on the slave's side of the line.

The slaveholder John Cooke viewed the driver as a "humble friend of the master." William Pettigrew of North Carolina, while consoling his driver Moses about the death of his uncle, reminded Moses that "our lot having been cast together her[e] [on earth] . . . I am a friend. . . ." Yet neither Pettigrew nor Cooke appeared to convey by this that the driver was a dupe. They expected him to be an individual who had confidence in himself to perform his assigned duties. If he did this—often having great leeway in his interpretation of them—he was eligible to receive rewards for "himself & his family" in money, clothing, or other things he selected. Thus, the driver's potential for acquiring influence over his fellows and his master's interests was greatly expanded. Regarding remuneration for services well performed, Cooke recalled, "I have known the monied annuity to very from $5 to $100 a year." Where this practice was followed the driver might aid his friends in getting badly needed additional clothing or even food. But he could, as well, withhold his beneficence in a display of displeasure with their behavior. Appropriately used, his "freedoms" could be the critical element in cementing his authority.

The slave Peter, identified in a letter from William Pettigrew to a relative as the one who "so well supplied the place of the worthless fellow [an overseer] you discharged," ran the North Carolina plantation of James C. Johnston in the mid-1840's. The letter continued, "there are some instances in which negroes are not inferior to white men . . ." Years before, in 1803, an ancestor, Charles Pettigrew, had commented that "the negroes at the Lake plantation have commonly done better by themselves with a little direction than with such Overseers, as we have had." James Johnston wrote in 1849: "I have three farms carried on entirely by colored men without the aid of a white and I think they are better managed than I ever had them when I employed white overseers. . . ." In each instance, select slaves apparently served as both overseers and drivers. The practice was not unusual, since many times the duties of overseer and driver were virtually the same. The practice appeared to add to plantation harmony. An additional consideration on the Pettigrew estates was that the bondsmen were furnished more of life's material goods than slaves obtained on many other plantations. But of far greater importance is the part these slave managers played in shaping the outcome. William Pettigrew summed up his feelings this way:

It is desirable, if the good conduct of my negroes will justify it not to employ a white overseer for preferring this I have several reasons . . . if one be so unfortunate as to employ a worthless man, then his negroes & his income both suffer; for the former with such a person soon settle into idleness. As far as I can, up to this time form an opinion, I think my people will, by the assistance of the two negro men who have heretofore been over them Henry at Magnolia & Moses at Belgrade, work faithfully, and conduct themselves well.

Any number of planters around the Old South would have agreed with this assessment. A South Carolina slaveholder, a friend of James Henry Hammond, certainly did. He wrote to Hammond about a slave auction where a slave driver was sold. He mentioned that he was a man 35 to 40 years of age and was "so intelligent & trustworthy that he had charge of a separate plantation & 8 or 10 hands, some 10 or 12 miles from home. . . ." He concluded, "Such a man would be invaluable to me. . . ."

Yet despite this evidence of his obvious importance to the slave scene, the driver has not received much attention from scholars, and in two recent studies about slave culture he garners only passing references. On large plantations the driver's influence in slave affairs was often of such importance as to alter many perceptions we have about the total slave community. He has to be an integral part of our examination of slavery.

It will perhaps serve to illustrate this point further if we focus on the experience of the slave driver George Skipwith, who has left us, in his own words, a rather unique and detailed account of his experiences. From Greensboro, Alabama, George wrote his master John Cocke in 1847, "i hav[e] a good crop on hand for you both of Cotton and corn this you knoe could not be don without hard work." For almost five years George managed the affairs of this particular plantation. He watched over the livestock, planting, and harvesting and handled the disciplining of his fellow slaves. This latter duty caused much animosity between him and his hands. He was also very protective of the authority he exercised and battled against whites and blacks who tried to compromise his position.

Admittedly, George Skipwith was an exceptional slave in many ways, not only by virtue of his status as a slave foreman. He and some of the other slaves on this Alabama plantation were among a group selected by John Cocke to be colonized from Virginia to Alabama and then, after a period of preparation, to be sent to Liberia in Africa. But many years were to pass before this began to happen, and in most cases these Alabama slaves did not escape bondage.

The Shadow of the Slave Quarters

Leslie Howard Owens

Throughout the world, both in the past and at present, most people leave for their homes after work. The homes may be a house, an apartment, a hotel, or a motel; the work may be anything from ruling a country to begging. The people who live together in a home, the activities they pursue once in a home, and the interaction between members of one home and another provide rich information for cultural and sociological studies of people. Such a study is provided in the following article "The Shadow of the Slave Quarters," another selection from the book *This Species of Property* by Leslie Howard Owens.

In reading this article, one has to exercise some caution in distinguishing facts from inferences drawn from those facts. Inferences with regard to human pathos are very often influenced by the perspective from which the facts are seen. Hence, it is possible that the reader may not agree with the inferences drawn by Mr. Owens.

The social arena in which bondsmen of every station—field hands, domestics, drivers, artisans—came face to face was the slave quarters. Here slaves held center stage, and the larger the farm or plantation the greater the odds that the roles they played here would go largely unnoticed by many masters. The influence of the quarters was a strong one, difficult to measure in direct terms, but frequently an important factor shaping the quality of the slave's personality, his private life, and his bondage itself.

Although slaves generally lived in huts arranged tightly together around an open expanse of ground, the dwellings themselves varied greatly from plantation to plantation. A slave has left us with this vivid description of the slave quarters on one of the larger estates:

> The houses that the slaves lived in were all built in a row, away from the big house. Just at the head of the street and between the cabins and the big house, stood the overseer's house. There was some forty or fifty of these two room cabins facing each other across an open space for a street. In them we lived. There was not much furniture. Just beds and a table and some stools or boxes to sit on. Each house had a big fire-place for heat and cooking.

This was the village-like setting he remembered, a physically tight community animated by the life within. In most settings the overseer's hut was not a part of this complex. When it was, of course, it was situated so that he might keep his eye on his charges. Perhaps an additional description is also worth noting. It comes to us from a slave, and in some ways describes the kind of living arrangement that was most widespread. Negro houses

> were constructed of logs, and from twelve to fifteen feet square; they had no glass, but there were holes to let in the light and air. The furniture consisted of a table, a few stools, and dishes made of wood, and an iron pot, and some other cooking utensils.

But what of the fabric of slave life, its disappointments and its joys? One historian has written that in the quarters "there was much hospitality and sociability, much dancing, laughing, singing and banjo playing when the day's work was done." A portion of his claim is correct, but his implications as to the bondsman's carefree existence are in need of revision.

For slaves, life in the quarters could be a welcome retreat from the prying eyes of overseer and master. To aid in securing this privacy many slave cabins had the conjurer's horseshoe brand or some other conjuring symbol on their doors to bar evil spirits and persons. And inside the door a "conjuring gourd" might be just within reach. A definite calm was often noticeable in bondsmen's deportment in this setting, as a result of their being here at leisure. The English traveler Captain Basil Hall once asked a master about happenings in the Quarters. "In answer to our question he told us that he interfered as little as possible with their domestic habits, except in matters of police." At times this widely followed practice nearly gave the bondsman a free hand. Robert Carter, the Virginia planter, once chastised his overseer for whipping the slave Jerry for a disturbance in the quarters. The "offense you Charged him with," he angrily pointed out, "was a matter in his own house, last Wednesday night when two Negro men [belonging to neighbors] were very much disposed to fight on acct of Negro Mary who lives at Jerry's house, but thro the means of Jerry these fellows were dispersed. . . ."

In all slave quarters, of course, the presence of slaves of varying duties, strengths, talents, and temperaments living and socializing together caused some personal and managerial difficulties. Skilled laborers might not have to start their work with the first sign of dawn like other slaves; they were more likely to labor at their own pace, and usually had longer rest breaks. They were "slaves of significance" to the plantation's operations, fully aware of their special status. Animosities quickly developed between them and other slaves during non-working hours. Finding himself an unwilling onlooker to an emerging rivalry, an overseer wrote to his employer that "i have bin oblige to tell your mill handes that they had to leave the quarter at the same time those people did that is in my Charge." The field hands did not believe that the mill laborers were working as hard as they. In a letter dated three days earlier, the overseer warned that if some slaves "see negroes around them Ideling why they want to doe so two" and would if given the chance, he believed.

Such disparities set the stage for the quarrels and fights that erupted in the quarters, sometimes becoming feuds that dragged on through the years, ending only when one or several of the feuding slaves died or were sold by the master. In a similar sense, a single slave could try to dominate the quarters scene, making life unpleasant for other bondsmen when he or she chose to. The Maryland slave Elisa was able to do this with some regularity. "Jane says," reads the diary of Susanna Warfield, that "she rules in the quarter—When she gets angry it is no use to Say any thing to Elisa—She will whip every child in the quarter until she satisfies her vengeance." With a slave like Elisa around, some difficult situations might develop between her and other bondsmen during their important leisure hours. Her impact, directly within the quarters, was probably more important at times than the Warfields'. Elisa worked steadily to consolidate her position, acting like a combatant to whom the engagement is new but the footpaths well worn.

Her position was different from, for example, that of the "old people" of the quarters, who with approaching age traditionally assumed places of respect among slaves. That this did not always hold true in a favorable sense, however, is clear from a runaway slave's unsympathetic words about "old Milla." He wrote to his former master in his own hand, "I expect [she] is dead & gone to the devil long ago, if she is not, I think the imps are close at her heels, & will soon put her where there are nothing else but *nasty stinking black dogs* a plenty." The emphasis is his own, and he perhaps alluded to supernatural forces because some of the old ones were known to be powerful practitioners of the occult. Throughout southern neighborhoods many were known as "oracles" of considerable influence.

For children and adults the old peoples' memories were the cultural storehouses of those tall tales that they loved to hear so much. As some huddled around a crackling fire in the evening (the fire was often used to ward off evil spirits), the old ones would frighten them with stories about snakes, their tails tucked neatly into their mouths, rolling in pursuit of human victims and upon catching them, stinging them to death with the end of the tail, or nearly so. Listeners followed the stories closely, for who knew when it might be *his* turn to retell them, winning the admiration of companions? In these settings, the slave's West African past frequently raised its head. "Most of these stories," remembered Charles Ball of his own experiences, "referred to affairs that had been transacted in Africa, and were sufficiently fraught with demons, miracles and murders to fix the attention of many hearers."

Sometimes slaves acted out various parts of the story, and often dancing, story, and music were blended into interesting folk operas. One visitor to Virginia was so enchanted with the folktales he heard that he not only argued, amidst some sarcasm, that slaves were "our ONLY TRULY NATIONAL POETS" but enthused, "A tour through the South, and a year or two of plantation life, would not fail to reward the diligent collector; and his future fame would be as certain as Homer's."

After these sessions slaves retired to their own huts where, depending on the season, "Sometimes we sit around the fire all night. We could have a big hot fire, as much as we wanted, and we would sit up sometimes to keep good and warm." Storytellers were usually elderly men as opposed to elderly women—the reason why is not clear—and they were important contributors to quarters harmony, especially during times when abuse accompanied by long hours of work and widespread disease escalated bondsmen's emotions and suffering to new peaks. This was the wonder of their folktales. The themes spanned a vast variety of circumstances and slave and master character. Frequently they combined a wide range of emotion in the same tale; good and bad, the happy and the sad were overlapping themes.

Keeping in mind sociologist Howard Odum's valuable perception that "treasures of folk-lore and song, the psychic religious, and social expression of the race, have been permitted to remain in complete obscurity," let us pursue some of the slaves' storytelling. Freedom and its necessary accompaniment within bondage, resistance, received extensive embellishment in the slave's folklore talk and give us insights into what slaves really thought concerning life's experience. And contrary to what some interpreters have written, the slave was not always the super-cunning winner in his tales. He was more real than that.

Bondsmen throughout the South told variations of the now-famous Br'er Rabbit stories, most of which have some particularly significant parallels in slave life. Important in this regard is the story "De Reason Br'er Rabbit Wears a Short Tail," found in South Carolina and elsewhere. In this account, Br'er Rabbit (the slave) learns that cunningness is not always rewarded. Br'er Rabbit plans to trick some fish away from brother wolf (the master) for use by his own family. So often in these stories the slave's attention turns to food, perhaps as an indication of a want of sufficient and varied edibles in his daily life. Br'er Rabbit gets the fish from the wolf by lying on the road pretending to be dead while the wolf, the dominant force in the neighborhood, puzzles over his sudden death and momentarily leaves his fish unattended. We cannot deny what some might call the lazy aspects of Br'er Rabbit's character, for he preys off others' efforts, though he does not victimize the weak or helpless. On the contrary, he is usually generous with his "rewards," sharing them with his friends. But in this instance the wolf takes revenge on Br'er Rabbit and his family. Discovering the loss of his fish, he goes to Br'er Rabbit's house and sets it on fire, driving Br'er Rabbit, his wife, and children to the rooftop. When the fire finally reaches them they are forced to leap off the roof one by one into the arms of the wolf, who viciously cuts them to pieces with an axe—an allegorical rendering of the splitting up of the family by the slave trade. Br'er Rabbit, of course, stays on the roof till the last moment when he leaps off into what seems certain death. But his wits save him. Just as the wolf is about to ax him, he spits some chewing tobacco—a familiar commodity of slave life and conjuration practices—into the wolf's eyes, with the result that the wolf's aim is deflected and only Br'er Rabbit's tail is chopped off.

The story is less amusing than most of the Br'er Rabbit variety, but perhaps this is because it bears a more realistic resemblance to slave life and experiences. The personal price that Br'er Rabbit has to pay merely to survive is a high one. The story recommends caution as a slave virtue, yet it also continues the theme of quick thinking and constant alertness, for it is only through these attributes that Br'er Rabbit manages to survive at all.

Indeed the Br'er Rabbit stories and other tales in the slave's folklore repertory are deeply concerned with power relationships. Beyond this concern with power and intertwined with it is the amazing amount of energy that Br'er Rabbit has to expend to accomplish his aims. He must often risk all to implement his cunning. He is, in effect, a rather daring personality, attuned to his own weaknesses and vulnerabilities as well as to those of others. Yet, Br'er Rabbit's triumphs are transitory. He outsmarts, but the powerful, momentarily outsmarted, still maintain their power. In contrast, Br'er Rabbit's power is momentary and totally dependent on the recognition and manipulation of transient opportunities. His view of his life is, in fact, an accurate one, and he sees behind life's surface realities to what may be possible for him even in his present condition. He possesses more human qualities than those who possess mere raw power; or, as an ex-slave storyteller noted in "Cooter an' Deer," "Cooter got de gal an' de whole county see him beat Deer in de ten-mile race for all Deer hab shich [such] long foot."

The slave turned his storytelling abilities to many topics, and mixed them with those endless coinments (aphorisms) that many bondsmen liked to make up on the spur of the moment. Especially in the quarters, they might sit back and momentarily reflect on their lives: "Tain't no use o' sp'ilin de Sat'day night by countin' de time to Monday mornin'."

By its nature the aphorism is a telling observation about one's existence. And the slaves made some interesting observations about their situation. Of their labors they said simply, "Sharp ax better'n big muscle." The hard labor of plowing on a hill received the comment, "Nigger don't sing much plowin' de hillside." And most slaves would have agreed, even when masters failed to understand, that "You can't medjer a nigger's wuk by de mount l' singin' he does at de shuckin'."

These examples make up, along with the slaves' other folklore (music, dance), a continual dialogue that slaves kept up with one another in the quarters and elsewhere. These were more than ingredients for "pep-talk"; they served to ease the bondsman's lot by promoting those images of themselves the slaves wished to assume in their own ranks. Children especially received this continual dict of images from the slave community, being in some measure reared on them. We can only speculate about the impact such accounts had on the slave's self-concept but, like many other things in his life, they clearly helped to shape the responses he made to his bondage.

Slaveholders' manuscript sources confirm that many of these accounts were told to white children by domestic slaves. What impact they had on young minds then and after slavery is hard to assess but should provide a fascinating field of exploration. Many of them are extremely revealing: "Tomorrow may be de carridge-driver's day for ploughin'." The slave turned his attention also to his very important spiritual life. In fact few things escaped his humorous jibes and telling comments: "De people dat stirs up de mos' rackit in de meetin' house ain't always de bes' kis'chuns." And they observed as well, "Folks dat go to sleep in de meetin' house do heap o' late settin' up at home."

The close living space in the quarters itself elicited some perceptive slave remarks. Probably because of the social events they sometimes held there, at which liquid spirits were served, they could see that "licker talks might loud w'en it git loose fum de jug." They also had this sage advice about the well-known practice of dirt-eating: "Ef you bleedzd ter eat dirt, eat clean dirt."

The settings that served as backdrops to the slave's folktales approximate his varied life situations. We know that these tales were told in the slave quarters and at work in the fields. They often turned into folksongs, helpful in cushioning slave labors. The slave John Parker remembered that bondsmen in a slave gang on the road just after an auction consoled themselves with stories and songs.

Folklorists of the slave past have uncovered a number of recurring themes; with further research into this rich reserve we will be able to advance considerably our understanding of slave culture, the African background, and the plantation system. One important theme concerns the cunning or intelligent slave who was frequently called John. The slaves of the John tales bear a resemblance to slave drivers (favored slaves) in that they often serve as mediators between Old Marster and the other slaves and escape the heaviest chores. In support of this interpretation it might be helpful to turn to an ex-slave driver who was something of a folklorist. He claimed that because he was the driver ". . . I aint hab for work so hard as de res'; some time I git mo' ration ebery mont' an' mo' shoe when dey share out de cloes at Chris'mus time. Well, dat com from usin' my sense." The parallel is not a precise one, and there is much of other slaves in John. But there is enough of the driver to suggest his hold on the slave imagination: "Old Marster had this main fellow on his farm he put his confidence in, John."

In the John and other folktales, unlike the Br'er Rabbit stories, the slave is not quite as successful in outsmarting his master. His triumphs take on a more deliberate note, for the tales granted masters their share of victories and kept the slave wisely aware of the realities of his situation.

Among the most interesting in the slave's stock of tales were many that had to do with relationships between slaves themselves. One of the most noteworthy in this regard is called "De Tiger An' De Nyung Lady." Recorded among South Carolina slaves along the seacoast, the story line, as backed up by other evidence, was certainly not unique to these bondsmen. The focus is on a brazen young woman who vows that she will marry no man "what gets a scratch on him back" from whipping. She is warned about her inflexible stand but steadfastly sticks to it. One day a tiger overhears her boast and with the help of a little conjuration determines to teach her a lesson. He turns into the perfect man, marries her and then carries her off to his lair in the swamps and leaves her for three days. She is eventually rescued by an Uncle Sambo, who, unlike the stereotype of that name, shows amazing courage before the tiger. But the tiger does not want to fight, and gives the moral of the story: "I aint gwine hu't her. I only married um for le' um know dat a woman isn't more dan a man, for de word dat she say, dat she 'Wouldn't married a man what gots a scratch on him back'." Uncle Sambo returns the girl home to her mother, who gives her this advice: "God had nebber made a woman for the head of a man."

Such slave traditions, elements of which now seem picturesque, were only slightly altered on the modest farms of less slaveholding whites. The scale of things was smaller, and one looks in vain for the Big House. There were, too, some physical differences in the layout of the slave quarters, if there was a place with that distinct identity. To be sure, that was the main difference. Seldom were there huts set apart on their own ground. Instead, a few unimposing shanties fanned out from the master's house—little more than a shanty itself sometimes—like fingers on a hand. The activities of the quarters were not entirely separate from farm life.

It was in the quarters, wherever they might be, that slaves learned the advantages of pooling their efforts and resources. During all seasons of the year bondsmen collected firewood, "and they often have to go to' the swamp for it." It was safer to travel with friends. Some slaves shared their fortune at hunting or fishing with others in exchange for reciprocal favors. The making of clothing is a case in point. During some evenings women sewed additional clothing for themselves, their men, and their children. They cooked together occasionally also, utilizing the skills and energies of the quarters in many joint efforts. In much of this, naturally, a few bondsmen sponged off the efforts of others and made a mockery of others' attempts at self-improvement, but this was exceptional.

A Slave Catechism

Frederick Douglass

Catechism as defined by the dictionary is "a short manual giving, in the form of questions and answers, an outline of principles of a religious creed." The reader is invited to examine the following selection by Frederick Douglass entitled "A Slave Catechism" to determine: (1) if it qualifies as a catechism, (2) why the term "slave" is introduced in the title, and (3) what distortions of religious principles are contained therein.

Q: Who keeps the snakes and all bad things from hurting you?
A: God does.
Q: Who gave you a master and a mistress?
A: God gave them to me.
Q: Who says that you must obey them?
A: God says that I must.
Q: What book tells you these things?
A: The Bible.
Q: How does God do all his work?
A: He always does it right.
Q: Does God love to work?
A: Yes, God is always at work.
Q: Do the angels work?
A: Yes, they do what God tells them.
Q: Do they love to work?
A: Yes, they love to please God.
Q: What does God say about your work?
A: He that will not work shall not eat.

Q: Did Adam and Eve have to work?
A: Yes, they had to keep the garden.
Q: Was it hard to keep that garden?
A: No, it was very easy.
Q: What makes the crops so hard to grow now?
A: Sin makes it.
Q: What makes you lazy?
A: My wicked heart.
Q: How do you know your heart is wicked?
A: I feel it every day.
Q: Who teaches you so many wicked things?
A: The Devil.
Q: Must you let the Devil teach you?
A: No, I must not.

Memoirs of a Monticello Slave

Rayford W. Logan

Political, economic, and social considerations placed the slaves and their white owners in two separate camps. However, since some of the slaves personally attended their masters day and night, they had entry into the private world of their white owners. The following article, which includes the memoirs of Isaac, one of Thomas Jefferson's slaves, as told to historian Charles Campbell, recounts the intimacy that existed between a black slave and a white master. Readers who like searching for authenticity in historical data will find the introduction to the memoirs quite fascinating.

INTRODUCTION

Thomas Jefferson bequeathed to posterity "the richest storehouse of historical information ever left by a single man." Scholars will draw upon this treasury in the definitive fifty-two volume edition of *The Papers of Thomas Jefferson* (Princeton University Press, 1950–), but even this repository will contain only the writings of Jefferson and of his correspondents. His full-limned portrait of himself and his contemporaries will undoubtedly lead to the publication of biographies and monographs which, added to those already available, should portray virtually every facet of the great Virginian. In the present volume, Jefferson and some of his contemporaries sit for their portraits by a slave—a unique and (so far as we have been able to discover) a hitherto unpublished etching.

Slaves and servants sometimes had the peculiar advantage of seeing the master under more intimate circumstances than anyone else except members of the family. The master might, indeed, be even more relaxed in the presence of his slaves than of his relatives. Relatives have been known to write biographies, with or without the assistance of their subject, but the master would hardly fear or hope for a sketch by a slave, especially if the slave could neither read nor write.

On the other hand, the value of the slave's observations and comments might be lessened by his limited intelligence. Within the area of his competent observation, however, his reminiscences might be as acute and as reliable as those of the more erudite.

Slave reminiscences constitute a recognized source in historical literature. The narratives of ex-slaves like Charles Ball, Lunsford Lane, J. W. Loguen, Josiah Henson, and Frederick Douglass, although they must be read with caution, are indispensable to offset the magnolia and wisteria tradition of some apologists for slavery in the United States. Ulrich B. Phillips and Frederic Bancroft quoted from ex-slaves to give divergent pictures of life and labor in the Old South; Professor Bell Irvin Wiley has enriched his study of *Southern Negroes, 1861–1865* by extensive use of the reminiscences of ex-slaves; and one of the most fully documented examples of the use of these reminiscences is Professor John B. Cade's "Out of the Mouths of Ex-Slaves."[1]

The credibility of testimony of slave and ex-slave witnesses must, of course, be judged by the standards applied to the testimony of other witnesses. How extensive were the witness's opportunities for observation? How capable was he of mirroring facts or passing judgement? Was he an admiring slave whose master could do no wrong, or had the slave led such a hard life that bitterness dominated his recollections? How good was his memory?

Isaac Jefferson, son of Great George and Ursula, was born at Monticello in December, 1775.[2] His earliest reminiscences date from the days of Thomas Jefferson's governorship and the British capture of Richmond in 1781. Taken to Yorktown by the British, Isaac apparently lived at Monticello after his release at the end of the Revolutionary War. He accompanied Jefferson to Philadelphia in 1790, returned to Monticello for about nine years, and then lived for more than twenty-five years with Jefferson's son-in-law, Thomas Mann Randolph. He helped nurse the ex-president in his old age. The last years of Isaac Jefferson's life were spent in Petersburg, where Charles Campbell came to know him and to record these reminiscences. The most exhaustive investigation by the late Professor Luther P. Jackson of Virginia State College failed to reveal any record that Isaac was a free man at that time.

The reminiscences are confined to what Isaac saw and heard. They recount the simple events which even an illiterate slave, possessed of normal sight and hearing at the time of the events, could intelligently observe. Isaac Jefferson was obviously not mistreated by his masters. He did not, however, indulge in nostalgia about the "good old days." The very simplicity of his story is its best watermark of authenticity.

His recollections about independently established facts give further credence to his narrative, for memory tricked him about only a few details. The manuscript states that "Isaac was one year's child with Patsy Jefferson: she was suckled part of the time by Isaac's mother." Patsy, the familiar name for Martha, was born, however, in 1772 and Isaac in 1775. Isaac also stated that in 1781 "The British reached Manchester about 1 o'clock." Campbell added a footnote: "They didn't come by way of Manchester." Isaac made a third slip when he declared: "The fust year Mr. Jefferson was elected President, he took Isaac on to Philadelphia." This reference was, of course, to the time that Jefferson went to Philadelphia as Secretary of State, for in 1800 the capital had been moved to Washington. Moreover, in 1790, when Jefferson became Secretary of State, Isaac was almost fifteen years old and the manuscript states that when he went to Philadelphia, he "was then about fifteen years old." Campbell for some reason failed to comment on this error about Jefferson's position. None of these mistakes, however, constitutes a serious slip. They do not discredit the narrative, nor do they measurably cast doubt upon the basic accuracy of Isaac's memory.

Charles Campbell, who recorded the reminiscences, was a scholar of considerable note. A lineal descendant of Governor Spotswood, he was born on May 1, 1807. He was a graduate of the College of New Jersey, an author and editor of various works, and a contributor to the *Southern Literary Messenger* and other periodicals. He was also a teacher, first conducting his own academy and later serving, from 1855 to 1870, as principal of Anderson Seminary in Petersburg. His voluminous papers at William and Mary College and Duke University further reveal a man of wide interests and scholarly attainments. Campbell died in the Staunton Lunatic Asylum July 11, 1876, after some years of invalidism, but the Isaac Jefferson manuscript was written many years before his breakdown, while he was engaged in other literary pursuits. He edited *The Bland Papers,* published by Edmund and Julian C. Ruffin at Petersburg, 1840–1843. His *Introduction to the History of the Colony and Ancient Dominion of Virginia* was published at Richmond by B. B. Minor in 1847, the date given in the Isaac Jefferson reminiscences for the interviews. Recognized as a solid contribution, Campbell's *History* was published in a considerably expanded form by Lippincott at Philadelphia in 1860. Joel Munsell, another well known publisher of historical works, brought out Campbell's *Some Materials to Serve for a Brief Memoir of John Daly Burk, Author of a History of Virginia,* in 1868.

Campbell prepared the Isaac Jefferson manuscript for publication in 1871, the year after he ceased to be principal of Anderson Seminary. The manuscript itself reveals a mind that is entirely lucid. The language is an interesting mélange of Isaac Jefferson's own words and of Campbell's editing. Campbell's instructions for the printer show not only that the manuscript was being prepared for publication but also that Campbell was in full possession of his mental powers. His handwriting is clear and steady. Comparison with other handwritten materials left by Campbell leaves no doubt that he wrote the manuscript that is in the McGregor Library as well as the fragment of another copy in the William and Mary Library.

The existence of the two manuscripts poses a problem that does not, however, impugn the authenticity of either. The University of Virginia manuscript, here published, consists of twenty chapters. The William and Mary manuscript goes almost to the end of Chapter 7, and with one omission, is almost literally identical as far as it goes. Accompanying the latter is a letter from Campbell to Dr. John Minge in Petersburg. Historians most familiar with Campbell's writings are convinced that the date of this letter is May 16, 1845. It contains this sentence: "I lent Isaac's life to a neighbour here & some one was so smitten with it as to carry it off 'unbeknown.' " But the texts of both manuscripts explicitly date the interview in 1847. It has been suggested that Campbell may have had a second interview with Isaac in 1847, that the University of Virginia manuscript was based upon this interview, and that the William and Mary manuscript is a partial copy of the former. This surmise would still leave unanswered the question: How did the Minge letter come to be attached to the William and Mary copy which also states in the text that it was recorded in 1847?

Whatever be the answer to this question, it is far more important to note that the McGregor manuscript published here contains one passage that was not included in the William and Mary copy. Since the former was clearly the one intended for publication, the passage in question bears witness to Campbell's meticulous concern for the responsibility of the historian. The passage dealt with a subject on which there was considerable sensitiveness. It reads as follows:

Sally Heming's mother Betty was a bright mulatto woman & Sally mighty near white: She was the youngest child. Folks said that these Hemingse's was old Mr. Wayles' children. Sally was very handsome: long straight hair down her back. She was about eleven years old when Mr Jefferson took her to France to wait on Miss Polly. She & Sally went out to France a year after Mr. Jefferson went. Patsy went with him at first, but she carried no maid with her. Harriet one of Sally's daughters was very handsome. Sally had a son named Madison, who learned to be a great fiddler. He has been in Petersburg twice: was here when the balloon went up—the balloon that Beverly sent off.

CHAPTER 1

Isaac Jefferson was born at Monticello: his mother was named Usler (Ursula[3]) but nicknamed Queen, because her husband was named George & commonly called King George. She was pastry-cook & washerwoman: Stayed in the laundry. Isaac toated wood for her: made fire & so on. Mrs Jefferson would come out there with a cookery book in her hand & read out of it to Isaac's mother how to make cakes tarts & so on.

Mrs Jefferson was named Patsy Wayles,[4] but when Mr Jefferson married her she was the widow Skelton, widow of Batter (Bathurst) Skelton. Isaac was one year's child with Patsy Jefferson: she was suckled part of the time by Isaac's mother. Patsy married Thomas Mann Randolph.[5] Mr Jefferson bought Isaac's mother from Col. Wm Fleming of Goochland. Isaac remembers John Nelson an Englishman at work at Monticello: he was an inside worker, a finisher. The blacksmith was Billy Ore; (Orr?) the carriage-maker Davy Watson: he worked also for Col. Carter of Blenheim, eight miles from Monticello. Monticello-house was pulled down in part & built up again some six or seven times. One time it was struck by lightning. It had a Franklin rod at one end. Old master used to say, "If it had'nt been for that Franklin the whole house would have gone." They was forty years at work upon that house before Mr Jefferson stopped building.

CHAPTER 9

Old master was never seen to come out before breakfast—about 8 o'clock. If it was warm weather he would'nt ride out till evening: studied upstars till bell ring for dinner. When writing he had a copyin machine: while he was a-writin he would'nt suffer nobody to come in his room: had a dumb-waiter: When he wanted anything he had nothin to do but turn a crank & the dumb-waiter would bring him water or fruit on a plate or anything he wanted. Old master had abundance of books: sometimes would have twenty of 'em down on the floor at once: read fust one, then tother. Isaac has often wondered how old master came to have such a mighty head: read so many of them books: & when they go to him to ax him anything, he go right straight to the book & tell you all about it. He talked French & Italian. Madzay[6] talked with him: his place was called Colle. General Redhazel

(Riedesel) stayed there. He (Mazzei) lived at Monticello with old master some time: Didiot a Frenchman married his daughter Peggy: a heavy chunky looking woman—mighty handsome: She had a daughter Frances & a son Francis: called the daughter Franky. Mazzei brought to Monticello Antonine, Jovanini, Francis, Modena & Belligrini, all gardiners. My old master's garden was monstrous large: two rows of palings, all round ten feet high.

CHAPTER 10

Mr Jefferson had a clock in his kitchen at Monticello; never went into the kitchen except to wind up the clock. He never would have less than eight covers at dinner —if nobody at table but himself: had from eight to thirty two covers for dinner: plenty of wine, best old Antigua rum & cider: very fond of wine & water. Isaac never heard of his being disguised in drink. He kept three fiddles: played in the arternoons & sometimes arter supper. This was in his early time: When he begin to git so old he did'nt play: kept a spinnet made mostly in shape of a harpsichord: his daughter played on it. Mr Fauble a Frenchman that lived at Mr Walker's— a music-man used to come to Monticello & tune it. There was a forte piano & a guitar there: never seed anybody play on them but the French people. Isaac never could git acquainted with them: could hardly larn their names. Mr Jefferson always singing when ridin or walkin: hardly see him anywhar out doors but what he was a-singin:[7] had a fine clear voice, sung minnits (minuets) & sich: fiddled in the parlor. Old master very kind to servants.

NOTES

1. *Journal of Negro History,* XX (July, 1935), 294–337.
2. Thomas Jefferson, Farm Book, manuscript, Massachusetts Historical Society.
3. There was a work published in 1862 by C. Scribner, at New York, entitled: "The Private Life of Thomas Jefferson from entirely new materials with numerous facsimiles, edited by Rev. Hamilton W Pierson DD President of Cumberland College, Kentucky. This work consists of the reminiscenses of a Captain Edmund Bacon who was overseer for Mr Jefferson at Monticello for 20 years. The Captain's reminiscenses were taken down from his lips by Dr Pierson. The Captain mentions Ursula among the house-servants & says—: "She was Mrs Randolph's nurse. She was a big fat woman. She took charge of all the children that were not in school. If there was any switching to be done. She always did it. She used to be down at my house a great deal with those children. They used to be there so much that we often got tired of them: but we never said so. They were all very much attached to their nurse: they always called her "Mammy." Isaac in 1847 by his own estimate upwards of seventy years old, was a big fat robust black man.
4. Martha youngest daughter of John Wayles, a native of Lancaster, England, a lawyer, who lived at "the Forest" in Charles City county, Va. He was married three times & dying in May 1773 left three daughters one of whom married Francis Eppes, (Father of John W. Eppes who married Maria daughter of Thomas Jefferson) & the other Fulwar Skipwith. Mr Jefferson inherited the Shadwell & Monticello estates. The portion that he acquired by marriage was encumbered with a (British) debt & resulted in a heavy loss. Martha Skelton was 23 years old in 1772 when She married Mr Jefferson.
5. Sometime Governor of Virginia.
6. Philip Mazzei—an Italian—author of "Recherches Sur Les Etats-Unis," 3 Vols. published at Paris, in 1788.
7. Capt. Bacon says: "When he was not talking he was nearly always humming some tune; or singing in a low tone to himself."

Night Riders in Black Folk History

Gladys-Marie Fry

An inescapable realization when one reads the book *Roots* is the crucial
contribution made by oral stories in instigating Alex Haley's search for his
ancestors and in providing several clues for a meaningful search. Oral stories
are not peculiar to black culture, but the historic nature of the stories and their
preservation through several generations seems striking in the culture. Why is
it so? The following selection by Gladys-Marie Fry, taken from her book, *Night
Riders in Black Folk History*, can lead to some hypotheses.

That Slave owners knew about—and tried to prevent—clandestine meetings of
the Blacks is a historical fact. Masters perceived these nocturnal gatherings as an
organizing force for the slaves, a very real threat to the slave system. What the
master did not understand, or perhaps even know, was that many of these secret
meetings were no more than the continuation of a practice deeply rooted in the
Blacks' African heritage and, in this strange land, the only way to preserve the
continuity with the past that would sustain them in the future. The Blacks needed
to talk to each other; quite simply, they met to tell stories. In so doing, they
continued their oral tradition, now the basis of this book. A former slave recalled
to this author the moving about at night from one plantation to another for
storytelling sessions at designated cabins:

> They used to sit nights and tell tales. One or two of them would come to the quarters,
> steal there after old marster and old mistress gone to bed. They would steal to the
> quarter and sit down and tell tales.[1]

During slavery, these gatherings for storytelling acted as a kind of clearing-
house of news concerning family members who had been sold or who had stolen
away from the plantation. Slaves learned of births, deaths, illnesses, and separations, as well as of approaching secret meetings and social events. Indeed, information concerning every facet of life, from the private world of the slave compound to the outside arena of local and national events, was verbally disseminated
in the quarters. Equally important, however, was the function of these sessions
in helping to preserve the slave's sense of self-identity, of knowing who he was
and how he perceived his world and objectified his experiences. These slaves who
risked so much to attend forbidden secret assemblies were driven by a strong need
to remember the past. Moments of conversation—fleeting though they must have
been at times—offered one of the few opportunities for transported Blacks to form
a verbal link with a long-remembered African past.

Stories told in the slave quarters were the first link in the storytelling tradition
in the newly formed Black community. In the post-Civil War period, Black
descendants channeled their need to remember their own side of the slavery
experience—the perspective of the victims rather than the perpetrators—into
frequent storytelling sessions at predetermined sites. Sometimes the storytelling
situation was occasioned by social events, such as a church revival, a housewarm-
ing, or a lull at a frolic. Indeed, any type of gathering sooner or later spontane-
ously turned to storytelling.

I recollect a good many stories told by my grandparents. As a matter of fact, when I was a child, my grandparents and other relatives of mine and people from the neighborhood used to go to my grandfather's house, and they would sit and talk on Saturdays and Sundays about what slavery was like, and I would sit and listen to them.[2]

These were frequent sessions open to a closely knit group of tellers. Within the family unit, time was often set aside nightly for reminiscences and stories. Such accounts either accompanied boring and tedious household routines or were the basis of afterwork leisure. Oral stories which provided an escape from stark reality were usually told while some form of food was being prepared, such as roasting sweet potatoes or chestnuts, pulling molasses candy, or cranking the ice-cream freezer.

Slave narratives frequently refer to the supernatural stories told by the fireside during the long winter months. The eerie light cast by burning embers, the puffs of curling smoke, and the crackling timbers provided a dramatic setting for stories about ghosts, witches, Jack o'Lantern, "the evil eye," and Raw Head and Bloody Bones. Listeners, especially those who had come from some distance, were known to have become so distressed by these stories that they refused to leave the security of the hearthside until morning. The Reverend Earl L. Harrison remembered that

My grandfather's sons would sit up until the wee hours of the night telling these stories. And they would tell some of the awfullest, most terrible ghost stories. Of course our houses would be built up on stilts, up off of the ground, where dogs slept under the house, and hogs too. We didn't have a fence at night. And there'd be cracks in the floor, like those down there, some of them bigger than that. And I've sat up many a night with my feet up on the chair like this, afraid that something would get me through those cracks. And then they would tell me to go to bed. We'd all be sitting before a fire, you know, a fireplace with logs on the fire. Just one fireplace and you had to go out in the cold room to go to bed. And I was scared to death.[3]

Whatever the storytelling situation, it was the constant repetition of these stories, year after year, that accounts for their tenacity in the memories of many Blacks. Individual members of the Black community became known as "good talkers" and were often identified with particular repertoires of stories. As the occasion required, these stories were repeated again and again in flawless and meticulous detail. The audience, acting as an unconscious preserving force, helped to maintain some stability of texts by calling attention to such story changes as substitutions of detail and omitted passages. Borrowing and exchanging stories occurred freely, with the storyteller usually beginning the borrowed story with the opening formula, "Old Man So and So used to tell the story about. . . ."

The role of children in these storytelling sessions is an aspect of folk tradition too long overlooked. Stories about the past seemed to have had a special kind of appeal for children of slave descendants, for they listened by the hour, fascinated by the history of their family. James C. Evans recalls that

In the evenings, we'd sit around. If it was the cool part of the weather, we'd sit around the fire, and if it was the warm summer time, just sit around the yard, and there would be two hours or more of just family talk. Maybe five of us there, maybe twenty-five of us. With the senior one always being respected as the moderator, or whatever it was. And this would go on every night.[4]

Old people, including favorite grandparents, were especially sought out by children because of their storytelling abilities. Such a person was

Old man Ben Jeanes [who] came up in slavery, and he used to have a lot of children to be around him. He was very amusing, and he'd tell stories about white folks and how they did him, and how he outplanned them.[5]

In public gatherings, however, children learned to sit as quietly as possible while their elders held forth. Assuming and maintaining an inconspicuous posture was essential, for there were certain types of sensitive stories which were felt by adult Blacks to be too delicate for children's ears. But older Blacks, often caught up in the atmosphere of re-created experience, simply forgot that children were present. These children then, listening mesmerized to countless tellings and retellings of a remembered past, learned of the fears, the horrors, the whole of the Black slave world. They learned, too, the storytelling-tradition and passed it on to their children, forging still another link in the chain of transmission between Africa, the slave situation in the New World, and the present Black experience. . . .

NOTES

1. Informant Alice Virginia Lyles, March 16, 1964.
2. Informant Floyd Wardlaw Crawford, Feb. 8, 1964.
3. Interview, March 19, 1964.
4. Interview, March 19, 1964.
5. Informant Samuel Chappell, March 7, 1964.

The Slave Sings Free

John H. Lovell, Jr.

The feelings of blacks are expressed in the universal language of song. Surely, lyrics that are in English lose their claim to universality. But then, what accounts for their widespread appeal? Can the aspirations, the dreams, the determinations, the hopes, the sorrows, the ideals in the songs be considered universals? Readers of the following selection by John Lovell, Jr.—taken from his larger work, *Black Song—The Forge and the Flame*—will probably arrive at different conclusions since each will reflect on the content of the songs from different perspectives. But it is hoped that all readers will share something of how black slaves felt when they sang the songs presented here.

Closely related to their [black slaves'] songs of fortitude are the songs demonstrating their commitment to freedom and democracy. All along we have been seeing various phases of their concepts of freedom. The songs we are about to display and interpret go much farther than concept. In Joseph Conrad's words, these are "the thing itself."

Far from the slave's religion being a calming influence, it was . . . one of the greatest stimulators of the slave's love for and determination to have his freedom. And thus, the commitment to freedom in spirituals begins, as one might say, with songs about Old Testament heroes and devils. The greatest hero is Moses; the greatest devil is Pharaoh. Nearly every song about Moses is intended to chide Americans, South and North, about permitting slavery and to issue a solemn warning that slavery will not be indefinitely tolerated. If this is not true, then the Southern states whose legislatures passed laws making it a crime for white or black to sing were bitterly deceived. And the many slaves freed by Harriet Tubman, partly through the use of this song, are hard to explain. Denmark Vesey, leader of the abortive Charleston revolt in 1822, also used the song.

Usually the song of freedom is a coin with two sides: the condemnation of the slaveholder and the insistence upon immediate freedom for the slave. One of the (anonymous) clergymen who strongly objected to the defense of slavery by Bishop Hopkins (in an article entitled "Bishop Hopkins' Letter on Slavery Ripped Up and His Misuse of the Sacred Scriptures Exposed") declared that whoever pleaded for heathen slavery deserved in justice, under the terms of Matthew 7:2, to be himself a slave. (Matthew 7:2 says that "with what judgment ye judge, ye shall be judged.") The spirituals do not go quite so far as this, but they do proclaim both sides of the coin. The Pharaohs are emphatically denounced, again and again. The claim for immediate freedom is put forth hundreds of times.

"Go Down, Moses" is direct statement all the way. It does not employ the undercurrent symbolism of "Steal Away to Jesus" and other such poems. Only a very obtuse listener can miss its point. It says flatly that Moses freed these Egyptian slaves boldly and justly because slavery is wrong. It clearly projects the principles of this experience to all the world: Wherever men are held in bondage, they must and shall be freed.

The "Let my people go!" refrain is thunderous. It does not argue economic, sociological, historical, and racial points. It does not concern itself with what the Pharaohs of the world shall do for substitute labor. It is one of the great freedom declarations of literature and history, as final and absolute as *The Trojan Women* is against war.

As a poem, it wastes no words and moves relentlessly toward its goal of filling every listener with a pervasive contempt for oppression and a resounding enthusiasm for freedom, wherever either one is found. It sets the penalty for violation as though it were a judge wearing a black cap. It makes arrangement for the immediate reimbursement to the slave for his unrewarded toil. When it is spoken or sung in anything close to the way it was conceived and composed, it leaves an indelible impression. The listener cannot be casual about slavery or freedom ever again.

The song is organized so that in each stanza the leader intones the first line, the chorus pronounces the second line, the leader returns with the third line, the chorus with the fourth, and both deliver the refrain. Although many songs, even famous ones, are adapted by arrangers, "Go Down, Moses" is about the same in nearly every book of spirituals.

When Israel was in Egypt's land,
Let my people go!
Oppressed so hard they could not stand,
Let my people go!

Go down, Moses, 'Way down in Egypt's Land,
Tell old [or "ole"] Pharaoh, Let my people go!

"Thus saith [spoke] the Lord," bold Moses said,
Let my people go!
"If not I'll smite your first-born dead,"
Let my people go!

No more in bondage shall they toil,
Let my people go!
Let them come out with Egypt's spoil,
Let my people go!

Go down, Moses, 'Way down in Egypt's land,
Tell old Pharaoh, Let my people go!

"Go Down, Moses" is only one of many freedom songs on this theme, but unquestionably the best. A song with at least a dozen stanzas in some versions is "Didn't Old Pharaoh Get Los'?" In one version, the story is told by stanzas, like this,

Stanza   1: Isaac's ransom; Moses' rescue by Pharaoh's daughter

Stanza   2: Joseph's rise; Samuel's predictions

Stanza   3: The Lord's first orders to Moses to go to Pharaoh

Stanza   4: Den Moses an' Aaron. To Pharaoh did go,
"Thus says de God of Israel, Let my people go."
Refrain: (same after each stanza)
Didn't old Pharaoh get los' get los', get los'
Didn't old Pharaoh get los' In de Red Sea.

Stanza   5: Pharaoh resists; Moses warns that the Lord hears his people pray

Stanza   6: The Israelites cry for bread; the downflow of manna

Stanza   7: Moses exhorts his people to stand fast

Stanza   8: Moses predicts the dispersal of the enemy

Stanza   9: Down came raging Pharaoh,
Dat you may plainly see,
Old Pharaoh an' his host
Got los' in de Red Sea.

Stanza 10: Smiting the rock, Moses gets water for his people

Stanza 11: An' de Lord spoke to Moses, From Sinai's smoking top,
Sayin', "Moses lead de people, Till I shall bid you stop."
Didn't old Pharaoh get los'.

In another version of "Go Down, Moses," which extends for twenty-five stanzas, Egypt is called "the proud oppressive land." When the Israelites finally get to the free side of the water, "They sang a song of triumph o'er." The cloud "cleaves" the way; "a fire by night, a shade by day." The children of Israel are promised that they will not be lost in the wilderness because they will have a lighted candle at their breast. The fall of the walls of Jericho and the possession of "fair Canaan's land" are predicted. At length, there are these lines.

O, let us all from bondage flee, . . .

And let us all in Christ be free, . . .

We need not always weep and moan, . . .

And wear these slavery chains forlorn, . . .

This world's a wilderness of woe, . . .

O, let us all to Canaan go, . . .

In "March On," two things are stressed, the victory and the resultant freedom. The fact that "you shall gain the victory!" and "you shall gain the day!" are repeated like a chant throughout this song which deals with adventures " 'way over in Egypt's land" [and] clearly portends the slave's expectations in his own land.

"He's Jus' the Same Today" combines Moses with another great freedom fighter, Daniel. The first stanza repeats one of the Moses episodes with a different and very important emphasis.

When Moses an' his soldiers f'om Egypt's lan' did flee,
His enemies were in behin' him, An' in front of him de sea,
God raised de waters like a wall, An' opened up de way,
An' de God dat lived in Moses' time is jus' the same today.

Once more in the spiritual is incontrovertible evidence that human slavery is doomed because God will not stand for it. The same God who delivered Moses and the enslaved Israelites, who ran from their masters to set up a free society, says the poet, will deliver slaves for the same purpose in the nineteenth century.

The slave admired Daniel because he would not submit to the tyrant no matter how much power the tyrant had. In the slave's eyes, he and Daniel were in the same boat; the slave would not submit in his heart to the institution of slavery, although he momentarily worked as a slave. In encouraging slaves everywhere to resist in the name of a God who supported resisters to tyranny, the second stanza of "He's Jus' the Same Today" is quite as insurrectionary as the first.

When Daniel faithful to his God, would not bow down to men,
An' by God's enemy he was hurled into de lion's den,
God locked de lion's jaw we read, An' robbed him of his prey,
An' de God dat lived in Daniel's time is jus' de same today.

The best song of freedom is, however, "Didn't My Lord Deliver Daniel?" It is as bold and explicit as "Go Down, Moses." It makes no reservations or allowances. The white people who heard it sung and permitted it must have been trusting souls indeed!

Didn't my Lord deliver Daniel, deliver
    Daniel, deliver Daniel,
Didn't my Lord deliver Daniel,
    An' why not-a every man!

He delivered Daniel f'om de lion's den,
    Jonah f'om de belly of de whale,
De Hebrew chillun f'om de fiery furnace,
    An' why not every man!

Obviously, these were all impossible deliverances. Only the Lord God could make them. Only an impossible deliverance could get the slave his freedom. But if the Lord God had done it several times already, why will he not continue? The clear implication is that he will. For those who hang on to the discredited notion that these songs deal with deliverance beyond the grave, how irrational is it that all the slave's models deal with people delivered from impossible situations here on earth, in the interest of further earthly living!

As we have shown in Chapter 19, the great champion of freedom was Jesus. Many times it is the Lord who sets the slave free ("I know my Lord has set me free, . . . /I'm in Him and He's in me"), but most often it is his son Jesus: "King Jesus died for ev'ry man," and

Oh, shout-a my sister for you are free, . . .
For Christ has bought yo' liberty,

and

Came down here and talked to me,
Went away and left me free.

The slave poet was fully aware that freedom in a democratic society imposed obligations.

You say the Lord has set you free, . . .
Why don't you let yo' neighbor be!

The terms *Jubilee, Canaan,* and *camp ground* are flat symbols for free land. Many times in the spiritual one sees lines like,

This is the day of jubilee, . . .
The Lord has set his people free.

and

Set my foot on de Gospel ship, an' de ship begin
    to sail,
It landed me over on Canaan's shore, An' I'll never
    come back no mo'.

Canaan was the free land of the chosen people who were, in many respects, a model for the slave: the parallelism is unarguable.

"Deep River," one of the most beautiful of spirituals, is also one of the most deadly to the institution of slavery. It talks about the promised land (Canaan) with very little disguise. The singer says again and again, "Lord, I want to cross over into camp-ground." Once more, the listener who thinks he means a land beyond the grave is either obtuse or not privy to the yearnings of the slave's heart. Into this song the slave poet poured his whole soul of desire for freedom, earthly freedom. As such, the song has irony and comes out more beautiful still than if it is interpreted as after death. Better still, let it mean both free land and heaven after death. The slave singer aimed at both.

In many of the songs so far has been an assurance of freedom that need only be noted here. When the poet, on behalf of his fellows, says,

One o' dese mornin's—it won't be long,
You'll look fo' me, an' I'll be gone,

or when he sings—

Git yo' bundle reddy I know it's time,

he doubtlessly means the words literally, although he "covers up" with talk about Judgment Day, as almost anyone would do in his shoes.

As reported by Thomas Wentworth Higginson, a white colonel of the Federal Army and a famous literary man, at the outbreak of the rebellion, black men were jailed in Georgetown, South Carolina, for singing "We'll Soon Be Free." A portion of this spiritual goes,

We'll soon be free, . . .
When de Lord will call us home.
My brudder, how long, . . .
'Fore we done sufferin' here?
It won't be long
'Fore de Lord will call us home.
We'll walk de miry road, . . .
Where pleasure never dies, . . .
We'll soon be free . . .
When Jesus sets me free.
We'll fight for liberty . . .
When de Lord will call us home.

As a black drummer boy told Colonel Higginson, "*de Lord* mean for say *de Yankees.*"

When real solid freedom finally came, the songs showed little change. One of the first "solid freedom" songs was "Many Tousand [thousands] Go,"

No more peck of corn for me, no more, no more;
No more peck of corn for me, Many tousand go.

No more driver's lash for me, . . .
No more pint o' salt for me, . . .
No more hundred lash for me, . . .
No more mistress' call for me.

Another is the famous "Free at Last." The song carries the same code of religious terms as many of the previous songs, even after the need for secrecy has been removed. This fact does not mean that the spiritual writer was not religious at all; it means that he was not just religious.

Free at last, free at last, I thank God I'm free at last;
Free at last, free at last, I thank God I'm free at last.
Way down yonder in the graveyard walk, . . .
Me and my Jesus goin' to meet and talk, . . .
On-a my knees when the light pass'd by, I thank
 God I'm free at last,
Thought my soul would rise and fly, I thank God
 I'm free at last.

Still another is "Done Wid Driber's Dribin',"

Done wid driber's dribin',
Done wid massa's hollerin', . . .
Done wid missus' scoldin', . . .
Roll, Jordan, roll.

To return to the slave's commitment to freedom, one finds an idea that is often found in freedom songs wherever they are composed and sung; namely, that the tree of liberty must be watered by the blood of patriots. Or, to state it more simply, freedom cannot be handed to an individual; the individual must fight for it.

Joshua at Jericho is a good example: "Dere's none like good ole Joshua." Usually, the emphasis is on his bringing down the walls with a shout from his army ("de chillun"). But when one considers what Joshua was really fighting for and the penchant of the spiritual poet to glorify only those who did things of significance to him and his code of values, one can read the deepest reason for the creation of the song.

Going back to the period just before Joshua, one poet has written of the children of Israel,

Yes, the children they did right, . . .
When they went and had that fight.

Not just the children of Israel, but every group and individual wishing to live the good life must fight, some of these poets say. The forces of evil are deeply entrenched and belligerent; you cannot win without fighting.

Marching up the heavenly road, (repeated)
I'm bound to fight until I die, . . .
My sister, have you got your sword and shield, . . .

I got 'em fo' I left the field,
Marching up the heavenly road.

Another song of the field shows the unyielding determination of a patriot and attempts to spread the contagion.

Oh, what-a you say, seekers, (repeated twice)
About dat Gospel war.
An' what-a you say, brothers,
Oh, what-a you say, brothers (repeated)
About dat Gospel war.
An' I will die in de fiel', will die in de fiel', will die in de fiel'
I'm on my journey home.
Sing it ovah—I will die in de fiel'.

The same spirit seems implicit in "Singin' Wid a Sword in Ma Han'," in which the creator and the fighter are joined, François Villon-style,

Singin' [Shoutin'] wid a sword in ma han', Lord,
Singin' wid a sword in ma han',
In ma han' Lord,
Singin' wid a sword in ma han'.

It is hard to see what quiet, peaceful interpretation the white listeners gave to this song, or to "Our bondage'll have an end, by and by, by and by."

That the spirit of the Underground Railroad providing transportation to freedom and the runaway slave pervaded and doubtless dictated some songs is unquestionable. A song like "Don't Be A-Stoppin' an' A-Lookin' " is almost certainly an invitation for travel to free land.

Oh! de song of salvation is a mighty sweet song,
Den don't be a-stoppin' an' -lookin'.

"Git on Board, Little Chillen" is a clear invitation to ride the train. It reiterates that plenty of room is available; that the train can be heard close by; that it is "rumblin' through de lan' "; that

De fare is cheap, an' all can go, De rich an' poor are dere,
No second class aboard dis train, No difference in de fare.

Perhaps the gospel train did refer to a train running from earth to heaven. It shows, however, a remarkable likeness to the Underground Railroad, which was running trains and transporting thousands from stations all over slavery land to free land. Had I been a slave with my knowledge of both trains and my right to choose, I think I would have unhesitatingly chosen the latter, with all its perils. Hundreds of slaves did so choose.

In "Same Train," the poet refers to a train, now "ablowin' at de station," which carried his mother, sister, and implicitly others to some desirable destination. You can easily deduce heaven as the destination. But Harriet Tubman was one of several who, after freeing herself, came back to free her relatives and friends among many others. "Be back tomorrer" has a far more pleasant ring if it refers to an earthly train with a free destination. One can always use the heavenly train later.

The same principle works for the ship. Just after "Didn't my Lord deliver, Daniel, An' why not-a every man" in one version are the lines,

I set my foot on de Gospel ship, an' de ship begin to sail,
It landed me over on Canaan's shore,
An' I'll never come back no mo'.

In the interpretive literature of the spiritual there are numerous references to the organs of freedom. Botkin asserts that trains are familiar in both the spiritual and the blues; the train is most frequently encountered as a symbol of freedom and vicarious expression. In a critique of Finkelstein is reference to the spiritual's drawing upon Biblical images in its yearning for freedom and in its defense against tyranny. He underscores the fact that these spirituals were employed as signals on the Underground Railroad. Haslam contrasts the oblique reference to freedom in "Go Down, Moses" with the open references in "No More Auction Block for Me." Long before emancipation, say Downes and Siegmeister, the slave sang of freedom. At first freedom was symbolized in such religious songs as "The Great Jubilee," "Dat Great Day of Mornin'," and "Kingdom Come." They also quote Frederick Douglass to the effect that a keen observer would have detected the freedom note in the repeated references in the songs to "O Canaan, sweet Canaan."

Freedom and democracy, fought and died for, confer certain rights in the spiritual. Eating at the welcome table, drinking at the crystal fountain, attending "the big baptizin' " were all proper rights of the sanctified.

But there were rights beyond these about which the slave poet sang. They are described in a number of songs, but one brilliant song, which reads like the Declaration of Independence, is a sufficient illustration. It is called "You Got a Right." Like the Declaration of Independence, it is rooted in divine justice. It sings,

You got a right, I got a right,
We all got a right to de tree of life.

De very time I thought I was los',
De dungeon shuck an' de chain fell off.

You may hinder me here. But you cannot dere,
'Cause God in de heav'n gwineter answer prayer.

O bretheren,
O sisteren, You got a right, I got a right,
We all got a right to de tree of life.

In the exercise of such rights, the man invested with freedom is invincible.

O no man can hinder me!
O no man, no man, no man can hinder me!

AWARENESS OF A JUST UNIVERSE

In spite of his slave condition, the brutalities of slavery, his recurring sense of personal insecurity, and the hazards of running to the freedom he felt he deserved, the slave poet proclaimed a just universe. The way he put it, justice did not emanate exclusively from the Deity. Under the eye of the Deity much of the injustice continued, although the slave poet did not blame the Deity for it. He did see the Deity as promulgating and administering just acts and just situations. The essential justice, however, was in the nature of things. People and things just naturally received the rewards and punishments they were due according to their character and behavior. Botkin quotes Alain Locke to the effect that the slave got his democratic sentiments not from the Bill of Rights, but from the moral justice of the Hebrew prophets. There is, however, another possibility. In Africa, strict justice was almost a religion. Africans had a law of reparation. Under this law, if a man steals, he or his family must give equal in value to the robbed person or his relatives. A murderer must give his own children to carry out the function of a murdered person. The underlying principle is a life for a life rather than a death for a death.

The rewards we have discussed in various connections. On the gospel train there was no second class because obviously all the sanctified are equal. When Heaven's pearly gates open, there will also be only first-class accommodations—welcome table, milk and honey, apartments on the golden streets. All of this arrangement follows the eternal principle which pervades life.

You shall reap jes' what you sow, Brother
    [Sister, Sinner],
You shall reap jes' what you sow,
On the mountain, in the valley,
You shall reap jes' what you sow.

He recognizes that it applies to him as much as to anyone else. "I'm gwine to jedgement bye an' bye."

Since his appeal is more to sinners than to the sanctified, the slave poet seems to spend more time on the punishments than on the rewards. In either case and in both cases he is advertising the natural justice in things.

Too late, too late, sinnah,
Hm—too late, too late, sinnah,
Carry de key an' gone home.
Massa Jesus' lock de do',
O Lord! too late; . . .

Too late, too late, false pretender,
Hm—too late; too late, too late, backslider,
Carry de key an' gone home.

Perhaps the workings of justice are just as strong on the other side when the key is in the hands of the man who says he is good.

I got a key to thuh Kingdom
I got a key, Oh, yes, I have-a now.
I got a key to thuh Kingdom
An' the worl' can't do me no harm.

Often, the message is a good deal more dramatic.

Oh, de sinner man he gambled an' fell, (repeat)
Oh, de sinner man gambled, he gambled and fell;
He wanted to go to hebben, but he had to go to hell,
Dere's no hidin' place down dere.

Even in the case of God's own son, justice was an irresistible force against strong earthly powers.

De soliahs der a-plenty, standin' by de do'
But dey could not hinder, De stone done roll away. . . .
Ol' Pilate an' his wise men, didn't know what to say,
De miracle was on dem, De stone done roll away.

No finer case of universal justice has been recorded than the story of Dives, the typical rich man, and Lazarus, the typical poor one, as related in numerous Afro-American spirituals. We have room for only one version:

Poor old Lazarus, poor as I, Don't you see? Don't you see?
Poor old Lazarus, poor as I, Don't you see? Don't you see?
Poor old Lazarus, poor as I, When he died had a home on high.
He had a home in-a that Rock, Don't you see?

Rich man, Dives, lived so well, Don't you see? Don't you see?
Rich man, Dives, lived so well, Don't you see? Don't you see?
Rich man, Dives, lived so well, When he died found home in hell,
Had no home in that Rock, Don't you see?

And so it happens that in the Afro-American spiritual, universal justice straightens all, clarifies all, judges all, at long last. It may allow distortions and deviations for seeming ages, but in the end it serves all men fairly according to their adherence to principle and right. It is no judge one can corrupt or bribe. It cares not at all for social or economic or political position, for class or rank, for bond or free. Eventually, it will give you what, in the rock, you have earned. Nothing less. Nothing more.
Don't you see!

DETERMINATION TO STRUGGLE, RESIST, AND HOLD FAST

Many people honestly do not believe that the spirituals use mask and symbolism. If they could accept symbolism, they would never accept a symbolism of resistance and struggle. Too many histories written by proponents of the plantation tradition have brainwashed them. Although they accept a handful of troublemakers, they believe in the docility of the slaves. They believe that slaves and their masters were sweet and loving partners.

The evidence offered in earlier portions of this book, taken from unimpeachable authorities, destroys these views. The great majority of slaves wanted to be free. If their masters had been utter darlings to them, they would still have wanted to be free. Besides their wanting to be free, their masters were the exact opposite of utter darlings. Thousands planned escapes from slavery, and a large percentage of these planners were successful. Where the slave could not escape, or until he could escape, he tolerated slavery and cooperated with it only to survive as long as he could. A few recklessly threw themselves into the mouth of the dragon and were burned in his flames. But most of them had resistance in their hearts; and they had resistance in their songs, most of the time carefully masked. Where it was not resistance, it was the determination to hold fast until help came.

The writings of Frederick Douglass and Booker T. Washington . . . clearly demonstrate the resistance and the spirit of freedom. Hundreds of other former slaves said the same things they said, felt the same way they felt. So far, under other headings, we have offered dozens of songs which express resistance and struggle; the point needs to be emphasized as an important outcome of the poetic experience of these slaves.

After hundreds of years of such mask and symbolism, the Southern white man had finally penetrated to the core. Ignoring the symbolism of "de Lord" and "Jesus," he at last realized that this spiritual, as hundreds of others before it, was blatantly opposing slavery and proclaiming freedom. Had the slaveholders throughout the South done similarly, and jailed every slave who sang of freedom and resistance, the plantation territory would have been covered with jails.

Since so many songs of this nature have already been given, only a few remarkable samples are necessary. Often songs about building upon rock are for the purpose of demonstrating the determination of the slave to hold fast in his personal antislavery feeling until he can manage a personal escape. Look at this one called "Bound to Go,"

I build my house upon de rock, O yes, Lord!
No wind, no storm can blow 'em down, O yes, Lord!
March on, member, Bound to go;
Been to de ferry, Bound to go;
Left St. Helena, Bound to go;
Brudder, fare you well.

The same general message is carried by "I've got a home in-a that Rock, Don't you see?"

We have already shown how the spiritual stressed the soldier theme. The mask of the Christian soldier was an excellent one for the kind of realistic war in which the slave realized he was engaged. As a soldier he could not only fight his necessary way, at least in his heart and in his songs; he could also develop his manhood. As a soldier he could build up his determination to resist. And so he sang,

O stay in the field, childeren-ah
Stay in the field, childeren-ah,
Stay in the field,

Until the war is ended.

I've got my breastplate, sword, and shield,
And I'll go marching thro' the field,
Till the war is ended.

And again he sang,

Oh, my feet are shod with the gospel grace,
And upon my breast a shield;
And with my sword I intend to fight
Until I win the field.

In "No Man Can Hinder Me," the slave poet once again uses the mask of Christianity to hide his personal determination to struggle. But the obvious buildup of the poem, its iteration and reiteration of a point which is not religious, its bringing in of "Saviour" and "Jesus" as sidelines, just as "We'll Soon Be Free" does, all prove the true meaning of the spiritual.

Walk in, kind Savior,
No man can hinder me!
Walk in, sweet Jesus,
No man can hinder me.

See what wonder Jesus done,
O no man can hinder me!
See what wonder Jesus done,
O no man can hinder me!
O no man, no man, no man can hinder me!
O no man, no man, no man can hinder me!

The singer, the member, the seeker is fixed in his plan. He will not allow himself to be frightened out of it.

I shall not, I shall not be moved,
I shall not, I shall not be moved,
Like a tree that's planted by the waters,
I shall not be moved.

If he does decide to move, then it will be irresistibly toward a new and free goal.

I'm on my way and I won't turn back, . . .
I'm on my way, Great God, I'm on my way.

I'm on my way to the heavenly land, . . .
I'm on my way, God knows, I'm on my way.

HEAV'M

The word heaven is spelled many ways by the various arrangers of the spirituals (heavem, heaven, heav'n, Heav'n, heab'n, hebben, hebb'n—to mention a few). When it is sung by a good chorus with good conductors, its sound depends to some extent upon its position in the series of words or sounds. When John W. Work, one of the outstanding arrangers and anthologists of spirituals, wrote instructions for singing "Heav'n, Heav'n" in the famous song, "Goin' to Shout All over God's Heav'n" (also known as "All God's Chillun Got Wings"), he said, "Let the last syllable of heav'n be a hum." This direction makes the words come out "Heav'm," and "Heav'm" is a topmost subject of the spiritual.

We will not belabor further the point that, since freedom is the slave's preoccupying thought, when he sang "when I get to heavb'm," he undoubtedly meant "when I get free." It is the belief of the present writer that most of the time he does mean "when I get free," but perhaps not every single time. Sometimes, he undoubtedly means the universe beyond the grave. It is possible that, at times, he means the free land first and the universe beyond the grave later. The songs were composed and popularized by many creators; they are entitled to a variety of views.

The solution to this problem interferes but little with the display of the evidence about heav'm, culled from hundreds of songs. No one concept so inspires him. No one concept better demonstrates the complete transformation he envisions, from the small organism he starts with to the gigantic thing he sees as the never-ending development if he is given the chance or under the omnipotent power it has been his good fortune to link up with.

If the reader thinks his heav'm is a theological or otherworldly thing, the evidence ought to disabuse him. The heav'm of the Afro-American spiritual speaks more to the slave's appreciation and criticism of the things and values of his earthly life than it does to anything else. When he mentions a heavenly thing or value, he more than likely has an earthly thing or value in mind—like Homer who had two names for certain characters, one for earth and one for the heavens —and the reader should take pains to search his meanings. The spiritual poet was no visionary or speculator in the usual senses.

*   *   *

And there, before you, is the Afro-American spiritual. It was Afro-American in three senses: strongly African, strongly American, and a curious and magnificent mixture of the two. No matter where it got its materials, like Shakespeare it was original in every fundamental way. It sang primarily of the life and aspirations of slaves. It was deeply realistic and, without paradox, full of irony and symbol. It was the expression of a folk community that had been singing its way through lives for at least two millenniums. It was religious in the total sense, not in the sense of the American white man. There was very little of camp meeting or Methodist hymn in it—very few slaves knew anything about camp meetings or Methodist hymn. There was very little of return to Africa. Besides the realism, there was the deep sorrow (occasioned by the contemplation of the human condition), the deep understanding of the human struggle (not just of the slave's struggle), and the deep joy of knowing that real manhood and faith could overcome *any* bad human condition. There was no revenge, although plenty of recognition of the grounds for revenge; no hopelessness, although plenty of recognition of great trouble in the world; and no inconsolable pain. There was no fear of death. There was humor and heartache, and the future was a mighty revolutionary dream, sure to come true.

Arthur Morton says that these songs are a new *Pilgrim's Progress* composed in the universal language of song. They appeal to many people who have no religion and no religious philosophy. They are "proof of the indestructible goodness and power to survive and conquer which exists not only in the Negro people but in all people everywhere. They give us a promise of victory in which we know we can have absolute trust."

Herein is the spiritual's prime greatness. These slaves did not stop with writing about the human soul on its journey to the stars. They brought in their personal experiences, but they did not sing for themselves alone. They sang faith and hope and truth for all mankind. They sang the triumph, however long it took, of freedom and justice. They sang the right of every man to his exalted portion of the tree of life.

And for these reasons, wherever they touch the world's people, who perpetually need to rebelieve in freedom and justice and man's individual greatness, the world's people sing! We all sing together:

Den my little soul's a-goin' t' shine, shine,
Yes, my little soul's a-goin' t' shine.

CHAPTER ELEVEN

Nonslave Status: Freedom vs. Quasi-Freedom

The selections in this chapter illustrate the variety of occupations in which free blacks engaged prior to the Civil War. As the chapter title implies, although there were numerous blacks who were not slaves, many experienced limitations of opportunity. For example, opportunities for formal education were limited; many blacks were either self-educated or received only some schooling. Among those who entered and achieved success in the professions, two examples are given—James Derham, physician, and Richard Allen, minister and church founder. Many others, such as Benjamin Banneker, could have been cited.

Surprisingly, some free blacks were slaveowners. Some operated large plantations worked by many slaves; others were townspeople who owned slaves. Occasionally, free blacks owned their wives or other members of their family.

Both free blacks and slaves achieved widespread reputations as skilled artisans. Some skilled slave artisans were able to purchase their freedom, whereas others operated businesses for their owners.

Free Negro Owners of Slaves, 1830

Carter G. Woodson

It comes as a surprise to many that blacks themselves were sometimes slaveowners. In the following report, first published in 1924, Carter G. Woodson explains the reasons why some free blacks bought and held slaves prior to the Civil War.

The aim of this report on the free Negro is to facilitate the further study of this neglected group. Most of these people have been forgotten, for persons supposedly well-informed in history are surprised to learn today that about a half million, almost one-seventh of the Negroes of this country, were free prior to the emancipation in 1865. It is hardly believed that a considerable number of Negroes were owners of slaves themselves, and in some cases controlled large plantations.

There were several reasons for selecting the census of 1830. In the first place, the earlier reports do not give as much information as the census of 1830. At that time, moreover, the free Negroes had about reached their highest mark as a distinct class. The reaction which set in earlier in the century restricted their freedom and in many cases expelled them from the South. This census, then, evidently reports the names of a larger number of representative free Negroes than any other census prior to their debasement to a lower status or their migration from the South. This trek reached its highest point between 1830 and 1835. Most of the free Negroes in the North in 1830, therefore, had been there for some years.

The census records show that the majority of the Negro owners of slaves were such from the point of view of philanthropy. In many instances the husband purchased the wife or vice versa. The slaves belonging to such families were few compared with the large numbers found among the whites on the well-developed plantations. Slaves of Negroes were in some cases the children of a free father who had purchased his wife. If he did not thereafter emancipate the mother, as so many such husbands failed to do, his own children were born his slaves and were thus reported by the enumerators.

Some of these husbands were not anxious to liberate their wives immediately. They considered it advisable to put them on probation for a few years, and if they did not find them satisfactory they would sell their wives as other slaveholders disposed of Negroes. For example, a Negro shoemaker in Charleston, South Carolina, purchased his wife for $700; but, on finding her hard to please, he sold her a few months thereafter for $750, gaining $50 by the transaction. The editor personally knew a man in Cumberland County, Virginia, whose mother was purchased by his father who had first bought himself. Becoming enamored of a man slave, she gave him her husband's manumission papers that they might escape together to free soil. Upon detecting this plot, the officers of the law received the impression that her husband had turned over the papers to the slave and arrested the freedman for the supposed offense. He had such difficulty in extricating himself from this complication that his attorney's fees amounted to $500. To pay them he disposed of his faithless wife for that amount.

Benevolent Negroes often purchased slaves to make their lot easier by granting them their freedom for a nominal sum, or by permitting them to work it out on liberal terms. John Barry Meachum, a Negro Baptist minister in St. Louis, thus came into possession of as many as twenty slaves by 1836. The exploitation type of Negro slaveholder, moreover, sometimes feeling the sting of conscience, liberated his slaves. Thus did Samuel Gibson, a Negro of Mississippi, in 1844, when he brought his six slaves to Cincinnati, Ohio, and settled them on free territory.

Having economic interests in common with the white slaveholders, the Negro owners of slaves often enjoyed the same social standing. It was not exceptional for them to attend the same church, to educate their children in the same private school, and to frequent the same places of amusement. Under such circumstances miscegenation easily followed. While those taking the census of 1830 did not generally record such facts, the few who did, as in the case of Nansemond County, Virginia, reported a situation which today would be considered alarming. In this particular County there appeared among the slaveholders free Negroes designated as Jacob of Read and white wife and Syphe of Matthews and white wife. Others reported with white wives were not slaveholders.

Practically all of these Negro slaveholders were in the South. Slavery, however, at that time had not been exterminated altogether in the North, and even there the Negro was following in the footsteps of the white man, as this report will show.

In the South where almost all of the Negro slaveholders were, moreover, we find some of them competing with the large planters in the number of slaves they owned. Most of such Negro proprietors lived in Louisiana, South Carolina, Maryland and Virginia, as did the majority of all such slave owners. There are, moreover, a few instances of confusing absentee ownership with Negro ownership. Sometimes a free Negro had charge of a plantation, but did not own the slaves himself, and the enumerator returned him as the owner.

Excepting those of Louisiana, one may say that most of the Negro owners of slaves lived in urban communities. In those parts of the South where the influence of the kind planter near the coast was not felt, the Negro owner of slaves did not frequently appear. The free Negroes themselves, moreover, encountered such difficulties in the lower South and Southwest that they had to seek more hospitable communities in free States.

By 1840 the trend toward degrading the free Negro to a lower status had become evident even in the apparently benevolent slaveholding States. Just before the outbreak of the Civil War the free Negro was receiving practically no consideration in the South and very little in the North. History here repeats itself, then, in showing the varying attitude of the whites toward the blacks in the cycles of national development.

Black Patterns of Employment, 1750–1820

Whittington B. Johnson

There was a period of about seventy years in America's formative era (1750–1820) when equal opportunity in employment might have been expected for blacks and whites. The period was one of practically full employment. The principle of "last-hired, first-fired" that prevails for millions of blacks today had not yet been practiced with any regularity. Whittington B. Johnson, in the excerpt presented below, points out that the occupational endeavors of African-Americans in colonial times closely parallel those of European-Americans, except at the professional and business ownership levels.

In the period 1750–1820, the demand for workers was growing, so much so that Europeans were unable to migrate in sufficient numbers to satisfy it. This led to an increase in the number of Africans forced into the American labor market as slaves.

Black workers in colonial times were very much a part of the blue-collar work force, obtaining employment as artisans, unskilled and semi-skilled industrial laborers, domestic servants, and farm hands.

Whittington Johnson has described the variety of black artisans who worked in the early period of this country's history. Of the various handicraft trades, woodworking was probably the first to have a sizable number of African-Americans. Coopers, carpenters, cabinet makers, sawyers, wheelwrights and shipwrights were the tradesmen who constituted the majority of the black woodworkers; and, of this group, carpenters and coopers tended to be in the majority, owing to the abundance of wood in the country during its formative years.

Leather, metal and stone workers constituted a group of tradesmen which was less numerous than woodworkers, but the quality of their work was just as high, and the standards of their trades were probably more demanding since they were required to convert raw materials into finished products more often than were the woodworkers. Certainly those who worked with leather, the tanners, curriers and shoemakers, were expected to demonstrate capabilities which exceeded those of menial workers.

Employing African-Americans as leatherworkers reflects, to some extent, one of the major reasons why African slavery was so attractive to the European settlers in British North America. Notwithstanding the claims of a few that Africans were of an inferior stock, the fact remains that New World Europeans needed skilled and unskilled laborers, not philosophers; and African laborers had the hands and skills needed, not the least of which was that of tanning, the act of converting skins and hides into leather by impregnating them with astringent matter. Asians and Africans had practiced this art for centuries before a scientific explanation for it had developed.

As the focus turns upon the metalworkers, the blacksmith, founders, finers, hammermen, goldsmiths, silversmiths and to a lesser extent, jewelers, attention is directed towards the groups of tradesmen having the greatest versatility and the highest market value. The blacksmith was the most versatile American craftsman; for there was hardly an economic endeavor which did not depend upon him. The farmer relied upon him for his utensils; the mechanic and other artisans depended upon him for their tools.

For that matter, scarcely a utensil, vehicle or tool could be named which did not come in part, either directly or indirectly from the blacksmith. He was the machine blacksmith, carriage and wagon ironer, trimmer, gunsmith, and wheelwright; and he often pared or honed hames, plowstocks, single trees and other necessities of farm life, and even shoed horses. The blacksmith also put edges with different degrees of sharpness on tools, erected lightening rods on ships and homes, made anchors for ships, and performed countless other tasks.

Further, the work of black artisans, whether slave or free, showed that color was not a bar to mastering the handicraft trade. Ironically, on slave plantations, the term "colored folks jobs," within the context of skilled jobs vis-a-vis menial tasks, had no meaning, for all the labor was done by slaves, the skilled as well as menial. Who performed the job was probably determined more by talent then, than now, for an owner could not afford to play favorites at the expense of increased productivity. In such an atmosphere, the gifted and talented tended to come to the forefront. Thus, during the periods 1750 to 1820, black artisans were a visible and viable force in the nation's economy.

As members of the professions, however, Negroes were few and far between. They included mainly clergymen, educators, and an occasional physician.

In the business field, the situation was even more barren of blacks. It is true that Negro labor dominated numerically in the iron and the tobacco industries, yet there was not one black owner among them. This condition has its counterpart today in certain sports businesses. Black athletes represent at least 30 percent of the players in football and an outright majority in basketball, but in neither of these sports businesses is there a black owner of a franchise.

Full employment, in the late 1700s and the early 1800s, did not mean a job worthy of the jobholder, especially if he or she happened to be black. Negroes were frequently, perhaps preponderantly, underemployed.

On the other hand, slaves who had been qualified as artisans were often kept on at these favored levels because it was in the best interest of their former masters to benefit by their skill.

Britain was, substantially, the mother country, and its needs largely shaped the economies of the colonies. English navigation laws created monopolies for crops of certain colonies, and as a maritime power England offered bounties to producers of naval supplies. North Carolina, South Carolina, and Georgia were among those colonies which diverted a sizable portion of their energies to producing naval stores, and there was heavy reliance on slave labor to perform the many and arduous tasks involved in producing pitch, tar, turpentine, and rosin.

In river boating and ocean shipping, as well as in marine-related jobs on land, Negroes had some of their best opportunities to earn a living. Most freight in the new and growing nation was transported by water. There was a need for seamen and boatmen, and African-Americans satisfied this need in large numbers, especially inasmuch as they were finding it hard to enter the trades and professions.

Almost 10 percent of the slaveowners in colonial Philadelphia were in work that was water related. A significant number of blacks manned the docks at Philadelphia, New York, and New Orleans. Approximately one free, adult male Negro in every four at Augusta, Georgia, was engaged in a marine occupation.

From these figures one might suppose that maritime-related work was favored among blacks, but this was not the case. In most instances they were obliged to accept these jobs by circumstances. The slave, of course, had to do as directed. The former slave in marine work found a job simply because many whites wouldn't accept such employment, which was often hazardous and poorly paid. Conditions on shipboard were often unwholesome, or even filthy, and sometimes required being away from home for prolonged periods, making the work especially unattractive to blacks, or whites, with a wife and family.

There is a common impression that mulattoes were spared the hardship of working in the hot sun because of their ancestry. Mulattoes were indeed among the thousands who worked in domestic service, but many more were employed in a variety of jobs ranging from the most menial and physically demanding to the exacting and responsible. Some, for instance, became barbers, performing such tasks as haircutting, shaving, hairdressing, and setting of wigs. Zamba, an African king who was kidnaped and sold into slavery in South Carolina, recalled that many of his fellow slaves were employed in Charleston barber shops, "soaping and shaving beards and cutting the hair of white gentlemen." Timothy Ford, a white Princeton University honor graduate who studied law under Robert Morris, colonial financier and statesman, told of seeing slaves in Charleston running the businesses of their barber owners, who used their own time to enjoy a life of "idleness and ease."

Another line of work for many blacks and mulattoes was in land transportation, which in those times meant horses or horse-drawn wagons and carriages. Teamsters and wagoners were practically indispensable. Coachmen needed a certain skill, of course, as did the hostlers, who handled horses, especially at inns, and the farriers, who were trained or practical veterinarians who also did black-smithing and handled various farm animals.

Once in a while a slave was fortunate enough to have a master who showed genuine appreciation for his loyalty and his labor, over and above the providing of mere subsistence. But few had the distinction of Frank Bird, a 57-year-old hostler at Buchanan's Inn in Bourbon County, Kentucky. He learned farriery, cooking, and hairdressing as a youth in England, prior to being shipped to the colonies and becoming the property of George Washington.

Bird not only accompanied General Washington but served with him during the Revolutionary campaigns. Evidently a warm relationship developed between the two men. Washington did not show his gratitude by freeing Bird at the conclusion of the war, although it is possible that the slave preferred remaining with a benevolent master rather than facing life on his own in his declining years. The nation's first President did, however, follow the practice of many of his contemporaries in specifying that, upon his death, the aging slave was to be freed and given a plot of land.

Within a generation after Washington's death in 1799, the chief commercial activities in the United States were shipping, shipbuilding, fishing, banking, the growing of various staples and food crops, and the raising of livestock. Blacks, however, whether free or slave, were as a rule connected with domestic services, groceries and taverns. Commercial opportunities were left almost totally to whites.

It may be asked, did blacks prefer small businesses to large ones, and why did they own barber shops instead of banks? The answer, probably, is that the nature of their business was more than likely determined for them, rather than by them. Apparently generations of viewing blacks almost solely as slaves or servants had impregnated whites with the concept that Negroes could only perform certain roles, and those whites who had money were seldom willing to lend it to blacks trying to start up sizable enterprises—no matter how capable the loan seeker may have been.

Economic prejudice fed upon and was fed by social, political, and religious prejudices which only now are slowly being overcome. The fact that African-Americans were not allowed to attend college, at least not as regular students, through many generations after their arrival in America did not make the situation any less difficult or unfair for Negroes.

All of this means, of course, that those who did manage to surmount the obstacles in their path and to equal or excel whites had intelligence and character fully commensurate with the members of any other race.

James Derham, Practitioner of Physics

Charles H. Wesley

During the latter part of the eighteenth century, few blacks practiced the profession of medicine. James Derham was an exception. After learning the medical routines and prescriptions of the time, he set up a practice in New Orleans as a free man. Derham was acquainted with some of the prominent figures of his time and was especially well informed in the treatment of tropical diseases.

The story of this black pioneer in the field of medicine is told by Charles H. Wesley in a work appropriately called *In Freedom's Footsteps.*

ACHIEVEMENTS IN SCIENTIFIC INQUIRY

Science was advancing in the United States toward the close of the eighteenth century. Many obstacles were faced by pioneer Americans in this field, and Negroes who were interested in the sciences were uncommon. Individuals with talent had little opportunity to become acquainted with scientific advances. There were a number of Negroes, nevertheless, who did show enthusiasm for scientific fields in spite of the peculiar obstacles in their way. Their beginnings, as elementary as they may now appear, do demonstrate the existence of a potential that might have been realized more fully had there been more opportunity for these thinkers in American intellectual life.

The art of practicing medicine developed very slowly in the period just before, during and after the Revolutionary War. There was a shortage of trained physicians; and even those who were trained were not informed of the causes and cures for most diseases. Harmful methods of healing were practiced. Charlatans peddled their nostrums from village to village. Among whites and Negroes, superstitions about sicknesses and their cures abounded.

The practice of medicine among the nation's blacks began with the transfer here and continuation of the practices of the medicine man in Africa. His conjuration was well known in many slave communities in the South. Some, however, discovered useful remedies. One of these men, known only as Caesar, developed a cure for poisoning in 1792, as well as many remedies using roots and herbs. The Assembly of South Carolina was so impressed with Caesar's value to the community that his freedom was purchased, and he was provided with an annuity of one hundred dollars. A slave in Charleston, South Carolina, in 1797, was known as a "Doctor" and practiced medicine in that city. Other Negroes who were barbers learned how to "bleed" and united these two functions in the practice of phlebotomy. Bleeding was the treatment given for many ailments, generally performed by those who knew the barber's trade. Since Negroes were the most numerous barbers in the southern states, they were also the most active users of this method of treating diseases.

James Derham, referred to as "a practicioner of physics," was born in Philadelphia in 1762. While a boy, he was transferred by his master to Dr. John Kearsley, Jr., who employed him in the mixing of medicines and in the routine duties of his practice. Following the death of Dr. Kearsley, Derham passed through the hands of several owners. Among these were Dr. George West, Surgeon in the Fifteenth British Regiment, and Dr. Robert Dove of New Orleans. Derham was employed by these physicians in ministering to their patients. After several years of service, Dr. Dove permitted Derham to purchase his freedom. He then became a practitioner in New Orleans, making use of his knowledge of medicine and becoming exceptionally proficient in treating the diseases prevalent in the city's tropical climate.

At the age of twenty-six, Derham's practice was bringing him the sum of three thousand dollars a year. Dr. Benjamin Rush, who was professor of the Institutes and Practice of Physics at the University of Pennsylvania, stated in an address to the Pennsylvania Society for Promoting the Abolition of Slavery, on January 5, 1789, that he had talked with James Derham concerning most of the diseases of the section of the country in which he was living and had found him acquainted with the modern methods for their treatment. Dr. Rush had expected to make suggestions to him regarding the medicines to be used; instead, Derham suggested others to him.

The Census of 1860

The census of 1860 is presented here for comparison purposes. Note that forty states, two territories, and the District of Columbia are included. Note, too, the number of states in which there were no slaves reported, and where there were neither slaves nor free blacks. Which states had the largest numbers of slaves? Which state had more slaves than whites? How do you account for these differences?

The United States Census of 1860, Showing the Number of Free and Enslaved Negroes in Each State

States	Total Negroes	Total whites	Negro slaves	Free Negroes
Alabama	437,770	526,271	435,080	2,690
Arkansas	111,259	324,143	111,115	144
California	4,086	323,177	−	4,086
Colorado	46	34,231	−	46
Connecticut	8,627	451,504	−	8,627
Delaware	21,627	90,589	1,798	19,829
District of Columbia	14,316	60,763	3,185	11,131
Florida	62,677	77,746	61,745	932
Georgia	465,698	591,550	462,198	3,500
Illinois	7,628	1,704,291	−	7,628
Indiana	11,428	1,338,710	−	11,428
Iowa	1,069	673,779	−	1,069
Kansas	627	106,390	2	625
Kentucky	236,167	919,484	225,483	10,684
Louisiana	350,373	357,456	331,726	18,647
Maine	1,327	626,947	−	1,327
Maryland	171,131	515,918	87,189	83,942
Massachusetts	9,602	1,221,432	−	9,602
Michigan	6,799	736,142	−	6,799
Minnesota	259	169,395	−	259
Mississippi	437,404	353,899	436,631	773
Missouri	118,503	1,063,489	114,931	3,572
Nebraska	82	28,696	15	67
Nevada	45	6,812	−	45
New Hampshire	494	325,579	−	494
New Jersey	25,336	646,699	18	25,318
New Mexico	85	82,924	−	85
New York	49,005	3,831,590	−	49,005

States	Total Negroes	Total whites	Negro slaves	Free Negroes
North Carolina	361,522	629,942	331,059	30,463
North Dakota	*	2,576	–	–
Ohio	36,673	2,302,808	–	36,673
Oregon	128	52,160	–	128
Pennsylvania	56,949	2,849,259	–	56,949
Rhode Island	3,952	170,649	–	3,952
South Carolina	412,320	291,300	402,406	9,914
South Dakota	*	*	–	–
Tennessee	283,019	826,722	275,719	7,300
Texas	182,921	420,891	182,566	355
Utah	59	40,125	29	30
Vermont	709	314,369	–	709
Virginia	548,907	1,047,299	490,865	58,042
Washington	30	11,138	–	30
Wisconsin	1,171	773,693	–	1,171
Total	4,441,830	26,922,537	3,953,760	488,070

Source: U.S. Bureau of Census, 1860.
*Dakota Territory.

The Founding of the African Methodist Episcopal Church

Richard Allen

The ministry early became a profession that attracted black Americans. The dramatic account of the founding of the African Methodist Episcopal Church is told by Richard Allen, a black minister in eighteenth-century America. Additionally, Allen describes the changing attitudes toward black members of officers and members of a Philadelphia congregation. The staunch convictions and dedication of these early ministers is part of our American heritage.

December 1784, General Conference sat in Baltimore, the first General Conference ever held in America. The English preachers just arrived from Europe were, Rev. Dr. Coke, Richard Whatcoat and Thomas Vassey. This was the beginning of the Episcopal Church amongst the Methodists. Many of the ministers were set apart in holy orders at this conference, and were said to be entitled to the gown; and I have thought religion has been declining in the church ever since. There was a pamphlet published by some person, which stated, that when the Methodists were no people, then they were a people; and now they have become a people they were no people; which had often serious weight upon my mind.

In 1785 the Rev. Richard Whatcoat was appointed on Baltimore circuit. He was, I believe, a man of God. I found great strength in travelling with him—a father in Israel. In his advice he was fatherly and friendly. He was of a mild and serene disposition. My lot was cast in Baltimore, in a small meeting-house called

Methodist Alley. I stopped at Richard Mould's, and was sent to my lodgings, and lodged at Mr. McCannon's. I had some happy meetings in Baltimore. I was introduced to Richard Russell, who was very kind and affectionate to me, and attended several meetings. Rev. Bishop Asbury sent for me to meet him at Henry Gaff's. I did so. He told me he wished me to travel with him. He told me that in the slave countries, Carolina and other places, I must not intermix with the slaves, and I would frequently have to sleep in his carriage, and he would allow me my victuals and clothes. I told him I would not travel with him on these conditions. He asked me my reason. I told him if I was taken sick, who was to support me? and that I thought people ought to lay up something while they were able, to support themselves in time of sickness or old age. He said that was as much as he got, his victuals and clothes. I told him he would be taken care of, let his afflictions be as they were, or let him be taken sick where he would, he would be taken care of; but I doubted whether it would be the case with myself. He smiled, and told me he would give me from then until he returned from the eastward to make up my mind, which would be about three months. But I made up my mind that I would not accept of his proposals. Shortly after I left Hartford Circuit, and came to Pennsylvania, on Lancaster circuit. I travelled several months on Lancaster circuit with the Rev. Peter Morratte and Irie Ellis. They were very kind and affectionate to me in building me up; for I had many trials to pass through, and I received nothing from the Methodist connection. My usual method was, when I would get bare of clothes, to stop travelling and go to work, so that no man could say I was chargeable to the connection. My hands administered to my necessities. The autumn of 1785 I returned again to Radnor. I stopped at George Giger's, a man of God, and went to work. His family were all kind and affectionate to me. I killed seven beeves, and supplied the neighbors with meat; got myself pretty well clad through my own industry—thank God—and preached occasionally. The elder in charge in Philadelphia frequently sent for me to come to the city. February, 1786, I came to Philadelphia. Preaching was given out for me at five o'clock in the morning at St. George church. I strove to preach as well as I could, but it was a great cross to me; but the Lord was with me. We had a good time and several souls were awakened, and were earnestly seeking redemption in the blood of Christ. I thought I would stop in Philadelphia a week or two. I preached at different places in the city. My labor was much blessed. I soon saw a large field open in seeking and instructing my African brethren, who had been a long forgotten people and few of them attended public worship. I preached in the commons, in Southwark, Northern Liberties, and wherever I could find an opening. I frequently preached twice a day, at 5 o'clock in the morning and in the evening, and it was not uncommon for me to preach from four to five times a day. I established prayer meetings; I raised a society in 1786 for forty-two members. I saw the necessity of erecting a place of worship for the colored people. I proposed it to the most respectable people of color in this city; but here I met with opposition. I had but three colored brethren that united with me in erecting a place of worship—the Rev. Absalom Jones, William White and Dorus Ginnings. These united with me as soon as it became public and known by the elder who was stationed in the city. The Rev. C———B——— opposed the plan, and would not submit to any argument we could raise but he was shortly removed from the charge. The Rev. Mr. W———took the charge, and the Rev. L——— G———. Mr. W———was much opposed to an African church, and used very degrading and insulting language to us, to try and prevent us from going on. We all belonged to St. George's church—Rev. Absalom Jones, William White and Dorus Ginnings. We felt ourselves much cramped; but my dear Lord was with us, and we believed, if it was his will, the work would go on, and that we would be able to succeed in building the house of the Lord. We established prayer meetings and meetings of exhortation, and the Lord blessed our endeavors, and many souls were awakened; but the elder soon forbid us holding any such meetings; but we viewed the forlorn state of our colored brethren, and that they were destitute of a place of worship. They were considered as a nuisance.

A number of us usually attended St. George's church in Fourth street; and when the colored people began to get numerous in attending the church, they moved us from the seats we usually sat on, and placed us around the wall, and on Sabbath morning we went to church and the sexton stood at the door, and told us to go in the gallery. He told us to go, and we would see where to sit. We expected to take the seats over the ones we formerly occupied below, not knowing any better. We took those seats. Meeting had begun, and they were nearly done singing, and just as we got to the seats, the elder said, "Let us pray." We had not been long upon our knees before I heard considerable scuffling and low talking. I raised my head up and saw one of the trustees, H———M———, having hold of the Rev. Absalom Jones, pulling him up off of his knees, and saying, "You must get up—you must not kneel here." Mr. Jones replied, "Wait until prayer is over." Mr. H———M——— said "No, you must get up now, or I will call for aid and force you away." Mr. Jones said, "Wait until prayer is over, and I will get up and trouble you no more." With that he beckoned to one of the other trustees, Mr. L———S——— to come to his assistance. He came, and went to William White to pull him up. By this time prayer was over, and we all went out of the church in a body, and they were no more plagued with us in the church. This raised a great excitement and inquiry among the citizens, in so much that I believe they were ashamed of their conduct. But my dear Lord was with us, and we were filled with fresh vigor to get a house erected to worship God in. Seeing our forlorn and distressed situation, many of the hearts of our citizens were moved to urge us forward; notwithstanding we had subscribed largely towards finishing St. George's church, in building the gallery and laying new floors, and just as the house was made comfortable, we were turned out from enjoying the comforts of worshipping therein. We then hired a store-room, and held worship by ourselves. Here we were pursued with threats of being disowned, and read publicly out of meeting if we did continue worship in the place we had hired; but we believed the Lord would be our friend. We got subscription papers out to raise money to build the house of the Lord. By this time we had waited on Dr. Rush and Mr. Robert Ralston, and told them of our distressing situation. We considered it a blessing that the Lord had put it into our hearts to wait upon those gentlemen. They pitied our situation, and subscribed largely towards the church, and were very friendly towards us, and advised us how to go on. We appointed Mr. Ralston our treasurer. Dr. Rush did much for us in public by his influence. I hope the name of Dr. Benjamin Rush and Robert Ralston will never be forgotten among us. They were the first two gentlemen who espoused the cause of the oppressed, and aided us in building the house of the Lord for the poor Africans to worship in. Here was the beginning and rise of the first African church in America. But the elder of the Methodist Church still pursued us. Mr. J———M——— called upon us and told us if we did not erase our names from the subscription paper, and give up the paper, we would be publicly turned out of meeting. We asked him if we had violated any rules of discipline by so doing. He replied, "I have the charge given to me by the Conference, and unless you submit I will read you publicly out of meeting." We told him we were willing to abide by the discipline of the Methodist Church, "And if you will show us where we have violated any law of discipline of the Methodist Church, we will submit; and if there is no rule violated in the discipline we will proceed on." He replied, "We will read you all out." We told him if he turned us out contrary to rule of discipline, we should seek further redress. We told him we were dragged off of our knees in St. George's church, and treated worse than heathens; and we were determined to seek out for ourselves, the Lord being our helper. He told us we were not Methodists, and left us. Finding we would go on in raising money to build the church, he called upon us again, and wished to see us all together. We met him. He told us that he wished us well, that he was a friend to us, and used many arguments to convince us that we were wrong in building a church. We told him we had no place of worship; and we did not mean to go to St. George's church any more, as we were so scandalously treated in the presence of all the congregation present; "and if you deny us your name, you cannot seal up the scriptures from us, and deny us a name in heaven. We believe heaven is free for all who worship in spirit and truth." And he said, "So you are determined to go on." We told him "Yes, God being our helper." He then replied, "We will disown you all from the Methodist connection." We believed if we put our trust in the Lord, he would stand by us. This was a trial that I never had to pass through before. I was confident that the great head of the church would support us. My dear Lord was with us. . . . Robert R. Roberts, the resident elder, came to Bethel, insisted on preaching to us and taking the spiritual charge of the congregation, [because] we were Methodists he was told he should come on some terms with the trustees; his answer was, that "He did not come to consult with Richard Allen or other trustees, but to inform the congregation, that on next Sunday afternoon, he would come and take the spiritual charge." We told him he could not preach for us under existing circumstances. However, at the appointed time he came, but having taken previous advice we had our preacher in the pulpit when he came, and the house was so fixed that he could not get but more than half way to the pulpit. Finding himself disappointed he appealed to those who came with him as witnesses, that "That man (meaning the preacher), had taken his appointment." Several respectable white citizens who knew the colored people had been ill-used, were present, and told us not to fear, for they would see us righted, and not suffer Roberts to preach in a forcible manner, after which Roberts went away.

The next elder stationed in Philadelphia was Robert Birch, who, following the example of his predecessor, came and published a meeting for himself. But the method just mentioned was adopted and he had to go away disappointed. In consequence of this, he applied to the Supreme Court for a writ of mandamus, to know why the pulpit was denied him. Being elder, this brought on a lawsuit, which ended in our favor. Thus by the Providence of God we were delivered from a long, distressing and expensive suit, which could not be resumed, being determined by the Supreme Court. For this mercy we desire to be unfeignedly thankful.

About this time, our colored friends in Baltimore were treated in a similar manner by the white preachers and trustees, and many of them driven away who were disposed to seek a place of worship, rather than go to law.

Many of the colored people in other places were in a situation nearly like those of Philadelphia and Baltimore, which induced us, in April 1816, to call a general meeting, by way of Conference. Delegates from Baltimore and other places which met those of Philadelphia, and taking into consideration their grievances, and in order to secure the privileges, promote union and harmony among themselves, it was resolved: "That the people of Philadelphia, Baltimore, etc., etc., should become one body, under the name of the African Methodist Episcopal Church." We deemed it expedient to have a form of discipline, whereby we may guide our people in the fear of God, in the unity of the Spirit, and in the bonds of peace, and preserve us from that spiritual despotism which we have so recently experienced—remembering that we are not to lord it over God's heritage, as greedy dogs that can never have enough. But with long suffering and bowels of compassion, to bear each other's burdens, and so fulfill the Law of Christ, praying that our mutual striving together for the promulgation of the Gospel may be crowned with abundant success. . . .

CHAPTER TWELVE

Abolition: The Antislavery Crusade

Who were the abolitionists? What were their motives in attacking institutionalized slavery?

Abolitionists were divided philosophically into two groups. The militant abolitionist advocated the eradication of slavery by any means necessary. The moderate abolitionist believed that attacks on slavery should be conducted within the spirit of the laws. In this chapter, both militant and moderate abolitionists articulate their philosophical positions regarding institutionalized slavery.

Nat Turner's Insurrection

Thomas Wentworth Higginson

Thomas Wentworth Higginson, a colonel of a black Union regiment during the Civil War, wrote the following article for the *Atlantic Monthly* in 1861. In it he describes the attempts of a group of slaves to change their status on a plantation in Jerusalem, Virginia. Led by Nat Turner, members of the group were either killed or captured and reenslaved. Nat Turner himself, after unsuccessfully trying to escape capture, was arrested, tried, convicted, and executed within a twelve-day period. This selection is the story of one leader of one group. The account represents, however, similar occurrences elsewhere, in which slaves actively tried to change their status by utilizing the same strategies for obtaining freedom that had made them slaves.

Near the southeastern border of Virginia, in Southampton County, there is a neighborhood known as "The Cross Keys." It lies fifteen miles from Jerusalem, the county-town or "court-house," seventy miles from Norfolk, and about as far from Richmond. It is some ten or fifteen miles from Murfreesboro' in North

Carolina and about twenty-five from the Great Dismal Swamp. Up to Sunday, the twenty-first of August, 1831, there was nothing to distinguish it from any other rural, lethargic, slipshod Virginia neighborhood, with the due allotment of mansion-houses and log-huts, tobacco-fields and "old-fields," horses, dogs, negroes, "poor white folks," so called, and other white folks, poor without being called so. One of these last was Joseph Travis, who had recently married the widow of one Putnam Moore, and had unfortunately wedded to himself her negroes also.

In the woods on the plantation of Joseph Travis, upon the Sunday just named, six slaves met at noon for what is called in the Northern States a picnic and in the Southern a barbecue. The bill of fare was to be simple: one brought a pig, and another some brandy, giving to the meeting an aspect so cheaply convivial that no one would have imagined it to be the final consummation of a conspiracy which had been for six months in preparation. In this plot four of the men had been already initiated,—Henry, Hark or Hercules, Nelson, and Sam. Two others were novices, Will and Jack by name. The party had remained together from twelve to three o'clock, when a seventh man joined them,—a short, stout, powerfully built person, of dark mulatto complexion and strongly-marked African features, but with a face full of expression and resolution. This was Nat Turner.

He was at this time nearly thirty-one years old, having been born on the second of October, 1800. He had belonged originally to Benjamin Turner,—whence his last name, slaves having usually no patronymic,—had then been transferred to Putnam Moore, and then to his present owner. He had, by his own account, felt himself singled out from childhood for some great work; and he had some peculiar marks on his person, which, joined to his great mental precocity, were enough to occasion, among his youthful companions, a superstitious faith in his gifts and destiny. He had great mechanical ingenuity also, experimentalized very early in making paper, gunpowder, pottery, and in other arts which in later life he was found thoroughly to understand. His moral faculties were very strong, so that white witnesses admitted that he had never been known to swear an oath, to drink a drop of spirits, or to commit a theft. And in general, so marked were his early peculiarities, that people said "he had too much sense to be raised, and if he was, he would never be of any use as a slave." This impression of personal destiny grew with his growth;—he fasted, prayed, preached, read the Bible, heard voices when he walked behind his plough, and communicated his revelations to the awe-struck slaves. They told him in return, that, "if they had his sense, they would not serve any master in the world." . . .

Whatever Nat Turner's experiences of slavery might have been, it is certain that his plans were not suddenly adopted, but that he had brooded over them for years. To this day there are traditions among the Virginia slaves of the keen devices of "Prophet Nat." If he was caught with lime and lamp-black in hand, conning over a half-finished county-map on the barn-door, he was always "planning what to do, if he were blind," or "studying how to get to Mr. Francis's house." . . .

The religious hallucinations narrated in his Confession seem to have been as genuine as the average of such things, and are very well expressed. It was quite like Jacob Behmen. He saw white spirits and black spirits contending in the skies, the sun was darkened, the thunder rolled. . . .

When he came, therefore, to the barbecue on the appointed Sunday, and found not these four only, but two others, his first question to the intruders was, How they came thither. To this Will answered manfully, that his life was worth no more than the others, and "his liberty was as dear to him." This admitted him to confidence, and as Jack was known to be entirely under Hark's influence, the strangers were no bar to their discussion. Eleven hours they remained there, in anxious consultation: one can imagine those terrible dusky faces, beneath the funereal woods, and amid the flickering of pine-knot torches, preparing that stern revenge whose shuddering echoes should ring through the land so long. Two things were at last decided: to begin their work that night, and to begin it with a massacre so swift and irresistible as to create in a few days more terror than many battles, and so spare the need of future bloodshed. "It was agreed that we should commence at home on that night, and, until we had armed and equipped ourselves and gained sufficient force, neither age nor sex was to be spared: which was invariably adhered to."

John Brown invaded Virginia with nineteen men, and with the avowed resolution to take no life but in self-defence. Nat Turner attacked Virginia from within, with six men, and with the determination to spare no life until his power was established. John Brown intended to pass rapidly through Virginia, and then retreat to the mountains. Nat Turner intended to "conquer Southampton County as the white men did in the Revolution, and then retreat, if necessary, to the Dismal Swamp." Each plan was deliberately matured; each was in its way practicable; but each was defeated by a single false step, as will soon appear.

We must pass over the details of horror, as they occurred during the next twenty-four hours. Swift and stealthy as Indians, the black men passed from house to house,—not pausing, not hesitating, as their terrible work went on. In one thing they were humaner than Indians or than white men fighting against Indians,—there was no gratuitous outrage beyond the death-blow itself, no insult, no mutilation; but in every house they entered, that blow fell on man, woman, and child,—nothing that had a white skin was spared. From every house they took arms and ammunition, and from a few, money; on every plantation they found recruits: those dusky slaves, so obsequious to their master the day before, so prompt to sing and dance before his Northern visitors, were all swift to transform themselves into fiends of retribution now; show them sword or musket and they grasped it, though it were an heirloom from Washington himself. The troop increased from house to house,—first to fifteen, then to forty, then to sixty. Some were armed with muskets, some with axes, some with scythes; some came on their masters' horses. As the numbers increased, they could be divided, and the awful work was carried on more rapidly still. The plan then was for an advanced guard of horsemen to approach each house at a gallop, and surround it till the others came up. Meanwhile what agonies of terror must have taken place within, shared alike by innocent and guilty! what memories of wrongs inflicted on those dusky creatures, by some,—what innocent participation, by others, in the penance! The outbreak lasted for but forty-eight hours; but during that period fifty-five whites were slain, without the loss of a single slave.

One fear was needless, which to many a husband and father must have intensified the last struggle. These negroes had been systematically brutalized from childhood; they had been allowed no legalized or permanent marriage; they had beheld around them an habitual licentiousness, such as can scarcely exist except in a Slave State; some of them had seen their wives and sisters habitually polluted by the husbands and the brothers of these fair white women who were now absolutely in their power. Yet I have looked through the Virginia newspapers of that time in vain for one charge of an indecent outrage on a woman against these triumphant and terrible slaves. Wherever they went, there went death, and that was all. Compare this with ordinary wars; compare it with the annals of the French Revolution. . . .

When the number of adherents had increased to fifty or sixty, Nat Turner judged it time to strike at the county-seat, Jerusalem. Thither a few white fugitives had already fled, and couriers might thence be despatched for aid to Richmond and Petersburg, unless promptly intercepted. Besides, he could there find arms, ammunition, and money; though they had already obtained, it is dubiously reported, from eight hundred to one thousand dollars. On the way it was necessary to pass the plantation of Mr. Parker, three miles from Jerusalem. Some of the men wished to stop here and enlist some of their friends. Nat Turner objected, as the delay might prove dangerous; he yielded at last, and it proved fatal.

He remained at the gate with six or eight men; thirty or forty went to the house, half a mile distant. They remained too long, and he went alone to hasten them. During his absence a party of eighteen white men came up suddenly, dispersing the small guard left at the gate; and when the main body of slaves emerged from the house, they encountered, for the first time, their armed masters. The blacks halted, the whites advanced cautiously within a hundred yards and fired a volley; on its being returned, they broke into disorder, and hurriedly retreated, leaving some wounded on the ground. The retreating whites were pursued, and were saved only by falling in with another band of fresh men from Jerusalem, with whose aid they turned upon the slaves, who in their turn fell into confusion. Turner, Hark, and about twenty men on horseback retreated in some order; the rest were scattered. The leader still planned to reach Jerusalem by a private way, thus evading pursuit; but at last decided to stop for the night, in the hope of enlisting additional recruits.

During the night the number increased again to forty, and they encamped on Major Ridley's plantation. An alarm took place during the darkness,—whether real or imaginary does not appear,—and the men became scattered again. Proceeding to make fresh enlistments with the daylight, they were resisted at Dr. Blunt's house, where his slaves, under his orders, fired upon them, and this, with a later attack from a party of white men near Captain Harris's, so broke up the whole force that they never reunited. The few who remained together agreed to separate for a few hours to see if anything could be done to revive the insurrection, and meet again that evening at their original rendezvous. But they never reached it.

Sadly came Nat Turner at nightfall into those gloomy woods where forty-eight hours before he had revealed the details of his terrible plot to his companions. At the outset all his plans had succeeded; everything was as he predicted: the slaves had come readily at his call, the masters had proved perfectly defenseless. Had he not been persuaded to pause at Parker's plantation, he would have been master before now of the arms and ammunition at Jerusalem; and with these to aid, and the Dismal Swamp for a refuge, he might have sustained himself indefinitely against his pursuers.

Now the blood was shed, the risk was incurred, his friends were killed or captured, and all for what? Lasting memories of terror, to be sure, for his oppressors; but on the other hand, hopeless failure for the insurrection, and certain death for him. . . .

There he waited two weary days and two melancholy nights,—long enough to satisfy himself that no one would rejoin him, and that the insurrection had hopelessly failed. The determined, desperate spirits who had shared his plans were scattered forever, and longer delay would be destruction for him also. He found a spot which he judged safe, dug a hole under a pile of fence-rails in a field, and lay there for six weeks, only leaving it for a few moments at midnight to obtain water from a neighboring spring. Food he had previously provided, without discovery, from a house near by. . . .

Worn out by confinement in his little cave, Nat Turner grew more adventurous, and began to move about stealthily by night, afraid to speak to any human being, but hoping to obtain some information that might aid his escape. Returning regularly to his retreat before daybreak, he might have continued this mode of life until pursuit had ceased, had not a dog succeeded where men had failed. The creature accidentally smelt out the provisions hid in the cave, and finally led thither his masters, two negroes, one of whom was named Nelson. On discovering the terrible fugitive, they fled precipitately, when he hastened to retreat in an opposite direction. This was on October 15th, and from this moment the neighborhood was all alive with excitement, and five or six hundred men undertook the pursuit.

It shows a more than Indian adroitness in Nat Turner to have escaped capture any longer. The cave, the arms, the provisions were found; and lying among them the notched stick of this miserable Robinson Crusoe, marked with five weary weeks and six days. But the man was gone. For ten days more he concealed himself among the wheat-stacks on Mr. Francis's plantation, and during this time was reduced almost to despair. Once he decided to surrender himself, and walked by night within two miles of Jerusalem before his purpose failed him. Three times he tried to get out of that neighborhood, but in vain: travelling by day was, of course, out of the question, and by night he found it impossible to elude the patrol. Again and again, therefore, he returned to his hiding-place, and during his whole two months' liberty never went five miles from the Cross Keys. On the 25th of October, he was at last discovered by Mr. Francis, as he was emerging from a stack. A load of buckshot was instantly discharged at him, twelve of which passed through his hat as he fell to the ground. He escaped even then, but his pursuers were rapidly concentrating upon him, and it is perfectly astonishing that he could have eluded them for five days more.

On Sunday, October 30th, a man named Benjamin Phipps, going out for the first time on patrol duty, was passing at noon a clearing in the woods where a number of pine-trees had long since been felled. There was a motion among their boughs; he stopped to watch it; and through a gap in the branches he saw, emerging from a hole in the earth beneath, the face of Nat Turner. Aiming his gun instantly, Phipps called on him to surrender. The fugitive, exhausted with watching and privation, entangled in the branches, armed only with a sword, had nothing to do but to yield; sagaciously reflecting, also, as he afterwards explained, that the woods were full of armed men, and that he had better trust fortune for some later chance of escape, instead of desperately attempting it then. He was correct in the first impression, since there were fifty armed scouts within a circuit of two miles. His insurrection ended where it began; for this spot was only a mile and a half from the house of Joseph Travis. . . .

When Nat Turner was asked by Mr. T. R. Gray, the counsel assigned him, whether, although defeated, he still believed in his own Providential mission, he answered, as simply as one who came thirty years after him, "Was not Christ crucified?" In the same spirit, when arraigned before the court, he answered, 'Not guilty,' saying to his counsel that he did not feel so." But apparently no argument was made in his favor by his counsel, nor were any witnesses called,—he being convicted on the testimony of Levi Waller, and upon his own confession, which was put in by Mr. Gray, and acknowledged by the prisoner before the six justices composing the court, as being "full, free, and voluntary." He was therefore placed in the paradoxical position of conviction by his own confession, under a plea of "Not guilty." The arrest took place on the thirtieth of October, 1831, the confession on the first of November, the trial and conviction on the fifth, and the execution on the following Friday, the eleventh of November, precisely at noon. He met his death with perfect composure, declined addressing the multitude assembled, and told the sheriff in a firm voice that he was ready. . . .

Editorial, *North Star,* Vol. 1, No. 1

Frederick Douglass

The short selection that follows is an extract of the first editorial in *North Star,* an antislavery newspaper founded in 1847. The editorial, written by abolitionist Frederick Douglass, is an example of one black American's attempt to incite other black Americans to action. Douglass argues that the entire burden for obtaining freedom cannot rest exclusively on the shoulders of the white man; it must be actively and cooperatively shared by the oppressed man himself, the American black.

We solemnly dedicate the "North Star" to the cause of our long oppressed and plundered fellow countrymen. May God bless the undertaking to your good! It shall fearlessly assert your rights, faithfully proclaim your wrongs, and earnestly demand for you instant and even-handed justice. Giving no quarter to slavery at the South, it will hold no truce with oppressors at the North. While it shall boldly advocate emancipation for our enslaved brethren, it will omit no opportunity to gain for the nominally free complete enfranchisement. Every effort to injure or degrade you or your cause—originating wheresoever, or with whomsoever—shall find in it a constant, unswerving and inflexible foe. . . .

Remember that we are one, that our cause is one, and that we must help each other, if we would succeed. We have drank to the dregs the bitter cup of slavery; we have worn the heavy yoke; we have sighed beneath our bonds, and writhed beneath the bloody lash;—cruel mementoes of our oneness are indelibly marked on our living flesh. We are one with you under the ban of prejudice and proscription—one with you under the slander of inferiority—one with you in social and political disfranchisement. What you suffer, we suffer; what you endure, we endure. We are indissolubly united, and must fall or flourish together. . . .

It is scarcely necessary for us to say that our desire to occupy our present position at the head of an Anti-Slavery Journal, has resulted from no unworthy distrust or ungrateful want of appreciation of the zeal, integrity or ability of the noble band of white laborers in this department of our cause; but, from the sincere and settled conviction that such a Journal, if conducted with only moderate skill and ability, would do a most important and indispensable work, which it would be wholly impossible for our white friends to do for us.

It is neither a reflection on the fidelity, nor a disparagement of the ability of our friends and fellow-laborers, to assert what "common sense affirms and only folly denies," that the man who has *suffered the wrong* is the man to *demand redress.*—that the man STRUCK is the man to CRY OUT—and that he who has *endured the cruel pangs of Slavery* is the man to *advocate Liberty*. It is evident we must be our own representatives and advocates—not exclusively, but peculiarly—not distinct from, but in connection with our white friends. In the grand struggle for liberty and equality now waging it is meet, right and essential that there should arise in our ranks authors and editors, as well as orators, for it is in these capacities that the most permanent good can be rendered to our cause. . . .

William Lloyd Garrison's Prospectus for the *Liberator,* 1831

Kenneth M. Stampp

The previous selection described a black man's efforts to abolish slavery. In this selection, Kenneth M. Stampp describes a white man's activities in the antislavery movement. Journalist William Lloyd Garrison launched a crusade against slavery in his weekly abolitionist newspaper, the *Liberator*. In the first issue, he stated clearly his demands for "the immediate enfranchisement of our slave population." Garrison's crusade ended in 1865 when the Thirteenth Amendment finally abolished slavery.

Emerson once asked: "What is man born for but to be a Reformer, a Remaker of what man has made; a renouncer of lies; a restorer of truth and good . . . ?" Many of Emerson's New England contemporaries agreed with him and devoted their lives to various movements for moral uplift or social reform, but none more fervently than William Lloyd Garrison.

Born in Newburyport, Massachusetts, in 1805, Garrison experienced both poverty and insecurity in his childhood. His father, a sailor, deserted the family when Garrison was an infant; his mother, an austere, pious Baptist, made her son aware of the prevalence of sin in the world but offered him neither warmth nor understanding. As a youth Garrison learned the printer's trade and developed a taste for polemical newspaper writing. He had considerable talent, and with it he combined a strong ambition to win public recognition—in order, as he once said, to have his name known "in a praiseworthy manner."

Reform journalism was Garrison's road to fame. In 1828 he went first to Boston to edit the *National Philanthropist,* a temperance weekly, then to Bennington, Vermont, to edit the *Journal of the Times,* in whose columns he preached temperance, world peace, and the gradual abolition of slavery. The survival of slavery in the southern states, he told a Boston audience on July 4, 1829, was a "glaring contradiction" of the American creed of liberty and equality. The free states had a right to demand gradual emancipation, because as long as slavery existed "they participate in the guilt thereof." Soon after making this speech, Garrison abandoned gradualism and began to demand the immediate abolition of slavery. Since slaveholding was a sin, to advocate gradual emancipation was like asking a thief gradually to abandon a life of crime.

In August, 1829, Garrison moved to Baltimore to join the gentle Quaker Benjamin Lundy in editing an antislavery newspaper, the *Genius of Universal Emancipation*. Two months later, in one of his editorials, Garrison violently upbraided Francis Todd, a Newburyport shipowner, for transporting a cargo of slaves from Baltimore to New Orleans. Men such as Todd, he said, were *"enemies of their own species—highway robbers and murders,"* and they deserved to be punished with solitary confinement for life. For this editorial a Baltimore grand jury indicted Garrison for libel, and he was tried, convicted, and fined $50. Since he could pay neither the fine nor court costs, he was jailed from April 17 to June 5, 1830.

After his release from jail, Garrison returned to Boston determined to awaken the northern people to the evils of slavery. "A few white victims must be sacrificed to open the eyes of this nation," wrote the young martyr. "I expect and am willing to be persecuted, imprisoned and bound for advocating African rights." Thus, at the age of twenty-five, Garrison was prepared for his life's work. On January 1, 1831, in a dingy room on the third floor of Merchants' Hall in Boston, he began to publish a weekly abolitionist newspaper, the *Liberator*. The prospectus, printed below, appeared in the first issue.[1]

In the month of August, I issued proposals for publishing *The Liberator* in Washington city; but the enterprise, though hailed in different sections of the country, was palsied by public indifference. Since that time, the removal of the *Genius of Universal Emancipation* to the Seat of Government has rendered less imperious the establishment of a similar periodical in that quarter.

During my recent tour for the purpose of exciting the minds of the people by a series of discourses on the subject of slavery, every place that I visited gave fresh evidence of the fact, that a greater revolution in public sentiment was to be effected in the free states—*and particularly in New-England*—than at the south. I found contempt more bitter, opposition more active, detraction more relentless, prejudice more stubborn, and apathy more frozen, than among the slave owners themselves. Of course, there were individual exceptions to the contrary. This state of things afflicted, but did not dishearten me. I determined, at every hazard, to lift up the standard of emancipation in the eyes of the nation, *within sight of Bunker Hill and in the birth place of liberty*. That standard is now unfurled; and long may it float, unhurt by the spoliations of time or the missiles of a desperate foe—yea, till every chain be broken, and every bondman set free! Let southern oppressors tremble—let their secret abettors tremble—let their northern apologists tremble—let all the enemies of the persecuted blacks tremble.

I deem the publication of my original Prospectus[2] unnecessary, as it has obtained a wide circulation. The principles therein inculcated will be steadily pursued in this paper, excepting that I shall not array myself as the political partisan of any man. In defending the great cause of human rights, I wish to derive the assistance of all religions and of all parties.

Assenting to the "self-evident truth" maintained in the American Declaration of Independence, "that all men are created equal and endowed by their Creator with certain inalienable rights—among which are life, liberty and the pursuit of happiness," I shall strenuously contend for the immediate enfranchisement of our slave population. In Parkstreet Church, on the Fourth of July, 1829, in an address on slavery, I unreflectingly assented to the popular but pernicious doctrine of *gradual* abolition. I seize this opportunity to make a full and unequivocal recantation, and thus publickly to ask pardon of my God, of my country, and of my brethren the poor slaves, for having uttered a sentiment so full of timidity, injustice and absurdity. A similar recantation, from my pen, was published in the *Genius of Universal Emancipation* at Baltimore, in September, 1829. My conscience is now satisfied.

I am aware that many object to the severity of my language; but is there not cause for severity? I *will be* as harsh as truth, and as uncompromising as justice. On this subject, I do not wish to think, or speak, or write, with moderation. No! no! Tell a man whose house is on fire, to give a moderate alarm; tell him to moderately rescue his wife from the hands of the ravisher; tell the mother to gradually extricate her babe from the fire into which it has fallen;—but urge me not to use moderation in a cause like the present. I am in earnest—I will not equivocate—I will not excuse—I will not retreat a single inch—AND I WILL BE HEARD. The apathy of the people is enough to make every statue leap from its pedestal, and to hasten the resurrection of the dead.

It is pretended, that I am retarding the cause of emancipation, by the coarseness of my invective, and the precipitancy of my measures. *The charge is not true.* On this question my influence,—humble as it is,—is felt at this moment to a considerable extent, and shall be felt in coming years—not perniciously, but beneficially —not as a curse, but as a blessing; and posterity will bear testimony that I was right. I desire to thank God, that he enables me to disregard "the fear of man which bringeth a snare," and to speak his truth in its simplicity and power.

And here I close with this fresh dedication:

"Oppression! I have seen thee, face to face,
And met thy cruel eye and cloudy brow;
But thy soul-withering glance I fear not now—
For dread to prouder feelings doth give place
Of deep abhorrence! Scorning the disgrace
Of slavish knees that at thy footstool bow,
I also kneel—but with far other bow
Do hail thee and thy herd of hirelings base:—
I swear, while life-blood warms my throbbing veins,
Still to oppose and thwart, with heart and hand,
Thy brutalizing sway—'till Afric's chains
Are burst, and Freedom rules the rescued land,—
Trampling Oppression and his iron rod:
Such is the vow I take—SO HELP ME GOD!"

The crusade that Garrison thus helped to launch lasted until 1865, when the Thirteenth Amendment finally abolished slavery and the *Liberator* was discontinued. In the intervening years many abolitionists proved to be better organizers, leaders, and strategists than Garrison, but none could match him as an agitator or polemicist. None ever penned a manifesto as stirring as the one that appeared in the first issue of the *Liberator*, and no other abolitionist document is so well remembered.

Garrison's severe indictment of slavery was hardly calculated to win converts among the slaveholders of the South. It was not meant to. Rather, the appearance of the *Liberator* and the organization of a northern abolitionist movement represented the abandonment of hope that slaveholders would voluntarily accept a program of gradual emancipation. With slavery flourishing in the South and spreading to the Southwest, few masters would tolerate criticism, however moderate, of the "peculiar institution." It can hardly be said that Garrison set back the cause of emancipation in the South, for there was no cause to set back.

Garrison's aim was to create massive moral indignation in the North, to isolate the slaveholders, to make the name slaveholder itself a reproach. But most Northerners were indifferent about slavery—"slumbering in the lap of moral death"—at the time the *Liberator* first appeared. In defense of Garrison, the Kentucky abolitionist James G. Birney expressed the belief that "nothing but a rude and almost ruffianlike shake could rouse . . . [the nation] to a contemplation of her danger."

Though Garrison's language was harsh, it was not his intention to achieve his goal by violence. Like most abolitionists he was a pacifist, and the New England Antislavery Society that he organized promised not to "operate on the existing relations of society by other than peaceful and lawful means." The violence was all in Garrison's words. He cried down slavery as the revivalist preachers of his day cried down other forms of sin. In the end, in spite of his pacifism, Garrison's chief contribution to the antislavery cause was to help give Northerners the moral strength to endure four years of civil war. That slavery died in the agony of this great conflict was in part due to the fact that Garrison had indeed been heard.

The prospectus for the *Liberator* is one among many protests against injustice that have from time to time been issued in the long and still unfinished struggle to achieve freedom and equality for American Negroes. This is a problem about which most white Americans have usually been apathetic, and whose solution they prefer to put off to a more convenient time. Each advance has usually been preceded by the shrill voice of a Garrison reminding us of the contradictions between American theory and practice. To this day it makes us uneasy to read Garrison, and few historians have shown much admiration for him. Garrison was a man of immense conceit, of overbearing dogmatism, of irritating self-righteousness. But he was also a man who gave himself wholly to the cause of the slave and who practiced the racial equality that he preached. He was, no doubt, a "fanatic."

Garrison's message has been a constant reminder to us as individuals of our moral responsibility in society. It was characteristic of the reformers of his age to feel directly involved in social injustices and to feel a personal obligation to work for their removal. What Garrison told his northern contemporaries was that there was no relief from guilt until slavery was destroyed. Today, in our mass society, the individual finds an escape from responsibility through a belief in his powerlessness. What possible difference could his small voice make? But Garrison tells us that as long as some men are not free all are bound with them. Each man must speak out for the sake of his own conscience, "till every chain be broken, and every bondman set free!"

NOTES

1. The text is reprinted here as it originally appeared in the *Liberator* of January 1, 1831.
2. I would here offer my grateful acknowledgments to those editors who so promptly and generously inserted my Proposals. They must give me an available opportunity to repay their liberality.

Letters Written During the Crisis

Carter G. Woodson

Correspondence is a valuable source of social and political commentary. Evidence of this can be found in Carter G. Woodson's *The Mind of the Negro As Reflected in Letters Written During the Crisis, 1800–1860.* The letters that follow were selected because they express a variety of attitudes toward slavery just prior to the Civil War. Try to imagine yourself as the writer or recipient of these letters.

LETTER TO REV. J. W. LOGUEN, FROM HIS OLD MISTRESS

The *Liberator* said on April 27, 1860:

The following letter was received a day or two since by Rev. Mr. Loguen, of this city, from his old mistress 'way down in Tennessee.' The old lady is evidently 'hard up,' financially, and attempts to frighten her former servant into the payment of $1,000 as 'hush money.' We imagine she sent to the wrong man, as Mr. Loguen needs no 'bill of sale' to secure himself from capture in this section of the State. Besides his own stalwart arm, he has hosts of friends who would make this region too hot to hold the manhunters who would venture on such an errand as the old lady hints at in her somewhat singular epistle. Her lamentations about the old mare are decidedly funny, (we may add womanly,) and all the misfortunes of the family are traced directly to the escape of 'Jarm.' But here is her letter:

MAURY COUNTY, STATE OF TENNESSEE, FEB. 20, 1860

To Jarm:—I now take my pen to write you a few lines, to let you know how we all are. I am a cripple, but I am still able to get about. The rest of the family are all well. Cherry is as well as common. I write you these lines to let you know the situation we are in,—partly in consequence of your running away and stealing Old Rock, our fine mare. Though we got the mare back, she never was worth much after you took her;—and, as I now stand in need of some funds, I have determined to sell you, and I have had an offer for you, but did not see fit to take it. If you will send me one thousand dollars, and pay for the old mare, I will give up all claim I have to you. Write to me as soon as you get these lines, and let me know if you will accept my proposition. In consequence of your running away, we had to sell Abe and Ann and twelve acres of land; and I want you to send me the money, that I may be able to redeem the land that you was the cause of our selling, and on receipt of the above-named sum of money, I will send you your bill of sale. If you do not comply with my request, I will sell you to some one else, and you may rest assured that the time is not far distant when things will be changed with you. Write to me as soon as you get these lines. Direct your letter to Bigbyville, Maury-County, Tennessee. You had better comply with my request.

I understand that you are a preacher. As the Southern people are so bad, you had better come and preach to your old acquaintances. I would like to know if you read your Bible. If so, can you tell what will become of the thief if he does not repent? and, if the blind lead the blind, what will the consequence be? I deem it unnecessary to say much more at present. A word to the wise is sufficient. You know where the liar has his part. You know that we reared you as we reared our own children; that you was never abused, and that shortly before you ran away, when your master asked you if you would like to be sold, you said you would not leave him to go with any body.

SARAH LOGUE

MR. LOGUEN'S REPLY

SYRACUSE, (N. Y.) MARCH 28, 1860

Mrs. Sarah Logue: Yours of the 20th of February is duly received, and I thank you for it. It is a long time since I heard from my poor old mother, and I am glad to know that she is yet alive, and, as you say, 'as well as common.' What that means, I don't know. I wish you had said more about her.

You are a woman; but, had you a woman's heart, you never could have insulted a brother by telling him you sold his only remaining brother and sister, because he put himself beyond your power to convert him into money.

You sold my brother and sister, Abe and Ann, and twelve acres of land, you say, because I ran away. Now you have the unutterable meanness to ask me to return and be your miserable chattel, or, in lieu thereof, send you $1000 to enable you to redeem the *land,* but not to redeem my poor brother and sister! If I were to send you money, it would be to get my brother and sister, and not that you should get land. You say you are a *cripple,* and doubtless you say it to stir my pity, for you knew I was susceptible in that direction. I do pity you from the bottom of my heart. Nevertheless, I am indignant beyond the power of words to express, that you should be so sunken and cruel as to tear the hearts I love so much all in pieces; that you should be willing to impale and crucify us all, out of compassion for your poor *foot* or *leg.* Wretched woman! Be it known to you that I value my freedom, to say nothing of my mother, brothers and sisters, more than your whole body; more, indeed, than my own life; more than all the lives of all the slaveholders and tyrants under heaven.

You say you have offers to buy me, and that you shall sell me if I do not send you $1000, and in the same breath and almost in the same sentence, you say, 'You know we raised you as we did our own children.' Woman, did you raise your *own children* for the market? Did you raise them for the whipping-post? Did you raise them to be driven off, bound to a coffle in chains? Where are my poor bleeding brothers and sisters? Can you tell? Who was it that sent them off into sugar and cotton fields, to be kicked and cuffed, and whipped, and to groan and die; and where no kin can hear their groans, or attend and sympathize at their dying bed, or follow in their funeral? Wretched woman! Do you say *you* did not do it? Then I reply, your husband did, and *you* approved the deed—and the very letter you sent me shows that your heart approves it all. Shame on you!

But, by the way, where is your husband? You don't speak of him. I infer, therefore, that he is dead; that he has gone to his great account, with all his sins against my poor family upon his head. Poor man! gone to meet the spirits of my poor, outraged and murdered people, in a world where Liberty and Justice are *Masters.*

But you say I am a thief, because I took the old mare along with me. Have you got to learn that I had a better right to the old mare, as you call her, than Mannasseth Logue had to me? Is it a greater sin for me to steal his horse, than it was for him to rob my mother's cradle, and steal me? If he and you infer that I forfeit all my rights to you, shall not I infer that you forfeit all your rights to me? Have you got to learn that human rights are mutual and reciprocal, and if you take my liberty and life, you forfeit your own liberty and life? Before God and high heaven, is there a law for one man which is not a law for every other man?

If you or any other speculator on my body and rights, wish to know how I regard my rights, they need but come here, and lay their hands on me to enslave me. Did you think to terrify me by presenting the alternative to give my money to you, or give my body to slavery? Then let me say to you, that I meet the proposition with unutterable scorn and contempt. The proposition is an outrage and an insult. I will not budge one hair's breadth. I will not breathe a shorter breath, even to save me from your persecutions. I stand among a free people, who, I thank God, sympathize with my rights, and the rights of mankind; and if your emissaries and venders come here to re-enslave me, and escape the unshrinking vigor of my own right arm, I trust my strong and brave friends, in this city and State, will be my rescuers and avengers.

YOURS, &C.,   J. W. LOGUEN

FROM SEVERAL FUGITIVES

"TORONTO, C. W., AUG. 17TH, 1856

Mr. Still:—Dear Sir—These few lines may find you as they leave us, we are well at present and arrived safe in Toronto. Give our respects to Mrs. S.——and daughter. Toronto is a very extensive place. We have plenty of pork, beef and mutton. There are five market houses and many churches. Female wages is 62½ cents per day, men's wages is $1 and york shilling. We are now boarding at Mr. George Blunt's, on Centre street, two doors from Elm, back of Lawyer's Hall, and when you write to us, direct your letter to the care of Mr. George Blunt,&c. (Signed), James Monroe Peter Heines, Henry James Morris, and Matthew Bodams."

FROM COLORED CITIZENS OF CHICAGO TO JOHN BROWN

CHICAGO, NOVEMBER 17

Dear Friend: We certainly have great reasons, as well as intense desires, to assure you that we deeply sympathize with you and your beloved family. Not only do we sympathize in tears and prayers with *you* and *them,* but we *will* do so in a more tangible form, by contributing material aid to help those of your family of whom you have spoken to our mutual friend, Mrs. L. Maria Child. How could we be so ungrateful as to do less for one who has suffered, bled, and now ready to die for the cause? "Greater love can no man have, than to lay down his life for the poor, despised, and lowly."

YOUR FRIENDS,

H. O. W., AND OTHERS.[1]

FROM A WOMAN OF THE RACE HE DIED FOR
KENDALVILLE, INDIANA, NOV. 25

Dear Friend: Although the hands of Slavery throw a barrier between you and me, and it may not be my privilege to see you in your prison-house, Virginia has no bolts or bars through which I dread to send you my sympathy. In the name of the young girl sold from the warm clasp of a mother's arms to the clutches of a libertine or a profligate,—in the name of the slave mother, her heart rocked to and fro by the agony of her mournful separations,—I thank you, that you have been brave enough to reach out your hands to the crushed and blighted of my race. You have rocked the bloody Bastile; and I hope that from your sad fate great good may arise to the cause of freedom. Already from your prison has come a shout of triumph against the giant sin of our country. The hemlock is distilled with victory when it is pressed to the lips of Socrates. The Cross becomes a glorious ensign when Calvary's page-browed sufferer yields up his life upon it. And, if Universal Freedom is ever to be the dominant power of the land, your bodies may be only her first stepping stones to dominion. I would prefer to see Slavery go down peaceably by men breaking off their sins by righteousness and their iniquities by showing justice and mercy to the poor; but we cannot tell what the future may bring forth. God writes national judgments upon national sins; and what may be slumbering in the storehouse of divine justice we do not know. We may earnestly hope that your fate will not be a vain lesson, that it will intensify our hatred of Slavery and love of freedom, and that your martyr grave will be a sacred altar upon which men will record their vows of undying hatred to that system which tramples on man and bids defiance to God. I have written to your dear wife, and sent her a few dollars, and I pledge myself to you that I will continue to assist her. May the ever-blessed God shield you and your fellow-prisoners in the darkest hour. Send my sympathy to your fellow-prisoners; tell them to be of good courage; to seek a refuge in the Eternal God, and lean upon His everlasting arms for a sure support. If any of them, like you, have a wife or children that I can help, let them send me word.

Yours in the cause of freedom,

F. E. W.

NOTES

1. James Redpath, *Echoes of Harper's Ferry,* p. 391.

CHAPTER THIRTEEN

Civil War: The Beginning of a New Era

No one wanted war—no one ever does. But it came—state against state, brother against brother—leaving scars that may not yet be completely healed. There should have been another way. The outcome of the war was strongly influenced by the slave from the perspective of immediate as well as long-range consequences. His contribution was both direct and strategic; for victory was ultimately to be determined by the availability of materials to pursue the war and by the success or failure of the South to gain international recognition as a separate nation built on slavery. Here, the slave as soldier or laborer, and the slave as an international moral issue influenced important decisions.

During the war, Lincoln issued the Emancipation Proclamation, a document of extraordinary importance in America's quest for freedom and equality. Though not strictly humanitarian in purpose, the language used by Lincoln is clearly that of a humanitarian. Blacks, newly freed by the Proclamation, recognized this. Their grief at his death is a poignant moment in history, a brief interval which perhaps captures the suffering that blacks would continue to experience in their search for the opportunities and responsibilities of freedom.

Although slaves were anxious for freedom and jubilant when it came, they could have had little notion of its true meaning. There were serious problems to be faced not only by the newly freed slaves but by the society into which they moved. For American blacks, the war signaled the beginning of an era—the era of freedom. As a result of the war, the first steps were taken on what would prove to be a long and arduous journey.

The General Strike

W. E. B. Du Bois

The role of the slave in the bloody war between the states is often poorly understood—just as causes and consequences of the war are often confused another. W. E. B. Du Bois defines the slave's role quite clearly in his *Black Reconstruction in America*. The chapter excerpted below describes causes of the war and the changing stance on slavery in the North as the war progressed. Careful thought should be given to Du Bois's analysis of the strategic importance of the slave from a political and economic perspective, his vivid description of the beginning of a new era, and his account of the frustrating and painful first steps into freedom.

How the Civil War meant emancipation and how the black worker won the war by a general strike which transferred his labor from the Confederate planter to the Northern invader, in whose army lines workers began to be organized as a new labor force

When Edwin Ruffin, white-haired and mad, fired the first gun at Fort Sumter, he freed the slaves. It was the last thing he meant to do but that was because he was so typically a Southern oligarch. He did not know the real world about him. He was provincial and lived apart on his plantation with his servants, his books and his thoughts. Outside of agriculture, he jumped at conclusions instead of testing them by careful research. He knew, for instance, that the North would not fight. He knew that Negroes would never revolt.

And so war came. War is murder, force, anarchy and debt. Its end is evil, despite all incidental good. Neither North nor South had before 1861 the slightest intention of going to war. The thought was in many respects ridiculous. They were not prepared for war. The national army was small, poorly equipped and without experience. There was no file from which someone might draw plans of subjugation.

When Northern armies entered the South they became armies of emancipation. It was the last thing they planned to be. The North did not propose to attack property. It did not propose to free slaves. This was to be a white man's war to preserve the Union, and the Union must be preserved.

Nothing that concerned the amelioration of the Negro touched the heart of the mass of Americans nor could the common run of men realize the political and economic cost of Negro slavery. When, therefore, the Southern radicals, backed by political oligarchy and economic dictatorship in the most extreme form in which the world had seen it for five hundred years, precipitated secession, that part of the North that opposed the plan had to hunt for a rallying slogan to unite the majority in the North and in the West, and if possible, bring the Border States into an opposing phalanx.

Freedom for slaves furnished no such slogan. Not one-tenth of the Northern white population would have fought for any such purpose. Free soil was a much stronger motive, but it had no cogency in this contest because the Free Soilers did not dream of asking free soil in the South, since that involved the competition of slaves, or what seemed worse than that, of free Negroes. On the other hand, the tremendous economic ideal of keeping this great market for goods, the United States, together with all its possibilities of agriculture, manufacture, trade and profit, appealed to both the West and the North; and what was then much more significant, it appealed to the Border States.

"To the flag we are pledged, all its foes we abhor,
And we ain't for the nigger, but we are for the war."

The Border States wanted the cotton belt in the Union so that they could sell it their surplus slaves; but they also wanted to be in the same union with the North and West, where the profit of trade was large and increasing. The duty then of saving the Union became the great rallying cry of a war which for a long time made the Border States hesitate and confine secession to the far South. And yet they all knew that the only thing that really threatened the Union was slavery and the only remedy was Abolition.

If, now, the far South had had trained and astute leadership, a compromise could have been made which, so far as slavery was concerned, would have held the abnormal political power of the South intact, made the slave system impregnable for generations, and even given slavery practical rights throughout the nation.

Both North and South ignored in differing degrees the interests of the laboring classes. The North expected patriotism and union to make white labor fight; the South expected all white men to defend the slaveholders' property. Both North and South expected at most a sharp, quick fight and victory; more probably the South expected to secede peaceably, and then outside the Union, to impose terms which would include national recognition of slavery, new slave territory and new cheap slaves. The North expected that after a threat and demonstration to appease its "honor," the South would return with the right of slave property recognized and protected but geographically limited.

Both sections ignored the Negro. To the Northern masses the Negro was a curiosity, a sub-human minstrel, willingly and naturally a slave, and treated as well as he deserved to be. He had not sense enough to revolt and help Northern armies, even if Northern armies were trying to emancipate him, which they were not. The North shrank at the very thought of encouraging servile insurrection against the whites. Above all it did not propose to interfere with property. Negroes on the whole were considered cowards and inferior beings whose very presence in America was unfortunate. The Abolitionists, it was true, expected action on the part of the Negro, but how much, they could not say. Only John Brown knew just how revolt had come and would come and he was dead.

Thus the Negro himself was not seriously considered by the majority of men, North or South. And yet from the very beginning, the Negro occupied the center of the stage because of very simple physical reasons: the war was in the South and in the South were 3,953,740 black slaves and 261,918 free Negroes. What was to be the relation of this mass of workers to the war? What did the war mean to the Negroes, and what did the Negroes mean to the war? There are two theories, both rather over-elaborated: the one that the Negro did nothing but faithfully serve his master until emancipation was thrust upon him; the other that the Negro immediately, just as quickly as the presence of Northern soldiers made it possible, left serfdom and took his stand with the army of freedom.

It must be borne in mind that nine-tenths of the four million black slaves could neither read nor write, and that the overwhelming majority of them were isolated on country plantations. Any mass movement under such circumstances must materialize slowly and painfully. What the Negro did was to wait, look and listen and try to see where his interest lay. There was no use in seeking refuge in an army which was not an army of freedom; and there was no sense in revolting against armed masters who were conquering the world. As soon, however, as it became clear that the Union armies would not or could not return fugitive slaves, and that the masters with all their fume and fury were uncertain of victory, the slave entered upon a general strike against slavery by the same methods that he had used during the period of the fugitive slave. He ran away to the first place of safety and offered his services to the Federal army. So that in this way it was really true that he served his former master and served the emancipating army; and it was also true that this withdrawal and bestowal of his labor decided the war.

The South counted on Negroes as laborers to raise food and money crops for civilians and for the army, and even in a crisis, to be used for military purposes. Slave revolt was an ever-present risk, but there was no reason to think that a short war with the North would greatly increase this danger. Publicly, the South repudiated the thought of its slaves even wanting to be rescued. The New Orleans *Crescent* showed "the absurdity of the assertion of a general stampede of our Negroes." The London *Dispatch* was convinced that Negroes did not want to be free. "As for the slaves themselves, crushed with the wrongs of Dred Scott and Uncle Tom—most provoking—they cannot be brought to 'burn with revenge.' They are spies for their masters. They obstinately refuse to run away to liberty, outrage and starvation. They work in the fields as usual when the planter and overseer are away and only the white women are left at home."

Early in the war, the South had made careful calculation of the military value of slaves. The Alabama *Advertiser* in 1861 discussed the slaves as a "Military Element in the South." It said that "The total white population of the eleven states now comprising the Confederacy is 5,000,000, and, therefore, to fill up the ranks of the proposed army, 600,000, about ten per cent of the entire white population, will be required. In any other country than our own such a draft could not be met, but the Southern states can furnish that number of men, and still not leave the material interest of the country in a suffering condition."

The editor, with fatuous faith, did not for a moment contemplate any mass movement against this program on the part of the slaves. "Those who are incapacitated for bearing arms can oversee the plantations, and the Negroes can go on undisturbed in their usual labors. In the North, the case is different; the men who join the army of subjugation are the laborers, the producers and the factory operatives. Nearly every man from that section, especially those from the rural districts, leaves some branch of industry to suffer during his absence. The institution of slavery in the South alone enables her to place in the field a force much larger in proportion to her white population than the North, or indeed any country which is dependent entirely on free labor. The institution is a tower of strength to the South, particularly at the present crisis, and our enemies will be likely to find that the 'Moral Cancer' about which their orators are so fond of prating, is really one of the most effective weapons employed against the Union by the South."[1]

Soon the South of necessity was moving out beyond this plan. It was no longer simply a question of using the Negroes at home on the plantation to raise food. They could be of even more immediate use, as military labor, to throw up breastworks, transport and prepare food and act as servants in camp. In the Charleston *Courier* of November 22, able-bodied hands were asked to be sent by their masters to work upon the defenses. "They would be fed and properly cared for."

In 1862, in Charleston, after a proclamation of martial law, the Governor and counsel authorized the procuring of Negro slaves either by the planter's consent or by impressment "to work on the fortifications and defenses of Charleston harbor."

In Mississippi in 1862, permission was granted the Governor to impress slaves to work in New Iberia for salt, which was becoming the Confederacy's most pressing necessity. In Texas, a thousand Negroes were offered by planters for work on the public defenses.

By 1864, the matter had passed beyond the demand for slaves as military laborers and had come to the place where the South was seriously considering and openly demanding the use of Negroes as soldiers. Distinctly and inevitably, the rigor of the slave system in the South softened as war proceeded. Slavery showed in many if not all respects its best side. The harshness and the cruelty, in part, had to disappear, since there were left on the plantations mainly women and children, with only a few men, and there was a certain feeling and apprehension in the air on the part of the whites which led them to capitalize all the friendship and kindness which had existed between them and the slaves. No race could have responded to this so quickly and thoroughly as the Negroes. They felt pity and responsibility and also a certain new undercurrent of independence. Negroes were still being sold rather ostentatiously in Charleston and New Orleans, but the long lines of Virginia Negroes were not marching to the Southwest. In a certain sense, after the first few months everybody knew that slavery was done with; that no matter who won, the condition of the slave could never be the same after this disaster of war. And it was, perhaps, these considerations, more than anything else, that held the poised arm of the black man; for no one knew better than the South what a Negro crazed with cruelty and oppression and beaten back to the last stand could do to his oppressor.

The Southerners, therefore, were careful. Those who had been kind to their slaves assured them of the bad character of the Yankee and of their own good intentions.

Thus while the Negroes knew there were Abolitionists in the North, they did not know their growth, their power or their intentions and they did hear on every side that the South was overwhelmingly victorious on the battlefield. On the other hand, some of the Negroes sensed what was beginning to happen. The Negroes of the cities, the Negroes who were being hired out, the Negroes of intelligence who could read and write, all began carefully to watch the unfolding of the situation. At the first gun of Sumter, the black mass began not to move but to heave with nervous tension and watchful waiting. Even before war was declared, a movement began across the border. Just before the war large numbers of fugitive slaves and free Negroes rushed into the North. It was estimated that two thousand left North Carolina alone because of rumors of war.

When W. T. Sherman occupied Port Royal in October, 1861, he had no idea that he was beginning emancipation at one of its strategic points. On the contrary, he was very polite and said that he had no idea of interfering with slaves. In the same way, Major General Dix, on seizing two counties of Virginia, was careful to order that slavery was not to be interfered with or slaves to be received into the line. Burnside went further, and as he brought his Rhode Island regiment through Baltimore in June, he courteously returned two Negroes who tried to run away with him. They were "supposed to be slaves," although they may have been free Negroes. On the 4th of July, Colonel Pryor of Ohio delivered an address to the people of Virginia in which he repudiated the accusation that the Northern army were Abolitionists.

"I desire to assure you that the relation of master and servant as recognized in your state shall be respected. Your authority over that species of property shall not in the least be interfered with. To this end, I assure you that those under my command have peremptory orders to take up and hold any Negroes found running about the camp without passes from their masters."[2]

Halleck in Missouri in 1862 refused to let fugitive slaves enter his lines. Burnside, Buell, Hooker, Thomas Williams and McClellan himself, all warned their soldiers against receiving slaves and most of them permitted masters to come and remove slaves found within the lines.

The constant charge of Southern newspapers, Southern politicians and their Northern sympathizers, that the war was an Abolition war, met with constant and indignant denial. Loyal newspapers, orators and preachers, with few exceptions, while advocating stringent measures for putting down the Rebellion, carefully disclaimed any intention of disturbing the "peculiar institution" of the South. The Secretary of State informed foreign governments, through our ministers abroad, that this was not our purpose. President Lincoln, in his earlier messages, substantially reiterated the statement. Leading generals, on entering Southern territory, issued proclamations to the same effect. One even promised to put down any slave insurrection "with an iron hand," while others took vigorous measures to send back the fugitives who sought refuge within their lines.

"In the early years of the war, if accounts do not err, during the entire period McClellan commanded the Army of the Potomac, 'John Brown's Body' was a forbidden air among the regimental bands. The Hutchinsons were driven from Union camps for singing abolition songs, and in so far as the Northern army interested itself at all in the slavery question, it was by the use of force to return to their Southern masters fugitives seeking shelter in the Union lines. While the information they possessed, especially respecting the roads and means of communication, should have been of inestimable service to the Federals, they were not to be employed as laborers or armed as soldiers. The North avoided the appearance of a desire to raise the Negroes from the plane of chattels to the rank of human beings."[3]

Here was no bid for the coöperation of either slaves or free Negroes. In the North, Negroes were not allowed to enlist and often refused with indignation. "Thus the weakness of the South temporarily became her strength. Her servile population, repulsed by Northern proslavery sentiment, remained at home engaged in agriculture, thus releasing her entire white population for active service in the field; while, on the other hand, the military resources of the North were necessarily diminished by the demands of labor."[4]

It was as Frederick Douglass said in Boston in 1865, that the Civil War was begun "in the interests of slavery on both sides. The South was fighting to take slavery out of the Union, and the North fighting to keep it in the Union; the South fighting to get it beyond the limits of the United States Constitution, and the North fighting for the old guarantees;—both despising the Negro, both insulting the Negro."

It was, therefore, at first by no means clear to most of the four million Negroes in slavery what this war might mean to them. They crouched consciously and moved silently, listening, hoping and hesitating. The watchfulness of the South was redoubled. They spread propaganda: the Yankees were not only not thinking of setting them free, but if they did anything, they would sell them into worse slavery in the West Indies. They would drive them from even the scant comfort of the plantations into the highways and purlieus. Moreover, if they tried to emancipate the slaves, they would fail because they could not do this without conquest of the South. The South was unconquerable.

The South was not slow to spread propaganda and point to the wretched condition of fugitive Negroes in order to keep the loyalty of its indispensable labor force. The Charleston *Daily Courier* said February 18, 1863: "A company of volunteers having left Fayette County for the field of action, Mr. Nance sent two Negro boys along to aid the company. Their imaginations became dazzled with the visions of Elysian fields in Yankeedom and they went to find them. But Paradise was nowhere there, and they again sighed for home. The Yanks, however, detained them and cut off their ears close to their heads. These Negroes finally made their escape and are now at home with Mr. Nance in Pickens. They are violent haters of Yankees and their adventures and experiences are a terror to Negroes of the region, who learned a lesson from their brethren whose ears are left in Lincolndom!"

The Charleston *Mercury,* May 8, 1862, said: "The Yankees are fortifying Fernandina (Florida) and have a large number of Negroes engaged on their works. Whenever the Negroes have an opportunity, they escape from their oppressors. They report that they are worked hard, get little rest and food and no pay."

The Savannah *Daily News* reports in 1862 that many stolen Negroes had been recaptured: "The Yankees had married a number of the women and were taking them home with them. I have seen some who refused to go and others who had been forced off at other times who had returned."

It was a lovely dress parade of Alphonse and Gaston until the Negro spoiled it and in a perfectly logical way. So long as the Union stood still and talked, the Negro kept quiet and worked. The moment the Union army moved into slave territory, the Negro joined it. Despite all argument and calculation and in the face of refusals and commands, wherever the Union armies marched, appeared the fugitive slaves. It made no difference what the obstacles were, or the attitudes of the commanders. It was "like thrusting a walking stick into an anthill," says one writer. And yet the army chiefs at first tried to regard it as an exceptional and temporary matter, a thing which they could control, when as a matter of fact it was the meat and kernel of the war.

Thus as the war went on and the invading armies came on, the way suddenly cleared for the onlooking Negro, for his spokesmen in the North, and for his silent listeners in the South. Each step, thereafter, came with curious, logical and inevitable fate. First there were the fugitive slaves. Slaves had always been running away to the North, and when the North grew hostile, on to Canada. It was the safety valve that kept down the chance of insurrection in the South to the lowest point. Suddenly, now, the chance to run away not only increased, but after preliminary repulse and hesitation, there was actual encouragement.

Not that the government planned or foresaw this eventuality; on the contrary, having repeatedly declared the object of the war as the preservation of the Union and that it did not propose to fight for slaves or touch slavery, it faced a stampede of fugitive slaves.

Every step the Northern armies took then meant fugitive slaves. They crossed the Potomac, and the slaves of northern Virginia began to pour into the army and into Washington. They captured Fortress Monroe, and slaves from Virginia and even North Carolina poured into the army. They captured Port Royal, and the masters ran away, leaving droves of black fugitives in the hands of the Northern army. They moved down the Mississippi Valley, and if the slaves did not rush to the army, the army marched to the slaves. They captured New Orleans, and captured a great black city and a state full of slaves.

What was to be done? They tried to send the slaves back, and even used the soldiers for recapturing them. This was all well enough as long as the war was a dress parade. But when it became real war, and slaves were captured or received, they could be used as much-needed laborers and servants by the Northern army.

This but emphasized and made clearer a truth which ought to have been recognized from the very beginning: The Southern worker, black and white, held the key to the war; and of the two groups, the black worker raising food and raw materials held an even more strategic place than the white. This was so clear a fact that both sides should have known it. Fremont in Missouri took the logical action of freeing slaves of the enemy round about him by proclamation, and President Lincoln just as promptly repudiated what he had done. Even before that, General Butler in Virginia, commander of the Union forces at Fortress Monroe, met three slaves walking into his camp from the Confederate fortifications where they had been at work. Butler immediately declared these men "contraband of war" and put them to work in his own camp. More slaves followed, accompanied by their wives and children. The situation here was not quite so logical. Nevertheless, Butler kept the fugitives and freed them and let them do what work they could; and his action was approved by the Secretary of War.

"On May twenty-sixth, only two days after the one slave appeared before Butler, eight Negroes appeared; on the next day, forty-seven, of all ages and both sexes. Each day they continued to come by twenties, thirties and forties until by July 30th the number had reached nine hundred. In a very short while the number ran up into the thousands. The renowned Fortress took the name of the 'freedom fort' to which the blacks came by means of a 'mysterious spiritual telegraph.'"[5]

In December, 1861, the Secretary of the Treasury, Simon Cameron, had written, printed and put into the mails his first report as Secretary of War without consultation with the President. Possibly he knew that his recommendations would not be approved, but "he recommended the general arming of Negroes, declaring that the Federals had as clear a right to employ slaves taken from the enemy as to use captured gunpowder." This report was recalled by the President by telegraph and the statements of the Secretary were modified. The incident aroused some unpleasantness in the cabinet.

The published report finally said:

"Persons held by rebels, under such laws, to service as slaves, may, however, be justly liberated from their constraint, and made more valuable in various employments, through voluntary and compensated service, than if confiscated as subjects of property."

Transforming itself suddenly from a problem of abandoned plantations and slaves captured while being used by the enemy for military purposes, the movement became a general strike against the slave system on the part of all who could find opportunity. The trickling streams of fugitives swelled to a flood. Once begun, the general strike of black and white went madly and relentlessly on like some great saga.

"Imagine, if you will, a slave population, springing from antecedent barbarism, rising up and leaving its ancient bondage, forsaking its local traditions and all the associations and attractions of the old plantation life, coming garbed in rags or in silks, with feet shod or bleeding, individually or in families and larger groups, —an army of slaves and fugitives, pushing its way irresistibly toward an army of fighting men, perpetually on the defensive and perpetually ready to attack. The arrival among us of these hordes was like the oncoming of cities. There was no plan in this exodus, no Moses to lead it. Unlettered reason or the mere inarticulate decision of instinct brought them to us. Often the slaves met prejudices against their color more bitter than any they had left behind. But their own interests were identical, they felt, with the objects of our armies; a blind terror stung them, an equally blind hope allured them, and to us they come."[6]

"Even before the close of 1862, many thousands of blacks of all ages, ragged, with no possessions, except the bundles which they carried, had assembled at Norfolk, Hampton, Alexandria and Washington. Others, landless, homeless, helpless, in families and in multitudes, including a considerable number of wretched white people, flocked North from Tennessee, Kentucky, Arkansas and Missouri. All these were relieved in part by army rations, irregularly issued, and by volunteer societies of the North, which gained their money from churches and individuals in this country and abroad. In the spring of 1863, there were swarming crowds of Negroes and white refugees along the line of defense made between the armies of the North and South and reaching from Maryland to Virginia, along the coast from Norfolk to New Orleans. Soldiers and missionaries told of their virtues and vices, their joy and extreme suffering. The North was moved to an extraordinary degree, and endless bodies of workers and missionaries were organized and collected funds for materials.

"Rude barracks were erected at different points for the temporary shelter of the freedmen; but as soon as possible the colonies thus formed were broken up and the people encouraged to make individual contracts for labor upon neighboring plantations. In connection with the colonies, farms were cultivated which aided to meet the expenses. Hospitals were established at various points for the sick, of whom there were great numbers. The separation of families by the war, and illegitimate birth in consequence of slavery, left a great number of children practically in a state of orphanage."[7]

This was the beginning of the swarming of the slaves, of the quiet but unswerving determination of increasing numbers no longer to work on Confederate plantations, and to seek the freedom of the Northern armies. Wherever the army marched and in spite of all obstacles came the rising tide of slaves seeking freedom. For a long time, their treatment was left largely to the discretion of the department managers; some welcomed them, some drove them away, some organized them for work. Gradually, the fugitives became organized and formed a great labor force for the army. Several thousand were employed as laborers, servants, and spies.

A special war correspondent of the New York *Tribune* writes: " 'God bless the Negroes,' say I, with earnest lips. During our entire captivity, and after our escape, they were ever our firm, brave, unflinching friends. We never made an appeal to them they did not answer. They never hesitated to do us a service at the risk even of life, and under the most trying circumstances revealed a devotion and a spirit of self-sacrifice that was heroic. The magic word 'Yankee' opened all their hearts, and elicited the loftiest virtues. They were ignorant, oppressed, enslaved; but they always cherished a simple and a beautiful faith in the cause of the Union and its ultimate triumph, and never abandoned or turned aside from a man who sought food or shelter on his way to Freedom."[8]

This whole move was not dramatic or hysterical, rather it was like the great unbroken swell of the ocean before it dashes on the reefs. The Negroes showed no disposition to strike the one terrible blow which brought black men freedom in Haiti and which in all history has been used by all slaves and justified. There were some plans for insurrection made by Union officers:

"The plan is to induce the blacks to make a simultaneous movement of rising, on the night of the 1st of August next, over the entire States in rebellion, to arm themselves with any and every kind of weapon that may come to hand, and commence operations by burning all the railroad and country bridges, and tear up railroad tracks, and to destroy telegraph lines, etc., and then take to the woods, swamps, or the mountains, where they may emerge as occasion may offer for provisions and for further depredations. No blood is to be shed except in self-defense. The corn will be ripe about the 1st of August and with this and hogs running in the woods, and by foraging upon the plantations by night, they can subsist. This is the plan in substance, and if we can obtain a concerted movement at the time named it will doubtless be successful."[9]

Such plans came to naught for the simple reason that there was an easier way involving freedom with less risk.

The South preened itself on the absence of slave violence. Governor Walker of Florida said in his inaugural in 1865: "Where, in all the records of the past, does history present such an instance of steadfast devotion, unwavering attachment and constancy as was exhibited by the slaves of the South throughout the fearful contest that has just ended? The country invaded, homes desolated, the master absent in the army or forced to seek safety in flight and leave the mistress and her helpless infants unprotected, with every incitement to insubordination and instigation, to rapine and murder, no instance of insurrection, and scarcely one of voluntary desertion has been recorded."

The changes upon this theme have been rung by Southern orators many times since. The statement, of course, is not quite true. Hundreds of thousands of slaves were very evidently leaving their masters' homes and plantations. They did not wreak vengeance on unprotected women. They found an easier, more effective and more decent way to freedom. Men go wild and fight for freedom with bestial ferocity when they must—where there is no other way; but human nature does not deliberately choose blood—at least not black human nature. On the other hand, for every slave that escaped to the Union army, there were ten left on the untouched and inaccessible plantations.

Another step was logical and inevitable. The men who handled a spade for the Northern armies, the men who fed them, and as spies brought in information, could also handle a gun and shoot. Without legal authority and in spite of it, suddenly the Negro became a soldier. Later his services as soldier were not only permitted but were demanded to replace the tired and rebellious white men of the North. But as a soldier, the Negro must be free.

The North started out with the idea of fighting the war without touching slavery. They faced the fact, after severe fighting, that Negroes seemed a valuable asset as laborers, and they therefore declared them "contraband of war." It was but a step from that to attract and induce Negro labor to help the Northern armies. Slaves were urged and invited into the Northern armies; they became military laborers and spies; not simply military laborers, but laborers on the plantations, where the crops went to help the Federal army or were sold North. Thus wherever Northern armies appeared, Negro laborers came, and the North found itself actually freeing slaves before it had the slightest intention of doing so, indeed when it had every intention not to.

The experience of the army with the refugees and the rise of the Departments of Negro Affairs were a most interesting, but unfortunately little studied, phase of Reconstruction. Yet it contained in a sense the key to the understanding of the whole situation. At first, the rush of the Negroes from the plantations came as a surprise and was variously interpreted. The easiest thing to say was that Negroes were tired of work and wanted to live at the expense of the government; wanted to travel and see things and places. But in contradiction to this was the extent of the movement and the terrible suffering of the refugees. If they were seeking peace and quiet, they were much better off on the plantations than trailing in the footsteps of the army or squatting miserably in the camps. They were mistreated by the soldiers; ridiculed; driven away, and yet they came. They increased with every campaign, and as a final gesture, they marched with Sherman from Atlanta to the sea, and met the refugees and abandoned human property on the Sea Islands and the Carolina Coast.

This was not merely the desire to stop work. It was a strike on a wide basis against the conditions of work. It was a general strike that involved directly in the end perhaps a half million people. They wanted to stop the economy of the plantation system, and to do that they left the plantations. At first, the commanders were disposed to drive them away, or to give them quasi-freedom and let them do as they pleased with the nothing that they possessed. This did not work. Then the commanders organized relief and afterward, work. This came to the attention of the country first in Pierce's "Ten Thousand Clients." Pierce of Boston had worked with the refugees in Virginia under Butler, provided them with food and places to live, and given them jobs and land to cultivate. He was successful. He came from there, and, in conjunction with the Treasury Department, began the work on a vaster scale at Port Royal. Here he found the key to the situation. The Negroes were willing to work and did work, but they wanted land to work, and they wanted to see and own the results of their toil. It was here and in the West and the South that a new vista opened. Here was a chance to establish an agrarian democracy in the South: peasant holders of small properties, eager to work and raise crops, amenable to suggestion and general direction. All they needed was honesty in treatment, and education. Wherever these conditions were fulfilled, the result was little less than phenomenal. This was testified to by Pierce in the Carolinas, by Butler's agents in North Carolina, by the experiment of the Sea Islands, by Grant's Department of Negro Affairs under Eaton, and by Banks' direction of Negro labor in Louisiana. It is astonishing how this army of striking labor furnished in time 200,000 Federal soldiers whose evident ability to fight decided the war.

General Butler went from Virginia to New Orleans to take charge of the city newly captured in April, 1862. Here was a whole city half-filled with blacks and mulattoes, some of them wealthy free Negroes and soldiers who came over from the Confederate side and joined the Federals.

Perhaps the greatest and most systematic organizing of fugitives took place in

New Orleans. At first, Butler had issued orders that no slaves would be received in New Orleans. Many planters were unable to make slaves work or to support them, and sent them back of the Federal lines, planning to reclaim them after the war was over. Butler emancipated these slaves in spite of the fact that he knew this was against Lincoln's policy. As the flood kept coming, he siezed abandoned sugar plantations and began to work them with Negro labor for the benefit of the government.

By permission of the War Department, and under the authority of the Confiscation Act, Butler organized colonies of fugitives, and regulated employment. His brother, Colonel Butler, and others worked plantations, hiring the Negro labor. The Negroes stood at Butler's right hand during the trying time of his administration, and particularly the well-to-do free Negro group were his strongest allies. He was entertained at their tables and brought down on himself the wrath and contempt, not simply of the South, but even of the North. He received the black regiment, and kept their black officers, who never forgot him. Whatever else he might have been before the war, or proved to be afterwards, "the colored people of Louisiana under the proper sense of the good you have done to the African race in the United States, beg leave to express to you their gratitude."

From 1862 to 1865, many different systems of caring for the escaped slaves and their families in this area were tried. Butler and his successor, Banks, each sought to provide for the thousands of destitute freedmen with medicine, rations and clothing. When General Banks took command, there was suffering, disease and death among the 150,000 Negroes. On January 30, 1863, he issued a general order making labor on public works and elsewhere compulsory for Negroes who had no means of support.

Just as soon, however, as Banks tried to drive the freedmen back to the plantations and have them work under a half-military slave régime, the plan failed. It failed, not because the Negroes did not want to work, but because they were striking against these particular conditions of work. When, because of wide protest, he began to look into the matter, he saw a clear way. He selected Negroes to go out and look into conditions and to report on what was needed, and they made a faithful survey. He set up a little state with its department of education, with its landholding and organized work, and after experiment it ran itself. More and more here and up the Mississippi Valley, under other commanders and agents, experiments extended and were successful.

Further up the Mississippi, a different system was begun under General Grant. Grant's army in the West occupied Grand Junction, Mississippi, by November, 1862. The usual irregular host of slaves then swarmed in from the surrounding country. They begged for protection against recapture, and they, of course, needed food, clothing and shelter. They could not now be reënslaved through army aid, yet no provision had been made by anybody for their sustenance. A few were employed as teamsters, servants, cooks and scouts, yet it seemed as though the vast majority must be left to freeze and starve, for when the storms came with the winter months, the weather was of great severity.

Grant determined that Negroes should perform many of the camp duties ordinarily done by soldiers; that they should serve as fatigue men in the departments of the surgeon general, quartermaster, and commissary, and that they should help in building roads and earthworks. The women worked in the camp kitchens and as nurses in the hospitals. Grant said, "It was at this point where the first idea of the Freedmen's Bureau took its origin."

Grant selected as head of his Department of Negro Affairs, John Eaton, chaplain of the Twenty-Seventh Ohio Volunteers, who was soon promoted to the colonelcy of a colored regiment, and later for many years was a Commissioner of the United States Bureau of Education. He was then constituted Chief of Negro Affairs for the entire district under Grant's jurisdiction.

"I hope I may never be called on again to witness the horrible scenes I saw in those first days of the history of the freedmen in the Mississippi Valley. Assistants were hard to get, especially the kind that would do any good in our camps. A detailed soldier in each camp of a thousand people was the best that could be done. His duties were so onerous that he ended by doing nothing. . . . In reviewing the condition of the people at that time, I am not surprised at the marvelous stories told by visitors who caught an occasional glimpse of the misery and wretchedness in these camps. . . . Our efforts to do anything for these people, as they herded together in masses, when founded on any expectation that they would help themselves, often failed; they had become so completely broken down in spirit, through suffering, that it was almost impossible to arouse them.

"Their condition was appalling. There were men, women and children in every stage of disease or decrepitude, often nearly naked, with flesh torn by the terrible experiences of their escapes. Sometimes they were intelligent and eager to help themselves; often they were bewildered or stupid or possessed by the wildest notions of what liberty might mean—expecting to exchange labor, and obedience to the will of another, for idleness and freedom from restraint. Such ignorance and perverted notions produced a veritable moral chaos. Cringing deceit, theft, licentiousness—all the vices which slavery inevitably fosters—were hideous companions of nakedness, famine, and disease. A few had profited by the misfortunes of the master and were jubilant in their unwonted ease and luxury, but these stood in lurid contrast to the grimmer aspects of the tragedy—the women in travail, the helplessness of childhood and of old age, the horrors of sickness and of frequent death. Small wonder that men paused in bewilderment and panic, foreseeing the demoralization and infection of the Union soldier and the downfall of the Union cause."[10]

There were new and strange problems of social contact. The white soldiers, for the most part, were opposed to serving Negroes in any manner, and were even unwilling to guard the camps where they were segregated or protect them against violence. "To undertake any form of work for the contrabands, at that time, was to be forsaken by one's friends and to pass under a cloud."[11]

There was, however, a clear economic basis upon which the whole work of relief and order and subsistence could be placed. All around Grand Junction were large crops of ungathered corn and cotton. These were harvested and sold North and the receipts were placed to the credit of the government. The army of fugitives were soon willing to go to work; men, women and children. Wood was needed by the river steamers and woodcutters were set at work. Eaton fixed the wages for this industry and kept accounts with the workers. He saw to it that all of them had sufficient food and clothing, and rough shelter was built for them. Citizens round about who had not abandoned their plantations were allowed to hire labor on the same terms as the government was using it. Very soon the freedmen became self-sustaining and gave little trouble. They began to build themselves comfortable cabins, and the government constructed hospitals for the sick. In the case of the sick and dependent, a tax was laid on the wages of workers. At first it was thought the laborers would object, but, on the contrary, they were perfectly willing and the imposition of the tax compelled the government to see that wages were promptly paid. The freedmen freely acknowledged that they ought to assist in helping bear the burden of the poor, and were flattered by having the government ask their help. It was the reaction of a new labor group, who, for the first time in their lives, were receiving money in payment for their work. Five thousand dollars was raised by this tax for hospitals, and with this money tools and property were bought. By wholesale purchase, clothes, household goods and other articles were secured by the freedmen at a cost of one-third of what they might have paid the stores. There was a rigid system of accounts and monthly reports through army officials.

In 1864, July 5, Eaton reports: "These freedmen are now disposed of as follows: In military service as soldiers, laundresses, cooks, officers' servants, and laborers in the various staff departments, 41,150; in cities on plantations and in freedmen's villages and cared for, 72,500. Of these 62,300 are entirely self-supporting—the same as any industrial class anywhere else—as planters, mechanics, barbers, hackmen, draymen, etc., conducting enterprises on their own responsibility or working as hired laborers. The remaining 10,200 receive subsistence from the government. 3,000 of them are members of families whose heads are carrying on plantations and have under cultivation 4,000 acres of cotton. They are to pay the government for their sustenance from the first income of the crop. The other 7,200 include the paupers—that is to say, all Negroes over and under the self-support-ing age, the crippled and sick in hospital, of the 113,650 and those engaged in their care. Instead of being unproductive, this class has now under cultivation 500 acres of corn, 790 acres of vegetables and 1,500 acres of cotton, besides working at wood-chopping and other industries. There are reported in the aggregate over 100,000 acres of cotton under cultivation. Of these about 7,000 acres are leased and cultivated by blacks. Some Negroes are managing as high as 300 or 400 acres."

The experiment at Davis Bend, Mississippi, was of especial interest. The place was occupied in November and December, 1864, and private interests were displaced and an interesting socialistic effort made with all the property under the control of the government. The Bend was divided into districts with Negro sheriffs and judges who were allowed to exercise authority under the general control of the military officers. Petty theft and idleness were soon reduced to a minimum and "the community distinctly demonstrated the capacity of the Negro to take care of himself and exercise under honest and competent direction the functions of self-government."[12]

When General Butler returned from Louisiana and resumed command in Virginia and North Carolina, he established there a Department of Negro Affairs, with the territory divided into districts under superintendents and assistants. Negroes were encouraged to buy land, build cabins and form settlements, and a system of education was established. In North Carolina, under Chaplain Horace James, the poor, both black and white, were helped; the refugees were grouped in small villages and their work systematized, and enlisted men taught in the schools, followed by women teachers from the North. Outside of New Bern, North Carolina, about two thousand freedmen were settled and 800 houses erected. The department at Port Royal continued. The Negroes showed their capacity to organized labor and even to save and employ a little capital. The government built 21 houses for the people on Edisto Island. The carpenters were

Negroes under a Negro foreman. There was another village of improved houses near Hilton Head.

"Next as to the development of manhood: this has been shown in the first place in the prevalent disposition to acquire land. It did not appear upon our first introduction to these people, and they did not seem to understand us when we used to tell them that we wanted them to own land. But it is now an active desire. At the recent tax sales, six out of forty-seven plantations sold were bought by them, comprising two thousand five hundred and ninety-five acres, sold for twenty-one hundred and forty-five dollars. In other cases, the Negroes had authorized the superintendent to bid for them, but the land was reserved by the United States. One of the purchases was that made by Harry, noted above. The other five were made by the Negroes on the plantations, combining the funds they had saved from the sale of their pigs, chickens and eggs, and from the payments made to them for work,—they then dividing off the tract peaceably among themselves. On one of these, where Kit, before mentioned, is the leading spirit, there are twenty-three fieldhands. They have planted and are cultivating sixty-three acres of cotton, fifty of corn, six of potatoes, with as many more to be planted, four and a half of cowpeas, three of peanuts, and one and a half of rice. These facts are most significant."[13]

Under General Saxton in South Carolina, the Negroes began to buy land which was sold for non-payment of taxes. Saxton established regulations for the cultivation of several abandoned Sea Islands and appointed local superintendents.

"By the payment of moderate wages, and just and fair dealing with them, I produced for the government over a half million dollars' worth of cotton, besides a large amount of food beyond the needs of the laborers. These island lands were cultivated in this way for two years, 1862, and 1863, under my supervision, and during that time I had about 15,000 colored freedmen of all ages in my charge. About 9,000 of these were engaged on productive labor which relieved the government of the support of all except newly-arrived refugees from the enemy's lines and the old and infirm who had no relations to depend upon. The increase of industry and thrift of the freedmen was illustrated by their conduct in South Carolina before the organization of the Freedmen's Bureau by the decreasing government expenditure for their support. The expense in the department of the South in 1863 was $41,544, but the monthly expense of that year was steadily reduced, until in December it was less than $1,000."[14]

Into this fairly successful land and labor control was precipitated a vast and unexpected flood of refugees from previously untouched strongholds of slavery. Sherman made his march to the sea from Atlanta, cutting the cotton kingdom in two as Grant had invaded it along the Mississippi.

"The first intimation given me that many of the freedmen would be brought hither from Savannah came in the form of a request from the General that I would 'call at once to plan the reception of seven hundred who would be at the wharf in an hour.' This was Christmas day, and at 4 P.M., we had seven hundred— mainly women, old men and children before us. A canvass since made shows that half of them had traveled from Macon, Atlanta and even Chattanooga. They were all utterly destitute of blankets, stockings or shoes; and among the seven hundred there were not fifty articles in the shape of pots or kettles, or other utensils for cooking, no axes, very few coverings for many heads, and children wrapped in the only article not worn in some form by the parents." Frantic appeals went out for the mass of Negro refugees who followed him.

A few days after Sherman entered Savannah, Secretary of War Stanton came in person from Washington. He examined the condition of the liberated Negroes found in that city. He assembled twenty of those who were deemed their leaders. Among them were barbers, pilots and sailors, some ministers, and others who had been overseers on cotton and rice plantations. Mr. Stanton and General Sherman gave them a hearing.

As a result of this investigation into the perplexing problems as to what to do with the growing masses of unemployed Negroes and their families, General Sherman issued his epoch-making Sea Island Circular, January 18, 1865. In this paper, the islands from Charleston south, the abandoned rice fields along the rivers for thirty miles back from the sea and the country bordering the St. John's River, Florida, were reserved for the settlement of the Negroes made free by the acts of war and the proclamation of the President.

General Rufus Saxton was appointed Inspector of Settlements and Plantations and was required to make proper allotments and give possessory titles and defend them until Congress should confirm his actions. It was a bold move. Thousands of Negro families were distributed under this circular, and the freed people regarded themselves for more than six months as in permanent possession of these abandoned lands. Taxes on the freedmen furnished most of the funds to run these first experiments. On all plantations, whether owned or leased, where freedmen were employed, a tax of one cent per pound on cotton and a proportional amount on all other products was to be collected as a contribution in support of the helpless among the freed people. A similar tax, varying with the value of the property, was levied by the government upon all leased plantations in lieu of rent.

Saxton testified: "General Sherman's Special Field Order No. 15 ordered their colonization on forty-acre tracts, and in accordance with which it is estimated some forty thousand were provided with homes. Public meetings were held, and every exertion used by those whose duty it was to execute this order to encourage emigration to the Sea Islands, and the faith of the government was solemnly pledged to maintain them in possession. The greatest success attended the experiment, and although the planting season was very far advanced before the transportation to carry the colonists to the Sea Islands could be obtained, and the people were destitute of animals and had but few agricultural implements and the greatest difficulty in procuring seeds, yet they went out, worked with energy and diligence to clear up the ground run to waste by three years' neglect; and thousands of acres were planted and provisions enough were raised for those who were located in season to plant, besides a large amount of Sea Island cotton for market. The seizure of some 549,000 acres of abandoned land, in accordance with the act of Congress and orders from the head of the bureau for the freedman and refugees, still further strengthened these ignorant people in the conviction that they were to have the lands of their late masters; and, with the other reasons before stated, caused a great unwillingness on the part of the freedmen to make any contracts whatever. But this refusal arises from no desire on their part to avoid labor, but from the causes above stated. . . .

"To test the question of their forethought and prove that some of the race at least thought of the future, I established in October, 1864, a savings bank for the freedmen of Beaufort district and vicinity. More than $240,000 had been deposited in this bank by freedmen since its establishment. I consider that the industrial problem has been satisfactorily solved at Port Royal, and that, in common with other races, the Negro has industry, prudence, forethought, and ability to calculate results. Many of them have managed plantations for themselves, and show an industry and sagacity that will compare favorably in their results—making due allowances—with those of white men."

Eventually, General Saxton settled nearly 30,000 Negroes on the Sea Islands and adjacent plantations and 17,000 were self-supporting within a year. While 12,000 or 13,000 were still receiving rations, it was distinctly understood that they and their farms would be held responsible for the payment. In other such cases, the government had found that such a debt was a "safe and short one."

Negroes worked fewer hours and had more time for self-expression. Exports were less than during slavery. At that time the Negroes were mere machines run with as little loss as possible to the single end of making money for their masters. Now, as it was in the West Indies, emancipation had enlarged the Negro's purchasing power, but instead of producing solely for export, he was producing to consume. His standard of living was rising.

Along with this work of the army, the Treasury Department of the United States Government was bestirring itself. The Secretary of the Treasury, Salmon P. Chase, early in 1862, had his attention called to the accumulation of cotton on the abandoned Sea Islands and plantations, and was sure there was an opportunity to raise more. He, therefore, began the organization of freedmen for cotton raising, and his successor, William Pitt Fessenden, inaugurated more extensive plans for the freedmen in all parts of the South, appointing agents and organizing freedmen's home colonies.

On June 7, 1862, Congress held portions of the states in rebellion responsible for a direct tax upon the lands of the nation, and in addition Congress passed an act authorizing the Secretary of the Treasury to appoint special agents to take charge of captured and abandoned property. Military officers turned over to the Treasury Department such property, and the plantations around Port Royal and Beaufort were disposed of at tax sales. Some were purchased by Negroes, but the greater number went to Northerners. In the same way in North Carolina, some turpentine farms were let to Negroes, who managed them, or to whites who employed Negroes. In 1863, September 11, the whole Southern region was divided by the Treasury Department into five special agencies, each with a supervising agent for the supervision of abandoned property and labor.

Early in 1863, General Lorenzo Thomas, the adjutant general of the army, was organizing colored troops along the Mississippi River. After consulting various treasury agents and department commanders, including General Grant, and having also the approval of Mr. Lincoln, he issued from Milliken's Bend, Louisiana, April 15th, a lengthy series of instruction covering the territory bordering the Mississippi and including all the inhabitants.

He appointed three commissioners, Messrs. Field, Shickle and Livermore, to lease plantations and care for the employees. He sought to encourage private enterprises instead of government colonies; but he fixed the wages of able-bodied men over fifteen years of age at $7 per month, for able-bodied women $5 per month, for children twelve to fifteen years, half price. He laid a tax for revenue of $2 per 400 pounds of cotton, and five cents per bushel of corn and potatoes.

This plan naturally did not work well, for the lessees of plantations proved to be for the most part adventurers and speculators. Of course such men took advantage of the ignorant people. The commissioners themselves seem to have done more for the lessees than for the laborers; and, in fact, the wages were from the beginning so fixed as to benefit and enrich the employer. Two dollars per month was charged against each of the employed, ostensibly for medical attendance, but to most plantations thus leased no physician or medicine ever came, and there were other attendant cruelties which avarice contrived.

On fifteen plantations leased by the Negroes themselves in this region there was notable success, and also a few other instances in which humanity and good sense reigned; the contracts were generally carried out. Here the Negroes were contented and grateful, and were able to lay by small gains. This plantation arrangement along the Mississippi under the commissioners as well as the management of numerous infirmary camps passed, about the close of 1863, from the War to the Treasury Department. A new commission or agency with Mr. W. P. Mellon of the treasury at the head established more careful and complete regulations than those of General Thomas. This time it was done decidedly in the interest of the laborers.

July 2, 1864, an Act of Congress authorized the treasury agents to seize and lease for one year all captured and abandoned estates and to provide for the welfare of former slaves. Property was declared abandoned when the lawful owner was opposed to paying the revenue. The Secretary of the Treasury, Fessenden, therefore issued a new series of regulations relating to freedmen and abandoned property. The rebellious States were divided into seven districts, with a general agent and special agents. Certain tracts of land in each district were set apart for the exclusive use and working of the freedmen. These reservations were called Freedmen Labor Colonies, and were under the direction of the superintendents. Schools were established, both in the Home Colonies and in the labor colonies. This new system went into operation the winter of 1864–1865, and worked well along the Atlantic Coast and Mississippi Valley. In the Department of the Gulf, however, there was discord between the treasury agents and the military authorities, and among the treasury officials themselves. The treasury agents, in many cases, became corrupt, but these regulations remained in force until the Freedmen's Bureau was organized in 1865.

By 1865, there was strong testimony as to the efficiency of the Negro worker, "The question of the freedmen being self-supporting no longer agitated the minds of careful observers."

Carl Schurz felt warranted in 1865 in asserting: "Many freedmen—not single individuals, but whole 'plantation gangs'—are working well; others are not. The difference in their efficiency coincides in a great measure with a certain difference in the conditions under which they live. The conclusion lies near, that if the conditions under which they work well become general, their efficiency as free laborers will become general also, aside from individual exceptions. Certain it is, that by far the larger portion of the work done in the South is done by freedmen!"

Whitelaw Reid said in 1865: "Whoever has read what I have written about the cotton fields of St. Helena will need no assurance that another cardinal sin of the slave, his laziness—'inborn and ineradicable,' as we were always told by his masters—is likewise disappearing under the stimulus of freedom and necessity. Dishonesty and indolence, then, were the creation of slavery, not the necessary and constitutional faults of the Negro character."

"Returning from St. Helena in 1865, Doctor Richard Fuller was asked what he thought of the experiment of free labor, as exhibited among his former slaves, and how it contrasted with the old order of things. 'I never saw St. Helena look so well,' was his instant reply; 'never saw as much land there under cultivation —never saw the same general evidences of prosperity, and never saw Negroes themselves appearing so well or so contented.' Others noticed, however, that the islands about Beaufort were in a better condition than those nearer the encampments of the United States soldiers. Wherever poultry could be profitably peddled in the camps, cotton had not been grown, nor had the Negroes developed, so readily, into industrious and orderly communities."[15] Similar testimony came from the Mississippi Valley and the West, and from Border States like Virginia and North Carolina.

To the aid of the government, and even before the government took definite organized hold, came religious and benevolent organizations. The first was the American Missionary Association, which grew out of the organization for the defense of the Negroes who rebelled and captured the slave ship *Amistad* and brought it into Connecticut in 1837. When this association heard from Butler and Pierce, it responded promptly and had several representatives at Hampton and South Carolina before the end of the year 1861. They extended their work in 1862–1863, establishing missions down the Atlantic Coast, and in Missouri, and along the Mississippi. By 1864, they had reached the Negroes in nearly all the Southern States. The reports of Pierce, Dupont and Sherman aroused the whole North. Churches and missionary societies responded. The Friends contributed. The work of the Northern benevolent societies began to be felt, and money, clothing and, finally, men and women as helpers and teachers came to the various centers.

"The scope of our work was greatly enlarged by the arrival of white refugees —a movement which later assumed very large proportions. As time went on Cairo (Illinois) became the center of our activities in this direction. It was the most northerly of any of our camps, and served as the portal through which thousands of poor whites and Negroes were sent into the loyal states as fast as opportunities offered for providing them with homes and employment. Many of these became permanent residents; some were sent home by Union soldiers to carry on the work in the shop or on the farm which the war had interrupted. It became necessary to have a superintendent at Cairo and facilities for organizing the bands of refugees who were sent North by the army. There was an increasing demand for work."[16]

New organizations arose, and an educational commission was organized in Boston, suggested by the reports of Pierce, and worked chiefly in South Carolina. Afterward, it became the New England Freedmen's Aid Society and worked in all the Southern States. February 22, 1862, the National Freedmen's Relief Association was formed in New York City. During the first year, it worked on the Atlantic Coast, and then broadened to the whole South. The Port Royal Relief Committee of Philadelphia, later known as the Pennsylvania Freedmen's Relief Association, the National Freedmen's Relief Association of the District of Columbia, the Contraband Relief Association of Cincinnati, afterward called the Western Freedmen's Commission, the Women's Aid Association of Philadelphia and the Friends' Associations, all arose and worked. The number increased and extended into the Northwest. The Christian Commission, organized for the benefit of soldiers, turned its attention to Negroes. In England, at Manchester and London, were Freedmen's Aid Societies which raised funds; and funds were received from France and Ireland.

Naturally, there was much rivalry and duplication of work. A union of effort was suggested in 1862 by the Secretary of the Treasury and accomplished March 22, 1865, when the American Freedmen's Union Commission was incorporated, with branches in the chief cities. Among its officers were Chief Justice Chase and William Lloyd Garrison. In 1861, two large voluntary organizations to reduce suffering and mortality among the freedmen were formed. The Western Sanitary Commission at St. Louis, and the United States Sanitary Commission at Washington, with branches in leading cities, then began to relieve the distress of the freedmen. Hospitals were improved, supplies distributed, and Yeatman's plan for labor devised. Destitute white refugees were helped to a large extent. But even then, all of these efforts reached but a small portion of the mass of people freed from slavery.

Late in 1863, President Yeatman of the Western Sanitary Commission visited the freedmen in the Mississippi Valley. He saw the abuses of the leasing system and suggested a plan for organizing free labor and leasing plantations. It provided for a bureau established by the government to take charge of leasing land, to secure justice and freedom to the freedmen; hospital farms and homes for the young and aged were to be established; schools with compulsory attendance were to be opened. Yeatman accompanied Mellon, the agent of the department, to Vicksburg in order to inaugurate the plan and carry it into effect. His plan was adopted by Mellon, and was, on the whole, the most satisfactory.

Thus, confusion and lack of system were the natural result of the general strike. Yet, the Negroes had accomplished their first aim in those parts of the South dominated by the Federal army. They had largely escaped from the plantation discipline, were receiving wages as free laborers, and had protection from violence and justice in some sort of court.

About 20,000 of them were in the District of Columbia; 100,000 in Virginia; 50,000 in North Carolina; 50,000 in South Carolina, and as many more each in Georgia and Louisiana. The Valley of the Mississippi was filled with settlers under the Treasury Department and the army. Here were nearly 500,000 former slaves. But there were 3,500,000 more. These Negroes needed only the assurance that they would be freed and the opportunity of joining the Northern army. In larger and larger numbers, they filtered into the armies of the North. And in just the proportion that the Northern armies became in earnest, and proposed actually to force the South to stay in the Union, and not to make simply a demonstration, in just such proportion the Negroes became valuable as laborers, and doubly valuable as withdrawing labor from the South. After the first foolish year when the South woke up to the fact that there was going to be a real, long war, and the North realized just what war meant in blood and money, the whole relation of the North to the Negro and the Negro to the North changed.

The position of the Negro was strategic. His was the only appeal which would bring sympathy from Europe, despite strong economic bonds with the South, and prevent recognition of a Southern nation built on slavery. The free Negroes in the North, together with the Abolitionists, were clamoring. To them a war against the South simply had to be a war against slavery. Gradually, Abolitionists no longer need fear the mob. Disgruntled leaders of church and state began to talk of freedom. Slowly but surely an economic dispute and a political test of strength took on the aspects of a great moral crusade.

The Negro became in the first year contraband of war; that is, property belonging to the enemy and valuable to the invader. And in addition to that, he became, as the South quickly saw, the key to Southern resistance. Either these four million laborers remained quietly at work to raise food for the fighters, or the fighter starved. Simultaneously, when the dream of the North for man-power produced riots, the only additional troops that the North could depend on were 200,000 Negroes, for without them, as Lincoln said, the North could not have won the war.

But this slow, stubborn mutiny of the Negro slave was not merely a matter of 200,000 black soldiers and perhaps 300,000 other black laborers, servants, spies and helpers. Back of this half million stood 3½ million more. Without their labor the South would starve. With arms in their hands, Negroes would form a fighting force which could replace every single Northern white soldier fighting listlessly and against his will with a black man fighting for freedom.

This action of the slaves was followed by the disaffection of the poor whites. So long as the planters' war seemed successful, "there was little active opposition by the poorer whites; but the conscription and other burdens to support a slave-owners' war became very severe; the whites not interested in that cause became recalcitrant, some went into active opposition; and at last it was more desertion and disunion than anything else that brought about the final overthrow."[17]

Phillips says that white mechanics in 1861 demanded that the permanent Confederate Constitution exclude Negroes from employment "except agricultural domestic service, so as to reserve the trades for white artisans." Beyond this, of course, was a more subtle reason that, as the years went on, very carefully developed and encouraged for a time the racial aspect of slavery. Before the war, there had been intermingling of white and black blood and some white planters openly recognized their colored sons, daughters and cousins and took them under their special protection. As slavery hardened, the racial basis was emphasized; but it was not until war time that it became the fashion to pat the disfranchised poor white man on the back and tell him after all he was white and that he and the planters had a common object in keeping the white man superior. This virus increased bitterness and relentless hatred, and after the war it became a chief ingredient in the division of the working class in the Southern States.

At the same time during the war even the race argument did not keep the Southern fighters from noticing with anger that the big slaveholders were escaping military service; that it was a "rich man's war and the poor man's fight." The exemption of owners of twenty Negroes from military service especially rankled; and the wholesale withdrawal of the slaveholding class from actual fighting which this rule made possible, gave rise to intense and growing dissatisfaction.

It was necessary during these critical times to insist more than usual that slavery was a fine thing for the poor white. Except for slavery, it was said: " 'The poor would occupy the position in society that the slaves do—as the poor in the North and in Europe do,' for there must be a menial class in society and in 'every civilized country on the globe, besides the Confederate states, the poor are the inferiors and menials of the rich.' Slavery was a greater blessing to the non-slaveholding poor than to the owners of slaves, and since it gave the poor a start in society that it would take them generations to work out, they should thank God for it and fight and die for it as they would for their 'own liberty and the dearest birthright of freemen.' "[18]

But the poor whites were losing faith. They saw that poverty was fighting the war, not wealth.

"Those who could stay out of the army under color of the law were likely to be advocates of a more numerous and powerful army. . . . Not so with many of those who were not favored with position and wealth. They grudgingly took up arms and condemned the law which had snatched them from their homes. . . . The only difference was the circumstance of position and wealth, and perhaps these were just the things that had caused heartburnings in more peaceful times.

"The sentiments of thousands in the upland countries, who had little interest in the war and who were not accustomed to rigid centralized control, was probably well expressed in the following epistle addressed to President Davis by a conscript. . . .

". . . 'It is with intense and multifariously proud satisfaction that he [the conscript] gazes for the last time upon our holy flag—that symbol and sign of an adored trinity, cotton, niggers and chivalry.' "[19]

This attitude of the poor whites had in it as much fear and jealousy of Negroes as disaffection with slave barons. Economic rivalry with blacks became a new and living threat as the blacks became laborers and soldiers in a conquering Northern army. If the Negro was to be free where would the poor white be? Why should he fight against the blacks and his victorious friends? The poor white not only began to desert and run away; but thousands followed the Negro into the Northern camps.

Meantime, with perplexed and laggard steps, the United States Government followed the footsteps of the black slave. It made no difference how much Abraham Lincoln might protest that this was not a war against slavery, or ask General McDowell "if it would not be well to allow the armies to bring back those fugitive slaves which have crossed the Potomac with our troops" (a communication which was marked "secret"). It was in vain that Lincoln rushed entreaties and then commands to Frémont in Missouri, not to emancipate the slaves of rebels, and then had to hasten similar orders to Hunter in South Carolina. The slave, despite every effort, was becoming the center of war. Lincoln, with his uncanny insight, began to see it. He began to talk about compensation for emancipated slaves, and Congress, following almost too quickly, passed the Confiscation Act in August, 1861, freeing slaves which were actually used in war by the enemy. Lincoln then suggested that provision be made for colonization of such slaves. He simply could not envisage free Negroes in the United States. What would become of them? What would they do? Meantime, the slave kept looming. New Orleans was captured and the whole black population of Louisiana began streaming toward it. When Vicksburg fell, the center of perhaps the vastest Negro population in North America was tapped. They rushed into the Union lines. Still Lincoln held off and watched symptoms. Greeley's "Prayer of Twenty Millions" received the curt answer, less than a year before Emancipation, that the war was not to abolish slavery, and if Lincoln could hold the country together and keep slavery, he would do it.

But he could not, and he had no sooner said this than he began to realize that he could not. In June, 1862, slavery was abolished in the territories. Compensation with possible colonization was planned for the District of Columbia. Representatives and Senators from the Border States were brought together to talk about extending this plan to their states, but they hesitated.

In August, Lincoln faced the truth, front forward; and that truth was not simply that Negroes ought to be free; it was that thousands of them were already free, and that either the power which slaves put into the hands of the South was to be taken from it, or the North could not win the war. Either the Negro was to be allowed to fight, or the draft itself would not bring enough white men into the army to keep up the war.

More than that, unless the North faced the world with the moral strength of declaring openly that they were fighting for the emancipation of slaves, they would probably find that the world would recognize the South as a separate nation; that ports would be opened; that trade would begin, and that despite all the military advantage of the North, the war would be lost.

In August, 1862, Lincoln discussed Emancipation as a military measure; in September, he issued his preliminary proclamation; on January 1, 1863, he declared that the slaves of all persons in rebellion were "henceforward and forever free."

The guns at Sumter, the marching armies, the fugitive slaves, the fugitives as "contrabands," spies, servants and laborers; the Negro as soldier, as citizen, as voter—these steps came from 1861 to 1868 with regular beat that was almost rhythmic. It was the price of the disaster of war, and it was a price that few Americans at first dreamed of paying or wanted to pay. The North was not Abolitionist. It was overwhelmingly in favor of Negro slavery, so long as this did not interfere with Northern moneymaking. But, on the other hand, there was a minority of the North who hated slavery with perfect hatred; who wanted no union with slaveholders; who fought for freedom and treated Negroes as men. As the Abolition-democracy gained in prestige and in power, they appeared as prophets, and led by statesmen, they began to guide the nation out of the morass into which it had fallen. They and their black friends and the new freedmen became gradually the leaders of a Reconstruction of Democracy in the United States, while marching millions sang the noblest war-song of the ages to the tune of "John Brown's Body":

Mine eyes have seen the glory of the coming of the Lord,
He is trampling out the vintage where the grapes of wrath are stored,
He hath loosed the fateful lightning of his terrible swift sword,
His Truth is marching on!

NOTES

1. *Public Opinion Before and After the Civil War,* p. 4.
2. Williams, *History of the Negro Race in America,* II, p. 244.
3. Oberholtzer, *Abraham Lincoln,* p. 263.
4. *Results of Emancipation in the United States of America* by a Committee of the American Freedman's Union Commission in 1867, p. 6.
5. *Journal of Negro History,* X, p. 134.
6. Eaton, *Grant, Lincoln and the Freedmen,* p. 2.
7. *Results of Emancipation in the United States of America* by a Committee of the American Freedman's Union Commission in 1867, p. 21.
8. Brown, *Four Years in Secessia,* p. 368.
9. Ashe and Tyler, *Secession, Insurrection of the Negroes, and Northern Incendiarism,* p. 12.
10. Eaton, *Grant, Lincoln and the Freedmen,* pp. 2, 3, 19, 22, 134.
11. Eaton, *Grant, Lincoln and the Freedmen,* p. 22.
12. Eaton, *Grant, Lincoln and the Freedmen,* p. 166.
13. Pierce, "Freedmen at Port Royal," *Atlantic Monthly,* XII, p. 310.

14. *Testimony Before Reconstruction Committee,* February 21, 1866, Part II, p. 221.
15. Taylor, *Reconstruction in South Carolina,* pp. 29, 30.
16. Eaton, *Grant, Lincoln and the Freedmen,* pp. 37, 38.
17. Campbell, *Black and White in the Southern States,* p. 165.
18. Moore, *Conscription and Conflict in the Confederacy,* p. 145.
19. Moore, *Conscription and Conflict in the Confederacy,* pp. 18–20.

Abraham Lincoln: The Emancipation Proclamation, 1863

John Hope Franklin

The political victory of the Civil War preserved the Union of the United States; the moral victory was the definitive statement to abolish slavery. Equality before the law and equality of opportunity were now promised to *all* Americans.

The Emancipation Proclamation played a significant role in the battle for freedom and equality, a battle still not completely won. Because it is such a vital part of American heritage, this document should be read carefully, taking note of the language used by Lincoln, particularly in the last paragraph. The complete text of the Proclamation is presented below. Accompanying notes by John Hope Franklin beautifully describe events leading to its issuance and summarize its consequences and relevance to issues that yet await resolution.

Once the Civil War had begun, there was never a time when the question of freedom for the slaves was not urgent. Abolitionists urged emancipation as a bold humanitarian step. Some military leaders favored it as a logical and necessary war measure. Many citizens, however, thought that the freeing of the slaves was not only inexpedient and impolitic but unconstitutional as well. For the first eighteen months of the war the debate was vigorous; and one delegation after another visited the President to advise him on what action to take.

President Lincoln had long been opposed to slavery, but he had grave doubts, even after the war began, that he possessed the necessary powers to abolish it. Even as he expressed these doubts he was seeking some opportunity and justification for taking action. By the late spring of 1862 he was convinced that he or Congress, perhaps both, should move against slavery. "Things had gone on from bad to worse," he said later, "until I felt that we had reached the end of our rope . . . and must change our tactics, or lose the game!" Action by Congress, in April and June, to abolish slavery in the District of Columbia and in the territories greatly encouraged him.

In June, during his regular visits to the telegraph room of the War Department, the President began to sketch out the main features of the Emancipation Proclamation. By June 18 he had completed a draft; he read this to Vice-President Hannibal Hamlin, who seemed quite pleased. A few weeks later he told Gideon Welles, Secretary of the Navy, and William H. Seward, Secretary of State, of his decision to issue a proclamation to free the slaves. After Congress passed the Second Confiscation Act of July 17, the President incorporated some of its provisions into his draft.

Within a few days the President was ready to share his plans w[...]
Cabinet. On July 22, 1862, he told the members of his decision, made it [...]
it was firm, and solicited their suggestions merely regarding language and t[...]
Some thought it unwise for Lincoln to make the Proclamation at all, while oth[...]
thought that he should wait to issue it when the military situation was more
favorable. The President made no promises, but he waited. When the news came
of the limited victory of the Union forces at Antietam on September 17, he felt
that the time had come. On that very evening he began reworking the draft and
putting it into final form in the quiet of Soldiers' Home near Washington. He
returned to the White House on the twentieth, and on the following day he
carefully rewrote the document that was the culmination of months of work and
worry.

On September 22, at a special meeting of the Cabinet, he read the document
and issued it the same day. This document, known as the Preliminary Emancipation Proclamation, announced that on January 1, 1863, all slaves in states or parts
of states then in rebellion against the United States would be "thenceforward, and
forever free."

For the next hundred days there was discussion throughout the country and
in many other parts of the world regarding the possible effect of emancipation by
presidential proclamation. Critics were bitter in their strictures. Abolitionists
were not altogether happy, but were encouraged at Lincoln's action. There were
some who doubted that the President would fulfill his promise to free the slaves;
but as the time approached, Lincoln was more determined than ever.

During the week following Christmas Day the Cabinet met almost daily, and
Lincoln had many opportunities to discuss with the members the final wording
of the Proclamation. At the meeting on December 29 he read a draft of the
Emancipation Proclamation on which he had been working, invited criticism, and
directed that copies be provided for each member of the Cabinet. During the
meetings of December 30 and 31 the Proclamation was one of the main items on
the agenda. Several members made suggestions for revision, largely of an editorial
nature. During the evening the President began the final writing of the Proclamation. He completed it on the morning of January 1, 1863, and sent it over to the
Department of State for the superscription and closing.

The New Year's Day reception at the White House had already begun when
the Secretary of State and his son, Frederick Seward, the Assistant Secretary,
returned with the Proclamation. After the reception the President went up to his
study, where, in the presence of a few friends, he signed the Emancipation
Proclamation. As he finished writing his signature, he said, "I never, in my life,
felt more certain that I was doing right than I do in signing this paper.

BY THE PRESIDENT OF THE UNITED STATES OF AMERICA:
A PROCLAMATION

JANUARY 1, 1863

Whereas, on the twenty-second day of September, in the year of our Lord
one thousand eight hundred and sixty two, a proclamation was issued by the
President of the United States, containing, among other things, the following,
to wit:

January, in the year of our Lord one thousand eight hundred
s held as slaves within any State or designated part of a State,
then be in rebellion against the United States, shall be then,
er free; and the Executive Government of the United States,
nd naval authority thereof, will recognize and maintain the
, and will do no act or acts to repress such persons, or any of
y may make for their actual freedom.

will, on the first day of January aforesaid, by proclamation,
designate ... d parts of States, if any, in which the people thereof, shall on that day be, in good faith, represented in the Congress of the United States by members chosen thereto at elections wherein a majority of the qualified voters of such State shall have participated, shall in the absence of strong countervailing testimony, be deemed conclusive evidence that such State, and the people thereof, are not then in rebellion against the United States.

Now, therefore, I, Abraham Lincoln, President of the United States, by virtue of the power in me invested as Commander-in-Chief, of the Army and Navy of the United States in time of actual armed rebellion against authority and government of the United States, and as a fit and necessary war measure for suppressing said rebellion, do, on this first day of January, in the year of our Lord one thousand eight hundred and sixty three, and in accordance with my purpose so to do publicly proclaimed for the full period of one hundred days, from the day first above mentioned, order and designate as the States and parts of States wherein the people thereof respectively, are this day in rebellion against the United States the following towit:

Arkansas, Texas, Louisiana, (except the Parishes of St. Bernard, Plaquemines, Jefferson, St. Johns, St. Charles, St. James, Ascension, Assumption, Terrebone, LaFourche, St Mary, St. Martin, and Orleans, including the City of New-Orleans) Mississippi, Alabama, Florida, Georgia, South-Carolina, North-Carolina, and Virginia (except the forty-eight counties designated as West Virginia, and also the counties of Berkley, Accomac, Northampton, Elizabeth-City, York, Princess Ann, and Norfolk, including the cities of Norfolk and Portsmouth, and which excepted parts are, for the present, left precisely as if this proclamation were not issued.

And by virtue of the power, and for the purpose aforesaid I do order and declare that all persons held as slaves within said designated States, and parts of States, are, and henceforward shall be free: and the Executive government of the United States, including the military and naval authorities thereof, will recognize and maintain the freedom of said persons.

And I hereby enjoin upon the people so declared to be free to abstain from all violence, unless in necessary self-defense; and I recommend to them that, in all cases when allowed they labor faithfully for reasonable wages.

And I further declare and make known that such persons of suitable condition, will be received into the armed service of the United States to garrison forts, positions, stations, and other places, and to man vessels of all sorts in said service.

And upon this act, sincerely believed to be an act of justice, warranted by the Constitution, upon military necessity, I invoke the considerate judgment of mankind, and the gracious favor of Almighty God.

In witness whereof, I have hereunto set my hand and caused the seal of the United States to be affixed.

Done at the City of Washington, the first day of January, in the year of our Lord one thousand eight hundred and sixty-three, and of the Independence of the United States of America the eighty-seventh.

BY THE PRESIDENT: ABRAHAM LINCOLN
WILLIAM H. SEWARD, SECRETARY OF STATE

Within a few hours, on the evening of January 1, 1863, the entire country knew that the President had signed the Emancipation Proclamation. Within a few days, the entire world knew that slavery in the United States was doomed. Emancipation celebrations, shared by Negroes and whites alike, were held from Boston to San Francisco. Bells were rung, poems written, hymns composed. One newspaper called the Proclamation "a great moral landmark, a shrine at which future visionaries shall renew their vows, a pillar of fire which shall yet guide other nations out of the night of this bondage. . . ." Almost overnight the war was transformed from a struggle to preserve the Union into one in which the crusade for human freedom became an equally important goal. The Proclamation sharpened the issues of the war. In Europe the opposition to the Union melted before the unequivocal position of the Proclamation. At home the proclamation provided the moral and humanitarian ingredient that had been lacking in Union attempts to subdue the rebellious South.

In later years the Emancipation Proclamation was to become a significant rallying point for freedom and equality. In pleading for the enfranchisement of the Negro in 1866, Senator Charles Sumner said that in the Proclamation Lincoln had promised to maintain freedom for the Negro "not for any limited period, but for all time." But when real freedom and equality eluded Negroes, some came to believe that gratitude for the Emancipation Proclamation did not require them to remain loyal to a party that had not kept the faith. Nevertheless, if Negroes became disillusioned with the party of Lincoln, they continued to show their gratitude to the man who had issued the Emancipation Proclamation. Throughout the country New Year's Day became and remained a day of commemoration; and the reading of the Emancipation Proclamation became a regular part of scores of annual observances.

As the nation prepared to celebrate the fiftieth anniversary of the Proclamation, many Americans expressed their understanding of the Document's continuing importance. One editor of a magazine said, "The emancipation of the Negro race was the act of the American people. The greatness of Abraham Lincoln was the greatness of a statesman who could lead them to that act, who could understand their unexpressed will calling for that act, and who dared to do the act in their name and on their behalf."

The Proclamation has remained, through more than a century, a vital factor in the movement to broaden and deepen the meaning of democracy and equality in the United States. Negroes themselves have always regarded it as a significant beginning of their quest for full citizenship, while the larger community has recognized it as an important milestone in the nation's program to make its early promises of equality meaningful. On many occasions it has been invoked by those who are full of pride for what the nation has achieved, as well as by those who are critical of the nation for what it has not done.

On the occasion of the centennial of the Emancipation Proclamation, most of the nation was acutely conscious of how much was yet to be done in order for all citizens to enjoy equality. On September 22, 1962, the centennial of the

Preliminary Emancipation Proclamation, more than 3,000 people gathered at the Lincoln Memorial in Washington. Governor Nelson Rockefeller of New York presented for public view the only known draft of the Preliminary Proclamation in President Lincoln's hand. In making the presentation he said, "May God give us the love, the courage, the understanding to see in perspective ourselves and the times in which we live—and to make the faith that lies behind this Proclamation truly live for all men in all places of our land." In a major address United Nations Ambassador Adlai Stevenson called individual freedom the "great unfinished business of the world today." He observed that the defense of freedom by the United States "will be all the stronger for being based not on illusions but upon the truth about ourselves and our world."

President John F. Kennedy, who sent a special message to the centennial observance, had occasion to refer later to the Emancipation Proclamation when he asked Congress to enact a new civil rights bill in 1963. On that occasion, he said, "No one has been barred on account of his race from fighting for America —there are no 'white' and 'colored' signs on the foxholes and graveyards of battle. Surely, in 1963, one hundred years after emancipation, it should not be necessary for any American to demonstrate in the streets for opportunity to stop at a hotel, or to eat at a lunch counter." Statements like this one and a growing awareness of the unfulfilled promises of the Emancipation Proclamation had much to do with the groundswell for civil rights that reached a new high during the centennial year.

Once the centennial of the Emancipation Proclamation had passed, there remained a sense of urgency to complete the long delayed task of extending equality to Negro Americans. The Civil Rights Act of 1964, with its far-reaching provisions that guaranteed equal enjoyment of public accommodations and facilities and its machinery to accelerate school desegregation, was a result—at least in part —of this sense of urgency. When it became clear that existing legislation was inadequate to guarantee to Negroes their right to vote, President Lyndon B. Johnson urged Congress to enact new laws to eliminate barriers to the right to vote. He showed that he had the unfulfilled promises of the Emancipation Proclamation in mind when he said, "There must be no delay, no hesitation, no compromise with our purpose. We cannot wait another eight months. We have already waited 100 years and more. The time for waiting is gone." Congress agreed, and with the enactment of the voting-rights legislation in 1965 it moved one step closer toward the complete freedom for Negro Americans that the Emancipation Proclamation had begun.

A Sleep and a Remembering

Benjamin Quarles

The war was over, but violence had not ended. One small gun was yet to be fired on April 14, 1865, in Ford's Theater.

A shocked nation reacted passionately to the assassination of President Lincoln. To American blacks, Lincoln was more than a president. His character assumed larger-than-life proportions perceived by many as verging on prophet or savior. In *Lincoln and the Negro,* Benjamin Quarles describes the unrelieved sorrow blacks experienced "when Abraham Lincoln's hour struck." Step back in time to share the grief, to move in imagination with the procession of mourners. The experience has a tragic ring of familiarity—for violence done in more recent days to other marchers on the road to freedom.

On the day that Lincoln died, the weather in Washington was bad, a cold rain falling. "Were you there when the sun refused to shine," runs an old spiritual in describing the kind of day it was when "they crucified my Lord." To Negroes it was a totally sunless day when Abraham Lincoln's hour struck.

The blow was harder to bear for having come without warning. On the preceding night, April 14, Lincoln had gone to Ford's Theatre for a few hours of relaxation. He was watching the comedy unfold when the door of his box quietly opened, and John Wilkes Booth let himself in. A professional actor casting himself in the real-life role of avenger of the defeated Southland, Booth pointed a derringer at the President's head and pulled the trigger. Lincoln's eyes closed, never to open again; he died a few minutes before seven thirty the next morning.

The news of Booth's deed stunned the Negroes of the city. Overwhelmed with grief, many of them walked up and down in front of the dwelling on Tenth Street where the dying President lay in the plain wooden bed of a rented room. Other Negroes had gone to the Executive Mansion and pressed their faces against the wet iron fence. "The Negroes who idolize Lincoln here line the sidewalk in front of the White House," wrote paymaster's clerk Charles A. Sanford. "Oh! how terrible!" Secretary Welles, afoot early that fateful morning, said that although strong men wept without shame, nothing moved him more deeply than the unrelieved sorrow of the Negroes.

Not far from the White House grounds that morning, Jane Gray Swisshelm heard one Negro woman express puzzlement that Lincoln should have met with violence in Washington after being down to Richmond where the danger supposedly was. Giving up trying to fathom such a mystery, the woman stamped her foot and shouted, "My good President! I would rather have died myself! I would rather have given the babe from my bosom! Oh, Jesus! Oh, Jesus."

Another colored woman whose grief was just as intense but whose manner was more restrained was Mrs. Keckley. Sent for by the inconsolable Mrs. Lincoln, she had snatched up her bonnet and shawl and hurried to the White House. Once there, she relieved Mrs. Gideon Welles, who had attended Mrs. Lincoln throughout the night. With Mrs. Keckley bathing her head, the bereaved First Lady became a little less violent. When Mrs. Keckley felt that she could be spared for a few minutes, she asked permission to view the body of the President, which had been escorted to the Executive Mansion at 9:30 A.M.

As the distinguished-looking and stylish mulatto entered the guest room where the lifeless form lay in state, the Cabinet officers and military commanders broke their circle so that she could make her way forward. Looking down into Lincoln's face, Mrs. Keckley's composure left her for a few moments; her eyes filled with tears and her throat suddenly became dry and tight. She recalled that the last time she had seen Lincoln, he had spoken kindly to her. But her feelings of personal bereavement soon merged into a more inclusive sense of loss: "No common mortal had died. The Moses of my people had fallen in the hour of triumph." When her bittersweet reflections had been brought under outward control, Mrs.

Keckley filed out of the room, her heart pounding and her footsteps not wholly steady.

In addition to the tens of thousands of personal lamentations by Negroes on that dread Saturday morning, there was one formal and official expression of sorrow, doubtless the first in the country. At Baltimore, the forty-eighth annual conference of the African Methodist Episcopal Church happened to be in session, having begun its deliberations on Thursday of that week. When the Saturday morning session was called to order, the presiding officer, Bishop Daniel A. Payne, "announced the death of Lincoln in a very feeling manner," as the *Baltimore Sun* reported it. There upon the delegates drew up a series of resolutions expressing their deep sorrow over the "cowardly assassination" of "the great and good Abraham Lincoln" and extending their profoundest condolences to his widow. Like most of the tens of thousands of resolutions, speeches, and sermons that would flood the country within the next few days, the resolutions bore a tone of outrage reaching the proportions of vengeance. Invoking the memory of John Brown (whose blood "was shed to inaugurate the meting out of justice to those who had long oppressed the Savior in the person of the bondmen"), the conference resolutions pledged to President Johnson two hundred thousand muskets to protect the flag.

As Washington prepared for the funeral exercises, the city's Negroes went into mourning. Many families went without a meal to buy a yard or two of black ribbon to hang above the door or window. By some means or other, most Negro women managed to procure mourning dresses, veils, and bonnets, while the Negro men faced a lesser problem of obtaining crepe bands for their hats. Such black-bedecked colored men and women were among the more than 25,000 visitors to the East Room on Tuesday, April 18, come to take a last solemn look as they filed past the President's bier.

On the following afternoon the impressive funeral services were held at the White House. Then came the procession to the Capitol, where the body was to lie in state. Forty thousand mourners were in the line of march following the long, black hearse and keeping a slow step to the dirges played by the regimental bands. Marching at the head of the line was a detachment of Negro soldiers, the Twenty-second U.S. Colored Infantry.

To have a Negro contingent lead the funeral procession had not been in the plans. It resulted, rather, from an accident of timing. Just up from Petersburg and hurrying down the avenue to be assigned to their proper place in the line of march, the Negro detachment reached the front of the procession just as it was about to move off, precisely at two o'clock. With the middle of the streets solidly filled with marchers, and with the sidewalks massed with onlookers, the three hundred soldiers could proceed no further. And since they could not be conjured away, the parade marshals, swallowing hard, decided to let them lead the way. Whereupon the black regiment wheeled about, reversed its arms, and "formed the advance of the whole."

If Negroes led the long parade, they also brought up the rear. Separated from the Negro regiment by over a mile in space, and by some two hours in time, were more than a dozen colored organizations and groups. Leading this contingent were the conference delegates of the A.M.E. Church, headed by Bishops Payne and W. A. Wayman, who had chartered a train and come over from Baltimore in a body that morning. A number of fraternal organizations were out in full strength, such as the Blue Lodge of Ancient York Masons and the Harmony

Lodge of Odd Fellows. The clergymen of the various Protestant denominations, other than the A.M.E.'s, marched in one group; the Catholic Benevolent Association marched in another. Regardless of the organization to which they belonged, all the colored marchers bore one basic similarity: "their walk and their mien," wrote a *New York Times* reporter, "were the very impersonation of sorrow."

Political Compromise: The Nadir of Black Americans

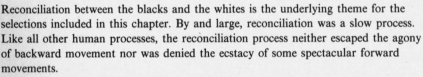

Reconciliation between the blacks and the whites is the underlying theme for the selections included in this chapter. By and large, reconciliation was a slow process. Like all other human processes, the reconciliation process neither escaped the agony of backward movement nor was denied the ecstacy of some spectacular forward movements.

The selections in this chapter describe the reconciliation process in political, economic, and educational contexts. More emphatically, they reflect the emotions of the people involved in the process during the late nineteenth century.

Reconstruction, the Negro, and the New South

La Wanda Cox and John H. Cox

Freedom is not simply the absence of slavery. Neither is equality before the law synonomous with true equality of life. Generally speaking, the latter is a slow process involving changes in the thinking of the masses, while the former is brought about by the thinking of a few. The brief selection below, taken from *Reconstruction, the Negro, and the New South,* sets the stage for an individual's contemplation as to when true reconciliation takes place.

In all modern history no development is more astounding than the attempt in the immediate post–Civil War years to raise over 4 million people just released from a legal servitude of special rigidity to a legal status of equality. By legislative enactment and constitutional amendment men who yesterday were property, subject to whatever discipline their owners might impose, were made the equal of their old masters in the right to due process of law, to contract freely, to hold property, to bear arms, to testify from the witness stand, to sit on juries, to enjoy public transportation, inns and theatres, to vote both for local and for national officials, and to themselves hold office. Moreover, the new rights and privileges were conferred upon a people of a distinctive race with the approval of an electorate who believed, except for an articulate dissenting minority, in the racial superiority of whites and the racial inferiority of blacks. The roots of this prejudice ran deep in the history of the country and of the Western world, and in the 1860s prejudice was dignified by the scientific authorities of the day. When the freedman was made equal citizen, the concept of racial inequality, unlike the institution of slavery which had become an anachronism, was still growing in vigor and malignancy. The documents presented in part one focus attention upon the problem of how the national commitment came to be made. They also explore what had been done by the close of the nineteenth century, at the national level, both to honor and to erode the promise of equal citizenship.

Recognition of the mid-nineteenth-century effort to establish civic equality has been equated in recent scholarship with a pledge by the nation to racial equality. This view embodies two misconceptions which can distort judgment of the past. Though a national commitment, it was not made by the nation as a whole. A consensus of white Americans was noticeably lacking; the legal changes were forced by one major political party, with almost no freely given support from Southern whites and in the face of nearly solid opposition in the North from the other major party. Equality was a commitment made for the nation by the Republican party. Nor was the promise an affirmation of racial equality. The pledge was to equality irrespective of race or past servitude in matters of public, as distinct from private, authority. Care need be taken not to assume that the Republican party was identical with "the North" or that the concept of equal citizenship is synonymous with that of the equality of races.

The Civil War Amendments: XIII–XV

Francis A. Allen

In the following selection edited by Francis A. Allen, one sees the continuation of the American nation's commitment to equality. The author traces the emergence of the post–Civil War amendments to the U.S. Constitution. He also points out the controversies arising out of ideological concepts being too general while implementation demanded some specifics. Inclusion in the amendments of terms such as "due process" continues to plague the nation's progress toward reconciliation between blacks and the whites. Living a century after these amendments were passed, one cannot escape some kind of personal assessment of the progress made in the reconciliation endeavors.

The American Civil War was, among other things, a struggle between competing ideas of constitutionalism and the rights of man. When the epic conflict ended with victory of the Union forces on the battlefield, it was inevitable that there would be efforts to consolidate the military victory by giving expression in our fundamental law to certain principles and propositions until then in dispute.

Between 1865 and 1870 three amendments were added to the Constitution which have ever since profoundly influenced our public law and policy.

The first problem demanding attention was the abolition of Negro slavery. The institution of slavery in the border states, as well as in the states in rebellion, created serious dilemmas for President Lincoln and Congress in the conduct of the war. The final proclamation of emancipation, issued by President Lincoln on January 1, 1863, left many fundamental issues unresolved. Even before the final proclamation was issued, President Lincoln had asked Congress to approve a constitutional amendment providing compensation to every state that abolished slavery before the beginning of the twentieth century. "In giving freedom to the slaves," he wrote, "we assure freedom to the free—honorable alike in what we give and what we preserve. We shall nobly serve or meanly lose the last best hope of earth." In the months following the final proclamation, Congress was offered various proposals for constitutional amendment. What was to become the Thirteenth Amendment passed the Senate on April 8, 1864, but the proposal received less than the requisite two-thirds vote in the House of Representatives. Only after the re-election of President Lincoln in November, 1864, did the amendment carry the House. The vote was 119 to 56—a margin so narrow that a shift of only three votes would have altered the result. The Thirteenth Amendment was declared adopted by Secretary of State Seward on December 6, 1865. Included among the ratifying states were eight of the former Confederacy.

At the end of the military hostilities, Congress and the nation were confronted by the myriad problems involved in restoring the southern states to the Union, giving protection to the rights of the recently emancipated Negro population, and establishing new patterns of political power. Issues so fundamental were thought by many to require further alterations in the fundamental law; and a great variety of proposals for constitutional amendment were advanced within a year of Appomattox. The purposes and motivation of those active in the drafting of the Fourteenth Amendment were many and complex. Because of the importance of the Fourteenth Amendment in our developing constitutional law, the adoption of the amendment has been closely studied by modern scholars. Although the main outlines are clear, many important matters remain in doubt and controversy. One of the important factors leading to the adoption of the Fourteenth Amendment was congressional reaction to the "black codes" adopted by southern state legislatures at the close of the war—laws severely restrictive of the civil rights of the emancipated slaves. As demonstrated by the Freedman's Bureau Act and the Civil Rights Law of 1866, many members of Congress felt that, unless vigorously defended by federal law, the rights of the Negro which the Thirteenth Amendment was intended to establish would prove illusory. The Civil Rights Law is particularly important, for it sought both to protect Negroes from discrimination in the enjoyment of certain basic rights, such as the right to acquire property, and to effect a legislative repeal of the famous *Dred Scott* decision which had denied the capacity of the Negro to become a citizen of the United States. Although the Act was vital to the program of the Radical group in Congress and was passed by a two-thirds vote of both Houses to override President Johnson's veto, many members, even among the Radicals, doubted its constitutional validity. One of the purposes of the first section of the Fourteenth Amendment was, accordingly, to establish the constitutional validity of the Civil Rights Law of 1866 and to guard against the consequences of its possible repeal by some subsequent Congress.

The text of the Fourteenth Amendment evolved slowly in the congressional joint committee on Reconstruction. The third and fourth sections relate to issues of immediate concern growing out of the Civil War and possess little but historical interest today. The second section represents an effort to protect rights of Negro suffrage, an effort soon perceived to be inadequate. The first and the fifth sections, however, remain among the most vital provisions of our public law. The Fourteenth Amendment was approved by Congress on June 13, 1866. Formal pronouncement of its ratification was made by Secretary Seward on July 28, 1868. Among the states counted as ratifying were two, Ohio and New Jersey, that had first adopted resolutions of ratification but later sought to withdraw consent and six southern states that were required to ratify the Fourteenth Amendment as a condition of their restoration in the Union.

The draftsmen of the Fourteenth Amendment sought to protect Negro rights of suffrage in Section 2, which, in effect, requires curtailment of congressional representation of any state in proportion to the number of persons disenfranchised in the state on grounds of race. Representative Thaddeus Stevens of Pennsylvania, a Radical leader, expressed the view that these provisions were the most important in the Fourteenth Amendment. Section 2 failed to achieve its purpose, however; and very soon proposals were advanced for constitutional amendment to provide more direct and effective protection of the Negro's right to vote. Various considerations underlay these proposals. To some it appeared that the civil rights of the Negro could be achieved only when he was accorded the right of full participation in the political life of the community. The proposals were also consistent with a general movement for expanded suffrage, which constituted one important aspect of nineteenth-century liberalism. Finally, it appears clear that some northern congressional leaders feared the rise of white political power in the South as a threat to their own political dominance in Congress and to the interests they represented. The Fifteenth Amendment was approved by Congress on February 26, 1869. Formal announcement of its ratification was made on May 30, 1870.

AMENDMENT XIII

Section 1. Neither slavery nor involuntary servitude, except as a punishment for crime whereof the party shall have been duly convicted, shall exist within the United States, or any place subject to their jurisdiction.

Section 2. Congress shall have power to enforce this article by appropriate legislation.

AMENDMENT XIV

Section 1. All persons born or naturalized in the United States and subject to the jurisdiction thereof, are citizens of the United States and of the State wherein they reside. No State shall make or enforce any law which shall abridge the privileges or immunities of citizens of the United States; or shall any State deprive any person of life, liberty, or property, without due process of law; nor deny to any person within its jurisdiction the equal protection of the laws.

Section 2. Representatives shall be apportioned among the several States according to their respective numbers, counting the whole number of persons in each State, excluding Indians not taxed. But when the right to vote at any election for the choice of electors for President and Vice President of the United States, Representatives in Congress, the Executive and Judicial officers of a State, or the members of the Legislature thereof, is denied to any of the male inhabitants of such State, being twenty-one years of age, and citizens of the United States, or in any way abridged, except for participation in rebellion, or other crime, the basis of representation therein shall be reduced in the proportion which the number of such male citizens shall bear to the whole number of male citizens twenty-one years of age in such State.

Section 3. No person shall be a Senator or Representative in Congress, or elector of President and Vice President, or hold any office, civil or military, under the United States, or under any State, who, having previously taken an oath, as a member of Congress, or as an officer of the United States, or as a member of any State legislature, or as an executive or judicial officer of any State, to support the Constitution of the United States, shall have engaged in insurrection or rebellion against the same, or given aid or comfort to the enemies thereof. But Congress may by a vote of two-thirds of each House, remove such disability.

Section 4. The validity of the public debt of the United States, authorized by law, including debts incurred for payment of pensions and bounties for services in suppressing insurrection or rebellion, shall not be questioned. But neither the United States nor any State shall assume or pay any debt or obligation incurred in aid of insurrection or rebellion against the United States, or any claim for the loss or emancipation of any slave; but all such debts, obligations and claims shall be held illegal and void.

Section 5. The Congress shall have power to enforce, by appropriate legislation, the provisions of this article.

AMENDMENT XV

Section 1. The right of citizens of the United States to vote shall not be denied or abridged by the United States or by any State on account of race, color, or previous condition of servitude.

Section 2. The Congress shall have power to enforce this article by appropriate legislation.

The Fourteenth Amendment is, without doubt, the most important addition made to the text of the Constitution since the adoption of the Bill of Rights in 1790. Of the five sections of the amendment, the first has proved to be of prime significance. Included in the language of Section 1 are the great protean phrases, "due process of law" and "equal protection of the laws." The draftsmen of the amendment provided no specific meanings for these grand generalizations. This is not to say that the language was wholly devoid of historical content. The powers of Congress are limited in the Fifth Amendment by a "due process" clause; and many state constitutions contained similar provisions that had frequently been interpreted by state courts. Moreover, "due process" suggests the traditions of Magna Carta and "the law of the land." "Equal protection," too, although less redolent of the past, invokes certain historical connotations.

Yet the great moral imperatives of due process and equal protection could not be confined to their historical understandings when applied to the emerging issues of modern American life. There is evidence that those who drafted Section 1 intended that the meanings of these phrases should evolve and expand with the passage of time and changes of circumstance. This, in any event, is what occurred. As a result, the history of Fourteenth Amendment interpretation reveals in sharp and accurate focus the principal public issues with which generations of Americans have been preoccupied in the past three-quarters of a century.

Two great issues, one political and the other primarily economic, dominate the first half-century of Fourteenth Amendment interpretation. Neither is directly or necessarily concerned with the rights of racial minorities. The first issue was: What changes did the Civil War and the postwar amendments effect in the fundamental structure of American federalism? At least some of the congressional proponents of constitutional change desired basic and far-reaching alterations and assumed that significant aggrandizement of federal power had been achieved by adoption of the postwar amendments. From the first, however, the Supreme Court made clear that the amendments had not replaced the essential features of the American system. The most important teaching of the *Slaughter-House Cases*, 16 Wall. 36, decided in 1873 when nationalist feeling was still high in Congress, is that the postwar amendments did not effect a revolution in the American form of government. Ten years later Justice Bradley maintained that the Fourteenth Amendment does not grant Congress power "to establish a code of municipal law." In the years that followed, a practical redistribution of authority between state and federal governments occurred, and the Fourteenth Amendment sometimes contributed to this development. Broader interpretations of the powers of Congress under Section 5 of the amendment may one day significantly accelerate these tendencies. For the most part, however, the new importance of federal power has evolved in response to conditions of the modern world that are largely independent of the Fourteenth Amendment and its interpretation.

The second great issue confronted by the nineteenth-century Court involved the scope of the regulatory powers of the states over the burgeoning economic activity of the nation. The response was at first tentative and restrained. Thus in the *Slaughter-House Cases*, Justice Miller, speaking of the "due process" clause, observes: "We doubt very much whether any action of a state not directed by way of discrimination against the Negroes . . . will ever be held to come within the purview of this provision." Only a short time later the Court's decision in *Munn* v. *Illinois*, 94 U.S. 113 (1876), recognized broad state legislative authority over the rates of public utilities. But beginning in the eighties a much more restrictive view of state authority was expressed, and in the four decades that followed much state legislation fell afoul of the Court's interpretation of the "due process" clause. Among the casualties were state laws seeking to regulate rates, prices, minimum wages of workers, maximum hours of labor, and other terms of employment. These decisions expressed the judicial view then dominant that the full promise of American life could be realized only through the release of creative energies in the economic sphere, largely unimpeded by government restraint, and that the attainment of civil and political liberty in all aspects depended upon the defenses of freedom of economic enterprise. At no time were these assumptions fully shared by all segments of American public opinion; and after the turn of the century criticism of the Court's role in these cases became more vocal and more organized.

It was not until the decade of the thirties that the Court fundamentally revised its views as to the permissible scope of state regulatory power. A majority of the Court has never wholly forsworn its authority to test the validity of state economic regulation against the requirements of due process, but today state legislation is not to be invalidated when supportable on any rational basis. The validity of state economic regulation is, therefore, no longer a central problem of Fourteenth Amendment interpretation.

The twentieth century brought to the nation new issues and new concerns, many of which found expression in judicial interpretations of "due process" and "equal protection." The years beginning with World War I may be regarded as a period of crisis for individual liberty, not only in the United States, but throughout the Western world. These concerns have been faithfully reflected in the work of the Supreme Court. Virtually all the constitutional law relating to the freedoms of expression, of association, and of religion, has been announced in the years since World War I. In 1925 the Court recognized that the imperatives of the First Amendment were part of the concept of "liberty" protected by the Fourteenth Amendment against invasion by the states, and many modern "due process" cases present such issues as the establishment of religion and freedom of speech. One of the most important questions of modern constitutional law has been whether the Fourteenth Amendment "incorporates" the provisions of the first nine amendments, traditionally understood to apply only to Congress and the federal government, and makes them applicable to the states. Efforts to interpret the "privileges and immunities" clause of the Fourteenth Amendment to achieve that end were frustrated by the Court in early cases arising under the amendment. No majority of the modern court has gone the entire distance of recognizing the full applicability of the Bill of Rights to the states. But a series of recent decisions dealing with particular rights has recognized that in most essential matters the states are subject to restraints comparable to those that limit the powers of the federal government.

Included in the modern judicial preoccupation with problems of civil liberty are the Fourteenth Amendment cases involving issues of fair procedure in state criminal proceedings. In the first half-century of the amendment's life, the Court had numerous occasions to consider the application of the "due process" clause to state criminal procedure. In virtually all these cases, the state procedures were upheld and a broad area of local self-determination was recognized. With the important decisions of *Powell* v. *Alabama,* 287 U.S. 45 (1932), however, a new era of "due process" interpretation began. The *Powell* case recognized that the appointment of counsel for the impoverished accused was, in the circumstances presented, an indispensable part of the fair hearing which the state court was required to provide. Since that time the Court has spoken on an impressive range of questions involving, not only the right to counsel, but coerced confessions, unreasonable search and arrest practices, and many other aspects of the criminal trial and police activity. The consequence has been the formulation of an extensive body of constitutional doctrine within the span of a single generation.

The rights and interests of the recently emancipated slaves were obviously matters of primary concern to the proponents of the Civil War amendments. This concern is manifest in the explicit language of the Thirteenth and Fifteenth Amendments. The Fourteenth Amendment undoubtedly encompassed other objectives; but here, too, the problems of race were central. In general, the judicial interpretation of "involuntary servitude" in the Thirteenth Amendment has been kept within rather narrow bounds. Efforts to find in that amendment legal protections for a broad range of civil rights, such as the right of access to public accommodations, were firmly rejected by a majority of the Court in cases arising in the early postwar period. The Fifteenth Amendment has received numerous applications, but social conditions and, until recently, the absence of valid and effective implementing legislation have frustrated full realization of the rights of Negro suffrage.

Despite the purposes of its framers and the circumstances out of which it evolved, the Fourteenth Amendment made surprisingly small contributions to the civil rights of the Negro population in the half-century following its adoption. Judicial holdings that the amendment's protections applied only to "state action," and not to the action of private persons, required invalidation of much protective legislation enacted by Congress in the postwar period. By the end of the century the Court found legally enforceable segregation of the races consistent with the requirements of equal protection of the laws, so long as "separate but equal" accommodations were provided. Not until the fourth decade of the twentieth century did stirrings of conscience in the American public and a new determination of Negro groups force substantial judicial consideration of racial discrimination as a Fourteenth Amendment problem. A series of decisions of the highest importance was handed down. The institution of the "white primary" in southern states was held to be in violation of the Constitution. Criminal convictions infected by racial discrimination were reversed. In *Shelley* v. *Kraemer,* 334 U.S. 1 (1948), enforcement of restrictive covenants barring Negroes from ownership and occupancy of dwellings was found to offend the "equal protection" clause. Beginning in the 1930's the Court entertained a succession of cases involving racial segregation in public education, culminating in the landmark decision of *Brown* v. *Board of Education,* 347 U.S. 483 (1954). There the Court confronted the "separate but equal" doctrine, established more than a half-century before, and laid it to rest. The *Brown* case represents only the beginning of the Fourteenth Amendment's serious involvement in the issue of admitting minority groups to full participation in American life. Once again the great generalizations of the Fourteenth Amendment—"due process" and "equal protection"—have identified and illuminated the central issues of the time.

Blanche Bruce, U.S. Senator

How many Americans know that in 1874, Blanche Bruce, a former slave, was elected to the U.S. Senate from the State of Mississippi? The next two articles highlight the spirit of this black Senator and his determination to achieve true freedom. The first selection below, which briefly describes his life, is taken from *The Spirit of '76,* a book about exemplary figures in American history. The second, from *Black Congressional Reconstruction Orators and their Orations, 1869–1879,* reflects the excellence in oratory exhibited by this black leader.

Speaking on voting practices in the State of Mississippi, Mr. Bruce reaffirmed his faith in the democratic process and in the country which is committed to such a process. Does commitment to national integrity run parallel to one's commitment to individual liberty and equality? Have the two hundred years of American experience answered the question either for the blacks or for the whites?

HIS LIFE

Reconstruction after the Civil War was the most bitter time in our history. Wounds inflicted by brothers are not easily remedied. Now, a former slave tried to heal those wounds. His name: Blanche Bruce of Mississippi.

After the Civil War, the South was divided into military districts by the Northern victors. Ex-Confederates were disfranchised and former slaves were given the vote. They were called free men but they desperately needed education and a chance to get started.

Blanche Bruce got a quick start on independence—he attended Oberlin College in Ohio, whose doors were open to all. Then he started Missouri's first school for blacks in Hannibal. But he wanted a new challenge. Bruce moved to Mississippi where he quickly became a successful planter and community leader.

In those early days of freedom, the odds were against the Negro. But judgment was being passed nevertheless. Could the black man govern himself, much less others? Some Southerners quickly pointed to a handful of black politicians who were corrupt. Blanche Bruce decided to go into politics.

Blanche Bruce soon proved that all the black man needed was an honest opportunity. He rose to heights almost unknown to the Negro, serving the state of Mississippi in one job after another. Then, in 1874, Blanche Bruce, former slave, was elected to the Senate of the United States.

The senior Senator traditionally accompanied a new Senator to be sworn in. But when Bruce's name was called, Mississippi's senior Senator remained seated. Blanche Bruce started to walk up alone. Then, one courageous man, Senator Roscoe Conkling of New York, stood and led him to the desk.

The powerful voice of Blanche Bruce soon rang out for human freedom and dignity everywhere. Bruce led the fight against unfair immigration quotas for the Chinese and spoke against the cruel treatment of the American Indian. Nor did he forget his own people. "I am a Negro and proud of my race," he said. And in an age of corruption, Bruce fought against election frauds in the South.

When Bruce was first paid the high honor of presiding over the Senate, the *New York Times* wrote: "Senator Bruce is universally respected by his fellow Senators."

Blanche Bruce never served a second term. The end of Reconstruction closed the door on the Negro. But Bruce proved that the door could not remain shut.

HIS WORK

I have confidence, not only in my country and her institutions, but in the endurance, capacity, and destiny of my people. We will, as opportunity offers and ability serves, seek our places, sometimes in the field of letters, arts, sciences, and the professions. More frequently mechanical pursuits will attract and elicit our efforts; more still of my people will find employment and livelihood as the cultivators of the soil. The bulk of this people—by surroundings, habits, adaptation, and choice—will continue to find their homes in the South, and constitute the masses of its yeomanry. We will there probably, of our own volition and more abundantly than in the past, produce the great staples that will contribute to the basis of foreign exchange, aid in giving the nation a balance of trade, and minister to the wants and comfort and build up the prosperity of the whole land. Whatever our ultimate position in the composite civilization of the Republic and whatever varying fortunes attend our career, we will not forget our instincts for freedom nor our love of country. Guided and guarded by a beneficent Providence, and living under the genial influence of liberal institutions, we have no apprehensions that we shall fail from the land from attrition with other races, or ignobly disappear from either the politics or industries of the country.

Mr. President, allow me here to say that, although many of us are uneducated in the schools, we are informed and advised as to our duties to the Government, our State, and ourselves. Without class prejudice or animosities, with obedience to authority as the lesson and love of peace and order as the passion of our lives, with scrupulous respect for the rights of others, and with the hopefulness of political youth, we are determined that the great Government that gave us liberty, and rendered its gift valuable by giving us the ballot, shall not find us wanting in a sufficient response to any demand that humanity or patriotism may make upon us; and we ask such action as will not only protect us in the enjoyment of our constitutional rights, but will preserve the integrity of our republican institutions.

Southern Cities: Economic Aspects

Hollis R. Lynch

The upward and downward movements experienced in the reconciliation process have continued to the present time; so too have the issues. In the following selection, the reconciliation process between the blacks and the whites is shown within the context of black urban conditions in the years 1861–1891. Using excerpts from various publications of the period, author Hollis R. Lynch charts the economic progress of blacks in Southern cities.

Despite their struggles, the blacks seem to have regarded the *church* as a unifying force. Several of the excerpts below tend to bolster this view.

CHARLESTON, S.C. (1869)

THE FREEDMEN'S LAND AND HOME SOCIETY[1]

. . . The question of permitting colored people to own land is of the greatest importance. In most places no obstacle appears if they have money . . . but as they have no money . . . the permission is of little importance.

Last year some 200 freedmen of Charleston formed a society for getting land and homes of their own. At a sale they bought a plantation of 600 acres on Remley's Point, opposite the city, for which they agreed to pay $6,000 or $10 an acre, which seems to me remarkably cheap. A part has been paid for and they have now 18 months to pay the remainder. Last year they planted 150 acres in cotton, but they got only one bale, because the cotton boll destroyed a part, and another part was stolen even after it was picked. This year they have put 30 acres in Sea Island cotton and about the same in corn. . . . They are doing their own work and are determined to watch the crop night and day until it is saved. The 30 acres of cotton of the Sea Island variety was cleared of timber during the Winter, and being too poor to buy a team, they dug up all this new ground with their hoes and planted it, and when I arrived I found 20 or more men and women busy hoeing it. . . .

GEORGIA AND SOUTH CAROLINA (1870)[2]

Amongst the better class of emancipated slaves in the South, I found . . . provident habits rapidly forming. Savings' banks, friendly societies, and building associations were springing up amongst them, and many were purchasing houses and land. In the single town of Macon, Georgia, they had purchased 200 buildings. In Savannah, during the month I was there, they laid past in the savings' bank $5,679, being $2,300 in advance of the previous year, notwithstanding the bad season. In their savings' banks throughout the South, they had deposited $1,500,000 since their emancipation three years before.

More recently the progress has been still more rapid. During this past year, 180 negroes have bought places around Augusta; 220 have built houses in Atlanta; at Columbia, where one black mechanic has already amassed a fortune of $50,000, forty heads of families have purchased city property for homes, at from $500 to $1,200 each, within six months; and on the islands near Charleston 2,000 freedmen's families have located themselves, built their houses and cabins, and paid for their little farms. I heard complaints from many colored men, who had saved some money and wanted to buy land, that landowners would not sell to negroes. But this evil is being remedied. The South Carolina Legislature, last year, appropriated $200,000 for the purchase of large estates, cut them up into farms, and offered them for sale to the freedmen and the poor of all colors. Forty thousand acres of this land have already been sold; and the Legislature has accordingly resolved on an appropriation this year of $400,000 more. . . . The freedmen's deposits in their savings banks have rolled up now to an aggregate of $12,000,000; and the cashiers who keep a note of the purpose for which sums are withdrawn report that in a large proportion of cases it is for the purchase of lands and houses. The deposited savings of the past year exceeded those of the year before to the extent of $558,000. And yet we are told the negroes are incurably thriftless.

AUGUSTA, GA. (1872)[3]

. . . Augusta contains about 15,000 inhabitants, one half of whom are colored, and of the remainder a large portion are of foreign origin, and many of them Germans. . . .

There are several banks in Augusta, one of which is the Freedman's Savings Bank; which is well patronized by the colored people. . . . These banks have been the means of great good to the colored people; having induced them to practise economy, and save their earnings to such a degree, that under their influence, great numbers of the freedmen have become the owners of houses and small farms. This bank occupies a large and handsome building in a prominent position on Broad street, which building was formerly owned by a Southern bank. . . .

The colored people in Augusta own four or five churches, principally of the Baptist order; and on Sundays these churches are well-filled with intelligent and well-dressed hearers. One of these churches was brilliantly lighted with gas, has a nice pulpit, with handsome cushions and a gallery on three sides; and will hold seven or eight hundred persons. Several of these churches were used for schools, and are hung around with maps, large mottoes, and supplied with other school appurtenances.

I am well acquainted with the pastors of two of these churches, the "Springfield" and "Central"; and am glad to be able to bear witness to the truly Christian character and eminently apostolic zeal of both of them. . . .

For several years there were eight or ten schools for the freedmen in Augusta, under the direction of the Am. Missionary Association. . . . So great was the desire for instruction on the part of the blacks that these teachers were often compelled to resume their task in the evening, after the labors of the day were over. . . .

The intelligence of the blacks in Augusta is so far beyond that of the plantation blacks, that one would hardly suppose that they belonged to the same race of beings. . . .

CHARLOTTE, N.C. (1889)[4]

Charlotte, the third city in size in the State of North Carolina, has a population of about 13,000, of whom a fraction more than one-half are negroes. . . .

Few of the negroes in and around Charlotte are prospering. There are about a dozen families of them thereabouts who have fine properties, but the land is too dear within a radius of five miles of the city for them to acquire much of it. In the town itself and in the suburbs, hundreds of them own their own homes—a lot or two and a cheap frame house. But the majority are as poor as Job's turkey, and have no prospects of rising from the depths of their penury. Many of them live in ramshackle cabins, of one or two rooms and in these squalid dwellings often a dozen persons crowd. . . .

In the town they follow the rudest vocations—laborers on the railroads, drivers of drays, stonebreakers on the roads, porters in stores, toilers at the cotton gins, etc. Whatever demands hard work and gives little compensation is theirs to do, although some of them are wheelwrights, carpenters, blacksmiths or shoemakers, and make out fairly well. One of them here is a physician. He is a graduate of Shaw University, at Raleigh, and appears to be building up a paying practice.

Labor is cheap in Charlotte, that is, negro labor. The men get from $20 to $25 a month; the women who live out as domestics get from $6 to $8 a month and dinner, and have to go home at night for supper and bed and return in the morning after getting their own breakfasts. Strapping big girls, from sixteen to thirty years, will give their services as children's nurses for two or three dollars a month and found. So keen is the competition for laundry work, that the negroes will offer to do the washing of an average family for seventy-five cents a week. . . .

The negroes have an excellent graded school in Charlotte, and in the Western suburbs Biddle University dominates the city, giving instructions to more than one hundred and fifty picked young colored men, who are nearly all aspiring to be teachers and preachers for their race. On Saturday afternoons, the colored people in the city and from the surrounding country take possession of the sidewalks of Charlotte. They assemble to do their "trading" and to hobnob with their acquaintances. Few whites go shopping on the day, consequently the town looks then as if it were inhabited almost exclusively by colored people.

ECONOMIC PROGRESS OF BLACKS IN THE SOUTH (1891)[5]

. . . In the vicinity of Birmingham, farms are owned ranging from fifty to two hundred acres.

The home-buying that is going on in the agricultural districts is going on also in the cities. In Montgomery, street after street is owned by colored people. In Chattanooga, one third of the colored people own their homes. Suburban lots range in cost from $350 to $400. A cottage costs in the neighborhood of $600 to $650. In Birmingham, colored people pay $10 or $12 a month rent. A number of householders have gardens with two or three acres of land. Some were fortunate enough to purchase land before the prices went up, and have profited by the rise.

The Negro is also venturing as a tradesman. In all the large cities, and even in the smaller towns, in the South, he is hanging out his sign. Two young men have engaged in the grocery business at Tuskegee, Alabama. Their credit is good at the bank. . . . The colored grocers in Birmingham are sharing the prosperity of this thriving city. . . . At Tuscaloosa, the livery stable man who drove me owns several horses and carriages, and is doing well. Thus, in whatever direction one goes, he can find Negroes who are rising by force of education and character. The influence of such schools as Hampton, Atlanta, and Tuskegee is felt all through the South in the stimulus given to industrial occupations. Tuskegee has turned out a number of printers, who have made themselves independent, and get patronage from both white and colored customers. One has a printing office in Montgomery. . . . In all the mechanical trades, colored men are finding places as blacksmiths, wheelwrights, masons, bricklayers, carpenters, tinsmiths, harnessmakers, shoemakers, and machinists. In Washington, colored brickmakers are earning from four to five dollars a day. Hod-carriers receive $1.50. . . . With industrial education and diversified mechanical pursuits, the Negro brain is becoming adaptive and creative. . . . A colored assistant examiner in the Patent Office department has . . . placed at my service a list of some fifty patents taken out by colored people, which show the scope of their inventive genius. In the list of things represented are an improved gridiron, a locomotive smokestack, a cornstalk harvester, a shield for infantry and artillery, a fire extinguisher, a dough kneader, a cotton cultivator, life-preserving apparatus, a furniture caster, a biscuit cutter, a rotary engine, a printing press, a file holder, a window ventilator for railroad cars, an automatic switch for railroads, and a telephone transmitter. The electric inventions are said to have a good deal of merit, and have been assigned to a prominent company. In Birmingham, a colored inventor is making money out of his patent.

With the purchase of homes and the accumulation of property, the colored people are gradually changing their condition of living. It is seen at its worst in the miserable one-room cabins of the country districts, and in the alley population of such cities as Washington and Baltimore. . . . Bad as the one-room cabin is, it is not so bad as the tenement house in the slums of the great cities. . . .

MONTGOMERY AND WASHINGTON

. . . The social progress of the Negro is well illustrated by two historic cities—the federal capital at Washington and the former capital of the Confederacy at Montgomery. The casual traveler, who sees the alley districts and the settlements around the railroads, forms no better idea of the social development of the Negro than he does of Northern whites, if he confines his inspection to similar localities. In Montgomery, under the guidance of Dr. Dorsette, a colored physician and a respected citizen, I had an opportunity to see the homes of the colored people at their best. In some of the streets, the whites occupy one side, and the blacks the other. Occasionally the colors alternate, like the squares on a checkerboard. It is not easy externally to tell one from the other. The interiors of these homes, especially of the younger and more progressive people, are comfortably and tastefully furnished. The rooms are as high as those of their white neighbors, well carpeted and papered, while the piano or the cabinet organ suggests loftier musical tastes than that of the plantation banjo. While in most respects the movement or development of the white and colored races runs on parallel lines, in music they seem to be going in opposite directions. Though I traveled all through the South, in urban, suburban, and agricultural districts, from Baltimore to New Orleans, the only banjo I heard was played in Atlanta by a white man. . . . In New Orleans, I was astounded at the strange phenomenon of a colored handorgan grinder. . . . It is estimated that there are from 250 to 300 pianos and cabinet organs in the homes of colored people in Montgomery. . . .

Immediately after the war I lived at the national capital. Thousands of destitute blacks from Virginia and further south had settled in the barracks around the city. They owned little more than the clothes on their backs, and most of these had been given to them. The change in these districts is remarkable. Large numbers of people live in their own homes. There is not much squalor outside of the alley population. Even the poorest houses have some comforts and show some endeavor to improve. A similar story may be told of Baltimore.

. . . There are no Negro millionaires that I know of; but there is growing up a class of men with fortunes ranging from $15,000 to $100,000. This accumulation has been going on in recent years with increasing rapidity. . . .

. . . Thus, in Montgomery, Alabama, a colored barber, originally a slave, has accumulated property amounting to $75,000 or $100,000. . . . In Baltimore, there are several colored men worth $15,000 each, three or four worth from $40,000 to $60,000, and the estate of a Negro recently deceased was appraised at $100,000. In Washington, also, colored men have profited by the rise of real estate, and a few are possessed of ample fortunes. These instances might be greatly multiplied from my notes.

RISE OF A PROFESSIONAL CLASS

The result of higher education is seen in the rise of a professional class. I remember the time when a colored doctor was a curiosity even in Washington; but colored physicians, lawyers, journalists, college professors, dentists, educated clergymen, and teachers are now to be found in all the large cities of the South.

In Montgomery, Dr. Dorsette has built up a thriving practice. He has erected a three-story brick building, on the lower floor of which are two stores, one of them a large and well-equipped drug store. A hall above is used for the physicians, one dentist, and one lawyer. At Selma, the practicing physician is a graduate of the university. There is also a pharmacist, owning his drug store, who studied at Howard University. There are six colored lawyers and seven colored physicians in Baltimore. The professional men command the confidence and support of their own people.

Journalism is growing slowly. There are now about fifty-five well-established Negro newspapers and journals. Thirty-seven are in the Southern States; seven are monthlies and two are semi-monthlies. The aggregate weekly circulation of all is about 850,000 copies. There are other ephemeral journals, not included in this list. The largest circulation, 15,000, is claimed for the *Indianapolis Freeman*.

The colored people are determined to have their churches, and they subscribe, in proportion to their means, large sums to sustain them. . . . In the comparatively new city of Birmingham, there are seven comfortable colored churches, ranging in cost from $2000 to $15,000. In Washington, two churches cost nearly $30,000 each, and the money has been raised almost exclusively by the colored people. In Baltimore, there are forty-four colored churches, holding a large amount of property. . . . The colored people are also ambitious to pay their preachers as much as the whites pay theirs. In Montgomery, one colored preacher has a salary of $1200 a year with a parsonage. In another city in Alabama, $1800 is paid.

BENEVOLENT AND FRATERNAL SOCIETIES

. . . The colored people have developed a laudable disposition to take care of their own poor. In addition to the Odd Fellows, Masons, and Knights of Pythias, benevolent and fraternal organizations are multiplying. The city churches are feeling a new impulse to such work. Brotherhoods, Good Samaritan societies, and mutual benefit organizations are established. Members of these organizations are allowed a regular stipend when sick. In New Orleans, the colored people have started a widows' home, and have collected enough money to buy a piece of ground and to put up a respectable building. In Montgomery, I visited the Hale Infirmary, founded by the late Joseph Hale and his wife, leading colored citizens. It is a large two-story building, especially designed by the son-in-law of the founder for hospital purposes. . . .

BUSINESS ASSOCIATIONS

. . . Small stock companies for various purposes exist in a number of cities. A little has been done in the way of building associations. There is one at Atlanta, with branches and local boards elsewhere; others at Tuskegee, Montgomery, Selma, Baltimore, and Washington. In Baltimore there are three or four such associations, but the German organizations, managed by white people, have had much more of their patronage. A daily paper of Charlotte, North Carolina, in speaking of the loan associations there, said that the colored shareholders were outstripping the white. It was noticeable that they paid more promptly. A penny savings bank, chartered under state law, was organized at Chattanooga about ten months ago. It has already one thousand depositors, the amounts ranging from two cents to one thousand dollars. The white as well as the colored children are being educated to save by this bank. In Birmingham, a similar institution was opened last October, and has about three thousand depositors. . . .

NOTES

1. *New York Tribune,* June 30, 1869.
2. David Macrae, *The Americans at Home,* Vol. II, pp. 55–57, Edinburgh: Edmonston and Douglas, 1870.
3. Charles Stearns, *The Black Man of the South and the Rebels,* New York: American News Company, 1872, p. 128.
4. *New York Tribune,* March 24, 1889.
5. Samuel J. Barrow, "What the Southern Negro Is Doing for Himself," *Atlantic Monthly,* June 1891, pp. 807–814.

Education

John H. Lovell, Jr.

Education in the reconciliation process is the focus of the following selection taken from the book *Black Song: The Forge and the Flame,* by John Lovell, Jr. Consider what the title of the book signifies. From Lovell's recount of the educational development of the blacks, one sees an image of human experience—the thirst for knowledge.

For thousands of slaves the desire for education was the strongest of desires. In many slave narratives and commentaries the point is made that facing the future without education was the most unbearable part of slavery. It motivated innumerable escapes and attempts to escape.

It is true that reading and writing were not generally a part of the educational system in Africa. This fact did not mean that there was no education. The African child was very carefully educated in the most exacting ways. Vocational training was pursued with systems of apprenticeship and other methods of inducting the young into gainful employments. Mungo Park, among many others, has told how deeply the Negro loved instruction. When education is defined as enlightened training for a place in society and for the individual's personal development, it was a thing highly respected in Africa. It must be remembered, also, that the slave came from the middle and upper classes of African society. And the Afro-American continued and intensified the respect for education.

The Afro-American's great desire to read and write was two things at least: It was recognition of what he would need to compete in the new world to which he had been brought and it was in line with his determination to develop his skills and talents. In the mid-eighteenth century the Reverend Samuel Davies wrote of the eagerness of the Negroes he had met to learn to read.

Several perceptive writers have drawn clear inferences about the educational outlook of slaves from an analysis of their lives. In John Rankin's work one reads that the African, by weathering slavery, has exhibited strong mental capacity. Russell Ames tells us that, if unlettered working people produce art of high quality, hard experience has hammered realism, wisdom, and ironic humor into their heads.

People with such skills as those we have just described had the implicit intelligence that warranted education. The power structure of the plantation South was determined, out of pure fear, to limit or prevent this deserved education. "Knowledge and slavery are incompatible," wrote a citizen in Woodville, Mississippi, in 1832. In the methods they used to deprive the slave, as Hildreth has shown, they set up a strong barrier against education for all whites.

The Maryland code in 1683 stated that "the inhabitants shall have all their rights and liberties according to the great charter of England"; and, further, "all Christian inhabitants (slaves excepted) to have and enjoy all such rights, liberties, immunities, privileges and free customs," et cetera! The fact that slaves were highly sensitive to this exception among Christian inhabitants all over slave country, and highly resentful too, has been often ignored even by Negro historians.

Shortly after the Nat Turner uprising a delegate arose in the Virginia legislature and frankly admitted,

We have as far as possible closed every avenue by which light may enter slaves' minds. If we could extinguish the capacity to see the light our work would be completed; they would then be on a level with the beasts of the field.

Out of one side of their mouths the slave owning powers said that such education would be useless, since the barbaric slave was utterly incapable of absorbing it. Out of the opposite side they worked hard to prevent education for fear it would lead to dissatisfaction, insurrection, rebellion, and "manifest injury of the citizens" (as an act to prevent the teaching of slaves, passed in North Carolina in 1830, put it). In late years of slavery, the fear that slaves would read abolitionist literature was given as a reason for preventing education. Punishments for teaching slaves to read ranged from fines for whites to death for Negroes in Alabama and Louisiana. As early as 1804 in Virginia it was no longer lawful for overseers of the poor to require master or mistress to teach black or mulatto orphans reading, writing, and arithmetic. Also in 1838 educated free Negroes were prohibited by law from returning to Virginia.

In spite of these restrictions John Hope Franklin reports that many slaves got educated. He quoted one observer who said that one of every fifty slaves in the Southwest could read and write, and another observer who estimated that five thousand of Georgia's four hundred thousand slaves were literate.

On the word of Francis Butler Simkins, in *A History of the South,* slaves overrode prohibitive laws and learned to read and write. Sydnor says that even in Mississippi many slaves learned to read. One Mississippian advertised in a weekly paper (in 1818) a school for blacks. He was told he could be fined $30 or be imprisoned for thirty days and given thirty-nine lashes. In Mississippi and elsewhere slaves were teaching themselves and receiving pointers from their fellows. Linda Brent tells of a black man, age 53, who all his life had wanted to read more than anything else. He begged her to teach him. She taught him. Allen W. Read concludes that during the colonial period the success of the black man in learning English was equal to that of any other immigrant body. And as C. L. R. James has reminded us, the Bible was the most readily available book. "It was," as he says, "a course in the alphabet, a first reader, and a series of lessons in the history of mankind." It is most ironic that the people who prided themselves so greatly on being a Christian nation and section should exert such brutal force to prevent their charges from learning to read the Bible.

Concerning the slave's ability to learn when given the opportunity, many writers have commented. Most say his learning power was considerable. Certainly one reason for this progress was an almost overwhelming motivation. Timothy Flint said that slaves were quick of apprehension and that they learned to read faster than whites. It would be difficult, though, he said, to teach them arithmetic.

Frederick Douglass and other ex-slaves who gained education, chiefly through self-teaching, have testified as to the desire of slaves to command the benefits and broad outlook which education conferred. They have also spoken of help they received from whites. It is notable that the laws often paid respect to such whites and, at the same time, threatened them with penalties. In Douglass's case, a kind mistress (Mrs. Auld) had taught him, out of sheer humanity, to read and write. When her husband convinced her that slavery and education were incompatible with each other, she tried to undo her teaching. She snatched away from him a newspaper or book he was quietly reading and scolded him for his persistence. But like many slaves with quick minds, Douglass had gone too far to turn back. As he puts it,

In teaching me the alphabet, in the days of her simplicity and kindness, my mistress had given me the "inch," and now, no ordinary precaution could prevent me from taking the "ell."

Douglass persisted most stubbornly, carrying a copy of Webster's spelling book in his pocket, having his white playmates "review" him in vocabulary, and otherwise enlarging his educational horizons. In these respects and in defiance of the stereotype, the comprehensive evidence shows him to be a sample of many thousands who learned by various means to read. Thousands more yearned for the opportunity.

The impact of education upon assembled Negroes was anticipated partly because of actual cases in which educated Negroes proved hard to handle or ran away, and partly because of assorted fears. Howell M. Henry in *The Police Control of the Slave in South Carolina* devotes a whole chapter to "Negro Gatherings for Religious and Social Purposes" and another to "Slave Insurrections." Under the latter he describes an act of 1800 which made all assemblages of slaves and free Negroes for mental instruction unlawful, even with whites present, if held behind closed doors. No meetings could be held between sunset and sunrise. This law interfered with Methodist meetings, especially class meetings. It was strengthened several times, particularly in 1837, obviously in response to growing anticipations. Hurd also lists an Alabama law of 1832 that prohibited the attempt to teach any slave or free person of color to spell, read, or write.

The most chilling fears about the slave's education arose from slave uprisings the leaders of which were often literate and sometimes well educated. Following the Nat Turner insurrection in 1831 and the dissemination of the information that Nat was an enormous reader who knew the Bible almost by heart, the state legislatures of the South were busy passing laws to forestall any semblance of slave education. The blood of each one of the sixty to eighty whites slaughtered by Nat's hand was assigned to the set of circumstances under which Nat had learned to read. Throughout the South slaves suspected of education were detected, tortured, and killed for no other reason than their dangerous literacy. Negro meetings were further restricted, even funerals, after it was learned that Nat had used funerals to reach three to four hundred slaves at a time; attendance at funerals was kept down to fifteen or twenty. Following the abortive Vesey revolt, free Negroes (Vesey was free) were denied the right to hold meetings.

On a smaller scale Jacob Stroyer testifies that his owners were shocked when they learned that he could read. After he had run away to freedom, he wrote a book and announced that the proceeds from sales would be used to further his education. Tom Fletcher relates that his grandmother's greatest ambition was to learn to read the Bible. Following the practice of many house servants, he was taught by white children.

The slave preacher has been often described as a man with an unusual storehouse of information, general and special, whether he could read or not. The very famous John Jasper, a black preacher of the late nineteenth century, tells how as a slave he "thusted for de bread uv learnin'." Although books were sealed to him, he longed to break the seal. A fellow slave finally taught him from the *New York Spelling Book.* He also learned to read the Bible. Several writers have said that the slave preacher was one of the first slaves to learn to read; one writer voices a strong suspicion that most spirituals were written by slave preachers.

Allison Davis wrote that the ancestors of the Afro-American left him this heritage, "the determination to survive and to wrest a home and education for their children from a hostile environment." And in his highly significant book, *The Education of the Negro Prior to 1861,* Carter G. Woodson has two compelling chapters, "Learning in Spite of Opposition" and "Education as a Right of Man." Both are directly in line with the predominant spirit of the slave folk community.

When the slave was unable to get formal education (and sometimes when he was able), he often cultivated memory as a substitute. Besides learning to read, Fletcher's grandmother would often select a chapter of the Bible and memorize it. Bernard Robb, in *Welcum Hinges,* writes of a former slave named Uncle Woodson who could not read, but who knew by heart large portions of the Bible and of the Episcopal service.

The slave preacher was famous for his memory, especially of great and dramatic portions of the Bible. Ball, Earnest, Sydnor, and others have cited innumerable cases. By embellishing these, he could maintain complete control of his service and congregation. No doubt many of the makers of spirituals were poets who remembered striking passages from the Bible and from other literature and used them effectively.

As Frederick Douglass proved, and delineates in his autobiography, learning to read and write and otherwise educating oneself were among the slave's sharpest weapons in his fight against slavery. Of course it was dangerous to be caught with a book. By using care and taking advantage of every opportunity, the slave could master reading. There was usually some friendly white person, or at times another slave or free Negro, who was willing to teach him how to write. Once he had captured writing and reading he was already on his way out of the most abject slavery. At the very least, he could write passes for himself and read signs on his route to freedom. Remember, though, that the everyday slave was not really an illiterate. His expression in conversation, story-telling, proverb, song, and other folklore were a strong form of literacy. Not only did he communicate; he left a sharp impression, often an impression of wisdom. The songs he created went far beyond the one language he was taught to use; they spoke, and still speak, in a universal tongue both in melody and in thought. Formal education the slave saw not as a means of getting started but as a weapon for intensifying and coordinating his natural gifts.

Charlotte Scott's Mite

Benjamin Quarles

One of the most heartwarming stories about Abraham Lincoln actually involved his death and the unimaginable sorrow of millions of blacks whom he had helped to liberate. In telling the story of the creation and dedication of the Lincoln Negro Monument, "Emancipation," Benjamin Quarles describes the intensity of the black response to freedom and to Lincoln as a man.

Once again it was Good Friday, April 14, the first Good Friday to fall on that date since the assassination of Abraham Lincoln eleven years earlier. What better date to unveil a monument to the martyred President? What better place than the nation's capital city, scene of his final, greatest years? And what better group to have raised the money for a bronze statue than those whom he had helped free?

The unveiling of the emancipation monument was recognized as something out of the ordinary. It was, wrote the Washington correspondent of the *Baltimore Sun,* "the event of the day." In its observance, Congress had passed a joint resolution setting aside that particular April 14 of 1876 as a general holiday so that "all persons desiring to do so should be given the opportunity of attending" the exercises. President Ulysses S. Grant, congressmen, and Supreme Court justices had accepted invitations to attend; members of foreign legations were also expected as guests; and the most prominent Negro of his times had been scheduled for the oration.

If the exercises at the unveiling of "Freedom's Memorial" were to be made newsworthy by the presence of high-ranking government officials, the origin of the monument was to be found in the sacrificing spirit of an obscure "washerwoman."

The original and foundation subscription for the Lincoln-Negro monument came from Charlotte Scott. Born a slave on a plantation near Lynchburg, Virginia, she had been given by her owner to his daughter, Mrs. William P. Rucker. When the Civil War broke out, William Rucker's sympathies for the Union cause led to his spending seventeen months in a Confederate prison, after which the family fled to Marietta, Ohio, taking Charlotte along. Freed in 1862, she stayed on with the Ruckers, living in their home. She was well thought of, according to Rucker, for her industry and her honesty.

Although over sixty when freed, she was still hale and active and had no trouble getting work washing clothes. She had just managed to scrape up her first small savings when the dread news of Lincoln's assassination reached Marietta.

On that mournful Saturday in April 1865, the deeply distressed Charlotte said to Mrs. Rucker, "The colored people have lost their best friend on earth. Mr.

Lincoln was our best friend, and I will give five dollars of my wages toward erecting a monument to his memory." The sympathetic Ruckers suggested that the money be placed in the hands of C.D. Battelle, a local clergyman. Taking this suggestion, Charlotte went to see Battelle and asked him to act as agent for the colored people, receiving their contributions and holding them for the time being.

Battelle bestirred himself at once: "I received her offering, and gave notice through the press that I would receive other donations, and cheerfully do what I could to promote so noble an object." The project quickly caught the fancy of Brigadier General T.C.H. Smith, in command of the military post at St. Louis, who hit upon the idea of turning it over to an organization that could best reach prospective Negro contributors, the Western Sanitary Commission whose headquarters was in the city. Late in June the Reverend C.D. Battelle sent Charlotte's mite to James E. Yeatman, president of the commission. In Yeatman's mail the same day came a letter from Rucker emphasizing that every dollar toward the monument should come from former slaves.

Now that the Western Sanitary Commission had become the active agent in collecting funds, the project got off the ground. In Negro circles the commission was well known. It had been founded in September 1861 to minister to the sick and wounded of the Western armies, but it had taken on the task of helping the needy former slaves along the Mississippi, who by the fall of 1863 had numbered some 50,000, from Columbus, Kentucky, to Natchez.

Upon receiving the letters about the Charlotte Scott proposal, Yeatman lost no time in sending notices to newspapers and to officers commanding Negro troops, informing them about the monument and inviting contributions. The black wearers of the blue quickly responded, subscribing some $12,000 in two months. The largest gift, $4770, came from the Sixth U.S. Colored Heavy Infantry ("those that Forrest's men did not murder at Fort Pillow," wryly added paymaster W.C. Lupton, in a covering letter to Yeatman). Another regiment in the District of Natchez authorized Lupton to deduct one dollar for each of its nearly 1700 men. At Rodney, Mississippi, where the Seventieth U.S. Colored Troops donated $2949.50, Colonel W.C. Earles felt it necessary to caution the officers "to check the noble generosity of my men rather than stimulate it." Before the winter snows fell on Lincoln's grave, the soldiers and freedmen along the Mississippi had sent a total of $16,242.00.

Once the money was collected, the task of the Western Sanitary Commission shifted to the erection of the monument. While a tribute to the generosity of its black donors, the sum raised was not nearly enough for a statue of large design. But the commission was in for a piece of luck. One of its five members, the clergyman-college president William G. Eliot, happened to be in Florence in 1869, where he visited the studio of Thomas Ball. Boston-born, although making his home in Italy, Ball was well known as a result of several excellent works, among them the equestrian statue of George Washington in the Boston Public Garden.

While at Ball's studio Eliot's attention was caught by a half life-size model of Abraham Lincoln and a liberated slave, a piece Ball had executed shortly after receiving the news of the President's death. Having difficulty in finding a good model for a slave, Ball had sat for himself and with the aid of mirrors had made "one of my best nude figures." (At least, wrote Ball, he could not have had a better model "for the money.")

The visiting Dr. Eliot observed the marble statuette very closely, storing up the details in his mind. Upon his return to America he told his fellow commissioners about the striking piece. Soon came a letter to Ball's studio asking him to furnish the Western Sanitary Commission with photographs of the emancipation duo and his terms for a nine- or ten-foot bronze. After examining the pictures Ball sent, the commission offered him the job, expressing the hope that he would accept such a small amount as $17,000 in light of the fact that it had been raised by former slaves. The commissioners had one other stipulation: in place of Ball's slave model of himself, they asked him to substitute the features of an actual Negro. To these terms Ball agreed. Thereupon Dr. Eliot sent him several photographs of the man who was to be the model for the slave, Archer Alexander.

If his past experiences give to a model's face the values the artist is seeking, Archer was a good choice. He was a man with a past, colorful if humble. A slave in Missouri when the war broke out, he had in February 1863 brought information to Union troops about a bridge over which they were scheduled to pass, but whose timbers had been sawed by Confederate sympathizers. Before his highly suspicious anti-Union master could punish him, Archer fled to St. Louis and took employment with Dr. Eliot.

Eliot let it be known publicly that he was willing to pay as high as $600 "ransom money" to Archer's master, but the offer was ignored. One afternoon, as Archer was working around the Eliot yard, he was seized by three of his master's henchmen and taken to the city jail—"the last fugitive slave taken in Missouri under the old laws of slavery." Before his master could rush him to Kentucky, Eliot managed to secure his release from jail and put him on a steamer to Alton, Illinois. Archer subsequently returned to St. Louis, where he became an organ-blower at Dr. Eliot's Church of the Messiah. He took a lasting pride in the memory of his son, Tom, who had been killed in battle.

It was, then, the face and figure of an ex-bondman that filled Ball's eye as he modeled his slave. Ball had some experience in working from photographs, having done so in executing a marble bust of Liszt. When the emancipation piece was finished, Ball sent it to Munich to be cast at the Royal Foundry. The statue then came to the United States, where Congress permitted it to pass the customs free of duty and also appropriated $3000 for a pedestal.

The bronze work was elevated into its position in Lincoln Park on April 13, being covered with American flags until the unveiling scheduled for the following day. The committee of five Negroes appointed by the Western Sanitary Commission to make arrangements for the exercises had done its job. All was in readiness for a day to remember.

It was eleven in the morning. The sun would not show itself, but the showers had held up although, as a reporter from an out-of-town newspaper put it, "the sky continued of that uncertain cast that made umbrellas the most satisfactory companions." Optimistic now that the rain had stopped, the celebrators went ahead with their plans.

Gathering at their places along a half-dozen blocks on K Street were some twenty Negro organizations—companies of the National Guard, benevolent and charitable societies like the Good Samaritans and the Sons of Purity, and workers' groups like the Labor League. All bore banners, and most were gaily attired, the Knights of St. Augustine sporting black hats with yellow plumes and blue, sword-ensheathed baldries. Interspersed between these groups were marching bands and the carriages bearing the orator of the day and his party. Heading the line of march was a yellow-sashed chief marshal, with a squad of mounted police a few paces behind.

The assembled line was soon ready to move. Passing through the streets, where flags were flying half-mast from the house tops, the marchers came to the Executive Mansion. They passed in review, after which they made their mile-long way up East Capitol Street to Lincoln Park. Here the grounds were "packed with human beings," fully half of them white, hiding the park's chain fence and posing a threat to its handful of slow-growing trees.

In front of the covered statue was a stand for the speakers and a railed platform for the dignitaries. At half-past one President Grant and his party of two—Ulysses S. Grant, Jr., and Secretary of the Interior Zachariah Chandler—got out of their carriage and were conducted to reserved chairs. Revolving around, finding seats on the platform, were some sixty figures of lesser importance.

Shortly before two o'clock the Marine Band struck up "Hail to the Chief," and the exercises were on. A bishop said a prayer. Then J. Henri Burch of Louisiana read Lincoln's message to Congress approving and signing the act freeing the slaves in the District of Columbia, which, as coincidence would have it, had taken place fourteen years ago to the day. The audience, taking advantage of its first opportunity to cheer, greeted the reading by Burch with "as much enthusiasm as if it had just been written." James E. Yeatman, representing the Western Sanitary Commission, then gave a sketch of the origin of the project, ending up by presenting the monument to John Mercer Langston, the presiding officer.

An Oberlin graduate, dean of the Howard University law department, and destined to be the only Negro ever to represent Virginia in the Congress, the slender, bearded, steady-eyed Langston was at home on the public platform. He responded to Yeatman by expressing the thanks of the Negro for the commission's work. Then, just as everyone was waiting for him to unveil the statue, Langston turned to President Grant and asked him to pull the cord. It was a very happy inspiration.

Whatever his shortcomings as a presidential leader, Grant could muster an impressive dignity. Rising and stationing himself in front of the flag-draped bronze, he paused for a moment to let the silence sink in. Then he gave a tug to the silken cord, the covering fell away, and the figures were finally exposed to view. The resultant din was deafening, compounded of spontaneous cries of admiration—a claque could have done no better—noisy handclapping, the booming of cannon, and the brassy strains of the Marine Band.

The statue that drew such applause was a twelve-foot bronze. It represented Lincoln standing beside a column bearing the face of George Washington, and upon which rested the Emancipation Proclamation, one corner of which Lincoln was fingering. Lincoln's face was turned toward a half-kneeling Negro, although his eyes seemed to be peering into the future, rather than focusing upon any object. Lincoln's left hand was poised over the Negro, as if in protection or benediction. His wrist shackles broken, the muscular former slave was in the act of rising, with one knee off the ground, like a sprinter getting set. His upward-looking face bore no pronounced expression. At the base of the piece was the single word EMANCIPATION in raised twelve-inch letters. The statue rested upon a ten-foot granite pedestal bearing two metal plaques, one telling of Charlotte Scott and the other quoting the final phrases of the Emancipation Proclamation.

When the applause had spent itself, the program proceeded with a poem,

"Today, O martyred chief, beneath the sun," by Cornelia Ray, which was read for her in her absence. Miss Ray's stanzas abounded in such passages as:

While Freedom may her holy spectre claim,
The world shall echo with "Our Lincoln's name."

But if the young New Yorker's eighty-line eulogy did not add notably to the Lincoln literature, it gave the audience time to settle back for the second and final high light of the overcast afternoon: the oration by Frederick Douglass.

To see that striking head again and to hear that rich baritone voice lifted in oratory would in itself attract an audience. Here was a man whose life read like a saga. After his escape from a Maryland slave master, he had become a polished speaker and a forceful writer, devoting his skills to reformist movements such as the abolition of slavery and equal rights for women. Like his career, his appearance was arresting. With a wealth of white hair and beard, a healthy glow to his skin, and a bit of a bulge around the middle, he gave one the initial impression of a Santa Claus in brownface. But a second look brought a different reaction: his piercing eyes, his formal bearing and no-nonsense air reminded one of an Old Testament patriarch.

As Langston, the presiding officer, completed his introduction of the "orator of the occasion," Douglass arose, manuscript in hand. He had brought to the writing of his address some firsthand knowledge of Lincoln, as he had had two White House audiences with the President. He owned a cane of Lincoln's, which Mrs. Lincoln had sent him and which he viewed as "an object of sacred trust."

In his lengthy address, however, Douglass let himself be swayed by no sentimental memories. After the opening congratulations to the assembled "friends and fellow citizens," he devoted his attention almost exclusively to one question: Was President Lincoln devoted to the welfare of the Negro, or were his actions on behalf of the colored man forced by the pressures of the times?

There was but one answer, said the unsparing Douglass, as he described Lincoln's slowness in coming around to the point of view held by those who had no patience with slavery. Lincoln "was preeminently the white man's President."

But, went on the orator of the day, this was far from the whole story. The Negro's faith was often taxed to the limit while the President "tarried in the mountain," but it never failed. And Lincoln finally proved himself worthy of this faith: "Though he loved Caesar less than Rome, though the Union was more to him than our freedom or our future, under his wise and beneficent rule we saw ourselves gradually lifted from the depths of slavery to the heights of liberty and manhood." In the person of Abraham Lincoln the hour and the man of "our redemption" had met.

It was on this latter, emancipating Lincoln that Douglass brought his oration to a close. The cheers of the audience indicated that this was the Lincoln they preferred to remember. The closing minutes of the program took on a fitting note of devotion, with the band playing Rossini's "Sicilian Vespers" Overture and Dr. J.P. Newman pronouncing the benediction. "The occasion," editorialized the *Washington Chronicle,* "could not fail to impress everyone with feelings of the most profound respect for a people in whom the sentiment of gratitude is so strongly ingrained as it is in those whose voluntary contributions paid for the magnificent memorial which commemorates the crowning act of Lincoln's life."

Dear, dear Charlotte Scott. In his address Douglass had not spoken her name.

But who more than she gave meaning to his words: "When now it is said that the colored man has no appreciation of benefits or benefactors, we may calmly point to the monument we have this day erected to the memory of Abraham Lincoln"—who, more than this former slave, who lived to be over a hundred, dying in 1892 at her birthplace four miles from Lynchburg?

Lorado Taft, art critic and himself a sculptor, had a high opinion of the Lincoln monument, describing it as one of the most inspired works produced by an American: "a great theme expressed with emotion by an artist of intelligence and sympathy, who felt what he was doing." Also impressed by the emancipation duo was Moses Kimball of Boston, businessman and long-time member of the state legislature, who commissioned Ball to do a replica. Kimball gave this copy to his native city, which held dedication exercises at Faneuil Hall on May 30, 1879. Attended by the governor of the state and opened with a prayer by Phillips Brooks, the exercises featured an oration by Mayor Frederick O. Prince and an occasional poem by John Greenleaf Whittier, who was "the slave's poet" of a bygone day but was still quick to point a moral:

Amidst thy sacred effigies
  Of old renown give place,
O city, Freedom-loved! to his
  Whose hand unchained a race.
Stand in thy place and testify
  To coming ages long,
That truth is stronger than a lie
  And righteousness than wrong.

The Kimball gift was erected in Park Square, where it was to stand, then as now, on a little plot of land completely engulfed by traffic.

The widest public knowledge of the Ball statue came in 1940 when the Post Office issued a three-cent-stamp reproduction of it, running off an initial order of forty million. The step was taken upon the urging of Negroes, who wanted the government to do something in observance of the seventy-fifth anniversary of the amendment abolishing slavery. Printed in deep violet, the stamp was first placed on sale at the New York World's Fair branch post office, on the occasion of the diamond jubilee celebration of the Thirteenth Amendment.

Despite the apparent popularity of the Ball monument, not all Negroes cared for it. Frederick Douglass found that it left him cold: "It showed the Negro on his knee when a more manly attitude would have been indicative of freedom." A subsequent critic, Freeman Henry Morris Murray, had a more inclusive bill of indictment against the piece in Lincoln Park.

Ball, said the dissenting Murray, had really not modeled his piece as an emancipation group, but as Lincoln and the kneeling slave. Hence the face of the sculptured Negro bears none of the elevated emotion of one who is and ought to be free; it was, rather, like that of a man who has just escaped the hangman's noose by a last-minute commutation of sentence. The statue reminded Murray of a conventional portrait of Jesus and the Magdalen, with the deified Lincoln saying, "Go, and sin no more." All in all, said Murray, the monument could have been improved, perhaps, by removing the ex-slave completely.

If many Negroes were destined to become lukewarm about the monument, this attitude was never transferred to Lincoln. In Negro circles his fame remained untarnished. In large measure this was due to former slaves, to whom Lincoln was a folk hero, legendary and semireligious. Typical of this mood was seventy-nine-year-old Bob Maynard, of Weleetka, Oklahoma: "I think Abe Lincoln was next to the Lord. He done all he could for the slaves; he set 'em free. 'Fore the election he travelled all over the South, and he come to our house and slept in Old Mistress' bed. Didn't nobody know who he was."

By no means was this worship of the Civil War President confined to the unlettered Negro. The cult of "Lincolnolatry" took firm root among the colored leaders, led by Booker T. Washington. Lincoln's was "almost the first name I learned," wrote this Negro who lunched with Theodore Roosevelt in the White House, and on whom Harvard University conferred an honorary degree. "I confess," said Washington, "that the more I learn of Lincoln's life the more I am disposed to look at him much as my mother and those early freedmen did . . ." To Kelly Miller, another listened-to spokesman for the colored man, Lincoln was "a genius of the first order," one who dwelt upon the "radiant summit." An executive director of the New York Urban League, James H. Hubert, found in Lincoln a familiar American theme, but one with especial appeal to minority groups. To Hubert, himself from a family of above-average achievement, the life of Lincoln said, "You may climb from the bottom to the top." And on one February 12, Mordecai Johnson, best known of the Negro clergyman-educators, gave a radio address entitled "The World-Significant Soul of Abraham Lincoln."

Most of these twentieth-century Negro leaders had succeeded in convincing themselves that Lincoln had been slow in striking at slavery because he had preferred to follow his own timetable, and not because he did not care about the slave. Now and then a Negro voice might cry out, "He was not our man," but such a minority report was not even discussed and died because no one would second the motion. Negroes of high degree, as well as of low, seemed to agree with the Lincoln sentiment expressed by their greatest poet, Paul Laurence Dunbar:

Earth learned of thee what Heav'n already knew,
And wrote thee down among her treasured few!

CHAPTER FIFTEEN

America: A Cultural Exchange

This final chapter takes us from a general discussion of the American black in American culture and society to descriptions of areas in which the black has excelled during the late nineteenth and early twentieth centuries, and finally presents descriptions of black accomplishments in all areas of American life since the 1930s. There is a statement in the headnote to the last selection in this chapter that "Since the articles represent only portions of the sources from which they were taken, you might be interested in going to the original sources for more information." Keep this thought in mind as you read Chapter Fifteen, since space limitations have restricted the amount of material that can be included here.

The Negro's Role in American Society

Margaret Just Butcher

The black person in America today continues to represent all minority groups in our society in the struggle for full and equal participation in American life. The Affirmative Action committees in business, industry, and education reflect one attempt our society is making to equalize opportunities for blacks and other minorities. Blacks have been, and continue to be, the catalysts in reducing political, social, and cultural discrepancies. The following article, excerpted from *The Negro in American Culture* by Margaret Just Butcher, traces some of these black attempts to obtain freedom and equal opportunity that have helped to advance democracy.

The right and most effective way to look at the Negro's relationship to American culture is to consider it not as an isolated race matter and minority group concern, but rather in the context of the whole of American culture. Thereupon one inevitably—and rightly—becomes involved with the history and fortunes of both the majority and the minority groups. These fortunes are not separate; nor can they be separately evaluated or understood. They overlap and interlock as, through successive generations, the lives of the Negroes and whites are intermingled. Together, and only together, they have interwoven the vital, sturdy patterns of American society. Together they have been responsible for both the basic characteristic structure of American society and the dynamic social changes that distinguish a democratic society from others. In short, to understand either the Caucasian majority or the Negro minority in America we must trace and follow the history, be it social or cultural, of each. To undertake, as we do here, a cultural history of the American Negro, it is as necessary to describe the impact of the Negro on America as it is to consider the impact of America on the Negro.

Whether the social or the artistic aspect of the culture be our focus of immediate interest, we shall discover on closer scrutiny that the two will be found vitally interrelated. To cope with a subject matter as involved in historical happenings and sociological complications as that which relates to the American Negro, one must constantly keep in mind American institutional life as it conditions artistic and intellectual activity. It would profit the historian and the sociologist to take this linkage into account more frequently; certainly in the study of the Negro it is a significant, though frequently neglected factor. For the culture historian consideration of the correlation is imperative. The literature of slavery, for example, throws much additional light on the nature of slavery. Yet there is an almost completely neglected body of fugitive-slave narratives. Consideration of the slave narratives, as well as of other available reflections of the slave mind and imagination, would supply a great lack in our history—a sufficient and adequate account of the Negro's own reaction to slavery. Again, the traditional stereotypes of the Negro, though in many instances contrary to fact, nevertheless reveal, more subtly than statutes and historical incidents, the inner complexes of the white mind in its attitudes and policies toward the Negro. A stubborn stereotype may block understanding and adjustment for decades because the way two groups of people think and feel about each other is often more influential and determinative than what the two groups actually are. Finally, changes of social attitude are at least as important as changes of social condition, and such changes, reflected in literature and art, are often the best barometers at hand to signal shifts in the character and quality of race relations.

The main approach in this book is from the side of ideological and artistic culture, but as frequently as possible an attempt has been made to correlate the parallel lines of social and artistic development. Indeed, though one of the main intentions is to document the considerable, but little known, contributions of the Negro to American arts and letters, we must include consideration of the Negro in his more fundamental connections with our social culture, and we must consider too his important impact upon the artistic culture of the nation. Although generally unrecognized, the Negro minority's counterinfluence upon the life and culture of the dominant white majority has been considerable in both degree and extent. Indeed, at several points in the national history the Negro's influence has exerted decisive effect upon the artistic and social culture of the nation as a whole.

Few would care to deny or even to minimize the momentous effects of slavery on our institutional culture. This assumption is valid, I think, whether one looks upon slavery as the moral, the humane, or the economic issue of the Civil War. Slavery challenged "head-on" two of the most basic of our national traditions:

political freedom and free labor. In his study *The American Philosophy of Equality,* T. V. Smith, a keen analyst, concurs: "Slavery proved to be the first great institutional test of the equality doctrine." Many would also understand, if they reflected deeply enough, the way in which the slow, consistently steady rise of the Negro's status since emancipation in 1863 has served as a base-level fulcrum for new freedom and wider foundations for American democracy. The Negro's progression from chattel to freedman, to legal citizenship, to increasing equality of rights and opportunities, to accepted neighbor and compatriot represents a dramatic testament to democracy's positive and dynamic character.

The Supreme Court Decision of May 17, 1954, is not to be interpreted as an isolated social, moral, or humanitarian phenomenon. It was a completely logical and foreseeable climax to the Negro's long struggle for equality of opportunity and for decisive recognition of the fact that color per se is not the measure of human worth or dignity. But here again the Decision was by no means a "Negro victory" in the literal sense. Those who recognize the insidious effects of segregation recognize them in reciprocal terms. Thus, the Education Decision of May 17 has significant and meaningful implications for the white majority. The progress of the Negro since his emancipation has in large measure involved, as the May 17 Decision exemplifies, revision or radically changed interpretation of the organic law of the land. Willis J. King sums up this point succinctly: "One of the significant contributions made by the Negro to American life has been the way in which his presence has helped in the development and extension of the American idea of Democracy." Stated differently, the test of a democracy's meaningfulness is to be found in the impact of its intrinsic philosophy upon minority groups. The shift in philosophy and intent of the Supreme Court, manifest in what Commager has described as "The New Jurisprudence," has paved the way for the formidable succession of affirmative civil-rights decrees in recent years. Finally, with reference to the Negro's influence upon America's culture, not many realize, but all should know how much evidence there is of the transforming effects of Negro folk idioms in such major areas of the American arts as music, dance, and folklore. These influences have been for the most part dominant, fundamental, and enduring, rather than merely superficial or transitory.

It may be safely concluded then, if these claims be successfully justified, that the Negro, in spite of his deprivations and handicaps—indeed in some respects because of them—has played two constructive roles in the course of his more than three hundred years in America. He has acted as what might be termed a potent artistic leaven in American arts and letters; he is serving, in the apt phrase of J. Saunders Redding, as a powerful "catalyst of American democracy." Recalling the extent of the Negro's physical and intellectual participation in the struggle for his own freedom as slave fugitive, slave insurrectionist, anti-slavery writer and orator, Union soldier in the Civil War, and civil-rights contestant thereafter, we might well add that the Negro is best identified as a proud collaborator in the advance of American democracy. Putting aside for the moment the matter of the Negro's artistic role and influence, let us turn to the even more important effect of the Negro in America on the social and institutional culture of the nation.

Really, it should be taken for granted that any minority as large and long-established as the American Negro would exert considerable influence on the national life. The Negro is America's largest and oldest minority group: for the past hundred years he has steadily averaged a fraction under or over one tenth of the population. In colonial times this percentage was higher; at the time of the first census (1790) Negroes comprised a full fifth of the population. In thinking of the situation realistically, we must add the factor of the Negro's heavy concentration in the southern states, in some of which ratios approximating half of the population have been and still are prevalent, and where in certain localities the Negro, on a strictly numerical basis, becomes an actual (though, of course, in matters of material power, an impotent) majority. Judging by relative rates of population growth, this racial ratio promises to remain nearly constant indefinitely, so that it has been reasonably suggested that to visualize the situation we think of the Negro as "America's tenth man." At the census figure for 1950, this was an impressive sum total of nearly fifteen million persons.

But the cultural and institutional importance of the Negro is not solely or even principally a matter of statistical ratios. His importance stems from his unusual historical experience as a group and from his peculiar position in American society. Both have paradoxically caused the Negro to exert an influence disproportionate to his numbers and his social status. To the extent to which the Negro was oppressed and segregated, his folk life became more distinct and its reactions more distinctive; the more slavery spread and deepened, the more the Negro became the concern and obsession of his enslavers. The more he was made an exception to the general condition, the stronger a moral contradiction he became in both the conscience and the institutional life of the country. As Gunnar Myrdal so penetratingly put it, the plight and predicament of the black minority became in time the "great American dilemma," a dramatic clash between incompatible ideologies and traditions: slavery and freedom, caste and consistent democracy.

Indeed, when the American colonists, in their hard task of conquering the new continent, reached out desperate hands to the African slave trade for conscripted labor, they took hold of one of the most fateful strands in American history. Simultaneously with the founding of a society destined to become a great political democracy, these men imported democracy's greatest antithesis—slavery and hereditary bondage. They could never have anticipated that the introduction of slave labor would in time produce civil war, precipitate American society's foremost social problem, and in recurring crises threaten American democracy's vitality and influence.

It was only by historical accident that a white indentured servant class did not bear the brunt of the labor load of the European settlement of this continent. In fact, the earliest Negro importees shared substantially the status and rights of the indentured English bondsmen and convict debtors, with the privilege of reselling their labor by contract and purchasing their freedom by individual enterprise. Hundreds of Negroes rose thereby to become free men and, sad to relate, in a few instances themselves became slaveowners. These facts show how basic the principle of economic caste was in the historical inception of American slavery and explain why, for both the Negro and the country at large, free labor was at stake with political freedom and citizenship in the issues that this antidemocratic tradition projected into the heart of American society. Only as it came into the American scheme, and again as it passed out in a life-and-death struggle over common human liberties, was slavery to be seen in its truest light, with the human issues dominant and the racial factor almost irrelevant. Indeed, the die of slavery was cast not primarily by difference of race, but by undemocratic ideas and class practices in the early scheme of American society. In two hundred and fifty years, however, slavery as the particular plight of the black man could mask its institutional inconsistencies behind the black exception thus protecting the expression of fundamental democratic principles which had been contradicted for many generations. Thomas Jefferson, clear-sighted democrat that he was, had the right emphasis when he said that when he considered slavery he "trembled for his country." The presence of the Negro, with outright purchase and an indelible color difference to confirm it, allowed this negation of democracy to develop into a deeper and more tragic scheme than that of mere class exploitation. The Negro took the brunt of transplanted feudalism, enabling it to be diverted from the backs of the poorer white settlers.

Too often, the American mind, lacking knowledge of these facts, and so without proper historical perspective on American slavery, follows the great cover-up tradition that makes the Negro bear the blame as well as the brunt of the situation; often it is assumed that his very presence in the body politic has constituted the race problem. J. Saunders Redding's shrewd pleasantry that Negroes were the only element of the American population which came by special invitation, passage paid, has scarcely sufficed to drive home the sober realization that the Negro was desperately needed and humbly but importantly effective in the settlement of the New World. His warrant for being here is beyond question, doubly so because his mass service of basic labor in the wide zone of the slave system was unrewarded for seven or eight generations. It is estimated that before 1800 the number of Negroes brought to America in the slave trade was more than twenty times that of all European immigrants combined. The terrific toll of lives taken may be realized from the fact that by the first census of 1790 the black population in the United States was only one fifth of the total. "The wealth of the New World," says Edwin Embree, "came largely by the sweat of this new race." In his *Gift of Black Folk*, W. E. B. Du Bois rightly rates the Negro's labor as his first substantial contribution. No matter how the benefits be reckoned, it remains a fact that the Negro's begrudged share in American civilization was dearly bought and paid for in advance of delivery.

Slavery, moreover, planted the Negro deep in the subsoil of American life and made him culturally a basic American. The domestic and rural form that slavery took necessitated particularly intimate group contacts and both forced and made possible the rapid assimilation of the white man's civilization, language, religion, and folkways. This cultural transfusion was considerably reinforced by wide interbreeding and admixture of blood: according to the rough evidence of the census count of mulattoes, about twenty per cent of the Negro population is of obviously mixed descent. In scientific investigation of sample Negro groups today, Melville J. Herskovits discovers an even higher percentage of mixture and estimates scarcely a one-third remnant of pure-blood Negroes in the total of fifteen million. On both physical and the cultural bases, American slavery is revealed as the institution directly responsible for undermining its own chief contentions about color and cultural difference. Originally there were wide physical and cultural differences between the two races. Now there is mainly a contrary-to-fact tradition of difference. Until quite recently this tradition was embraced by those who stubbornly tried to deny the trends and consequences of slavery's own handiwork.

While breaking down these natural barriers, slavery and its supporting code of prejudice erected artificial and tyrannical substitutes. Doctrines of race difference and inferiority and a rigid etiquette of color caste were formulated. The sense of difference operated most forcefully in situations where actual difference was least in evidence; the white majority became fanatical wherever the Negro claimed the rewards of conformity or the privileges of assimilation. Out of these peculiar paradoxes the characteristic American variety of race prejudice was born or, rather, manufactured. In the official apologia for slaveholding, a doctrine was needed to offset every real and potential claim for the Negro's rights as a human being and citizen: it was necessary to devise counterclaims that nullified any expression of humanitarian or civil concern for the slave.

Against the country's debt to the Negro for service and labor was set the Negro's presumably incalculable indebtedness for the benefits of the white man's civilization. Christianity represents a strong case in point. It was indeed a spirit-saving solace, but emphasis on its moral benefactions was used both to inculcate submissiveness and to rationalize slavery as a social practice. Eventually, in the "Bible argument for slavery," Christianity was demeaned into justifying the very institution itself. Furthermore, to discount the Negro's really remarkable assimilation of the rudiments of American civilization, the legend of his "nonassimilability" was popularized. This legend wrote off the Negro's accomplishments as mere "imitativeness" and thwarted further effort on the score of "inherent mental inferiority." The doctrine attributing to inherent inferiority the Negro's imposed handicaps and disabilities has developed so strong a hold upon the American public mind that only in the last decade or so have scientific study and objective comparisons made any headway in correcting it. There persists also the fallacious doctrine of the Negro's childlike dependence upon a guiding paternalism. Rarely is there a frank recognition of the fact that the feudal system of slavery and its semifeudal aftermath depended in large measure upon the perpetuation of paternalistic bonds. Fortunately, the Negro has resisted this old dependence with increasing vigor, and his present-day attitude renders the "doctrine" completely specious.

The worst paradox and perhaps the saddest irony of all, in the pattern of masking the facts of racial admixture and insulating its social consequences, was the promulgating of the doctrine of white ethnic integrity. The promulgation and arbitrary maintenance of this unscientific concept negated the normal claims of the mixed-blood group—claims that generally have been recognized in every other culture where considerable miscegenation has taken place. This last policy needs close analysis. It has been crucial in determining the patterns of the social and intellectual culture of the United States. It is the historical reason for the absence of a buffer mulatto group in the North American racial situation, and so constitutes the great cultural divide between the Anglo-Saxon and the Latin cultures in the matter of race relations. However, it is a difference we should approach objectively, for it has both good points and bad. Among the former, one may mention that because in the United States any traceable degree of Negro blood has classified a person as "sociologically" a Negro, a most unusual—an almost solid—psychological solidarity of the whole Negro minority has been produced.

These rationalizing dogmas of "race integrity" and "pure" Anglo-Saxon culture have had wide, deep consequences that must for a moment give us pause. In the first place, they have concealed the actual facts of the historical development of a mixed race and a composite culture. By becoming traditional in American ways of thinking, these dogmas have been the taproot of our most characteristic variety of chauvinism, the stock notion of American culture as exclusively Anglo-Saxon. This bias has affected a much wider area of group relations than those between white and Negro, and has indeed until quite recently disparaged many other non-Anglo-Saxon strains and traditions in the national culture. Further, the same attitudes have unquestionably fed and intensified the mind-sets of race prejudice and have extended themselves into a more generalized color complex. This complex has adversely dominated our external cultural relations, particularly those with the entire non-white world.

There are other more immediate reasons for keeping in mind the sharp difference between the Latin and the Anglo-Saxon racial attitudes and codes in America. First of all, it explains why emancipation by no means eradicated race prejudice. Under different circumstances it might have been wiped out in a generation or so; instead, in some instances emancipation actually intensified race prejudice. Racial dogmas became chronic; they could not die a natural death with the death of the system that had produced them. This psychological aftermath of slavery, persisting as the philosophy of the color line, has had the most serious consequences in the period from emancipation to the present. It still offers more resistance to the Negro's progress than all the practical difficulties of social advance combined, and it still obstructs many normal realignments of social, political, and economic adjustment. "Keeping the Negro in his place," or its compromise form of compartmentalized "segregation," amounts to prolonging in clandestine form the regime of slavery and leads to the same negative results for the Negro and for American society at large. Dual standards and biracial partitioning add up to the denial of democracy in actual practice and have led inevitably to an undemocratic and self-frustrating policy of keeping one tenth of the population in a condition of artificially arrested development.

These generalizations, basically true, must not give the misleading impression that there was no counterpoint of dissent and protest on the matter of slavery among the Anglo-Saxons of American society. From early colonial days, there were anti-slavery thought and anti-slavery action. The earliest of these came from Quaker sources: John Woolman, Anthony Benezet, and others urged the Friends to have no part in slaveholding. They were followed by a small dissenter minority, north and south, expressing the awakening conscience of the more radically evangelical Christian churches. Notable were Bishop Asbury and the proselyting Wesleyans. Here were the beginnings of what in several generations would culminate formidably as the organized protest of the abolitionists.

Significantly, too, in 1789, the very year of the nation's founding, Negro protest began with the anonymous publication of an anti-slavery pamphlet, *On Slavery*. The author was a Negro freeman who discreetly hid his identity under the pen name "Othello." Researchers surmise that he may have been the phenomenal Benjamin Banneker, who, in 1791, addressed a long letter in similar vein to Thomas Jefferson. The little-known but significant exchange of correspondence (for Jefferson replied civilly and sympathetically, stating that he had sent a copy to M. de Condorcet, Secretary of the Academy of Sciences at Paris and a member of "The Philanthropic Society," "because I consider it a document to which your whole colour had a right for their justification against the doubts which have been entertained of them") may have had much to do with Jefferson's doubts and fears about the rectitude and wisdom of slavery. Negro protest continued bravely but sporadically until it climaxed a generation later in the noteworthy collaboration of men like Samuel Ringold Ward, Charles Lenox Remond, Henry Highland Garnet, and Frederick Douglass. But all this was at best representative of only a small segment of the population, the majority of which in the North tacitly acquiesced in slavery. The South, despite a brave but minute quota of Southern abolitionists, was, of course, overwhelmingly committed to "the peculiar institution."

There is not only the interesting divergence between the Anglo-Saxon and Latin attitudes toward differences of race; there are also important divergences in their typical social and cultural consequences. The Latin tradition is happily free from a priori prejudice: there is more likelihood of individuals being judged on their merits rather than in terms of categories. The triple inheritance of the French Revolution, Catholic universalism, and Latin social tolerance doubtless is responsible for this democratic attitude, without which outstanding accomplishments and the ready recognition of individual Negroes according to merit in Latin and Latin-American societies could never have taken place. One need only recall the Chevalier Saint-Georges; General Dumas and his even greater son, Alexandre Dumas, in France; such pioneer patriots as Plácido, Calixto García, and José Martí in Cuba; Machado de Assis, founder of realism in Brazilian letters, and Mario de Andrade, until recently Brazil's leading contemporary novelist.

It is evident that the Anglo-Saxon code of race is based on a priori prejudice, and really pre-judges the individual on the arbitrary basis of the mass status of his ethnic group. It does make occasional exceptions, often grudgingly and as "exceptions." More often, however, it forces the advancing segments of the group back to the level and limitations of the less advanced. This hard code has led to some unforeseen and unintended democratic consequences. By forcing the advance-guard of a minority back upon its people, it eventually forges mass organization for group progress out of the discipline of solidarity. The outstanding individual, in the majority of instances still linked to the common lot, is impressed into group leadership, and as he achieves recognition, becomes a human shuttle threading a binding strand of progress. Should his social conscience relax in the satisfactions of success, discrimination would resaddle him with his moral obligation to the group.

So the Latin code, while it metes out readier justice to the individual, does so at the price of an unhappy divorce of the elite from the masses. On the other hand, the Anglo-Saxon code, seriously handicapping the individual and his immediate chances for success, forces, despite its intentions to the contrary, a bond of group solidarity, and unavoidable responsibility for and toward the group. This is a necessary though painful, condition of mass progress. Oddly enough, in this hemisphere, both policies were laid down by slaveowning societies before the abolition of slavery. One saw in the more favorable condition and aspiration of the mulatto a menacing advance that must be firmly blocked by a solid wall of prejudice. The other, for the most part, saw in the differential treatment of the *mestizo* the strategy of the buffer class, and therefore granted him considerably more opportunity and recognition than was allowed the blacks, but always something less than was standard for privileged whites. Neither was really democratic in intention. One policy produced an out-and-out race problem; the other policy contributed to a class problem. One system, the Latin, has vindicated a basic condition of cultural democracy: the open career for talent and relatively unhampered mobility and recognition for rising individual aspiration and achievement. The Anglo-Saxon developments have, however, taught an increasingly important essential of a democratic social order: the responsibility of the elite for the masses.

Instead of gradually liquidating prejudice after emancipation, our American behavior, based on the intransigent, rigid, Anglo-Saxon tradition, has tended to intensify racial tensions as the white majority faced the ever-increasing challenges of minority progress. Yet in spite of this compounded discouragement and opposition, the career of the Negro in the United States since 1863 has shown an epic achievement, only some of which—the cultural and artistic—falls within the scope of this book. Broadly regarded, this achievement is American as well as Negro: the common dynamic of American life and civilization has entered into its making. As already pointed out, the Negro is typically American in his group values and objectives, in his spirit and motivations; perhaps he is more American than several other minority groups, by virtue of his long residence and intimate contacts. Discrimination and undemocratic treatment have often operated as goads and special pressures instead of as the intended discouragement and handicaps. The net outcome has been a gradually increased rate and range of progress. Partly through his own patient endurance and effort, and partly through saving alliances with the forces of moral and social liberalism, the Negro has been able to make phenomenal advances in both material and immaterial culture.

The American dilemma deepens with such continued progress of the Negro minority; its paradoxes increasingly defy concealment as the older justifications of backwardness and incompetence disappear. In the light of the rapid general advance of the whole society, weaknesses stand out the more conspicuously. With slavery's obvious inequalities outlawed and largely overcome, disfranchisement, unequal civil privileges, segregation, and discriminatory treatment loom up as even greater contradictions. The economic and cultural aspects of the inconsistency become equally obvious: the shortsightedness of the effort to maintain economic caste in a highly mobile and open-enterprise society, and the futility, in an essentially composite culture, of a chauvinism that blindly prefers an ethnically flattering fiction. Cultural democracy is an important and inescapable corollary of political and social democracy, and it involves an open door for the acceptance of minority contributions and for the full recognition of the minority contributors.

Under such circumstances the Negro minority retains today, as in the past, its significant and symbolic position at the center of America's struggle for the full development of the tradition of freedom. For the core of the issue is wherever undemocratic inconsistencies exist, and the majority stakes in its progressive solution are fully as great as those of the minority.

We must, finally, take note of the fact that today the critical frontier of racial issues is no longer domestic, but in a vital and pressing sense international. Indeed, in the opinion of all competent observers, the international front of race has been permanently joined to the home front of race, with America's moral leadership completely dependent upon the consistency of our democratic practices with our democratic creed and professions. The United States is already under heavy past-and-present suspicion of inveterate and unrenounced racialism. Any discrepancy—political, social, or cultural—threatens to undermine American prestige and moral authority by alienating the confidence, respect, and collaboration of the warrantably sensitive and skeptical non-white world. With all our national power and present strength, over against the huge two-thirds majority of the human race we are in the long run ourselves a rather hapless minority. It must be conceded, and can no longer be concealed, that racial differentials on any level of group living amount to a self-contradicting double standard of democracy.

In 1860, when democracy's vital frontier was the Mason and Dixon dividing line, fate cast the Negro in the role of a critical test of the domestic consistency of democracy in the national Union; today, with the Atlantic, the Pacific and the Rio Grande as cultural boundaries, the Negro is cast very similarly in an international role, involving American democracy's moral and cultural integrity on a world scale and with world influence and leadership at stake. A review of the cultural status of the Negro and the historical steps in its progressive improvement is without doubt the most accurate way to determine the achieved realizations and further prospects of spiritual and cultural democracy among us.

The Negro in American Culture

Margaret Just Butcher

This selection, while tracing the American blacks' "acculturation," perhaps reinforces some of the stereotypes present in much of our literature. Margaret Just Butcher describes black accomplishments in American culture primarily in terms of art, music, and humor. After reading this selection, decide whether or not black folk art and music are, in fact, as relevant to the black in American culture today as they might have been during the late nineteenth and early twentieth centuries.

In a consideration of the Negro folk, we fortunately can leave the risky though necessary level of all-inclusive generalization about "the Negro." At best, such generalization can give us only the barest common denominators, the broadest trends, and the diffuse features characteristic of all composite portraits. The subject of the Negro folk, on the other hand, has flesh-and-bone concreteness, and promises to reveal more of the human reality and texture of Negro life and character. The Negro folk products also reflect most vividly the basic group experience and, as anonymous and unsophisticated mass reactions, possess the substance and flavor of what was the common life of more than three fifths of the whole Negro population during more than two thirds of its group history. These folk expressions, of which unhappily we have only a chance-preserved remnant, give us the generic Negro as nothing else can. Paradoxically enough, because of their deeply original and creative character, American culture is most indebted, above all other folk sources, to this lowly but distinctive level of Negro peasant experience.

Even the life of the ante-bellum Negro had wide contrasts and diversities: it was not confined wholly to the common lot of the plantation slave and field laborer. Completely different and separate, of course, was the life of that very considerable group of free Negroes, who after 1790 constituted over one fifth of the Negro population and by 1860 totaled almost a half-million (488,000). Most of these were safely concentrated in the North, but there were a few on the frontier and in upland settlements. Still fewer were precariously located in the mid-South and in oasis sanctuaries like Charleston, Savannah, Mobile, and New Orleans, where by right of free papers and "passes" they somehow held their status. They clung to this precious and often dearly bought station with desperate middle-class conviction and respectability. Often they were so jealous of their privileges and so fearful of the threat of slavery that they remained stiffly apart from their slave brethren, outwardly indifferent to their predicament. They were, as might be expected, desperate conformists, staunchly conventional and Puritan for the most part, disdainful of the manner, speech, and what were to them the demeaning relaxations of the shouting, boisterous, uninhibited, openhearted Negro peasant. In the North, free Negroes were occasionally engaged in fellowship with liberal whites either in open abolitionist protest or in underground anti-slavery action. But except for such few brave souls, the free Negroes were fully preoccupied in cautious, conservative, conventional living.

There was, next, at the top level of the larger slave society, a small, anomalous segment of household retainers and servitors who lived apart in comfort, symbiotically absorbed in upper-class manners and values. They shared the life, the refinements, and the outlooks of the master class and upheld at a respectful distance the foibles, feuds, and substantial traditions and interests of "their" families. Often, though far from always, they were natural sons and daughters of the masters, and were discreetly conscious of their fathers and half-sisters and half-brothers. They carefully cultivated proper, restrained manners and conservative standards, disdaining the boisterous, carefree ways of the other slaves, whom they regarded as "common field hands." More than they despised these black "pariahs of the big gate" they despised the poor whites, who, as "white trash," became the scapegoats of their own humiliations. Proudly parasitic, these "house Negroes" were culturally sterile, cultivating the airs of "ladies" and "gentlemen," though generally in a bad imitation of the conduct of the masters. From time to time a few, manumitted, became detached to join (usually with a small patrimony) the more useful class of free Negroes. At times, too, this group, with its education by contact, bred such an outstanding talent as that developed by Phillis Wheatley. Yet, inevitably, a Phillis Wheatley was labeled "an exception" and was usually haunted by the superstition that all talents came from white-inherited characteristics. Phillis Wheatley herself, being pure African, did not suffer this embarrassment, but rather was credited as being imitative—of the whites. Typical, then, with this stratum of Negro life, was its perplexity and confusion of "belonging" and "not belonging," alternating moods of pride and boasting with moods of silent shame. How could they have been expected to escape the cynicism and bitterness that illegitimacy and its imposed badge of psychic and social separateness levied on them? Only occasionally was there a full acceptance of being a Negro on the part of one who usually ripened into a crusading, militant Negro, a race-organizer, and a bitter, implacable foe of slavery.

Below this thin upper level there was a thicker mid-class layer of lower servants and artisans, considerably privileged except on those symbolic occasions when slavery exacted its ceremonial rituals. The artisans had necessary exemption from the common lot by virtue of their skills and usefulness; they built and mended, worked and even supervised, like trusties in their institutional prison. In old age, after years of faithful service, they became privileged characters and prize exhibits of slavery's benevolence. In the household, with the exception of the chore underlings, they, too, had status: there were the "Mammy" nurse, the cook, the gardener, and even the most useful supernumerary, the messenger and tattletale, who often doubled as plantation spy. They knew their rank and held it except when they were subject to punishment. They enjoyed open favor of personal intimacy (after etiquette obeisance) and had a natural security of things by right of the appetites to which they catered. The exception was the ill-fated concubine, whom a Puritan culture condemned to an anomalous status. At the lowest level, and really supporting all on his bent and lash-scarred back, was the Negro peasant. He sank deeper and deeper into the subsoil of plantation slavery as slavery's weight became harsher and heavier. Harried by day in the fields, and only half relaxed in slave quarters except on festive occasions, the masses of Negro slaves toiled, suffered, and, by some miracle of emotional endurance and compensation, survived. As they shared their burdens, their folk living took on the most intimate sort of collective community. From these depths and pressures arose crude folk reactions expressive in an elemental fashion. These folk products have preserved for us the unique quality of the Negro's mass experience.

It must be understood that slavery was not, even on the average plantation, quite so manorial as this; but such was its basic model. Although it ran a realistic gamut from the frontier holding of a single proprietor with one or two slave helpers to the late-period cotton barony with over one thousand slaves and a corps of driver-overseers, the South's "peculiar institution" assumed the characteristic form here indicated wherever prosperity permitted.

Throughout the many generations of mutually dependent living, contacts between black and white, though not so acknowledged, were close and intimate because of the domestic character of the American slave system. Blacks and whites were also actively reciprocal despite a great outer show of social distance and an elaborate etiquette of social untouchability. Southern tradition has never denied the closeness, but has always rejected any notion of reciprocal exchange. It is a fallacy to assume that the overlord influences the peasant, but remains uninfluenced by him. In this particular historical instance, the undeniable intimacies of the Southern scheme of living, reinforced by considerable crossbreeding, forged bonds too vital to be negated by caste custom and etiquette and too humanly contagious not to transcend "official" color prejudice. Ironically enough, the Old South itself and its insistently intimate domestication of the Negro were mainly responsible. And so, even in his lowly condition of servitude, with its imposed condition of cultural unawareness and intellectual illiteracy, the Negro became a potent folk influence. By planting him in the heart of its domestic life, Southern society provided the base for the Negro's clandestine and unforeseen effect upon its own folkways and institutions.

The orthodox version of race contacts in the South assigns to Negroes solely a one-way direction of cultural traffic and influence, on the understandable but hardly warranted assumption that the Negro, deliberately cut off from the sustenance of his native African culture and fed on the crumbs of an adopted one, had no cultural assets with which to make a contribution. With regard to formalized culture, this was indeed true, but folk culture is another sort of social plant. It has an atmospheric mode of growth and propagation. Within little more than the first generation after his arrival, sturdily surviving slavery's rude transplanting, the Negro rapidly assimilated the basic rudiments of a complex and very alien culture: its English language, its Christian religion, and its Anglo-Saxon mores. The nearly complete loss of his original culture and the resultant vacuumlike emptiness undoubtedly speeded the absorption. The Negro, traditionally credited in this respect with only a "most unusual degree of imitativeness," is really to be credited with phenomenal flexibility and adaptive capacity.

This hasty acculturation, crude as it was, is the outstanding feat of the Negro's group career in America. Considering its handicapped start, one may well concede that it is quite without parallel in human history—certainly on such a mass basis. It is even more significant that within another generation the Negro became originally and vigorously productive at the folk level, and that before very long vital influences from Negroes were weakening the barriers of caste and prejudice. By his characteristic humor, emotional temper, mystic superstitions, contagious nonchalance, amiability, and sentimentality—all of which were later to find expression in typical modes of folk art—the Negro observably colored the general temper and folkways of the American South.

The master class, proud and prejudiced, could, however, under no circumstances take the Negro seriously enough to acknowledge any indebtedness. Its members felt committed to reject one who to them was a legal chattel as well as a hapless, childlike dependent. They even resented any Negro influence that could be recognized as such. But the same society that shut its front doors so relentlessly and raised such formidable barrier of caste, naïvely left its psychological rear doors unguarded. Negro influences came creeping, indeed often crowding, in.

Let us consider a typical instance, that of the humble but triumphant invasion of Negro humor. Behind the humor, seemingly so simple and natural, are a very complex pattern and a complicated social history. Frequently masking sorrow, and sometimes impotent resentment, the Negro's laughter was certainly more often contrived and artificial than natural and spontaneous, despite contrary Southern conviction. Grasping with a desperation that an instinct for survival developed, the Negro early learned the humble, effective art of placating his capricious masters. In time, with the masters' hearty and constant encouragement, the Negroes became established as the South's official jesters. We need assume in this interpretation nothing more sophisticated than the mere adroitness of mother wit, nothing more premeditated than the anticipation of ready rewards for ingratiating behavior. Despite the sad fact that it also led to the most ingrained and contrary-to-fact of all the Southern stereotypes—that of the "happy, contented slave"—this protective mimicry of laughter was for generations an almost infallible psychological weapon of appeal and appeasement for the otherwise defenseless Negro. The South itself occasionally suspected this, as its jocular anecdotes of the Negro's "possum-playing" fully attest. But it yielded, preferring not to spoil the fun by questioning it too deeply. The Southern spirit must often have craved not merely amusement, but also contentment and ease of conscience. Without hurt to its pride and arrogance it often achieved shrewd penance in the capricious kindliness and familiarity evoked by the comradeship of laughter.

Because the comic side of the Negro offered no offense or challenge to the South's tradition of the Negro's subordinate status, it richly colored Southern local and regional culture, and eventually that of the whole nation. The improvised plantation entertainment of ragamuffin groups of dancing, singing, jigging, and grinning slaves, staple amusement of the theaterless South, was the genesis of a major form of the American theater: blackface minstrelsy and its later stepchild, vaudeville. Together they dominated the national stage for a period of at least seventy years (1830–1900). Negro minstrelsy was also destined to become one of America's famous native-culture exports during the latter half of that same period. Despite its broad and frequently misrepresentative caricature, minstrelsy, with its basic idioms of song, dance, and humor, patently reflects its Negro folk origins. It also records the far-reaching consequences of the naïve devices of the Negro folk temperament.

What is of particular interest for the moment is the far different fate of another and even more representative aspect of the Negro folk genius. It must not be overlooked that the comic "jig-song and dance" and the serious, almost tragic "spirituals" were plantation contemporaries. The South that gleefully heard the one must at least have overheard the other. However, the religious folk songs, though equally odd and attractive, did not meet a receptive Southern mood: in fact they ran counter to the stock conception of the Negro's character and status. They are barely mentioned in the whole range of literature of the Pre-Civil War South; in its post-bellum letters they receive only the most casual and indifferent notice. Southerners had been listening to plaintive and rhapsodic fold-singing for generations, but because they listened with cavalier condescension and amused bewilderment they could dismiss the music as just the Negro's "way of carrying on." Although now recognized even by the South as one of its most distinctive regional folk products and as among the rare elements of American native culture, the spirituals could not find recognition and proper appreciation for many years.

At the close of the Civil War, a Northerner, spurred by the sensitive interest of Thomas Wentworth Higginson (colonel of one of the black regiments that served heroically on the Union side), explored with sympathetic curiosity the group life of the Negro freedmen in refugee camps. Noticing what he called "these peculiar but haunting slave songs," he took them seriously and thereby made the momentous discovery of the American Negro's now universally recognized musical genius. He was William Allen, and in 1867, he published *Slave Songs of the United States,* a transcribed collection of the melodies he heard. Out of such chance recovery from generation-long neglect and belittlement, these "slave songs," the unique spiritual portrait of the Negro folk temperament, rose to final recognition and universal acclaim as the incomparable "Negro spirituals."

Even in the Allen transcriptions the precious folk products were only half revealed, for Allen was unable to give adequate notation to the unique folk way of singing them. Only in 1879 was proper interpretation given them by the choral singing of the Fisk Jubilee Singers, a Negro university group. The Jubilee Singers themselves, so under the hypnotism of white disparagement of things wholly and distinctively Negro that they hesitated to put the spirituals on their regular programs, at first gave them as experimental encores and only on request. Not until after the revelation of their profound effect upon musically enlightened audiences, American and European, were the spirituals finally launched on their triumphant career of revealing and vindicating the extraordinary folk genius they so clearly reflect.

Here, then, in epitome, is the story of the Negro as art influence, and of the career of the folk elements in American culture. Negro expression, when flattering and obsequiously entertaining to the majority ego, is readily accepted, and becomes extremely popular in a vulgarized, stereotyped form. When more deeply and fully representative, with undiluted idioms, it has invariably been confronted with apathy and indifference and has been faced with a long struggle for acceptance and appreciative recognition. In the minstrel role, for instance, where at best the Negro was only half himself, at the worst a rough caricature, he was instantly popular and acceptable. The spirituals, in which he was seriously self-expressive, met with long-standing disinterest and misunderstanding. In the arts, as in matters political, economic, and social, the Negro advance has been a slow, tortuous journey from slavery toward freedom. Step by step, and from one province to another, Negro genius and talent have plodded a hard road to freer and more representative artistic self-expression.

In many fields the goal of maturity and freedom has now been achieved or nearly achieved; in some areas the Negro artist is on a parity with his white fellow artists. In a few fields, as in music, the dance, and acting, by reason of an unrivaled quality of expressive control, he has staked out areas of distinctive originality and pre-eminence. But on the whole, the Negro's conquest of the more formal and sophisticated arts—fiction, playwriting, literary and art criticism, and the like— has been slow and hazardous, in part because of his limited cultural opportunities and contacts. Faster progress, as might be expected, has been made in those areas where there was an early start in well-developed folk art. This explains very obviously why the Negro was outstanding in vocal and choral music earlier than he was successful with instrumental music; again, there was a great skill and preference for improvisation as opposed to formal musical composition. The Negro has, in fact, many generally recognized qualities of special excellence in the arts. His talents, however, are best understood and interpreted as the cumulative effects of folk tradition and group conditioning. This interpretation belies the popular hypothesis that some mysterious "folk traits" or native ethnic endowment are responsible for Negro artistic capabilities and expression. What might be called, for lack of a better term, "folk virtuosities" must be credited to the special character and circumstances of the Negro group experience. The artistic "virtuosities" have been passed on by way of social heritage; they are just that: a heritage, not an endowment.

Among these artistic virtuosities may be mentioned what is often referred to as the "gift of spontaneous harmony." This is really a transmitted musical ear-mastery based on group choral singing, and is very like that of the Welsh or Russian peasants. Similarly to be explained is the Negro musician's instrumental versatility in improvisation and inventive sound and rhythm, lying back of the resourceful impromptu musicianship and extraordinary techniques of jazz. Like the phenomenal, unorthodox resources of the gypsy performer, the techniques go back to the ready skills and tricks of the humble folk musician. Other outstanding Negro artistic "gifts" include an unusual fluency of oral expression, both forceful rhetoric and spectacular imagery. The Negro has, also, a marked, almost intuitive, skill in mimicry, pantomime, and dramatic projection. Above all, he has a virtuoso facility in rhythm, both formal and spontaneous, which is the taproot of his notable aptitude in dance and body-control. These, and others to be examined later in greater detail, are indeed characteristic Negro folk qualities, but they have no need of the trite, pseudoscientific explanations so frequently given of them. On the contrary, they suffer from such unscientific and unrealistic implications.

The few but significant African cultural survivals and carry-overs in American Negro life have likewise been too magically conceived as transmissions by heredity. They also have a realistic social explanation. Their supposed innate character is disproved by their relative or complete absence among Negroes in localities where, as in the northern and western United States, the environment favorable for their survival is lacking. The converse proof is the greater prevalence and intensity of such traits in areas like the Caribbean and Brazil, where native African culture was not so ruthlessly broken down, where the racial concentration was denser, and where, most important of all, the more lenient attitudes of Latin culture did not suppress Africanisms as "horribly" venal and pagan.

Negro folk influences have generally exerted themselves with more immediate and lasting effect in the zone of the more tolerant Latin culture, though even there in degrees varying according to local circumstances. In those areas characteristic African patterns in folklore, music, and ritualistic folk customs still survive recognizably intact. For the same reason, as aftereffect of the French tradition in New Orleans, we still find in Louisiana strong survivals both of musical idioms and of such ritualistic customs as "voodoo." On the other hand, broadly speaking, within the radius of the rigid, less tolerant Anglo-Saxon zone (which characteristically reinforced its racial prejudice with cultural disdain) Negro cultural influence, though by no means negligible, is much more indirect. Here, in most cases, the African elements survive only fragmentarily.

There are, however, surviving Africanisms within the borders of Anglo-Saxon communities—the coastal islands of Georgia and the Carolinas and even the vicinity of Charleston, South Carolina, are examples. But these are amply explained—in the case of the islands by their relative isolation and the dense and stable character of their Negro population, in the case of the Charleston region possibly by the cultural differential of its French Huguenot stock, which, though Protestant, was Latin in social attitudes.

With the exception of New Orleans, the United States lacks almost completely the interesting mixed or "creole" cultures so typical of Latin-American contacts with the Negro and, for that matter, with the Indian peoples also. Although biologically the mulatto is conspicuously present in our society, that parallel phenomenon, which Manuel Gonzales so aptly calls the "mulatto culture," is just as conspicuously absent. In marked contrast also with the many *patois* language mergers to the south of us, language crossing has rarely occurred in the United States, again with the exception of New Orleans Creole. Carolina "Gullah," which at one time promised to spread as a Negro pidgin English, is now only an exceptional reservoir of African linguistic survivals with no cultural outlet or influence. The chauvinism and exclusiveness of the Anglo-Saxon code of culture, mainly responsible for this, are deeply ingrained and characteristic. Its aftereffects, resulting in the late maturing and delayed influence not only of the Negro, but also of other minority-group cultures, have thus considerably affected American art and letters. Until comparatively recently this rigid snobbishness has kept the upper levels of American culture "pure," but also, as many are now willing to admit, thin and anemic. Meanwhile, at all other less-guarded levels, as our anthropologists have been discovering, the inevitable osmosis of culture contact has been taking place constantly.

For the double reason of such inhospitable attitudes and the lack of any vitally intact ancestral culture, the American Negro's folk products have had to be fashioned almost wholly from forms and ingredients borrowed from the majority culture. This has had advantages and disadvantages. The compensating advantage has been that, without substantial loss of racial character, Negro folk expression is also characteristically American and, when adopted, has circulated as indigenous to the national culture. Unlike the products of Creole and *patois* culture, it is not felt to be alien or exotic, but is sensed as just another emotional dialect of a common heritage and tradition. Even when the Negro producer has himself not received comparable acceptance, his creations have often been widely and openheartedly accepted. Some indeed, like minstrelsy and jazz, have been so completely and congenially shared that they have taken on national representativeness, and when exported have become known as "American," and not particularly as American Negro, products. After all, this is in accord with our type of composite and democratic culture, especially when, as is now more frequently the case, the Negro artist is being acknowledged and credited along with his own creative productions.

There is the disadvantage: that of being subject, as hybrids of one degree or another, to endless vulgarized exploitation. Jazz and ragtime are obvious examples. As another, the folk sagas of Uncle Remus and others have been watered down to tawdry sentiment and pale banality, their fine folk speech and imagery effaced by insipid, badly transcribed dialect. In spite of all this, the admixture of the Negro temperament and its folk idioms has usually produced something recognizably characteristic by virtue of a distinctive emotional stamp and flavor. In rare cases like the spirituals, the subtle folk alchemy has transformed the borrowed materials into an end-product so uniquely intimate and typical as almost—but not completely—to defy imitation. Even the spirituals have not been entirely exempt from attempted imitation, although fortunately a synthetic spiritual usually rings counterfeit after the first few phrases. More typically, however, the creative Negro folk fusions have fallen, for better or worse, into the public artistic domain. Most notable in this last instance are the style and patterns of ragtime and jazz, which for at least two generations have dominated popular American music and our stage and popular dance. Associated with them has been that contagious succession of new and compelling dance idioms which have enjoyed similar vogue. Only slightly less influential have been the matchless folk balladry of the "blues" and the popularity of many of the secular work songs and folk-tale ballads. Some of them, like *John Henry,* are Negro originals; others, like *Casey Jones* and *Frankie and Johnny,* are remodeled from general American folklore and often have greater power and wider currency than their originals.

The more the cultural rather than the sociological approach to the Negro is emphasized, the more apparent it becomes that the folk products of the American Negro are imperishably fine, and that they constitute a national artistic asset of the first rank. They have survived precariously; much has been lost. Modern research, especially the folk-music-archives project of the Library of Congress, has retrieved a noteworthy remnant. But Uncle Remus and the spirituals are enough to establish the high quality of the unadulterated product. The folk-story background was recovered by such discerning Southern writers as Thomas Cable and Joel Chandler Harris. But modern scholarship has yet to delete the sentimental additions that glossed over the real "folkiness" of the originals. Grateful as we must be to Harris for his timely preservation of the most organic body of Negro folk tale American literature possesses, we cannot help wishing that he had been a more careful and less improvising amanuensis for the mid-Georgia Negro peasant whom he knew and liked so well. For when the contemporary folklorist arrived on the scene with his scientific attitudes and skills, Uncle Remus and his kind had all but vanished.

The heritage of the religious and secular folk song and dance was saved by the Negroes themselves, beginning, as we have already seen, with the work of the Fisk Jubilee Singers. Their effort, dating from 1878, has culminated since 1900 in the work of an outstanding succession of such Negro musicians as Harry T. Burleigh, Nathaniel Dett, Rosamond and James Weldon Johnson, John Work, Jr., Roland Hayes, and Hall Johnson, all of whom have labored to preserve and promote the folk music. Some have done it through careful transcriptions of Negro folk song; others have created elaborate formal composition based on folk themes. Through the creative work of the musicians and in increasingly competent musicology, critically interpreting this most important folk phase of American music, we are now in a position to appraise its genuine worth. Rated as finely representative of its historical source and setting, this folk treasure is regarded as even more precious in its potential value as material for fresh artistic reworking. Consequently, contemporary musicians and folklorists, Negro and white, are turning back more and more to early Negro folk music. For the Negro musician it has served as a special asset, especially since the onset in the 1920's of the "New Negro" movement, which established as a basic objective the artist's return to Negro folk materials.

This claim to being the most important body of American folk music is well supported by comparison with the competitor traditions: the so-called "hillbilly" tunes, dances, and ballads of the "mountain white," the "cowboy" songs and ballads of the ranch country, and the less-known but richly potential Spanish-Indian folk materials of the Southwest border. Without minimizing any of these, one may easily concede that none is comparable in either range of artistry or scope of influence to the many-sided, perennially influential Negro tradition. The balladry of the mountain culture is of great value and interest, particularly as a fine survival of old Scotch-Irish and English lore and folkways, but its musical and dance idioms are, in comparison with Negro idioms, mediocre and monotonously shallow. By right of kinship and racial affinity, however, the mountain culture should have been the preference of the South. But the Southern patricians looked down on the "poor whites" and disdained their culture. Only in the upland retreats away from the pressures of this condescension did the Appalachian culture become assertive enough to flourish, and even there it was inbred and somewhat anemic.

Paradoxically, then, the South, by culturally rejecting the "poor whites" and patriarchically accepting the Negro (on its own terms, which included keeping the Negro "in his place"), paved the way for Negro folkways to become the peasant culture of nearly three fourths of its geographic area. The plantation system dominated the entire lowland agrarian region and, with its semifeudal regime and the relation of the Negro masses to it, provided the closest approximation in American social history to the conditions and social climate of peasantry. The United States has never possessed a true peasant class: the geographic and the class mobility of almost all elements of the population precluded the slow compounding of one generation on the other. Even the Negro, whose masses did live for generations in a static, stratified way, shared, to a reduced degree, the typical American experience and privilege of place and class mobility. After emancipation, he underwent wave after wave of migration, intersectional to the North and Midwest, intrasectional from the plantations and farms to the Southern cities. But certainly during slavery, and in many of the more rural areas of the South thereafter, it was the Negro's hard lot to remain static from one generation to the next and thus to approximate a peasant class. This social experience, if analyzed in some detail, can explain both the peculiar character and the unusual strength of the Negro folk influence.

This fate, which was and to some extent still is the Negro's basic ordeal and handicap, had one lone compensation. The immobility, reinforced by the psychological weight of prejudice, developed an unusual degree of group solidarity, tended to preserve the characteristic folk values, and intensified the Negro's traditional modes of expression. Out of rejection and oppression there evolved emotional distinctiveness; out of persecution and suffering there evolved unique compensatory ways of making life livable. Until recently, then, caste prejudice has considerably insulated the Negro folkways from the powerful standardizing processes of general American living. With the aboriginal Indian folkways pushed to the periphery of American society and concentrated on reservations (which did not occur in Central and South America), the Negro folk offerings stand out in the rather colorless amalgam of the general population as among the most distinctive spiritual elements in American culture.

By virtue of these folk qualities and their artistic manifestations, the foundations of which were well laid before the end of slavery, the Negro has made America considerably his cultural debtor. For here in the United States there has been no exception to the historical rule that the roots of a national culture are in its soil and its peasantry. Accordingly, some of the most characteristic features of American culture are derivatives of the folk life and spirit of this darker tenth of the population. This claim, first made in 1922 by James Weldon Johnson in this famous preface to *The Book of American Negro Poetry* has never been challenged seriously. The inventory of this humble but influential contribution is impressive: the spirituals, Uncle Remus, a whole strain of distinctive humor, some of the most typical varieties of Southern folk balladry, a major form and tradition of the American theater (the minstrel and vaudeville), and practically all of the most characteristic idioms of modern American popular music and dance. Many of these idioms, of course, have been blended with elements from the majority culture, sometimes for the better, sometimes for the worse; but their Negro origin and distinctive uniqueness are now universally acknowledged. This adds up to a patterning of a substantial part of the native American art forms and to an unusually large share in molding and sustaining the entertainment life of the whole nation. Strange trick of destiny this, that the group of the population most subject to oppression and its sorrows should furnish so large a share of the population's joy and relaxation!

These contributions stretch out, of course, over a wide span of time and a variety of social conditions, but divide naturally into two phases. The first is a true folk period of slavery, the second a post-slavery period in which, in addition to continued folk production, creative artists, Negro and white, have engaged in extensive elaboration and reworking of the folk materials. Only a small, precious remnant of the first phase survives: much more was undoubtedly produced and then irretrievably lost. Nevertheless, the scant fragments of Uncle Remus, the spirituals, and a few older-generation seculars give us a revealing portrait of the ante-bellum Negro and his composite folk temperament.

The post-slavery crop, much more extensive and varied, as well as more adulterated, gives us the important picture of the interaction of Negro folk idioms and materials with the rest of American culture. Indeed, as we approach our own times, we discover Negro influences operating simultaneously on three cultural levels: the folk, the popular, and the formally artistic. Production still continues in very reduced volume on the folk level, while influences like ragtime music and jazz expand importantly in the popular arts, and still other strains of influence work constructively on the sophisticated levels of formal American music, art, and literature—a rare cultural phenomenon indeed. Research in remote, undisturbed areas has unearthed creative folk artistry still active, producing contemporary religious and secular folk balladry only slightly different from the spirituals and blues that are their traditional prototypes. Though in imminent danger from an advancing technological civilization, the folk well-springs are not yet quite exhausted. After nearly a generation of most profitable and creative use, the artistic potentials of Negro materials in popular and formal American art seem still considerable and promising.

The most deeply characteristic folk qualities, which even today are sources of artistic strength and appeal, are registered perhaps most clearly in the earliest folk products. Of course, we find in them only a dated portrait of the ante-bellum Negro and his outlook, but they nonetheless supply a key to later phases of Negro creative expression. For the Negro experience during slavery, and to a modified degree ever since, has involved abnormal degrees of emotional stress and strain, and has evoked deep, elemental, though far from primitive, reactions. Not all of these have been somber and tragic: indeed, as we have seen, some have been exuberantly lighthearted and joyful. But all of them in some aspect or other have been compensatory. Alongside that serious, mystical, and other-worldly catharsis of religious escape and ecstasy, there existed, quite as usefully for successful survival, the emotional exhausts of laughter, ridicule, and even mockery, of which Uncle Remus is such a good example. Indeed, there would be much more of this comic relief of satire and laughter on record if Negro folk humor could have had an inside instead of an outside reporting. But the scheming, relentless "Br'er Fox" and the patient, cunningly resourceful "Br'er Rabbit" remain to tell a sly, meaningful allegory and to display the crafty comic consolation they once afforded.

The spirituals naturally reflect the most serious and intimate aspects of the slave Negro. Under the crucible-like pressures of slavery, with semiliterate but deep absorption of the essentials of Christianity, the slave Negro found with remarkable intuition and insight his two main life-sustaining aspirations: the hope of salvation and the hope of freedom. This was a creative reaction of the first magnitude, for it did much to save his spirit from breaking. It was also a triumph of folk art. From the episodes and imagery of the Bible, the Negro imaginatively reconstructed his own versions in musical and poetic patterns both highly original and of great emotional vitality. The borrowed materials were transformed to new fervor and a deepened mysticism, stemming very unexpectedly from a naïve and literal acceptance of Bible truths and a translation of them into the homeliest, most vividly concrete sort of imagery. Sober evangelical hymns became rhapsodic chants, and the traditional Bible lore came alive again in such new colloquial phrases as the "deep river that chills the body but not the soul," "De morning star was a witness, too," "Dese bones gwine to rise again," "Bright sparkles in de churchyard give light unto de tomb," and "My Lord is so high you can't get over Him,/He's so low you can't get under Him,/You gotta come in an' through de Lamb."

At the same time, from Old Testament sources, the slaves' imagination singled out the episodes relevant to their own condition, and used Jewish parallels to nourish their own hopes of physical freedom and to chide shrewdly and challenge their masters with their own beliefs. There was social point as well as religious faith to such exhortations as "Go down, Moses, tell ole Pharaoh to set my people free" and "Didn't my Lord deliver Daniel and why not every man?" "Steal away to Jesus" was sometimes a plea for revival conversion, at others, a password for camp-meeting assemblies, and, it is said, occasionally an encouraging signal for slave fugitives. Rescued from the disesteem of slavery and properly appraised, these first-crop folk creations fully justify James Weldon Johnson's estimate: "The Uncle Remus stories constitute the greatest body of folklore America has produced, and the spirituals are its greatest single body of folk-song." Although reactions to the Negro's own specific situation and experience, they are so profoundly intense as to become significantly universal; there are no finer expressions than these Negro folk utterances of the belief in freedom and immortality or of the emotional essences of Christianity native to the American soil. A brilliant ex-slave, Frederick Douglass, aptly called slavery "the graveyard of the mind," but happily it did not turn out to be the tomb of the Negro spirit.

Negro Contributions to American Life

Mabel Morsbach

The selection below, taken from Mabel Morsbach's *The Negro in American Life*, reaches beyond the stereotypes presented in the previous article. It describes the American blacks' contributions in all areas of American life from the 1930s to 1967. As you read this selection, remember that the figures noted in the table (which identifies the percentage of blacks in a variety of occupations and professions) were based on the 1960 census. One might speculate an increase in the percentages in a number of areas. It is also interesting to note that, although sports is the first area in which black participation is discussed, it is not a category noted in the table. In fact, as you read the selection, be aware that the listing of occupations and professions in the table does not correspond directly to the headings within the selection itself.

From the middle of the 1930's to the present time, Negroes have built successful careers in every field of American life. Better job opportunities in large cities resulted in higher wages and a higher standard of living for many Negro families. Educational opportunities had also increased, and college education was no longer beyond the reach of most ambitious students. In ever-increasing numbers, Negroes have entered professional occupations. Opportunities, both for training and for practice, have weakened some of the long-standing barriers of discrimination in the professions. The 1960 census shows the number of Negroes in certain professions and technical occupations and gives the percentage of Negroes compared to all other U.S. citizens in the same profession:

Occupations	Negro Citizens in Occupation	Percentage of Total Occupation
Accountants and auditors	3,662	.77
Architects	1,878	1.84
Clergymen	15,852	3.04
Lawyers and judges	2,180	1.02
Musicians and music teachers	9,305	4.84
Physicians and surgeons	4,706	2.05
Social scientists	2,059	2.07
Social welfare and recreation workers	14,276	10.72
Teachers	130,658	7.81
Medical and dental technicians	9,767	7.06
Dietitians and nutritionists (women only)	3,507	14.46

Librarians (women only)	3,144	4.37
Professional nurses (women only)	27,034	4.76

Higher standards of living and education are factors which have increased Negro interest and participation in the arts, sciences, and professions. Important, also, have been a greater acceptance and appreciation of Negro achievements by all Americans. Talented Negroes proved that they had the ability to excel in many professions. By doing so, they won a greater respect for themselves and their race.

SPORTS

In the sports world, there is an impressive list of Negro athletes who have won fame because of exceptional performance. Many of the individuals are still regarded as champions in their field. Their rise to success made them popular heroes of the day.

Track. Perhaps because speed and distance are carefully measured, it is hard to discriminate against a track man, and track was the first major sport in which Negroes won wide recognition. Jesse Owens stands out as one of the greatest American athletes of all times. Born in Alabama, Jesse Owens moved to Cleveland, Ohio, with his family when he was still a boy. When he was in junior high school, he excelled in running and jumping. His track coaches in junior and senior high school encouraged his development by giving special training to their star athlete. At Ohio State University, he became a star.

In 1936, Jesse Owens was a member of the United States track team that played in the Olympic games. Since Berlin, Germany, was the host city for the Olympic games that year, the event attracted worldwide attention. Germany had recently come under the rule of Adolf Hitler, whose violent speeches against racial minority groups disturbed the world. This intolerance was apparent to the members of the United States Olympic team since the Negro athletes were treated with contempt.

It was here that Jesse Owens had his most spectacular success. He set three records in Olympic competition in the 100-meter dash, the 200-meter dash, and the broad jump. Hitler himself watched the superb performance of Jesse Owens as the world's fastest runner. But the dictator quickly left the stands before four gold medals were presented to the great American athlete. The fourth gold medal was for placing first in the 400-meter relay. Ralph Metcalf teamed with Owens in the relay and placed second to him in the 100-meter dash at the Berlin Olympics. Negroes took seven gold medals that year.

Meredith Gourdine, an outstanding broad jumper from Cornell won a second place silver medal for the broad jump in the 1952 Olympics at Helsinki. Gourdine is now an engineering physicist working under a government grant to devise cheaper means of generating electricity.

In the 1960 Olympics at Rome, three Negro track stars took gold medals. Wilma Rudolph, often called the world's speediest woman, won her three gold medals for the women's 100-meter and 200-meter runs and for the 400-meter relay. Miss Rudolph did not begin to run, even to walk, until the age of eight, being a victim of various crippling diseases in her earliest years. Rafer Johnson set a world record to win the Decathlon at Rome. He is considered one of the greatest athletes on record. Ralph Boston picked up his gold medal at Rome for the broad jump. He placed second instead of first at the Tokyo Olympics in 1964, but is preparing for the 1968 Olympics in Mexico City.

In the 1964 Olympics, Bob Hayes won two gold medals, one for the 100-meter run and one for the 400-meter relay. The National Academy of Sports voted him the outstanding male track and field athlete of 1964. He went from track to football, playing end for the Dallas Cowboys.

Boxing. Boxing is a sport that has produced many Negro champions. But none captured the public imagination or became a popular hero as quickly as Joe Louis. His life story leads from dire poverty to worldwide fame. Joe Louis Barrow was born in Alabama in 1914 of parents who were sharecroppers. Like many other rural families, the Barrows moved to Detroit to try to make a better living. Joe Louis started working out in local gyms, and in 1933 he won the heavyweight championship in the Detroit Golden Gloves tournament.

After that, he rose quickly in the boxing world. He was aiming for world championship and defeated a number of heavyweight boxers in his campaign to reach the top. One bout he lost. In 1936, he was knocked out by Max Schmeling, the German boxer, who later boasted about his victory over the "inferior Negro fighter." The world championship finally came to Joe Louis in 1937 when he defeated James Braddock for the title. He remained world champion for twelve years, longer than any other individual. During these years, he defended his title twenty-five times. One of the most dramatic fights was a rematch with Max Schmeling in 1938. It was one of the shortest fights in Louis's career. He knocked out the German fighter in the first round.

Joe Louis won the respect of his countrymen not only because of his boxing skill, but also because of his modesty and his sportsmanship. He demonstrated his patriotism by serving as a private in the Army. More than that, he donated his share of the earnings from two of his fights to Army and Navy relief. Asked why, Joe Louis replied, "I'm fighting for my country."[1] Joe Louis retired undefeated and was followed by such future Negro champions as Ezzard Charles, Sugar Ray Robinson, Floyd Patterson, Sonny Liston, and Cassius Clay.

Baseball. It was not until after World War II that Negro athletes had the chance to play in professional team sports. Jackie Robinson, the first Negro to play in major league baseball, succeeded on two counts. He made an excellent career for himself, and he led the way for other Negro athletes to play professional baseball. Although he had some unpleasant experiences with discrimination, his top-quality performance on the ball field won the respect of his teammates, of opposing teams, and of the baseball fans.

Even as a child, Jackie Robinson had been good at games. When he attended high school in Pasadena, California, he was a member of the football, basketball, baseball, and track teams. His interest in athletics continued when he went to college. In 1939 at UCLA, he was a well-known football star, and during the next two years he won recognition for his ability in basketball.

After college, Jackie Robinson joined the Army. He qualified for Officers' Candidate School, and after intensive training, he became a lieutenant. He remained in the Army until 1944.

Following his military service, young Jackie Robinson was faced with choosing a career. His chances in professional baseball were limited because he was a Negro. In 1944, major league teams were closed to Negro athletes, no matter how talented they were. Negro athletes played in segregated, all-Negro leagues with little chance to become nationally recognized. Jackie Robinson chose baseball anyway, and he played with the Kansas City Monarchs, an all-Negro team. His career seemed settled.

Changing attitudes toward the Negro after World War II brought changes to the sports world, too. Newspaper articles questioned racial segregation in the major leagues. Sports writers suggested that Negro players be given a chance to compete in the big leagues. Branch Rickey, president of the Brooklyn Dodgers, became interested in adding a Negro ballplayer to his organization. Because he realized that any Negro would probably meet discrimination on and off the ball field, Rickey wanted a player with character and intelligence, as well as athletic ability. When baseball scouts repeatedly mentioned Robinson's name as an outstanding player, Rickey checked on his background. Everything seemed in Robinson's favor: he had college training; he had played in sports competition with both Negro and white athletes; and he was a good ballplayer. Jackie Robinson was called in for an interview. After being offered the opportunity to join the Brooklyn organization, he was told very frankly of some unpleasant situations that he would probably face if he took the job. With the clear understanding that his success or failure would influence the future of other Negro ballplayers, Jackie Robinson signed a contract. On October 15, 1945, Branch Rickey made the startling announcement to the newspapers that Jackie Robinson, Negro ball-player, would play regularly with the Dodger farm club, the Montreal Royals.

The choice of Jackie Robinson as a pioneer Negro in major league baseball was an excellent one. He met and refused to be upset by such unpleasant experiences as name calling, Jim Crow accommodations, and crank notes. His baseball record was impressive from the beginning. During his first year with Montreal, the Royals were first in the International League, and Robinson was their outstanding player. In his second year with Rickey, Jackie Robinson entered the big leagues by becoming the regular first baseman for the Brooklyn Dodgers. At the end of the season, he was voted the Rookie-of-the-Year. In 1947, he led the National League in stolen bases and even succeeded in stealing home on five different occasions. Later, as second baseman, his brilliant playing continued throughout his career with the Dodgers. He was twice honored with the Most Valuable Player of the Year Award. He retired in 1956, and became vice-president of a chain of restaurants in New York City and a vigorous spokesman for the NAACP.

Within a few years, Negroes were playing on every major league team. Twelve years after Jackie Robinson had paved the way, there were fifty-seven Negro major leaguers in both the National and American Leagues. Many became outstanding stars. Besides Jackie Robinson, the following Negro athletes have won the Most Valuable Player Award: Roy Campanella, Willie Mays, Don Newcombe, Hank Aaron, Ernie Banks, Frank Robinson, and Maury Wills.

Professional Basketball and Football. Professional basketball and football teams have also been strengthened by the outstanding performances of Negro players. The skill and speed of such players as Wilt Chamberlain, Elgin Baylor, and Oscar Robertson have brought loud cheers from basketball fans. In 1966, Bill Russell, star player for the Boston Celtics, was chosen to manage the team for the following season. This was another first: the first Negro manager of a professional team in organized sports. In professional football, "Night Train" Lane, Lenny Moore,

Jimmy Brown, Bobby Mitchell, and Roosevelt Greer are just a few of the stars whose exploits are well known to sports fans.

Tennis.   Tennis, as a sport, has produced few Negro stars. Althea Gibson, who grew up in Harlem, was the first exceptional Negro performer in this sport. Growing up in the 1940's when national competition was closed to Negroes, she became champion of the American Tennis Association, composed largely, but not exclusively, of Negro players. In 1950, the color ban in tennis competition was relaxed. Althea played for the first time against other national tennis stars. In 1957, she reached the peak of her career, winning three important championships to become the world's best woman tennis player. She later wrote an autobiography, *I Wanted to Be Somebody.* She is.

Arthur Ashe, Jr., placed first in the South Australian Tennis Championship matches in December 1966, graduating that year from the University of California at Los Angeles. Two years earlier in 1964 Ashe was rated among the nation's top ten amateur players and was the first Negro to make the United States Davis Cup team. Born in Richmond, Virginia, Ashe was sponsored by Dr. Robert Johnson of that city and sent to St. Louis for his senior year in high school so that he could play in integrated tournaments. At the age of 17, he was the first Negro to win the United States Lawn Tennis Association's Interscholastic championship.

THE ARTS

The Harlem Renaissance had sparked Negro enthusiasm and participation in all the arts during the 1920's. The depression years which followed made it difficult for artists, musicians, and writers to work, but national programs like WPA gave the talented a chance to develop their creative abilities. Negro contributions to the arts continued through the 1940's, 50's, and 60's.

The Visual Arts.   Horace Pippin was a self-taught artist who overcame many obstacles in his rise to success. His family was poor. The future artist left school after the elementary grades to work in a number of menial jobs. He loved to draw and paint and took his sketching pad with him wherever he went. In World War I, he served overseas and was severely wounded. Upon his discharge from the Army, Horace Pippin received the French Croix de Guerre and the American Purple Heart.

Still interested in art, Horace Pippin found it hard to hold a paint brush in his hand. His war wound prevented him from raising his right hand as high as his shoulder. But he was determined to paint. At first he held a wooden board in his lap. With a hot poker he drew outlines for his pictures on it and then filled in the outlines with house paint. Gradually he recovered the use of his right arm and could paint on canvas with artist's paints. Although it took him three years to complete his first canvas, he continued with the work he loved. In 1940, he had a successful one-man art show in New York City. Four of his paintings were exhibited in the Museum of Modern Art in that city.

Charles White, born in Chicago, now lives in California where he has been involved in preaching, teaching, and art. His drawings are strong and moving. He portrays Negro personalities with fine daughtsmanship and great vitality.

Jacob Lawrence lives in New York City. He spent much of his free time in a neighborhood settlement house where he was encouraged to draw and paint. He studied at the American Artists' School in New York. Examples of his work come from his panels on Negro history: "The Life of Frederick Douglass," "The Life of Harriet Tubman," and "The Migration of the Negro."

Many other contemporary artists of note could be named, among them Hale Woodruff, John Biggers, and Philip Hampton.

Gordon Parks rose from poverty to become a successful photographer. Born on a small farm in Kansas in 1912, he moved to St. Paul, Minnesota, in his late teens. When he left high school, Parks worked at numerous jobs before choosing a career in photography in 1937. He then moved to Chicago, where he was encouraged by the artists at the South Side Community Art Center. He was given a dark room in which to work, and eventually held a one-man exhibit. Parks became a staff photographer for *Life* magazine in 1949, and was named "Magazine Photographer of the Year," in 1961. Parks has also composed several pieces of classical music, and has written a book on photography and a novel, *The Learning Tree.*

Music and Dancing.   Negroes with musical talent followed careers on the concert stage and in the Metropolitan Opera Company. In the footsteps of Marian Anderson and Roland Hayes, a number of young singers achieved fame as serious musicians. Among them were Dorothy Maynor, Carol Bryce, Gloria Davy, William Warfield, and Leontyne Price. Even more recent arrivals are George Shirley, Grace Bumbry, and Shirley Verrett. André Watts, a pianist, has played with the New York Philharmonic Symphony and other nationally known orchestras.

Outstanding musical performance demands training. Each of the talented musicians who rose to fame had excellent musical training, either from well-known teachers or from conservatories of music. Each had also attended college before beginning a professional study of music. Most had received help from a sponsor who had both the wealth and interest in seeing a great talent developed.

William Warfield's life serves as an example of a young musician's progress toward achievement. He grew up in Rochester, New York, where his father was a minister. A good student, young Warfield was also liked by his classmates, who elected him vice-president of the student council. His voice already showed great promise during high school, and his music teacher gave him private voice lessons without charge. The whole community was proud of William Warfield's talents and predicted a bright future for him.

While still in high school, he was entered in a national contest sponsored by the Music Teachers' Association. The only Negro contestant, William Warfield emerged as the winner. The prize in the contest had a marked influence over his future. It was a full scholarship to the music conservatory of his choice. William Warfield attended the Eastman School of Music in Rochester.

After three years of military service, Warfield turned to music to earn a living. At first he worked in night clubs, singing all kinds of music from classical to jazz. When he was appearing in Toronto, Canada, his voice made a deep impression on a man in the audience. This man, Walter Carr, made arrangements for the young baritone to give a concert at Town Hall, and his musical career was launched.

Another singer, Leontyne Price, was born in Mississippi, earned a B.S. degree from Central State College in Wilberforce, Ohio, and studied at the Juilliard School of Music in New York. Her first success followed her singing of the role of Bess in the 1952 revival of *Porgy and Bess.* Renown in opera followed her singing of the lead in *Aïda* on a European tour in 1959. After that, she landed a starring role in the Metropolitan Opera's production of Verdi's *Il Trovatore* in 1961 and was named "Musician of the Year" by a group of editors and critics. The peak of her career, so far, came when she opened the new Metropolitan Opera House in New York, in 1966, singing the lead in Samuel Barber's new opera, *Antony and Cleopatra.* In 1964, she was one of thirty Americans receiving the Freedom Medal, the highest American civil honor.

In popular music the roster is full of famous names. The late Nat King Cole and the late Billie Holliday will long be noted for their singing of popular music and blues. Ella Fitzgerald, Harry Belafonte, Lena Horne, Pearl Bailey, Eartha Kitt, Sammy Davis, Jr., and The Supremes, Diana Ross, Mary Wilson, and Florence Ballard offer a wide range of talents and styles. Mahalia Jackson is probably the most famous of the gospel singers.

In the 1930's Negro jazz gained great popularity over the radio. Fletcher Henderson, Duke Ellington, and Count Basie played pianos and directed bands. The last two, as well as Louis Armstrong, Coleman Hawkins, Jelly Roll Morton, Earl Hines, and Dizzy Gillespie, on their various instruments, span the 1920's to the 1960's. Cool jazz, seldom danced to, as opposed to the older music, characterizes the most recent jazz, and familiar names are those of Miles Davis playing the trumpet, Charlie Mingus on the bass, Thelonius Monk on the piano, and John Coltrane on the saxophone.

Arthur Mitchell of the New York City Ballet has won an international reputation in the field of dance. He is the first Negro to attain the distinction of becoming a leading dancer of one of the world's great ballet companies. Mitchell was encouraged to pursue his talent for the dance by a guidance teacher who urged him to enroll in the High School of the Performing Arts in New York. There, Mitchell majored in modern dance but decided to try classical ballet after being offered a scholarship to study at the School of American Ballet. Arthur Mitchell has devoted much of his spare time to work with Negro children in the hope of inspiring them to follow careers in ballet.

During the 1940's and 1950's Katherine Dunham was one of the nation's foremost dancers and choreographers. Pearl Primus was well known in the 1950's. Eleo Pomare and his dance company are becoming known in the 1960's.

Acting. Ossie Davis and Ruby Dee are listed among the most versatile Negro actors. Sidney Poitier won an Academy Award as the best actor in 1963 for his performance in *Lilies of the Field.* Diahann Carroll starred in a successful Broadway musical, *No Strings,* in 1962. Gloria Foster has won acclaim for her role in New York productions of *In White America* and *Medea;* she is now a member of the repertory theatre at Lincoln Center, in New York.

Literature. The success of Negro authors in the 1920's continued and grew in the years that followed. A whole new generation of authors began to gain recognition. Many of the young authors wrote from their own experience, and their works often dealt with racial themes. Richard Wright wrote powerful novels that protested against discrimination in American life. Arna Bontemps found success in different kinds of writing: history, fiction, poetry, and biography. Frank Yerby turned his back on the racial theme and wrote best-seller novels of swashbuckling adventure and romance, including *Foxes of Harrow,* which became a movie. Willard Motley gained prominence with his books, *Knock on Any Door,* 1947, and *Let No Man Write My Epitaph,* 1958.

Ralph Ellison won the National Book Award in 1953 for his novel *The Invisible Man.* The late Lorraine Hansberry wrote *Raisin in the Sun,* which ran on Broadway for a year beginning in 1959, was taken on a tour of the country, and eventually was made into a movie.

James Baldwin has spoken and written strongly for the protest movement with his *Nobody Knows My Name,* 1961, and *Fire Next Time,* 1963. His provocative play *Blues for Mr. Charlie* was written in 1964.

Gwendolyn Brooks is one of the noteworthy American poets of today. She is the only American Negro who has ever won the Pulitzer prize for excellence in writing. Her first volume of poetry, *A Street in Bronzeville,* received high praise from book reviewers. *Annie Allen,* her second book, was awarded the Pulitzer prize for poetry.

SCIENCE

Among today's Negro scientists is Percy Julian, whose work in chemical research has brought him recognition and wealth. His life story is a dramatic example of the progress that has been made by one Negro family in just three generations. Percy Julian's grandfather was a slave, who was punished severely for learning to read. His father was a railway clerk in Montgomery, Alabama. Percy Julian left the family to enter DePauw University in Indiana. When he graduated as valedictorian of his class, his family was delighted. They were determined to give the same opportunity to the other children in the family. So Mrs. Julian moved to Greencastle, Indiana, with her three daughters and two sons. Mr. Julian remained in Montgomery and sent the necessary money so that the young people could have a college education. Their hopes and ambitions were realized. Both of Percy Julian's brothers became doctors, and each of his three sisters earned a Master's degree.

After his graduation from DePauw, Percy Julian received a scholarship to study at Harvard University, where he earned the degree of Master of Science. He then attended the University of Vienna in Austria, where he earned a Ph.D. After teaching a number of years at DePauw, he entered the field of chemical research. He became the director of research for a large firm in Chicago. In 1953, he formed his own company, the Julian Laboratories. This company produced hormones, products from soy beans, and various drugs. After the first year of operation, the Julian Laboratories showed a profit of exactly $71.70. After the second year, however, the profit was an impressive $97,000, and these earnings have continued to increase. Percy Julian's contribution to American science has been great. His name has been listed for many years in *Who's Who in America.*

LAW

Modern Negro lawyers have been active in protecting Negro rights. Nationally known lawyers have worked with such organizations as the NAACP in advancing the Negro's cause. Thurgood Marshall's work in overcoming segregation in public schools was described earlier in this chapter. He went on to become a federal judge in the United States Court of Appeals for the Second Circuit. In 1965, he became the Solicitor General for the United States, the first Negro to serve in this capacity. As he took the oath of office in the White House, President Lyndon Johnson had high praise for him: "Mr. Marshall symbolizes what is best in our society: the belief that human rights must be satisfied through the orderly processes of law." In June, 1967, President Johnson bestowed an even higher honor on Thurgood Marshall by appointing him to the United States Supreme Court, thus making him the first Negro Justice of the highest court in the land.

William Hastie's talent and training prepared him for a career of service as judge and government official. After taking his legal training at the Harvard University Law School, Mr. Hastie received his first federal appointment from President Franklin Roosevelt. He served as Assistant Solicitor in the Department of Interior. In 1937, he was appointed as a United States District Judge for the Virgin Islands. Resigning from this position in 1939, he became Dean of the Law School at Howard University in Washington, D.C.

William Hastie's career was developing during the crisis years of World War II. In 1940, he was once more appointed to serve in a federal position. He became a civilian aide to the Secretary of War. While he held this position, he worked unceasingly for integration in the armed forces. In 1944, William Hastie was appointed Governor of the Virgin Islands. The high point in his distinguished career came in 1949 when he became Judge of the United States Circuit Court of Appeals, Third Circuit. This was the highest judicial office that had been held by a Negro, up to this time.

RELIGION

The church has always been an important force in the Negro community. It has often done more than provide religious and moral leadership. Negro churches, particularly in large cities, have given practical help in their community. Some churches organized summer camps, playgrounds, family counseling services, or evening industrial schools. Others became centers for political action. The church also provided many opportunities for developing Negro leaders. Some ministers are well known for their leadership outside the church.

The man who founded the largest Negro church in the United States was Adam Clayton Powell, Sr. He retired from the ministry of his Abyssinian Baptist Church in New York in 1937, when the church had a membership of 15,000 persons. During his twenty-nine years as pastor, Mr. Powell had made the Abyssinian Church an active influence in Harlem life. In the depression years, the church helped thousands of jobless and hungry people. It gave coal, clothing, and medicines to the needy. A food kitchen was opened in the gymnasium of the church's community house, and approximately two thousand people were fed there every day.

POLITICS

Adam Clayton Powell, Jr., took over the leadership of his father's Abyssinian Baptist Church in 1937. In 1944 he was elected to Congress as the first Negro Representative from the East. Still representing New York at Washington in

1961, Powell became Chairman of the Education and Labor Committee of the House of Representatives. In 1966, Powell was charged with contempt of court for failure to pay the assessment in a libel case which he had lost earlier. He came under further criticism for his use of public funds. Early in 1967 he lost his committee chairmanship and in March of the same year the House voted to exclude him from his seat in Congress. At a special election in April, he was voted back into Congress by his constituency.

Carl Rowan was named Deputy Assistant Secretary of State for Public Affairs in 1961. In 1963 he was appointed ambassador to Finland and, in 1964, Director of the United States Information Agency. In 1965 he joined the Marshall Field chain of newspapers as a syndicated columnist.

The elections of 1966 produced two more firsts for Negroes in politics. Lucius Amerson of Macon County, Alabama, became the first Negro sheriff in the South since Reconstruction days. Edward W. Brooke won the first U.S. Senate seat to be held by a Negro since Reconstruction days. Brooke, who grew up in a middle-class home in Washington where his father was a Veteran's Administration lawyer, was formerly State Attorney General in Massachusetts and represents that state in Washington.

FOREIGN SERVICE

Ambassadors to foreign countries serve as representatives of our government wherever they are stationed. Appointed to their position by the President of the United States, they have a responsible role in government service. To date, not many Negroes have represented the United States as ambassadors to foreign nations. In recent years, Edward Dudley served as Minister to Liberia from 1949 to 1953. In 1953 Jesse Locker replaced him as Ambassador to Liberia.

In 1965 President Johnson selected a Negro lawyer, Mrs. Patricia Roberts Harris, as Ambassador to Luxembourg. Other Negro ambassadors serving in 1965 included Mercer Cook, Senegal; Clinton Knox, Dahomey; Hugh Smythe, Syria; Franklin Williams, Ghana; Elliott P. Skinner, Upper Volta; and James Nabrit, Jr., United States Mission to the United Nations. Mr. Nabrit resigned from his diplomatic post in 1967 to return to the presidency of Howard University.

BUSINESS

America's wealth is tied to the development of industry and business. Since World War II, many different jobs have been opened to Negroes for the first time. Qualified men and women have become stewardesses and pilots. They have worked in television studios as actors, stage managers, and cameramen. They have been employed as chemists and engineers in large industrial companies. Some have started and operated thriving businesses of their own.

In North Carolina, Charles Clinton Spaulding started to work in a small life insurance company. His untiring efforts caused the firm to grow into the huge North Carolina Mutual Life Insurance Company. Spaulding himself served as president of the company from 1923 until his death in 1952.

In Birmingham, Alabama, Arthur Gaston rose from a three-dollar-a-day laborer to a millionaire owner of several successful businesses. His business enterprises have included an insurance company, a chain of funeral homes, a business college, a chain of motels, a housing development, a savings and loan association, a realty and investment corporation, and a cemetery.

One of the most successful business ventures of recent years has been the development of Negro magazines. The *Negro Digest, Jet,* and *Ebony* all owe their existence to the efforts of John Johnson. Born in 1919, John Johnson spent his early life under conditions of great poverty. His family moved to Chicago when the boy was of high school age. He worked hard at school, determined to take advantage of every opportunity. He was editor of the school newspaper, president of the student council, and manager of the yearbook. He was also a tireless reader, studying particularly the lives of Negro leaders.

After high school, John Johnson worked for a while in an insurance company in Chicago. In 1942, with borrowed money, he started his career in the publishing business. He printed the *Negro Digest,* a small magazine about Negro affairs. The new magazine was an immediate success and by 1943, over fifty thousand copies were sold every month.

In 1945, *Ebony* made its appearance. This magazine contained stories emphasizing the achievement and success of Negroes. Articles about Negro history have pointed out their continuing contributions to American life. This magazine has a circulation which reaches into the hundreds of thousands every month. After the success of *Ebony,* the Johnson Publishing Company started printing three more magazines: *Jet, Hue,* and *Tan.*

John Johnson's remarkable career as a self-made man has left him with an appreciation of the United States as a land of opportunity. In one interview he expressed his feeling that the United States is the world's best home for Negroes.

CONCLUSION

The Negro's record in American life has been long and exciting. The history of the race is rich in achievement and constant efforts to overcome barriers of prejudice. It has been a story of both abrupt and gradual changes. Racial discrimination is gone from many areas of American life, but not from all. Today's newspapers describe the challenges being made against existing barriers. What occurs now will become tomorrow's history, for history is a living thing, an account of the events that affect our present and future lives.

The history of the Negro American is an important part of the history of our entire nation. The development of the United States has been profoundly influenced by the Negro and his position in America. Negro slavery provided the manpower for the plantation system of agriculture in the South. The lives of whites, as well as Negroes, became tightly bound to this rural way of life. Later, westward expansion into new territories raised the question whether or not the new states were to permit slavery. The Civil War, which started as an effort to keep the country united, brought about the end of slavery. Historic documents, like the Emancipation Proclamation and the Thirteenth, Fourteenth, and Fifteenth Amendments to the Constitution, defined Negro citizenship and became a part of the American heritage. Court decisions and laws dealt with Negro rights and brought changes to traditional patterns of living. In recent years, thousands of people have organized to end racial discrimination and the prejudice from which it stems.

The history of any nation pays tribute to its leaders and heroes. The United States has been enriched by a variety of contributions from prominent Negro citizens. Throughout the years, individuals with talent and determination have reached new goals of excellence in many areas of American culture: education, religion, literature, art, music, sports, entertainment, politics, government, business, science, and law. In many cases, these persons were the Negro pioneers in their chosen work, the first of their race to earn recognition for outstanding achievement. In overcoming handicaps of prejudice, the talented leaders succeeded in opening unseen doors of opportunity. By their courage and efforts, they made it easier for others to follow in their footsteps. Through their talents and skills, they built greater understanding and respect among all American citizens.

NOTES

1. Roi Ottley, *New World A-Coming* (Boston: Houghton Mifflin Company, 1943), p. 200.

Mary McLeod Bethune: My Last Will and Testament

Rackham Holt

Mary McLeod Bethune's work in education made her famous among both blacks and whites. Her last will and testament, reproduced here, is poetic, humanitarian, and vital to all Americans.

Sometimes I ask myself if I have any legacy to leave. My worldly possessions are few. Yet, my experiences have been rich. From them I have distilled principles and policies in which I firmly believe. Perhaps in them there is something of value. So, as my life draws to a close, I will pass them on to Negroes everywhere in the hope that this philosophy may give them inspiration. Here, then, is my legacy:

I Leave You Love.   Injuries quickly forgotten quickly pass away. Personally and racially, our enemies must be forgotten. Our aim must be to create a world of fellowship and justice where no man's color or religion is held against him. "Love thy neighbor" is a precept which could transform the world if it were universally practiced. It connotes brotherhood and to me, brotherhood of man is the noblest concept of all human relationships. Loving your neighbor means interracial, interreligious, and international.

I Leave You Hope.   Yesterday, our ancestors endured the degradation of slavery, yet they retained their dignity. Today, we direct our economic and political strength toward winning a more abundant and secure life. Tomorrow, a new Negro, unhindered by race taboos and shackles, will benefit from this striving and struggling.

I Leave You a Thirst for Education.   More and more, Negroes are taking full advantage of hard-won opportunities for learning, and the educational level of the Negro population is at its highest point in history. We are making greater use of the privileges inherent in living in a democracy. Now that the barriers are crumbling everywhere, the Negro in America must be ever vigilant lest his forces be marshaled behind wrong causes and undemocratic movements. . . . He must not lend his support to any group that seeks to subvert democracy.

I Leave You Faith.   Faith is the first factor in a life devoted to service. Without faith, nothing is possible. With it, nothing is impossible. Faith in God is the greatest power but great faith, too, is faith in oneself. The faith of the American Negro in himself has grown immensely, and is still increasing. The measure of our progress as a race is in precise relation to the depth of the faith in our people held by our leaders.

I Leave You Racial Dignity.   I want Negroes to maintain their human dignity at all costs. We, as Negroes, must recognize that we are the custodians as well as the heirs of a great civilization. As a race, we have given something to the world, and for this we are proud and fully conscious of our place in the total picture of mankind's development.

I Leave You a Desire to Live Harmoniously with Your Fellow Men.   The problem of color is world wide, on every continent. I appeal to all to recognize their common problems, and unite to solve them. So often our difficulties have made us supersensitive and truculent. I want to see my people conduct themselves in all relationships, fully conscious of their responsibilities and deeply aware of their heritage. We are a minority of fifteen million living side by side with a white majority of 177 million. We must learn to deal with people positively and on an individual basis.

I Leave You Finally a Responsibility to Our Young People.   Our children must never lose this zeal for building a better world. They must not be discouraged from aspiring to greatness, for they are to be the leaders of tomorrow. We have a powerful potential in our youth, and we must have the courage to change old ideas and practices so that we may direct their power toward good ends.

Faith, courage, brotherhood, dignity, ambition, responsibility—these are needed today as never before. We must cultivate them and use them as tools for our task of completing the establishment of equality for the Negro. We must sharpen these tools in the struggle that faces us and find new ways of using them. The Freedom Gates are half ajar. We must pry them fully open.

If I have a legacy to leave my people, it is my philosophy of living and serving. As I face tomorrow, I am content. I pray now that my philosophy may be helpful to those who share my vision of a world of peace.

The Negro Almanac

Harry A. Ploski and Roscoe C. Brown, Jr.

The Negro Almanac, published in 1967, lists the accomplishments of famous black personalities in areas such as government, the fine arts, science and technology, the performing arts, and sports. An entire section of the *Almanac* is devoted to the role of the black woman in American life. The following excerpt presents descriptions of some of the personalities mentioned in an earlier selection, although it does not include as many categories of accomplishment as are included in "Negro Contributions to American Life."

Are there other personalities or areas that should have been included in this chapter? Since the articles represent only portions of the sources from which they were taken, you might be interested in going to the original sources for additional information.

THE NEGRO IN THE FEDERAL GOVERNMENT

The role played by the Negro in the federal government has expanded dramatically in recent years, with Negroes experiencing a particularly significant upsurge in middle- and upper-level posts at the executive level. For the first time in our nation's history, Negroes are beginning to exercise authority and responsibility in positions which have nothing whatsoever to do with race.

For the Negro, this favorable trend stands in marked contrast to the time when members of his race were mainly clerks in various governmental agencies, notably in the postal service. In the pre-Roosevelt years, however, the financial security afforded the Negro by such minor federal posts often enabled him to send his children to colleges and universities which proved to be the fertile training ground for the leaders of a new generation.

During the Roosevelt years, Negro professionals were, as it were, moved up in the ranks, being induced to serve the government as "specialists" in Negro affairs, or as race relations "advisers." Ultimately, the most influential members of this cadre of Negro leaders formed what came to be known as the "Black Cabinet." Headed unofficially by Mary McLeod Bethune, the group was able to facilitate the entry of other young and energetic Negroes into government service, and also helped break down several established patterns of racial exclusion operative at various governmental levels.

Since then, particularly during the Kennedy and Johnson Administrations, prospects have broadened considerably for the Negro interested in a government career, and many Negroes have passed far beyond the "honorific" positions—i.e. those of racial or secondary importance only—to the more substantial, policy-making echelons of government service.

Numerous Negroes now occupy important sub-cabinet positions, and one—Robert Weaver—has become the first to be named to a presidential cabinet. Numerous Negroes serve as key members of the president's personal staff, in positions ranging from Associate Special Counsel to military and social aides. Others serve as U.S. ambassadors to foreign countries (not all of which inevitably are African), while still others serve in federal regulatory agencies like the Export-Import Bank, the National Labor Relations Board, and the Federal Reserve Board.

At the present time, there is only one Negro in the Senate, but prospects appear bright that Edward A. Brooke, once Republican Attorney General of the State of Massachusetts (then the highest state office held by a Negro), will become the standard bearer for a new breed of responsible political leaders. To date, Negro presidential and vice-presidential candidates have been confined to minority parties. (Clifton DeBerry ran for the nation's highest office on the Socialist Workers ticket in 1964, whereas James B. Ford ran for the vice-presidency three times— in 1932, 1936, and 1940.)

Our review of the Negro in the federal government is necessarily a comprehensive one which attempts to take into account a representative cross-section of an imposing roster of important personalities. . . .

THE NEGRO IN THE FINE ARTS

A. AFRICAN ANTECEDENTS

The role of the Negro in the fine arts in America has been one of discovery and re-discovery.

Cut off from his African artistic heritage, and often forced to believe that the fine arts lay outside his province, the American Negro underwent his early period of development as an artist independent of an ancestral foundation.

In Africa, manual arts such as woodcarving, bone-carving, and metal-work had reached great heights during the Middle Ages but, in America, these same arts were largely lost to the Negro. The slave artisan, for instance, was limited in his work to the creation of practical implements, tools, and household equipment. In the wrought-iron industry, he was able to display some of his artistic facility, but never on a par with the representative material created by his predecessors.

B. NEGRO PAINTING

The first American Negro painter was probably Scipio Morehead, who is known as an allegorical landscapist by virtue of a dedicatory poem written by Phillis Wheatley some time before 1773. What little Negro painting there was in the Revolutionary era was largely imitative of the far from memorable work of most American artists. With the exception of a few outstanding colonial painters, America produced no really great painters until the decade of the 1870's when Whistler and Homer emerged.

In his "apprenticeship period" (1865–1890), the Negro artist was not far behind the general level of the age. In his "journeyman period" (1890–1914), he gained a greater degree of international attention, but he did not begin to realize his true potential until the coming of the Negro Renaissance in the 1920's. The pseudo-classical imitations and the stilted, overly formal approach once typical of him gave way in this decade to an abundant use of subject matter close at hand —Negro historical themes, domestic scenes, and symbolism filled with the vitality and thrust of the "New Negro." Then, too, the greatness of African art was re-discovered, not only by the Negro artist, but by a number of white artists (among them, Picasso), and by the art-loving public as well.

At the present time, there are no boundaries to the creative vistas of the American Negro artist. The forms which his work takes range from primitive simplicity to sophisticated complexity; the subject matter, from personal evocations, to Negro thematic statements, to the most avant-garde abstractions. It seems likely that the American Negro's achievements in the fine arts will one day —if, indeed, they have not already done so—rival those of his musical heritage.

NEGRO INVENTORS AND SCIENTISTS

In 1870, more than 80% of the Negroes in the United States were illiterate and, even 40 years later, more than one-third of the Negro population over 10 years of age had still never been to school. It is against this background of systematic educational deprivation that the achievements of the Negro inventor and scientist can be seen in their sharpest perspective.

In addition to this lack of formal schooling, the Negro inventor and scientist also encountered innumerable legal and social obstacles. In pre-Civil War days, for example, slaves were unable to obtain patents with the result that, today, there is no way of determining the actual number of Negro inventors who had their work expropriated by their masters. Even the inventions of free Negroes were often refused acceptance once the racial identity of the inventor became known. . . .

Many inventions by Negroes have not, therefore, been identified as such; nonetheless, even if one considers only the *verifiable* ones, the total still runs into the thousands, ranging from simple household conveniences to more complex mechanical devices which have proved to be of vital importance to business and industry. Some are as familiar as the potato chip of Hyram S. Thomas, a Saratoga chef; the ice cream of Augustus Jackson, a Philadelphia confectioner known as the "man who invented ice cream" (1832); the golf tee of George F. Grant; the mop-holder of Thomas W. Stewart, and the player pianos of J. H. and S. L. Dickinson.

On the other hand, no commentary on Negro inventors and scientists could fail to make mention of the major accomplishments of such men as Granville Woods (the synchronous multiplex railway telegraph); Elijah McCoy (the automatic lubricator), and Jan Matzeliger (the shoe-last machine).

Nor should one forget that most of these achievements—whether large or small —were often made in the face of overwhelming odds, and frequently greeted with hostility and derision.

THE NEGRO IN THE PERFORMING ARTS

A. THE SLAVE EXPERIENCE

The Negro has made a truly prodigious contribution to the world of American entertainment. His presence has been felt to a degree far greater than could normally be expected given the clear population minority which he represents and the barely peripheral place which American society often provides him.

For more than a century, the most formidable obstacle faced by the Negro entertainer was the fact that he was often excluded—both as spectator and participant—from those public places of entertainment which are the logical training ground for any performer. Nevertheless, from the earliest days of slavery, entertainment was one of the few avenues of expression open to the Negro. As singers, dancers, or bones players, slaves were often called upon to perform for their masters and, if talented enough, were even hired out by them to entertain others. Such slave performers as "Blind Tom," a talented pianist, gained national fame in this manner.

Slaves also used the medium of religious songs (considered "safe" by the masters) to express their dissatisfaction with their lot. In this fashion, *Go Down Moses, Oh Freedom, God's Gonna Cut You Down* and many other spirituals have become part of the vast oral tradition created by the Negro musical artist. (After the Civil War, the Fisk Jubilee Singers extended the realm of the Negro spiritual to the international arena by going on a tour of Europe with "Negro" music as the basis of their repertoire.)

B. DRAMA AND THEATRE

The Negro's entrance into serious drama was first attempted in 1821. For 11 years after that, a group of free Negroes maintained a theatre called *The African Grove* on New York's Bleecker Street, performing such Shakespearean vehicles as *Othello* and *Richard III.* (Young Ira Aldridge, who was to become the greatest Negro tragedian, played small roles in these productions.) Local thugs eventually forced the venture to close, whereupon 50 years were to pass before Negro actors had access to theatres where they could perform regularly.

On April 5, 1917, the production of three one-act plays by poet Ridgely Torrance, with music conducted and performed by Negroes, marked "the first time anywhere in the United States for Negro actors in the dramatic theatre to command the serious attention of the critics, the general press and public." Three years later, Charles Gilpin starred in Eugene O'Neill's *Emperor Jones* and, from then on, the Negro actor became a more accepted part of the American theatre. (Nevertheless, only 11 Negro playwrights have been presented on Broadway in its entire history.)

C. VAUDEVILLE

In the field of variety entertainment, the earliest commercial successes lay not with Negro song-and-dance men, but with white men performing their material in "blackface." Such groups as The Virginia Minstrels headed by Dan Emmett (the composer of *Dixie*) became popular in the 1840's and, for the next half century, America was entertained by the stereotyped image of the laughing, cake-walking, chicken-stealing, gin-guzzling, crap-shooting, razor-wielding Negro wearing any number of outlandish costumes. This is an image which the American Negro has been trying to overcome for many years. To cap the irony, when Negro performers did begin to share some of the commercial rewards of the variety stage, they too often worked in "blackface," thus imitating whites who were themselves imitating Negroes!

D. MOVIES

Until recent years, the Negro's role in movies has been a perpetuation of the clown figure. (The scene of the shiftless Negro walking through the graveyard rolling his eyes in terror and trying to whistle at the same time to allay his fears was for decades an American comedy staple.) This ludicrous image has probably been more damaging to the Negro in the long run than the threatening image of him as a terrorist. (In *The Birth of a Nation,* for example, one scene involves a Negro—played by a white man in blackface—who makes a fatal assault on the honor of a Southern white girl.)

Nowadays, more and more Negro actors in movies and television are being given opportunities to portray doctors, lawyers, mailmen—in short, the complete spectrum of available roles reflecting Negro life in the United States. Movie Oscars have been won by Negroes in both supporting and starring roles. On the concert stage, in grand opera, and in musical comedy, the Negro has also made notable strides toward the realization of his full potential.

Any list of outstanding performers could, therefore, run into the hundreds, and include great talents whose audience has been largely limited to Negro theatres. The list finally chosen by our editors represents an attempt to suggest the spectrum of talent ranging from concert, to theatre, to variety stage, as well as to most popular media of importance today.

THE NEGRO IN SPORTS

It is possible to discuss the sports specialties of the American Negro largely in terms of two causes: economics, and the desire for individual recognition. In those sports which are generally fostered in more affluent circles—such as golf, tennis, or even swimming—the Negro has not produced many outstanding performers. (There are some exceptions, of course, like Althea Gibson and Arthur Ashe in tennis, as well as PGA golf pro Charlie Sifford, but they are admittedly few and far between at the moment.) Conversely, in sports such as boxing, basketball and track which in varying degrees are accessible even to the poorest ghetto child, the Negro has made progress to the point of dominance. The Negro engaging in these sports has often found that his feats have had to be prodigious in order for him to gain the kind of attention he desires. (As related to track, this—along with the harsh nutritional facts of life—may well be advanced as a reason for his having chosen the more glamorous sprints over the distance events.)

Apart from the underlying causes for the Negro's performance in sports, however, the fact remains that he has a vital and impressive history in this area of human endeavor—one filled with long lists of champions and record holders. Negro "stars" become too numerous to catalog, with the result that we are compelled, in this section, to include only those personalities who must be rated "superstars"[1] in their respective fields. They are household names to the widest public, and must stand as being representative of the hundreds of other performers whom it is impossible to include. In addition, they are almost all 20th-century figures.

Since we are concerning ourselves with contemporary athletes, it is perhaps important to pause momentarily and give some attention to the place of the American Negro in organized sports from a historical point of view. In earliest days, although no records were kept, it is safe to assume that Negroes indulged in the conventional athletic activities native to the society in which they lived. It is significant, however, that the first sport in which they are known to have come to the fore was in boxing.

In 1777, a British officer took back to England with him one Bill Richmond, a Negro who became the first famous American prizefighter. In the early 1800's,

Tom Molineaux, an ex-slave who had earned his freedom by defeating the champion of a neighboring plantation, proclaimed himself America's first heavyweight champion, although he was twice beaten by the English champion, Tom Crib.

In more modern times, Negroes were systematically excluded from many other sports, although they were able to participate by subterfuge or by forming their own counterpart leagues. In 1887, for example, Moses Fleetwood was a catcher for the Toledo team (then considered to be in the major leagues) but, after that, those Negroes who did play claimed to be Indians, Cubans, or Mexicans. (John McGraw of the New York Giants once tried to employ a Negro player named Grant by maintaining that he was really an Indian but, when the Giants played in Baltimore, the city's Negro sports public showed up in such droves that the rest of the league soon pressured the Giants into dismissing Grant.)

When Jackie Robinson finally broke the color barrier in 1947, the pattern was followed in other major sports. In professional football, for instance, a recent survey indicated that there were 140 players in the National Football League and 80 in the American Football League. In professional basketball, the Negro role is also significant, with Negroes accounting for from 30 to 40% of the players on most teams. Negro participation in hockey, horse racing and wrestling continues to be minimal, although there are some Negroes represented in these sports as well.

THE NEGRO IN THE UNITED NATIONS

The basic blueprint for what was to become the United Nations was first drawn up at Dumbarton Oaks in Washington, D. C. in 1944. It was thought then that the five leading powers (the United States, Russia, Great Britain, China and France) should be permanently united as members of a single body which would dedicate itself to the preservation of world peace.

In 1945, the delegates of 50 nations assembled in San Francisco for the purpose of drawing up a charter which would embody the preliminary agreements reached at Dumbarton Oaks. Ratification of this charter by the "Big Five" in October of the same year paved the way for the establishment of the most comprehensive international organization in the history of mankind—the United Nations.

For the American Negro (as indeed for Negroes in other parts of the world), the United Nations immediately became a symbol of mankind's highest aspirations to create a world order based on principles of liberty and justice. Called upon to offer concrete evidence of its preparedness to adhere to these same principles, the United States soon began to assign a number of qualified Negroes to serve on its delegations—even as a host of other nations dispatched men and women of all races and creeds to represent them in the world body.

Slowly at first, but then in ever-increasing numbers, Negroes began to take their places alongside their white counterparts as members of the American delegation, and in other key staff and advisory positions. With the emergence of such major figures as Ralph Bunche, William Dean, Edith Sampson, Franklin Williams, and James M. Nabrit, Jr.—to name but a handful—there can be little doubt that the Negro has played a vital role in the development of the U.N., and in the progress it has made toward the extension of basic human rights to all men.

THE NEGRO WOMAN

A. HISTORICAL PERSPECTIVE

The civil rights struggle in the United States—often thought of as an attempt to allow the Negro male to assume his rightful place in American society—has at times tended to obscure the role of Negro women in shaping America's culture.

Historically, the roots of Negro women go back as far as any on American soil. Of the 20 African Negroes who arrived in Jamestown in 1619, at least two— Antony and Isabella—are reported later to have been married and, in 1624, to have become the parents of the first Negro child born in the English colonies of mainland America (William Tucker, named in honor of a local planter).

Until 1863, the Negro woman was as much governed by the slave system as the Negro man. Without rights of any kind, it was impossible for her to function as a woman—even to hold her own family intact when her children became old enough to be sold to other slaveowners. Nor could she assume her natural role as the emotionally supportive personality of the family, particularly since she herself was often forced to engage in such rigorous physical labor that the care of her own children became an immense burden. (Ironically, she was given special status as the nurse and confidante of her mistress' children, but was often deprived of the opportunity to shower the same appropriate attentions on her own children.)

Defined by countless stereotypes, the Negro woman was often denounced as an insensitive creature by the very people subjecting her to the oppressive circumstances which made such a generalization appear to be accurate.

If it is true that a woman has often had to work harder than a man to achieve the same recognition and earn the same money, then surely the Negro woman has often labored under a double burden. She has had to struggle for the emancipation of her race as a whole, while at the same time fighting for her rights as a woman as well.

On many occasions, the currents of these two streams—Negro rights and women's rights—crossed and merged with each other. The battles for the Negro vote and the vote for women, for Negro education and education for women, were often fought on the same ground. In the mid-19th century, for instance, Frederick Douglass and the Forten sisters, all Negroes, were fighting for Negro emancipation and the rights of women, and were aided in their work by a number of white abolitionists (e.g. Sarah and Angelina Grimké). In Philadelphia and Boston especially, many Negro and white families united to form anti-slavery societies dedicated to the common cause of emancipation and education.

After Emancipation, one of the first discernible trends among Negro women was the development of a strong club movement, designed to improve their overall welfare and broaden the horizons open to them. At that time, such leading Negro educators as Fannie Jackson Coppin, Charlotte Hawkins Brown and Nannie Helen Burroughs came into prominence, only to be joined later by Mary McLeod Bethune and Mary Church Terrell, among others. These women were eventually to become famous among members of both races.

B. MATRIARCHY AND CURRENT TRENDS

Much has been written of the matriarchal structure of Negro society—from the post-war era down to the present day. Whatever conclusions are drawn, there can be little doubt that the Negro woman has often been called upon to compensate for the failure (through no fault of his own) of the Negro man to find suitable, dependable employment in an intensely competitive society. Cases in which women become the marginal family breadwinner—the sole financial support of the group—inevitably involve a certain reversal of roles for both partners, and assuredly contribute in some measure to the psychological hazards faced by the Negro family as a whole.

Nevertheless, Negro women have strengthened their positions considerably in the 20th century by their entry into more skilled and better-paying jobs made possible through higher educational achievement. As opportunities have opened up, the Negro woman has been quick to make the transition from low-paid, unskilled domestic, farm and operative jobs to employment in clerical, professional, technical, sales and service jobs.

Today, the role of the Negro woman in American life is as significant as it ever was, and more people than ever are becoming aware of the implications of this role. The last 20 years have seen important advances not only in the rights of the Negro in general, but also in the status of the Negro woman. The women included in our section are representative of a truly vast number which have been unavoidably omitted due to spatial limitations.

NOTES

1. Satchel Paige is included, although he reached his peak as a player while in Negro baseball. The Globetrotters, a star team, also receive mention here.